SECURING THE FUTURE THROUGH SUSTAINABILITY, HEALTH, EDUCATION, AND TECHNOLOGY

SECURING THE FUTURE THROUGH SUSTAINABILITY, HEALTH, EDUCATION, AND TECHNOLOGY

Proceeding for 14th International Annual Research Conference at Symbiosis Institute of Management Studies (SIMS), 2023

Edtitors
Brig Dr Rajiv Divekar
Dr. Komal Chopra
Dr. Pravin Dange
Dr. Smita Mehendale

Routledge
Taylor & Francis Group

First published 2024
by Routledge
4 Park Square, Milton Park, Abingdon, Oxon OX14 4RN

and by Routledge
605 Third Avenue, New York, NY 10158

Routledge is an imprint of the Taylor & Francis Group, an informa business

British Library Cataloguing-in-Publication Data
A catalogue record for this book is available from the British Library

ISBN: 978-1-032-95921-4 (hbk)
ISBN: 978-1-032-95922-1 (pbk)
ISBN: 978-1-003-58720-0 (ebk)

DOI: 10.1201/9781003587200

Typeset in Times LT Std
by Aditiinfosystems

Securing the Future through Sustainability, Health, Education, and Technology –
Brig. Dr. Rajiv Divekar et al. (eds)
© 2024 Taylor & Francis Group, London, ISBN 978-1-032-95922-1

CONTENTS

Securing the Future through Sustainability, Health, Education, and Technology –
Brig. Dr. Rajiv Divekar et al. (eds)

List of Figures

Securing the Future through Sustainability, Health, Education, and Technology – Brig. Dr. Rajiv Divekar et al. (eds)
© 2024 Taylor & Francis Group, London, ISBN 978-1-032-95922-1

List of Tables

Securing the Future through Sustainability, Health, Education, and Technology –
Brig. Dr. Rajiv Divekar et al. (eds)

Foreword

It was an immense pleasure to participate in SIMSARC 23 which aimed to invite presentations on Sustainability in many areas. The conference also invited papers from other researchers from all over India. It was a very successful attempt as many high-quality papers were prepared and presented in the three-day conference. I am very happy to see the collection of these articles to be published in this book. As I skim through these papers, I witness the tremendous efforts put in the preparation. Editors have done a magnificent job of selecting the relevant, applied, and scholarly works. I wish a great success for this publication.

Kishore G. Kulkarni, Ph.D.,
Distinguished Professor of Economics,
College of Business, Metropolitan State University of Denver
Chief Editor, International Review of
Business and Economics, (www.irbejournal.com),
President, Society of Indian Academics in America (SIAA),
Indian Institute of Finance (www.IIF.edu)

*Securing the Future through Sustainability, Health, Education, and Technology –
Brig. Dr. Rajiv Divekar et al. (eds)
© 2024 Taylor & Francis Group, London, ISBN 978-1-032-95922-1*

Preface

Today's era is an era of seismic disruptions—disruptions introduced by emerging technologies affecting business, education and society. The singularities have had a devastating effect on our ability to predict what lies ahead. Trend-lines have lost their relevance in the imminent context, best described as BANI (Brittle, Anxious, Non-linear and Incomprehensible). The magnitude of disruptions coupled with their non-linearity is creating havoc across all walks of life and sectors including business, society, heath and technology too, leading to severely compromised ability of humanity to predict futuristic scenarios and consequent strategy-building to address the same.

The massive disruptions have challenged the very fundamentals on which the current structures of business and society are built and have raised several questions on the ability of not just the current social and economic structures but also of humanity at large, to set the terms of survival. In such a context, it's important that we secure our future and explore ways and means of sustaining be it business, health, education or society including its socio-economic structures. Secure before we lose it and require discussing retrieval as it would unfold,

Aptly capturing the essence, this 14th edition of SIMSARC was dedicated to the theme "Securing the Future - Sustainability, Health, Education, Technology and Society". This book is a compilation of select articles presented at the conference that encompass a variety of topics revolving around the theme. Each study is authored by different researchers and covers a specific aspect of their respective fields, contributing to the overall understanding and advancement of knowledge in these areas. The articles aim to provide insights, analysis, and assessments to address various challenges and opportunities in different sectors and thus, contribute to the cause of a more sustainable future.

The research articles cover a wide range of topics including the importance of sustainability, the critical role of the Indian Armed Forces in disruptive times, the effectiveness of alcohol-based hand sanitisers, the integration of artificial intelligence in healthcare management, customer satisfaction analysis using the Kano model, understanding customer response in omnichannel grocery shopping, the value of internships for experiential learning in MBA programs, the impact of overconfidence bias on market efficiency, the perception of the workforce for labour laws rejuvenation, and producers' perceptions of consumer price control in the agri-food supply chain. Each study provides valuable insights and analysis to contribute to the existing knowledge base in their respective fields.

The studies aim to address current challenges and future trends in various sectors such as sustainability, healthcare management, customer satisfaction, market efficiency, labor laws, and consumer price control. The research articles provide a comprehensive analysis of different aspects of these topics, offering valuable insights and recommendations for policymakers, practitioners, and researchers. The diverse range of topics covered in the studies reflects the multidisciplinary nature of research and the need for holistic approaches to address complex issues in different sectors.

The research articles contribute to the ongoing discourse on these topics and provide a foundation for further research and exploration in these areas. This book will be of help to a variety of target groups. For the research community, it will help in understanding current trends in research, relook into existing theories in different areas of study in the context of endemic situations, and identify new research areas. The book will help the academic community incorporate research inputs into classroom teaching, which will help prepare students for their future careers. Behavioral changes in consumers and employees and their high adoption of digital technology at all levels of life have business implications that call for deeper understanding and articulation of the phenomenon.

Securing the Future through Sustainability, Health, Education, and Technology –
Brig. Dr. Rajiv Divekar et al. (eds)

Acknowledgements

Symbiosis Institute of Management Studies would like to thanks the authors, editors, reviewers, and Ms Dipali More, organising secretary, for their constant support in publication process.

Securing the Future through Sustainability, Health, Education, and Technology –
Brig. Dr. Rajiv Divekar et al. (eds)
© 2024 Taylor & Francis Group, London, ISBN 978-1-032-95922-1

About the Editors

1. Brig. (Dr.) Rajiv Divekar

Brig (Dr.) Rajiv Divekar is the Director of Symbiosis Institute of Management Studies for the last 12 years. SIMS is amongst the top ranked B-schools in India which is over 27 years old. Prior to this he was Head of Faculty Strategic and Operational Studies at Army War College and Faculty member in Defence Strategic Studies at Defence Services Staff College, Wellington. He has done his PhD from Symbiosis International University. He is a M. Phil from D A V V University and MSc from Madras University. A Gold medallist in BE (civil), he has done his MBA specializing in Human Resource Management. He has rich experience of strategy, planning, logistics and human resource management based on his service with multinational teams as part of United Nations Force in both Somalia and Lebanon. He has served in Kargil and Leh on the LoC where he was responsible for the Logistics and Supply Chain Management for soldiers located on posts at 17,000- 22,000 feet in the Siachen Glacier.

He has a large number of research publications in National & International Journals & also in Scopus listed Journals. He is also a reviewer for a journal which is indexed in SCOPUS.

Under his leadership and guidance, SIMS has been organising an Annual International Research Conference for last 11 years. He teaches Strategy, Human Resource and Leadership to MBA students and has been invited to deliver talks at various organisations and institutes as also to deliver key note address in conferences.

He is a recipient of many awards in the field of education. He has been awarded "The Rashtriya Vidya Gaurav Gold Medal" by the Indian Solidarity Council, the "Rajiv Gandhi Education Excellence Award" by International Institute of Education and Management and the "Education Leadership Award" by Education Leadership Awards, Dubai.

2. Dr. Komal Chopra

Dr. Komal Chopra is an Associate Professor of Marketing at Symbiosis Institute of Management Studies, Symbiosis International (Deemed University), Pune, India. He has more than 16 years of experience in academics. Dr. Komal Chopra has taught subjects such as Retail Management, Consumer Behaviour, and

Essentials of Marketing to post-graduate students. He has conducted management development programmes for Godrej & Boyce, Wipro, John Deere, Cognizant and Directorate General of Resettlement, Government of India. He has also delivered guest sessions at the University of Witwatersrand, South Africa, and Kathmandu University. He has done research and consultancy projects for Ministry of Corporate Affairs, ICSSR, Tata Motors, Springer Nature and Bilcare Research. He has published many research papers in ABDC and Scopus ranked journals and is a reviewer for Asia Pacific Journal of Marketing and Logistics, International Journal of Emerging Markets, Sage OPEN, Emerald Emerging Markets Case Studies, International Journal of Retail & Distribution Management, Journal of Applied Research in Higher Education, Foresight and Health Education. He has also won the best research paper award at international conferences. He is a PhD guide at Symbiosis International (Deemed University) and PhD referee at the University of Witwatersrand, South Africa. He is an ISO 9001:2015 certified auditor and Co-Convener of SIMS Annual Research Conference.

3. Dr. Pravin Dange

Dr Pravin Dange is an associate professor at Symbiosis Institute of Management Studies in the area of Marketing and Strategy. An agricultural engineer and Ph.D. from BIT Mesra, he brings along more than 30 years of experience in Academics and Industry. In the past he has handled several profiles including teaching, academic administration, consultancy. He has several research papers and project assignments to his credit. He has been recognised for his teaching contribution at the 17th Dewang Mehta B-School Awards and Higher Education forum. His research interests include Corporate Social Responsibility, Sustainability and Higher Education.

4. Dr Smita Mehendale

Dr. Smita Mehendale is an Assistant Professor with Symbiosis Institute of Management Studies, Symbiosis International (Deemed University), Pune She has 18+ years of experience in diverse functions like finance, marketing and HR and across industries and educational institutions. She has worked in manufacturing, service sector and consultancy before stepping into academics. She has done her PhD from SPPU, Pune in online retailing. She teaches Research Methodology, Retail Management and Marketing Research at SIMS. She is passionate about training and has conducted sessions for FMCG, healthcare, financial services and educational institutions like Cargill, L&T, Nikita Distributers, SVM, St. Mira's, BMCC, SVIMS. She has presented numerous papers in international conferences and won best paper awards. She has conducted Faculty Development Programmes and is the co-convener of SIMSARC22

Securing the Future through Sustainability, Health, Education, and Technology – Brig. Dr. Rajiv Divekar et al. (eds)
© 2024 Taylor & Francis Group, London, ISBN 978-1-032-95922-1

1 A Bibliometric Analysis of Sustainability Literature: Benefits, Implications and Future Trends

Ankit Kumari[1]
Research Scholar,
Mittal School of Business, Lovely Professional University,
Phagwara, Punjab

Razia Nagina[2]
Associate Professor,
Mittal School of Business, Lovely Professional University,
Phagwara, Punjab

Mandakini Paruthi[3]
Assistant Professor,
Chaitanya Bharthi Institute of Technology,
Gandipet, Hyderabad

Hirak Das Gupta[4]
Associate Professor,
Symbiosis Institute of Management Studies,
Symbiosis International (Deemed University), Pune

Abstract

The study provides a comprehensive analysis of trends in the global scientific exploration on the sustainability reporting disclosures. Since the last decade, concept of Sustainability received increasing attention from research scholars, students, and academician's institutions globally. Previous researchers have broadly studied the concept of Sustainability worldwide and with the period of time this concept is getting matured. Therefore, the main theme of this is to deploy bibliometric techniques for analyzing the related literature. The study sustains review of literature along with bibliometric analysis methodology and Vosviewer. Publications data output was identified based on Scopus database's research articles from 2005 to 2023. This bibliometric review of research analyzes 472 articles related to Sustainability. The researchers analyzed the current papers,

[1]ankitaduhan712@gmail.com, [2]razia.23646@lpu.co.in, [3]paruthi.mandakini@gmail.com, [4]hirak.dasgupta@sims.edu

DOI: 10.1201/9781003587200-1

authors, countries, and keywords using Biblioshiny software. The goal of this paper is to document the volume of Sustainability literature, identify pioneer journals, publications, influential authors, and highlight emerging themes and various research issues related to the field of study. In addition, bibliometric analysis has been developed to obtain further understanding regarding the importance of Sustainability impacts to the individuals, firms, and entire economy. The present study is useful for the researchers who will pursue research on Sustainability field. The study helps not only researchers but practitioners also, in order to understand this topic and its development over a period of time. It also highlights the beneficial and challenged side that being faces by organizations.

KEYWORDS: Bibliometric analysis, Biblioshiny, Disclosures, Sustainability, Sustainability reporting

1. Introduction

1.1 Sustainability Disclosures

The word sustinere is where the word sustainability comes from. The word "to sustain" can also mean to hold up, support, or endure. During the late 1980s, the United Nations made a significant contribution to the growth of the global sustainability movement. The United Nations' Brundtland Commission, also known as the World Commission on Environment and Development, issued a report in 1987 titled "Our Common Future." In this report, a universal definition of Sustainable Development has been established "It refers to the development that meets the needs of the present without compromising the ability of future generations to meet their own needs". As organizations become conscious about the concept of sustainability, most of them nowadays are trying to make their activities sustainable. Research using bibliometric analysis on sustainability reporting specifically in banking sector remains scarce. This a bibliometric study delivers a holistic picture of this domain through the exploring of the evolution of hot spots in the field. To achieve the aim of the study, Vosviewer software is used to visualise and analyse trends and patterns in scientific literature which based on the Scopus citation index. The methodology portion of the study elaborates on the specifics of the data gathered and software utilized. The co-author and co-country network analysis, followed by the co-citation analysis, will be presented after the statistical analysis of the data. Finally, the researchers summarize our key findings before summarizing the current study's limitations and suggesting directions for further research.

The study conducted on sustainability disclosure on organization financial performance. Sustainable also related as investing in things that are not destructive. Concept of sustainability has acquired greater importance over some time. The sustainability concept does not deal only in terms of the ecological, economic and social environment but also in terms of related to the quality of life. Today, due to this mindset everyone wants to value resources and currently, develop their organizations in achieving effectively and efficiently their objectives (Di Fabio, 2017). It is an attempt for achieving long-term goals and objectives which the organizations aimed to achieve within a specific period (Jerome, 2013). By emphasizing the literature, it was coming to know that sustainable disclosure composes an integral part that could be helpful for an organization in becoming efficient and in obtaining competitive recognition (Kaur & Rani, 2020). The study of Sustainability disclosures has become an area of study that catches huge interest from the scholars, researchers, academicians and policy maker's viewpoint, because of which researchers have written enormously about this particular field. However, the progress in the sustainable disclosures field unfolds various unique exploration areas. Due to the invention of a new research area, there is a need to analyze the literature review by highlighting the overall progress of this particular field over a while. The novelty of the research lies in the fact that through this bibliometric analysis, the researchers have added to existing literature development of sustainable disclosure concept over a period of time. The researchers have presented the existing literature thorough various charts and graphs by using Biblioshiny software. Moreover, major factors contributing, key benefits, barriers in successful implementation of Sustainable disclosure are also discussed. In the last, implications for the various stakeholders are highlighted. So, through this bibliometric review, the major objective is to present a comprehensive analysis of the published literature of sustainable disclosure through the database Scopus.

Our research in this particular field provides us with the current trends in this field. Along with this, key gaps were also identified; emerging themes were also discussed in the upcoming sections of this article (Sanchez et al., 2020). To attain the objectives of our study, the researchers divided the research into four sections. The first section includes the literature review of all the articles generated through biblioshiny software. The next section includes the methodology used to select the reference study. The upcoming section elaborated results and findings of the study. The last section ends with the conclusion, implications and limitations of the investigation.

1.2 Need of Sustainability Disclosure

Sustainability is meeting the needs of the present without compromising the needs of the future or ensuring a balance between economic growth, environmental protection, and social well-being. Sustainability disclosures practices provides so many benefits to a firm be its related to better risk management, cost and savings optimization, decision-making facilitation, and increased corporate confidence etc. In addition to this, businesses that successfully implement sustainability strategies may also profit financially and achieved high social benefits result from improving the environment and meeting human needs. The long-term survival of a corporation can be improved by employing sustainable resources.

1.3 Research Objectives

1. To examine the year-wise growth in the publication of sustainable concept.
2. To identify the most influential journals, most pioneer authors in sustainability impacts literature, most frequently studied topics, most frequently used author keywords, and emerging and basic research themes in the sustainable disclosure in the research field.
3. To identify the benefits of and barriers to the implementation of these practices, and its implications for future research.

Achieving our main objectives of the study will help in will help in bringing back the respect for communities through the implementation of sustainable concept and contributed towards uniform incorporation of practices.

2. Literature Review

Sustainable corporate performance and disclosures need to be assessed on the basis of triple bottom line parameters that include economic viability of firm in terms of creation of wealth for shareholders, environmental sustainability and social sustainability of business line (Dyllick and Hockerts, 2002). Between the pre- and post-disclosure reform periods in India, sustainability reporting had an impact on several aspects of financial performance; it had a positive impact on the financial parameters of return on sales, return on equity, and Tobin's Q in the pre-reform period, but had no discernible impact in the post-reform period (Goel, 2021). Scholars and development agencies, especially in developing countries, had advised that sustainability practices to be embraced as a method of enhancing financial service access, (Bongomin et al., 2018). Sustainability development creates inclusive growth (Wang et al., 2023). Despite this importance, the sustainability reporting level is very less in worldwide, especially among the developing countries (DemirgüçKunt et al., 2018; Klapper et al., 2015). Gálvez-Sánchez et al. (2021) conducted a bibliometric analysis on financial institutions from the Scopus databaseA scientific literature review of the studies in this field still needs to be explored in the literature. As a result, in order to be able to provide insights into the existing research, the researchers identify the relevant research areas and future trends of research in the field of sustainability reporting disclosure impacts, which will address the current problems existing in this field that still need to be studied.

3. Research Methodology

3.1 Sources of Data

'R package' and 'Biblioshiny software are used for the analysis of this research work (Chae, Yim, Lee, Jo, & Oh, 2020). The major purpose of performing a bibliometric review on this emerging concept is to identify, organize, and analyze the main components and dimensions, annual growth of this topic over a period of time (Kumar, Sureka, & Colombage, 2020). In recent years, the bibliometric analysis and review have earned ample attention from academicians and scholars as they provide us with a piece of information that is based on an over a period of data (Battour, Barahma, & Al-Awlaqi, 2021). Bibliometric analysis is a method that allows future scholars to get knowledge about the past trends and fluctuations in the publications of a particular topic (Donthu, Kumar, Mukherjee, Pandey, & Lim, 2021). Along with this, the new trend of the literature review also throws light on the future growth of a particular concept.

Fig. 1.1 Data sources and methodology

Source: Authors' work

3.2 Identification of Sources and Search Strategy

In the initial stages of the bibliometric analysis, we require the perfect database from which we get the necessary research articles for further analysis. We have selected the Scopus database as it is one of the most noticeable databases that are used by most researchers globally. Scopus database has the largest coverage of social science studies for identifying highly qualified, reliable, and relevant research documents for analysis.When conducting this research, we took all the documents published on sustainability impacts regardless of date. In the 'type of documents', the review includes research articles only published in English language. We have excluded the conference papers and book chapters. For the initial search of documents in Scopus database we used the various keywords string like ("Sustainability Reporting" OR "Sustainability Disclosures" OR "Sustainability Index"). The system showed 472 articles documents related to sustainability impacts after entering the above sting. Further, the searches of the articles only related to the sustainability impacts were included.

4. Analysis and Findings

4.1 Bibliometric Maps and Measurement

In this study, we used R software and Biblioshiny application for analysis. Bibliometric maps through the tables and graphs presents the related knowledge about a particular concept, frequently used keywords, authors, and collaboration between different authors (Alberto, Lordelo, Monaliza, & Nogueira, 2021).

Before moving ahead for the analysis, Table 1.1 show the necessary sustainability disclosure literature which acquainted with all the concept.

Table 1.1 Main information about the data

S. No.	Description	Results
1	Time span	2005-2023
2	Sources (Journals, Books)	217
3	Documents	218
4	Average years from publication	4.15
5	Average citations per documents	16.96
6	Average citations per year per documents	3.32
7	References	15479
8	Document type (Article)	218
9	Documents content (Keyword plus)	285
10	Documents content (Author's Keyword)	695
11	Authors of single authored documents	38
12	Authors of multi authored documents	489
13	Authors per document	2.42
14	Co-authors per document	2.71
15	Collaboration index	2.81

Source: Data from Scopus database, Created by Biblioshiny

4.2 Year Wise Trend of Publication

Figure 1.2 shows the publication trend of sustainability disclosure impacts literature in Scopus from 2005-2023. It shows an increasing trend in terms of number of publications in year 2005-2023. The graph represents that the sustainability disclosure impacts concept is still in its emerging stage.

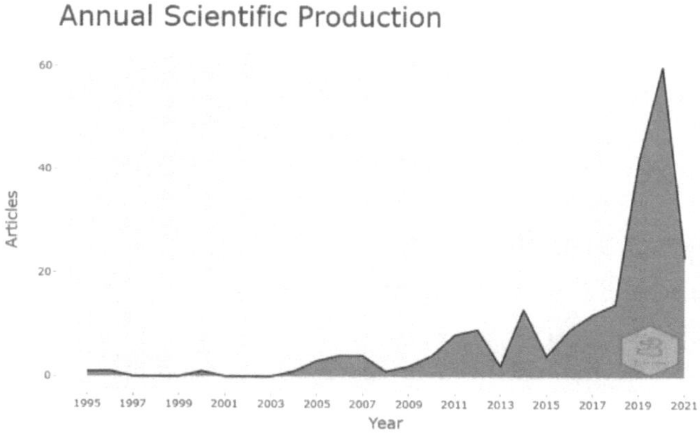

Fig. 1.2 Annual scientific production

Source: Data from Scopus database, Created by Biblioshiny

4.3 Top Contributing Journals Publishing Sustainability Disclosures

The research question (RQ3) was to articulate the pioneer journals and the documents produced by them. Figure 1.3 shows the 10 most influential journals. The social responsibility journal has the highest number of publications that is 20 on yearly basis.

4.4 Most Relevant Authors

Figure 1.4 represents the most relevant authors in the sustainable disclosure literature with respect to the Scopus database is presented in the Figure 1.4.

4.5 Country Wise Production

The Figure 1.5 depicts that overall trend in the field of sustainability disclosure research which is majorly dominated by India. Similarly, in the other countries the frequency of publishing articles are few like in USA,France, Malaysia and in United Kingdom as compare to India. Figure 1.5 shoes the worldwide distribution of literature.

4.6 Country Scientific Production

The Fig. 1.6 depicts the country scientific production in the field of sustainability disclosure research. In, country wise specific production trend, India is the one which dominated in sustainability disclosure research comparative to others countries.

4.7 Author Keywords

For answering the one of research objective, we used the frequency of occurrence of Keywords plus as shown in Fig. 1.6 through Vosviewer software. Vosviewer is a software tool for constructing and visualizing bibliometric networks which represents the major themes of sustainability. From the figure, this is observed that words like- sustainability, financial performance, Sustainable development, and corporate governance features prominently as author's keywords. Words with high frequency are more in size. The higher frequency means that these words are highly used as their keywords by the authors in the literature of sustainability disclosure field. Fig. 1.7 depicts the word cloud of authors' keywords.

4.8 Thematic Map

Thematic analysis is one of the most common form of analysis which emphasizes in identifying, analyzing, and interpreting patterns of themes in the research. We have observed the emerging and basic research themes in the sustainable disclosure for answering the one of research objective. We have done categorization of the identified themes through a map for the analysis and development of a particular research theme. The density of these motifs is depicted on the y-axis in Fig. 1.7

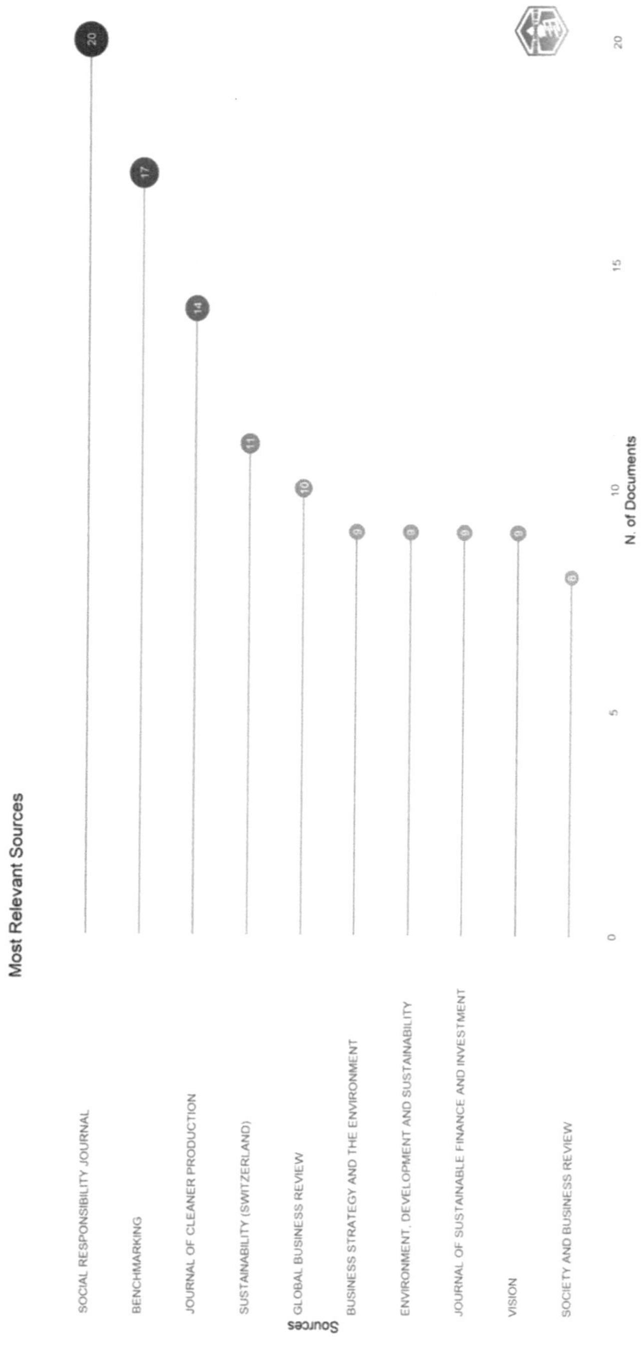

Fig. 1.3 Most relevant sources

Source: Data from Scopus database, Created by Biblioshiny

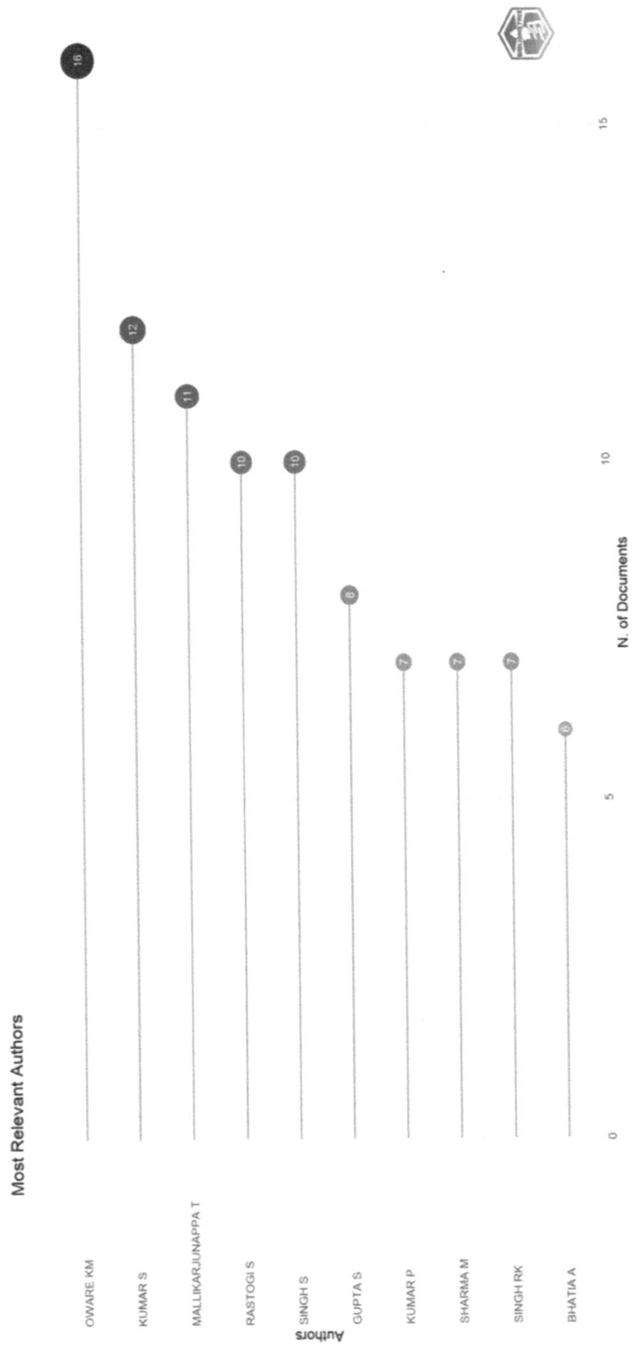

Fig. 1.4 Top authors of the present study

Source: Data from Scopus database, Created by Biblioshiny

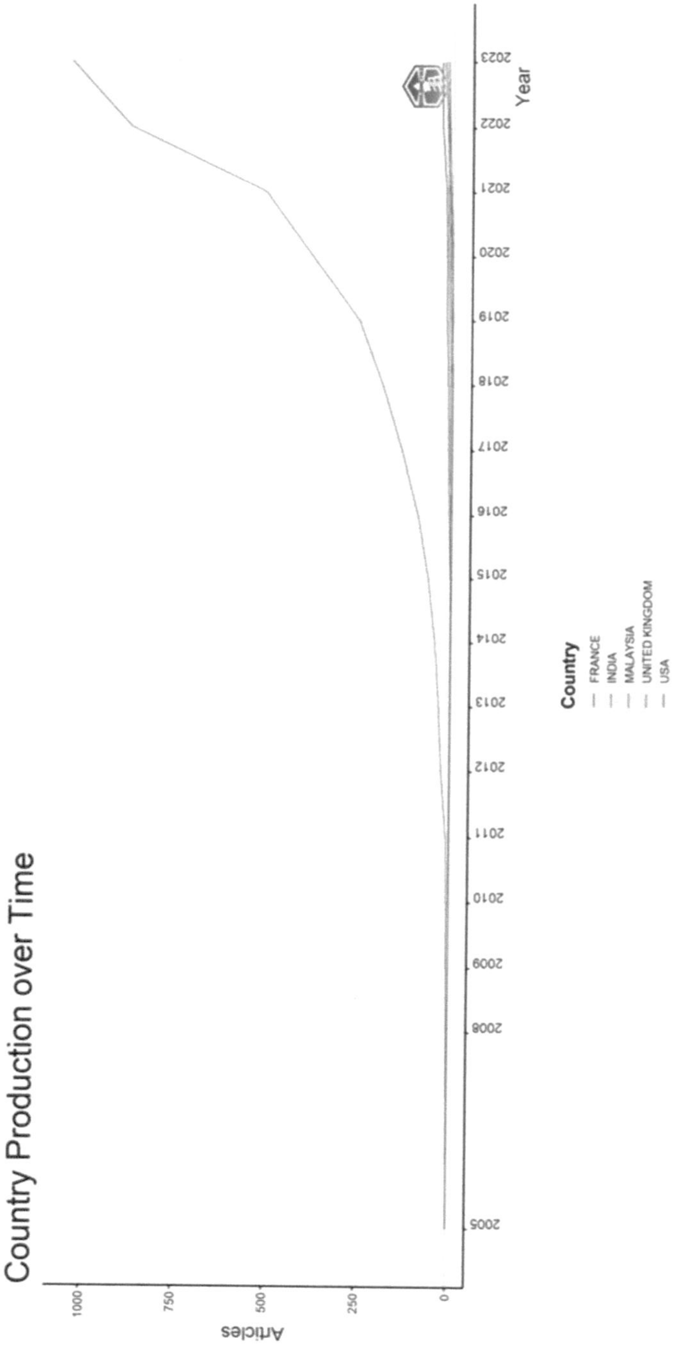

Fig. 1.5 Country production over time

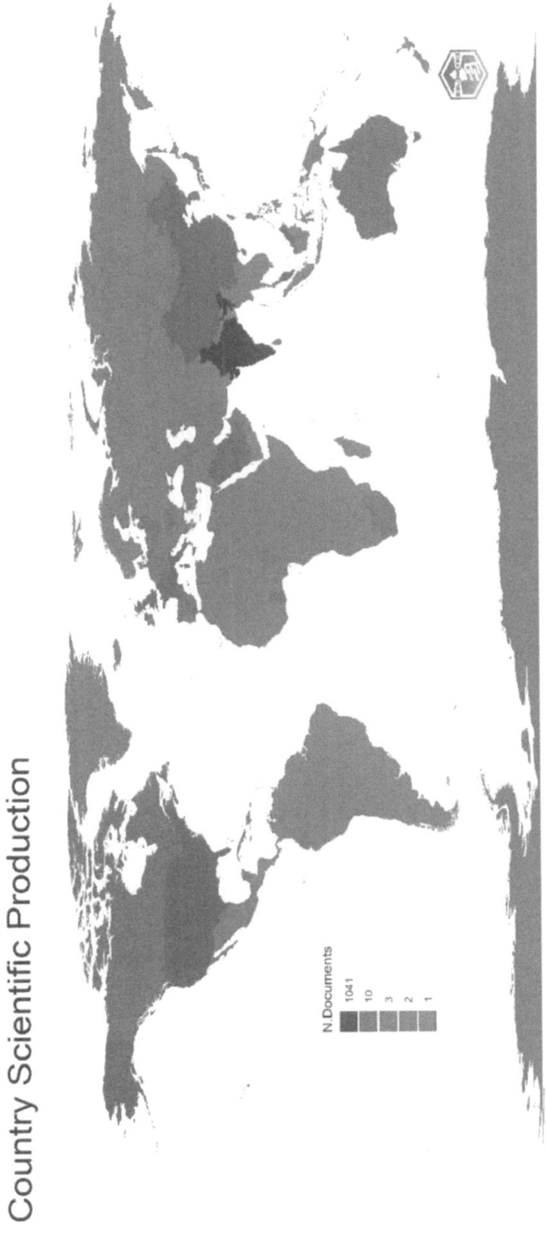

Fig. 1.6 Country scientific production

Source: Data from Scopus database, Created by Biblioshiny

Fig. 1.7 Authors keywords

Source: Data from Scopus database, Created by Vosviewer

below, while their centrality is shown on the x-axis. The centrality means worth of a particular theme, and density measures the progress of chosen theme over a certain time period (Nasir et al., 2020). We have divided the graph into four parts. Lower left part of the graph represents emerging themes. These are those themes that represents their ability to adapt to new ideas, concepts, or findings. The lower right corner of the thematic map highlights the basic themes. It highlights that the particular keywords have their worth in research but lower level of progress with respect to these themes. Similarly, upper left corner represents high density but lower centrality, which means that particular keyword is less important to the sustainable disclosure literature, but research on this topic is increasing in numbers day by day. Figure 1.8 shows the thematic map.

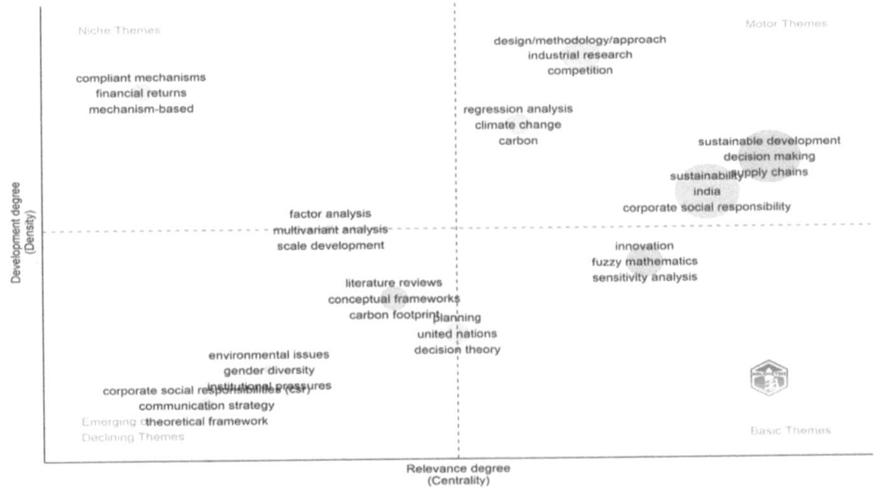

Fig. 1.8 Thematic map

Source: Data from Scopus database, Created by Biblioshiny

4.9 Co-occurrence Network

The author keyword co-occurrence network is shown in Fig. 1.8. The co-occurrence of networks demonstrates that there are four clusters of sustainability disclosures literature in the social sciences: red, blue, green, and purple. Thematically, blue and green clusters are related to one another. Sustainable development contain the highest centrality and is linked to other clusters namely sustainability performance, social responsibility. Figure 1.8 represents the co-occurrence network using author keywords. The figure below represents the trending topics in the literature of sustainability disclosures. The term 'sustainable development' is the most emergent topic in this field, as this term is used forty five times in the year 2005-2023. 'Sustainability' is the second most trending theme in this research field with frequency of twenty six.

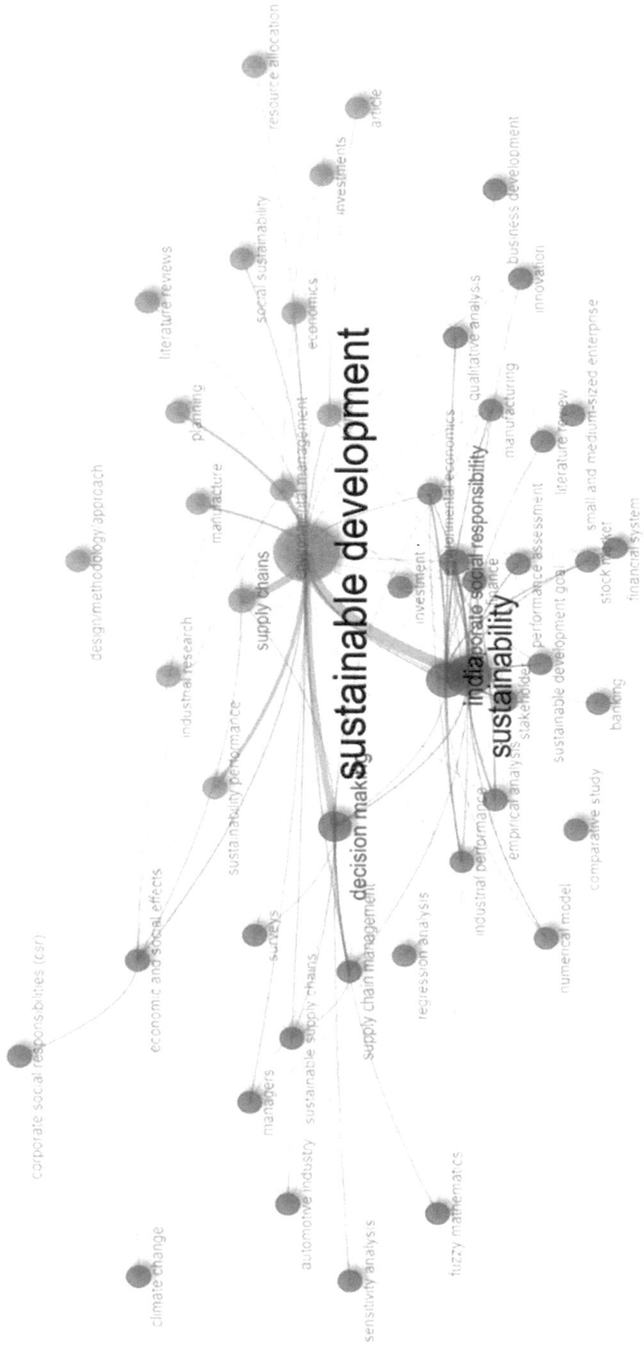

Fig. 1.9 Co-occurrence network

Source: Data from Scopus database, Created by Biblioshiny

4.10 Major Findings

Sustainability disclosures is considered as a new humanistic paradigm in analyzing performance. It is beneficial for both the organizations and its stakeholders. There are different factors which are contributing towards the Sustainability disclosures impacts approach as discussed in figure below which represents the factors contributing sustainable reporting.

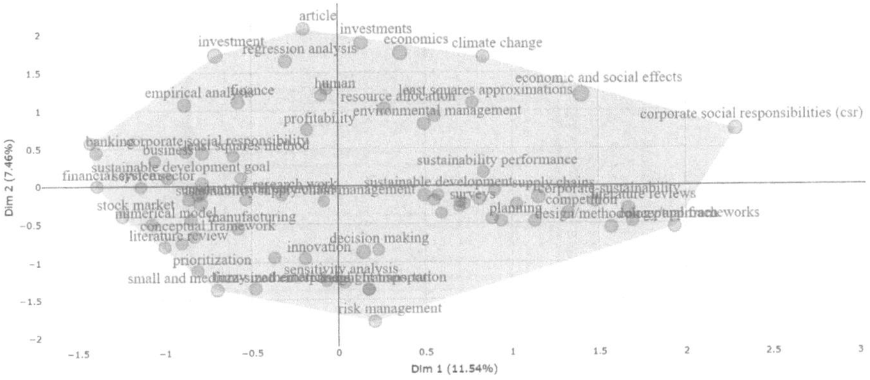

Fig. 1.10 Factors contributes to sustainability reporting

Source: Compiled from Review of Literature

5. Benefits of Adopting Sustainability Disclosure Practices

This upcoming section of the research discussed about the benefits of sustainability disclosure practices. This section state the benefits associated with implementation of sustainability disclosure practices. The adoption of these practices would lead to maintain a balance between the clashing expectations of distinct stakeholders such as- employees, society, customers, shareholders, and government by creating a positive impact on firms economical, environmental, and financial performance (Ja, 2016), (Chams & García-Blandón, 2019). From the past research studies, it has been also explored that companies having good social, financial, and ecological practices will create a positive impact on their financial performance (Nadeem & Garza-reyes, 2020).

6. Barriers to the Implementation of Sustainability Reporting Disclosure Practices

In the literature review, various previous studies have stated the core dimensions of the sustainability disclosure practices that are considered necessary to follow for smooth functioning of firm performance. One the other side, there are fewer of studies that have highlighted the barriers to and challenges faced by firms in the sustainability disclosure practices implementation. Through this current research work, we have explored certain hurdles in the way of successful implementation of Sustainability disclosures as in Fig. 1.11. Figure 1.9 depicts the barriers in the implementation of sustainable disclosure practices.

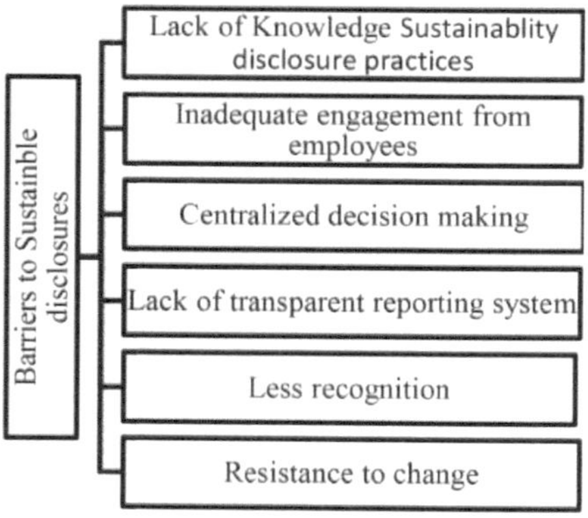

Fig. 1.11 Barriers to the implementation of sustainability reporting disclosure practices

Source: Compiled from Literature Review

7. Conclusion, Implications and Future Scope

This paper emphasized that bibliometric analysis is a scientific method that can be useful for both experienced and rising scholars who seek to conduct research from such a broad perspective. The study presents a literature review and bibliometeric overview of the publications related to sustainability reporting disclosure practices. The bibliometric analysis shows the progression of research articles on sustainability disclosure practices at global level from the year 2005 till the date. The ultimate goal of sustainability reporting is to drive positive social and environmental change. By disclosing sustainability performance organisations can identify areas for improvement and track progress towards a more sustainable future. With regard to the growth of a particular journal, Sustainability journal has been the highly influential during the period from 2005 to 2023. The study has theoretically outlined the overall development of this concept over a period of time. It also highlights the benefits, barriers and implications of sustainable disclosures impacts in firm's context. Thus the study concludes that sustainable reporting disclosure practices provides an imperative view towards linking different aspects of social responsibility, economic effectiveness and safeguarding the environment.

Table 1.2 Implications of sustainability reporting disclosures

S. No.	Categories	Implications	Source
1.	Stockholders	• Increase in shareholder value	• (Lombardi, Manfredi, Cuozzo, & Palmaccio, 2020)
2.	Society	• Employment availability • Better quality of life • Development of society	• (Van Buren, 2022) • (Goc & Kusku, 2020)
3.	Organization	• High Performance work system • Learning for growth • Life harmony Decisions	• (Rao, 2020) • (Perspectives, 2010) • (Chillakuri & Vanka, 2020)
4.	Environment	• Adopting to green initiatives • Effective and efficient use of natural resources • Global Reporting Initiative	• (Saeed et al., 2019) • (Puri & Agrawal, 2020) • (Ehnert, Parsa, Roper, Wagner, & Muller-, 2016)

Source: From Review

8. Limitations

The limitations of the study imply the need for future research directions. First off, bibliometric analysis-related publications are not typically included in databases like Scopus or Web of Science, and if they are, they usually contain inaccuracies. In our research paper, we have only considered the quantitative figures and data to present the results, so qualitative aspects are not considered. If, the qualitative aspects are considered in future it may provide slightly variant results. One of the flaws also includes the inclusion of only the publication of scientific articles which are published during the time span 2005-2023, not considering the participation's in the conference, book chapters, book publications as well as other time span. Future studies can fill these gaps by considering other databases for the search of studies.

9. Acknowledgement

I would like to thank Dr. Razia Nagina, my research supervisor, for her sustained guidance, persistent support, and constructive criticism of this study. I would also like to express my gratitude to Dr. Mandakini Paruthi and Dr. Hirak Das Gupta for their unwavering guidance and support. I am especially extremely grateful to my daddy for supporting me and my wonderful friend,Yashu,Priyanka and Manpreet who are a source of great inspiration for me.

REFERENCES

1. Arora, A., & Sharma, D. (2022). Do environmental, social and governance (ESG) performance scores reduce the cost of debt- Evidence from Indian firms. *Australasian Business, Accounting and Finance Journal, 16*(5), 4–18.

2. Alatawi, M. S., & Daud, Z. B. M. (2022). Integrated reporting practices and firm performance: A review study. *Corporate and Business Strategy Review*, *3*(2), 96–111.
3. Alshehhi, A., Nobanee, H., & Khare, N. (2018). The impact of sustainability practices on corporate financial performance: Literature trends and future research potential. *Sustainability*, *10*(2), 494.
4. Agarwal, A., Aggarwal, S. P., & Gupta, S. (2019). Sustainable earnings: A new eye for emerging finance. *Journal of Sustainable Finance and Investment*, *9*(4), 325–348.
5. Bhatia, A., & Tuli, S. (2018). Sustainability reporting: An empirical evaluation of emerging and developed economies. *Journal of Global Responsibility*, *9*(2), 207–234.
6. Bodhanwala, S., & Bodhanwala, R. (2018). Does corporate sustainability impact firm profitability? Evidence from India. *Management Decision*, *56*(8), 1734–1747.
7. Bhatia, A., & Tuli, S. (2018). Sustainability reporting practices in US and UK: An empirical comparison. *International Journal of Law and Management*, *60*(4), 1034–1056.
8. Bhattacharya, S., & Sharma, D. (2019). Do environment, social and governance performance impact credit ratings: A study from India. *International Journal of Ethics and Systems*, *35*(3), 466–484.
9. Bhuvaneskumar, A., Sivakumar, V. J., & Pushparaj, N. (2023). Performance assessment and ranking of socially responsible companies in India using FAHP, TOPSIS and Altman Z-score. *Benchmarking: An International Journal*, *30*(3), 736–765.
10. Bodhanwala, S., & Bodhanwala, R. (2022). Exploring relationship between sustainability and firm performance in travel and tourism industry: A global evidence. *Social Responsibility Journal*, *18*(7), 1251–1269.
11. Bhimavarapu, V. M., Rastogi, S., Gupte, R., Pinto, G., & Shingade, S. (2022). Does the impact of transparency and disclosure on the Firm's valuation depend on the ESG? *Journal of Risk and Financial Management*, *15*(9), 410.
12. Bodhanwala, S., & Bodhanwala, R. (2019). Relationship between sustainable and responsible investing and returns: A global evidence. *Social Responsibility Journal*, *16*(4), 579–594.
13. Bhargava, A., & Ligade, P. (2023). Corporate social responsibility (CSR) and sustainability – A scientometric analysis of the interrelationship. *Journal of Indian Business Research*, *15*(1), 110–124.
14. Bahuguna, P. C., Srivastava, R., & Tiwari, S. (2023). Two-decade journey of green human resource management research: A bibliometric analysis. *Benchmarking: An International Journal*, *30*(2), 585–602.
15. Bhimavarapu, V. M., Rastogi, S., & Kanoujiya, J. (2023). Ownership concentration and its influence on transparency and disclosures of banks in India. *Corporate Governance*, *23*(1), 18–42.
16. Biswas, S., Bhattacharya, M., Sadarangani, P. H., & Jin, J. Y. (2022). Corporate governance and earnings management in banks: An empirical evidence from India. *Cogent Economics and Finance*, *10*(1), 1.
17. Bansal, M., Samad, T. A., & Bashir, H. A. (2021). The sustainability reporting-firm performance nexus: Evidence from a threshold model. *Journal of Global Responsibility*, *12*(4), 491–512.
18. Chalissery, N., Tabash, M. I., Nishad T, M., & Saleh Al-Faryan, M. A. (2023). A bibliometric analysis of socially responsible investment based on thematic clustering. *Cogent Business and Management*, *10*(1), 1.
19. Charumathi, B., & Ramesh, L. (2020). Impact of voluntary disclosure on valuation of firms: Evidence from Indian companies. *Vision*, *24*(2), 194–203.

20. Chatterjee, S., Chaudhuri, R., & Vrontis, D. (2023). Investigating the impacts of microlevel CSR activities on firm sustainability: Mediating role of CSR performance and moderating role of top management support. *Cross Cultural and Strategic Management*, *30*(1), 123–141.
21. Das Gupta, R., & Roy, A. (2023). Firm environmental, social, governance and financial performance relationship contradictions: Insights from institutional environment mediation. *Technological Forecasting and Social Change*, *189*, ISSN 0040-1625.
22. Deb, D., Gillet, P., Bernard, P., & De, A. (2022). Examining the impact of corporate social responsibility on the financial performance of Indian companies. *FIIB Business Review*, *0*(0).
23. Das, M., & Rangarajan, K. (2020). Impact of policy initiatives and collaborative synergy on sustainability and business growth of Indian SMEs. *Indian Growth and Development Review*, *13*(3), 607–627.
24. Gangwar, H., Mishra, R., & Kamble, S. (2023). Adoption of big data analytics practices for sustainability development in the e-commerce supply chain: A mixed-method study. *International Journal of Quality and Reliability Management*, *40*(4), 965–989.
25. Gill, S., Kohli, M., & Satija, P. (2022). Materiality in sustainability disclosures and investment portfolio performance in the Indian context. *Journal of Sustainable Finance and Investment*, 1–23.
26. Goel, P., & Misra, R. (2017). Sustainability reporting in India: Exploring sectoral differences and linkages with financial performance. *Vision*, *21*(2), 214–224.
27. Goel, P. (2021). Rising standards of sustainability reporting in India: A study of impact of reforms in disclosure norms on corporate performance. *Journal of Indian Business Research*, *13*(1), 92–109.
28. Ghosh, D., Dutta, A., & Dutta, M. (2022). Impact of financial performance on environmental sustainability in the presence of credit constraints: Evidence from Indian manufacturing firms. *Journal of Sustainable Finance and Investment*, 1–17.
29. Jain, N. K., Choudhary, P., Panda, A., Jain, S., & Dey, P. K. (2022). Impact of institutional pressures and dynamic capabilities on sustainability performance of oil and gas sector. *International Journal of Energy Sector Management*, Vol. ahead-of-print No. ahead-of-print.
30. Gupta, H., Lawal, J. N., Orji, I. J., & Kusi-Sarpong, S. (2023). Closing the gap: The role of distributed manufacturing systems for overcoming the barriers to manufacturing sustainability. *IEEE Transactions on Engineering Management*, *70*(5), 1754–1773.
31. J., S., K.r., S., & Prasad, K. (2023) Does GRI compliance moderate the impact of sustainability disclosure on firm value. *Society and Business Review*, *18*(1), 152–174.
32. Jain, K., & Tripathi, P. S. (2023). Mapping the environmental, social and governance literature: A bibliometric and content analysis. *Journal of Strategy and Management*, Vol. ahead-of-print No. ahead-of-print.
33. Jain, S., & Raithatha, M. (2022). Risk disclosures and firm value: The role of governance in an emerging market. *International Journal of Productivity and Performance Management*, *71*(8), 3205–3227.
34. Jaisinghani, D., & Sekhon, A. K. (2022). CSR disclosures and profit persistence: Evidence from India. *International Journal of Emerging Markets*, *17*(3), 705–724.
35. Kumar, S., Sharma, A., Mishra, P., & Kaushik, N. (2023). Corporate social responsibility disclosures and earnings management: A bibliometric analysis. *International Journal of Disclosure and Governance*, *20*(1), 27–51.

36. Kumar, S., & Dua, P. (2022). Environmental management practices and financial performance: Evidence from large listed Indian enterprises. *Journal of Environmental Planning and Management*, *65*(1), 37–61.
37. Kumar, D. (2022). Economic and political uncertainties and sustainability disclosures in the tourism sector firms. *Tourism Economics*, *0*(0).
38. Kumar, K., Kumari, R., Poonia, A., & Kumar, R. (2023). Factors influencing corporate sustainability disclosure practices: Empirical evidence from Indian National Stock Exchange. *Journal of Financial Reporting and Accounting*, *21*(2), 300–321.
39. Kumar, S., Pandey, N., & Kaur, J. (2023). Fifteen years of the Social Responsibility Journal: A retrospective using bibliometric analysis. *Social Responsibility Journal*, *19*(2), 377–397.
40. Kalia, D., & Aggarwal, D. (2023). Examining impact of ESG score on financial performance of healthcare companies. *Journal of Global Responsibility*, *14*(1), 155–176.
41. Khan, P. A., Johl, S. K., & Akhtar, S. (2022). Vinculum of sustainable development goal practices and firms' financial performance: A moderation role of green innovation. *Journal of Risk and Financial Management*, *15*(3), 96.
42. Kumar, K., & Prakash, A. (2019). Developing a framework for assessing sustainable banking performance of the Indian banking sector. *Social Responsibility Journal*, *15*(5), 689–709.
43. Laskar, N., & Maji, S. G. (2016). Corporate sustainability reporting practices in India: Myth or reality? *Social Responsibility Journal*, *12*(4), 625–641.
44. Laskar, N., Chakraborty, T. K., & Maji, S. G. (2017). Corporate sustainability performance and financial performance: Empirical evidence from Japan and India. *Management and Labour Studies*, *42*(2), 88–106.
45. Laskar, N. (2018). Impact of corporate sustainability reporting on firm performance: An empirical examination in Asia. *Journal of Asia Business Studies*, *12*(4), 571–593.
46. Laskar, N. (2019). Does sustainability reporting enhance firms profitability? A study on select companies from India and South Korea. *Indian Journal of Corporate Governance*, *12*(1), 2–20.
47. M. R., F. K. (2021) Socially Responsible Investing and Sustainable Indices: A Sustainability Agenda. *Indian Journal of Corporate Governance*, *14*(2), 209–225.
48. Maji, S. G., & Lohia, P. (2023). Environmental, social and governance (ESG) performance and firm performance in India. *Society and Business Review*, *18*(1), 175–194.
49. Maji, S. G., & Kalita, N. (2022). Climate change financial disclosure and firm performance: Empirical evidence from Indian energy sector based on TCFD recommendations. *Society and Business Review*, *17*(4), 594–612.
50. Munjal, P., & Sharma, D. (2023). Determining the managerial perception on triple bottom line performance. *Journal of Financial Reporting and Accounting*, *21*(2), 322–343.
51. Oware, K. M., & Mallikarjunappa, T. (2023). Financial performance and gender diversity: The moderating and mediating effect of CSR disclosure and expenditure of listed firms in India. *Vision*, *27*(2), 243–255.
52. Oware, K. M., & David Kweku Botchway, K. (2023). Exchange and moral capital of CSR disclosure and financial distress likelihood of family management firms: Evidence from India. *Management Research Review*, *46*(4), 625–646.
53. Oware, K. M., & Iddrisu, A.-A. (2022). Moral capital of CSR and firm performance: Does a shift from voluntary to mandatory policy matter in an Indian context? *Society and Business Review*, *17*(1), 3–21.

54. Oware, K. M., Valacherry, A. K., & Mallikarjunappa, T. (2022). Do third-party assurance and mandatory CSR reporting matter to philanthropic and financial performance nexus? Evidence from India. *Social Responsibility Journal, 18*(5), 897–917.
55. Popli, M., & Raithatha, M. (2022). Implications of overwhelmed leadership: How executive job demands hinder corporate sustainability performance. *Business and Society*, *0*(0).
56. P., F., & Busru, S. A. (2021) CSR disclosure and firm performance: Evidence from an emerging market. *Corporate Governance*, *21*(4), 553–568.
57. Pratihari, S. K., & Uzma, S. H. (2018). Corporate social identity: An analysis of the Indian banking sector. *International Journal of Bank Marketing*, *36*(7), 1248–1284. https://doi.org/10.1108/IJBM-03-2017-0046
58. Prashar, A. (2023). Moderating effects on sustainability reporting and firm performance relationships: A meta-analytical review. *International Journal of Productivity and Performance Management*, *72*(4), 1154–1181.
59. Rastogi, S., & Singh, K. (2023). The impact of ESG on the bank valuation: Evidence of moderation by ICT. *Journal of Global Responsibility*, *14*(2), 273–288.
60. Singh, A. K., Zhang, Y., & Anu, . (2023). Understanding the evolution of environment, social and governance research: Novel implications from bibliometric and network analysis. *Evaluation Review*, *47*(2), 350–386.
61. Sekhon, A. K., & Kathuria, L. M. (2019). Analyzing the impact of corporate social responsibility on corporate financial performance: Evidence from top Indian firms. *Corporate Governance*, *20*(1), 143–157.
62. Saha, R., & Kabra, K. C. (2020). Corporate governance and voluntary disclosure: A synthesis of empirical studies. *Business Perspectives and Research*, *8*(2), 117–138.
63. Sharma, G. D., Talan, G., Bansal, S., & Jain, M. (2021). Is there a cost for sustainable investments: Evidence from dynamic conditional correlation. *Journal of Sustainable Finance and Investment*, 1–21.
64. Sinha, N., Sachdeva, T., & Yadav, M. P. (2018). Investigating relationship between corporate social responsibility and financial performance using structural equation modelling. *Management and Labour Studies*, *43*(3), 175–191.
65. Sehgal, V., Garg, N., & Singh, J. (2023). Impact of sustainability performance and reporting on a firm's reputation. *International Journal of System Assurance Engineering and Management*, *14*(1), 228–240.
66. Saha, R. (2023). Corporate governance, voluntary disclosure and firm valuation relationship: Evidence from top listed Indian firms. *Journal of Accounting in Emerging Economies*, Vol. ahead-of-print No. ahead-of-print.
67. Soriya, S., & Rastogi, P. (2023). The impact of integrated reporting on financial performance in India: A panel data analysis. *Journal of Applied Accounting Research*, *24*(1), 199–216.
68. Sharma, A., Kaushik, K., Awasthy, P., & Gawande, A. (2022). Leveraging text mining for trend analysis and comparison of sustainability reports: Evidence from Fortune 500 companies. *American Business Review*, *25*(2).
69. Shoeb, M., Aslam, A., & Aslam, A. (2022). Environmental accounting disclosure practices: A bibliometric and systematic review. *International Journal of Energy Economics and Policy*, *12*(4), 226–239.
70. Soriya, S., & Rastogi, P. (2022). A systematic literature review on integrated reporting from 2011 to 2020. *Journal of Financial Reporting and Accounting*, *20*(3/4), 558–579.

71. Saha, R., & Kabra, K. C. (2022). Corporate governance and voluntary disclosure: Evidence from India. *Journal of Financial Reporting and Accounting*, *20*(1), 127–160.
72. Suresha, B., Srinidhi, V. R., Verma, D., Krishna, T. A., & T. A. (2022). The impact of ESG inclusion on price, liquidity and financial performance of Indian stocks: Evidence from stocks listed in BSE and NSE ESG indices. *Investment Management and Financial Innovations*, *19*(4), 40–50.
73. Tripathi, V., & Kaur, A. (2020). Socially responsible investing: Performance evaluation of BRICS nations. *Journal of Advances in Management Research*, *17*(4), 525–547.
74. Vig, S. (2023). Environmental disclosures by Indian companies: Role of board characteristics and board effectiveness. *International Journal of Disclosure and Governance*.
75. Vig, S., & Datta, M. (2021). The impact of corporate governance on sustainable value creation: A case of selected Indian firms. *Journal of Sustainable Finance and Investment*, 1–19.
76. Vinod, M. S. S., Umesh, P., & Sivakumar, N. (2023). Impact of COVID-19 on corporate social responsibility in India – A mixed methods approach. *International Journal of Organizational Analysis*, *31*(1), 168–195.

Securing the Future through Sustainability, Health, Education, and Technology – Brig. Dr. Rajiv Divekar et al. (eds)

2 Beyond the Call of Duty for Securing Future: Analyzing the Vital Role of Indian Armed Forces in Response to Disruptive Times

Anupama Munshi[1]
Indian Army Officer and Faculty
Sneha Kumari[2]
Symbiosis School of Economics, Symbiosis International (Deemed University), Pune, India
Suruchi Pandey
Symbiosis Institute of Management Studies, Symbiosis International (Deemed University), Pune, India

Abstract

Purpose India has faced unprecedented consequences and challenges. This paper aims to highlight the unflinching support of Indian armed forces in the fight against COVID-19. The Indian Armed Forces have created COVID facilities on a war footing. This mission was accomplished by setting up the COVID hospitals in a very short duration, providing medical specialists, adding beds to the existing numbers, air evacuating the critical patients in emergency by transshipments of cryogenic oxygen containers and tankers, and stranded Indian citizens in other countries. **Design/methodology/approach** An extant and systematic literature review was carried out to develop a model/framework that was empirically tested/validated. The study is exploratory in nature. Questionnaires have been emailed to the armed forces personnel for data collection. 196 respondents from the armed forces have been selected for data collection. Snowball sampling has been selected for data collection. Data has been further analyzed using statistical software. The analyzed data has been further discussed and interpreted in the result and discussion. **Findings** Drawing from our model view, our results revolve around highlighting the key role, preparedness, and commitment of Indian armed forces, which is significant in response to the unprecedented pandemic COVID-19. However, negligence on the part of human beings has had a negative impact on relief measures for COVID 19 which resulted in increased COVID cases and disrupted disaster relief safety measures. Network building among the

[1]munshianu.17@gmail.com, [2]snehakumari1201@gmail.com

DOI: 10.1201/9781003587200-2

government, armed forces, and officials during COVID-19 led to disaster relief safety measures. **Research limitations/implications** The study is limited to the armed forces and the pandemic scenario. The study adds to the knowledge of the role of armed forces and paves the way for policy implications. The different stages of COVID–19 with different variants moderated the linkages with disaster relief safety measures. The Armed forces managed the internal as well as external security threats. External and Internal security threats lead to moderate linkages between disaster relief measures. **Originality** The study is a unique contribution toward understanding the impact of stages and severity of threats in the country during the pandemic disaster.

KEYWORDS: Disaster, Humanitarian, COVID-19, Armed forces, Social capital, Resource

1. Introduction

The first case of coronavirus was reported in India on 31st January 2020 in a student who returned to Kerala from China. COVID-19 started affecting people in March 2020, when the country had to announce a strict lockdown. There has been a rise in the number of patients affected by the Coronavirus from March to August. This has made it difficult and unpredictable for many states to strategize to control the economy. Amid all these challenges, the armed forces have been struggling to build a better economy for the country. The Indian Air Force (IAF) airlifted innumerable oxygen containers and tankers with huge capacities in numerous sorties from other nations and within India as well. Indian Navy transported oxygen to various locations in the country and carried out repairs of oxygen plants in innumerable state hospitals. IAF aircraft did sorties all over the country and crisscrossed the entire nation through its length and breadth to carry medical experts and equipment (April, 2021.instagram.com; Indian airforce). The armed forces have been involved since the beginning of the lockdown period when the country had to face difficult times from the agriculture supply chain, affected patients, transportation of essential goods, medicinal support, and sustaining livelihood. The humanitarian role of the armed forces cannot be overlooked at present. While the armed forces may find it difficult to maintain social distancing being the primary mission for the country, they have been showing their vital contribution towards controlling the virus spread in society. They have been involved in engaging themselves in supplying food resources, building up medical facilities, or providing shelters for the homeless, they have been the responders ready to indulge themselves with the external and internal threats. With resources under strain, the country's ability to sustain the economy is stressful. The period has imposed several threats be it the terrorist attacks or floods across, locust attacks, and the tension at China and India borders where the contribution of the Armed Forces cannot be explained in words. Despite facing difficult times/ situations, there has been a scarcity of research on the humanitarian role of the armed forces The research gap has driven us to study the research question What is the Humanitarian role of Armed forces in securing the future during disruptive times? The study aims to explore the role of armed forces using resource-based theory in securing the future during disruptive times.

The study is divided into nine sections. After defining the objectives of the study, the authors have undergone an extensive literature review in the next section. The third section explains the underpinning theory taken to study the objective of the study. This section is followed by results and discussions, conclusion, limitations, and implications of the study.

2. Literature Review

On April 23^{rd,}2021, the Ministry of Defence granted an extension to all the Short Service Commissioned doctors in the Armed Forces Medical Services who were due to retire on 31st December 2021. It enhanced the number of doctors by 238. On April 30th the number of oxygenated beds was supplemented to 4220 from 1821since 19 April 2021(Indian army.nic.in; Indian Express; TOI,30Apr 2021; May 7, 2021Abhishek Bhalla)

In addition to providing extensive medical assistance to veterans and their dependents, Military Hospitals (MIL)across the country are now supporting the civil administrations also (Siddiqui Huma, May 03, 2021, Financial Express Online). Indian armed forces (Army, Air Force and Navy) have launched operation CO-JEET to help and support the civil administration to restore oxygen supply chains, strengthen medical infrastructure, and safeguard the mental wellness of people. Indian armed forces appealed to its medical services veterans to register themselves on one sehat portal which is an online triservice teleconsultation and provide their teleconsultation to the countrymen (1 May2021, Indian army.nic.in). The Ministry of Defence has approved 50 Armed Forces Medical Services hospitals (42 Army, 5 Airforce, 3 Navy) as dedicated and mixed COVID hospitals where civilians can also be admitted on being referred by state health authorities (2 May, 2021, Indian army.nic.in).

Given the calamitous second wave of COVID-19 in India, doctors and other medical staff from key bases, different recruitment offices, National Cadet Corps, and those on staff appointments have been recalled to assist civil authorities in dealing with the unexpected surge in coronavirus infections (4May2021, Indian army.nic.in). Indian army mobilized two Field hospitals from Northeast to Patna by air to assist the state govt in fighting the sudden surge of COVID cases in the state by establishing a 500-bed hospital in Patna and 100 ICU beds. (6 May2021, Indian army.nic.in). Through the online portal Sehat opd.in, the Indian army provided 5151 consultations for 696 hours with 3-minute average waiting period. Because of sudden surge of COVID in the month of April 2021, 400 Ex AMC /SSC medical officers were recruited under tour of duty on a contract basis for 11 months (Indian army.nic.in). Indian Army operationalized fully oxygenated 750-bed hospitals in Delhi, Ahmedabad & Lucknow, and 250 beds in Varanasi. Western Command of the Indian army operationalized 100 bed COVID Hospital in Chandigarh.

Western Command of Indian Army operationalized a 100-bed hospital for COVID at Sh. Atal Bihari Vajpayee Govt Medical college in Haryana.(11May2021). Towards the fight against COVID - 19, Surya command of the Indian Army set 50 bed COVID Care Centers at Joshimath, Pithoragarh, Lansdowne & Ranikhet(13May). Eastern command of the Indian army established 5 ICU and 45 Oxygen beds in Tezpur Medical College. Indian Army reactivated a non-operational oxygen plant at Meerut district of 20T capacity on daily basis (18May,202, 2021, Indian army.nic.in). Corps of Engineers developed a low-pressure oxygen system that converts liquid oxygen to oxygen gas and ensures its availability to patients. Indian army provided 100 bullnose fillings for oxygen cylinders to Goa medical college on 19 May2021 2021, Indian army.nic.in). Indian armed forces augmented the medical infrastructure of Karnataka state administration and assisted in setting up a 100-bed COVID care center at Bengaluru.). Army Engineer task force in Odisha & West Bengal was involved in rescue & relief operations during cyclone tauktae and extending required aid to the locals. (26 May, 2021,Indian army.nic.in). Indian Army also rescued 384 persons from an avalanche site in Uttarakhand. (24 April,2021, 2021, Indian army.nic.in). IAF aircraft, C-17 Globe master -III and IL-76 airlifted 39 oxygen containers of 670 MT capacity from UAE and Singapore. Aircraft IL-76's were also involved in carrying equipment and medical personnel of the army from Delhi, for setting three oxygen plants in Dimapur and ferrying about 15 T of supplies for establishing a COVID Hospital in Lucknow.

Four cryogenic oxygen containers were airlifted from Singapore to India in an IAFL-17. Aircraft C-17 airlifted cryogenic oxygen tankers from Hindan airbase and Bhopal to Ranchi. (23,24 April2021, instagram.com/indianairforce). IAFC -17 shuttled between 7 cities across the country for airlifting cryogenic oxygen containers to Jamnagar, Ranchi and Bhubneshwar. In addition to aircraft within the country, containers were being airlifted from Singapore, Dubai, and Bangkok (29 April 2021, instagram.com/indianairforce). IAFL-17s were engaged in airlifting cryogenic oxygen containers from Frankfurt, Germany to Hindan and Oxygen cylinders from the UK to Chennai. (1 May 2021) Till 02 May 2021, IAF undertook 192 domestic and 30 international sorties. They airlifted 134 oxygen cylinders domestically and 50 internationally. The airlifting of O_2 containers, medical personnel and equipment continued 24/7 throughout the country. (03 May 2021, instagram.com/ indianairforce). On 4th May2021, aircraft IAFL-17 air transported oxygen cylinders from the UK to Chennai (instagram.com/ Indian air force).

Airlifting of oxygen containers by AIFL-17 from Australia to Chennai and airlifting of oxygen cylinders from Singapore to India by IL-76 was carried out on 05thMay 2021.100 bed COVID Care facility was made operational for the general public at Air Force Station Jalehalli, manned by medical personnel of

Airforce hospital Bengaluru. IAF medical personnel were augmented at COVID Hospital set up by DRDO exclusively for civilians at Delhi, Ahmedabad, and Lucknow to manage cases of COVID pneumonia.(06 May2021, instagram.com/indianairforce).

IAFL-17 airlifted cryogenic oxygen containers and medical equipment from Israel. IL-76 ferried oxygen containers from Singapore to Panagarh. Pan India airlifting of oxygen concentrating ventilators, medicines and essential COVID19 medical equipment was underway by IAF, AN-32, and C-130 aircraft. (08 May,2021, instagram.com/indianairforce).IAF, IL-76 airlifted cryogenic oxygen containers from Indonesia, oxygen generators from France, and medical equipment from Germany by IAFL-17s.The various countries from where airlifting has been done include Australia, Singapore, Indonesia, Thailand, UAE, Israel, France, Germany, UK, Belgium, Netherland, and Qatar.(instagram.com/indianairforce). During cyclone Tautkae in May 2021,two C-130 aircraft airlifted 3 NDRF teams of 126 people and equipment for Bhubaneshwar to Jamnagar. (15,16 May2021,instagram.com/indianairforce). IAF aircraft were engaged in the transportation of NDRF teams and helping with cyclone Yaas. As of 06 June 2021, IAF had undertaken numerous sorties & loads, and flying hours & covered air miles as shown in Table 2.1 (instagram.com/indianairforce).

Table 2.1 Sorties and flying hours of IAF

		Domestic	International
Sorties	1796	1587	209
Flying hours	3554	2550	1004
Loads (T)	14898	12898	2000
Tankers /Containers	840	690	150
Air Miles	1397014	975439	421575

Source: Indian Navy

On May 5th, a 200-bed COVID care center was set up at Naval Dockyard Visakhapatnam for the treatment of defense civilians with mild to moderate symptoms of COVID-19. For the transportation of liquid medical oxygen-filled cryogenic containers and medical equipment through the Indian ocean, the Indian navy launched Operation Samudra Setu. Patients were airlifted from L & M islands and admitted to INHS Sanjeevani, the naval hospital at Kochi. INHS Sanjeevani offered 10 jumbo oxygen cylinders of 7000 litre capacity to taluk hospital in Ernakulam district of Kerala. INS Chilka was set up with a 10-bed isolation center for patients with mild COVID symptoms.(04 May 2021, Indian navy.nic.in).The three warships INS Trikand, Tabar & Kochi ferried 140 T liquid medical oxygen tanks and 1400 oxygen cylinders from Kuwait and Doha (07 May,2021, Indian navy.nic.in).On 10th May 2021 INS Airavat got 216 MT cryogenic oxygen tanks about 4000 MT oxygen cylinders,10000 rapid antigen test kits, and other critical COVID medical stores from Singapore. INS Kochi and Tabar brought five 135 MT, liquid medical oxygen-filled containers and 1200MT oxygen cylinders from Kuwait.60 bed COVID care center with 12 oxygen support beds, 2 beds with oxygen concentrators, and 46 beds with nebulizers and steamers was set up at INS Kalinga for the civilian population in Bheemunipatnam region (11 May 2021, Indian navy.nic.in). INS tarkash brought 54 MT liquid medical oxygen containers and 230 plus oxygen cylinders through French mission as part of oxygen solidarity bridge and oxygen from the India diaspora in Qatar(12 May). On 13 May, the first batch of ten civilians was trained by the public health officer of INS Venduruthy. Two teams from Karwar audited oxygen infrastructure at Govt hospitals in all 12 talukas of Uttara Indian Navy was involved in search and rescue operations in cyclone tauktae in west Bengal, Kochi, and Gujrat.INS Jalashwa got essential supplies from Brunee and Singapore. Indian navy assisted civil administration in disaster relief operations to mitigate damages caused by cyclone tauktae. They did road clearance and rescued villages by clearing fallen trees and electric poles.(19 May,2021, Indian navy.nic.in).

Vaccination centers were set up for the local population in Goa by the Indian Navy. Mobile oxygen generation plants (oxygen on wheels) were designed and developed by naval dockyard Visakhapatnam.National Disaster technical team conceived and developed two oxygen generation plants, each having capacity of 100 liters/minute to provide a direct feed to any hospital's pipeline system(21May2021,Indian navy.nic.in). Samudra Setu II launched by INS Tarkash reached Mumbai carrying 2 containers of 40 MT liquid medical oxygen and 760 oxygen cylinders along with other medical supplies from Qatar and Bahrain. (24 May 2021, Indian navy.nic.in). 270 MT of liquid medical oxygen from Kuwait & UAE, comprising of 11 ISO containers, 2 semitrailers, and 1200 oxygen cylinders were shipped to India by the Indian navy.Indian navy transported oxygen on wheels plant to Palasa COVID care center and trained staff in the operation of the plant (25 May 2021, Indian navy.nic.in). INS Karanja, a COVID designated hospital treated civilian patients in addition to defense personnel and ex-servicemen and their dependents (26 May 2021, Indian navy.nic.in). As a part of Op Samudrasetu II,INS Shardul of the Indian Navy carried 4 ISO,80 MT liquid medical oxygen containers to supplement oxygen requirements in the country. The Indian Navy's disaster relief team was deployed in the distribution of food packets and assisting people in Balasore in coordination with state authorities. (28,29May2021, Indian navy.nic.in) INS Kolkatta and Airavat were transshipped from Kuwait and Singapore with 4000 plus oxygen cylinders,40 MT oxygen-filled containers and tankers. INS Sharda and MPV Meghna were deployed as oxygen Express for ferrying oxygen cylinders to and fro from L& M islands along with doctors, assistants, medical supplies, PPE kits, RADT kits. masks, gloves, nebulizers and SPO2 probes. Triservice medical team of approx. 380 personnel were deputed to a 100-bed childcare hospital in Ahmedabad and provided yeoman service.The naval medical team of 170 personnel comprising of administrative components, medical specialists, medical officers and naval hospitals provided support to the entire nation. Indian Navy's disaster relief team was deployed in the distribution of food packets and assisting people in Balasore coordination with state authorities (30May 2021,Indian navy.nic.in). Installation of a Medical Intensive Care Unit (MICU) was done on board all-weather aircraft (ALH) in INS Hansa by HAL, enabling the Indian Navy to undertake the medical evacuation of critical patients by air even in unfavourable weather conditions. Indian Navy launched operation Samudra Setu II to ship COVID relief material which included filled medical oxygen cryogenic cans, cylinders and associated medical equipment from various countries to India. Naval teams of Naval area Karnataka were deployed for ensuring sustained functioning of medical oxygen infrastructure with COVID-19 hospitals of all 12 talukas of Uttara Kannada district for May, which included attending to defects in leakage of the oxygen distribution system in various hospitals in the district. They ensured sustained availability of oxygen in rural areas of the state. (06 June 2021,Indian navy.nic.in; 24 June2021, Indian navy.nic.in).

3. Theoretical Framework and Hypothesis Development

Resource-based Theory involves tangible and intangible resources. Tangible resources include Physical resources, Human capital resources, and Organizational resources. Intangible resources include knowledge, skills, and competency.

3.1 Tangible Resources

The humanitarian supply chains suggest that tangible, intangible resources, social participation, network, and contingent factors can propose a framework for sustainable humanitarian supply chain management. In our framework, we propose that more the tangible resources like finance, technology, and organization, the better will be the relief operations.

3.2 Intangible Resources

The intangible resources like knowledge, skills, and competency may also have an impact on sustainable humanitarian supply chains. Training should be provided to humanitarian aid workers. To complete any work successfully it is essential to make a strategy. During humanitarian disasters, human capital uses their knowledge and skills more intensively than the producers of tangible resources. Knowledge and experience sharing needs to happen across NGOs from different regions. This helps in better management during humanitarian disasters.

3.3 Social Capital Theory

Social Capital is the goodwill and trust available within a group of people (Muller, 2014). Despite the vague nature of the theory, there is growing consensus among authors for exploring different aspects of social capital. Social capital consists of 3 dimensions namely structure (social intentions), relational (trust), and cognitive (common goal) (Nahapiet,1998). These dimensions contribute to the performance gains of any organization. The dimensions result in information sharing, information volume, and information diversity (Tantardini & Kroll, 2015). In each humanitarian operation, different organizations take a lead role in planning, coordinating, and distributing aid. The organization may be a military, government, local or international NGO. This results in a common goal to provide shared representation, interpretation, and system for humanitarian supply chain management (HSC) in the disaster area. The management of any deadliest disaster is based on the social participation, network building, and collaboration of the stakeholders. As stated earlier in the guidelines for managing HSC, smaller disasters can be managed at the local level, medium disasters at the regional level, and for big disasters, global networks can be leveraged for resources (Samii et al., 2017). The global network involves social relationships and trusts with a common cause of restoring the economic standing of the community affected by the disaster in the shortest possible time. Fawcett and Fawcett (2013) have reported in their study that HSC enables efforts to reduce human suffering. For any HSC to succeed, collaboration among participants plays an important role. Thus, social capital is an important component of the proposed framework.

4. Theoretical Framework

The section shows the theoretical framework as shown in Fig. 2.1. The linkages between the constructs have been further explained.

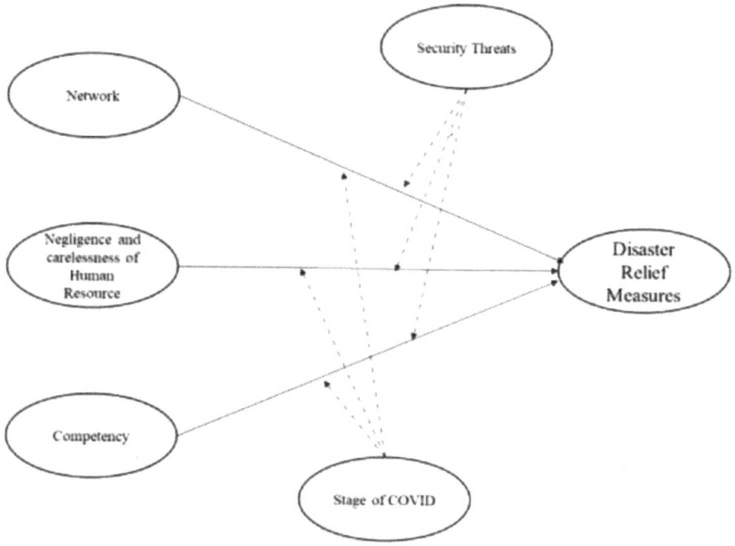

Fig. 2.1 Theoretical framework

4.1 Linkage between Competency and Disaster Relief Safety Measures

Armed Forces are enriched with knowledge, skills, and competency. The competency of the Indian Armed Officers has resulted in disaster relief safety measures. Indian Armed Forces are well equipped with knowledge, skills, and capability for giving their best for disaster relief safety measures. The militaries across the globe have gone through important changes in technology and transformation in their organization. This has changed how militaries organize and fight (Munshi & Pandey,2017). The military forces could provide additional resources that are deployed if the pandemics have the potential to impact the economy significantly.

H1: Competency of the Armed Forces has a strong positive impact on Disaster relief safety measures

4.2 Linkage between negligence by Humans and Disaster Relief Safety Measures

The negligence by humans during COVID-19 has led to ignorance of the safety measures to be followed during COVID. The negligence by humans has increased the number of COVID cases and disrupted disaster relief safety measures. Seybolt (2009), writes that Humanitarian military intervention has saved life by applying different methods and techniques in various circumstances. He also highlights that humanitarian military intervention is not justifiable without some fair prospect of success. However Humanitarian military intervention will be an exception and not the rule for the future.

H2: Negligence by the human resources led to an adverse negative impact on Disaster relief safety measures

4.3 Linkage between Network and Disaster Relief Safety Measures

Network among the government, armed forces, and officials during COVID-19 can result in disaster relief safety measures. Svoboda (2014) mentions that though the field of operation for military and humanitarian actors has been the same for a long, their objectives and the means to achieve them differ considerably. The dialogue between the military and humanitarian actors must take place to provide effective and timely aid in conflict and disaster-affected areas. It is also necessary that they are consistently and strategically engaged at the headquarters level as well as in the field to agree on core issues of competence and responsibility and recognize the differences in their approach and aim.

H3: Network building led to Disaster relief safety measures

4.4 Moderating Effect of Stages of COVID and Disaster Relief Safety Measures

COVID-19 affected the population at different stages. Stage 1 came with the first phase of COVID-19 and led to a national lockdown accompanied by the trend of patients. Stage 2 came up with the second phase of COVID-19 which led to an increase in the number of patients and mortalities. Stage 3 came up with the third phase of COVID-19 leading to the occurrence of the delta variant virus. The stages of COVID have influenced disaster relief safety measures.

H4: Stages of COVID–19 with different variants moderated the linkages with disaster relief safety measures

4.5 Moderating Effect of security threats and Disaster Relief Safety Measures

The country was affected by external and internal security threats. The Armed forces managed the internal as well as external threats. The period was influenced by the increasing growth of COVID-19 and the attacks at the Indo-China border.

H5: External and Internal security threats lead to moderate linkages between disaster relief measures

Table 2.2 explains the constructs and items.

Table 2.2 Constructs and Variables

Sr.	Construct	Variables	Author (Year)
1	Negligence of Humans	Ignorance of the COVID rules by Human Population Break of the safety precautions Increase in the Crowd and travels.	Dhar et al., 2021
2	Competency	Knowledge Skills Capability	Barney, 1991; Chomilier, 2002; Grant, 1991; Shih and Pierson, 2017; Kumari et al., 2017 & Kumari, 2017
3	Network	Trust Coordination Social Participation	Schniederjans et al., 2016; Pateman, 2013; Samii et al. (2002)

5. Research Methodology

The study is exploratory in nature. Literature review and experts have been consulted to draw questionnaires for the study. The questionnaire has been pretested from 5 experts including government officers and bureaucrats. Questionnaires have been emailed to the armed forces personnel for data collection. 196 respondents from the armed forces have been selected for data collection. Snowball sampling has been selected for data collection. Data has been further analyzed using statistical software. The analyzed data has been further discussed and interpreted in the result and discussion.

6. Data Analysis and Findings

The data collected has been checked for reliability and normality. Reliability has been checked through Cronbach's alpha. It was found that the Cronbach alpha was 0.7, which shows that the responses are consistent (Table 2.3). Composite Reliability and Average Variance Error have been tested for validity. The average Variance Error is greater than 0.5. The composite validity for the data has been found to be greater than 0.7. The Average Variance extracted and Composite Reliability are shown in Table 2.3.

Table 2.3 Reliability and validity of the construct

Construct	Cronbach alpha	Composite Reliability	Average Variance Extracted	Full collinearity VIFs
Network	0.558	0.736	0.40	1.487
Negligence of HR	0.778	0.872	0.70	2.266
Competency	0.700	0.817	0.53	2.064
DRSM	0.789	0.848	0.50	1.334

Discriminant Validity has been further checked using Fornell & Larcker, 1981. The square root of the Average Variance Error has been found greater than the correlation among the factors.

Table 2.4 Discriminant validity

	Network	Negligence of HR	Competency	DRSM
Network	0.616			
Negligence of HR	0.288	0.834		
Competency	0.360	0.580	0.729	
DRSM	0.299	-0.034	0.264	0.671

Figure 2.2 shows the validation of the model. It has been found that 43 percent of the variation in disaster relief safety measures is influenced by the negligence of HR, competency, and network.

Table 2.5 shows the result of hypothesis testing. The path coefficients are mentioned in Table 2.5.

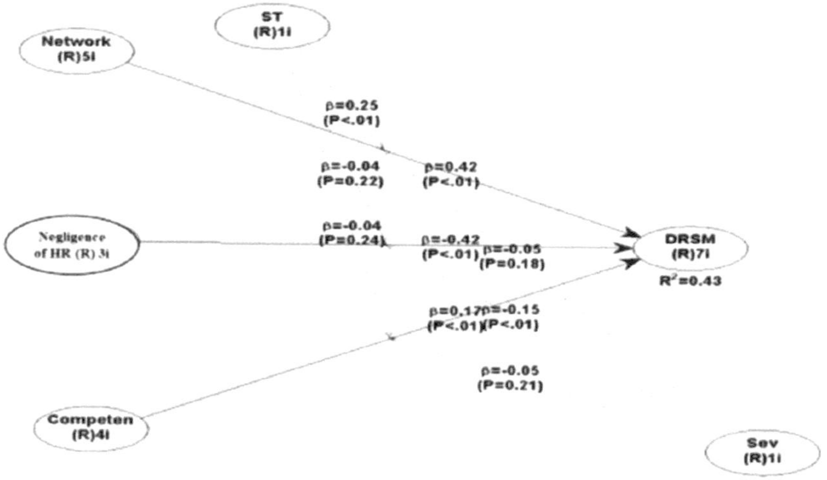

Fig. 2.2 Validation of the model

Table 2.5 Path coefficients and hypothesis results

Linkages		Path Coefficients	P-Value	Results
Network	DRSM	0.424	<0.001	Hypothesis Accepted
Neg HR	DRSM	-0.425	<0.001	Hypothesis Accepted
Competency	DRSM	0.173	0.001	Hypothesis Accepted
ST*Netw	DRSM	0.252	<0.001	Hypothesis Accepted
ST*MPan	DRSM	-0.044	0.220	Hypothesis Rejected
ST*Comp	DRSM	-0.040	0.243	Hypothesis Rejected
Sev*Net	DRSM	-0.051	0.185	Hypothesis Rejected
Sev*MPa	DRSM	-0.152	0.003	Hypothesis Accepted
Sev*Com	DRSM	-0.046	0.206	Hypothesis Rejected

The network and social capital have supported monitoring the COVID cases. The result shows that the network and competency have a significant impact on humanitarian relief measures. However, the Stages of COVID along with the severity have moderated the linkages to the relief measures. The ignorance shown by the people towards the disaster has led to a negative impact on the relief safety measures.

The Table 2.6 shows the effect size of the coefficients. The linkages in network, and negligence of humans have a large effect as the effect size is greater than 0.14. It has been found that the quality indices for model fitness are in the acceptable range.

Table 2.6 Effect size of the coefficients

Linkages		Effect Size of the Coefficients
Network	DRSM	0.190
Neg HR	DRSM	0.160
Competency	DRSM	0.053
ST*Netw	DRSM	0.072
ST*MPan	DRSM	0.012
ST*Comp	DRSM	0.009
Sev*Net	DRSM	0.006
Sev*MPa	DRSM	0.041
Sev*Com	DRSM	0.007

7. Discussions

There is no doubt that the knowledge, work culture and awareness of Indian armed forces have resulted in a significant and extensive impact on their humanitarian role during pandemic situations. The disciplined, skilled and committed human resource of the Indian military has always helped in building knowledge, competency and skills. Round the clock, they operated quarantine facilities and hospitals, and took on procurement and repair of equipment and materials, besides provisioning of various services and works essential to support the ongoing effort against of the nation to fight the pandemic COVID-19. They set up the COVID hospitals, ICU beds and trauma centers in record time and contributed for decantation and distribution of oxygen, the production and distribution of PPE kits, masks, oximeters, surgical gloves, hand sanitizers. They worked tirelessly to strategize and monitor steps to provide relief to COVID-19 patients. The Indian Air Force with their aircraft has assisted to transport doctors, men, and materials to and from remote parts of the nation and other countries.15 tons of medical assistance was provided to Wuhan in February 2020. People were also provided assistance to reach back to their countries. The second aircraft departed to Tehran for bringing five hundred and twenty-nine samples for COVID-19 investigation and fifty-eight Indian citizens. 6.2 tons of medicines were also brought by C-130J Super Hercules to the Maldives. Medical assistance was provided every now and then to foreign countries. AN 32 aircraft airlifted personnel on 6th Apr 2020 and thirty-five hundred kg of medical equipment of the Indian Council of Medical Research from Chennai to Bhubaneshwar. The medical equipment were used to set up a testing lab and other medical facilities in Orissa. Crisis Management Cells (CMC) have been set up for providing quick responses at headquarters. Indian navy launched Operation Samudra Setu to augument the national effort to fight COVID 19. Indian Naval Ships, carried thousands of filled oxygen cylinders, oxygen concentrators, tons of liquid medical oxygen (LMO) from all over the world to India as a part of the operation Samudra setu. Their technical teams repaired and audited oxygen plants in the remotest hospitals and also provided training for the same to the people in the hospitals.

8. Implications

The study is a pioneer work highlighting the importance of the armed forces during the pandemic situation. The study has listed out the extensive and consistent work done by the armed forces and has a theoretical contribution to academicians and researchers. The study paves a way for managerial implication in designing the road map for building a future strategy for the humanitarian role of armed forces during such disastrous situations. *First*, it highlights the significance of the Armed Forces in monitoring the external and internal threats to the nation. Despite the external threats in the country armed forces have showed a significant contribution towards controlling the pandemic scenario. *Second*, the study paves the importance of armed forces which need to be explored. The work should be highlighted so that the human population can come to know their vital contributions to the nation. *Third*, the study through the resources and social capital highlights that there is a need for policy interventions to make the working conditions better. There is a need to provide significant facilities to the armed forces. *Fourth*, the study explores that the Armed Forces are always ready for any national threat which shows their commitment towards the nation. There is a need to understand the fact nationwide that the country cannot sustain itself without the indispensable role of the Armed Forces.

9. Conclusion, Limitations and Future Scope

The armed forces have provided much-needed aid to the civil authorities through tangible and intangible resources during the unprecedented situation brought in by COVID-19 in the country. Through primary and secondary data, the study has tried to map the resource-based theory with the humanitarian role of the Armed Forces. It has been studied that the Armed Forces have supplied the essential commodities across the borders and have successfully overcome the internal and external challenges in the face of the country. The integration of the resources and the humanitarian role has been studied by undertaking data collection from the Armed Forces personnel. The Indian Army, Navy, and Air Forces have been consistently and simultaneously fighting with the internal enemy in the form ofCOVID-19 pandemic and external security threats on across borders. The Armed Force Personnel have tried to utilize their tangible and intangible resources. They are rich in knowledge, skills, and competency. The Armed Forces have been able to monitor the internal and external challenges by utilizing their intangible resources. These resources as shown in the results have led to a significant positive impact on the humanitarian logistics role of the Armed Forces during pandemic situations. The present study is limited to the armed forces personnel. The study can be further extended by comparing the perception of civil personnel and armed force personnel towards the humanitarian logistics role of the Armed Forces in pandemic relief operations to find out the gap.

REFERENCES

1. Pandit, R. (2021), COVID-19: Emergency financial powers granted to armed forces, https://timesofindia.indiatimes.com/india/armed-forces-get-emergency-financial-powers-amid-COVID-crisis/articleshow/82330049.cms, as retrieved on 1st May, 2021.
2. Curran, P. J., West, S. G., & Finch, J. F. (1996). The robustness of test statistics to non-normality and specification error in confirmatory factor analysis. *Psychological methods*, 1(*1*), 16.
3. Dubey, R., Gunasekaran, A., & Ali, S. S. (2015). Exploring the relationship between leadership, for green supply chain. *International Journal of Production Economics*, 160, 120–132.
4. Eva Svoboda (April 2014),The interaction between humanitarian and military actors: where do we go from here? Humanitarian Policy Group, https://www.odi.org/sites/odi.org.uk/files/odi-assets/publications-opinion-files/8929.pdf.
5. Global aid, Indian Armed Forces help in fighting COVID -19, Huma Siddiqui | ,May 03, 2021
6. Farnell, C. & Larcker, D. F. (1981). Evaluating structural models with unobservable variables and measurement error. *Journal of Marketing Research*, 28, pp. 39–50.
7. Vardhan, H. (2021) Negligence towards COVID-19 norms behind rising cases: Vardhan, https://www.business-standard.com/article/current-affairs/negligence-towards-COVID-19-norms-behind-rising-cases-vardhan-121031501039_1.html, as retrieved on 3rd May, 2021.
8. Coronavirus in India: Is public negligence causing surge in cases?https://www.dw.com/en/coronavirus-in-india-is-public-negligence-causing-surge-in-cases/a-54394810, as retrieved on 3rd May, 2021.
9. Negligence towards COVID-19 appropriate behaviour behind rising cases: Vardhan, https://m.economictimes.com/news/politics-and-nation/negligence-towards-COVID-19-appropriate-behaviour-behind-rising-cases-vardhan/articleshow/81514214.cms, as retrieved on 3rd May, 2021.
10. Pandit, R. (2021). COVID-19: Emergency financial powers granted to armed forces, http://timesofindia.indiatimes.com/articleshow/82330049.cms?utm_source=contentofinterest&utm_medium=text&utm_campaign=cppst, as retrieved on 3rd May, 2021.
11. Armed forces recalling medical officers from key bases for deployment at COVID care facilities, https://economictimes.indiatimes.com/news/defence/armed-forces-recalling-medical-officers-from-key-bases-for-deployment-at-COVID-care-facilities/articleshow/82382441.cms, as retrieved on 3rd May, 2021.
12. Pubby, M. (2021). How the Ministry of Defence is fighting COVID-19, https://economictimes.indiatimes.com/news/defence/ministry-of-defences-contribution-to-fight-COVID-19/articleshow/75075456.cms, as retrieved on 3rd May, 2021.
13. Armed Forces given emergency financial powers to combat COVID, https://indianexpress.com/article/india/armed-forces-given-emergency-financial-powers-to-combat-COVID-7297395/, as retrieved on 3rd May, 2021.

14. COVID-19: Armed forces swing into action in battle against pandemic, https://timesofindia.indiatimes.com/india/COVID-19-armed-forces-swing-into-action-in-battle-against-pandemic/articleshow/82225134.cms, as retrieved on 3rd May, 2021.
15. IAF conducts 160 sorties to facilitate oxygen supply across India, https://timesofindia.indiatimes.com/india/iaf-conducts-160-sorties-to-facilitate-oxygen-supply-across-india/articleshow/82328792.cms april 2021, as retrieved on 3rd May, 2021.
16. Indian Air Force, Official Instagram Page Of IAF, https://www.instagram.com/indianairforce/ as retrived on 3rd May, 2021.
17. Indian Air Force, https://www.instagram.com/indianarmy.adgpi/ as retrieved on 3rd May, 2021.
18. Humanitarian Military Intervention The Conditions for Success and Failure Taylor B. Seybolt,https://www.sipri.org/sites/default/files/2018-10/sipri08seybolt.pdf, as retrieved on 3rd May, 2021.
19. Indian Army sets up COVID cell to coordinate aid with civil authorities, May 7, 2021Abhishek Bhalla, as retrieved on 3rd May, 2021.
20. Indian Express, Armed forces in coronavirus outbreak battle: their role, procedures for requisition, 10 April,2020, ttps://indianexpress.com/article/explained/indian-army-coronavirus-outbreak-role-procedures-requisition-6355513/, as retrieved on 3rd May, 2021.
21. Kapucu,N.(2011).The role of the military in disaster response in the U.S. *European Journal of Economics and Political studies*,4(2),6–33.
22. Manu Pubby, ET Bureau (April 10 ,2020) ,How the Ministry of Defence is fighting COVID-19, https://economictimes.indiatimes.com/news/defence/ministry-of-defences-contribution-to-fight-COVID-19/articleshow/75075456.cms?from=mdr, as retrieved on 22nd June 2021.
23. Munshi,A. And Pandey, S. (2017). Perspective of Indian soldiers towards leadership and inclusion of women in Army. *Research journal of Management sciences*, 6(*3*), 24–30.
24. *Narayanan CS Dr (Lt Gen)*,Coronavirus: Armed forces' response to the COVID-19 pandemic in India, April 22, 2020,https://www.financialexpress.com/defence/coronavirus-armed-forces-response-to-the-COVID-19-pandemic-in-india/1936604/, as retrieved on 2nd April 2021.
25. Nomani, M. Z. M. & Sherwani, F. (2020). Security and Safety of Health Care Professionals During COVID-19 Pandemic in the Context of Epidemic Diseases (Amendment) Ordinance, 2020. *International Journal on Emerging Technologies*, 11(*4*): 23–26.
26. Regional Humanitarian Civil-Military Coordination (UN-CMCoord) - Operational Guidance on the Interaction with Armed Actors in the Context of the COVID-19 Response for Asia-Pacific Region,9 Apr 2020, https://reliefweb.int/report/world/regional-humanitarian-civil-military-coordination-un-cmcoord-operational-guidance, as retrieved on 22nd June 2021.
27. The Role of the Military in Humanitarian Emergencies, University of Oxford, 29-31 October 1995.
28. Dhar, R., Pethusamy, K., Talukdar, J., Karmakar, A., Kumar, A., & Karmakar, S. (2021). The curious case of COVID-19: Its murky origin, negligence and a botched international attempt for a cover-up. Asian Journal of Medical Sciences, 12(7), 146–148.
29. The use of military assets in the humanitarian response to natural disasters, Report on Wilton Park Conference 994,September 2009.
30. www.indianarmy.nic.in, https://indianarmy.gov.in/home, as retrieved on 2nd August 2021.

Note: All the figures and tables in this chapter were made by the authors.

*Securing the Future through Sustainability, Health, Education, and Technology –
Brig. Dr. Rajiv Divekar et al. (eds)*
 ISBN 978-1-032-95922-1

3 Assessment of Efficacy of Alcohol Based Hand Sanitizers

Vanishree Pabalkar[1]
Symbiosis Institute of Management Studies,
Symbiosis International (Deemed University) Pune, India

Ruby Chanda[2]
Symbiosis Institute of Management Studies,
Symbiosis International (Deemed University) Pune, India

ABSTRACT: Purpose/objectives: Hand Sanitizer has become an important part of our life even Post COVID-19 and a large number of people in India have started using Hand Sanitizers for the first time. The study intends to study on the efficacy of sanitisers that are equipped with alcohol as a base, along with the factors motivating consumers' purchase intention regarding hand Sanitizers with help of consumption values theory, subjective norms and health consciousness, and also to investigate whether consumption values, subjective norm, health consciousness and purchase intention significantly differ between Pre and Post COVID-19 consumers of Hand sanitizers. Though there are several studies conducted on the usage process of Hand sanitisers, there is no study that has focussed on assessing the efficacy of alcohol-based hand sanitisers. Hence, the current study has been undertaken to assess the efficacy.

Research Methodology: Analytical tools of the Scopus database and Web of Science were used to conduct the research and to draw analysis. An investigation of the literature was carried out from reputed journal publications. The data was analysed using techniques like Hypothesis testing and one-way analysis of variance. An online questionnaire survey was used to gather the data by convenience sampling method. According to the results of ANOVA Pre COVID-19 consumers show greater purchase intention compared to Post COVID-19 consumers. This research indicated that the key influencing factors on Hand Sanitizer purchase intention include emotional value, social value, subjective norms, health consciousness, conditional value, and functional value.

Findings/Conclusion: This research adds to the preliminary yet critical insights for successful hand sanitizer promotion as there is no prior research in this area.

[1]vanishree.p@sims.edu, [2]ruby.chanda@sims.edu

DOI: 10.1201/9781003587200-3

These findings have implications for the hand sanitizer companies, industry, and retailers.

Originality/contribution to the body of knowledge: The study has sought to make an original contribution to the existing body of knowledge by way of literature. A thorough quantitative analysis has been carried out through SPSS.

Limitation/scope: The research included research papers from the databases that include Scopus and Web of Science. The primary data has been collected and the quantitative data extends to draw the concrete analysis.

Practical/social/managerial implications: The current study would provide valuable insights for the prospective researchers. The guidelines on the theories would provide the basis for their research.

KEYWORDS: COVID-19, Efficacy, Consumption Values, Hand Sanitizer, Alcohol based Hand Rub, Purchase intention, Subjective norms, Health Consciousness, Consumer behaviour

1. Introduction

1.1 Consumer Behaviour

Consumer behaviour is defined as the study of an individual's decision to spend their time, money, and efforts to buy a product. According to Schiffman & Kanuk, (2014) consumer behaviour is the behaviour displayed by a consumer seeking, buying, using, assessing, and disposing of goods and services which they believe will meet their requirement.

COVID-19 previously known as novel coronavirus originated from Wuhan, China in late 2019 and by March 11, 2020 was declared as a pandemic by World Health Organisation (WHO). Pandemic was declared as the life-threatening virus, (WHO, 2010). Soon it spiralled across 213 countries affecting 22.6 million people across the world (WHO,2020). As of 21 August 2020, India is the 3rd worst-hit country with 2.19 million affected cases (Business Standard, 2020). During this COVID-19 pandemic, consumers all around the world adopted unusual buying behaviour. For example, surging demand for a lot of fmcg products in almost each country around the world, and unprecedented purchasing of tissue rolls in Hong Kong and Australia (Altsdter & Hong, 2020). A similar kind of behaviour was also noticed among Indian Consumers (Singh and Rakshit, 2020). Another item that saw the spike in sales is Hand sanitizer (Nielsen, 2020; Svenska Dagbladet, 2020).

1.2 The Originality of the Study

A similar kind of spike in sales of Hand sanitizer was first observed worldwide when 60 million people were infected by H1N1 Flu in the USA in the year

2009 and WHO and CDC guidelines recommended the use of Hand Sanitizers. (Livemint, 2020). More than 150 manufacturers have started producing Hand Sanitizers looking at the sudden surge of demand (Bloomberg Quint, 2020).

Consumers today spend millions of dollars each year on the hand sanitizer. (Qureshi,2019) found in their study that hand and body care category was bought on Impulse the most amongst the personal hygiene purchases under hair care, facial care, along with body care. According to a forecast by a company Fior Markets which does market research, the demand could reach 2.1 billion Dollars by the year 2027 for hand sanitizer and notices the lingering impact of the COVID-19 on the sector's growth potential. Along with the world, India has also witnessed an increase in sales of hand sanitizers.

1.3 Research Questions

RQ 1. Will there be any difference in the purchase of Hand sanitizers pre and post COVID-19

1.4 Research Objectives

This research is conducted with the following objective:

- To assess the efficacy of Alcohol based hand sanitisers
- To measure the factors influencing consumer purchase intention towards hand sanitizers
- To determine whether female and male consumers buying decision of hand sanitizer differ significantly
- To determine whether pre and post COVID-19 consumers buying decision of hand sanitizer differ significantly

2. Literature Review

2.1 Hand Sanitizers

Given the above background, it is important to find out the factors that are motivating individuals to purchase hand sanitizers. Will consumers continue to use hand sanitizers even after the COVID-19 pandemic is over? In the previous studies on hand sanitizer by different researchers, the focus was on the germ-killing activity or effectiveness of hand sanitizers (Kampf, G. & Ostermeyer, C.,2005) (Pickering et al. 2010) (Picheansathian et al 2004), or encouraging the usage of hand sanitizers among different groups of people. Also, Extensive Research has been done on hand hygiene compliance with alcohol-based hand rub (**Bissett, L.** 2002) (Hugonet et al 2002) (Keller et al 2020) or attitudes towards alcohol-based hand rub (Kingston et al,2017). Very little or no research has been done on the factors that encourage/motivate the customer in India to buy and use a hand sanitizer and whether they will continue using it even after the pandemic gets over, so these are the things we are trying to understand through this research paper.

This research provides insights into how hand sanitizer companies can focus on different aspects to cater to different consumers. As post-COVID-19 consumers show less purchase intention, Companies and businesses can make better use of different strategies to retain this new segment of consumers. This study also shows that subjective norms and social value plays a major role thus word of mouth becomes an important source.

Knowing the factors that affect customer purchasing behaviour helps marketers build marketing opportunities to influence customers with their products (Karunakaran, 2013).

Hand sanitizers can be classified depending on the active ingredient used: Alcohol-based or alcohol-free. Also, they come in different forms like gel, foam, and liquid. In this study, both types and all the forms are taken into consideration and collectively termed as Hand sanitizers without any further differentiation.

3. Background

"Hand hygiene is a core component of a healthy home and community hygiene practices and can benefit significantly in terms of reducing the occurrence of respiratory diseases, alimentary tract infections, and skin infections." (Bloomfield, et al, 2007). According to Whitby et al., 2007; Pittet et al., 2000 "Hand hygiene is known as the most crucial way to minimize and prevent the spread of infection." Hand hygiene can be achieved by various types of products like washing hands with water, plain soap, antimicrobial soap, or using hand sanitizers containing ethanol, triclosan, or benzalkonium chloride (BAC), etc.

During this Covid-19 outbreak, WHO and CDC recommended the use of hand sanitizers as they do not require water and can be easily carried along while traveling. The CDC wrote in 2002 that hand sanitizers require lesser time than washing hands and a medical attendant can save one hour in an eight-hour shift by using hand sanitizer. It was also observed by Hammond et al. (2000) that approximately 20% absenteeism reduced due to infection in school kids after the usage of hand sanitizer.

Plain soaps or antibiotic was considered as the first choice for decontamination of hands for decades in many countries but at the same time, many central European countries started using alcohol-based hand rubs (Rotter and Skopec,2003). This is mainly because of their better skin tolerance (Rotter,2001) and a faster and broader spectrum of antimicrobial activity (Rudolf and Kampf, 2003)

There is a lot of debate regarding the history of hand sanitizers. Even though GermX and Purell, the two well-known Hand Sanitizer companies entered the market in the late 1990s, sales of hand sanitizers did not begin until the 2000s. In fact, it was not until 2002 that the Centre of Disease Control and Prevention updated its hand hygiene recommendations to advise hand sanitizer as a potential substitute for health care workers along with individuals seeking to remove germs when water and soap are not available, or for saving time. WHO also updated its guidelines in 2009 after Dr. Didier Pittet who is a specialist of infectious diseases suggested hand sanitizer as an alternative to health care workers particularly those in third world countries where there is a dearth of clean water?

3.1 Conceptual Background and Research Hypothesis

Theory of consumer values and that of Reasoned Action are used to develop the conceptual framework in this paper, which by previous research has been successfully applied for the purpose of understanding consumer behaviour regarding a variety of products and services including personal care products (Candan, Ünal and Erciş, 2013) were used. According to Holbrook (1996), these values are implicit criteria for choice and assessment and help to steer the attitude and behaviours of consumers (Long and Schiffman, 2000). Therefore, according to Turel et al., 2010 "the effect of multiple value dimensions should be taken into consideration simultaneously as predictors of behaviour such as purchase intention".

Seven independent variables were identified: functional value, emotional value, health consciousness, subjective norm, conditional value, and social value were identified. The data collected these variables will be assessed to determine their importance in consumers' buying behaviour of Hand Sanitizers.

3.2 The Theory of Consumption Values

The Consumption Values Theory was developed by Sheth et al, which explains why consumers chose to purchase some goods over others. They suggested that consumer behaviour can be predicted as well as described and explained using this theory. According to this theory, comprising of the consumption values that could influence consumer choice: social value, functional value, conditional value, emotional value, and epistemic value. Furthermore, "the theory has three options (1) consumer choice behaviour is a function of various consumption values, (2) consumption values have different contributions in any given choice situation, and (3) consumption values are independent." The theory can be applied to consumer purchases involving durable to non-durable products as well as services. For example: on the basis of consumption value theory, Sweeney and Soutar (2001) had come up with perceived value scale. Consumption value theory was used by Long and Schiffman (2000) to find the values motivating consumer's reactions to Flights frequent flyer programs.

Consumption value theory implies that consumers can associate different values to different goods, which will finally affect their purchase intention (Ramkissoon et al., 2009). Ramayah, Rahman & Ng (2018) showed in their study the positive effect of consumption values on purchase intention. According to Kamakura and Novak (1992), a consumer can associate different interpretations to one "value". Yeonsoo et al. (2002) asserted that the Theory of Consumption values allows greater understanding as it explores the fundamental factors for the customer decision-making cycle. So, Theory of Consumption Values can help identify main values motivating consumers to purchase Hand Sanitizers.

3.3 Functional Value

Functional value derives from goods utilitarian, functional, or physical attributes such as reliability, durability, and price also it is believed to be the key factor of consumer preference (Sheth et al., 1991). "Functional values are about conveying the functional benefits of the good or brand, e.g., the products superior performance, lower cost, quality, price or better owing's value" (Doyle and Stern, 2006; Melin, 1999; Bergstrom, 2000.

H1: Consumers' perception of the functional value of hand sanitizers will positively effect their purchase intention.

3.4 Social Value

Sheth et al., 1991 mentioned the social value as the perceived utilisation through an alternative's association with one or more particular social groups. According to Sweeney and Soutar (2001) "Social value is the utility derived from the product's ability to enhance social self-concept". Consumers tend to get involved in purchases, along with purchase pattern in order to elicit a favourable response from their peer groups (Grubb and Grathwohl, 1967). According to Maslow (1943) Individuals are motivated to purchase products and services that can help to meet their higher social needs and desire for self-actualization. Therefore, hypothesis 2 is proposed as follows:

H2: Consumers' perception of the social value of hand sanitizers will positively affect their purchase intention.

3.5 Epistemic Value

Epistemic value is "the perceived utility acquired from an alternative's capacity to arouse curiosity, provide novelty, and/or satisfy a desire for knowledge" (Sheth et al., 1991). Berlyne (1960, 1970) study tells us that people are inclined to keep their stimulation level optimal. According to Hirschman (1980) study of innovative purchase tendency of consumers concluded that the consumers look for variety and they are exploratory. A consumer may also choose alternatives cause he/she is bored and may try out new things to feel different or satisfy curiosity. Hypothesis 3, is therefore proposed as follows:

H3: Epistemic value of hand sanitizers will positively affect the consumer's purchase intention.

3.6 Conditional Value

"Conditional value is the perceived utility derived from an alternative as the result of a particular situation or set of circumstances encountered by the decision-maker" (Sheth et al., 1991). Conditional values are capable of promoting or restraining a decision (Hung and Hsieh, 2010). (Hansen, 1972; Belk,1974:428) considered the variables of "time, location, and environment" to be the key determinants in identifying conditional factors. Mclaughlin and Walsh (2012) found in their research that the use of hand sanitizer was situational: the environment and products allowed and promoted the use of hand sanitizer. In the context of hand sanitizers, conditional value seems important as Indian consumers didn't use hand sanitizers as much as they are using due to the COVID-19 pandemic. With the onset of Pandemic, customer's attitudes are likely to change (Xu & Peng, 2015). As there is no research on the conditional value in the past with regards to Hand Sanitizers, the COVID-19 pandemic situation will be examined in this study as it could be one of the reasons motivating consumers to buy and use hand sanitizers. Hypothesis 4 is, therefore proposed as follows:

H4: Consumer perceptions of the conditional value of hand sanitizers will positively affect their purchase intention.

3.7 Emotional Value

Emotional value is defined by Sweeney and Soutar, (2001) as "the utility derived from the feelings or affective states that a product generates." According to Xiao, Kim, 2009, the benefit obtained as an outcome of sentimental and emotional conditions is emotional value. This value is related to the consumers' reactions that they show against a commodity. Emotional responses are frequently associated with products and services (Sheth et al., 1991). Hypothesis 5, therefore, is proposed as follows:

H5: Emotional value of hand sanitizers will positively impact the consumers' purchase intention.

3.8 Subjective Norms

Azjen and Fishbein, (1970) developed a Theory of Reasoned Actions whereby they said that subjective norms are one of the variables that can explain consumer behaviour. "Subjective norm depicts an individual's perceived social stress to pursue a certain behaviour". Consumers are inclined to purchase a product for e.g., Hand sanitizer if their significant others find it good. Evidence was provided by Finlay, Trafimow & Jones (1997) that in the health domain subjective norms are particularly important. Consumer's purchase intention is positive for a purchase when they are significant for the outlook towards that product (Teng and Wang, 2015). According to Hillhouse et al., 2000 subjective norm significantly effects ones' behavioural intention related to skin management. Hypothesis 6 is therefore proposed as follows:

H6. Subjective norms will positively impact customer's purchase intention towards hand sanitizers.

3.9 Health Consciousness Value

Health consciousness, according to Becker et al., 1977 encourages people to involve in healthy patterns. According to (Newsom et al.,2005) customers aspire to maintain a healthy life and an ideal state of well-being. Several prior research has depicted that health consciousness does predict a range of health perceptions and behaviours. (Schafer, Schafer, Bultena, & Hoiberg, 1993; Jayanti & Burns, 1998; Michaelidou & Hassan, 2008; Furnham & Forey, 1994; Gould, 1988, 1990). In a study conducted by Wall and Smiddy (2017) on therapeutic students, the most important reason for following hand hygiene was that students felt that the practice of overall health with hygiene helps in preventing the transmission of infections. Fahmy and Sohany (2020) found in their research that the consumer's health consciousness increased due to the COVID-19 pandemic and they purchased more hygienic products. Hypothesis 7 is therefore proposed as follows:

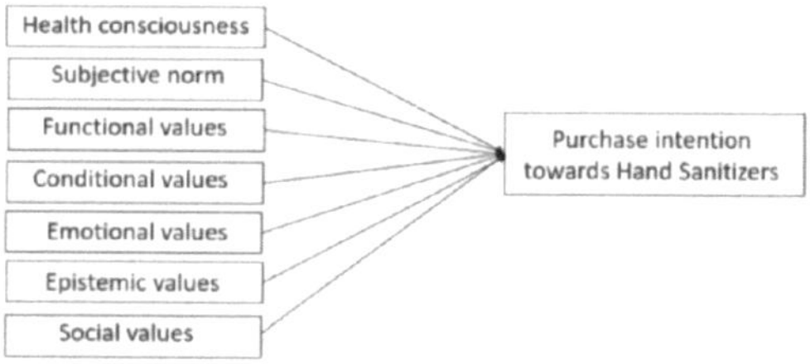

Fig. 3.1 Conceptual model for purchase intension towards hand sanitizers

Source: Made by Author using Scopus Database

H7. Health consciousness will positively affect the customers' purchase intention towards hand sanitizers.

4. Methods

4.1 Source of Data

Using Cochran's Formula, our required sample size is calculated to be 385. A pilot study with 25 respondents through the online method of survey was conducted initially. Based on pilot study questionnaires were revised and modified. The technique adopted was convenience sampling for this research and total 415 questionnaires were distributed among the respondents through online mode. We got total 386 responses after discarding invalid responses yielding a response rate of 93.01%, which were finally used for the analysis. A convenience sampling method was used. The sample demographic characteristics are as follows: (Table 3.1) in all, 52.33% of the respondents were male and 47.67% were female. All ages were equally represented by the 386 subjects and 91.97 % were college-educated. The reasons for not purchasing hand sanitizers before COVID-19 were "didn't think it was useful" (7.26%), "didn't think it was required" (76.54%), "didn't know about Hand sanitizers" (8.94%), and "Hand sanitizers were costly" (7.26%).

4.2 Measures

For the questionnaire, most of the constructs with items that had been picked from literature but measures were also taken to have a sync between the objectives and questions. Four measures in subjective norms were taken from (Bauer et al., 2013) (Chen, 2007; Teng and Wang, 2015) (e.g., "People who are important to me can influence my decisions of purchasing hand sanitizer"). Health consciousness measures the consumers' concern towards their health for purchasing Hand sanitizers, four measures were adapted from (Bauer et al., 2013) (e.g., "The

Table 3.1 Demographics

		Size of sample	Frequency distribution (%)
Sex	Male	202	52.33
	Female	184	47.67
Age	56 Years and above	8	2.07
	46-55	10	2.59
	36-45	12	3.11
	26-35	106	27.46
	16-25	250	64.77
Education	Postgraduate	194	50.26
	Undergraduate	161	41.71
	Senior Secondary	23	5.96
	Senior High	8	2.07
Occupation	Student	235	60.88
	Businessman/Businesswoman	11	2.85
	Private Sector	90	23.32
	Government	14	3.63
	Housewife	19	4.92
	Not Working	17	4.40
Purchased Hand Sanitizer before COVID-19	Yes	207	53.63
	No	179	46.37
the reason for not purchasing before COVID-19	I didn't think it was required	137	76.54
	Unaware of its use	16	8.94
	I didn't think it was useful	13	7.26
	Sanitizers were costly	13	7.26
most Important Source of Information used for buying Hand sanitizer	Ads on social media	33	8.55
	Advices from family members or close friends	114	29.53
	Newspaper ads	11	2.85
	Personal experiences	160	41.45
	TV ads	71	18.39
	Web sites of brands	7	1.81

Source: Made by Author using Scopus Database

use of Hand Sanitizer enhances my health"). The social value measures (e.g., "Purchasing Hand Sanitizers makes me feel acceptable") were adapted from Sweeney and Soutar (2001). In the epistemic value, three measures (e.g., "Using hand sanitizer makes me feel different") were adapted from Hirschman (1980), Lin and Huang (2012). The functional value measures include "germ-killing activity" and "quick and easy to use". Initially, four items were included in functional value but later due to low factor loadings two items were dropped. The emotional value measures (e.g., "Purchasing Hand Sanitizer makes me feel good") consumer feeling towards Hand Sanitizer and was adapted from Lin and Huang (2012), Sweeney and Soutar (2001). To measure the purchase intention 3 items were included from Michaelidou and Hassan (2008) (e.g., "It is likely I will purchase Hand Sanitizer in the upcoming year"). Five points Likert's type scale was used in the questionnaire to measure the items where 1 stood for strongly disagree and 5 for strongly agree.

5. Analysis and Synthesis of Findings

5.1 Descriptive Analysis

Using SPSS 21.0 and AMOS 20.0 the reliability and validity of the scale were analysed. As suggested by Griethuijsen et al. (2015) and Taber (2018) the accepted value of Cronbach's alpha is 0.7; however, values above 0.6 are also accepted and all the constructs Cronbach's Alpha is above 0.65. As the Composite Reliability of all constructs is above 0.7, this means the scales are adequately reliable. The recommended value of average variance extracted (AVE) is more than 0.5 and all constructs AVE is higher than the of 0.5, indicating good convergent validity. The items factor loading and mean of the constructs are also shown in Table 3.2.

Table 3.2 Reliability and validity

Constructs	Item	Factor Loading	Mean	Cronbach's Alpha	Ave	Composite Reliability
Purchase Intention (PI)	PI1 PI2 PI3	0.854 0.881 0.812	4.53	0.87	0.72	0.89
Social Value (SV)	SOV1 SOV2 SOV3 SOV4	0.762 0.805 0.860 0.821	3.30	0.87	0.66	0.88
Subjective Norms (SN)	SN1 SN2 SN3 SN4	0.692 0.826 0.842 0.689	4.08	0.80	0.59	0.85
Health Consciousness (HC)	HC1 HC2 HC3 HC4	0.823 0.830 0.811 0.680	3.71	0.88	0.62	0.87
Emotional Value (EMV)	EMV1 EMV2 EMV3 EMV4	0.775 0.805 0.765 0.750	3.93	0.88	0.60	0.86
Conditional Value (CV)	CV1 CV2 CV3	0.768 0.828 0.803	3.60	0.74	0.64	0.84
Epistemic Value (EV)	EPV1 EPV2 EPV3	0.733 0.782 0.732	3.05	0.68	0.56	0.79
Functional Value (FV)	FV1 FV4	0.840 0.809	4.40	0.68	0.68	0.81

Source: Made by Author using Scopus Database

Note: Items FV2 and FV3 were dropped due to low factor loadings

5.2 Hypothesis Tests

The hypotheses were tested using SPSS AMOS 20. Table 3.3 provides the estimates and significance level. The results show that emotional value, social value, subjective norms, health consciousness, and functional value positively influence respondents' purchase intention whereas contrary to our hypothesis conditional value negatively influences purchase intention. When the consumers have higher emotional value, social value, subjective norms, health consciousness, and functional value with Hand Sanitizer, the likelihood that they will purchase hand Sanitizer is higher. Therefore, hypotheses H1, H2, H5, H6, and H7 were accepted. Hypotheses H3 and H4 were not significant thus rejected.

Table 3.3 Results of hypothesis testing

Constructs	Estimate	S.E.	C.R.	P	Significance	Hypothesis
Social value	0.084	0.024	3.442	0.000***	Significant	Accepted
Emotional value	0.062	0.028	2.238	0.025*	Significant	Accepted
Health consciousness	0.069	0.028	2.476	0.013*	Significant	Accepted
Subjective norms	0.1	0.034	2.99	0.003**	Significant	Accepted
Conditional value	-0.081	0.027	-2.991	0.003**	Significant	Rejected
Functional value	4.653	2.306	2.018	0.044*	Significant	Accepted
Epistemic value	-0.055	0.03	-1.847	0.065	Not Significant	Rejected

Source: Made by Author using Scopus Database

Note: Dependent variable: purchase intention; ***$p< 0.001$, **$p < 0.01$, *$p < 0.05$

The effect of gender on consumption values, subjective norms, health consciousness and purchase Intention

A one-way ANOVA had been carried out, with gender as the independent variable and with purchase intention, epistemic value, emotional value, functional value, conditional value, social value, subjective norms, and health consciousness as dependent variables. As shown in Table 3.4 emotional value between male and female respondents differed significantly. According to the averages of dependent variables, female consumers are more inclined towards the emotional value of Hand Sanitizers than male consumers.

The effect of Pre and post Covid-19 purchase of hand Sanitizer on consumption values, subjective norms and health consciousness

A one-way ANOVA was conducted with pre and post Covid-19 consumers as the independent variable along the purchase intention, functional value, conditional value, health consciousness social value, epistemic value, emotional value, and subjective norms as dependent variables. One-way ANOVA depicts (Table 3.5) show Pre and post Covid-19 Consumer of hand Sanitizer differ significantly

Table 3.4 The result of one-way ANOVA in the Gender

Dependent variable	Males (N=202)	Females (N=184)	P-Values
Purchase intention	4.52	4.54	0.748
Conditional value	3.66	3.54	0.321
Subjective norms	4.06	4.11	0.510
Health consciousness	3.63	3.80	0.112
Social value	3.27	3.33	0.596
Functional value	4.35	4.45	0.181
Emotional value	3.82	4.04	0.017*
Epistemic value	3.06	3.04	0.816

$*p < 0.05$
Source: Made by Author using Scopus Database

in all the dependent variables except Emotional, Social, and Epistemic value. Dependent variables showing a positive p-value lesser than 0.05 (Table 3.5), suggests that subjective norms, health consciousness, functional value, conditional value, and purchase intention regarding hand sanitizers differed between Pre and post Covid-19 Consumer. According to the averages for dependent variables, respondents who purchased hand sanitizers Pre COVID 19 were in stronger agreement with four dependent variables: subjective norms, health consciousness value, functional value, and purchase Intention for Hand sanitizers is far more apparent (mean 4.67) among them than among those individuals who started purchasing after COVID-19 (mean 4.37). On the other hand, the post-COVID-19 Consumers of hand Sanitizers were in a stronger agreement with the conditional values.

Table 3.5 Pre and post Covid-19 consumers' one-way ANOVA result

Dependent variables	Pre Covid-19 Consumer (N=207)	Post Covid-19 Consumer (N= 179)	P-Values
Purchase intention	4.67	4.37	0.000***
Conditional value	3.18	4.09	0.000***
Subjective norms	4.18	3.97	0.014*
Health consciousness	3.82	3.58	0.023*
Emotional	3.99	3.84	0.089
Social	3.32	3.27	0.742
Functional	4.50	4.27	0.002**
Epistemic value	3.10	2.99	0.321

$***p < 0.001$, $**p < 0.01$ and $*p < 0.05$.
Source: Made by Author using Scopus Database

Effect of Gender on the Product Attributes

Table 3.6 shows the 6 attributes of Hand sanitizers and their relative importance. The reliability of the constructs was checked through Cronbach alpha which came out to be 0.844 above the required value of 0.7. The relative significance of each attribute is determined by the average attribute score. The table is based on these average scores.

An attributes higher mean score indicates that it is more important to them. A one-way ANOVA had been conducted along with gender as the independent variable and with Packaging, smell/odour, Irritation, Ease of Use, Speed drying, colour, and texture as dependent variables. Table 3.6 shows that males and females differed significantly in product attributes like Irritation, Ease of Use, Speed drying, and texture. On the basis of the mean scores, it implies that female consumers are more inclined towards product attributes like Irritation, Ease of Use, Speed drying, and texture than males.

Table 3.6 The result of one-way ANOVA in the Gender for product attributes

Dependent variables	Males (N=202)	Females (N=184)	P-Values
Packaging	2.88	3.06	0.183
Irritation	3.79	4.17	0.005**
Ease of use	3.72	4.03	0.010**
Speed Drying	3.63	3.89	0.030*
Smell/Odour	3.51	3.76	0.064
Texture	3.26	3.70	0.001***
Color	2.09	2.24	0.213

*$p < 0.05$, **$p < 0.01$ and ***$p < 0.001$.*

Source: Made by Author using Scopus Database

6. Discussion

The theories used for the current study included, Consumption Values theory, health consciousness, and subjective norms. Additionally, respondents were separated into four Groups: Male and Female Consumers, Pre and post Covid-19 Consumers according to their responses. One-way ANOVA was applied to test whether health consciousness, subjective norms, consumption values, and Purchase intention differ significantly between these groups.

The data analysis shows that the reasons for not buying Hand Sanitizers before Covid-19 were "didn't think it was useful" (7.26%), "didn't think it was required" (76.54%), "didn't know about Hand sanitizers" (8.94%), and "Hand sanitizers were costly" (7.26%). This shows, 43%(approx.) of the respondents lacked an understanding of the use and requirement of Hand Sanitizers before COVID-19.

Emotional value plays a crucial role in influencing the customer's intention towards hand sanitizer. Lee, Lee, and Choi's research (2010) confirms that emotion acts as a catalyst.

In this study, functional value positively influences consumers' purchase intention towards hand sanitizer. This is in line with the findings by (Ramayah, Rahman & Ng 2018) Engstrom et al. (2015) and Hur et al. (2012). The functional value derives from an entity's perceived utility in the choice situation (Pope, 1998) so the benefits of using hand sanitizer do motivate consumers to purchase them. According to the results, Subjective norms positively influence purchase intention which aligns with other researcher's findings (Chen, 2007; Asif et al, 2013; Teng and Wang, 2015; Kim and Chung 2011). This study also found that health consciousness positively influences consumers' purchase intention towards hand sanitizer. These findings are in line with Ghazali et al. 2017; Bauer et al., 2013 research which showed consumers are concerned about their physical well-bein.

Conditional value affected it negatively so the hypothesis was rejected. This is contrary to the research findings of Lin and Huang,2008 who showed that conditional values have a positive effect. Further research will need to explore the possible reasons or the probable effects of other factors on the final direct effects of conditional value on Purchase intention.

The study indicates that epistemic value does not significantly impact the purchase intention. The reason could be that Epistemic values relate to the potential of a product to stimulate attention, deliver novelty or fulfil the demand for information, which may be of significance to customers who are seeking different and new experiences and are more likely applicable to services of experiential nature such as vacations, or even shopping trips (Babin, Darden & Griffin, 1994; Sheth et al., 1991a) and is perhaps less relevant when contemplating the purchase of a durable product." such as hand sanitizer.

References

1. A. Altstedter, J. Hong, (2020) Why rational people are panic buying as Coronavirus spreads. Retrieved from: https://eds-b-ebscohostcom.ezproxy.uow.edu.au/eds/detail/detail?vid=0&sid=8c57fd62-6c6a-46e6-9536-50feaa61b283%40pdc-vsessmgr03&bdata=JnNpdGU9ZWRzLWxpdmU%3d#AN=142168142&db=heh, (accessed 7 April 2020).
2. Ajzen, I. and Fishbein, M. (1977), "Attitude-Behavior Relations: A Theoretical Analysis and Review of Empirical Research," *Psychological Bulletin*, 84, 888–91.
3. Asif, M., Xuhui, W., Nasiri, A., Ayyub, S. (2013) Determinant Factors Influencing Organic Food Purchase Intention and the Moderating Role of Awareness: A Comparative Analysis, *Food Quality and Preference* (2017), doi: http://dx.doi.org/10.1016/j.foodqual.2017.08.006
4. BBC (2020). https://www.bbc.com/news/stories-52126847. Retreived on 24 August 2020

5. Becker, M., Maiman, L., Kirscht, J., Haefner, D. and Drachman, R. (1977), "The health belief model and prediction of dietary compliance: a field experiment", *Journal of Health and Social Behavior*, Vol. 18 No. 4, pp. 348–66.
6. Belk, R. W. (1975) Situational Variables and Consumer Behavior. *Journal of Consumer Research*. Vol.2. December.
7. Bergstrom, A. (2000) Cyberbranding: leveraging your brand on the internet. Strategy and Leadership, 28(4), pp. 10–15.
8. Berlyne, D. E. (1960) ***Conflict, Arousal, and Curiosity,*** McGraw-Hill New York.
9. Berlyne, D. E. (November 1970) Novelty, Complexity, and Hedonic Value. ***Perception Psychophysics 8*** : 279–286.
10. **Bissett, L.** (2002) Can alcohol hand rubs increase compliance with hand hygiene? Br. J. Nurs. **11:**1074–1077.
11. Bloomberg Quint (2020): https://www.bloombergquint.com/business/how-indias-sanitiser-market-grew-after-coronavirus-outbreak. Retrieved on 23 August 2020
12. Bloomfield, S.F., Aiello, A.E., Cookson, B., O'Boyle, C., Larson, E.L. (2007) The effectiveness of hand hygiene procedures in reducing the risks of infections in home and community settings including handwashing and alcohol-based hand sanitizers American Journal of Infection Control, 35 (10 SUPPL. 1), pp. S27–S64. Cited 123 times. DOI:10.1016/j.ajic.2007.07.001
13. Business Standard (2020). https://www.business-standard.com/article/current-affairs/coronavirus-live-updates-india-total-cases-over-29-lakhs-global-death-toll-delhi-maharashtra-tamil-andhra-up-delhi-cases-latest-news-120082100048_1.html. retrieved on 24 August 2020
14. Candan B., Ünal S., Erciş A. (2013) Analysing the relationship between consumption values and brand loyalty of young people: A study on personal care products European *Journal of Research on Education, 2013*, Special Issue: Human Resource Management, 29–46
15. Chen, M.-F. (2007) Consumer attitudes and purchase intentions in relation to organic foods in Taiwan: moderating effects of food-related personality traits. Food Qual. Prefer. 7 (18), 1008–1021.
16. CNBC (2020). https://www.cnbc.com/2020/03/27/coronavirus-the-history-of-hand-sanitizer-and-why-its-important.html , Retrieved on 24 August 2020
17. Doyle, P. and Stern, P. (2006) Marketing management and strategy. Edinburgh Gate, Harlow: Pearson Education.
18. Engstrom, A., Styven, M. E., Wallstrom, A., & Salehi-Sangari, E. (2015). Developing an attractive mobile service: A comparison of desired consumption values of three different services *The Sustainable Global Marketplace,* 454–456.
19. Fahmy T. & Sohani A. (2020) The impact of a pandemic on brand preference in purchasing decisions of food and hygiene products: a COVID-19 perspective. www.hkr.se
20. Finlay, K. A., Trafimow, D., & Jones, D. (1997). Predicting health behaviors from attitudes and subjective norms: Between-subjects and within-subject's analyses. *Journal of Applied Social Psychology*, 27, 20 15–203 1.
21. Furnham, A., & Forey, J. (1994). The attitudes behaviors and beliefs of patients of conventional vs. complementary (alternative) medicine. *Journal of Clinical Psychology*, 50(3), 458–469.
22. Furukawa, H Matsumura, K, Harada, S. (2019) Effect of Consumption Values on Consumer Satisfaction and Brand Commitment: Investigating Functional, Emotional,

Social, and Epistemic Values in the Running Shoes Market. *International Review of Management and Marketing*, 9(6), 158–168.
23. Ghazali, E., Soon, P. C., Mutum, D. S., & Nguyen, B. (2017). Health and cosmetics: Investigating consumers' values for buying organic personal care products. *Journal of Retailing and Consumer Services, 39*, 154–163. doi: 10.1016/j.jretconser.2017.08.002
24. Gould, S. J. (1988). Consumer attitudes toward health and health care: A differential perspective. *Journal of Consumer Affairs*, 22(1), 96–118.
25. Gould, S. J. (1990). Health consciousness and health behavior: the application of a new health consciousness scale. *American Journal of Preventive Medicine*, 6(4), 228–237.
26. Grubb, E.L., Grathwohl, H.L. (1967). Consumer self-concept, symbolism and market behavior: a theoretical approach. *J. Mark.* 31 (4), 22–27.
27. Greenaway, RE, Ormandy, K, Fellows, C, . Impact of hand sanitizer format (gel/foam/liquid) and dose on its sensory properties. J Hosp Inf 2018; 2: 411–416. Google Scholar
28. Hammond, B., Ali, Y., Fendler, E., Dolan, M., Donovan, S. (2000). Effect of hand sanitizer use on elementary school absenteeism *American Journal of Infection Control*, 28 (5), pp. 340–346. Cited 109 times. 10.1067/mic.2000.107276
29. Han, T.-I., Chung, J.-E. (2014). Korean consumers' motivations and perceived risks toward the purchase of organic cotton apparel. Cloth. Text. Res. J. 32 (4), 235–250.
30. Hansen, Flemming. (1972). Consumer Choice Behavior: A Cognitive Theory, *The Free Press*, New York.
31. Hansen, Flemming. (June 1981) Hemispheral Lateralization: Implications for Understanding Consumer Behavior. *J. Consumer Res. 8:* 23–36.
32. Hillhouse, J., Turrisi, R. and Kastner, M. (2000), "Modeling tanning salon behavioral tendencies using appearance motivation, self-monitoring and the theory of planned behavior", Health Education Research, Vol. 15 No. 4, pp. 405–14.
33. Hirschman, Elizabeth C. (December 1980) Innovativeness, Novelty Seeking, and Consumer Creativity. *J. Consumer Res. 7*: 283–295.
34. Holbrook, M.B. (1996) "Customer value—A framework for analysis and research". *Advances in Consumer Research.* 23.1: 138–142.
35. Hugonnet S, Perneger TV, Pittet D. (2002). Alcohol-based handrub improves compliance with hand hygiene in intensive care units. *Arch Intern Med.* ;162(9):1037 –43.
36. Hung, C.L. and Hsieh, C.Y. (2010). Searching the fit pattern between cultural dimensions and consumption values of mobile commerce in Taiwan. *Asia Pacific Management Review*, 15(2), pp. 147–165.
37. Hur, W.-M., Yoo, J.-J., & Chung, T.-L. (2012). The consumption values and consumer innovativeness on convergence products. *Industrial Management & Data Systems*, 112(5), 688–706.
38. Jayanti, R. K., & Burns, A. C. (1998). The antecedents of preventive health care behavior: An empirical study. *Academy of Marketing Science*, 26(1), 9–15.
39. Kamakura, W.A. and Novak, T.P. (1992). Value-system segmentation: exploring the meaning of LOV. *Journal of Consumer Research*, 19(Jun), pp. 119–132.
40. Kampf, G. & Ostermeyer, C. (2005). Efficacy of two distinct ethanol-based hand rubs for surgical hand disinfection—A controlled trial according to prEN12791. *BMC Infectious Diseases, 5,* Retrieved June 10, 2020 from http://www.biomedcentral.com/1471-2334/5/17

41. Karunakaran. (2013). Marketing Management, Text and Cases in Indian Context. Mumbai: Himalaya Publishing House.
42. Keller, J., Wolfensberger, A., Clack, L., Kuster, S. P., Dunic, M., Eis, D., . . . Sax, H. (2018). Do wearable alcohol-based handrub dispensers increase hand hygiene compliance? - A mixed-methods study 11 medical and health sciences 1117 public health and health services. *Antimicrobial Resistance and Infection Control, 7*(1) doi:10.1186/s13756-018-0439-5
43. Kim, G. & Kim, J. (2009). The Investigation of Chinese Consumer Values, Consumption Values, Life Satisfaction, and Consumption Behaviors. *Psychology & Marketing*. Vol. 26(7): 610–624 (July 2009).
44. Kingston LM, Slevin BL, O'Connell NH, Dunne CP. (2017). Attitudes and practices of Irish hospital-based physicians towards hand hygiene and hand rubbing using alcohol-based hand rub: a comparison between 2007 and 2015. *Journal of Hosp Infect* 2017b, http://dx.doi.org/10.1016/j.jhin.2017.05.010 Accessed 07 Jul 2017.
45. Lee, J.-S., Lee, C.-K., & Choi, Y. (2010). Examining the role of emotional and functional values in festival evaluation. *Journal of Travel Research, 19.* https://doi.org/10.1177/0047287510385465.
46. Live mint (June, 2020). https://www.livemint.com/mint-lounge/features/the-truth-about-hand-sanitizers-11594912340434.html. Retrieved on 23 August 2020
47. Lin, Huang. (2012) The influence factors on choice behavior regarding green products based on the theory of consumption values. *Journal of Cleaner Production*. 22.: 11–18
48. Long, M. M., & Schiffman, L. G. (2000). Consumption values and relationships: Segmenting the market for frequency programs. Journal of Consumer Marketing, 17,214–232.
49. Maslow A.H. (1943) A theory of human motivation Psychological Review., 50 (4) , pp. 370–396
50. McLaughlin, A. C., & Walsh, F. (2012). Self-reported reasons for hand hygiene in 3 groups of health care workers. *American Journal of Infection Control, 40*(7), 653–658. doi: 10.1016/j.ajic.2011.08.014
51. Michaelidou, N., & Hassan, L. M. (2008). The role of health consciousness, food safety concern and ethical identity on attitudes and intentions towards organic food. International Journal of Consumer Studies, 32(1), 163–170
52. Nielsen. (2020). *Key Consumer Behavior Thresholds Identified as the Coronavirus Outbreak Evolved*. Retrieved April 1, 2020, from Nielsen: https://www.nielsen.com/us/en/insights/article/2020/key-consumer-behavior-thresholds-identified-as-the-coronavirus-outbreak-evolves/
53. Newsom, J., McFarland, B., Kaplan, M., Huguet, N. and Zani, B. (2005), "The health consciousness myth: implications of the near independence of major health behaviors in the North American population", *Social Science & Medicine*, Vol. 60 No. 2, pp. 433–7.
54. Pavlou, P.A. and Chai, L. (2002). What drives electronic commerce across cultures? a cross-cultural empirical investigation of the Theory of Planned Behaviour. *Journal of Electronic Commerce Research*, 3(4), pp. 240–53.
55. Picheansathian W., 2004. A systematic review on the effectiveness of alcohol based solutions for hand hygiene. Int *J Nurs Pract* ;10(1):3–9.
56. Pickering, A. J., Boehm, A. B., Mwanjali, M., & Davis, J. (2010). Efficacy of waterless hand hygiene compared with handwashing with soap: A field study in Dar es Salaam, Tanzania. *American Journal of Tropical Medical Hygiene*, 82, 270–278.

57. Pittet, D., Hugonnet, S., Harbarth, S., Mourouga, P., Sauven, V., Touveneau, S. and Perneger, T.V. and members of the Infection Control Programme (2000), "Effectiveness of a hospital wide programme to improve compliance with hand hygiene", *The Lancet*, Vol. 356 No. 9238, pp. 1307–1312.
58. Pope, N. (1998). Consumption values, sponsorship awareness, brand and product use. *Journal of product & brand management*, 7(2), 124–136
59. Qureshi, A. A., & Vakkassi, H. (2019). Factors Affecting In-store Impulse Buying Behavior: An Analysis of Personal Care Products. *International Journal of Entrepreneurial Research*, *2*(4), 7–11. https://doi.org/10.31580/ijer.v2i4.1091
60. Ramayah, T., Rahman, S. A., & Ng, C. L. (2018). How do consumption values influence online purchase intention among school leavers in Malaysia? Review of Business Management, 20(4), 638–654. https://doi.org/10.7819/rbgn.v0i0.3139
61. Ramkissoon, H., Nunkoo, R. and Gursoy, G. (2009). How consumption values affect destination image formation, in Woodside, A.G., Megehee, C.M. and Ogle, A. (Eds), Perspectives on Cross-Cultural, Ethnographic, Brand Image, Storytelling, Unconscious Needs, and Hospitality Guest Research (Advances in Culture, Tourism and Hospitality Research Volume 3), Emerald Group Publishing Limited, Bingley, pp. 143–168.
62. Rotter M, Skopec M. (2003) Entwicklung der Ha¨ndehygiene und die Bedeutung der Erkenntnisse von Ignaz Ph. Semmelweis. In: Kampf G, editor. Ha¨nde-Hygiene im Gesundheitswesen, Berlin: Springer. p. 1–27.
63. Rotter ML. (2000) Arguments for the alcoholic hand disinfection. J Hosp Infect; 48(Suppl. A): S4–S8.
64. Rudolf M, Kampf G. Wirkstoffe (2003) In: Kampf G, editor. Ha¨ndehygiene im Gesundheitswesen. Berlin: Springer; p. 71–104.
65. Schafer, R. B., Schafer, E., Bultena, G., & Hoiberg, E. (1993). Coping with a health threat. *Journal of Applied Social Psychology*, 23(5), 386–194.
66. Schiffman, L., & Kanuk, L. (2014). Consumer Behaviour.Pearson/PHI.
67. Sheth, J.N., Newman, B.E. and Gross, B.L. (1991). Why we buy what we buy: a Theory of Consumption Values. *Journal of Business Research*, 22(2), pp. 159–170.
68. Smith-Spangler, C., Brandeau, M.L., Hunter, G.E., Bavinger, J.C., Pearson, M., Eschbach, P.J., Sundaram, V., et al. (2012). Are organic foods safer or healthier than conventional alternatives? a systematic review. Ann. Intern. Med. 157 (5), 348–366.
69. Singh. C. K and Pushpendu Rakshit (2020). A Critical Analysis to comprehend Panic buying behaviour of Mumbaikar's in COVID-19 era. *UGC Care journal*
70. Svenska Dagbladet. (2020, March 3). *Coronaoro driver upp försäljningen av krisvaror*. Retrieved July 1, 2020, from https://www.svd.se/coronaoro-driver-upp-forsaljning-av-krisvaror
71. Sweeney, J.C., Soutar, G.N., (2001). Consumer perceived value: the development of a multiple item scale. *J. Retail.* 2 (77), 203–220.
72. Taber, K. S. (2018). The use of Cronbach's alpha when developing and reporting research instruments in science education. *Research in Science Education*, 48(6), 1273–1296.
73. Teng, C.-C., Wang, Y.-M. (2015). Decisional factors driving organic food consumption: generation of consumer purchase intentions. Br. Food J. 117 (3), 1066–1081.
74. van Griethuijsen, R.A.L.F., van Eijck, M.W., Haste, H. *et al* (2015). Global Patterns in Students' Views of Science and Interest in Science. *Res Sci Educ* **45,** 581–603 https://doi.org/10.1007/s11165-014-9438-6

75. Vox (2020). https://www.vox.com/the-goods/2020/3/5/21164673/hand-sanitizer-coronavirus-pocketbac-purell. retrieved on 24 August 2020
76. Wall, O.M. and Smiddy, M.P. (2017), "Factors that influence hand hygiene practice amongst occupational therapy students", *Irish Journal of Occupational Therapy*, Vol. 45 No. 2, pp. 112–122. https://doi.org/10.1108/IJOT-02-2017-0009
77. Whitby, M., McLaws, M.L. and Ross, M.W. (2006), "Why health care workers don't wash their hands: a behavioural explanation", *Infection Control and Hospital Epidemiology*, Vol. 27No. 5, pp. 484–492.
78. WHO. (2010). *WHO | What is a pandemic?* Retrieved July 1, 2020, from World Health Organization: https://www.who.int/csr/disease/swineflu/frequently_asked_questions/pandemic/en/
79. WHO. (2020, March 11). *Coronavirus disease 2019 (COVID-19) Situation Report - 51.* Retrieved July 1, 2020, from World Health Organization.
80. Yeonsoo, L., Jinwoo, K., Inseong, L. and Hoyong, K. (2002). A cross-cultural study on the value structure of mobile internet usages: comparison between Korea and Japan. *Journal of Electronic Commerce Research*, 3(4), pp. 227–239.
81. Xu, J., & Peng, Z. (2015). People at Risk of Influenza Pandemics: The Evolution of Perception and Behavior. *PloS One, 10*(12), 1–14.

*Securing the Future through Sustainability, Health, Education, and Technology –
Brig. Dr. Rajiv Divekar et al. (eds)*

4 Transforming Health Care Management through Artificial Intelligence

Reena (Mahapatra) Lenka*
Symbiosis Institute of Management Studies,
Symbiosis International (Deemed) University, Pune

ABSTRACT
Artificial intelligence (AI) aspires to mimic human intelligence. The rapid progress of examination techniques and the increased accessibility of medical information are changing how people view medical treatment. The current study examines how AI is used in medical services and discusses potential future uses. Information on many types of medical services may be processed using artificial intelligence (organized and unstructured). As is customary for language handling for unstructured information, well-known AI approaches also contain AI techniques for organized information. Malignancy, nervous system science, and cardiology are important illness areas that use AI technology. In the three significant areas of right-on-time detection and analysis, therapy, outcome prediction, and diagnostic assessment, we further explore the nuances of AI applications in stroke. Overall, the research shows that early AI frameworks, like IBM Watson, can make it challenging to implement AI in real-world settings.

KEYWORDS: Artificial intelligence, Vector machine, Stroke, AI frameworks

1. Introduction

Constantly monitoring a patient under specific situations involves assuring the best possible action by a medical professional or a doctor to commence the correct procedure or regulate the needed medicine. Cardiology, obstetrics, nervous system science, and brain research are just a few fields where constant remote patient surveillance is required for patient care and involves high-risk patients. (Davahli, M. R.et,.al, 2021)

*reena.lenka@sims.edu

DOI: 10.1201/9781003587200-4

Framework and method for observing patients at high risk via remote reasoning. Most high-risk patients may be followed concurrently without involvement from the patient. The patient hears the specialist's inquiries during each observing encounter and answers. The replies from the patient are recorded at a distance focal checking station and are available for subsequent review or online. (Quinn, T. P et.al, 2021) To provide the patient with specified query options. Artificial intelligence (AI) and voice innovation (DEC voice) have been combined from most recorded inquiries. AI uses parsing to choose the patient's queries depending on their response. The screen might be made of various objects, including uterine movement strips, glaucoma circulatory strain sleeves, beat screens, electroencephalographs, etc. (Bajwa, J.,et, al 2021) The optimal number of phone lines for every understanding would be four: one for the screen, one for the voice, one as a backup, and one to keep track of disappointments. The connection between a device that disperses stimulating drugs and various medical service devices, such as beat screens, thermometers, pulse screens, etc., can be seen by using double-tone grid recurrence signals (DTMF), which can transmit checked signs and other data that DEC voice, which is still under development, can understand. (Wang, A.,et,al, 2021) The customer must be expressly informed when to take the readings or what to do with the results.

There should be at least one source of clinical data, about one source of individual clinical information for roughly one patient, and at least one server where the clinical data and the individual clinical information are accessible to the server as part of a framework for individual clinical consideration, philosophical investigation, and conclusion (s). The server(s) might have an artificial intelligence (AI) component for analyzing each patient's clinical data and at least one interface for continuing bi-directional correspondence with at least one approved external element. (Haque, A., Milstein, A., & Fei-Fei, L. (2020)

An electronic medical services consistency assistance framework comprises a client device and a host station utilized by a healthcare professional to assist the patients regarding the method and process for filling the required drugs from the datasets and periodic check-ups. It uses packed computerized conversation to provide comprehensible and natural-sounding audio communications. (World Health Organization. (2016) The host station is used by a healthcare professional to create and maintain a database of discourse messages and related information. Information is delivered from the host station to the client device to establish a redone process. A line structure makes it easier to identify pharmaceuticals with usual dosage intervals in communications. (United States Government Accountability Office. (2020). Allowing flexible message rescheduling is what a boundary is described. When a message is prepared to play, the client device alerts the client via flexible and intelligent visible and visual signals. A satellite device may be used to produce such prompts to alert the client to advise the client device for the message. (Sendak, M. P,et.al 2020) To play messages, repeat messages, verify that the desired task has been done, or play messages providing help, client-worked keys are offered. The client device records each client's activities and inactions to send the information to the host station later, which collects the information into a report for medical care providers. (University of Leeds. (2020)

Early electronic clock and medication compliance alarms frequently required the user to configure the device using a variety of switches and fasteners. Even with the guidance of text prompts on an LCD. Some patients, particularly the elderly, find it difficult and dangerous to remember the grouping of activities and which meanings of the buttons. This is because the little fastens are difficult for them to operate. (Xie, Y., Nguyen, Q. D., Hamzah, H., et al. (2020)

Moreover, it is up to the patient to remember and accurately reassemble the device each time the routine changes. According to U.S. Patent No. 5,088,056, the client must operate a different mode switch depending on whether the medication is taken as directed, early, or in response to the circumstance. Hence, the customer experiences increased complexity and debilitation due to the enhanced usefulness. (Simonite, T. (2020).

Moreover, complete reliance on instant messaging causes problems for the elderly, customers with limited competence, and persons who are visibly disabled. Such problems might result from the LCD's use of glare or the relatively small type size required for such "versatile" devices. In the unlikely event that the presentation size is increased to improve comprehension, the updated gadget gets more extensive and less valuable. The amount and type of information transmitted in text design simultaneously in a practical device is still constrained. (Oktay, O.et, al. 2020)

In other instances, the visual cues go on forever without a response from the client. Many illustrations show that a persistent warning that shuts off when the client reacts might utilize too much force. Hence, under some previous craftsmanship licenses, the client can only reply to the alarm before the perceptible brief is terminated. Some do the detectable short repeatedly, on cue, or at regular intervals for a predetermined period, like 10. (Alverez-Valle, J., & Moore, G. J. (2020)

Even if these and similar devices will leave an LCD message or LED pointer to remind the user to take a pill, the customer still wants additional information. For instance, LED shows how to prevent overeating by instructing a client not to take a with too little time separating it from the next portion. A client should receive more detailed instructions regarding taking prescription measurements after the schedule and doing so close to the hour of the next scheduled dose. (Senior, A. W. et al. (2020)

Medication updates allow former employers' clients a suitable way to communicate with them. Yet, research indicates that different customers have varying levels of intellectual capacity, necessitating a range of communication strategies. (The AlphaFold team. (2020)

The system enables a doctor-client to get updates on each sick patient by the doctor's preferred standards, subject to AI limitations. (Turea, M. (2019)

A framework, technique, and computer program item that may be changed to provide a patient with a practical, complex clinical record that the patient may send is needed to ensure that access to the patient's clinical data is always available. This previously unmet need is more common in crises since it takes longer for a healthcare practitioner to assess a patient's condition and give them the care they require. (Reardon, S. (2019)

2. Review Literature

This paper talks about Artificial intelligence (AI), a subfield of computer science, which has the potential to dramatically change how healthcare is delivered and how medicine is performed. In this review paper, we provide a road map for developing effective, trustworthy, and safe AI systems, discuss current advancements in the application of AI in healthcare, and speculate on the potential future of AI-enhanced healthcare systems. (Topol, E. J. (2019)

In this paper, the author talks about the healthcare-related processes, right from diagnosis, operations, and pathological findings of the patients, which are done with the help of Artificial Intelligence. The critical healthcare processes can be done quickly and efficiently with few human interventions and with utmost accuracy leading to a correct time-saving diagnosis and immediate addressing of the problem. This leads to more saving of life. All these benefits lead to increased dependency on Artificial intelligence in the healthcare sector. (Kelly, C.et al 2019)

Artificial intelligence is "the theory and development of computer systems able to do activities ordinarily requiring human intellect, such as visual perception, speech recognition, decision-making, and language translation." Darrell M. West (2018), John McCarthy was the first to introduce the phrase "artificial intelligence" to respond to Alan Turing's query from the early 1950s, "Can machines think?" The area of computer science known as artificial intelligence seeks to recreate or duplicate human intellect in machines. Artificial intelligence (AI) algorithms can make morally sound judgments in addition to the usual mechanical and planned reactions from robots. (Panch, T., Mattie, H., & Celi, L. A. (2019).

Recently more researchers have giving more attention to Artificial intelligence in the healthcare sector. Previously research related to the importance of AI in different sectors like decision sciences, Management, Business, and Finance has been done. (NHSX. (2019). The use of AI in healthcare and ethical concerns are discussed by Wiens, J.et al. (2019).

It is possible to identify patterns and correlations with the use of AI, which leads to actionable insights for bettering healthcare delivery. Although there have been several contributions to the literature on this subject, we still need a clear picture of how research and application are doing right now. This essay aims to evaluate the material that is already out there to give scholars data that enables nurturing more advancement in this field. (Nachev, P, et al.2019)

Evaluating the literature to give the researchers information. The healthcare sector is adopting impactful technologies to enhance patient care. Artificial intelligence (AI) in healthcare and medicine has been a hot issue recently. (Strodthoff, N., & Strodthoff, C. (2019)

Healthcare AI replaces all of the regular duties that doctors, administrators, and even patients once perform in less time and with lower costs. This served as the main support structure for the expanded use of AI in healthcare. (Bellemo, V.et al. (2019)

From radiography to tumor identification, physicians benefit from AI-driven tools and applications. Applications of artificial intelligence in healthcare uncover fresh approaches to creating new medications. One of the most essential advantages of AI in healthcare (Ting, D. S., et al. (2019). Lashinsky has discussed that the focus of AI has also been on looking for the possible advantages and challenges of integrating AI into healthcare. (Lashinsky, A. (2017)

This paper talks about how healthcare as well as the fields of medical and dental education are being quickly transformed by artificial intelligence (AI). The application of AI in healthcare will be examined in the first section of the article, along with its effects on patient care, diagnosis, and treatment, as well as the advantages it offers both patients and medical professionals. The application of AI in medicine will next be discussed, along with how it affects instructional strategies and student learning, as well as the advantages and disadvantages it offers teachers and students. (Feeley, D. (2017)

3. Problem Statement

AI may use specially developed algorithms to "learn" structures from a vast amount of medical information and then put the newfound understandings to use in supporting medical practice (Davahli, M. R.et,.al, 2021). Moreover, it is strengthened with learning and self-correcting abilities to advance its response-based accuracy (Quinn, T. P et.al, 2021). Moreover, AI systems can assist clinicians by providing up-to-date medical information from research books, journals, and clinical settings to illuminate optimal patient treatment (Bajwa, J.,et, al 2021) Moreover, a system using artificial intelligence (AI) can reduce therapeutic and diagnostic errors inherent in human medical practice. A schematic representation of the hybrid healthcare architecture was shown (Fig. 4.1). Also, an AI system extracts valuable information from a large patient population to enable real-time implications for health danger awareness and wellness. (Wang, A. et,al, 2021)

Fig. 4.1 Schematic representation of healthcare hybrid cloud architecture

Figure 4.2 The diagram talks about the various data which starts with a patient who goes to Private clinics and goes to the medical where their various reports like CT, and Lab are collected in the reception and with the help of the IT department preserved in the public cloud. AI then fetches data from the public cloud and makes the information available to the patients and the doctor for further processing and treatment this leads to smoother and error-free diagnosis and treatment.

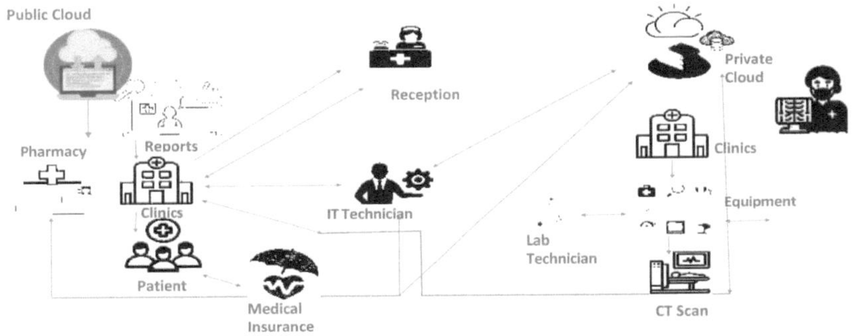

Fig. 4.2 General schematic view of the process flow of AI in the healthcare sector

Figure 4.3 describes the medical staff and patient remote access process where patients with the help of AI can have restricted access to the medical staff anywhere in the globe. The patient can discuss their various health-related issues by uploading their queries and reports in the cloud which is protected and get suggestions from medical staff and the entire discussion is again protected from outsiders leading to better and more timely treatment.

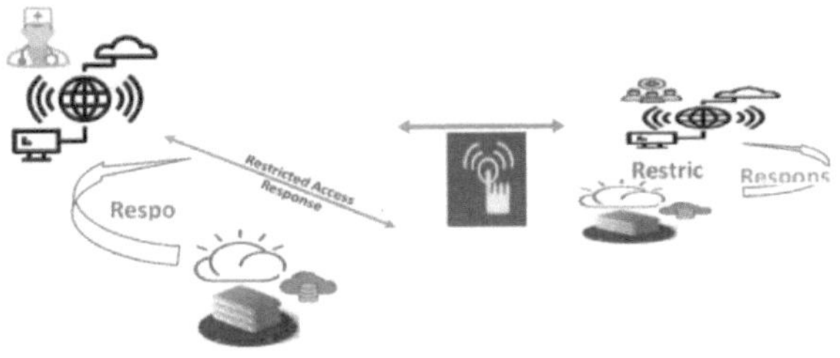

Fig. 4.3 Medical staff and patient remote access

The most common use of classical machine learning in healthcare is accuracy medicine, which predicts which treatment procedures are likely to be successful on a patient based on several patient characteristics and their medical history.

4. Result

A training dataset for which the outcome variable (such as the onset of illness) is known is required for the extreme majority of machine learning and precision medicine demands; this is known as controlled learning (Fig. 4.4). The literature gathered from the study articles also revealed that the application of AI was high in the year of 2019-2020. According to the current survey, the impact of AI in the health care system is reliant mainly on recent years as compared to the prior six year

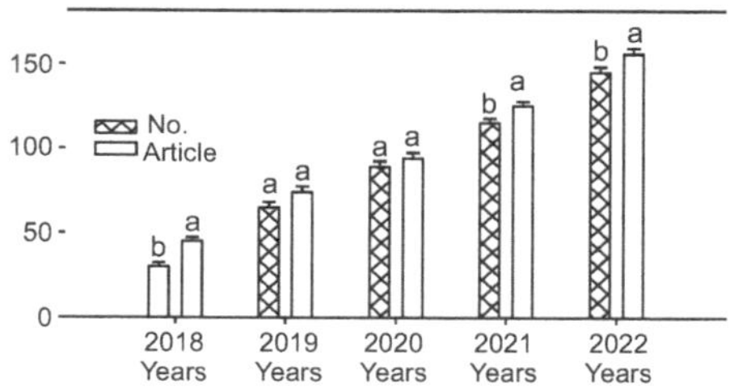

Fig. 4.4 Application of AI and their trend line from the year 2018-2022

For a while, it was believed that patient commitment and adherence were the final hurdles between poor health outcomes and effective treatment. The better the usage, financial outcomes, and part experience, the more patients actively participate in their well-being and treatment. Enormous data and AI are increasingly taking care of these components.

5. Authors Contribution/Novelty

Different from the previous type of brain organization, profound learning incorporates additional secret layers with the purpose that the computations can deal with complicated information with varied structures. Convolution neural organization (CNN), intermittent neural organization, profound conviction organization, and profound neural organization are the commonly used deep learning computations in clinical applications.

A modern improvement on the traditional neural organizing method is deep learning. Deep learning may be compared to a multi-layered neuronal structure (Fig. 4.5). Modern computing has advanced quickly, making creating complex neural networks with many layers—impossible for older neural networks.

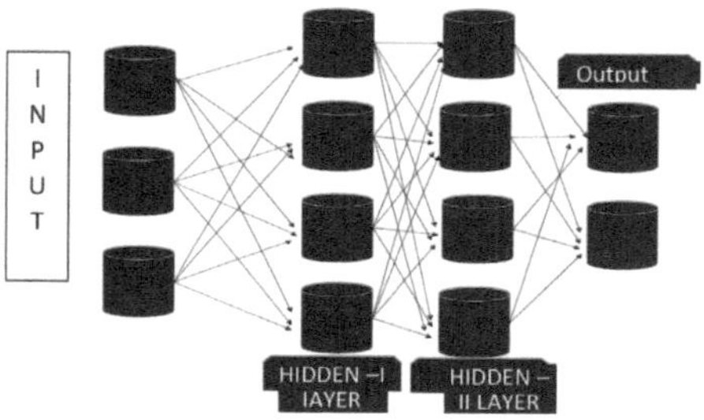

Fig. 4.5 Schematic view of deep learning with two hidden layers in the health care system

Deep learning may therefore examine more complex non-direct instances in the data. Because of the growth in the amount and complexity of knowledge, profound learning continues to enjoy popularity.

6. Discussion & Conclusion

The present finding points to the fact that "the use of Machine learning and AI" is the need of the hour. Nowadays, most healthcare-related processes, right from diagnosis, operations, and pathological findings of the patients, are done with the help of Artificial Intelligence.

The critical healthcare processes can be done quickly and efficiently with few human interventions and with utmost accuracy leading to a correct time-saving diagnosis and immediate addressing of the problem. This leads to more saving of life. All these benefits lead to increased dependency on "Artificial intelligence in the healthcare sector".

AI in healthcare is transforming the future of healthcare in a big way. AI technologies are helping healthcare become more accurate, predictive, and time-saving. The patients are being handled with utmost care leading to a more positive impact on the patients' minds. The diagnosis and operations are becoming more accurate and less invasive, leading to quick relief from hospitals and a fast recovery rate. Time-saving, according to NHS, can help doctors and nurses to give time to patients' care so that the patient has an overall good healthcare experience.

AI applications in healthcare are a boon, but many challenges have to be addressed to make AI-enabled healthcare a success. The steps that should be implemented are as follows:

- Training for Healthcare administrators related to digital capability and proficiency in operating AI-enabled healthcare machines.
- Prior domain knowledge related to dataset operations for healthcare administrators is necessary.
- Everyone should know that healthcare administrators should know knowledge regarding the lawful use of available datasets so that they can be used for research and make the system much better.

REFERENCES

1. Davahli MR, Karwowski W, Fiok K, Wan T, Parsaei HR. Controlling safety of artificial intelligence-based systems in healthcare. *Symmetry* 2021;13:102. [Google Scholar]
2. Quinn TP, Senadeera M, Jacobs S, Coghlan S, Le V. Trust, and medical AI: the challenges we face and the expertise needed to overcome them. *J Am Med Inform Assoc* 2021;28:890–4. [PMC free article] [PubMed] [Google Scholar]
3. Muoio D. *Google's next-gen Nest Hub debuts with contactless sleep monitoring and analysis features*. Mobi Health News, 2021. www.mobihealthnews.com/news/googles-next-gen-nest-hub-debuts-contactless-sleep-monitoring-and-analysis-features [Google Scholar]
4. Wang A, Nguyen D, Sridhar AR, et al.. Using smart speakers to contactlessly monitor heart rhythms. *Commun Biol* 2021;4:319. [PMC free article] [PubMed] [Google Scholar]
5. Haque A, Milstein A, Fei-Fei L. Illuminating the dark spaces of healthcare with ambient intelligence. *Nature* 2020;585:193–202. [PubMed] [Google Scholar]
6 World Health Organization. *Working for health and growth: Investing in the health workforce*. WHO, 2016. http://apps.who.int/iris/bitstream/10665/250047/1/9789241511308-eng.pdf [Accessed 31 January 2020]. [Google Scholar]

7. United States Government Accountability Office. *Artificial intelligence in health care: Benefits and challenges of technologies to augment patient care*. GAO, 2020. [Google Scholar]
8. Sendak MP, D'Arcy J, Kashyap S, et al.. A path for translation of machine learning products into healthcare delivery. *EMJ Innov* 2020;10:19–00172. [Google Scholar]
9. University of Leeds. *NPIC - Northern Pathology Imaging Co-operative*. University of Leeds, 2020. www.virtualpathology.leeds.ac.uk/npic [Google Scholar]
10. Xie Y, Nguyen QD, Hamzah H, et al.. Artificial intelligence for teleophthalmology-based diabetic retinopathy screening in a national programme: an economic analysis modelling study. *Lancet Digit Health* 2020;2:e240–9. [PubMed] [Google Scholar]
11. 45. Simonite T. *The US government will pay doctors to use these AI algorithms*. Wired, 2020. www.wired.com/story/us-government-pay-doctors-use-ai-algorithms [Google Scholar]
12. 46. Oktay O, Nanavati J, Schwaighofer A, et al. Evaluation of deep learning to augment image-guided radiotherapy for head and neck and prostate cancers. *JAMA Netw Open* 2020;3:e2027426. [PMC free article] [PubMed] [Google Scholar]
13. 47. Alverez-Valle J, Moore GJ. *Project InnerEye open-source deep learning toolkit: Democratizing medical imaging AI*. Microsoft, 2020. www.microsoft.com/en-us/research/blog/project-innereye-open-source-deep-learning-toolkit-democratizing-medical-imaging-ai [Google Scholar]
14. 48. Senior AW, Evans R, Jumper J, et al.. Improved protein structure prediction using potentials from deep learning. *Nature* 2020;577:706–10. [PubMed] [Google Scholar]
15. 49. The AlphaFold team. *AlphaFold: a solution to a 50-year-old grand challenge in biology*. DeepMind, 2020. https://deepmind.com/blog/article/alphafold-a-solution-to-a-50-year-old-grand-challenge-in-biology [Google Scholar]
16. *Satya Nadella announces strategic collaboration with Novartis*. You Tube, 2019. www.youtube.com/watch?v=wMfsQE-D2q4
17. Turea M. *How the 'Big 4' tech companies are leading healthcare innovation*. Healthcare Weekly, 2019. [Google Scholar]
18. 13. Binns R, Gallo V. *Trade-offs*. Information Commissioner's Office, 2019. https://ico.org.uk/about-the-ico/news-and-events/ai-blog-trade-offs
19. Reardon S. Rise of robot radiologists. *Nature* 2019;576:S54–8. [PubMed] [Google Scholar]
20. Topol EJ. High-performance medicine: the convergence of human and artificial intelligence. *Nat Med* 2019;25:44–56. [PubMed] [Google Scholar]
21. Kelly CJ, Karthikesalingam A, Suleyman M, Corrado G, King D. Key challenges for delivering clinical impact with artificial intelligence. *BMC Medicine* 2019;17:195. [PMC free article] [PubMed] [Google Scholar]
22. Panch T, Mattie H, Celi LA. The 'inconvenient truth' about AI in healthcare. *NPJ Digit Med* 2019;2:77. [PMC free article] [PubMed] [Google Scholar]
23. NHSX. *Artificial intelligence: How to get it right*. NHS, 2019. [Google Scholar]
24. Wiens J, Saria S, Sendak M, et al.. Do no harm: a roadmap for responsible machine learning for health care. *Nat Med* 2019;25:1337–40. [PubMed] [Google Scholar]
25. Nachev P, Herron D, McNally N, Rees G, Williams B. Redefining the research hospital. *NPJ Digit Med* 2019;2:119. [PMC free article] [PubMed] [Google Scholar]
26. Strodthoff N, Strodthoff C. Detecting and interpreting myocardial infarction using fully convolutional neural networks. *Physiological Measurement* 2019;40:015001. [PubMed] [Google Scholar]

27. Bellemo V, Lim ZW, Lim G, et al.. Artificial intelligence using deep learning to screen for referable and vision-threatening diabetic retinopathy in Africa: a clinical validation study. *Lancet Digit Health* 2019;1:e35–
28. Ting DSW, Pasquale LR, Peng L, et al.. Artificial intelligence and deep learning in ophthalmology. *Br J Ophthalmol* 2019;103:167–75. [PMC free article] [PubMed] [Google Scholar]
29. Raumviboonsuk P, Krause J, Chotcomwongse P, et al.. Deep learning versus human graders for classifying diabetic retinopathy severity in a nationwide screening program. *NPJ Digit Med* 2019;2:25. [PMC free article] [PubMed] [Google Scholar]
30. The Health Foundation, Nuffield Trust, The King's Fund. *The health care workforce in England: make or break?* The King's Fund, 2018. [Google Scholar]
31. Feeley D. *The Triple Aim or the Quadruple Aim? Four Points to Help Set Your Strategy*. Institute for Healthcare Improvement, 2017. www.ihi.org/communities/blogs/the-triple-aim-or-the-quadruple-aim-four-points-to-help-set-your-strategy. [Google Scholar]
32. Lashinsky A. *Tim Cook on how Apple champions the environment, education, and health care*. Fortune, 2017. [Google Scholar]
33. Bejnordi BE, Veta M, Van Diest PJ, et al.. Diagnostic assessment of deep learning algorithms for detection of lymph node metastases in women with breast cancer. *JAMA* 2017;318:2199–210. [PMC free article] [PubMed] [Google Scholar]
34. Grazia Dicuonzo, Francesca Donofrio, Antonio Fusco, Matilda Shini, Healthcare system: Moving forward with artificial intelligence, Technovation, Volume 120,2023,102510,ISSN 0166-4972,https://doi.org/10.1016/j.technovation.2022.102510.
35. Dave, M., & Patel, N. (2023). Artificial intelligence in healthcare and education. *British Dental Journal, 234*(10), 761–764.

Note: All the figures and tables in this chapter were made by the authors.

Securing the Future through Sustainability, Health, Education, and Technology –
Brig. Dr. Rajiv Divekar et al. (eds)

5 Kano Model Analysis for Understanding Customer Satisfaction

Ruby Chanda[1],
Vanishree Pabalkar[2], Manisha Singh[3]
Symbiosis Institute of Management Studies,
a Constituent of Symbiosis International (Deemed University),
Range Hills Road, Khadki, Pune, India

Abstract

Purpose: This study is proposed as a background for the real estate industry to understand how and where the brand can improve customer service at the sales centers.

Methodology: The study covers three crucial aspects. Firstly, it talks about the competitor analysis done by visiting the sales centers of other developers in the market. The research ranks the brand and its competitors on nine parameters of customer experience. Secondly, the customer's emotional journey of house buying is mapped to understand their phases while buying a house and their goals, activities undertaken, emotional response, and metrics to measure the company's performance in these phases. The third part of the research covers applying the Kano model to measure customer satisfaction on all the current services in the market.

Findings: The model classifies fourteen service attributes into four major categories, and hence, final suggestions are made based on the importance given to these attributes by respondents, competitor analysis, and customer journey mapping.

Implications: The study highlights the attributes of customer service that are important for customers in the luxury real estate market and provides suggestions to improve customer service

Originality: The methodology and the analysis adopted in this study are quite focused as the Kano model is followed, which is more in line with aiming specific attributes and their contribution towards overall customer satisfaction.

Keywords: Kano model, Customer satisfaction, Customer emotional journey, Customer services, Customer experience, Real estate, Consumer buying behavior

[1]ruby.chanda@sims.edu, [2]vanishree.p@sims.edu, [3]manisha.na2020@sims.edu

DOI: 10.1201/9781003587200-5

1. Introduction

Making a positive client experience is now a top managerial goal (Lemon and Vehoef 2016). Customer experience is one of the Marketing Science Institute's top research challenges for the foreseeable future (Lemon and Vehoef 2016). The complexity of customer touchpoints, which is growing, and the idea that providing strong, positive customer experiences will increase revenue by boosting word-of-mouth advertising and customer loyalty, as well as performance throughout the customer journey at various touchpoints, are likely to be the causes (Lemon and Vehoef 2016; Edelman 2010; Homburg, Jozi'c, and Kuehnl 2015). Superior customer experiences can give businesses a competitive edge when designed and delivered. Due to the proliferation of potential customer touchpoints and the condensed control of the experience, businesses must integrate a wide range of business functions, including information technology (IT), service operations, logistics, marketing, and even external partners, to create and deliver positive customer experiences (Lemon and Vehoef 2016). Businesses are finding it harder to create, manage, and try to control each customer's journey Edelman, 2010; Rawson, Duncan, and Jones, 2013). The consumer's intellectual, behavioral, emotional, social, physical, and responses to the company's value offers are all included in the holistic customer experience (Grewal et al. 2017).The elements that influence the customer experience include those that are under the company's control as well as those that are not (such as the customer's personality, the influence of others, the type of product, and the purpose of the purchase), such as the service interface, retail environment, assortment, and price) (Verhoef et al. 2009, Grewal et al. 2017).

This study is about the services and experience provided to the customer in the Realty sales center across various touchpoints and how this experience can lead to higher customer satisfaction and increased conversion rates. Understanding the demand & importance of customer services is extremely important for developers to pitch their products quickly. The study is aimed to develop a strategy to improve the customer experience at Realty's sales centers.

Research Objective thus emerged as Comprehensive determination of customer service requirements at the sales center & their impact on customer satisfaction

2. Material and Method

Current Customer Journey in the Real Estate Industry

Looking at customer experience from a holistic view in the real estate industry, the convenience for the customer to understand the project aspects like area, buildings, house size, amenities, connectivity furnishings, etc., and how we can achieve customer delight in the customer journey. The hospitality, convenient pricing & payment plans also determine customer satisfaction. The customer journey at a sales center includes the following major stages:

Pre-sales call: Inbound calls are received from the customer on the contact numbers seen on websites, hoardings, print ads, etc., whereas outbound calls are done by the call center executives on the database.

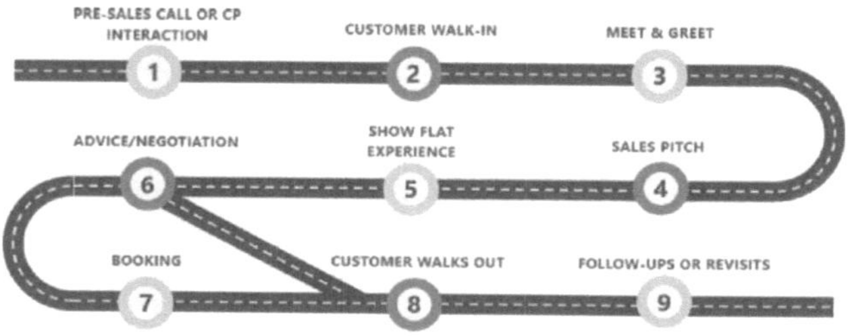

Fig. 5.1 Steps in customer journey in the real estate sector

Channel partner interaction: Channel Partners are those who assist the developers in getting clients for the project. As per the real estate business model, channel partners get a percentage-based commission for every client and buy a product from the developer.

Customer walk-in: The stage in which a customer walks in the sales center, primarily located at the project site, to understand the project, meet the sales manager, and book the flat.

Meet & greet: The stage in which the first face-to-face interaction happens between the customer and sales staff. This stage involves welcoming the customer, providing them with welcome drinks, and filling the customer information form.

Sales pitch: The sales pitch involves pitching the USPs, benefits, values to the customer by the sales manager and making them understand everything about the project from connectivity to possession timelines. This stage involves sub-stages like project model, audio-visual, interactive screen, etc., to aid the sales pitch.

Show flat experience: The customer is shown either a show flat (fully furnished flat in exact dimensions considered a representative of how their home would like once they start living there) or a sample flat (representative of how exactly the flat will be delivered to the customer i.e. without any extra décor & furniture).

Advice/negotiation: The stage to make the customer aware of the price, all-inclusive price, price break-up, taxes & duties, payment plans, etc. This stage also involves suggesting the customer a floor and flat number based on their requirements & Vaastu compliance.

Booking: This stage involves the sale closure with the customer booking a flat, handing- over a cheque, and completing all the formalities.

Customer walk-out: When a customer walks out of the sales center, what is the exit like, what collaterals are he taking with him? The branding on the ways plays an important role.

Follow-ups or re-visits: Most customers choose to explore projects by competitors and hence, not to book the flat on the first visit. The sales manager follows up with these customers on phone calls, text messages, and emails. The customers also re-visit their shortlisted projects with other members of their families.

Table 5.1 Customer emotional journey

Stage	IAwareness	II Consideration - Pre-sales	III Desire to buy - Customer Walk-in	IV Meet & greet
Customer activities	Hears from friends, sees ads, referrals	Searches online, contacts channel partner	Reaches the sale center to see the property	Interaction with CED
Customer goals	No goals at this point	Wants to buy a house	Find the best place/property to buy home in	To meet the contacted person or to meet someone who can explain the project
Touch Points	Call, OOH & digital advertising, WOM, Referrals	Google search, website, Pre-sales call, CP, social media	All physical evidences & employees at sales center	Security, Reception CED exec & other Staff Interiors Branding/AV/Books Information form F&B
Experience	Hygiene	Hygiene	Feel good	Delight
Emotional Response	None, unsure	Requires effort but curious, interested "I want a new house"	Excited, Keen to view/know everything but uncertain where to buy "Let's see properties!"	Overwhelmed, happy, yet confused "Thank you"
Metrics	No. of people reached	Online presence, CP relations	No. of walk ins	
Improvement/ Goal	Increase awareness & interest Creative OOH advertising	NA	Convenience in locating Accessibility of sales center Branding	Make the customer feel comfortable while filling the info form Engage in the waiting time

Stage	V Sales Pitch	VI Show Flat Experience	VII Negotiation	
Customer activities	Interacting, asking questions, observing, understanding the offering	Roaming inside the show flat, interacting, raising queries	Move to closing table with SM	
Customer Goals	to get a proper understanding of the project, pricing & payment plan	To know how the house would look like Understanding the flat specs & fixtures	Get the understanding of pricing, taxes, duties, price break-up etc. Getting discounts	
Touch Points	Sales Manager AV & Interactive screen 3D Model	Show Flat interiors Sales Manager Other staff: Darbaan Branding & music	Sales Manager Other staff: Pantry boy Collaterals F&B	
Experience	Hygiene	Feel good	Hygiene	
Emotional Response	Eager, Inquisitive "Where is the gym?"	Awestruck, aspirational & curious "Beautiful, but they won't give all this."	Anxious & apprehensive "Can I afford it?" "Why so expensive?"	
Metrics	Ease of understanding - Net Effort Score Conversion Rate		Customer Satisfaction Score Conversion Rate	
Improvement/Goal	Increase ticket size Better Need analysis Personalization More tech integration for ease of understanding	Providing show flat of all configurations & SA Setting the right expectations Integrating VR if show flat not available	Make the customer feel comfortable in the moment of anxiety: Highlight value, savings, better offering than competitors	

Stage	VIII Closing	IX Follow-ups	X Loyalty/Advocacy	
Customer activities	Closing the deal, make the booking payment	Expecting & attending the calls, checking mails & messages, comparing properties	Waiting for possession, making payments, keeping a track of completion	
Customer Goals	Paying as little as possible	To make the best decision after evaluating all To be in continuous touch to know about offers	Want to shift to new house or start earning ROI from investment	
Touch Points	Sales Manager Documentation Payment procedures	Sales Manager through: phone call, text, WhatsApp, mail Channel Partner	CRM team through: CRM tool, phone call, text, WhatsApp, mail Customer Re-visits	
Experience	Hygiene	Feel good	Delight	
Emotional Response	Nervous & anxious	Cautious, hopeful, optimistic	Confident & ecstatic "I would suggest you to buy house in Piramal" Nervous of timely payments	
Metrics		TAT No. of follow ups Conversion Rate	NPS CSAT No. of complaints	
Improvement/Goal	Replacing anxiety with celebration of his achievement together Proper hand holding with CRM team	Increase trustworthiness: Providing sales team with more official communication in email & images Show more concern to customer's issues & help him solving them	Give them reasons to talk about us more	

Customer Emotional Journey Map

- *The experience is divided into three categories: hygiene, feel good, and delight.*
- *The moments of anxiety are marked in red, whereas the moments with positive emotional response are highlighted in yellow*

Quantifying the results based on factors chosen:

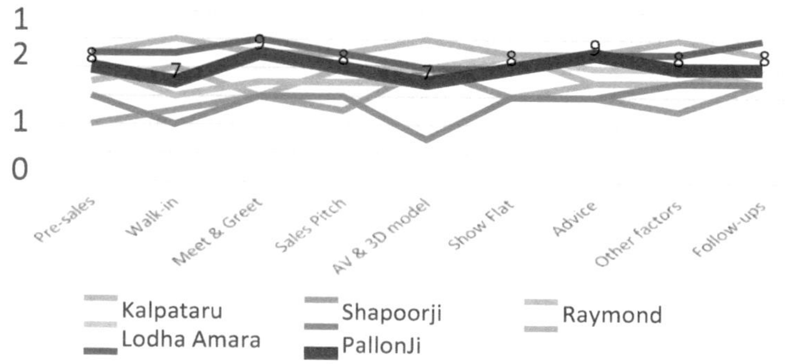

Fig. 5.2 Scoring of competitor analysis

3. Results

The data collection method for a quantitative Kano analysis study is survey forms filled by regular walk-ins. Hence, the quantitative research covers Thane's real estate micro-market. Respondents were selected among the walk-ins in April 2019. They received the link to the survey form based on their willingness to participate. The questionnaires had two groups, with the first part including demographic characteristics. The central part of the survey consisted of questions on 14 customer services provided in the real estate industry, which form the customer experience. Based on the Kano model, this part measured customers' expectations using a three-question functional, dysfunctional & self-stated importance. The researcher obtained 240 valid surveys (more than 10% of monthly walk-ins).

3.1 Six-level Kano Questionnaire

In the original Kano model classification, the questionnaire is constructed through two parts: how do you feel if the particular attribute is present in the product/service (Functional form of the question), and how do you feel if the particular attribute is not present in the product/service (Dysfunctional form of the question). In this study, the respondent was asked a set of three questions on each attribute. For the first two questions, the respondent selects one of the five alternatives on a Likert scale: "like it," "expect it," "don't care," "live with it," and "dislike it.". The third question evaluated the self-stated importance of the attribute on a scale of 1-9. The perceptions were then assessed based on Pouliot's revised evaluation table (see figure below) to classify customer perceptions into six categories, namely:

- Must-be (M)
- Performance (P)
- Attractive (A)
- Indifferent (I)
- Reverse (R)
- Questionable (Q)

		Dysfunctional (X)				
Functional (Y)		Like	Expect It	Don't Care	Live With	Dislike
		-2	-1	0	2	4
Like	4	Q	A	A	A	P
Expect It	2	R	Q	I	I	M
Don't Care	0	R	I	I	I	M
Live With	-1	R	I	I	Q	M
Dislike	-2	R	R	R	R	Q

Fig. 5.3 Evaluation table

Category R stands for Reversible Quality, which signifies that the customer wants the product and that the customer expects the opposite. Category Q stands for Questionable suggesting the question was expressed incorrectly or the respondent misunderstood the question.

14 service attributes used for the study are:

Table 5.2 Fourteen attributes chosen for kano analysis

Code	Description
F1	Pre-visit phone call
F2	Convenience in locating the sales center
F3	Sales center look & feel
F4	Welcomed & attended in time
F5	Hospitality (Beverage & snacks)
F6	Knowledge of sales manager
F7	Project explanation using 3D Model
F8	AV or Interactive Screen
F9	Overview of amenities
F10	Show flat furnishing (furniture & decor)
F11	Ease of understanding price & payment plans
F12	Ease of choosing floor & unit
F13	Factual & pictorial brochure
F14	Regular follow-ups

Firstly, discrete analysis is used on the obtained data. The Discrete study categorizes each respondent using Pouliot's evaluation table, leading us to how many respondents have been numerically classified into each category. Each attribute's final category is the most frequent response (i.e., the Model).

To overcome the limitations of the discrete analysis, like softer answers getting the same weightage as the harder ones (e.g., Attractive with a dysfunctional "expect it" vs. "live with"), the researcher uses the continuous analysis by Bill DuMouchel (DuMouchel, 1993) Hence, the suggestions to improve the services at Piramal projects are based on quantitative and qualitative studies done in 6 weeks, i.e., competitor analysis, customer emotional journey mapping, and Kano analysis of customer satisfaction.

Table 5.3 Gender distribution of respondents

Gender	Male	Female	Total
	193	47	240

Respondents Demographic Profile

Interpretations:

55% of them are working in the service sector, 17% have their own business.53% of the respondents are upgraders which means they are looking to upgrade their lifestyle by buying a new home. It could be shifting from 1 BHK to 2 BHK, or 2 BHK to 3 BHK, etc. 67% of respondents are looking for 2BHK. A high number of customers come in search of buying a 2 BHK, i.e., 67%.

Discrete Analysis

The discrete analysis gives a brief understanding of where the real estate marketers need a rigorous approach while providing customer experience at the sales center. The attributes marked "Must-be" like Pre-visit phone call, convenience in locating the sales center, knowledge of the sales manager, and project explanation using 3D Model need to be given high importance to be executed perfectly. Otherwise, they would lead to significant dissatisfaction.

According to discrete analysis carried out to determine the frequency of repetition, 5 out of 14 attributes were identified as Attractive attributes, 4 out of 14 attributes were identified as Must-be attributes, 3 out of 14 attributes were identified as Performance attributes, one attribute as Reverse and one as indifferent.

Table 5.4 Discreet analysis

	Discrete Analysis							
	M	P	A	I	R	Q	Total	Category
F1	**32.50%**	22.50%	15.00%	25.00%	0.00%	5.00%	100%	M
F2	**35.00%**	17.50%	15.00%	30.00%	0.00%	2.50%	100%	M
F3	5.00%	15.00%	**52.50%**	25.00%	0.00%	2.50%	100%	A
F4	7.50%	15.00%	**47.50%**	22.50%	2.50%	5.00%	100%	A
F5	12.50%	10.00%	**37.50%**	35.00%	0.00%	5.00%	100%	A
F6	**45.00%**	20.00%	17.50%	15.00%	2.50%	0.00%	100%	M
F7	**37.50%**	10.00%	22.50%	22.50%	0.00%	7.50%	100%	M
F8	7.50%	15.00%	**47.50%**	22.50%	2.50%	5.00%	100%	A
F9	27.50%	**40.00%**	17.50%	12.50%	0.00%	2.50%	100%	P
F10	12.50%	5.00%	15.00%	27.50%	**37.50%**	2.50%	100%	R
F11	20.00%	**42.50%**	15.00%	22.50%	0.00%	0.00%	100%	P
F12	12.50%	17.50%	**35.00%**	30.00%	2.50%	2.50%	100%	A
F13	20.00%	**30.00%**	27.50%	20.00%	2.50%	0.00%	100%	P
F14	15.00%	25.00%	15.00%	**37.50%**	2.50%	5.00%	100%	I

The attributes marked "Performance" are Overview of amenities, Ease of understanding price & payment plans, and Factual & pictorial brochure. These features need to be executed at high functionality for higher satisfaction. The attributes marked “Attractive” are F3, F4, F5, F8, and F12. These attributes lead to customer delight even at low execution. Hence to achieve higher customer satisfaction, the primary focus should be on elevating the customer experience in these touchpoints. Attribute F10 show flat furnishing turned out to be a reverse feature that customers like more when it is not there.

Most of the customers are indifferent towards attribute F14; regular follow-ups.

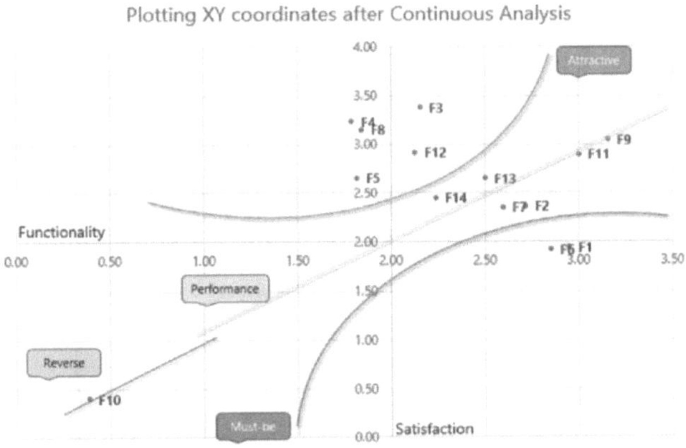

Fig. 5.4 Application of kano analysis on 14 attributes

Continuous Analysis

The final distribution of attributes into four categories as per the continuous analysis by Bill DuMouchel is as below:

Table 5.5 Continuous analysis

	Continuous Analysis						
Feature	**Dysfunctional (X)**	**Functional (Y)**	**Importance (Z)**	**Category**	**Std Dev X**	**Std Dev Y**	**Std Dev Z**
F3	2.15	3.38	7.49	A	1.14	1.15	0.84
F1	2.95	1.95	7.08	M	1.35	2.05	1.26
F4	1.79	3.24	7.26	A	1.81	1.17	1.20
F5	1.82	2.66	7.42	A	1.66	1.62	1.04
F2	2.72	2.36	7.72	P	1.54	1.50	1.13
F6	2.85	1.93	7.90	M	1.79	1.98	0.89
F7	2.59	2.35	7.59	P	1.57	1.71	1.12
F8	1.84	3.16	6.84	A	1.58	1.60	1.23
F9	3.15	3.05	7.97	P	1.55	1.27	0.84
F10	0.38	0.41	6.72	R	2.16	2.28	1.43
F11	3.00	2.90	8.10	P	1.43	1.48	0.83
F12	2.13	2.92	7.82	A	1.57	1.47	0.99
F13	2.50	2.65	7.53	P	1.77	1.86	1.02
F14	2.24	2.45	6.92	P	1.76	1.67	0.85

Table 5.6 Attributes categorized in Kano categories

Must Be		Attractive		Performance		Reverse	
F1	Pre-visit phone call	F4	Welcomed & attended in time	F2	Convenience in locating the sales center	F10	Show flat furnishing
F6	Knowledge of the sales manager	F5	Hospitality (Beverage & snacks)	F7	Project explanation using 3D Model		
		F8	AV or Interactive Screen	F9	Overview of amenities		
		F3	Sales center look & feel	F11	Ease of understanding price & payment plans		
		F12	Ease of choosing floor & unit	F13	Factual & pictorial brochure		
				F14	Regular follow-ups		

For Must-be attributes:

Competitive intelligence reports: It is advised that two sales managers visit competitors on weekdays and present detailed information to other employees. The same will be done with two different managers next week. This would enhance the industry & competitor knowledge among sales managers and a great employee engagement activity.

Personalization of pitch: After getting the phone no & email id of the customer in CIF, the sales manager receives a notification regarding the new customer being allotted. The social media links (LinkedIn, Facebook, Twitter, Instagram) should be displayed on the same salesforce page. The sales manager can click the links and analyze the customer profile to pitch the property's good feature/amenity/USP. (E.g. if the customer has many pictures with their pet, the sales manager can include this information in their sales pitch and highlight a 1 km long pathway & gardens inside the project to walk the pet.)

Internal quality measures for pre-sales call executives for attractive attributes:

Maintain the current look of the sales center: It is premium, cozy, and easily recallable since it is different from all other sales centers in the micro-market.

Maintain the same quality of hospitality: Don't over-invest in the quality of hospitality that we are providing (support staff behavior, food & snacks facilities, comfortable seating)

Greeting manual for the support staff and their uniforms based on the theme colors of the project

Enhance ease of choosing floor & unit: 3D Model to light up all the flats of the same configuration in the building, showing which one is available in green light. The Model should be well placed according to directions

Include an AV: Audio-visual will be shown in the waiting time between CIF filling and first interaction with sales manager to engage the customer within that time with the brand

Make a kids' zone: 54% of walk-ins are with family, a group, or friends, and around 80% of bookings happen in re-visits, making it necessary to have a kid zone at site.

For performance attributes:

Include interactive project 3D model: The 3D Model should highlight each part of the project when AV or sales manager speaks about it. This creates an immersive experience for the customer and makes it easy to recall amenities.

Make it easy to locate: Pre-sales executive to mandatorily send a message to the customer with GPS location of the site. Signages should be installed on the roads. The entrance should have noticeable huge branding showcasing amenities.

Enhance ease of understanding of price & payment plans: Equip the sales managers/financial assistant with ready to use tools on

- Eligibility amount of the loan for the customer
- Cash flows in payment (especially first one year)
- Regular vs. modified payment plans NPV

Project book to be kept in the waiting area highlighting the ideology behind the project, international partners, and lifestyle that company offers.

Follow-ups:

- Official images from the company should be sent to clients personally by the sales managers at for new launches and offers. The media like WhatsApp, text messages, and emails should be used for this.
- Companies should add blogs to their website about loans, RERA guidelines, possession, etc. Sales managers can easily send to potential clients they are trying to convert. The brand appears like an expert in the sector and is always ready to serve the customers with the right information.
- Create a brand property for customer testimonials & referrals in videos & images, which can be sent to clients to remind and reinforce the brand Piramal Realty.

For reverse attribute:

- Reduce the heavy furnishing inside the show flat and use minimalistic yet classy décor
- Provide lift & gallery experience for flats whose USP is an unshared gallery and lift on that floor
- Use of mirror in decorations to extend the eye-sight making it appear more spacious
- Inform the customer before showing flat walk-in that it is a representative of how your home would look like once you start living here
- Keep a sample flat as an option if the customer wants to see it

Other suggestions

360° Need Analysis Model: A model to do complete need analysis of the customer and modify the sales pitch accordingly. The customer should leave the sales site with one particular flat number in mind, which should arrive based on the 8 factors suggested in the Model.

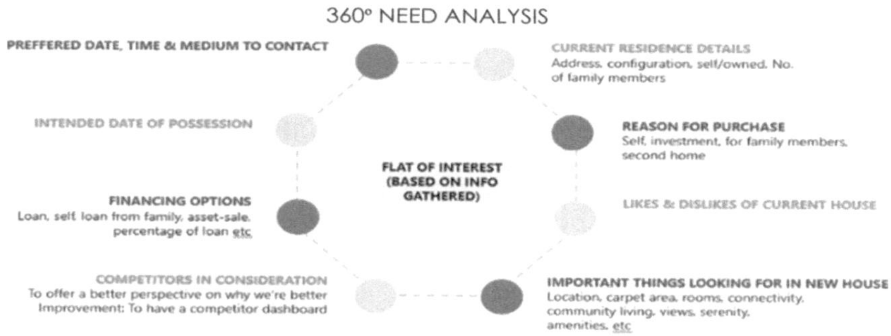

Fig. 5.5 360° need analysis for sales pitch

Create social proof:

Make the closing area and waiting area nearby, so the customer sees more of the other customers buying the flat or in the process of buying. Create a customer wall where customers book the flat sign and leave a message. The other customers should be able to see it. Comfort the customer in the moment of anxiety by celebrating his achievement of buying a new house. All employees gather nearby to clap and congratulate. The other customers shall also see this upheaval of celebration.

Booking gifts should be something they would want to keep on the center table of their house. It should make the customer feel like a proud flat owner in the project. It should also act as a conversation starter with their guests and induce positive Word of Mouth.

Virtual Reality Tour for outstation and NRI clients

A virtual reality tour of the project and show flat should be provided to showcase yet-to-be-constructed properties in an immersive experience to outstation and NRI clients who can't visit the sales center. It can easily simulate actual life walk-throughs using virtual staging of fixtures, interiors, amenities, etc. This would help in reducing NRI & outstation sales cycle time.

4. Discussion and Limitations

Customer Satisfaction

Customer satisfaction was described by (Tse and Wilton,1988, p. 204) as "The consumer's response to the evaluation of the perceived discrepancy between prior expectations and the actual performance of the product as perceived after consumption." Since it is the focal point of marketing as a crucial relationship concept, customer happiness has been discussed (Fournier & Mick, 1999). The importance of customer happiness to marketers stems from the fact that it plays a vital role in determining a company's overall success and reputation among consumers. A company's competitive advantage in the market is also tied to customer satisfaction (Anderson, Fornell, & Lehmann, 1994), which motivates marketers to use trust-based strategies. It is reasonable to suppose that satisfaction is multifaceted, including social and interaction elements like utility, expectation, usability, and performance. Brunner, Stöcklin, and Opwis (2008) talk about overall customer satisfaction, which covers all supplier-client interactions. This confines all client's psychological responses depending on their experience Olsen and Johnson, 2003). Therefore, it is safe to infer that pleased customer are engaged consumers (Brodie et al., 2011; Hollebeek 2011) and that overall satisfaction serves as the foundation for both existing and possible new customer engagement processes.

Customer Engagement

Engagement is a key concept for studies on consumer behavior, despite the imprecise and surprising operationalization (Brodie et al. 2013). Customer engagement is the combination of behavioral responses with emotional context claims (Vivek et al., 2012, p. 131). The emotional context is assurance and commitment, and as a result, the behavioral context is action. As a result, it entails using the internet to browse or log onto websites, conducting business, and frequently conversing. It takes into account my brand. As a result, some of them are quantifiable, while others are more challenging. Customer engagement behaviors, according to Doorn et al. (2010), "go beyond transactions and may specifically define as a customer's behavioral manifestations that have a brand or firm focus, beyond purchase, resulting from motivational drivers." Customer engagement might be positive or negative.

Numerous researches pertaining to the media, advertising, entertainment, and brands consider customer involvement. brand (Calder et al., 2009; Higgins and Scholer, 2009; Scott and Craig-Lees, 2010; Bowden, 2009). Cheung et al. (2011) have further divided involvement into three categories.:

- consumer engagement is classified as a behavioral expression that goes beyond the purchase (Scott and Craig-Lees, 2010).
- and as a psychological process that results in consumer loyalty (Bowden (2009).
- Customer engagement is a psychological state characterized by zeal, commitment, engrossment, and connection with products or brands (Patterson, P., 2016).

Kano Model of Customer Satisfaction

Customer satisfaction measures how emotionally and logically customers rate their interactions with a product or service (Gronholdt, Martensen, & Kristensen, 2000). Customers may base their standards for evaluating their experiences on requirements, individual objectives, prior encounters, expectations, encounters with rival businesses, etc. Customer joy, brand loyalty, readiness to pay more or make repeat purchases, and favorable word-of-mouth recommendations are all influenced by higher customer satisfaction. The Kano model, which categorizes product characteristics based on how customers perceive them and their impact on customer happiness, is one of the methods used to quantify customer satisfaction. (Di Paula, 1999). These divisions serve as a roadmap for design choices because they show when something is enough and when more is preferable (Spool, 2011). The Japanese researcher Noriaki Kano and his colleagues developed the Kano model of customer satisfaction, which classifies service elements into four groups: performance, must-have, indifferent & alluring, or delighters. To determine consumer expectations & relevance with regard to service qualities, the Kano model is used. Customer happiness and service/quality qualities have an asymmetrical, non-linear relationship (Feng-Han Lin et al., 2017). The Kano model employs a graph with X and Y dimensions and two dimensions for customer happiness and attribute functioning.

To gauge consumer satisfaction and therefore make decisions about adding new features, expanding and enhancing certain components, and other things (Barutçu et al.,2015), the features of the good or service are categorized into the aforementioned categories. The qualities in each category are chosen by creating a functional and dysfunctional attribute matrix based on consumer reaction. In light of this, the characteristics may be classified into five different sorts of classes, as follows:

Performance: The linear attributes wherein the satisfaction increases as the attribute's functionality.

Must-be: Product/service attributes that customers expect. If these are not provided, the customer experiences extreme dissatisfaction.

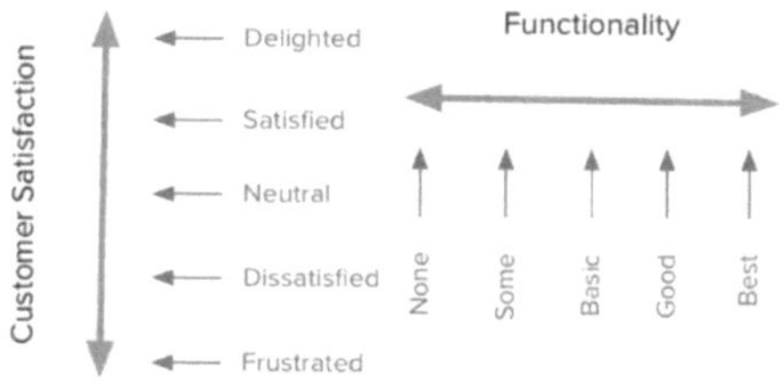

Fig. 5.6 Two-axis of the kano model

Attractive: The unexpected attributes that result in high satisfaction even at less functionality. These bring customer delight and hence give a competitive advantage.

Indifferent: The attributes toward which customers feel indifferent. Their presence or absence doesn't clearly make a difference to satisfaction.

The core premise is that by comprehending how various aspects affect customer happiness, resources may provide the best degree of satisfaction, resulting in customer loyalty (Velikova, Slevitch, and Mathe-Soulek, 2017). One of the recent studies (Wu et al., 2020) explored service quality using the Kano model for analyzing customer satisfaction of luxury housing service management. The Kano model was combined with IPA(Importance Performance Analysis) to overcome the limitations of the Kano Model. The article discussed the customers'

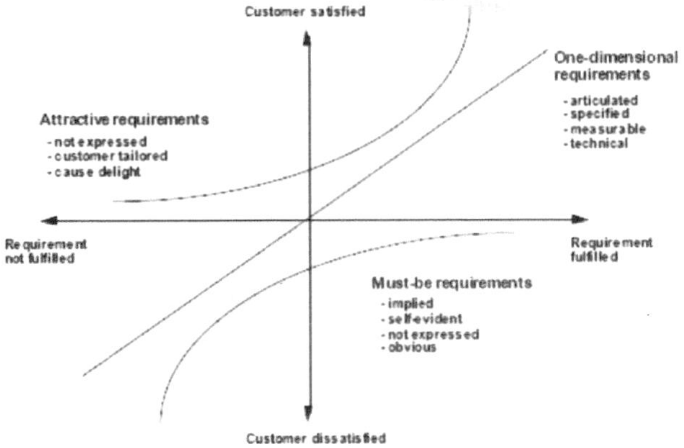

Fig. 5.7 Kano's model of customer satisfaction

perception regarding the service/product attributes for luxury apartments in Taiwan. The researchers also highlighted that we could not only measure and expect service attributes in one dimension. A combined model or approach would be more appropriate to understand customer satisfaction regarding the services.

The research highlights the attributes of customer experience that the company needs to focus on to achieve a minimum level of customer satisfaction, i.e., all must-be attributes like a good overview of amenities. The study also identifies attributes that bring extreme customer delight that is attractive attributes of service like food & beverage, welcomed & attended in time, sales center look & feel even a tiny level of execution. The findings of the research have both theoretical & practical implications.

The research adds to the highly scarce literature on customer experience in the real estate industry. The findings will help the premium & luxury market real estate players optimize business decisions to deliver a delightful customer experience. Measuring & providing what HNI customers want will help companies understand which value attributes matter more than others. Moreover, the suggestions like integrating virtual reality and better financial assistance will help in easier & faster conversions. Personalization of pitch and 360° need analysis will help sales managers to pitch the product in an improved way. The study tried to determine to what extent the customers' expectations are high for each attribute in the considered market. This tells the real estate sellers where to concentrate more. Ultimately, customer satisfaction can only be created by combining all the characteristics at the right execution level. Creating a wow experience makes the real estate player stand out in such a hyper-competitive market. The whole customer experience journey can be mapped, and the marketers can develop strategies to pull the customer interest towards the project during different stages of the trip.

Specifically, from an Indian perspective, buying a house is not solely decided by the Project brand or the price. It is primarily a one-time investment. Customers are emotionally attached to buying a home, and this is generally the decision of the whole family. Thus, it is essential to focus on all the members involved in the purchase to have better customer satisfaction afterward.

The research was done on clients who visited the sites, and hence the sample size was dependent on the number of clients who visited the site on a particular day. Therefore, the data gathered in the given time frame was limited to how many walk-ins were interested in filling the surveys.

References

1. Anderson, E. W., Fornell, C., & Lehmann, D. R. (1994). Customer satisfaction, market share, and profitability: *Findings from Sweden. Journal of marketing*, 58(3), 53–66.
2. Barutçu, S., Akgün, A. A., & DİNÇER, H. U. A. (2015). An assessment of m-customer satisfaction drivers and levels from m-shopping applications with Kano's Model. MANAS Sosyal Araştırmalar Dergisi, 4(5), 244–262
3. Bowden, J. L. H. (2009). The process of customer engagement: A conceptual framework. Journal of marketing theory and practice, 17(1), 63–74.
4. Brodie, R. J., Hollebeek, L. D., Jurić, B., & Ilić, A. (2011). Customer engagement: Conceptual domain, fundamental propositions, and implications for research. Journal of service research, 14(3), 252–271.
5. Brodie, R. J., Ilic, A., Juric, B., & Hollebeek, L. (2013). Consumer engagement in a virtual brand community: An exploratory analysis. Journal of business research, 66(1), 105–114.
6. Brunner, T. A., Stöcklin, M., & Opwis, K. (2008). Satisfaction, image and loyalty: new versus experienced customers. European journal of marketing.
7. Calder, B. J., Malthouse, E. C., & Schaedel, U. (2009). An experimental study of the relationship between online engagement and advertising effectiveness. Journal of interactive marketing, 23(4), 321–331.
8. Cheung, C., Lee, M., & Jin, X. (2011). Customer engagement in an online social platform: A conceptual model and scale development.
9. Di Paula, A. (1999). Assessing customer values: stated importance versus derived importance. Marketing News, 33(12), 39.
10. DuMouchel, W. (1993). Thoughts on Graphical and Continuous Analysis" on "Kano's Methods for Understanding Customer-defined Quality. *Center for Quality of Management Journal*. 2(4), pp. 20–23.
11. Edelman, D.C. & Singer, M. (2015). Competing on Customer Journeys. *Harvard Business Review*, 93 (11), 88–100.
12. Feng-Han Lin, Sang-Bing Tsai, Yu-Cheng Lee, Cheng-Fu Hsiao, Jie Zhou, Jiangtao Wang, & Zhiwen Shang.(2017). Empirical research on Kano's Model and customer satisfaction. PLoSONE, 12(9), p.e0183888.
13. Fournier, S., & Mick, D. G. (1999). Rediscovering satisfaction. *Journal of marketing*, 63(4), 5–23.
14. Grewal, D., Roggeveen, A.L., & Nordfält, J. (2017). The Future of Retailing. *Journal of Retailing*, *93*(1), 1–6
15. Gronholdt, L., Martensen, A., & Kristensen, K. (2000). The relationship between customer satisfaction and loyalty: cross-industry differences. Total quality management, 11(4-6), 509–514.

16. Heitmann, M., Lehmann, D. R., & Herrmann, A. (2007). Choice goal attainment and decision and consumption satisfaction. *Journal of marketing research*, 44(2), 234–250.
17. Higgins, E. T., & Scholer, A. A. (2009). Engaging the consumer: The science and art of the value creation process. Journal of Consumer Psychology, 19(2), 100–114.
18. Homburg, C., Jozić, D., & Kuehnl, C. (2015). Customer Experience Management: Toward Implementing an Evolving Marketing Concept. *Journal of the Academy of Marketing Science*, *45*(3), pp.377–401
19. Hollebeek, L. D., Glynn, M. S., & Brodie, R. J. (2014). Consumer brand engagement in social media: Conceptualization, scale development and validation. Journal of interactive marketing, 28(2), 149–165
20. Lemon, K. N. & Vehoef, P. C. (2016)/ Understanding Customer Experience throughout the Customer Journey. *Journal of Marketing,* 80(6), 69–96.
21. Olsen, L. L., & Johnson, M. D. (2003). Service equity, satisfaction, and loyalty: from transaction-specific to cumulative evaluations. Journal of Service Research, 5(3), 184–195.
22. Patterson, P. (2016). Retrospective: tracking the impact of communications effectiveness on client satisfaction, trust and loyalty in professional services. Journal of Services Marketing.
23. Rawson, A., Duncan, E., & Jones, C. (2013). The Truth about Customer Experience. *Harvard Business Review*, 91(September), 90–98.
24. Schultz, D. E., & Peltier, J. J. (2013). Social media's slippery slope: challenges, opportunities and future research directions. Journal of research in interactive marketing.
25. Scott, J., & Craig-Lees, M. (2010). Audience engagement and its effects on product placement recognition. Journal of Promotion Management, 16(1-2), 39–58.
26. Spool, J. (2011). Understanding the Kano Model – A Tool for Sophisticated Designers. Retrieved from uie: http://www.uie.com/articles/kano_model/
27. Tse, D. & Wilton, C. (1988). Models of consumer satisfaction: An extension. *Journal of Marketing Research*, 25(2), 204–212.
28. Van Doorn, J., Lemon, K. N., Mittal, V., Nass, S., Pick, D., Pirner, P., & Verhoef, P. C. (2010). Customer engagement behavior: Theoretical foundations and research directions. Journal of service research, 13(3), 253–266.
29. Verhoef, P., Lemon, K., Parasuraman, A., Roggeveen, A., Tsiros, M., & Schlesinger, L. (2009). Customer Experience Creation: Determinants, Dynamics and Management Strategies. *Journal of Retailing,* 85(1), 31–41.
30. Vivek, S. D., Beatty, S. E., & Morgan, R. M. (2012). Customer engagement: Exploring customer relationships beyond purchase. Journal of marketing theory and practice, 20(2), 122–146.
31. Velikova, N., Slevitch, L., & Mathe-Soulek, K. (2017). Application of Kano model to identification of wine festival satisfaction drivers. International Journal of Contemporary Hospitality Management.
32. Wu, T. H., Weng, S. J., Pan, R. B., Kim, S. H., Gotcher, D., & Tsai, Y. T. (2020). Exploring service quality combining Kano model and importance-performance analysis-customer satisfaction of luxury housing service management. International Journal of Services, Economics and Management, 11(1), 71–95.

Note: All the figures and tables in this chapter were made by the authors.

Securing the Future through Sustainability, Health, Education, and Technology –
Brig. Dr. Rajiv Divekar et al. (eds)

6 Internships for Experiential Learning in MBA Curriculum

Pradnya Vishwas Chitrao*
Professor,
Symbiosis Institute of Management Studies (SIMS),
A Constituent of Symbiosis International Deemed University, Pune

Pravin Kumar Bhoyar
Deputy Director,
Symbiosis Institute of Management Studies (SIMS),
A Constituent of Symbiosis International Deemed University, Pune

Brig(Retd) Rajiv Divekar
Director,
Symbiosis Institute of Management Studies (SIMS),
A Constituent of Symbiosis International Deemed University

ABSTRACT

Internships are now becoming an integral part of the MBA curriculum. They are increasingly being seen as beneficial to both the student managers as well as the companies where internships are executed. From understanding the practical applications of the concepts learned in the classroom to understanding corporate culture and developing certain essential competencies required for a business life, student managers need internships. Companies also find it lucrative as they get fresh perspectives from the interns and can develop talent in some interns for absorbing them as prospective employees at low hiring costs and also at the same time utilize the internships to create a good reputation of giving an enriching experience to the interns.

The study sought to find out how the student managers benefitted from internships and whether they really were prepared for corporate life through these internships. Student managers from management institutes in Pune were surveyed. The findings show that the internship experience is average and that more training and support is required from the companies where the internships happened.

KEYWORDS: Summer internships, Practical learnings, Feedback, Support from host company, Corporate culture, Corporate related competencies

*Corresponding author: pradnyac@sims.edu

DOI: 10.1201/9781003587200-6

1. Introduction

An internship is a kind of experiential learning which is being now accepted as vital for imbibing new competencies and knowledge. It helps candidates understand the knowledge and concepts learned from books and in the classroom through their practical application in a corporate setting. So, student managers get valuable applied experience and also get opportunities for networking in the corporate world which in turn helps them in their placements. Internships also give employers an opportunity to guide talent for future. It aids freshers to compete with candidates having prior experience for corporate positions. Many of the candidates joining management institute are engineers having corporate experience in engineering. When they apply for different specializations like marketing, HR, etc. they are often viewed as not having the relevant experience. So, internships help them get the needed experience in their respective specializations

2. Literature Review

The 21st C is witnessing immense progress in different fields. Old skillsets as a result are fast becoming obsolete. Business practices are undergoing massive changes as also laws governing the business world. The business world consequently has become even more competitive and uncertain which requires competent and versatile management graduates to handle situations. Given these circumstances, even academic institutions have realized the need to offer their student managers an opportunity to get hands on experience in the corporate world. An internship is a short-term opportunity which is provided to students where the main aim is to apply theoretical knowledge into workplace. It can be paid or unpaid. Internship helps the students to apply what they have learnt in various courses at relevant places and gain work experience that would add value to the future role. Thus, it is a crucial part in determining a student's professional worthiness.

Previous research sought to see the impact of internships on student managers' career progress.

3. Advantages for the Student Managers

A major advantage of working as an intern is that it connects a student manager with many people working in the same field. These connections do aid in securing a better job as well. Building networks and nurturing them is one key skill for a manager. Meeting Co-interns from other B-schools also provides for relevant interaction from similar educational institutes. The internship program provides several benefits to students not only in terms of giving clarity related to their career but also helps in making them confident and satisfied with the lifelong learning experience. Many students who have been a part of the internship program have experienced that the internship was the most important experience as the students got to learn much more and beyond the classroom knowledge in the entire academic administration preparatory cycle (Fry et al., 2005). Morrison (2005) found that this program provides leadership experiences to students, as they are given problems to resolve which gives them a true experience as to what business executives do daily. In a study done by Renganathan, Krim and Chong Su Li (2012) on students' views about the corporate internship program, it was revealed that the internship program is designed in such a way that the students have work experience which is very different to the experiences gained by students through classroom sessions. Hess and Kelly, 2005 also realized that the internship program gives students the opportunity to experience real business world environment and to use the theoretical knowledge learned to it and thereby relate to the authentic working sites. They learn the dissimilarity between the conventional classroom learning process and learning amidst the corporate world (Trotskovy and Sabag, 2010).

Akomaning, E. (2019) in a study of internships concluded that learning happens in an internship when both the parties are equally involved in the process and the learnings of classroom can be utilized at workplace. Quite often, internships are initiated by job-seekers themselves for the purpose of gaining contacts or filling out a resumé. Such internships are often called 'open market' internships. But whatever the category, internships are basically work-based schemes which try to provide corporate competencies and concepts (Jeannet-Milanovic et al 2017, 143), but usually are not of long duration and are a combination of hands-on work and concepts perceived as the most suitable version of latest apprenticeships.

The marketability of student managers increases when they have an exposure to the industry. The reason is that businesses are on the lookout for students with high academic knowledge and can also display varied competencies which they use to tackle any issues as and when they arise at the workplace (India Skills Report 2022). Some of these skillsets are ability to work in teams, presentation skills, and problem solving (Okay & Sahin 2010). Other globally recognized market skills which are seen as essential are: communication, ability to manage time, improving confidence, and getting motivated (Narayanan et al. 2010). A few other skills like leadership, team building and relationship management are also developed through internships and which are also preferred by recruiters who work in the consumer products organization (Semedo et al., 2010).

A study by Gerard Beenen (2008) of MBA interns pre and post internship showed that interns had before the internship clear learning and performance goals and wanted to be a good resource to the company besides getting a great company and career learning. Post internship these interns learned more about the company and the career. They were also found to have a stronger learning orientation that improved performance-approach goal orientations. The students who learned a lot during their course of internship were found to receive and accept the job offers. Relevant feedback from the company supervisor was found to improve considerably the performance of the students (Binder et al 2014). Feedback maintains the essence of the internship and increases the confidence of the interns (Anjum, S 2020).

4. Advantages for the Organizations

Internships not only help the students but also the organizations as they can use the "try before you buy", approach so that they can select the potential employees (McCracken, M. et al, 2015). Employers can offer future job opportunities to the interns who perform really well during the internship and are also seen as a good "fit" with the organization (Inceoglu, I. et al 2019). Today, employers are enhancing their repute as sought-after companies to work for by giving interns enriching experiences (Pandita, D. and Ray, S. 2018). Organizations save on hiring costs when the interns and further screen them in order to fully understand whether the intern would be a better fit and can become a prospective employee of the organization. Interns sometimes bring fresh insights thereby helping organizations (Petrie, K. A., et al 2017).

In short, previous studies show that internships are mostly win-win situations for both the companies as well as the interns.

5. The Indian Scenario

Management education in India was found by some researchers to be mainly theoretical. Also most Indian Business schools follow a curriculum designed for Western business cultures. Today as a result, MBA graduates often face employment issues. The Associated Chambers of Commerce & Industry of India (ASSOCHAM) found that only 7% of them are employable on account of the gap between theories and practice (ASSOCHAM2016). Many of the students enrolling for these management programs do not have prior work experience. Many universities do not update their curriculum regularly according to the need of the hour. Students consequently do not possess skillsets like analytical skills, good communication skills, and cognitive skills which result in poor employability (Confederation of Indian Industry, 2017). The solution to this according to many experts is putting management students through internship programs which help them to apply concepts to practice and impart experiential learning (Rahman, Khatun, & Mezbah-ul-Islam, 2008). In fact, critical thinking and strong communication skills were found to be necessary for improving employability in India and which can be improved through internships. ASSOCHAM(2016) also strongly advocated the updating and training of management faculty so that they become knowledgeable about global current perspectives.

Narayan, Olk and Fukami (2010) found that success of the internship depends to a great extent on the way the corporate project study is designed for the student. There is thus a need for B-Schools to provide a robust orientation to both its faculty as also the corporate mentors to help them provide maximum learning chances to the students. So, internships should involve all the concerned stakeholders in the planning and implementation phase so that collective ownership is created for making the SIP relevant and enriching (Shrivastava et al., 2022).

A lot of studies observed the financial benefits of pursuing MBA education but very few studies focus on skills learned through these internships and the employers' perception of their usefulness to their business.

6. Objectives of the Study

The study was undertaken as internships carry a lot of weightages in the course curriculum of most B-Schools. Recruiters also were observed to ask a lot of questions related to the internships done by the student managers. So, the stakeholders interdependency theory was the basis of the research conducted. The study tried to find out in what manner the internships help MBA students understand the theories learned in the curriculum. It also tried to understand how the internships helped the interns develop the skills required for corporate life. The researchers also sought to find out the involvement of the hiring organizations in the internship programs.

7. Research Methodology

The researchers interviewed management students from different management institutes in Pune who had undergone internships. Stratified sampling technique was used. This is because student managers from different management institutes in Pune having different educational, cultural, and language of school instruction were administered the questionnaire. The identities of the respondents and the institutions to which they belonged have been kept anonymous to avoid ethical issues. The total sample size was 196 respondents out of which 78 were males and 118 were females.

Simple linear regression analysis was done. Over here, satisfaction with or fulfilment of expectation regarding the corporate project study is the dependent variable and the developmental support, host company's support, academic skills, personal skills, and enterprise skills are the independent variables.

The effectiveness of the internship program was taken on a 5-point Likert scale which varied from strongly agree, agree, neutral, disagree and strongly disagree.

In addition, some company mentors were asked questions in semi structured interviews. But these were very few in number. The researchers did want to also conduct qualitative research but most of the company executives who were mentoring interns from different institutes did not have time either for a one-on-one discussion or agree to a mutually convenient day and time for a focused group discussion. The researchers did not ask the respondents to put them across to their company mentors on ethical grounds. Also, it was easier to administer the questionnaire and get their responses rather than detailed personal interviews which would have been more time consuming for which the student managers did not have the time or inclination.

8. Hypothesis

Some studies showed that students were satisfied with their internship while some internships failed to live upto the interns' expectations. (Gautam, PK 2017, Maaravi et al 2021, Savitha, GR & Nair , J.R. 2018).

So the researchers came up with the following hypotheses:

The null hypothesis: The MBA students were not satisfied with their internship

The alterative hypothesis: The MBA students were satisfied with their internship

9. Significance of the Study

The study will help students acquire good training and reduce gaps in expectation. The study also aims to help the institution in understanding the expectations of the students, and also objectively look into the internship matters and think of ways of improving the internship program.

10. Findings

Simple linear regression was used. The value of R square was 0.625 and the p-value was less than 0.05

Further, mean was also calculated for each of the independent variables:

The obtained scores are neither very high nor very low for any of the key variables. The highest mean score is that of developmental support and the lowest mean score obtained is of academic skills

Table 6.1 Mean scores of the key variables

Variable	Mean
Developmental Support	3.458
Host Company Support	3.343
Academic Skills	3.187
Personal Skills	3.410
Enterprise Skills	3.450

Table 6.2 This table shows the questions that have been clubbed under the head 'Developmental support'

Developmental Support	Strongly agree/ Agree
My reporting manager was available and accessible when I had questions/concerns	83%
I had a great working relationship with my colleagues	93%
I was treated on the same level as the other employees	75%

93% of the respondents said that they had a great working relationship with their fellow colleagues. But, only 75% felt that they were treated the same as the employees.

Table 6.3 This table consists of the questions that are clubbed under the head 'Host Company Support' which shows the involvement of the hiring company with their interns

Host Company Support	Strongly agree/ Agree
I was given adequate training or explanation about the project before assigning the tasks	61%
I regularly met my reporting manager and was continuously given practical feedback	65%
The experience gave me a real picture of the relevant career field	68%

All the questions related to Company's involvement, work relevance and engagement have been rated low. 35% of the interns felt that they did not receive any inputs or feedback from their reporting managers which could contribute to their dissatisfaction.

Table 6.4 The third division of questions is based upon the Learning and knowledge enhancement for an intern because of the internship

Academic	Strongly agree/ Agree
On account of my corporate project study, I understand better the concepts, theories, and skills in my curriculum	54%
There were ample opportunities for learning	67%
My internship helped me in developing critical thinking skills	72%

Only half of the total respondents felt that the internship later contributed to their academics back in college and they could connect to the concepts and theories. 67% agreed that they received ample opportunities for learning but it was not relevant to their institute's curriculum. 72% of the respondents did feel that they were able to develop critical thinking skills. So, it is pertinent to note that a major number of students (67%) said that they had a lot of learning opportunities but only 54% said that the summer internships made them understand their theoretical concepts. So, the learnings were more of a practical nature which are not incorporated in the curriculum.

Table 6.5 The fourth group of questions aimed to explore the personal expectations of the interns

Personal skills	Strongly agree/ Agree
The work I performed was challenging and stimulating	75%
The internship gave me an opportunity to interact with people of other cultures	71%
I feel more confident and prepared to enter the world of work after this experience	79%

They measure the contribution of the programme to an intern's personal skills. All the three questions have received similar responses, i.e., more than 70% of the interns felt that the internship contributed to their personal skills.

Table 6.6 The last group 'Enterprise' is based on the projects undertaken by the interns

Enterprise	Strongly agree/ Agree
I was assigned tasks consistent with my ability and given additional responsibilities as my understanding increased	80%
I would recommend others to join this company for future internships	68%
I am clearer about my career goals after this internship	78%

68% of the interns would recommend others to intern with the same company while 80% found the tasks given to them, matching their ability and understanding.

11. Analysis

The students perceive the positive learning experiences of the internship program as an opportunity to pursue future education and the career of their choice. This perception comes when they can execute various problem-solving activities, become confident, strengthen interpersonal skills, acquire the industry work culture and also efficiently prioritize activities on account of the internships. The internship program gives students a chance to apply concepts to workplace situations.

The regression analysis indicated that R square value obtained was 0.625, which indicates the goodness of fit model. This statistical output reflects the percentage of variance in the dependent variable that the independent variable explains collectively. Hence, one can say that there is an overall satisfaction among the students regarding the internship programme in terms of developing various skillsets and meeting their expectations. The p-value obtained is less than 0.05 thereby showing that the null hypothesis can be rejected. In other words, we can accept the alternative hypothesis and the students were found to be satisfied with their internship programm. The mean scores (Table 6.1) were derived to find out whether the students have a favourable or poor view about the internship programme. As a five-point Likert scale was used, a mean score of more than 3 is treated as an indicator of a positive perception on the part of the students.

Developmental Support: The students rated their developmental support with an overall mean score of 3.458 which was found to be the highest mean among all the variables. This indicates that the majority of them neither agree nor disagreed that their organization supported them. Table 6.2 indicates that the students rated 75% for the item "I was treated on the same level as the other employees", which shows that the students felt that they were not given equal responsibility on the tasks or were not trusted enough when given any task or shared any inside information. This could also be due to the short duration of the internship programme, as it has been suggested that the minimum of six months is the accurate time for any individual to become an 'employee' of the organization. However, 93% of the rating is also given to the statement "I had a great working relationship with my co-worker", In other words, the majority of the students did share a warm and a helping relationship with their co-workers. One can infer that the contrasting views on the two statements led to an average mean score on the variable

Host Company's Support: The students rated the host company's support variable with an overall mean score of 3.343, which is neither a very high nor a very low score. Table 6.3 indicates that the students rated 61% for the item "I was given adequate training or explanation about the project before assigning the tasks". From this percentage it is clear that the students had very less opportunity and were not given proper training before the tasks were assigned. For a successful, meaning internship experience for students it is very important that they get centralized work unit and have clear guidelines and training provided to them, which according to the respondents was not given to them. This can also be linked to the statement of regular and ongoing feedback as not a lot of students rated a very high percentage (65%) regarding the same and also in providing a real-life picture of the career field (68%). Giving feedback of both which includes the performance and the learning opportunities, are the key predictors about internship satisfaction. The quality of any internship programme can only be maintained if constructive feedback is given to the interns on their tasks performed.

Academic Skills: The mean score for this key variable obtained was 3.187, which is also the lowest among all the key variables. Table 6.4 indicates that only half of the respondents (54%), feel that they were able to utilise and apply the theories and concepts learnt in class to their work environment and vice-versa. The reason for this could be the fact that many organizations do not have a proper internship programme and also that the situations presented in textbooks are more theoretical and not practical and that what is studied in class differs greatly from what is seen in the industry. The information and the experience gained in classrooms differs from the industrial internship experience. Classroom learning is found to be more formal and uniform for all students, however, the internship experience might differ for each student. On the other hand, 72% of the respondents did feel that they were able to develop critical thinking skills. So, the researchers conclude that internships do help in developing critical thinking due to the varied situations faced by the students and the probable solutions derived due to the situations faced. This also helps the students to be more adept in identifying the differences between the conventional learning procedure and the actual design environment as well.

Personal Skills: 3.410 was the overall mean score obtained for this key variable; this also indicates that the students rated this variable as an "average". As per

Table 6.5, a majority of the students (79%) rated the statement for feeling more confident after the internship and entering the real world. Researchers have found this to be true due to the experiences students face either good or bad. They are able to develop various skills such as leadership, relationship management etc. The internship programme does help the students to gain a real time experience and have a better clarity regarding their area of expertise and the course of field they want to pursue. This can also be linked by saying that the students did perform tasks which were stimulating and creative in nature (75%). Also, they did get a chance to work with people from other cultures (71%) which helped in relationship management which is an important personal skill to be developed when working in large teams in the industry

Enterprise Skill: The last key variable obtained an overall mean score of 3.450. This variable was also found to be average, indicating that the students neither strongly agree or disagree with it. From Table 6.6, one can see that the majority of the students (80%) of the respondents did strongly concur that they were given responsibilities which were consistent with their ability and the level increases as and when it was required. This can be linked to increase in confidence levels (personal skills) and also getting a clearer picture of the real design industry world. This programme helps in providing leadership experiences to students, as they are given problems to resolve which enables a true experience as to what administrators do on a daily basis. However, only 68% of the respondents agreed to recommend others to join their organization. This could be due to the fact that the respondents did not get feedback on time, they felt that they were not given enough training before the tasks were assigned to them.

12. Conclusions and Recommendations

On the basis of the results obtained, namely the mean score of the overall learning experience of the students as 3.5, one may conclude that the students did not feel that their overall internship experience at the industry was "good" or "excellent". Also mean scores of developmental supports, host company's support, academic skills, personal skills, and enterprise skills stand at 3.343, 3.458, 3.187, 3.410, 3.450 respectively. Therefore, it can be concluded that the support and the training provided by the host company is 'average' and hence there needs to be a more effective programme which needs to be developed for the students.

The researchers therefore recommend that both the industry and the educational institutions should collaborate to make an internship programme for students which is clearer and the students don't feel a discrepancy between what is taught in the classrooms and what is seen on the job-site. It is important for student managers to have an overall training for a period of at least 3 months. In order to have a successful training programme, a well-established and structured training programme must be designed that will cover all areas and departments of the organization. In fact, with the implementation of NEP's mandate of upgrading undergraduate three years' courses to four years courses, management institutes may soon find it necessary to go in for a reduced duration class room sessions and an extended six months' internship course structure.

Since internships provide a chance to apply theory- based learning into practice, it is very important that the organisation is more concerned about developing student's skills. The organizations should give special focus to creativity-based learning, help in building presentation skills, increase communication at all levels, and maintain transparency at all times. Also, it is very important that the college institutions link themselves with industry to set up a good equation among other factors so as to create effective internship programmes. Organizations need to draw up a plan for enhancing innovation and enriching both the students' experience as also benefitting from their creativity. Student managers must develop discovery skills in addition to professional skills. Management institutes must recreate their internship programs. It is also the responsibility of the students to establish a favourable connect between the organisation and the industry as they are the middle source of the internship programme.

13. Limitations of the Study

The research was carried out in Pune city of Maharashtra. Also, the researchers did not get an equal number of male and female respondents. Further, they could not conduct qualitative research

References

1. Akomaning, Edward (2019) Improved Internship Practices as a Result of Collaborative Curriculum Design, Collaborative Curriculum Design for Sustainable Innovation and Teacher Learning pp 265–284
2. Anjum, Sadia (2020) Impact of Internship Programs on Professional and Personal Development of Business Students, A case Study from Pakistan
3. ASSOCHAM. (2016). B and C category B-schools producing un-employable pass-outs. Retrieved from http://www.assocham.org/newsdetail.php?id=5651
4. Beenen, Gerard (2008) Exploring Internship Effectiveness: Intern Goals and Outcomes
5. Binder, Jens Florian, Baguley, Thom, Crook, Chris, & Miller, Felicity (2014) The Academic Value of Internships: Benefits Across Disciplines and Student Backgrounds
6. Confederation of Indian Industry (2017). Indian skills report 2017, CII (India). Retrieved from https://www.undp.org/content/dam/india/docs/india-skills-report-2017.pdf
7. Fry, B., Bottoms, G. and O'Neill, K. (2005), The Principal Intern: How Can We Get it Right? Southern Regional Education Board (SREB), Atalanta, GA.
8. Gautam, P.K.,2017 Satisfaction from Internship Program and Changing Attitude: A Perceptual Survey from Hotel Management Students, The International Research Journal of Management Science Vol. 2 No. 1 Decm.2017/ ISSN 2542–2510

9. Hess, F.M. and Kelly, A.P. (2005), Learning to Lead? What Gets Taught in Principal Preparation Programs, American Enterprise Institute, Washington, DC, PEPC-05-02.
10. Inceoglu, I., Selenko, E., McDowall, A. and Schlachter, S. (2019), "(How) do work placements work? Scrutinising the quantitative evidence for a theory-driven future research agenda", Journal of Vocational Behavior, Vol. 110, pp. 317–337.
11. India Skills Report 2022, Re-engineering Education and Skilling: Building for the Future of Work
12. Jeannet-Milanovic, A.; O'Higgins, N.; Rosin, A. 2017. "Contractual arrangements for young workers" in N. O'Higgins, Rising to the youth employment challenge: new evidence on key policy issues, ch. 6 (Geneva, International Labour Office).
13. Maaravi, Yossi, Heller, Ben, Hochman, Guy, Kanat-Maymon, Yaniv 2021 Internship Not Hardship: What Makes Interns in Startup Companies Satisfied? Journal of ExperientialEducationVolume44,Issue3https://doi.org/10.1177/1053825920966351
14. McCracken, M., Currie, D. and Harrison, J. (2015), "Understanding graduate recruitment, development and retention for the enhancement of talent management: sharpening 'the edge' of graduate talent", The International Journal of Human Resource Management, Vol. 27 No. 22, pp. 2727–2752.
15. Morrison, E.C. (2005), "Trial by fire", Supporting New Educators, Vol. 62 No. 8, pp. 66–8.
16. Narayanan, V.K, Olk, P.M. and Fukami, C.V., 2010. Determinants of internship effectiveness: An exploratory model. Academy of Management Learning & Education, 9(1), 61–80.
17. Okay, S. and Sahin, I. 2010, "A study on the opinions of the students attending the faculty of technical education regarding industrial internship", International Journal of the Physical Sciences, Vol. 5 No. 7, pp. 1132–46.
18. Pandita, D. and Ray, S. (2018), "Talent management and employee engagement – a meta-analysis of their impact on talent retention", Industrial and Commercial Training, Vol. 50, pp. 185–199.
19. Petrie, K. A., Carnahan, R. H., Brown, A. M., & Gould, K. L. (2017). Providing experiential business and management training for biomedical research trainees. CBE—Life Sciences Education, 16(3), ar51. doi: 10.1187/cbe.17-05-0074
20. Rahman, A.I.M., Khatun, M., & Mezbah-ul-Islam, M. (2008). Library education in Bangladesh: Strengths, problems, and suggestions. Library Philosophy and Practice.
21. Renganathan, S., Abdul Karim, Z.A.B. and Li, C.S. (2012), "Students' perception of Industrial internship programme", Education + Training, Vol.54 No.2/3, pp. 180–191.
22. Savitha, G.R., & Nair, Jai Raj. 2018. Effectiveness of Summer Internship In Indian Management Education, IOSR Journal of Business and Management (IOSR-JBM) e-ISSN: 2278-487X, p-ISSN: 2319-7668. Volume 20, Issue 8. Ver. VI (August. 2018), PP 46–48 www.iosrjournals.org
23. Semedo, L., Newman-Ford, L., Lloyd, S. and Thomas, S. (2010), "HoneyBee: evaluating Glamorgan's work-based learning initiative"
24. Shrivastava, S., Bardoel, E.A., Djurkovic, N., Rajendran, D., Plueckhahn,T. (2022). Co-Creating curricula with industry partners: A case study, International Journal of Management in Education, 20 (2) (2022), Article 100646
25. Trotskovy, E. and Sabag, N. (2010), "Internship in engineering design at hi-tech industries: theory and practice", paper presented at the IEEE-IBM TEE 2010 – Transforming Engineering Education Conference, Dublin, p. 5.

Note: All the tables in this chapter were made by the authors.

Securing the Future through Sustainability, Health, Education, and Technology –
Brig. Dr. Rajiv Divekar et al. (eds)

7 Impact of Overconfidence Bias on Perceived Market Efficiency—The Mediating Role of Investment Decision-Making of Indian Individual Investors

Ankita Bhatia[1]
Symbiosis Institute of Management Studies,
Symbiosis International (Deemed University), Pune, India
Arti Chandani[2]
Jaipuria Institute of Management Studies, Lucknow, U.P. India
Rajiv Divekar[3]
Symbiosis Institute of Management Studies,
Symbiosis International (Deemed University), Pune, India

Abstract

Purpose: This paper investigates how overconfidence bias influences investment decision making and how this in turn impacts market efficiency of Indian individual investors. A set of questions sheet has three sections including 1) Behavioural Biases and 2) Market Efficiency and 3) Investment decision making. To test the suitability among unobserved factors and underlying observed variables Exploratory Factor Analysis (EFA) was performed for exploring important factors and then CFA (Confirmatory Factor Analysis) and Mediation analysis was carried out to achieve the research goal. The uncovering of this study reveals that investment decision making has a complete mediation effect between overconfidence bias and decision making.

Keywords: Bootstrapping, Confirmatory factor analysis, Individual investors, Market efficiency, Mediation analysis, Overconfidence bias

1. Introduction

There have been continuous ongoing debates on market efficiency for more than several decades now. Since Fama (1960) has spoken about Efficient Market

[1]ankita.bhatia@sims.edu, [2]arti.chandani@jaipuria.ac.in, [3]director@sims.edu

DOI: 10.1201/9781003587200-7

Hypothesis (EMH) for financial markets it has always been a topic of theoretical and empirical debates (Ackert and Deaves, 2010; Shefrin et al., 2007). In modern finance paradigm as per EMH (Efficient Market Hypothesis) markets are efficient, however, as per behavioural finance paradigm there is an AMH (Adaptive Market Hypothesis), which postulates that markets are adaptively efficient.

Many researchers have been consistently raising their voices that if investors are trading in market, markets can never be efficient. This is because investors are normal humans. Every human being has emotions and fears. This emotion leads to short lived financial craze, enthusiasm and despondency (Sanford, 1994; Slezak, 2003). If market inefficiency is to be seen from behavioural finance paradigm, it could be due to behavioural risks stemming out of biases, investors as human being possesses. These are more imperative to study in developing countries like India where financial markets are seemingly more prone to volatility and instability (Kim & Nofsinger, 2008). According to Shah et al., (2018) overconfidence bias influences market efficiency, however, they have also proposed that mediating and moderating relationships should be formed and tested to check their influence on investment patterns.

This paper has tried to test the mediation impact of investment decision making on overconfidence bias and market efficiency. A good amount of quantitative and qualitative researches is being carried out in large number to check for prevalence of overconfidence biases in Indian context. This motivates the researchers to explore how determinants of overconfidence bias can directly and indirectly impacts Indian stock market efficiency considering investment decision making as control variable.

2. Literature Review

2.1 Psychological Perspectives

Big five personality traits, innovation and conscientiousness, negative emotion, extraversion, masculinity and risk propensity influence investment decisions (Durand et al., 2013). Salience is most important measures of heuristics in decision making followed by mental accounting and representativeness (Yalcin et al., 2016).

An investor's sentiment influences investment decision making. The major factors influencing investor sentiment were market effect and herding. Internet is the least preferred when it comes to awareness than that of social media and social interaction.

Perceptions and beliefs together lead to biases in an individual. Some biases arise from an emotional and logical perspect (Arora et al., 2013). Formation of bias also varies with an investor's demographic variables like gender, age, experience (Zahera et al.,2019; Filbeck et al., 2017).

2.2 Investment Decisions and Market Efficiency

American Economist and Professor Eugen Fama in his seminal work "Efficient Capital Market," spoke about Market Efficiency. This theory tells that financial markets can never be inefficient (Fama, 1997; Lo, 2007).

I. **Weak Form of Market Efficiency**—In efficient markets all investors act prejudicially (Hayat et al., 2006).

II. **Semi – Strong Form of Efficiency**—In this category security prices not only reflects historic prices but also reflects publicised information in the form of secondary data like financial reports, dividend announcements, price earnings announcements, monetary policies and so on.

III. **Strong Form of Efficiency—**Fundamental values of securities are the result of competition of earning abnormal returns between different profit-oriented investors like financial investors and decision makers (Ritter, 2003). Fundamental asset prices deviate because irrational people invest in the market (Barberis and Thaler, 2003). Markets behave inefficiently because of the heuristic biases which leads irrational behaviour of individual investors (Shah et al., 2012). According to (Pompian, 2006), not any of the markets can be 100 percent efficient nor cent percent unpredictable. Anomalies does exist in market but can also be overcome by investors with them enhance proficiency (Fama,1997).

2.3 Overconfidence Bias

Overconfidence heuristic bias stems out of cognitive abilities, intuitive reasoning, and memory abilities (Pompian, 2006). Over precision, overestimation and over placement are some attributes that investors suffer from which is nothing but overconfidence bias (Moore and Healy, 2008). Overestimation and locus of control, chance of success is some of the attributes of overestimation (Shiller, 2003). Lack of initial assessment and revising them periodically as per the latest information leads to overconfidence (Simon et al., 2000). Over-precision also occurs when investors predict ignoring risk factors (Odean, 1999).

Overconfidence Bias and Investment Decisions

Four behavioural factors heuristics, herding, market and prospect impacts investment decision making (Kengatharan et al., 2014). Investors with confirmation bias are highly prone to display overconfidence bias as well as expecting higher returns from investments lead them to trade excessively.

Overconfidence Bias and Market Efficiency

Numerous studies carried out for overconfidence bias and market efficiency. Few research studies postulated that both phenomena are directly proportional. It directly means that if market efficiency increases overconfidence bias also increases. According to Shah (2012) in a way overconfidence indulges investors to collect more information which in turn helps them to supersede stock market.

The process of overdoing something doesn't always leads to decreased market efficiency (Ko and Huang, 2007).

2.4 Hypothesized Research Model

Following Hypotheses derived explicitly on the comprehensive literature review (Fig. 7.1)

H1: Overconfidence Bias influences the decision making of Indian indivisual investors;

H2: Investment decision making influences the Indian stock market efficiency;

H3: Overconfidence bias influences the Indian stock maret efficiency

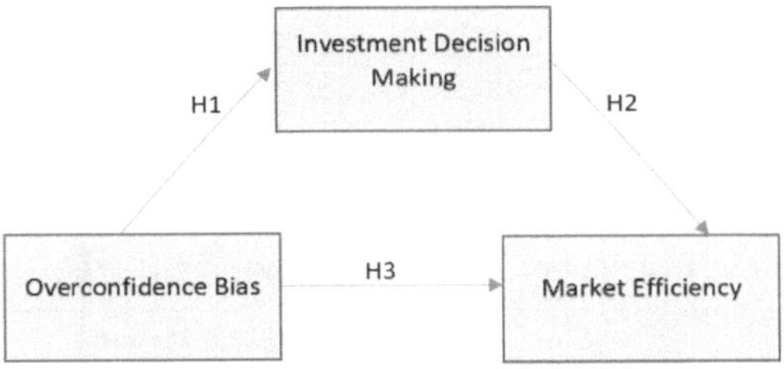

Fig. 7.1 Hypothesised conceptual framework

3. Research Methodology and Design

It is a complete layout plan used to apply statistical techniques in order to achieve research objectives.

3.1 Sample and Data Collection

Sample, data collection has been done suitably

3.2 Questionnaire and Scales used

Questionnaire comprised of three sections.

Market Efficiency

In total of 5 items were considered to evaluate this variable. Below are sample questions framed by Luong and Ha (2011).

Overconfidence Bias

Some of the six sample questions are taken from study by Odean (1999) and Odean (2000).

Investment Decision Making

Six items from the study of Nyamute (2016) are being considered to measure the endogenous construct of Investment Decision making. Some of its items embrace:

"I have considerable amount of knowledge about investing" and "I invest to meet my financial goals" and "I invest to meet my short-term goals."

4. Analysis and Discussion

4.1 Demographic Information

Demographic Information was suitably noted

4.2 Exploratory Factor Analysis

Exploratory Factor Analysis was carried out before CFA

Sample Size Consideration

0-150 is an adequate sample size when it comes to the factors having communalities of more than 0.6. Furthermore, each construct should have minimum of 3 or more items when it comes to applying SEM techniques (McDonald et al., 1988).

Correlation and KMO Barlett's Test of Latent Constructs

KMO and Barlett's Test values between 0.5 to 1 model is adequately good. Barletta value significant so we can perform CFA. It can also be observed that Barlett's Test variables identified are correlated to each other and a structure can be detected out of this as shown in Table 7.1.

Table 7.1 KMO and bartlett's test

Kaiser-Meyer		0.612
Bartlett's Test	Chi-Square	30.46
	Df	3
	Sig.	0

4.3 Confirmatory Factor Analysis

Reliability Analysis is performed using Cronbach's alpha.

Table 7.2 Reliability scores

Overconfidence, Cronbach alpha = 0.829, no of items =6	Invest Dec, Cronbach alpha = 0.786 no of items =6	Overconfidence, Cronbach alpha = .768, no of items =5

Model Fit Indices

The variance estimates of all three latent constructs ranges from 0.2 to 0.7. The CMIN/df (2.297), RMR (0.103), GFI (0.957) and RMSEA (0.087) (root mean square approximation) are considered as goodness of fit indices for testing a measurement model. Secondly, (Hu and Bentler,1999) has recommended some threshold values for Goodness of Fit model, should be greater than 0.9.

4.4 Mediation Analysis

Confirmatory Factor Analysis (CFA) empirically test the significance of all the measurement models (Gudergan et al., 2008). Mediation analysis method was proposed by Baron and Keny (1986).

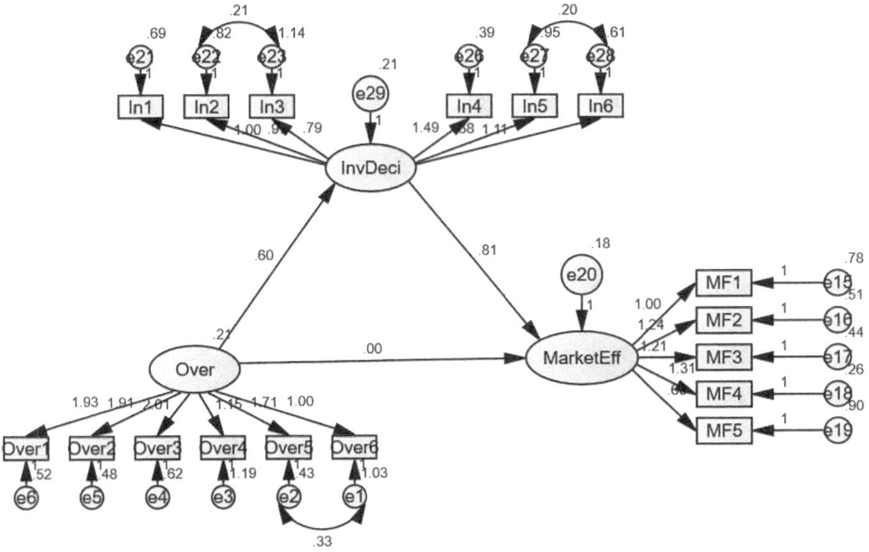

Fig. 7.2 Path diagram of confirmatory factor analysis

Regression Analysis and Bootstrapping

Mediation analysis is performed using Process v3.5 by Andrew F Hayes. at 95 percent confidence and 5000 interval Bootstrap samples. These results are reported in line with the bias corrected bootstrapping method (Preacher and Hayes,2008). The results clearly indicate that direct effect significance is reduced as compared to that of total effect of predictor on outcome. Indirect effect results are Bootstrap samples lower and upper bound range are (0.0100,0.910). It can be clearly drawn that 0 doesn't lies between this interval so investment decision making has full mediation effect on predictor and outcome.

Total effect of X on Y

Effect	se	t	p	LLCI	ULCI	c_ps	c_cs
.2160	.0632	3.4172	.0008	.0912	.3407	.2720	.2528

Direct effect of X on Y

Effect	se	t	p	LLCI	ULCI	c'_ps	c'_cs
.1698	.0637	2.6643	.0085	.0440	.2956	.2139	.1988

Indirect effect(s) of X on Y:

	Effect	BootSE	BootLLCI	BootULCI
InDMean	.0461	.0216	.0100	.0950

Fig. 7.3 Direct and indirect effects of bootstrapping results

Mediation Analysis in AMOS

To validate again mediation analysis in AMOS was performed to test the influence of overconfidence bias on predictor and outcome and it turned out that overconfidence bias is a significant predictor ($\beta = 0.429$, $p < 0.01$) of investment decision making which suffices Hypothesis H1. When the influence of investment decision making on market efficiency was evaluated it turned out to be significant (β = 0.823, op < = 0.01) which suffices Hypothesis H2. However, when the direct influence of overconfidence bias on market efficiency was tested without mediating variable it has a significant influence on market efficiency (β = 0.361, p <0.01). However, when overconfidence bias on market efficiency was tested keeping investment decision as mediating variable it turned out to be insignificant (β= 0.018, p> 0.05) as shown in below Table 7.6. From this it can be concluded that investment decision making has full mediation impact between overconfidence bias and market efficiency.

5. Conclusion, Limitations and Scope of Future Work

The aim of the research was to assess whether investment decision making mediates the relationship between overconfidence bias and market efficiency. Consistent with findings that overconfidence bias impacts investment decision making (Odean,1999) and investment decision making of Indian individual investors impact Indian stock market efficiency (DeBondt and Thaler,1995), it is also found that investment decision making significantly mediates the relationship between these two. Placing emphasis on investment decision making is likely to assure that improved market efficiency (Kahneman and Tversky, 1973; Bazerman 1998) because it is the consequent of investment decision making arising after taking care of behavioural bias of Indian investors. This finding suggests that investor bias, investment decision making and market efficiency process are cyclical in nature. If all steps are taken care efficiently then it is likely to improve the Indian stock market efficiency.

5.1 Limitations and Directions for Future Research

Due to time constraints sample size taken is small and even single bias is considered for mediation analysis. Different biases can be taken into consideration and can be carried out in different socio-cultural backgrounds. Gender, Salary, Professions, Advisory services can be taken as moderating variables to check their effects.

References

1. Ackert, L. F., & Deaves, R. (2010). Behavioral finance. South-Western Cengage.
2. Aren, S., Aydemir, S. D., & Şehitoğlu, Y. (2016). Behavioral biases on institutional investors: a literature review. *Kybernetes*.
3. Baker, H. K., & Nofsinger, J. R. (Eds.). (2010). Behavioral finance: investors, corporations, and markets (Vol. 6). John Wiley & Sons.
4. Barberis, N., & Thaler, R. (2003). A survey of behavioral finance. Handbook of the Economics of Finance, 1, 1053–1128.

5. Daniel, K. D., Hirshleifer, D., & Subrahmanyam, A. (2001). Overconfidence, arbitrage, and equilibrium asset pricing. *The Journal of Finance*, *56*(3), 921–965.
6. De Bondt, W. F., & Thaler, R. H. (1995). Financial decision-making in markets and firms: A behavioral perspective. *Handbooks in operations research and management science*, *9*, 385–410.
7. Fama, E. F. (1960). *Efficient market hypothesis* (Doctoral dissertation, Ph. D. dissertation, University of Chicago, Graduate School of Business).
8. Fama, E. F., & French, K. R. (1997). Industry costs of equity. *Journal of financial economics*, *43*(2), 153–193.
9. Filbeck, G., Ricciardi, V., Evensky, H. R., Fan, S. Z., Holzhauer, H. M., & Spieler, A. (2017). Behavioral finance: A panel discussion. *Journal of Behavioral and Experimental Finance*, *15*, 52–58.
10. Hair, J. F., Black, W. C., Babin, B. J., Anderson, R. E., & Tatham, R. L. (1998). *Multivariate data analysis* (Vol. 5, No. 3, pp. 207-219). Upper Saddle River, NJ: Prentice hall.
11. Hu, L. T., & Bentler, P. M. (1999). Cutoff criteria for fit indexes in covariance structure analysis: Conventional criteria versus new alternatives. *Structural equation modeling: a multidisciplinary journal*, *6*(1), 1–55.
12. Kim, K. A., & Nofsinger, J. R. (2008). Behavioral finance in Asia. Pacific-Basin Finance Journal, 16(1–2), 1–7.
13. Odean, T. (1998). Volume, volatility, price, and profit when all traders are above average. *The journal of finance*, *53*(6), 1887–1934.
14. Pompian, M. M., & Wood, A. S. (2006). *Behavioral finance and wealth management:* How to build optimal portfolios for private clients.
15. Preacher, K. J., & Hayes, A. F. (2008). Asymptotic and resampling strategies for assessing and comparing indirect effects in multiple mediator models. *Behavior research methods,* 40(3), 879–891.
16. Ritter, J. R. (2003). Behavioral finance. Pacific-Basin finance journal, 11(4), 429–437.
17. Shah, S. Z. A., Ahmad, M., & Mahmood, F. (2018). Heuristic biases in investment decision-making and perceived market efficiency. *Qualitative Research in Financial Markets*.
18. Shefrin, H., & Belotti, M. L. (2007, June). Behavioral finance: biases, mean-variance returns, and risk premiums. In CFA Institute Conference Proceedings Quarterly (Vol. 24, No. 2, pp. 4–12).
19. Shiller, R. J. (2003). From efficient markets theory to behavioral finance. Journal of economic perspectives, 17(1), 83–104.
20. Simon, M., & Houghton, S. M. (2003). The relationship between overconfidence and the introduction of risky products: Evidence from a field study. *Academy of Management Journal*, *46*(2), 139–149.
21. Slezak, S. L. (2003). On the impossibility of weak-form efficient markets. *Journal of Financial and Quantitative Analysis, 38(3), 523–554.*
22. Tversky, A., & Kahneman, D. (1973). Availability: A heuristic for judging frequency and probability. *Cognitive psychology*, *5*(2), 207–232.
23. Zahera, S. A., & Bansal, R. (2019). A study of prominence for disposition effect: a systematic review. *Qualitative Research in Financial Markets*.

Note: All the figures and tables in this chapter were made by the authors.

Securing the Future through Sustainability, Health, Education, and Technology – Brig. Dr. Rajiv Divekar et al. (eds)

8 Perception of Workforce for Rejuvenation of Labour Laws

Prakash Yerragola[1]
Associate Professor, NIMS School of Business,
NIMS University, Jaipur, India
Charwak Bojja[2]
Assistant Professor, School of Management Studies,
Jawaharlal Nehru Technological University Kakinada, Kakinada, India
Sagarika Yerragola[3]
Assistant Professor, Department of Management,
Bhoj Reddy Engineering College for Women, Hyderabad, India

ABSTRACT

Code of conduct at the factory level has become need of the hour as the buyers (the firms buying the raw materials at national and international level) have made it mandate before purchase of the goods from the suppliers (manufacturer of the goods). In this context, a multistage sampling method is adopted to study on 3 textile industrial units with a sample size of workforce (n=1008). Correlation, Factor analysis and Regression analysis is used to find the correlation, identified the significant factors and prediction of dependent variable. This study reveals that the employers, managers, executives of the organization have to give high priority to those factors that influence the robust industrial relations. Thus, boost the economy of the country with higher workforce participation, increase in productivity and harmonious relations in industrial units.

KEYWORDS: Rejuvenation of labour laws, Textile industries, Labour reforms, Workforce well-being, Employment relations

1. Introduction

Indian textile industry positioned second in terms of manufacturing and third as exporter in the world. Indian textile and clothing industry has 10.5% share in total

[1]y.prakash@nimsuniversity.org, [2]bcharwak@gmail.com, [3]yerragola.sagarika@slv-edu.in

DOI: 10.1201/9781003587200-8

exports during 2021-22 and 4.6% share of global trade in textile and clothing industry. Major export destination to Indian textile and apparel are European Union (EU-27), United States of America (USA) and United Kingdom (UK) for approximately 50% of total textile and apparel exports. Textile industry in India stands second largest employment provider after the agriculture. More than 45 million people were directly employed and 10-crore people were indirectly employed. There is a decrease in exports of textile and apparel including handicrafts from India from US$ 31.5 billion to US $44.4 billion during 2020-2021 to 2021-22. Despite a 15% decline in overall exports during April-December 2022 compared to the same period in the previous year, the export of readymade garments exhibited a positive growth of 6% in 2022-23 (April 2022 to December 2023) when compared to 2021-22 (April 2021 to December 2022) vis-a-vis its competitors (Ministry of Textiles, 2023). Table 8.1 shows the percentage of increase or decrease in the export of textile and apparel products.

Table 8.1 Exports details of Indian textile and apparel

Particulars	Percentage (%)				
	2019-20	2020-21	2021-22	2021-22 (April-Dec)	2022-23 (Apr-Dec) Provisional
% Share of Textiles and Apparel Exports (Including Handicrafts) of Overall Merchandise exports	11.2%	10.8%	10.5%	10.5%	8.2%

Source: Author's compilation

The relationship between employer and employee due to the contractual relations is termed as industrial relations. There is an obligation on part of the employer to comply with code of conduct when they entered with the domestic and international firms (those who purchases the finished, semi-finished products). When there is a breach of code of conduct or contract by the firms (those who supplies the finished, semi-finished products) they will lose the opportunities in exporting the goods at domestic and international market. In this regard, these is a need to rejuvenate the labour laws to meet the international standards for the robust industrial relations.

1.1 Research Objectives

Agriculture is the backbone of rural India, which is a labour-intensive sector that generates huge employment. The textile and apparel sector contributes 2% to the Indian economy. Based on this background information, the research objectives have been formulated.

1. To study the perception of workforce on robust industrial relations.
2. To inquiry into the perception of workforce for rejuvenation of labour laws.

3. To identify the factors that contributes for rejuvenation of labour laws.
4. To examine the perception of workforce for rejuvenation of labour laws and its effects on robust industrial relations and
5. To evaluate the efforts of the government in rejuvenation of labour laws and suggest the measure to enhance the robust industrial relations.

2. Literature Review

The establishment of the new Economic Governance aimed to introduce a new European Labour Market Policy, which, unfortunately, falls short of adhering to the principles initially set forth. Notably, this policy has a direct or indirect impact on wage regulation, particularly in France. The influence factor involves dominant fractions of French capitalists seeking to disrupt the balance of forces at the national level and assert their specific interests. Consequently, trade unions have significantly weakened, and the influence of French capitalists over labour market and wage policies has become pronounced (Syrovatka, 2021). Workers employed in import-competing sectors will try to resist trade liberalization since the employment protection legislation applies only to formal sector workers as observed in almost 140 countries (Campos et al. 2018).

Labour market and collective bargaining (Bulfone and Tassinari, 2021), reforms on industrial relations (Peetz, 2021), Investment in state capacity in building labour market institutions (Deakin and Haldar, 2015), reform labour laws (Datta and Sil, 2007), Social safety nets and labour market condition (Hoynes and Stabile, 2019), women into the economic productive activities (Kennedy, 2018), reforms on apprenticeship contract (Albanese et. al. 2021), fixed-term employment, de-dualization and deregulation of dismissal (Eichhorst and Marx, 2021), labour market policy (Branco and Cardoso, 2020), labour market reforms (Wang et al. 2021), reforms in labour regulations (Hasan et al. 2021), flexible labour market (Sharma, 2006). Hence, a comprehensive labour market and labour reform is required to address the needs of both employers and workers.

Power relationships, policy settings that affect the health of workers (Lipscomb et al. 2006). There is a need for analysis on policies relates to occupational safety and health, regulation and enforcement, labour market equity and welfare reforms relates to occupational safety, health and health disparities research. Improvements in design and implementation of active labour market (Anant et al. 2006), universal social protection (Srivastava, 2008), promotion of freedom of association (Gokhan and Fransen, 2009), flexible labour regulations (Amin, 2009), meditation between labour and capital (Hill, 2009). The failure of both industrial system and the union movement to understand and accommodate the needs of workers becomes challenging for the industrial relations in India.

Wages paid were less than the minimum wage, overtime is unpaid and is compulsion to do overtime. Unaware of trade union rights and lack of minimum occupational safety to the workers (Singh, 2009), Labour legislation on working conditions needs to be equitable, more responsive and more inclusive that facilities the Indian firms competitive (Deb, 2010). The impact of globalized competition and export-oriented economic growth in China, Korea, and Japan is such that it undermines the state's ability to intervene effectively, ultimately granting more power to employers (Cooke, 2010). Women participation in labour market (Bala, 2012), Gender inequality at workplace (Tavora and Rubery, 2013). The Tripartite consultation, amendments to labour laws through deliberate discussions by actors of industrial relations (Ministry of Labour and Employment, 2013). In response to safety concerns, the European Union (EU) has urged Bangladesh to enhance worker safety standards. Subsequently, government officials, textile factory employers, and workers convened with International Labour Organization (ILO) representatives and collectively committed to implementing measures aimed at improving the well-being of workers. (Ruma and Serajul, 2013).

Inconsistency in frequency of data to impress upon the state authorities to take appropriate measures for policy making (Labour Bureau, 2014). Simplification of forms for various statutory and voluntary returns results in timely collection of data that can improve compliance of labour returns. The European Union (EU) emphasizes that all governments must adhere to ILO Conventions, addressing issues such as long working hours, low wages, lack of regular contracts, and systematically hazardous conditions. In response, European Parliament resolutions recommend that Asian governments take steps to improve these conditions. Additionally, international brands and importing countries are urged to promote greater union rights, regular work, cooperative audits, and stable purchasing practices through legally binding guidelines and principles. These efforts aim to exert pressure on Asian authorities to better uphold workers' human rights (D' Ambrogio, 2014). Lack of terms and conditions of employment and contract agreement, delayed settlements of unpaid wages and severance benefit settlement (International Labour Organization,2015) are being practiced.

Wage issues and implementation of agreed minimum wage (Apparel Resources, 2015), US Department of Labour's Wage and Hour Division resolved the wage violation by devising a news strategy to counter the low wages paid to garment workers. The strategy is by analysing the prices that retailers pay for clothing, and tracing those prices to supply chain (Apparel Resources, 2016). The blame game by the contractors, manufacturers will end can be learned through the judgement against a Vernon-based clothing manufacturer called YN Apparel. Wage disparities between low-cost productions, more expensive labour force within ASEAN expressed their concerns to reduce such disparities and exploitation of labour. (ASEAN Briefing, 2016). As per Clean Clothes Campaign, the workers in garment industry are not meeting the basic needs, excessive overtime, unhealthy and workers forced to live apart from their families (Apparel Resources, 2016), demand for minimum wages (The Hindu, 2017), workers unrest (Express News Service, 2017), denial of workers right to form association (Industrial Union, 2017).

2.1 Research Gap

From the available literature, rejuvenation of labour laws is required for employment and wage protection, collective bargaining and industrial relations for harmonious industrial relations. Hence, a study is done to predict the perception of workforce for rejuvenation of labour laws for robust industrial relations.

3. Research Methodology

3.1 Data Collection

Data was collected on the perception of workforce for rejuvenation of labour laws that effects robust industrial relations. Table 8.2 shows the collection of secondary data.

Table 8.2 Collection of secondary data

S.No.	Sources of secondary data	Referred (in numbers)
1	International Journals	23
2	Reports of national and international agencies	9
3	Books/Edited books	4
4	Annual reports	1
5	Thesis	1
6	Online Newspaper/Websites	9

Source: Author's Compilation

A multistage sampling technique is adopted to select the sample for the collection of data from the textile industrial units. Primary data is collected from a sample (n=1008) respondent consists of 2 large and 1 medium scale textile industries of Mahaboobnagar district in Telangana State, India out of 1201 respondents where the questionnaire is distributed. There are 34 items in the study as suggested (Nunnally, 1994) 10 times the variables would be the sample size (i.e., 340 Sample size), 300 sample size as good, 100 as poor and 1000 as excellent (Comrey and Lee, 1992).

The average age of the respondents is 38 years, gender, 52.6% or 530 were males, 47.4% or 478 were females, marital status, 82.6% or 833 were married, 17.4% or 175 were unmarried. When it comes to the employment type, 7.5% or 76 were employees, 92.5% or 932 were workers. The nature of job, 3% or 30 were administrators, 13% or 132 were Skilled, 67% or 675 were semi-skilled, 17% or 171 were unskilled. Five points rating scale has been used for the psychometric analysis on perception of workforce for rejuvenation of labour laws and perception of workforce on robust industrial relations starting with *5-Strongly Agree, 1-Strongly disagree* were used to get the responses from the workforce. The correlation statistics is performed to know the positive, negative or no relationship between the factors that measures the perception of workforce on the variables. Exploratory Factor analysis with Regression statistics is performed to know the influence of independent variable upon dependent variable.

3.2 Perception of Workforce for Rejuvenation of Labour Laws

The government enacts new legislation or amendments to the existing laws where the workforce perceives and respond to such reforms or rejuvenation of labour laws.

3.3 Perception of Workforce on Robust Industrial Relations

The workforce includes the employees, workers in the industrial units who perceives the healthier or stronger relationship between employer and workforce is called as perception of workforce on robust industrial relation.

3.4 Test of Hypothesis

H1 (Null Hypothesis): There is no significance influence in perception of workforce for rejuvenation of labour laws category 1 (PWRLL1) and has no effect on the perception of workforce on robust industrial relations (PRIR).

H2 (Null Hypothesis): There is no significance influence in perception of workforce for rejuvenation of labour laws category 2 (PWRLL2) and has no effect on the perception of workforce on robust industrial relations (PRIR).

H3 (Null Hypothesis): There is no significance influence in perception of workforce for rejuvenation of labour laws category 3 (PWRLL3) and has no effect on the perception of workforce on robust industrial relations (PRIR).

4. Results and Discussion

This section gives the information on the results and discussion on primary data and the factors affecting the perception of robust industrial relations.

The Table 8.3 shows the measure of sampling adequacy for the perception of workforce on robust industrial relations (PRIR) is greater than .50 where p value of .884 (Kaiser, 1974) recommends the accepting value greater than .5 as barely acceptable. It is also suggested that .5 to .7 are medicore, .7 to .8 are good, .8 to .9 are great and .9 are superb (Hutcheson and Sofroniou, 1999). The Bartlett's test of sphericity significance is less than .01 for n=1008 with the degrees of freedom 66.

Table 8.3 KMO and bartlett's test

Kaiser-Meyer-Olkin Measure of Sampling Adequacy		0.884
Bartlett's Test of Sphericity	Approx. Chi-Square	25425.882
	df	66
	Sig.	0.000

Source: Primary data

The Table 8.4 shows the communalities for all the items extracted with Principal axis factoring methods has the value above the .40. The Factor matrix explains the total variance by 84.250% as against the 50% by one factor.

Table 8.4 Communalities

Item code	Extr	Item code	Extr	Item code	Extr
FS1	0.904	FS5	0.858	FS10	0.920
FS2	0.901	FS7	0.904	FS11	0.753
FS3	0.885	FS8	0.834	FS12	0.873
FS4	0.717	FS9	0.679	FS13	0.882

Source: Primary data. Note. Extr = Extraction

The Table 8.5 provides the information about perception of workforce on robust industrial relations (PRIR) factor that was extracted using the Principal Axis factoring method with oblique (Promax with Kaiser normalization) rotation. All the

Table 8.5 Perception of workforce on robust industrial relations (PRIR) scale (n=1008)

Item Code	Attributes	PRIR Loadings
FS10	Superior and subordinate relationship influences industrial relations.	0.959
FS1	Wage fixation based on national agreements ensures harmonious industrial relations.	0.951
FS7	Employee Association/Trade union affiliated with political parties influence industrial relations.	0.951
FS2	Social security contributes to the stability of employment and industrial relations.	0.949
FS3	Re-employment of retrenched workers improves employer-employee relationship	0.941
FS13	Collective bargaining ensures industrial peace.	0.939
FS12	Fixation of timely action (viz., daily/weekly/monthly) can avoid loss of production instead of pressure tactics.	0.934
FS5	Enforcement of agreements reached due to industrial disputes maintains industrial peace.	0.926
FS8	Government, employers and workforce (employee and workers) contributes to the economic growth of the country due to harmonious industrial relations.	0.913
FS11	Company Service rules and the model standing orders maintain healthy industrial relations.	0.868
FS4	Compensation to workforce i.e., employees and workers, in case of transfer of establishment (i.e., mergers and acquisitions) promotes industrial relations.	0.847
FS9	Professional leadership in employee association / trade unions ensures lasting relations with employer and workforce.	0.824
Internal Consistency (α)		.98
α^2 explained (%)		84.250
Measure of Sampling Adequacy		.884
Bartlett's Test of Sphericity significance		.000

Source: Primary data

Factor loadings are above .70. Three items have been removed for the purification of the scale (F6, F14 and F15). The variance captured and internal consistency reliability for the perception of workforce on robust industrial relations (PRIR) is .842 and .984 (Cronbach, 1951), (Hair et al. 2013), (Kline,2013). The measure of sampling adequacy on the perception of workforce for the rejuvenation of labour laws (PWRLL) is greater than .50 where p value is .980. (Kaiser, 1974) recommends the accepting value greater than .5 as barely acceptable. It is also suggested that .5 to .7 are medicore, .7 to .8 are good, .8 to .9 are great and .9 are superb (Hutcheson and Sofroniou, 1999). The Bartlett's test of sphericity significance is less than .01 for n=1008 with the degrees of freedom 231.

The Table 8.6 shows the communalities for all the items extracted with Principal axis factoring methods has the value above the .40. The Factor matrix explains the total variance by 81.358% as against the 50% by three factor.

Table 8.6 Communalities

Item Code	Extr.	Item Code	Extr.	Item Code	Extr.
ES1	0.880	ES9	0.888	ES17	0.841
ES2	0.850	ES10	0.772	ES18	0.594
ES3	0.868	ES11	0.885	ES19	0.888
ES4	0.811	ES12	0.913	ES20	0.514
ES5	0.595	ES13	0.919	ES21	0.896
ES6	0.886	ES15	0.914	ES22	0.656
ES7	0.877	ES16	0.874	ES23	0.909
ES8	0.666				

Source: Primary data. Extr. = Extraction

The Table 8.7 provides the information about perception of workforce for rejuvenation of labour laws category 1 (PWRLL1), category 2 (PWRLL2) and category 3 (PWRLL3) Factors that was extracted using the Principal Axis factoring method with oblique (Promax with Kaiser normalization) rotation. All the factor loadings are above .70. Two items ES14 and ES24 were excluded. The variance captured and internal consistency reliability for the perception of workforce for rejuvenation of labour laws C1 (PWRLL1) is .837 and .963. The variance captured and internal consistency reliability for the perception of workforce for rejuvenation of labour laws C2 (PWRLL2) is .748 and .959. The variance captured and internal consistency reliability for the perception of workforce for rejuvenation of labour laws C3 (PWRLL3) is .585 and .875 (Cronbach, 1951), (Hair et al. 2013), (chu and Murrmann, 2006).

4.1 Regression Analysis

This section deals with the regression analysis for the variable's perception of workforce for rejuvenation of labour laws and perception of workforce on robust industrial.

Table 8.7 Perception of workforce for the rejuvenation of labour laws (PWRLL) scale

Item Code	Attributes	Factor Loading		
		1	2	3
ES12	A provision on group housing under EPF Scheme benefit to the contributors (employees and workers).	0.957		
ES7	Universal Account Number (UAN) benefits the workforce to make contribution to a single account even after re-employment in another organization.	0.924		
ES11	An increase in compensation to the dependents in the event of total permanent disablement, partial disablement resulting from personal injury leads to industrial peace as per Employees Compensation Act	0.921		
ES15	It is not desirable to encourage multiplicity of trade unions in the organization.	0.917		
ES19	Profit sharing and co-partnership schemes affects relations between management and workforce (employees and workers)	0.915		
ES16	Fact-finding enquiries can improve industrial relations.	0.912		
ES1	A Statutory National Minimum wage for different geographical areas can fix wage/salary related issues.	0.903		
ES13	Enhancement in Employees deposit Link Insurance Scheme to Rs.6 Lakhs under EPF Scheme benefits to the contributors (employees and workers).	0.902		
ES21	Punishments to the employee association or trade union leader to be introduced in case of illegal strikes.	0.884		
ES23	Executives (Government) should be given powers to make amendments so as not to delay in specific Labour laws by proper notification.		0.931	
ES9	Increase to 50 or more women workers instead of 30 or more women workers is appropriate to set up a Creche as per Factories Act.		0.920	
ES6	Universal Account Number (UAN) has given relief in retrieval of passbook download from employee provident fund or through UMANG app.		0.868	
ES17	Formulation of Standing orders should be done in consultation with the workers/ employee association or trade union.		0.848	
ES2	Equal Remuneration Act Prohibits gender discrimination at work place		0.846	
ES10	Increase of maternity leave benefit to 26 weeks from the present 12 weeks is appropriate as per Maternity Benefit Act.		0.838	
ES3	Payment of wages act has to ensure time limit (viz., daily/ weekly/monthly) payment of wages/salaries.		0.832	
ES4	A National Social Security Council has to administer Social Security in India.		0.829	

Item Code	Attributes	Factor Loading		
		1	2	3
ES8	A Central Board of Social Security has to perform certain functions to protect the interests of certain members of Social Security schemes in India.			0.830
ES22	A separate Labour legislation should be set up for large, medium and small-scale enterprises.			0.800
ES18	Employee Association/Trade Union or workers must be involved in normal domestic enquiries.			0.794
ES5	Pehachan card ensures timely action to the insured person and his or her dependents			0.700
ES20	Retention of adjudication system plays an important role in maintaining industrial peace			0.693
Internal Consistency (α)		.973		
α^2 explained (%)		81.358		
Measure of Sampling Adequacy		.968		
Bartlett's Test of Sphericity significance		.000		

Source: Primary data

Table 8.8 shows the influence of perception of workforce for rejuvenation of labour laws category 1 on the perception of workforce on robust industrial relations. The coefficient of determination (R^2), which stands at 0.942, signifies that the predictors account for 94.20% of variance observed in the outcome variable. This relationship was statistically highly significant and positively predicts the perception of the workforce on robust industrial relations ($\beta = 0.971$, $p < 0.001$). Hence, **Accept the alternate hypothesis.** Thus, increase in perception of workforce for rejuvenation of labour laws category 1 will improve the perception workforce on robust industrial relations. There is no collinearity as the VIF is less than 3 (Hair et al. 2014). The regression equation is written as:

$$Y_{PRIR} = b + wX_1$$

Table 8.8 Summary of perception of workforce for rejuvenation of labour laws on robust industrial relations

Factors	PWRLL1	PWRLL2	PWRLL3
R^2	0.942	0.569	0.108
F value	*F* (1,1006) = 16460.874	*F* (1,1006) = 1327.756	*F* (1,1006) = 121.899
Constant	0.173	-0.15	0.908
Beta Coefficient	0.941	0.961	0.672
β	0.971*	0.754**	0.329**
p value	Less than .01	Less than .001	Less than .001
VIF Value	1.000	1.000	1.000

Source: Author's Compilation; *: Highly Significant; **: Significant;

Where Y_{PRIR} = Perception of workforce on robust industrial relations (Dependent variable)

$b = constant$

$w = beta\ coefficient\ for\ X_1$

X_1 = perception of workforce for rejuvenation of labour laws category 1 (PWRLL1 - independent variable)

Therefore, $Y_{PRIR} = 0.173 + 0.941\ (PWRLL1)$

From the Table 8.8 The coefficient of determination (R^2), which stands at 0.569, indicates that the predictors account for 56.90% of the variance observed in the outcome variable. This relationship was statistically significant and positively predicts the perception of the workforce regarding robust industrial relations ($\beta = 0.754$, $p < 0.001$). Hence, **Accept the alternate hypothesis.** Thus, increase in perception of workforce for rejuvenation of labour laws category 2 will improve the perception workforce on robust industrial relations. There is no collinearity as the VIF is less than 3 (Hair et al. 2014). The regression equation is written as:

$$Y_{PRIR} = b + wX_2$$

Where Y_{PRIR} = Perception of workforce on robust industrial relations (Dependent variable)

$b = constant$

$w = beta\ coefficient\ for\ X_2$

X_2 = perception of workforce for rejuvenation of labour laws category 2 (PWRLL2 – independent variable)

Therefore, $Y_{PRIR} = -0.15 + 0.961\ (PWRLL2)$

Table 8.8 shows the partial influence of perception of workforce for rejuvenation of labour laws category 3 on the perception of workforce on robust industrial relations. The coefficient of determination (R^2), which stands at 0.108, indicates that the predictors account for 10.80% of the variance observed in the outcome variable. This relationship was statistically significant and has a positive effect on the perception of the workforce regarding robust industrial relations ($\beta = 0.329$, $p < 0.001$). Hence, **Accept the alternate hypothesis**. Thus, increase in perception of workforce for rejuvenation of labour laws category 3 will improve the perception workforce on robust industrial relations. There is no collinearity as the VIF is less than 3 (Hair et al. 2014). The regression equation is written as:

$$Y_{PRIR} = b + wX_3$$

Where Y_{PRIR} = Perception of workforce on robust industrial relations (Dependent Variable)

$b = constant$

$w = beta\ coefficient\ for\ X_3$

X_3 = perception of workforce for rejuvenation of labour laws category 3 (PWRLL3 - independent variable)

Therefore, $Y_{PRIR} = 0.908 + 0.672\ (PWRLL3)$

4.2 Multiple Regressions

This section further deals with multiple regression between the variables the perception of workforce for rejuvenation of labour laws reflects the perception of workforce on robust industrial relations.

Table 8.9 shows that the R^2 value of 0.942 indicates that the predictors account for 94.2% of the variance observed in the outcome variable. The statistical analysis, based on an F-statistic with degrees of freedom (3, 1004), yielded a value of 5482.772 with a p-value less than 0.001. The findings reveal that PWRLL1 is highly significant and has a positive effect on the perception of workforce regarding robust industrial relations ($\beta = 0.966$, $p < 0.001$). Although PWRLL2 is non-significant, it still has a positive effect on the perception of workforce regarding robust industrial relations ($\beta = 0.010$, $p > 0.05$). Similarly, PWRLL3 is non-significant, but it has a negative effect on the perception of workforce regarding robust industrial relations ($\beta = -0.009$, $p > 0.05$). These findings provide valuable insights into the relationship between labour laws and workforce perceptions in the context of robust industrial relations. There is no collinearity among the factors as the (VIF) is less than or equal to the 3 (Hair et al. 2014). Thus, the multiple regression equation is written as:

$$Y_{PRIR} = l_1X_1 + l_2X_2 + l_3X_3 + c$$

Table 8.9 Summary of multiple regression

Factors	PWRLL1	PWRLL2	PWRLL3
R^2		0.942	
F value		*F* (3,1004) = 5482.772	
Constant		0.218	
Beta Coefficient	0.937	0.012	-0.02
B	.966**	0.10*	-0.009*
p value	Less than .001	Greater than .05	Greater than .05
VIF Value	2.52	3.00	1.35

Source: Author's Compilation; **: Highly Significant; *: non-significant;

Where PRIR = Perception of workforce on robust industrial relations (Dependent Variable)

$$l_1 = beta\ coefficient\ for\ X_1$$
$$l_2 = beta\ coefficient\ for\ X_2$$
$$l_3 = beta\ coefficient\ for\ X_3$$

$c = constant$

$X_1 = $ *Perception of workforce for rejuvenation of labour laws category 1 (PWRLL1)*

$X_2 = $ *Perception of workforce for rejuvenation of labour laws category 2 (PWRLL2)*

$X_3 = $ *Perception of workforce for rejuvenation of labour laws category 3 (PWRLL3)*

Therefore, $Y_{PRIR} = 0.937\,(PWRLL1) + 0.012\,(PWRLL2) - 0.02\,(PWRLL3) + 0.218$

5. Conclusion

The following are the conclusions that have drawn from the study:

Model 1: We identified that the perception of workforce for rejuvenation of labour laws category 1 factor is highly significant and positively predicts the perception of workforce on robust industrial relations ($\beta = 0.971, p < .001$).

Model 2: We identified that the perception of workforce for rejuvenation of labour laws category 2 factor is significant and positively predicts the perception of workforce on robust industrial relations ($\beta = 0.754, p < .001$).

Model 3: We identified that the perception of workforce for rejuvenation of labour laws category 3 factor is significant and positively predicts the perception of workforce on robust industrial relations ($\beta = 0.329, p < .001$). Therefore, we deduce that the workforce perception regarding the rejuvenation of labour laws in categories 1, 2, and 3 significantly and positively influence their perception on robust industrial relations. Multiple regression indicates that all predictors collectively account for 94.20% of the variance in the outcome variable. The statistical analysis, based on an F-statistic with degrees of freedom (3, 1004), yielded a value of 5482.772 with a p-value less than 0.001. Specifically, Category 1 and Category 2 factors exhibit a significant and positive effect on robust industrial relations. However, the Category 3 factor, despite its significance, has a negative effect on the perception of workforce on robust industrial relations. Consequently, we conclude that the provisions related to Category 3 in labour laws adversely impact the perception of workforce regarding robust industrial relations.

5.1 Limitations, Managerial Implications and Future Directions of the Study

Exploratory analysis with simple and multiple regression statistics was employed to predict the dependent variable. Time constraint and application of this model in a practical manner will suffice the study. This study is helpful to the policy makers, managers, executives to understand the significance of factors for rejuvenation labour laws to better manage the robust industrial relations. Their main focus should be on category 1 factor that is highly significant and has positively predicted the perception of workforce on robust industrial relations. Most importantly they need to focus on category 2 and category 3 factors that are significant but category 3 variable has negative effect on the perception of workforce on robust industrial relations. Hence, enough care has to be taken on the policies relates to rejuvenation of labour laws that has negative effect on the perception of workforce on robust industrial relations which results in unrest across industrial sector can affect the economy of the country.

REFERENCES

1 Albanese, A., Cappellari, L. and Leonardi, M., (2021). The effects of youth labour market reforms: evidence from Italian apprenticeships. Oxford Economic Papers, Vol. 73, No.1, pp. 98–121.

2 Amin, M., (2009) Labor regulation and employment in India's retail stores. Journal of Comparative Economics. Vol. 37, No.1, pp. 47–61. DOI: 10.1016/j.jce.2008.07.001

3 Anant T.C.A., Hasan R., Mohapatra P., Nagaraj R., Sasikumar S.K. (2006). Labor Markets in India: Issues and Perspectives. In: Felipe J., Hasan R. (eds) Labor Markets in Asia. Palgrave Macmillan, London. DOI: 10.1057/9780230627383_5.

4 Annual Report (2023). Ministry of Textiles, Government of India. https://texmin.nic.in/sites/default/files/English%20Final%20MOT%20Annual%20Report%202022-23%20%28English%29_0.pdf

5. Apparel Resources (2015). ASEAN nations gear up for single market http://news.apparelresources.com/trade-news/asean-nations-gear-up-for-single-market/

6. Apparel Resources (2016). Bangladesh garment workers get one-fifth of living wage: AFWA.http://www.news.apparelresources.com/trade-news/bangladesh-garment-workers-get-one-fifth-of-living-wage-afwa/

7. Apparel Resources (2016). US garment factories violating labour laws: Report. http://news.apparelresources.com/sustainability-news/us-garment-factories-violating-labour-laws-report/

8. ASEAN Briefing (2016). Indonesia Promotes ASEAN Minimum Wage. http://www.aseanbriefing.com/news/2016/06/06/indonesia-promotes-asean-minimum-wage.html

9. Bala, S., (2012). Implementation of Maternity Benefit Act. NLI Research Studies Series. Vol. 99, p. 2012.

10. Branco, R. and Cardoso, D., (2020). The Politics of Change. Coalitional politics and labour market reforms during the sovereign debt crisis in Portugal. Journal of Social Policy, pp. 1–19. DOI: 10.1017/S0047279420000653.

11. Bulfone, F. and Tassinari, A, (2021). Under pressure. Economic constraints, electoral politics and labour market reforms in Southern Europe in the decade of the Great Recession. European journal of political research, Vol. 60, No.3, pp. 509–538, DOI: 10.1111/1475-6765.12414.

12. Campos, N.F., Nugent, J.B., Campos, N.F., Grauwe, P. and Ji, Y. (2018). The Dynamics of the Regulation of Labour in Developing and Developed Countries. The political economy of structural reforms in Europe. pp. 75–91. DOI: 10.1093/oso/9780198821878.003.0003.

13. Chu, K.H.L. and Murrmann, S.K., (2006). Development and validation of the hospitality emotional labor scale. Tourism Management. Vol. 27, No.6, pp. 1181–1191, DOI: 10.1016/j.tourman.2005.12.011

14. Comrey, A. and Lee, H., (1992). Interpretation and application of factor analytic results. A first course in factor analysis. Hillsdale, NJ: Lawrence Erlbaum Associates 10, pp. 240–262, p.9781315827506.

15. Cooke, F.L., (2010). Women's participation in employment in Asia: a comparative analysis of China, India, Japan and South Korea. The international journal of human resource management. Vol. 21, No.12, pp. 2249–2270. DOI: 10.1080/09585192.2010.509627.
16. Cronbach, L.J., (1951). Coefficient alpha and the internal structure of tests. Psychometrika. Vol.16, No.3, pp. 297–334. DOI: 10.1007/BF02310555.
17. D'Ambrogio, E., (2014). Workers' conditions in the textile and clothing sector: Just an Asian affair. Issues at Stake after the Rana Plaza Tragedy. European Parliamentary Research Service http://www.europarl.europa.eu/EPRS/140841REV1-Workers-conditions-in-the-textile-and-clothing-sector-just-an-Asian-affair-FINAL.pdf
18. Datta, R.C. and Sil, M., (2007). Contemporary Issues on Labour Law Reform in India. An Overview. ATLMRI (Adecco TISS Labour Market Research Initiatives) Discussion Paper.https://kalsatrust.org.in/images/pdf/LAWS_ACTS/KALSA%20RESERCH%20INSTITUTE%20%20LAWS%20&%20ACTS%20412.pdf
19. Deakin, S. and Haldar, A., (2015). How should India reform its labour laws? Economic and Political Weekly. pp. 48–55. DOI: 10.2139/ssrn.2601039.
20. Deb, T., (2010). Reforming labour legislation on working conditions for competitive advantage: an empirical study. Indian Journal of Industrial Relations. Vol. 46, No.2 pp. 201–219. DOI: http://www.jstor.org/stable/41149441.
21. Eichhorst, W. and Marx, P., (2021). How stable is labour market dualism? Reforms of employment protection in nine European countries. European Journal of Industrial Relations. Vol.27. No.1. pp. 93–110. DOI: 10.1177/0959680119899199
22. Express News Service (2017). Agitation at Textile mill: Worker's 'block' mill official's car, says police shot at them. http://indianexpress.com/article/cities/kolkata/agitation-at-textile-mill-workers-block-mill-officials-car-says-police-shot-at-them/
23. Gokhan Kocer, R. and Fransen, L., (2009). Codes of conduct and the promise of a change of climate in worker organization. European Journal of Industrial Relations. Vol. 15. No.3. pp. 237–256.
24. Hasan, R., Mehta, A. and Sundaram, A., (2021). The effects of labor regulation on firms and exports: Evidence from Indian apparel manufacturing. Journal of Comparative Economics. Vol. 49. No.1. pp. 183–200. DOI: 10.1016/j.jce.2020.04.007.
25. Hill, E., (2009). The Indian industrial relations system: Struggling to address the dynamics of a globalizing economy. Journal of Industrial Relations. Vol. 51. No.3. pp. 395–410.
26. Hoynes, H. and Stabile, M., (2019). How do the US and Canadian social safety nets compare for women and children? Journal of Labor Economics. Vol. 37. No. S2. pp. S253–S288.
27. Hutcheson, G.D. and Sofroniou, N., (1999). The multivariate social scientist: Introductory statistics using generalized linear models. Sage Publication.
28. Industrial union (2017). Bangladesh: garment workers fight for their union to be legally registered. http://www.industriall-union.org/bangladesh-workers-fight-for-their-union-to-be-legally-registered
29. International Labour Organisation (2015). Insight into working conditions in India's garment industry. International Labour Organization. http://www.ilo.org/global/topics/forced-labour/publications/WCMS_379775/lang--en/index.htm.
30. Joseph Jr, F. Hair Jr, William C. Black, Barry J. Babin, Rolph E. Anderson. (2013). Multivariate data analysis (2014). Pearson New International edition., ISBN 13: 978-1-292-02190-4 pp. 123–124.

31. Joseph Jr, F. Hair Jr, William C. Black, Barry J. Babin, Rolph E. Anderson. Multivariate data analysis (2014). Pearson New International edition., ISBN 13: 978-1-292-02190-4 pp. 196–201.
32. Kaiser, Henry F (1974). An index of factorial simplicity. Psychometrika. Vol. 39. No.1. pp. 31–36. DOI: 10.1007/BF02291575
33. Kennedy, S., (2018). Irish women and the Celtic Tiger economy. In The end of Irish history? Manchester University Press.
34. Kline, P., (2013). Handbook of psychological testing. (2nd ed.). Routledge. DOI: 10.4324/9781315812274
35. Labour Bureau (2014). Ministry of Labour & Employment. Collection of Labour Statistics through statutory and voluntary returns. http://labourbureaunew.gov.in/UserContent/Report_on_Simplification_of_Returns.pdf
36. Lipscomb, H.J., Loomis, D., McDonald, M.A., Argue, R.A. and Wing, S., (2006). A conceptual model of work and health disparities in the United States. International Journal of Health Services. Vol. 36. No.1. pp. 25–50. DOI: 10.2190%2FBRED-NRJ7-3LV7-2QCG.
37. Ministry of Labour and Employment (2013). 39th session of the Indian Labour Conference, Report of the Second National Commission on Labour with emphasis on rationalization of Labour Laws and Unorganized labour (2013). https://labour.gov.in/sites/default/files/39ilcagenda_1.pdf
38. Nunnally, J.C., (1994). Psychometric theory 3E. Tata McGraw-Hill education.
39. Peetz, D., (2021). Is industrial relations reform the road to recovery in monopsonistic labour markets? The Economic and Labour Relations Review. p.10353046211015786.
40. Ruma, P, and Serajul Q., (2013). Bangladesh urges no harsh EU measures over factory deaths.https://www.reuters.com/article/us-bangladesh-factory-idUS-BRE94304420130504.
41. Sharma, A.N., (2006). Flexibility, employment and labour market reforms in India. Economic and Political Weekly. pp. 2078–2085.
42. Singh, S., (2009). Richer Bosses, Poorer Workers, Bangalore's Garment Industry. CIVIDEP and SOMO. https://www.somo.nl/wp-content/uploads/2009/07/Richer-Bosses-Poorer-Workers.pdf
43. Srivastava, R., (2008). Towards universal social protection in India in a rights-based paradigm. Indian Journal of Human Development. Vol.2. No.1. pp. 111–132.
44. Syrovatka, F. (2021). Labour market policy under the new European economic governance: France in the focus of the new European labour market policy. Capital & Class. Vol. 45 No.2. pp. 283–309. DOI: 10.1177/0309816820943177.
45. Tavora, I. and Rubery, J., (2013). Female employment, labour market institutions and gender culture in Portugal. European Journal of Industrial Relations. Vol. 19. No.3. pp. 221–237.
46. The Hindu (May 10, 2017). Weavers call off strike in Textile Park. http://www.thehindu.com/news/national/telangana/weavers-call-off-strike-in-textile-park-in-sircilla/article18416341.ece
47. Wang, F., Milner, C., & Scheffel, J. (2021). Labour market reform and firm-level employment adjustment: Evidence from the hukou reform in China. Journal of Development Economics. 149. 102584.

Securing the Future through Sustainability, Health, Education, and Technology – Brig. Dr. Rajiv Divekar et al. (eds)

9 Agri-food Supply Chain (AFSC) Producers' Perceptions of Consumer Price Control—An Assessment using MCDM Technique

Pramod K. Mishra[1]
Assistant Professor, School of Management Studies,
University of Hyderabad, Hyderabad, Telangana, India

Satyaranjan Sahu[2]
Research Assistant, School of Management Studies,
University of Hyderabad, Hyderabad, Telangana, India

Chinmaya Behera[3]
Associate Professor, Goa Institute of Management,
Sanquelim, Poriem, Sattari, Goa, India

Pratap K. Jena[4]
Assistant Professor,
Maharaja Sriram Chandra Bhanja Deo University,
Baripada, Odisha, India

B. Raja Shekhar[5]
Professor, School of Management Studies,
University of Hyderabad, Hyderabad, Telangana, India

Abstract

In any supply chain, production plays a vital role and so is the role of the producers. The production cost and the other costs related to the material flow in the supply chain greatly control the prices paid by the customers at the end. In this study, we consider six different agri-food supply chains (AFSCs) namely, rice, wheat, sugarcane, tomato, turmeric, and potato, and assess the producers' perceptions of the consumer price control. The data were primarily collected through a survey from about 1,183 respondents in the supply chain and analyzed using a Multi-Criteria Decision Making (MCDM) algorithm, The Technique for Order of Preference by Similarity to Ideal Solution (TOPSIS), to rank various factors of price control. In the later part, the inferences drawn were cross-validated with the

[1]pramod.mishra@uohyd.ac.in, [2]satyaranjansahu835@gmail.com, [3]chinmaya@gim.ac.in, [4]jenapratapkumar@gmail.com, [5]brsmsuh@gmail.com

DOI: 10.1201/9781003587200-9

inferences drawn from the consumer data. It was found that system transparency, hoarding (artificial), and transportation costs are the top three indicators of consumer price control in the downstream markets. However, technology adoption, storage, higher production volume, etc. are found to be the other major indicators controlling consumer prices in the markets. As the paper holds it the perceptions of producers which are further validated through the perceptions of consumers, policy implications related to price control are expected to be more sustainable in the long run.

KEYWORDS: Agri-food supply chains (AFSCs), Prices, MCDM, Price control, Validation

1. Introduction

Agri-food supply chains (AFSCs) play a very vital role in any individual's life. Irrespective of the taste and preferences of the consumers, food above all is one of the indispensable parts of every single life on the earth. Making the food items reach the right time, right place, and right quantity in the downstream market is the basic function of the AFSCs and in the process, it faces formidable challenges. As supply chains (SCs) deliver consumer value at a price (Simchi Levi et al., 2008; Chopra and Meindl, 2014), incompatible prices lead to customer dissatisfaction without compromising on product consumption. The majority of the products that AFSCs deliver fall under the need-based items and are normally driven by push strategies (Fisher, 1997). The performance of the AFSCs is greatly influenced by the production volume, production costs, transportation costs, perishability, system transparency etc. The performance is not only influenced by the right time, right place and right quantity delivery rather it is also greatly influenced by the right price delivery. As the AFSCs mostly are scattered and heterogeneous across the world, strict control of the volatile markets is extremely difficult. The two major endpoints of the AFSCs, the producers (farmers) and the consumers are highly vulnerable. The producers lack in terms of their bargaining power in the supply chain and get less than half of the value that they add to it. On the other hand, as the food items are need-based, consumers desperately need them at any cost to make a living. However, exception cases are there for dairy and non-vegetarian items.

The work is theoretically motivated by the transaction cost economics (TCE) proposed by Williamson (1975) and the value chain concept proposed by Porter (1980). In this piece of work, the perceptions of the two endpoints on price control have been rigorously analysed and ranked which needs the attention of the AFSCs. The various price performance indicators have been ranked and cross-validated to draw some meaningful inferences. In the following Section I, we discuss the literature review while in Section II, we discuss the research methodology, Section III talks about data analysis. The results and discussions have found a place in Section IV. Finally, we conclude the work in Section V citing the limitations of the work and the direction for the future work.

2. Literature Study

In the following section, we focus on two aspects the performances of the AFSCs in terms of the price and measure of the performance using the MCDM technique. Christopher and Towill (2000) presented various models of supply chain performance considering quality conformance, delivery reliability, total chain cost, purchasing price, and flexibility (mix) of production indicators. Huang, Sheoran and Wang (2004) demonstrated the key supply chain operations reference (SCOR) metrics while Aramyan (2007) and Aramyan et al. (2007) considered efficiency, responsiveness, flexibility, product quality and process quality in their study of "performance measurement in agri-food supply chains".

AFSCs face many challenging situations while making the products flow from the upstream to the downstream supply chains (markets). These situations are oftentimes influenced by multiple criteria as well as alternatives which are confusing but important. Given the constraints in decision-making, it is very difficult for the practising managers to make the right decision, at the right time with reasonable accuracy. In this context, the MCDM tools and techniques help managers to make effective decisions. The MCDM techniques can resolve choice problems, sorting problems, ranking problems, elimination problems etc. Several MCDM techniques, namely, Analytic Hierarchy Process (AHP), Technique for Order of Preference by Similarity to Ideal Solution (TOPSIS), VIKOR (VIseKriterijumskaOptimizacija I KompromisnoResenje meaning Multi-criteria Optimization and Compromise Solution), ELECTRE (ÉLimination Et Choix Traduisant la REalité meaning Elimination and Choice Translating Reality), DEMATEL (Decision making trial and evaluation laboratory), etc. are greatly used in the social scienceworks (Saaty, 1980; Hwang and Yoon, 1981; Hwang, Lai and Liu, 1993; Chen and Chen, 2010; Ishizaka and Nemery, 2013; Rajput and Singh, 2019). The MCDM techniques are robust and try to minimize the possible biases through data transformations. In this study, the TOPSIS algorithm has been used elaborately.

The Technique for Order of Preference by Similarity to Ideal Solution (TOPSIS) is a simple but practical MCDM technique greatly used in Multiple Attribute Decision Making (MADM) environments in various fields (Hwang and Yoon, 1981). Further developments in this method were done by Yoon (1987), Hwang, Lai and Liu (1993), and Opricovic and Tzeng (2004). As per the pioneering works of the researchers stated above, "the TOPSIS is based on the concept that the chosen alternative should have the shortest geometric distance from the positive ideal solution and the longest geometric distance from the negative ideal solution".

An assumption of TOPSIS is that the criteria are monotonically increasing or decreasing.

3. Research Methodology

The study is descriptive research based on cross-sectional data collected during March – June 2023 from eight places in India. As far as the upstream supply chain is concerned, the data have been collected from 10 locations – six locations were considered for producers' responses while four locations were considered for customers' responses. In the process of the data collection, we contacted about 1,300 respondents of which 9% of schedules were either not filled or not responded at all and hence they were not considered for the data analysis, resulting in 1,183 complete schedules. The breakups of 1,183 respondents have been stated in the following Table 9.1.

Table 9.1 Sample size break-up

Sl. No.	State	Commodity	Location	Respondent	Sample size
1	West Bengal	Rice	Medinipur	Farmer	189
2	Uttar Pradesh	Wheat	Hardoi	Farmer	129
3	Uttar Pradesh	Sugarcane	Kanpur Nagar	Farmer	359
4	Andhra Pradesh	Tomato	Chitoor	Farmer	140
5	Telangana	Turmeric	Jagitial	Farmer	85
6	Uttar Pradesh	Potato	Agra	Farmer	92
7	Telangana	Mixed	Urban	Customer	50
8	Telangana	Mixed	Rural	Customer	50
9	Madhya Pradesh	Mixed	Shivpuri	Customer	39
10	Uttar Pradesh	Mixed	Kanpur Nagar	Customer	50

3.1 The TOPSIS Algorithm

The steps executing the method are hereby briefly represented in the following paragraphs.

Step 1: Calculate Normalized Matrix:

The decision matrix A is normalized with the following computation to generate the matrix R:

$$\overline{X}_{ij} = \frac{X_{ij}}{\sqrt{\sum_{i=1}^{n} X_{ij}^2}} \tag{1}$$

Where X_{ij} is the value of the jth criterion for the ith alternative of the decision matrix A

Step 2: Calculate Weighted Normalized Matrix:

The weighted normalized decision matrix is obtained by using the normalized decision matrix and weights assigned to criteria:

$$V_{ij} = \bar{X}_{ij} \times W_j \tag{2}$$

Step 3: Calculate the Ideal Best (V_j^+) and Ideal Worst (V_j^-) Values:

At this stage, the ideal best and ideal worst, based on minimum or maximum criterion, are found and used in the subsequent analysis.

Step 4: Calculate the Euclidean Distances from the Ideal Best and Ideal Worst:

$$S_i^+ = \left[\sum_{j=1}^{m}\left(V_{ij} - V_j^+\right)^2\right]^{0.5} \tag{3}$$

$$S_i^- = \left[\sum_{j=1}^{m}\left(V_{ij} - V_j^-\right)^2\right]^{0.5} \tag{4}$$

Step 6: Calculate the Performance Scores:

The relative closeness of each alternative to the Ideal Solution is computed as follows:

$$P_i = \frac{S_i^-}{S_i^+ + S_i^-} \tag{5}$$

Based on the performance scores the indicators/metrics can be ranked.

4. Data Analysis

In the following section, we discuss the performance indicator scores of producers (farmers) as perceived by them and what the customers are facing about price control. Further, at the later stage, we discuss the consumer's perceptions of price control of agri-products and then the comparison is made to validate the results.

4.1 Producers' Perception Scores

The six different supply chains, namely, Rice, Wheat, Sugarcane, Tomato, Turmeric and Potato are taken into consideration and analysed in the following section. The decision matrix (Table 9.2) is the original data obtained from the respondents.

The data above have been normalized using equation (1) to give the following Table 9.3. Normalization is one essential step to control the possible response bias.

Table 9.2 The decision matrix

Factors	Rice	Wheat	Sugarcane	Tomato	Turmeric	Potato
Production volume	3.0741	3.8182	3.0377	3.2000	3.7083	4.1765
Production cost	4.0000	3.8000	3.0063	3.2429	3.7500	4.2941
Transportation cost	3.9894	3.6667	3.9937	3.3286	3.9583	4.3235
Storage cost	3.1534	3.7500	3.0377	3.4000	3.2500	3.7941
Processing cost	3.2540	3.8571	2.9937	3.1000	3.2083	3.5882
Controlling losses	4.1111	4.0000	3.0314	3.1000	4.0417	3.9706
Govt. support	4.9683	4.2000	2.9937	3.2714	3.7917	3.8235
Stopping shortages	4.8889	4.0000	3.0000	3.1571	3.7500	3.5882
Technological support	4.9947	4.0000	4.0000	3.0571	3.2917	3.0588
System transparency	5.0000	5.0000	3.0314	3.1500	5.0000	3.1471

Table 9.3 The normalized decision matrix

Factors	Rice	Wheat	Sugarcane	Tomato	Turmeric	Potato
Production volume	0.0742	0.0952	0.0946	0.1000	0.0982	0.1106
Production cost	0.0965	0.0948	0.0936	0.1013	0.0993	0.1137
Transportation cost	0.0963	0.0915	0.1243	0.1040	0.1049	0.1145
Storage cost	0.0761	0.0935	0.0946	0.1062	0.0861	0.1005
Processing cost	0.0785	0.0962	0.0932	0.0969	0.0850	0.0950
Controlling losses	0.0992	0.0998	0.0944	0.0969	0.1071	0.1051
Govt. support	0.1199	0.1048	0.0932	0.1022	0.1004	0.1012
Stopping shortages	0.1180	0.0998	0.0934	0.0986	0.0993	0.0950
Technological support	0.1205	0.0998	0.1245	0.0955	0.0872	0.0810
System transparency	0.1207	0.1247	0.0944	0.0984	0.1325	0.0833

In the following Table 9.4 the weights have been calculated using the equations (6), (7) and (8):

$$W_i = \frac{e_i}{1-e_i}, i = 1,2, \dots \dots m \tag{6}$$

Where:

$$e_i = -\left(\frac{1}{\ln(m)} * \sum_{j=1}^{n} X_{ij}\right), i = 1,2, \dots \dots m \quad (7) \text{ and}$$

$$X_{ij} = X_{ij} * \ln(X_{ij}) \tag{8}$$

Table 9.4 The computation of weights W_i

Factors	Rice	Wheat	Sugarcane	Tomato	Turmeric	Potato	Total	e_i	$1-e_i$	W_i
Production volume	-0.1930	-0.2239	-0.2230	-0.2302	-0.2279	-0.2435	-1.3416	0.5827	0.4173	0.1039
Production cost	-0.2257	-0.2233	-0.2217	-0.2320	-0.2294	-0.2472	-1.3793	0.5990	0.4010	0.0998
Transportation cost	-0.2253	-0.2188	-0.2592	-0.2354	-0.2365	-0.2481	-1.4233	0.6181	0.3819	0.0950
Storage cost	-0.1960	-0.2216	-0.2230	-0.2382	-0.2111	-0.2309	-1.3208	0.5736	0.4264	0.1061
Processing cost	-0.1998	-0.2252	-0.2211	-0.2261	-0.2095	-0.2236	-1.3055	0.5670	0.4330	0.1078
Controlling losses	-0.2292	-0.2300	-0.2228	-0.2261	-0.2392	-0.2368	-1.3841	0.6011	0.3989	0.0993
Govt. support	-0.2543	-0.2363	-0.2211	-0.2331	-0.2308	-0.2319	-1.4076	0.6113	0.3887	0.0967
Stopping shortages	-0.2522	-0.2300	-0.2214	-0.2285	-0.2294	-0.2236	-1.3850	0.6015	0.3985	0.0992
Technological support	-0.2550	-0.2300	-0.2594	-0.2243	-0.2127	-0.2036	-1.3850	0.6015	0.3985	0.0992
System transparency	-0.2552	-0.2596	-0.2228	-0.2282	-0.2678	-0.2071	-1.4406	0.6256	0.3744	0.0932

Using equation (2), the following Table 9.5 have been found.

Table 9.5 The normalized weighted decision matrix

Factors	Rice	Wheat	Sugarcane	Tomato	Turmeric	Potato	Wi
Production volume	0.2308	0.2999	0.2968	0.3160	0.3080	0.3476	0.1039
Production cost	0.3004	0.2985	0.2937	0.3202	0.3115	0.3574	0.0998
Transportation cost	0.2996	0.2880	0.3902	0.3287	0.3288	0.3598	0.0950
Storage cost	0.2368	0.2946	0.2968	0.3357	0.2699	0.3158	0.1061
Processing cost	0.2444	0.3030	0.2925	0.3061	0.2665	0.2986	0.1078
Controlling losses	0.3087	0.3142	0.2962	0.3061	0.3357	0.3305	0.0993
Govt. support	0.3731	0.3299	0.2925	0.3230	0.3149	0.3182	0.0967
Stopping shortages	0.3671	0.3142	0.2931	0.3118	0.3115	0.2986	0.0992
Technological support	0.3751	0.3142	0.3908	0.3019	0.2734	0.2546	0.0992
System transparency	0.3755	0.3928	0.2962	0.3111	0.4153	0.2619	0.0932

Equations (3), (4) and (5) stated above, the following table has been found. Finally, the scores for each indicator have been depicted in the last column of Table 9.6.

Table 9.6 The computation of euclidean distances and performance scores

Factors	Rice	Wheat	Sugar-cane	Tomato	Turmeric	Potato	S_i^+	S_i^-	P_i
Production volume	0.0240	0.0312	0.0308	0.0328	0.0320	0.0361	0.0193	0.0142	0.4237
Production cost	0.0312	0.0298	0.0293	0.0320	0.0311	0.0357	0.0164	0.0143	0.4659
Transporta-tion cost	0.0311	0.0274	0.0371	0.0312	0.0312	0.0342	0.0151	0.0158	0.5117
Storage cost	0.0246	0.0313	0.0315	0.0356	0.0286	0.0335	0.0199	0.0126	0.3882
Processing cost	0.0254	0.0327	0.0315	0.0330	0.0287	0.0322	0.0194	0.0111	0.3642
Controlling losses	0.0321	0.0312	0.0294	0.0304	0.0333	0.0328	0.0152	0.0136	0.4717
Govt. sup-port	0.0387	0.0319	0.0283	0.0312	0.0305	0.0308	0.0157	0.0167	0.5151
Stopping shortages	0.0381	0.0312	0.0291	0.0309	0.0309	0.0296	0.0158	0.0156	0.4977
Technologi-cal support	0.0390	0.0312	0.0388	0.0299	0.0271	0.0252	0.0177	0.0186	0.5125
System transparency	0.0390	0.0366	0.0276	0.0290	0.0387	0.0244	0.0175	0.0207	0.5415
Ideal best (V+)	0.0390	0.0366	0.0388	0.0356	0.0387	0.0361			
Ideal worst (V-)	0.0246	0.0274	0.0276	0.0290	0.0271	0.0244			

4.2 Customers' Perception Scores

The four different downstream supply chains (consumers' markets), namely, Hyderabad (Urban) (Cluster – A), Hyderabad (rural) (Cluster – B), Gwalior (Cluster – C) and Kanpur (Cluster – D) are taken into consideration and analysed in the following section. The decision matrix is the original data obtained from the respondents.

The data above (Table 9.7) have been normalized using equation (1) to give the following Table 9.8. Normalization is one essential step to control the possible response bias.

Table 9.7 The decision matrix

Factors	Cluster - A	Cluster - B	Cluster - C	Cluster - D
Production volume	2.8367	3.0800	3.9250	3.8600
Production cost	3.4286	3.2600	3.7750	3.9200
Transportation cost	3.4490	3.3600	3.7436	3.6000
Storage cost	3.1429	3.4800	3.0000	3.5200
Processing cost	3.3061	3.4200	3.6500	3.6200
Controlling losses	3.0000	3.4800	3.7750	4.1400
Govt. support	3.2449	3.5200	3.7000	3.9600
Stopping shortages	2.8980	3.7200	3.7500	3.6000
Technological support	3.3878	3.6200	3.6500	3.6600
System transparency	3.1020	3.4600	3.5750	4.0600

Table 9.8 The normalized decision matrix

Factors	Cluster - A	Cluster - B	Cluster - C	Cluster - D
Production volume	0.0892	0.0895	0.1074	0.1017
Production cost	0.1078	0.0948	0.1033	0.1033
Transportation cost	0.1085	0.0977	0.1024	0.0949
Storage cost	0.0988	0.1012	0.0821	0.0928
Processing cost	0.1040	0.0994	0.0999	0.0954
Controlling losses	0.0944	0.1012	0.1033	0.1091
Govt. support	0.1021	0.1023	0.1012	0.1044
Stopping shortages	0.0911	0.1081	0.1026	0.0949
Technological support	0.1065	0.1052	0.0999	0.0965
System transparency	0.0976	0.1006	0.0978	0.1070

In the following Tables 9.9, 9.10 and 9.11 the weights have been calculated using the equations (6), (7) and (8):

Table 9.9 The computation of W_i

Factors	Cluster - A	Cluster - B	Cluster - C	Cluster - D	Total	e_i	$1-e_i$	W_i
Production volume	-0.2156	-0.2161	-0.2396	-0.2325	-0.9038	0.3925	0.6075	0.1012
Production cost	-0.2402	-0.2233	-0.2345	-0.2345	-0.9325	0.4050	0.5950	0.0991
Transportation cost	-0.2409	-0.2272	-0.2334	-0.2235	-0.9250	0.4017	0.5983	0.0997
Storage cost	-0.2287	-0.2318	-0.2052	-0.2206	-0.8863	0.3849	0.6151	0.1025
Processing cost	-0.2354	-0.2295	-0.2301	-0.2242	-0.9191	0.3992	0.6008	0.1001
Controlling losses	-0.2227	-0.2318	-0.2345	-0.2417	-0.9307	0.4042	0.5958	0.0992
Govt. support	-0.2329	-0.2333	-0.2319	-0.2359	-0.9339	0.4056	0.5944	0.0990
Stopping shortages	-0.2183	-0.2405	-0.2336	-0.2235	-0.9160	0.3978	0.6022	0.1003
Technological support	-0.2386	-0.2369	-0.2301	-0.2256	-0.9312	0.4044	0.5956	0.0992
System transparency	-0.2271	-0.2310	-0.2274	-0.2392	-0.9246	0.4016	0.5984	0.0997

Table 9.10 The normalized weighted decision matrix

Factors	Cluster - A	Cluster - B	Cluster - C	Cluster - D	W_i
Production volume	0.2815	0.2828	0.3389	0.3212	0.1012
Production cost	0.3403	0.2993	0.3260	0.3262	0.0991
Transportation cost	0.3423	0.3085	0.3233	0.2996	0.0997
Storage cost	0.3119	0.3195	0.2591	0.2929	0.1025
Processing cost	0.3281	0.3140	0.3152	0.3013	0.1001
Controlling losses	0.2977	0.3195	0.3260	0.3445	0.0992
Govt. support	0.3220	0.3232	0.3195	0.3296	0.0990
Stopping shortages	0.2876	0.3415	0.3238	0.2996	0.1003
Technological support	0.3362	0.3324	0.3152	0.3046	0.0992
System transparency	0.3079	0.3177	0.3087	0.3379	0.0997

4.3 Summary of Findings

After a thorough analysis, we draw the following inferences. From Table 9.12 it is evident that producers' perceptions of the customers' prices are close to customers' perception scores with a correlation of 0.57 (statistically significant at 5%). To validate the results and elicit a scientific rating of the price control indicators, we assessed the gap between the two scores and then rated the indicators. The minimum gap got the highest rating and the maximum gap to the lowest rating.

Table 9.11 The computation of euclidean distances and performance scores

Factors	Cluster - A	Cluster - B	Cluster - C	Cluster - D	S_i^+	S_i^-	P_i
Production volume	0.0285	0.0286	0.0343	0.0325	0.0081	0.0083	0.5038
Production cost	0.0337	0.0297	0.0323	0.0323	0.0054	0.0079	0.5975
Transportation cost	0.0341	0.0307	0.0322	0.0299	0.0060	0.0078	0.5673
Storage cost	0.0320	0.0327	0.0265	0.0300	0.0092	0.0044	0.3221
Processing cost	0.0328	0.0314	0.0315	0.0302	0.0058	0.0066	0.5341
Controlling losses	0.0295	0.0317	0.0324	0.0342	0.0056	0.0076	0.5755
Govt. support	0.0319	0.0320	0.0316	0.0326	0.0044	0.0069	0.6109
Stopping shortages	0.0289	0.0343	0.0325	0.0301	0.0069	0.0075	0.5200
Technological support	0.0334	0.0330	0.0313	0.0302	0.0052	0.0073	0.5842
System transparency	0.0307	0.0317	0.0308	0.0337	0.0056	0.0063	0.5311
Ideal best (V+)	0.0341	0.0343	0.0343	0.0342			
Ideal worst (V-)	0.0289	0.0297	0.0265	0.0299			

Table 9.12 Comparison of producers' and customers' performance scores

Sl. No.	Factors	Producers' ranking (P_R)	Customers' ranking (C_R)	Gap ($P_R - C_R$)	Final Rank (F_R)
1	Production volume	0.4237	0.5038	0.0801	6
2	Production cost	0.4659	0.5975	0.1316	9
3	Transportation cost	0.5117	0.5673	0.0556	3
4	Storage cost	0.3882	0.3221	0.0661	4
5	Processing cost	0.3642	0.5341	0.1698	10
6	Controlling losses	0.4717	0.5755	0.1038	8
7	Govt. support	0.5151	0.6109	0.0957	7
8	Hoarding	0.4977	0.5200	0.0223	2
9	Technological support	0.5125	0.5842	0.0717	5
10	System transparency	0.5415	0.5311	0.0104	1

$R = 0.57$ (statistically significant at 5%)

4.4 Policy Implications

Increasing food prices have impacted consumers' buying behaviour in a variety of ways. Ranging from stopping of consumption of certain goods to reduction in consumption of goods are some of the critical aspects recently observed in the markets. The very example of tomato is no deviation in this regard. To make the prices more stable and sustainable in the market, it is imperative to think about the pricing mechanism from both production and consumption perspectives. This study has tried to examine the producers' as well as consumers' perceptions of the price control mechanism in India for need-based items i.e., food. This paper has taken all the significant factors which are normally considered while framing the policies for food inflation. As the producer and the consumer are complementary to each other, the decisions regarding price control cannot be effective by keeping one side in isolation. In this regard, the producers' perceptions of consumer price control (i.e., the downstream supply chain prices) are thoroughly analysed and cross-validated to conclude the arguments cited in the paper. The results suggest that system transparency, minimizing artificial hoarding and controlling transportation costs are some of the top priorities for controlling consumer prices in the downstream markets. However, technology adoption, adoption of scientific storage practices, increasing volume of production etc. are also found to be the other significant indicators of consumer price control in the markets. The governments (both the centre & the state) and the regulatory bodies should keep a close watch on various aspects of price rises and intervene as per the need for better market stability.

5. Conclusion

Food supply chains are mostly fragmented and hence price fluctuations are quite common in the marketplaces. The performances of the producers greatly depend upon the consumers buying behaviour and expectations (Fritz et al., 2008; Beske et al., 2014; León-Bravo et al., 2018). What the producers feel about the price rises in the market is not completely independent of what the consumers feel about the daily price rises, in the sense that one stakeholder gets affected when the decisions of the other. So, broadly, the pricing sustainability issues are interrelated and hence need the intervention of multiple players on a typical problem, say price rise. In this piece of work, we look at the price rise (inflation) from both ends and cross-validated the results to avoid any possible bias. With the outputs of this research, we expect that the producers (i.e., the upstream stakeholders) will keep in mind the hardships of the customers while setting prices for the downstream markets.

AFSCs play a vital role in every individual's life. The performance of the AFSCs in the process greatly affects the daily expenses of customers. Higher costs of essential goods and services reduce the saving potential of the customers. In this study, we tried to assess the price control mechanism from two important stakeholders of the supply chain namely, producers and the customers. The inferences drawn from the producers' data analysis were cross-validated with the inferences drawn from the customers' data analysis. There were some disagreements traced in terms of the ranking while all agreed with the indicators stated in the analysis. To minimize the bias and elicit the scientific ranking the gaps in the performance scores were calculated and then the ranks were given.

The lowest gaps got the higher rating while the highest gap got the lowest ranking. The output of this piece of work has paramount importance in the AFSCs and bears in its ability to provide implications to the policymakers, especially in the developing and emerging economies in the world.

Acknowledgements

The paper titled, "Agri-food Supply Chain (AFSC) Producers' Perceptions of Consumer Price Control – An Assessment using MCDM Technique", a part of the Research Project "The Causal Link between Supply Chain Management Practices and Food Inflation in India (IoE/RC1/RC1-2020-035)", is fully funded by the Institution of Eminence (IoE), University of Hyderabad, Hyderabad, India.

References

1. Aramyan, L. H. (2007). Measuring supply chain performance in the agri-food sector. Wageningen University, Wageningen, Netherlands.
2. Aramyan, L. H., Lansink, A. G. J. M. O., Van der Vorst, J. G. A. J., and Van Kooten, O. (2007). Performance measurement in agri-food supply chains: A case study. Supply Chain Management: An International Journal. 12(4): 304–314.
3. Beske, P., Land, A., and Seuring, S. (2014). Sustainable supply chain management practices and dynamic capabilities in the food industry: a critical analysis of the literature. Int. J. of Production Economics. 152(2014): 131–143. https://doi.org/10.1016/j.ijpe.2013.12.026
4. Chen J. K., and Chen I. S. (2010). Using a novel conjunctive MCDM approach based on DEMATEL, fuzzy ANP, and TOPSIS as an innovation support system for Taiwanese higher education. Exp. Syst. Appl. 37(3): 1981–1990.
5. Chopra, S., and Meindl, P. (2014). Supply chain management: Strategy, planning and operation. New Delhi: Pearson Education.
6. Christopher, M., and Towill, D. (2000). Supply chain migration from lean and functional to agile and customised. Supply Chain Management: An International Journal. 5(4): 206–213.
7. Fisher, M. (1997). What is the right supply chain for your product? Harvard Business Review. March – April(1997): 1–13.
8. Fritz, M., and Schiefer, G. (2008). Food chain management for sustainable food system development: a European research agenda. Agribusiness. 24(4): 440–452. https://doi.org/10.1002/agr.20172
9. Huang, S. H., Sheoran, S. K., and Wang, G. (2004). A review and analysis of the supply chain operations reference (SCOR) model. *Supply Chain Management: An International Journal.* 9(1): 23–29.
10. Hwang, C. L., and Yoon, K. (1981). Multiple attribute decision making: methods and applications. New York, USA: Springer - Verlag.
11. Hwang, C. L., Lai, Y. J., and Liu, T. Y. (1993). A new approach for multiple objective decision making. Computers and Operational Research. 20(8): 889–899. doi:10.1016/0305-0548(93)90109-v

12. Ishizaka, A., and Nemery, P. (2013). Multi-criteria decision analysis: methods and software (1st ed.). New Delhi: John Wiley & Sons, Ltd.
13. León-Bravo, V., Caniato, F., and Caridi, M. (2018). Sustainability in multiple stages of the food supply chain in Italy: practices, performance and reputation. Operations Management Research. 2019(12): 40–61. https://doi.org/10.1007/s12063-018-0136-9
14. Opricovic, S., and Tzeng, G. H. (2004). Compromise solution by MCDM methods: a comparative analysis of VIKOR and TOPSIS. European Journal of Operational Research. 156(2004): 445–455.
15. Porter, M. E. (1980). Competitive strategy: techniques for analyzing industries and competitors. New York: Free Press.
16. Rajput, S., and Singh, S. P. (2019). Identifying Industry 4.0 IoT enablers by integrated PCA-ISM-DEMATEL approach. Management Decision. 57(8): 1784–1817.
17. Saaty, T. L. (1980). The Analytic Hierarchy Process. New York: McGraw-Hill.
18. Simchi-Levi, D., Kaminsky, P., Simchi-Levi, E., and Shankar, R. (2008). Designing and managing the supply chain. New Delhi: Tata McGraw Hill.
19. Williamson, O. E. (1985). The economic institutions of capitalism. New York: Free Press.
20. Yoon, K. (1987). A reconciliation among discrete compromise situations. Journal of the Operational Research Society. 38(3): 277–286. doi:10.1057/jors.1987.44

Note: All the tables in this chapter were made by the authors.

Securing the Future through Sustainability, Health, Education, and Technology – Brig. Dr. Rajiv Divekar et al. (eds)
© 2024 Taylor & Francis Group, London, ISBN 978-1-032-95922-1

10 Behavioural Patterns of Indian Shoppers in Tier II Cities of South Asia: A Confirmatory Factor Analysis Approach

Pooja Khanna[1], Mohd Farhan[2]
Associate Professor,
Mittal School of Business, Lovely Professional University,
Punjab, India

Komal Chopra[3]
Associate Professor,
Symbiosis Institute of Management Studies,
Symbiosis International (Deemed University), Pune, India

ABSTRACT

The study was undertaken to understand the consumer behaviour of shoppers in Tier II cities of India. The study intends to recognize the factors that are crucial to the sustainability of malls in South Asian countries. Exploratory factor analysis (EFA) has been used to condense the data, that resulted into five factors- Convenience to Shoppers, Marketing focus, Economic Deals, Accessibility Issues and Merchandize that are crucial for the viability of malls in Tier II cities. Results were confirmed using Confirmatory Factor Analysis. Outcomes of this research give an insight into the psychology of non- metropolitan shoppers in South Asian Countries and gives significant contribution to the sparse literature pool in this area with special reference to Tier II cities in India. Results of this study are applicable to Tier II cities. The study makes strong argument for the changes that need to be incorporated in the brick-and-mortar stores located in malls keeping in mind the threat faced by them from local retailers. Shopping malls in India have seen a spiralling growth in the recent decade, but all of them have not survived the test of time. Tier II cities have witnessed a relatively larger investment in mall development. This research analyses the syndrome of struggling malls in Tier II cities by focusing on the behavioural pattern of small-town shoppers in South Asian cities.

KEYWORDS: Shopping malls, Tier II cities, Factor analysis, Confirmatory factor analysis, Shoppers, Consumers, Regression, Consumer behaviour, Indian shoppers

[1]Pooja.28675@lpu.co.in, [2]mohdfarhan7@gmail.com [3]chopra.k@sims.edu

DOI: 10.1201/9781003587200-10

1. Introduction

The well-entrenched mall culture in South Asian countries has faced many challenges since its advent. Though shopping malls are mushrooming across the country, but only a handful are running successfully. Insignificant number of them are bereft of customers and are in crisis and struggling hard to survive, thus giving a gloomy picture. Hit by high rentals, low footfall and matured markets in metros, retailers are now targeting Tier II cities as they promise better returns. Lower operational costs, relatively less competition and high growth potential in Tier II cities, attract mall developers and retailers as they show a strong growth momentum and promise golden opportunities. Rising incomes, increasing awareness and high aspirations of consumers in small cities spell big opportunities for retailers. Besides, these cities also have uncharted opportunities and unexplored novelty value that allure retailers to invest. The market size in these cities is also likely to grow from US$ 5.7 billion to US$ 80 billion by 2026. In the last few years, the malls that have not been performing well, are either getting transformed into office spaces or the buildings are destroyed to pave way for new venues. The challenges faced by malls are relatively on a higher side than the ones faced by an individual retail tenant in the mall. Malls have to do much more to entice shoppers to visit. They face the pressure of creating an experience that shoppers would relish forever.

Earlier, retailers and builders were not well versed with the tastes and preferences of consumers, especially in metros. Now mall developers in Tier II cities are facing the same problem. Shoppers in small cities do not have income levels as their counterparts in metropolitans. Hence, they have their own definition of shopping experience. Shopping malls in small cities promote the lifestyle of shoppers to a different level thus promising to transform shopping and recreation. Shoppers in small cities consider the concept of malls with great admiration because of limited leisure and entertainment options available in these cities. The air-conditioned ambience with world class infrastructure of malls is viewed as a perfect place for family outings to get together, to shop, to dine and watch a movie. Though malls have opened a new dimension to entertainment and shopping in small cities yet consumers are more inclined towards local retailers. The inability on the part of Mall developers, managers and retailers to recognize this fact is a shortcoming that needs to be addressed. Shopping malls are hugely capital-intensive ventures and have long gestation periods. Mall developers in Tier II cities need to emphasize less on investing heavily in making them more ornate and more on operations of these properties so that they do not neglect the real sentiments of the target segment. The productivity of any mall depends on the research carried out to study the consumer behaviour of shoppers in that area. It is extremely important to adapt to the demands of Millennials, failing which can be disastrous for underperforming malls. Mall developers and retailers need to introspect into the reasons that impact the profitability and sustainability of mall.

This paper studies the shopping orientation of shoppers of Tier II cities in Punjab (India). This research leads the researchers towards getting a deep insight into the factors that govern the viability of shopping malls in Tier II cities. By attending to these mall attributes, mall developers can develop multi-pronged strategies to attract and retain customers in South Asian countries. The study is carried out with the objectives that are described in the following section.

2. Research Objective

Plethora of studies on management orientation of shopping malls, touch various dimensions of shopping malls – financing pattern, mall development and operations, satisfaction, perception etc. Focus of some of these studies has been on dimensions that impact the perception and satisfaction of shoppers about shopping malls. There are studies that also talk about the expectations of retailers from mall developers (Khanna and Seth, 2018). Despite the higher growth potential and untapped novelty value in Tier II cities, consumers' response to shopping malls in these cities is luke-warm. It's not that small town shoppers are not enthusiastic about shopping, but a decent number of them are inclined towards local retailers. Do the local retailers have a better understanding of the taste of their indigenous customers or the mall developers have not been able to catch the pulse of their target market, this is the question that needs to be pondered up-on. This research has been conducted to investigate the factors that determine the viability of malls considering the expectations of shoppers in Tier II cities. It is primarily an exploratory study that would help the mall developers in non-metropolitans to devise strategies and make the necessary structural and operational changes to add life to the aging malls.

3. Review of Literature

Marketing processes and actions of any organization are customer centric and revolve around the response of consumers. Many studies have been carried out to explore different aspects of shopping malls. Gamut of antecedent factors influencing holistic experience of shoppers have been heavily examined and cover all the relevant evaluative criterions. Prashar et al. (2016) analysed the relationship between various components constituting shopping experience with reference to Indian shopping malls. The study provided a better understanding of various shoppers' segments and empirically explored the complete shopping experience that adds value to the shopping spree of shoppers and not just the act of purchasing the product. Great deal of literature focuses on Tier I cities and reveal the consumption pattern and orientation of metropolitan shoppers. There is a need to explore the dimensions that influence the consumer behaviour of small-town shoppers. Gupta et al. (2020), developed a theoretical framework for the assessment of the dimensions that impacted the experience of customers.

The study focused on the customer experience in Tier II and Tier III cities and classified the variables associated with retail experience.

Many studies have been conducted in the last decade measuring the dimension of customer satisfaction in shopping malls. Utilitarian and Hedonic values were analysed and portrayed to be significant in driving customer satisfaction by Kesari & Atulkar (2016). Khanna & Seth (2018), in their study on shopping malls in Tier II cities, examined the factors that impacted the shoppers' satisfaction in malls. They analysed six factors that were substantial to customer satisfaction in malls – mall infrastructure, convenience, customer service, time saving, promotional offers and stress reliever. Recent contribution in this field was done by Ali et al. (2021), the study investigated the association between utilitarian and hedonic shopping value, mall personality, and shoppers' wellbeing. Results revealed that both, utilitarian and hedonic values are influenced positively by mall personality.

Extending the concept of Customer Satisfaction further, researchers took another dimension into consideration i.e. customer service, that holds relevance in creating customer satisfaction and loyalty. Eid & Adly (2016) explored the relationship between the shopping environment, customer perceived value, customer satisfaction and customer loyalty in context to malls in the United Arab Emirates (UAE). They posited eight dimensions of MALLVAL – hedonic, self-gratification, utilitarian, epistemic, social interaction, spatial convenience, transaction and time convenience value. Highlighting the importance of MALLVALL, the study concluded that MALLVALL has a substantial positive impact on customer satisfaction and customer loyalty. Khanna & Seth (2018) explored and validated six factors that primarily contributed to customer satisfaction in malls in Tier II cities. These factors were Mall Infrastructure, Convenience, Customer Service, Time Saved, Promotional Offers and Stress Reliever. Rather et al. (2018) based their study on the premise that value congruity affected consumer brand identification, customer brand engagement and affective brand commitment, thus focusing on dynamics of customer relationship management.

Generation of footfall was another pertinent attribute that was profusely studied by various researchers as it significantly impacts the profitability and sustainability of any mall. Bhatt *et al.*, (2020) in their study posited, attractive store stimuli indicated affective and sensory store brand experience which further predicted store satisfaction. Many studies have tried to explore relationship between the factors that are controlled by retailers and influence shoppers' buying behaviour. Kushwaha et al. (2017) in an exploratory study on consumer perception tried to explore the factors that influenced selection of shopping malls. They identified seven factors that impacted the decision to select any shopping mall. Aragoncillo & Orus (2018) analysed the phenomena of impulse buying in the fashion industry and results depicted that shopping behaviour of consumers was more influenced by offline channels (retail outlets) than various online platforms. The scope of these studies is limited to developed economies like UK, USA, UAE and Europe. There is limited research on developing countries in South Asia like India.

Yi & Kang (2019) in their study postulated the effects of music on customer satisfaction, behaviour intention and emotional response and concluded that background music increased individuals' positive evaluation of the environment. Katrodia et al. (2018) in their study identified that there was significant influence of factors like sales dynamics, and service accessibility on buying behaviour of consumers.

Review cited above depicts that, to shoppers, shopping is not the only criterion for visiting malls. It's the recreational activities and overall experience that drives people to them. Consumers in small cities visit malls because they are fascinated by superior facilities, world class infrastructure and wide merchandize. However, we demonstrate that there is a strong need to study the dimensions that impact consumer behaviour in small cities of South Asian countries. Variables considered in this study are the ones that any small-town shopper would consider while shopping, irrespective of the place, whether malls or local retailers. Bargaining, economic purchases, home delivery, merchandize and credit facility are some of the variables that demonstrate the orientation of small-town shoppers and thus these variables have been taken into consideration while conducting this research. An attempt has been made through this paper to highlight those dimensions, so that mall managers can offer the most meaningful and relevant proposition to their customers.

4. Research Methodology

4.1 Instrument Design

A tentative list of attributes determining the behavioural pattern of Indian small-town shoppers was prepared from the review of literature cited above. This list thus prepared was sent to a panel of academicians and industry experts. The recommendations of the panel members were considered and certain inclusions and modifications were made in some attributes. For example, variables like credit facility and home delivery were added to the construct 'convenience'. Final instrument comprised of 16 variables. The questionnaire was found to be reliable after checking its validity and reliability. Details of the demographics of the respondents were also recorded in the questionnaire. This research is an empirical investigation based on the primary data that was collected from the shoppers who came to the malls. Three cities of Punjab were considered for this research. Mall intercept survey was used to collect data, to get on-site feedback.

4.2 Sampling

The research aimed at understanding the consumer behaviour and identifying the factors that impacted the viability of shopping malls in Tier II cities. Mall intercept and store intercept techniques were used to fetch information from shoppers using a structured questionnaire. Data was collected from people who visited shopping malls in Jalandhar, Ludhiana and Amritsar. The cities were selected based on population density which was maximum in Ludhiana followed by Amritsar and then Jalandhar. Random convenience sampling was used on a sample size of 177 shoppers.

5. Data Analysis and Interpretation

The demographic profile of the consumers (Table 10.1) was prepared from the information collected through the questionnaire. Data collected was subjected to factor analysis using SPSS.

Table 10.1 Profile of respondents

Demographic Group	Demographic Sub-group	Number	Percentage
Age Group	Less than 18	23	12.99
	19-30	58	32.77
	31-40	32	18.08
	41-50	34	19.21
	51-60	23	12.99
	61 and above	7	3.95
Gender	Male	98	55.37
	Female	79	44.63
Education Level	Under-Graduate	57	32.20
	Graduate	49	27.68
	PG and above	71	40.11
Monthly Income	less than 25K	18	10.17
	25K -40K	67	37.85
	40K-60K	48	27.12
	60K-1 Lac	23	12.99
	Above 1 Lac	21	11.86
Marital Status	Single	58	32.77
	Married	91	51.41
	Any other	28	15.82
Area of Residence	Rural	56	31.64
	Urban	121	68.36

Source: Author's Calculations

6. Reliability and Suitability Test of Data

The newly constructed instrument was treated with Chronbach's Alpha. SPSS was used to check the reliability of the factor output. Reliability of all the factors was confirmed by alpha value which was more than 0.7. Exploratory Factor Analysis was used to explore factors that impacted the sustainability of shopping malls in Tier II cities. Data was initially tested and KMO was generated. KMO value of .791 supports the usage of factor analysis on the sample considered for this research. The Barlett's test of sphericity, depicts chi square value of 851.421, which is significant at 1% level of significance. Table 10.2 depicts the results of KMO and Barlett's test of sphericity. Five factors were extracted after performing a series of deletions.

Table 10.2 KMO & barlett's test of sphericity

Kaiser-Meyer- Olkin Measure of Sampling Adequacy		0.791
Barlett's Test of Sphericity	Approx. Chi-Square	851.421
	Df	403
	Sig.	.000

Source: Author's Calculations

7. Factor Output

Results of Factor Analysis revealed five factors that explained 73.44 %variance regarding the factors that determine the fate of shopping malls in Tier II cities. All these values showed that the data was fit for factor analysis. Tabulated factor output of the extracted factors is presented in Table 10.3.

Table 10.3 Tabulated factor output

Factor No.	Factor title	Variables included	Factor loading
F1	Convenience to Shoppers $\alpha = 0.891$	Home delivery	.845
		Credit facility not available	.816
		Spatial, temporal	.793
		Utilities	.765
F2	Marketing Focus $\alpha = 0.845$	Unattractive ambience	.593
		Refrain buying perishable goods from malls	.654
		Lifts and escalators	.641
F3	Economic Deals $\alpha = 0.814$	More expensive	.921
		No bargaining	.876
		More economic deals-online	.854
		Shopping	
F4	Accessibility Issues $\alpha = 0.746$	Location	.761
		Distance from Home/office	.732
		Security and Parking space	.612
F5	Merchandize $\alpha = 0.723$	Better variety in local market	.843
		High end brands	.632
		More variety of ethnic wear	.911
		In local shops	

Source: Author's Calculations

7.1 Factor 1 – Convenience to Shoppers

First factor extracted in this study was named 'Convenience to shoppers'. It comprised of variables like home delivery (.845), credit facility (.816), temporal and spatial factors (.793), and utilities (.716) offered at the mall while shopping (Table 10.3). Significantly higher factor loadings of .845 and .816 of two variables- home delivery and credit facility in malls is an indication that shoppers in Tier II cities look forward to such facilities in Malls. This can be attributed to the fact that, the retail sector in small cities is still dominated by local retailers and malls so far have not been able to captivate the hearts of shoppers despite their glitzy appearance and world class ambience. Reimers & Clulow (2014) posited the significance of convenience in shopping. The study considered factors like spatial convenience, temporal convenience, parking and various services while shopping. Non-availability of services like home delivery and credit facility in malls demotivates consumers from visiting the same mall again.

7.2 Factor 2 – Marketing Focus

Marketing Focus, the second factor comprises of variables like ambience (cleanliness, hygiene, lighting, odour, temperature and aesthetic appeal), shoppers' orientation towards purchasing perishable goods from malls and condition of lifts and escalators having factor loadings of .593, .654 and .641 respectively. Small town shoppers feel dejected by the absence of any of these elements and refrain buying from such malls.

Shoppers in Tier II cities perceive shopping malls as one stop destination where they can get diverse range of products under one roof, be it branded clothes, foot-wears, and electronics or even vegetables and fruits. But they refrain buying vegetables and fresh fruits from malls because they are highly sceptical about freshness of these commodities. A small-town shopper feels that he can get fresh fruits and vegetables from a street hawker and that too at a relatively cheaper rate, so why to purchase it from malls where they are doubtful about the packaging and even rates also. Malls, not getting a good rating on these parameters do not serve as attractive destinations for consumers. Another factor to be highlighted here is, the pleasant appeal of store environment which retailers ought to pay attention (Wirtz et al. 2007). Bäckström (2006) also supports this finding by positing that ambience of the mall has a major influence on the engagement of shoppers. On the other hand, unattractive ambience acts as a major repelling factor that pushes customers to other shopping destinations like local retailers. Other studies that support the importance of eye-catching ambience in enhancing mall patronage are given by De Juan (2004) & Michon et al. (2005). We cannot imagine a mall without lifts and escalators today but are they in working condition that's the question. If they are not operational, then again that disappoints the shoppers and they have another reason to avoid that mall. A higher factor loading of .641 to this parameter depicts that shoppers in small cities have strong expectations of getting world class amenities in malls that adds a new dimension to their shopping experience thus, also impacting their emotional and mental processes while shopping.

7.3 Factor 3 – Economic Deals

'Economic Deals' comprised of three variables- More expensive products (.921), No bargaining (.876) and more economic deals in local shops and online (.854). A higher factor loading for the three variables indicates a high level of correlation between the variables and the concerned factor. This also signifies that shoppers in small cities are more price conscious and take utmost care while spending money. The lifestyle of small-town shoppers cannot be generalized with that of bigger cities, reason being, the inability to spend large amount of money on global brands or recreation in malls because of the lower disposable income. Shoppers in these cities consider malls to be relatively an expensive venture because of factors like air-conditioned atmosphere, aesthetic ambience, high- end brands, décor, aroma and impressive physical layout. They believe that bargaining over the price of products, which is perceived by them as an integral component of shopping, is not possible in branded outlets. This again, is a significant determinant of the fate of any mall in Tier II cities. Consumers in Tier II cities have an orientation towards savings, be it shopping or large investment (Khare, 2011). Shoppers here believe that shopping in local stores and online sites offer relatively more economic deals (Khanna & Seth, 2018). Though malls offer rebates and discounts to shoppers, but they are mostly seen during festivals. Shoppers in small cities are elated to bargain with shopkeepers at local shops and believe that with this practice the price of goods can be reduced and they can get a more economic deal (Tauber,1972), which also gives them psychological satisfaction. The monetary savings and economical purchases in the local market of Tier II cities adds to the utilitarian value which is lacking in shopping malls.

7.4 Factor 4 – Accessibility Issues

'Accessibility' is the fourth factor extracted and location, distance from home/ office and security and parking space are the variables that contribute mainly to this factor with factor loadings of .761, .732 and .612 respectively. There are other variables that contribute to this factor, but, to a lesser extent. Shoppers in small cities do not prefer a mall that is located far off from their home or work station. It can be related to the behaviour to seek proximity while going for shopping as shoppers in Tier II cities are used to travelling less while going for shopping to local market. Shopping in malls entails lot of walking and shoppers in small cities are accustomed to visiting local bazars where they neither have to travel much nor walk more. Locational convenience plays a significant role in the decision to select a mall for shopping in small towns. Malls that are located far off and are not easily accessible to consumers. They may either have to take local conveyance or a keep a car, which further raises doubts about convenient parking. Non-Metropolitan shoppers have an orientation to seek proximity and lesser inter-store distances while shopping (Stassen et al. 1999). Because of the accessibility issues, shoppers in Tier II cities may opt for shopping in local market where they feel that their time is saved. Huff & Rust (1984) in a dedicated study illustrated significance of distance and travel time with the help of retail gravity model, which demonstrated and predicted the significance of store size and distance in retail patronage. Another variable that catches our attention here is Safety and hassle-free parking. Shoppers are very conscious of parking their vehicles in malls and their safety at the same time. This can be attributed to the increasing number of theft and robbery of cars in small cities. Shoppers in non- metro cities find it safer and more convenient to visit local shops where they can go on a two-wheeler, this also saves their time.

7.5 Factor 5 – Merchandize

This factor comprises three variables – better variety in local market, high end brands and more variety of ethnic wear in local shops. Factor loadings in this case are .843, .632 and .911 respectively. These variables indicate that undoubtedly, malls offer a wide range of high-end brands (Solomon, 1983), still shoppers in non-metropolitan cities have a mind-set of getting more variety of products at local shops. Significantly higher factor loading to variable 'more variety of ethnic wear in local shops' holds great importance as shoppers feel that traditional shops in the market are flooded with wide variety of merchandize in ethnic wear. Shopping malls, despite having high end brands do not offer wide assortment in ethnic wear. Shoppers in small towns find malls to be suitable for casual, chic clothes and other products but unsuitable for traditional wear.

8. Validity and Reliability of Factor Output

On checking the reliability and validity of factors extracted, value of Chronbach's Alfa was found to be greater than 0.7, which indicated that factor output was reliable. Variance Extracted for all the factors was more than 0.5 (Table 10.4).

Table 10.4 Variance extracted

S no.	Factor no. & Label	Variance Extracted (VE)
1	Convenience to shoppers	0.841
2	Marketing Focus	0.758
3	Economic Deals	0.724
4	Accessibility Issues	0.654
5	Merchandize	0.612

Source: Author's calculations

Discriminant validity check was done by comparing the Average Variance Extracted (AVE) with the squared correlation for each of the constructs. Final factor output showed absence of any cross loadings as there was only one significant factor loading per variable.

9. Confirmation of Factor Structure

Factor output as indicated by EFA is portrayed in Table 10.3 and highlights five factors that were extracted in this model. The model represents the measurement model indicating the factors which can be the cause of failure of malls in Tier II cities. It depicts co-variance amongst various factors along with the error variance related to each variable. The model also represents group of variables associated with corresponding factors. This model was subjected to Confirmatory Factor Analysis (CFA) using AMOS (Fig. 10.1). Number of variables (Table 10.6) given as per this model was 15, of which 9 were exogenous and 6 were endogenous. The goodness of fit statistics indicated that the proposed model was adequate.

Table 10.5 Fit statistics of the measurement model

Goodness of Fit Index (GFI)	**0.923**
Adjusted Goodness of Fit Index (AGFI)	0.91
Normed Fit Index (NFI)	0.90
Relative Fit Index (RFI)	0.96
Comparative Fit Index (CFI)	0.93
Tucker Lewis Index (TLI)	0.98
Root Mean Square Error of Approximation (RMSEA)	.06

Source: Author's Calculations

Table 10.6 List of variables used in Fig. 10.1

Label	**Description**	**Label**
F1	Convenience to shoppers	V6 Utilities
F2	Marketing Focus	V7 Better variety in local Market
F3	Economic Deals	V8 More economic deals online/local stores
F4	Accessibility Issues	V9 Non availability of credit facility
F5	Merchandize	V10 Spatial & Temporal Factors
V1	Unattractive Ambience	V11 Distance from Home / Office
V2	No bargaining	V12 Parking & other services
V3	Refrain buying fresh	V13 Lifts and escalators
	Vegetables and fruits	V14 Tenant Mix
V4	High End Brands in Malls	V15 More variety of ethnic wear in local shops
V5	Location of the Mall	V16 Security and Parking Space

Source: Author's Calculations

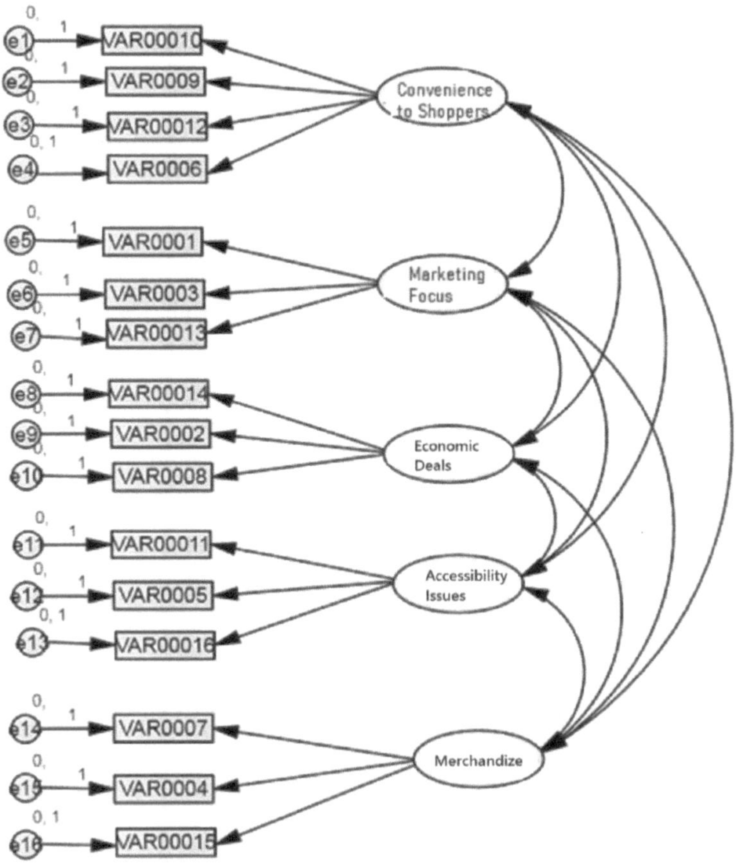

Fig. 10.1 Results of confirmatory factor analysis

Source: Made by Author

Goodness of Fit Index (GFI) attained is 0.923 as against recommended value of 0.90 (Table 10.5). The Adjusted Goodness of Fit Index (AGFI) is 0.91 as against the acceptable value of above 0.90 as well. The Normed Fit Index (NFI), Relative Fit Index (RFI), Comparative Fit Index (CFI), Tucker Lewis Index (TLI) are 0.96, 0.93, 0.97, 0.98 respectively as against the recommended level of above 0.90. Root Mean Square Error of Approximation (RMSEA) is .06. All these values are indicators of a good fit and the model stood validated.

10. Regression Analysis

Regression model has been employed to quantify the impact of these five factors on the expectations of customers in shopping malls. Following model has been developed in order to measure the impact of five factors identified:

$$CE = \alpha + \beta_1 ED + \beta_2 MF_I + \beta_3 C + \beta_4 A + \beta_5 M + \varepsilon \qquad (1)$$

Where, CE is the Customer Expectation (Dependent Variable), α is the constant and β_1 to β_5 are the slopes associated with different independent variables which have emerged from factor analysis. The specifications of regression have been depicted in Table 10.7.

Table 10.7 Results of stepwise regressions conducted on various combinations of independent variables that determine the expectations of small-town shoppers

	(i)		(ii)		(iii)		(iv)		(v)	
Independent Variable	**t-stat**	**R^2**	**t-stat**	**R^2**	**t-stat**	**R^2**	**t-stat**	**R^2**	**t-stat**	**R^2**
Economic Deals	6.194	0.344	7.581	0.497	8.110	0.574	**8.317**	0.633	8.124	0.6 56
	0.000		0.000		0.000		**0.000**		(0.000)	
Marketing Focus			4.664		5.038		**5.389**		5.217	
			0.000		0.000		**0.000**		(0.001)	
Convenience to Shoppers					3.603		**3.854**		3.953	
					0.001		**0.000**		0.000	
Accessibility										
							3.353		3.439	
							0.001		0.001	
Merchandize									2.151	
									0.035	

Source: Author's own calculations

The results of the stepwise regression are depicted in Table 10.7. It is evident from the table that the factor Economic Deals, exerts a significant impact on the expectations of shoppers in Tier II cities (t-stat of 6.194 with p-value of 0.000) and commands a strong position in impacting the expectations of small town shoppers to a considerable extent with t-stat 8.317 and significance level of 0.000. The findings are supported by the study of Khare (2011), which mentioned that consumers in Tier II cities are more inclined towards savings, be it shopping or any large investment.

Second factor that can be an important predictor of expectations of shoppers is Marketing Focus, having t-stat 5.389 and significance level of 0.000. Variables that contribute to this factor, to a great extent are pivotal in attracting customers and serving them comprehensively and comfortably. Yavas (2003) posited the importance of world class amenities and the way it impacts the emotional processes of consumers, indicating the importance of marketing-oriented efforts.

Convenience to shoppers and Accessibility are the factors that showed t-stat 3.854 and 3.353 respectively This is supported by earlier studies by Kirkup & Rafiq

(1994), which states that convenience has a substantial impact on the success of any shopping mall.

Mercahndize showed t-stat 2.151 and significance level of 0.035. Results show that 5 factors considered in the study collectively explain 65.6 percent of the variance in customer expectations in small cities. It can be inferred that out of the five factors extracted in EFA; Economic Deals, Marketing Focus and Shoppers' convenience are the factors that have significant impact on the expectations of small-town shoppers. This paves way for mall managers to focus more on these areas, to offer more meaningful proposition to small town shoppers.

11. Conclusion

Results of this study support the notion that shopping spree of consumers in Tier II of Indian cities is an orchestration of various factors. Observations presented above highlight the need to relook into the designing and management of shopping malls in Tier II cities, so that malls in these cities do not run out of business. The economic potential of India depends on the growth momentum of small cities. Nonmetropolitan cities are showing growth and development on all fronts –urban housing, infrastructure, offices and retail. Retail being the key component of development, can drive the future growth and add value to the infrastructure of small cities. They ought to invest on giving a more holistic shopping experience to shoppers in Tier II cities. Efforts made on promotional events go in vain, if the tenant mix of the mall does not satiate the shoppers who visit them. Mall operators need to keep pace with preferences of consumers and think on giving wholesome experience to the shoppers. Another point to ponder here is, the preference given by small town consumer to credit facility and home delivery in malls. They compare shopping in malls to the experience they have with local retailers where they feel that their utilitarian and emotional needs are satisfied. Lack of credit facility and home delivery service in malls are considered to be major shortcomings by small town consumers, as they are used to such expediencies while shopping in local market. Retailers in local market not only stock products according to the choices of their customers, but they also provide them with shopping assistance and customised services. Supplementing shopping in malls with these services would help mall developers to create a community experience which will further help them survive and thrive. An interesting point in the results relates to the marketing focus of shopping malls. 'Marketing focus' here covers dimensions like ambience, lifts/escalators and attitude towards purchasing perishable goods like fruits and vegetables from malls. These dimensions could be different from those in metropolitan cities. Escalators and lifts undoubtedly are aesthetically appealing but their performance puts a question mark in the mind of consumers. Results posit that lifts and escalators should be functioning and well maintained so that consumers do not have to think twice before shopping in that mall. Similar observations have been observed in case of Accessibility where shoppers have assigned almost similar weightage to all the three variables. Other than the location of the mall, shoppers are also concerned about the safety and security in parking areas. Parking lot in a mall should be well lit and should have security guards, so that consumers, especially females and children can go, park their vehicle safely and move around freely.

Consumers in Tier II cities are attracted to malls because of attractive designs, multiplex, food court and showrooms filled with well recognized brands. Favourable design elements, no doubt attract and persuade consumers to visit malls, but if they do not get the desired variety in merchandize, they are compelled to visit local retailers, which is not a good sign for malls. Not being able to haggle in malls is another major factor that impacts the sustainability of malls. Consumers in small cities are not willing to spend large amount of money on branded products. They are also reluctant to spend relatively more money on high end entertainment venues in malls. Shoppers in Tier II cities relish the experience of bargaining with shopkeepers believing that by doing so the price of the goods can be reduced and they can get a rebate on the products. The same may not be possible in the branded showrooms of malls, thus demotivating consumers to revisit the malls. Consumers in Tier II cities seek more of experiential benefit in shopping and mall location plays an important role in influencing consumer's shopping behaviour.

Location of the mall also acts as a deterrent for visiting it for routine shopping, if located in the outskirts or is far off from the residential of office premises. There is a need for them to change their vision from being competition centric to customer centric.

12. Managerial Implications

Malls have opened up new dimensions for consumers in Tier II cities, but their sustainability is a big challenge. The research analyses the syndrome of struggling malls in Tier II cities, with an attempt to comprehend the orientation of small-town consumers towards shopping malls. Small town shoppers in Tier II cities have for years craved for global brands, cineplexes, world class ambience which their counterparts in metropolitans have enjoyed. Small town consumers have the notion that shopping malls would bring them a new lease of life. Generally consumer in a Tier II or Tier III city is well travelled and is exposed to more brands leading to a larger scope in retail spending. Shopping Malls in small cities are seen as peaceful hassle-free places that are temperature controlled and free from pollution. Tier II shoppers take pride in calling malls the modern temples of small cities because of their novelty value. It gives them immense pleasure in showing off products they bought from their neighbouring mall.

Shopping Malls in small cities are bound to shift the lifestyle of shoppers and promise to give them an experience they have never experienced before. Small town consumers are attracted to shopping malls because of variety of retail outlets, superior ambience and international brands. However, they think twice before spending money there, as shopping dynamics in Tier II cities are different than in metro cities. Mall shopping behaviour of small-town shoppers cannot be generalised with metropolitan shoppers. Consumers in metropolitan cities are exposed to global brands and better-quality products through organized retail formats and they consider shopping in malls to be a leisure activity and status symbol. On the contrary, small-town shoppers consider malls a place where they connect to the society, friends and relatives socially and shopping in malls is a family activity for them. This preference for family-oriented shopping persuades the developers and managers to devise a proposition that fosters more footfall and offer something more relevant to shoppers. Malls in small cities are an entertainment destination, where they go with their dear ones and spend quality time because of relatively lesser entertainment options. Results of this study envisage re-inventing strategies for shopping malls to strengthen their positioning in the ever-changing digital marketing scenario. Mall developers should work on multi-pronged strategies to ensure that there is enough excitement in malls to attract people keeping in mind the profile of consumers in Tier II cities. The study makes strong argument for the changes that need to be incorporated in the retail outlets in malls keeping in mind the threat faced by them from local retailers. For small town shoppers, malls are recreation place where they can visit not only over weekends but also spend evenings over the weekdays. This wave of change in the consumption pattern of small-town shoppers as compared to metropolitan shoppers is building a humungous retail appetite thus creating eye popping business opportunities.

The outcomes of the study give an insight to mall managers about the antecedent factors and their relative significance. Findings of the study will also help the managers and retailers in allocating resources to the most critical factors thus, having resource optimization implication also. Struggling malls can focus on critical success factors to bounce back on the adversities. After taking into consideration the requirements and shopping behaviour of small-town shoppers in South Asian countries, mall developers can introduce novelty, add new attractions and can make a significant change thereby regaining the lost lustre.

13. Limitations and Future Research

Findings of the study are applicable to the Tier II cities of North Region as the sample was taken from these cities. Carrying out the similar research in other countries of South Asia would give thought provoking outcomes about the differences between various markets, thus depicting the reasons for the same. This would help the mall developers to devise logical strategies for the tastes and preferences of consumers. As, the study was catered to consumers of Tier II cities in India, hence a limited scale of variables was used, as mentioned earlier in this paper. A wider scale, having more variables, can be used to carry out the similar kind of research that can be extended to other geographical boundaries. Further, a comparative study can also be carried out between online shopping and malls. This would give retailers and mall developers an insight into the changing buying behaviour of shoppers. These results are applicable for tier ii cities of Punjab and can be generalized to the whole of India, only if corroborated by studies that are alike. Further comparative research may be undertaken between Tier II and Tier III cities to get a deeper insight into the behaviour of consumers in these cities. Research can also be directed on different age groups to understand their buying behaviour. Another study focusing on the preference of consumers for malls and local retailers can also be carried out.

References

1. Ali, S., Mishra, M., & Javed, H. M. U. (2021), The impact of mall personality and shopping value on shoppers' well-being: moderating role of compulsive shopping. *International Journal of Retail & Distribution Management*, *49*(8), 1178–1197. DOI: 10.1108/IJRDM-07-2020-0272.
2. Bhatt, G., Sarkar, A., & Sarkar, J. G. (2020). Attractive and facilitating store atmospheric stimuli: validating the scales. *International Journal of Retail & Distribution Management*. DOI: https://doi.org/10.1108/IJRDM-07-2020-0272.
3. Gupta, A., Mishra, V., & Tandon, A. (2020). Assessment of Shopping Mall Customers' Experience through Criteria of Attractiveness in Tier-II and Tier-III Cities of India: An Exploratory Study. *American Business Review*, 23(1), 70–93, DOI: https://doi.org/10.37625/abr.23.1.70-93.4.
4. Katrodia, A., Naude, M. J., & Soni, S. (2018). Determinants of shopping and buying behaviour: a case at Durban shopping malls. *African Journal of Business and Economic Research*, *13*(1), 219–241.
5. Kushwaha, T., Ubeja, S., & Chatterjee, A. S. (2017). Factors influencing selection of shopping malls: an exploratory study of consumer perception. *21*(3), 274–283, DOI: https://doi.org/10.1177/0972262917716761.
6. Kesari, B. and Atulkar, S., 2016, Satisfaction of mall shoppers: A study on perceived utilitarian and hedonic shopping values. *Journal of Retailing and Consumer services*, 31(C), 22–31, DOI: https://doi.org/10.1016/j.jretconser.2016.03.005.
7. Khanna, P. and Seth, S., 2018, Factors influencing customer satisfaction towards shopping malls: evidence from tier II cities. *International Journal of Business Competition and Growth,* 6(3), 206–224, DOI: https://doi.org/10.1504/IJBCG.2018.097772.
8. Khanna, P. and Seth, S., 2018, Expectations of Retailers: An Empirical Investigation of Malls in Tier II Cities, *IUP Journal of Marketing Management*, 17(4),7–29.
9. Khanna, P. and Seth, S., 2018, Consumer perception towards shopping malls: Evidence from a Tier II city, *Indian Journal of Marketing*, 48(4), 47–59, DOI: http://doi.org/10.17010/ijom/2018/v48/i4/122625.
10. Orus Carlos, Aragoncillo Laura, (2018), Impulse buying behaviour: an online-offline comparative and the impact of social media, *Spanish Journal of Marketing - ESIC*, 22(1), 42–62, DOI: https://doi.org/10.1108/SJME-03-2018-007.

11. Prashar, S., Gupta, S., Singh, H., Vijay, T.S. and Parsad, C., 2016, Clustering shoppers by mall experience for emerging Indian city, *Asian Academy of Management Journal*, 21(2), DOI: http://doi.org/10.21315/aamj2016.21.2.3.
12. Rather Raouf Ahmad, Shehnaz Tehseen, Shakir Hussain Parrey,(2018), Promoting customer brand engagement and brand loyalty through customer brand identification and value congruity", *Spanish Journal of Marketing* - ESIC, 22(3),319–337, DOI: http://doi.org/10.1108/SJME-06-2018-0030.
13. Reimers, V. and Clulow, V., (2014), Spatial convenience: bridging the gap between shopping malls and shopping strips, *International Journal of Retail & Distribution Management,* 42(10), 864–883, DOI: https://doi.org/10.1108/IJRDM-08-2013-0153.
14. Yi, F. and Kang, J., (2019), Effect of background and foreground music on satisfaction, behavior, and emotional responses in public spaces of shopping malls, *Applied Acoustics*, 145, 408–419, DOI: https://doi.org/10.1016/j.apacoust.2018.10.029.

Securing the Future through Sustainability, Health, Education, and Technology – Brig. Dr. Rajiv Divekar et al. (eds)
© 2024 Taylor & Francis Group, London, ISBN 978-1-032-95922-1

11 Customer Advocacy in Value Co-creation Space in Context to Customers' Perceptions

Shanul Gawshinde[1]
Symbiosis Institute of Management Studies,
Symbiosis International University, Pune, India

Ajay Khurana[2]
University School of Business, Chandigarh University,
Mohali, Mohali, Chandigarh

Rakhi Arora[3]
University School of Business, Chandigarh University,
Mohali, Mohali, Chandigarh

ABSTRACT: Purpose/Objective

According to exciting marketing and service research developments, the frontiers between companies and their clientele are becoming increasingly porous. "customer engagement" (CE) refers to a collection of varied consumer activities beyond simple transactional influence. CE influences value co-creation, but neither academics nor practitioners know this because the concept is still relatively new. This is the first study to attempt to conceptualize CEB's function within an MSO.

Study Design: Our findings examine the value outcomes encountered, four categories of CEB, drivers for CEB, and causes for CEB by various allies. The argument made in the paper is that CEB influences value co-creation because customers contribute a variety of resources to the target company and other stakeholders, which alter, enhance, or transform the product as well as the opinions, tastes, expectations, or behaviors of various stakeholders about the business or its offerings. By insisting on more comprehensive resource integration, CEB elevates value co-creation to the level of a system-level activity.

Findings: The linkages between CEB and value co-creation between customers of the target audience, the target industry, and other stakeholders are described in nine study hypotheses that we provide.

[1]Shanul.gawshinde@sims.edu, [2]Ajayp.khurana@gmail.com, [3]rakhi_arora5@yahoo.com

DOI: 10.1201/9781003587200-11

Originality/Value: According to our research, businesses Should put greater emphasis on the finances that clients may provide, consider bringing diverse stakeholders together around a single goal, and use steadily expanding platforms that enable broader value-creation collaboration.

KEYWORDS: Co-creation, Customer advocacy, Customer engagement, SEM-PLS, Consumer behaviour

1. Introduction

SD, which represents service-dominant marketing logic proposed by Lusch and Vargo (2004, 2006), presented an alternate paradigm for marketing literature. SD Logic provided functional concepts and a basis for organization-wide philosophy (Crowther & Donlan, 2011). One of the foundation premises emphasizes value proposition and asserts that "enterprise can only make value proposition" (Vargo & Lusch, 2004). This was a significant departure from the conventional value in exchange philosophy and its role in marketing, which has been limited to 'value addition' (Porter, 1985). The research focuses primarily on SD logic's value-creation aspect (Grönroos, 2012). In the literature on the value component, numerous propositions have been made. These propositions can be divided into three groups according to their relevance to value creation, market offerings, and marketing (Grönroos, 2008).

The notion that customers' perceptions of service quality are a component of value creation has long been held (Hansen, A.V.) and has been influenced by streams of research on SD logic, service logic, and CD logic. SD theory suggests that firms and their customers are working together in an indirect way to create new value by drawing on each other's collective expertise and experience (Vargo, S.L); companies no longer view customer involvement in production and decision-making as a passive aim (Tapscott et al., A.D.). In a highly developed version of this phenomenon called "crowdsourcing," companies employ the pooled knowledge of their consumers to deliver precise and well-crafted assignments (Helms, R.; Booij, E.; Spruit, M.).

This paper examines the interaction sphere within the value creation sphere. The literature has discussed the value creation space and impact of organizational events (Crowther & Donlan, 2011), joint interaction space in the value creation process, where customers and service providers interact to co-create value (Grönroos, 2012). However, the literature does not specify ways and means to expand this interaction space. Our attempt here is to find out if marketers can control this space and, if so, investigate possible ways to expand this space. This paper specifies two fundamental propositions

- Can the value co-creation space be controlled by marketers?
- How the interaction space can be increased in value co-creation

2. Literature Review

In early service literature, co-production was discussed as the firm-customer interaction that utilizes resources to derive the service (Langeard & Eiglier, 1987). Benefits obtained during or after the consumption of a good or service are valued. (Grönroos, 2008). The conceptualization in SD logic is derived as the promises created independently by the firm or in conjunction with the customer and involving actors, integrating the resources (Skålén et al., 2014). The advancement of the literature creation domain has allowed firms to approach the service experience differently. The focus has shifted to understanding how these (outcomes) are experienced and interpreted by customers in a given context (Jaakkola et al., 2015). Putting the customer at the center of the co-creation process rather than understanding their need is a significant deviation from the extant marketing literature.

2.1 Lit on Value Co-Creation

Value creation happens when a supplier's product information, support staff, logistics, and other backend services are integrated with specific customer processes. Integration of resources is, therefore, critical for value co-creation. The conceptual framework proposed by Payne, Storbacka, and Frow (2008) considers the aspect of customer learning, which is critical for value creation. Additionally, the relationship experience enables the client and the organization to engage in value generation. The mapping of supplier and customer processes is necessary for co-creation to be effective (Payne et al., 2008).

3. Value Co-creation and Interaction Space

However, in the value creation process, it is not easy to ascertain who created the value. The argument provided by Gronroos indicated that the term "value co-creation" is misleading and it is value creation initiated by the customer, and the firm facilitates it (Gronroos, 2011). A systematic and analytical explanation of the nature of value and its generation and co-creation was provided by the customer-grounded view of value creation, which views value creation and co-creation from the customer's perspective. This view, contrary to the prevailing SD Logic view, argues for greater involvement of service providers in customer's life as the *locus* of value is argued to be in the *customer* sphere. The long-held belief that value creation is a whole process has been challenged as metaphorical, hindering further analytical thinking. This research addresses two fundamental problems: how value-in-use originates and how value production might be managed. (2012) Gronroos conceptualized value creation spheres in which the divergent roles of provider and customer in different spheres have been articulated. From a value creation perspective, it is argued that the provider's role varies from being a value facilitator in the provider sphere to engaging in a role where the customer is argued to be an independent value creator. In addition to capturing spatial variation, the definition of value production spheres also encompasses temporal contexts.

An instinctual argument for augmenting the service provider's role would be to broaden the joint sphere. Gronroos (2012) discusses two ways of moving the joint sphere's perimeter: (a) inviting the customer to join as the provider took a co-producer. (b) customer-initiated conversation following a dissatisfactory service experience (customer calling to complain about service failure). The provider-initiated move could be a '*double-edged sword.*' Direct interactions are necessary as without them, no value creation is possible. However, interactions generated by the provider that are unsolicited by the customer could risk value destruction. The first research question thus can be answered as:

P1: Value co-creation space can be controlled by the firm, but there exists a danger of value destruction as firms do not know the emotional state of consumers

Therefore, the central question is, 'How can firms augment customer interactions, thereby expanding the boundaries of the joint sphere without value destruction'? If the potential to destroy or create value implies a firm's engagement with the customer, then what kind of engagement would be viewed positively from the value creation point of view?

Unsolicited or interactions uninvited by the customer are grimaced upon, irrespective of the intent. Such unsolicited interactions symbolize the push marketing mindset. Therefore, the solution lies in creating an environment where the customer not only looks forward to interacting with the firm but also welcomes such interactions, thereby broadening the value co-creation platform. If viewed from a slightly higher level of abstraction, the philosophy of customer advocacy offers a way forward.

4. Customer Advocacy in Value Co-creation Space

This wish is mainly realized as Internet usage becomes commonplace. According to Urban and Hauser (2004), the rise in consumer power, one of the many manifestations of which is the desire to define value in one's terms, is primarily due to technology like the Internet. According to the consumer-grounded perspective of value, the idea that customers independently combine resources to create their value (in the customer sphere) is consistent with this approach.

More and more research points to the fact that traditional push-based marketing strategies are losing their effectiveness since they emphasize the loyalty of high-value clients while ignoring their relational demands (Maklan et al., 2011). Therefore, conventional push-based marketing is being repealed by customers wanting to self-create value. The argument that unwelcomes interactions created by the firm could result in value destruction (as reasoned in the customer-grounded view of value) is congruent with this view. In contrast to traditional push-based marketing, the advocacy relationship philosophy argues for a consultative approach in which the firm is encouraged to provide customers with balanced information and objective advice, thus elevating the relationship to a much higher level (Jayasimha & Billore, 2015).

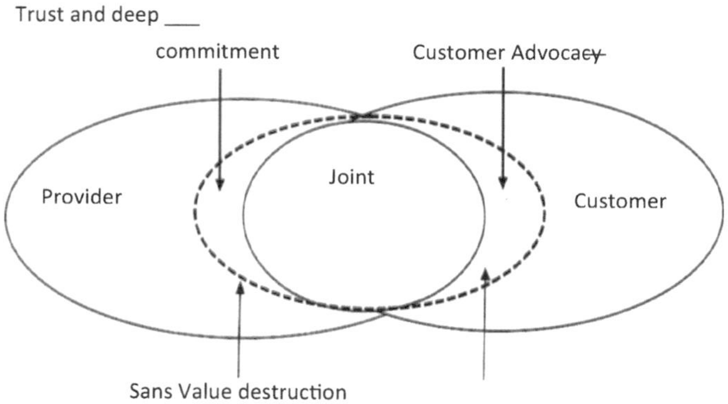

Fig. 11.1 A broadened value co-creation platform

Source: Authors Creation

Customer Role: Generate C2C dialog; Positive word of mouth, Referral

In our view, the philosophy of customer advocacy and grounded view of value co-creation is concomitant for the following reasons;

a. Customer-centric
b. Swear by mutual interaction (dialogical process)
c. Developing knowledge and creating partnerships

According to Urban (2005), advocacy "has duality." It is mutual and reciprocal. This assertion is based on anecdotal evidence. This is instinctively understandable, as the higher levels of trust generated due to customer advocacy are expected to give the company economic benefits through repeat business, willingness to pay a premium, and referrals.

In a nutshell, customer advocacy is based on the following premises;

a. Placing customers' interest ahead of firms' interest
b. Providing customers with truthful information
c. Using advocacy to increase levels of accountability, openness, and trust.
d. Formation of deeper relationships is due to renewed trust and commitment earned by the firm through truthful dialogue with the customers.

Given the virtues of customer advocacy, it is our firm belief that it is possible to expand the boundaries of the joint sphere without value destruction by practicing customer advocacy. As opposed to the firm playing a passive role, it could actively engage in value-creating interactions without the fear of being perceived as an intruder and, hence, value destruction. It is just a *"function of discrete events, but multiple episodes in an overall relationship"* Kleinaltenkamp et al. (2012). Customer advocacy could build trust-based deeper relationships that would sustain the multiple episodes required for successful value creation. The second research question thus can be answered with the proposition: *P2a: Customer advocacy presents an opportunity to expand the interaction space:*

Worth assessments with interactions with clients in use are divided into individual and communal phases in the customer-centered perspective of value. Further, consumer social networks and ecosystems can impact independent value generation (in the customer sphere). It has been found that an unintended but desirable consequence of higher levels of trust due to customer advocacy is referrals to friends and relatives and positive word of mouth (Roy, 2013), including on review sites (sources of customer power) that could make the firm part of the social network. In our view, customer advocacy is a potent way of expanding the boundaries of the joint sphere sans value destruction. On the other end of the spectrum, the provider side can be expanded by providing the necessary resources for customers for value co-creation. This can be achieved by adopting the one-stop-shop approach. *P2b: Firms can expand the interaction space by playing the role of resource integrator and - stop-shop*

5. Research Methodology

Since the study's main objective is to create the working hypotheses from an operational standpoint, the research uses an exploratory research design. These kinds of investigations put much emphasis on identifying concepts and insights. Therefore, the research design offers the chance to consider many aspects of the studied subject.

5.1 Data Collection

For the study, primary and secondary data were both gathered. The primary data was gathered using a standard scale questionnaire, and the secondary data was gathered using the literature and readily available resources.

5.2 Data Analysis Tool

Using PLS-SEM 3.0, the gathered data was examined. The tool has gained widespread acceptance because it can function with smaller samples, makes no assumptions about how data will be distributed and has greater.

5.3 Research Methodology

As a result, PLS-SEM is a suitable option for data analysis. Before evaluating the structural models, analytical results were evaluated. Details of the analytical model can be found in Table 11.1. The acceptable level of composite dependability (CR), which goes from 0 to 1, is over 0.70. These findings indicate that the measurement model's convergent validity is adequate overall (Table 11.2). The conditions for discriminant validity have been met because all the diagonal values are more significant than the remaining column values. The variance inflation

Table 11.1 Convergent validity and measurement model results in brief

Construct	Items	Cronbach's Alpha (CA)	Composite Reliability (CR)	Average Variance Extracted (AVE)
Customer Engagement	3	0.632	0.740	0.671
Trust	2	0.712	0.810	0.511
Deep Commitment	3	0.601	0.735	0.714
Word of Mouth	2	0.617	0.717	0.612
Customers Perceptions	2	0.734	0.721	0.683

Source: Authors Creation

Table 11.2 Discriminant validity

	Customer Engagement	Trust	Deep Commitment	Word of Mouth	Customer Perceptions
Customer Engagemment	0.701				
Trust	0.612	1			
Deep Commitment	0.603	0.687	1		
Word of Mouth	0.510	0.732	0.689	1	
Customers Perceptions	0.781	0.578	0.661	0.718	1

Source: Authors Creation

factor (VIF) values address the multicollinearity issue. Referring to Table 11.3, it can be concluded that the data is collinearity-free because all of the VIF values are less than 10 (Hair, Ringle, & Sarstedt, 2011). The data can, therefore, be used for additional analyses.

Table 11.3 VIF values

	Customer Engagement	Trust	Deep Commitment NT	Word of Mouth	Customer Perceptions
Customer Engagement	1				
Trust	1.913	1			
Deep Commitment	1.814	0.894	1		
Word of Mouth	2.121	2.214	1.841	1	
Customers Perceptions	1.901	0.984	1.927	1.720	1

Source: Authors Creation

5.4 Test Result for Hypothesis

The entire proposed hypothesis for this investigation is displayed in Table 11.4.

Table 11.4 Hypothesis testing

	Original Sample (O)	Sample Mean (M)	Standard Error (STERR)	T Statistics (IO/STERR I)	P Values
Customer Advocacy	0.510	0.142	0.905	3.712	0.000
Trust	0.321	0.210	0.137	2.101	0.181
Deep Commitment	2.107	1.231	0.412	2.310	1.641
Word of Mouth	0.437	0.742	0.930	2.720	1.951
Customers Perceptions	1.786	2.410	0.812	2.417	1.487

Source: Authors Creation

5.5 Analysis & Results

The two-stage study created a structural model that includes scale items and components. The structural model's validity and the proposed causal connections between the seven components were examined. The examination of structural equation modeling results and the testing of hypotheses are described below:

1. Acceptable structural model fitness has been identified. The CFI, GFI, and RMSEA fit indices produced acceptable results, showing that the study's model effectively describes customer advocacy characteristics.
2. According to the R2 values of the dependent variables in the framework, the research's analysis can predict and explain the effectiveness of lobbying for customers in co-creating consumer perceptions.

6. Conclusion and Discussion

Customers can derive value from any offer, as mentioned in the article's beginning if they are involved in co-creation. In many cases, the supplier company initiates the possibility of co-creation. However, value erosion is risky due to the service provider's multiple interactions. It is argued that the one-stop-shop solution provided by the customer advocacy and services provider safeguards and encourages value co-creation. Assessing product or service excellence, modern consumers now evaluate a company's social responsibility (Mukherjee & Althuizen, 2020; Hong & Li, 2021). Our research backs up this claim and emphasizes how critical the condition above is. Companies need to become brand advocates and get people engaged with their brands if they want to position themselves to base their marketing and communication decisions on societal challenges.

7. Acknowledgment

We sincerely thank our research team members for their dedication and hard work. Their collaboration and collective effort have significantly enriched the content and execution of this paper. Furthermore, we wish to acknowledge Symbiosis Institute of Management Studies, Pune's generous assistance in facilitating access to necessary resources and data, without which this research would not have been possible. Thank you to all those mentioned above and others who have contributed in various ways to complete this research paper.

REFERENCES

1. Crowther, P., & Donlan, L. (2011). Value-creation space: the role of events in a service-dominant marketing paradigm. *Journal of Marketing Management*, *27*(December), 1444–1463. doi:10.1080/0267257X.2011.626786
2. Grönroos, C. (2008). Service logic revisited: Who creates value? And who co-creates? *European Business Review*, *20*(4), 298–314. doi:10.1108/09555340810886585
3. Gronroos, C. (2011). Value co-creation in service logic : A critical analysis. *Marketing Theory*, (3), 279–301. doi:10.1177/1470593111408177
4. Grönroos, C. (2012). Conceptualizing value co-creation: A journey to the 1970s and back to the future. *Journal of Marketing Management*, *28*(13-14), 1520–1534. doi:1 0.1080/0267257X.2012.737357
5. Gronroos, C. (2013). 'Critical Service Logic: Making sense of value creation and co-creation, Journal of the Academy of Marketing Science, 41:133–150
6. Hong, C., Li, C., (2021). Will consumers silence themselves when brands speak up about sociopolitical issues? Applying the spiral of silence theory to consumer boycott and buycott behaviors. J. Nonprofit & Public Sect. Mark. 33 (2), 193–211.
7. Jaakkola, E., Helkkula, A., & Stenroos, L. A. (2015). Service experience co-creation : Conceptualization, implications, and future research directions. *Journal of Service Management*, *26*(2).
8. Jayasimha, K. R., & Billore, A. (2015). I complain for your good? Re-examining consumer advocacy. Journal of Strategic Marketing, 1–17.
9. Kleinaltenkamp, M., Borkie J., Rodrick., Frow, P., Hughes, T., Peters. D., Linda & Woratschek, Herbert. (2012), 'Resource Integration', Marketing Theory, 12(2): 201–205
10. Lawer, C. And Knox, S. (2006), 'Customer advocacy and brand development, Journal of product and brand management, 15(2): 5–25
11. Lusch, R. F., & Vargo, S. L. (2006). Service-dominant logic: reactions, reflections and refinements. Marketing theory, 6(3), 281–288.
12. Maklan, S., Knox, S., & Pepparad, J. (2011). 'Why CRM fails and how to fix it,' Sloan Management Review, Mukherjee, S., Althuizen, N., 2020. Brand activism: Does courting controversy help or hurt a brand? Int. J. Res. Market. 37 (4), 772–788
13. Payne, A. F., Storbacka, K., & Frow, P. (2008). Managing the co-creation of value. *Journal of Academy of Marketing Science*, *36*(1), 83–96. doi:10.1007/s11747-007-0070-0
14. Porter, M. E. (1985). Competitive advantage: creating and sustaining superior performance, 1985.
15. Roy, S.K. (2013). 'Consequences of Customer Advocacy', Journal of Strategic Marketing, 21(3): 260–276
16. Sheth, J.N., Sisodia, R.S., and Sharma, A. (2000). 'The antecedents and consequences of customer-centric marketing', Journal of Academy of Marketing Science, 28 (1): 55–66

17. Skålén, P., Gummerus, J., von Koskull, C., & Magnusson, P. R. (2014). Exploring value propositions and service innovation: a service-dominant logic study. *Journal of the Academy of Marketing Science*, 1–22. doi:10.1007/s11747-013-0365-2
18. Urban L. Glen and John R. Hauser (2004). 'Listening in' to find and explore new combinations of customer needs, Journal of Marketing, 68(2): 72–87
19. Urban L. Glen (2005). 'A New Era in Marketing?', Journal of Public Policy & Marketing,24(1): 155–159
20. Vargo, S. L., & Lusch, R. F. (2004). Evolving to a New Dominant Logic. *Journal of Marketing*, *68*(January), 1–17.

Securing the Future through Sustainability, Health, Education, and Technology – Brig. Dr. Rajiv Divekar et al. (eds)

12 A STITCH IN TIME: A Study on the Latent Factors of Awareness and Perception of Sustainable Estate Planning Among Millennials in Urban Bengaluru

Padma Nandanan[1], Amudhan[2]
Asst. Professor, St. Josephs University, Bengaluru, India

ABSTRACT

The primary objective of the study was to identify the cardinal factors in the awareness and the perception of millennials in Urban Bengaluru towards estate planning. Estate plans are concrete plans that helps in the distribution of an individual's assets or estate after his death. The data was collected using stratified sampling method from over 387 respondents. An exploratory factor analysis was done to reduce the variables and identify the princip factor determinants of awareness and perception of estate planning. It was found from the analysis that the construct awareness had 2 latent factors namely consciousness and cognition whereas the construct perception also had 2 factors namely discernment and acuity.

KEYWORDS: Awareness, Estate planning, Consciousness, Perception

1. Introduction

The only certain aspect of life is death, and it is inevitable. Thus, it becomes imperative for all individuals to understand this and be prepared for the same and estate planning finds its relevance here. Estate planning is a systematic exercise of planning, preparing and arranging for the efficient dissemination of an individual's assets and wealth in the event of their death or incapacity. The common mindset among people is that estate planning is only for elderly individuals but that's not the fact. No individual can unfortunately predict the time of one's death and an accident or illness can happen to individuals of all ages. These further necessitates the need for and importance of estate planning.

Estate planning involves planning in advance, the management of an individual's assets and properties in case of the death or incapacitation of the individual. It

[1]Padma.nandanan.research@gmail.com, [2]Amudhan.s@sju.edu.in

DOI: 10.1201/9781003587200-12

ensures that the assets and properties of an individual are managed efficiently in accordance with the wishes of the individual. This ensures to provide a sense of clarity, control, and security for both the individual and their loved ones.

Studies have proved that proper estate planning has both therapeutic and antitherapeutic characteristics (Glover, n.d.).Without proper estate planning, the distribution of assets can be an ordeal for the loved ones. A proper estate planning in place helps to do away with unnecessary taxes and expenses associate with the transfer of properties to the rightful heirs. (Alma'Amun & Kamarudin, 2014) in their paper have highlighted the impending challenges associated with the significant increase in the number of unclaimed inheritances especially in Malaysia and Singapore.

Estate planning is a multidimensional endeavour that goes beyond merely distributing assets. It encompasses a range of legal tools and strategies to guarantee the smooth transfer of wealth, protect assets, ensure healthcare preferences are respected, and maintain control over one's legacy. With a well-crafted estate plan, individuals can find solace in knowing that their wishes will be upheld, their loved ones will be cared for, and their hard-earned assets will continue to benefit generations to come. By consulting legal and financial professionals and staying attuned to changes in laws and personal circumstances, individuals can create a dynamic estate plan that evolves alongside their life journey. Studies have placed relevance on the need of a person to plan and decide for his estate for the financial protection of beneficiaries (Choi et al., 2019), reducing family disputes (Garber, 2019) and avoid tax complications (Venter, 2014).

1.1 Instruments of Estate Planning

A very crucial element of estate planning is the creation of a 'will'. While there are many instruments that aid a person in Estate planning, the most popular and typically used instrument is the 'will'. A 'will' is a legal document that explains and specifies the modalities of distribution of assets and properties of an individual after his death. This document ensures that one's assets are allocated according to their desires and can encompass properties, investments, personal belongings, and even digital assets in today's digital age. The 'will' also designates an executor, responsible for overseeing the distribution process and adhering to the stipulated wishes.

A 'will' is used in isolation or in combination with the other tools of Estate planning (Rollison, 1961). "Wills", as defined under Section 2(h) of the ISA is 'the legal declaration of the intention of a testator with respect to his property which he desires to be carried into effect after his death.' Literatures have proved that despite the awareness of the need for estate planning, a vast majority of individuals over the age of 55 still didn't have a valid will (James, 2015).

While the 'Will' is a very crucial document of estate planning, an equally important instrument are trusts. They are more flexible and the scope for customisation is also more as compared to wills. Trusts can serve various purposes, such as protecting assets from creditors, supporting charitable causes, providing for minors or individuals with special needs, and minimizing estate taxes.

Another noteworthy tool of estate planning is the 'Power of Attorney'. A power of attorney assigns another individual the power to make financial and legal decisions on behalf of the individual if they become incapacitated. It ensures that important financial matters can be managed without the need for court intervention.

Healthcare Directive (Living Will): A living will is gaining popularity in recent days, It is a directive given by an individual regarding medical treatment and end-of-life care if they are unable to communicate.

Beneficiary Designations: These beneficiary designations or nominations are an integral tool of estate planning. These designations give a clarity to financial institutions and retirement account administrators regarding who should receive the assets upon the account holder's death. Common accounts with beneficiary designations include life insurance policies, retirement accounts, and payable-on-death bank accounts.

Guardianship Designation: In the event of minor children, a will or separate document can designate a guardian who will care for the children if both parents pass away.

These tools can be used individually or in combination to create a comprehensive estate plan that reflects an individual's unique financial situation, family dynamics, and personal goals. Consulting with legal and financial professionals is crucial to ensure that the estate plan aligns with current laws and achieves the desired outcomes.

2. Statement of the Problem

Investments are an important part of financial planning. Equally important is Estate planning. It is an integral part of financial planning and retirement planning (Ismail et al., 2013). Estate planning is a systematic exercise of planning, preparing and arranging for the efficient dissemination of an individuals assets and wealth in the event of their death or incapacity. Various market studies and reports have emphatically highlighted the increase in the number of unclaimed assets lying idle with the Government due to the absence of a legal will. Reports have claimed that the value of such assets are a staggering amount of Rs.50,000 crores. As a relief to this, (Abhinav Singh 2023)(www.the week.in) in his report throws light on the fact that will writing and succession planning are slowly gaining popularity in India. This prompted the researcher to study the awareness and perception of informed individual towards estate planning and to determine its determinants.

3. Objectives of the Study

To understand and identify the latent factors in the awareness and perception of estate planning of working millennials in Urban Bengaluru

4. Methodology

The study was conducted among the millennials in Urban Bengaluru. Them millennials are the generation of people who are born between 1981 and 1996 and hence their age would range between 27 and 42. The above age group was considered for the study since it would include a wide extent of the working population . An initial pilot study was conducted with around 37 respondents and the data collected therein was used to check the reliability of the questionnaire. With mild modifications there in, a structured questionnaire was distributed to around 387 respondents who were identified using stratified sampling method where the strata was divided according to the taluks in Urban Bengaluru. Thereafter an EFA was done on the data collected after ensuring that the minimum requirements of KMO test and the Bartley's test of Sphericity is met. SPSS 29.0 was used for this.

5. Literature Review and Gap

(Kling, 2012) in his study opined that the fear associated with the care for dependants after death can be to an extent reduced through effective estate planning. The primary step to ensure that an individuals assets/wealth are completely utilised for the benefit of their deserving heirs is to create an efficient estate plan (Mui'zz Abdullah et al., n.d.). Estate planning not only involves transferring of estate but also focuses on creating and building it through regular savings and investments(Ismail et al., 2013). (Mark E. Lee,2014), emphasizes on the importance of having a trusted advisor, such as an attorney or financial planner, to help guide individuals through the estate planning process and avoid common mistakes.

The benefits of having an estate plan are immense but the main ones include ensuring protection, safety and security of the dear ones in case of an unfortunate event of death or incapacitation, have ones wishes carried out and also ensuring sufficient liquidity of the estate for effective management of taxes (Horkey, 2009). While the former focussed on the need for estate planning in general, (Bahr, 2014) conducted a study on the women's status with regards to estate planning. The researcher states that women need to make adequate arrangements for the welfare of their family members to be financially prepared for an event of death or disability. Three primary reasons, namely, women being the tutelary parent in most of the cases, lower average earnings, and lengthy longevity, were cited by Bahr for the women to be financially independent. A popular misconception is that estate planning is meant only for the rich and affluent sections of the society. (Ismail et al., 2013) in his study, emphasises on the need for estate planning by all the economic segments of the society. Yet another misunderstanding rampant in the society is that estate planning is meant only for the elderly. It is interesting to note that individuals over 65 years of age are more likely to have a will as against the younger generation (Fellows et.al,1978; Schwartz, 1993).It is a noteworthy fact that by the year 2025, around 75% of the global workforce would be millennials (Schawbel, 2012) and hence it becomes very important and essential to understand, gauge and assess their financial knowledge (Kim et al., 2019).

Limited studies have been conducted to understand the awareness of estate planning in millennials and their perception of the same.

6. Analysis and Discussion

6.1 Factor Identification for the Construct Awareness

The KMO test and the Bartlett's test of sphericity was done as a pre determinant for EFA for the construct 'Awareness of Estate Planning'. The KMO test (Table 12.1) revealed a test value of 0.862 that satisfied the requirement of sampling adequacy. The construct 'Awareness of Estate planning' consisted of around 9 items . The significance level of 0.000 for the Bartlett's test of sphericity (Table 12.1) highlighted the interdependency among these 9 items of the construct. All the 9 items of the construct were involved in the factor analysis. The Principal component analysis was used for the reduction of the dimension of the construct. The details of the variance explained by each factor and also the items falling under each of these three factors along with their corresponding factor loadings and the cumulative factor loadings are seen in Table 12.2.

Table 12.1 Sampling adequacy

KMO and Bartlett's Test		
Kaiser-Meyer-Olkin Measure of Sampling Adequacy.		.862
Bartlett's Test of Sphericity	Approx. Chi-Square	3443.027
	df	36
	Sig.	.000

Table 12.2 Total variance

Total Variance Explained						
	Initial Eigenvalues			Rotation Sums of Squared Loadings		
Component	Total	% of Variance	Cumulative %	Total	% of Variance	Cumulative %
1	5.448	60.531	60.531	5.263	58.478	58.478
2	1.604	17.824	78.355	1.789	19.877	78.355
3	.731	8.120	86.475			
4	.426	4.732	91.207			
5	.252	2.800	94.007			
6	.214	2.382	96.389			
7	.166	1.846	98.235			
8	.116	1.283	99.518			
9	.043	.482	100.000			
Extraction Method: Principal Component Analysis.						

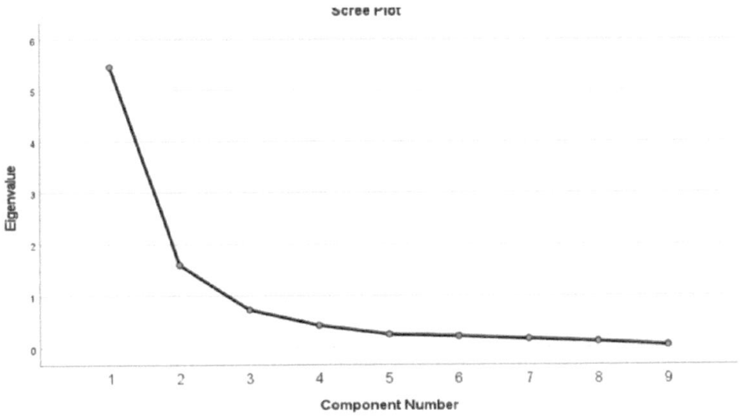

Fig. 12.1 Scree plot

The EFA on the construct 'Awareness of Estate planning' resulted in 2 latent factors with significant Eigenvalues of more than 1. These 2 latent factors collectively contributed to a cumulative variance of 78.355%.The percentage of individual variances contributed by the 2 factors are 58.478 and 19.877. The latent factors identified were further named as 'Estate planning consciousness' and 'Estate planning Cognition. The latent factor 'Estate planning consciousness' had 7 items whereas the latent factor 'Estate planning Cognition' had 2 items. The division of the items into the latent factors was done based on the Rotated Component Matrix. (Table 12.3).

Table 12.3 Rotated component matrix

Rotated Component Matrix[a]		
	Component	
	1	2
I am aware of "estate planning"	.855	-.260
I am aware of the importance of making a will	-.070	.873
I have made a "will"	.859	-.309
I am aware of a "power of attorney"	.887	-.157
All my financial assets have designated nominees	-.089	.831
I have documented all my financial and leagl documents	.854	-.290
I am aware of the risks associated in the absence of an estate plan	.857	.158
I am capable of managing my estate efficiently	.860	.169
I have discussed estate planning with my family members	.889	-.106
Extraction Method: Principal Component Analysis. Rotation Methods: Varimax with Kaiser Normalization.		

[a]Rotation converged in 3 iterations.

6.2 Factor Identification for the Construct Perception

Table 12.4 Sampling adequacy

KMO and Bartlett's Test		
Kaiser-Meyer-Olkin Measure of Sampling Adequacy.		.911
Bartlett's Test of Sphericity	Approx. Chi-Square	4107.105
	df	55
	Sig.	.000

Table 12.5 Total variance

Total Variance Explained						
	Initial Eigenvalues			Rotation Sums of Squared Loadings		
Component	Total	% of Variance	Cumulative %	Total	% of Variance	Cumulative %
1	6.672	60.652	60.652	6.365	57.865	57.865
2	1.338	12.164	72.816	1.645	14.951	72.816
3	.823	7.484	80.300			
4	.540	4.908	85.208			
5	.432	3.928	89.136			
6	.348	3.168	92.303			
7	.333	3.027	95.330			
8	215	1.951	97.281			
9	.175	1.589	98.869			
10	.096	.869	99.738			
11	.029	.262	100.000			
Extraction Method: Principal Component Analysis.						

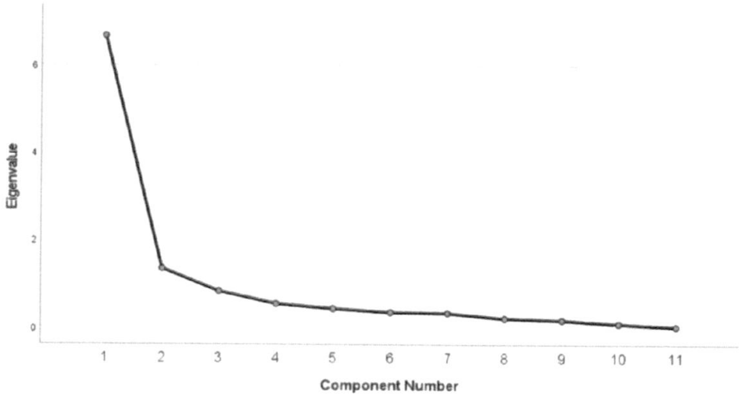

Fig. 12.2 Scree plot

Table 12.6 Rotated component matrix

Rotated Component Matrix[a]		
	Component	
	1	2
Estate planning is crucial for financial success	.865	272
I consider estate planning as a priority	.936	-.035
I find estate planning intimidating	.931	-.049
It is too early for me to make an estate plan	.745	-.089
I dont have enough assets to make an estate plan	-.273	.633
Estate planning is only for the rich	.891	.009
Estate planning is only for the aged	.876	.249
I have no interest in what happens to mmmy assets after my death	.728	.338
Estate planning is time consuming and expensive	.842	.366
The benefits of estate planning are worth the effort	-.296	-.745
Estate planning reduces stress and worry	.597	.541
Extraction Method: Principal Component Analysis. Rotation Method: Varimax with Kaiser Normalization.		

[a]Rotation converged in 3 iterations

The KMO test and Bartlett's test of sphericity are essential preliminary steps before conducting an EFA. These tests help researchers evaluate the suitability of their dataset for factor analysis, ensuring that the underlying assumptions are met and the analysis yields meaningful and interpretable results. The KMO test and the Bartletts test of sphericity as seen in Table 12.4 yielded favourable results validating the application of EFA to the construct "Estate planning perception". While the KMO test resulted in a value of 0.911signifying the sampling adequacy, the Bartletts test of sphericity also resulted in a value of 0.000 validating the interdependence of the items in the construct.

There was a total of 11 items under the construct 'Estate planning Perception'. The principal component methos of EFA resulted in the identification of 2 latent factors with significant Eigen values. These factors collectively explained a cumulative variance of 72.816 % whereas the individual factors explained variations of 57.865% and 14.951%. (Table 12.5) These factors are further grouped based on the return Eigen value and combination of different variables under the group are identified and named properly.

The first latent factor was named "Discernment" and it had 9 items whereas the second factor was named 'acuity' and had 2 items. The grouping of the items under the latent variables were done according to the Rotated Component Matrix. (Table 12.6)

7. Conclusion

Estate planning is of supreme importance in the personal financial management of individuals. This comprehensive process involves creating legal documents such as wills, trusts, powers of attorney, and healthcare directives, among others, to safeguard the financial security of loved ones and ensure the smooth transfer of wealth to future generations. The study aimed at identifying the latent factor determinants in the awareness and perception on estate planning among millennials. The study revealed that the awareness on estate planning was determined by latent factors namely Consciousness and cognition; and the perception about estate planning had discernment and acuity as the main determining factors. While consciousness about the need for Estate planning is the fundamental requirement ,an attempt should be made by the millennials to acquire and improve their cognition on this as well. A lack of discernment should be avoided and this would in turn help the millennials to have an acuity over estate planning. An attempt to understand and identify these factors will help millennials realize the importance of estate planning and do the needful.

References

1. Alma'Amun, S., & Kamarudin, M. K. (2014). Nomination of insurance policy for Singaporean Muslims. *Jurnal Pengurusan*, *42*, 63–73. https://doi.org/10.17576/pengurusan-2014-42-06
2. Basir, F. A. M., Ahmad, W. M. W., & Rahman, M. (2023). Estate Planning Behaviour: A Systematic Literature Review. *Journal of Risk and Financial Management*, *16*(2), 84. MDPI AG. Retrieved from http://dx.doi.org/10.3390/jrfm16020084
3. Choi, S. L., McDonough, I. M., Kim, M., & Kim, G. (2019). Estate planning among older Americans: The moderating role of race and ethnicity. *FINANCIAL PLANNING REVIEW*, *2*(3–4). https://doi.org/10.1002/cfp2.1058
4. Fellows, M. L., Simon, R. J., & Rau, W. (1978). Public attitudes about property distribution at death and intestate succession laws in theUnited States. *American bar Foundation Research Journal*, 3(2), 19–391. https://doi.org/10.1111/j.1747-4469.1978.tb00848.x
5. Garber, Julie. 2019. *5 Reasons You Need an Estate Plan. Available online*: https://www.thebalance.com/top-reasons-why-you-need-an-estate-plan-3505444
6. Glover, M. (n.d.). *A Therapeutic Jurisprudential Framework of Estate Planning*.
7. Horkey, C. (2009). Estate planning documents in Virginia among adults 50 and over with at least one adult child.
8. Ismail, S., Hashim, N., Kamis, R., Harun, H., Nadiah, N., & Samad, A. (2013). *Procedia Economics and Finance 00 (2013) 000-000 Determinants of Attitude towards Estate Planning In Malaysia: An Empirical Investigation*. www.sciencedirect.com
9. James, R. N. (2015). The new statistics of estate planning: Lifetime andpost-mortem wills, trusts, and charitable planning. *Estate Planning & Community Property law Journal*, 8, 1–40.
10. Kim, K. T., Anderson, S. G., & Seay, M. C. (2019). Financial Knowledge and Short-Term and Long-Term Financial Behaviors of Millennials in the United States.

Journal of Family and Economic Issues, *40*(2), 194–208. https://doi.org/10.1007/s10834-018-9595-2
11. Kling, C. H. (2012). Estate Planning For Parents of Young Children. Retrieved June 1, 2012 from http://www.ext.colostate.edu/pubs/consumer/09102.html/
12. Mui'zz Abdullah, M., Mohamad Nasir, N., Teknologi Malaysia, U., Muhammad Ridhwan Ab Aziz, utmmy, Bari Awang, A., Mui'zz, M., Mohamad, N., Muhamad, N., Hisyam, N., Aziz, A., Ridhwan, M., Bari, A., & Wok, M. (n.d.). *A Literature Review on Islamic Estate Planning From Year 2014 to A Literature Review on Islamic Estate Planning From Nasrul Hisyam Nor Muhamad.* https://digitalcommons.unl.edu/libphilprac
13. Rollison, W. D. (1961). Issue 2 Article 4 12-1-1961 Dame L. In *Rev* (Vol. 37). http://scholarship.law.nd.edu/ndlr/vol37/iss2/4

Note: All the figures and tables in this chapter were made by the authors.

Securing the Future through Sustainability, Health, Education, and Technology – Brig. Dr. Rajiv Divekar et al. (eds)
© 2024 Taylor & Francis Group, London, ISBN 978-1-032-95922-1

13 The Impact of Russian and Ukrainian Conflict on Indian Stock Returns

Mohit Boralkar[1]
SBM, Assistant Professor, Christ University, Bangalore
Harshal Anil Salunkhe[2]
SBM, Associate Professor, Christ University, Bangalore
Mehak Sharma[3]
SBM, Christ University, Bangalore
Parameswaran. S.[4]
SBM, Associate Professor, Christ University, Bangalore

ABSTRACT

In February 2022, Ukraine was invaded by Russia, the biggest conventional military assault since World War II; this event is significant for the world economy. Considering the India-Russia strategic alliance so far in terms of technology, nuclear power, diplomacy, and the defense sector, the Indian government chose to take a neutral stand on the prevailing global issue. Russia has contributed mainly to the nation-building process of India since the time of independence. As a result of this back-dated alliance with Russia, it could not keep India from the consequences of the Russia-Ukraine conflict. The article studies the impact of the Russia-Ukraine conflict on the Indian stockmarket. Predominantly, an adverse effect was witnessed on the Indian stock markets just as the rumors of the crisis started spreading because of the rise in political unpredictability. It can be inferred that the Indian market was quite efficient and started adjusting to the situation just after the event day, i.e., February 24, 2022. In this case, average abnormal returns were only for a short period; hence, the market was semi-strong. The impact on the market post-event was positive.

KEYWORDS: Russia-Ukraine crisis, Event study, Stock returns, Abnormal returns

[1]mohit.boralkar@christuniversity.in, [2]harshal.salunkhe@gmail.com,
[3]mehaksharma1598@gmail.com, [4]parameswaran.s@christuniversity.in

DOI: 10.1201/9781003587200-13

1. Introduction

The event study method is a great way to do market-based analysis in finance. The events study tests are also called abnormal performance index tests (APIs) or residual analysis, which includes looking at asset/security price movements around the news announcement or event (Brown, 1972). It has been observed as a standard practice to determine the reaction of securities' prices to specific announcements or events. In general, the event study methodology has been used for two primary purposes: 1) for testing the null hypothesis that the market incorporates information for a summary of this evidence efficiently and 2) for analysing the impact of the event on the wealth of the security holders, at least concerningpublicly available information, under the maintained hypothesis of market efficiency (Binder & Merges, 2001).

What constitutes an event has a fairly broad interpretation. Most of the research has been conducted in the purview of the event declaration, with the announcement usually coming from a company. However, outside-of-firm announcements and more general "happenings" might be considered events (Brown, 1972). The broad research category, event studies, can have various goals and methodological adaptations(Bowman, 2006). The event research literature's diversity regarding the themes covered and the specific technique options offered can be bewildering.

2. Literature Review

The event study methodology can be broken down into micro and macro events. A micro event is an event that is specific to a particular company. For example, an annual accounting report, an accounting principal change, a big block trade, a business merger, a stock split, et cetera. For example, we saw a lot of tweets about asset price changes. We asked ourselves, "Do these tweets have any meaningful information or are they just noise?" (Shutes et al., 2016). On 8 November 2016, the government of India announced the demonetization of ₹500 ₹1000 banknotes. Following this announcement, the Indian stock market went into a bearish spiral. The ban on higher-denomination currencies or "demonetization" harmed most industries. However, the public sector banking, pharmacy, energy, and I.T. sectors saw positive returns(Chellasamy & K.M., 2017). On the event day, currency demonetization was significantly influenced by indices like Sensex, Nifty, and BSE100 (Sathyanarayana & Gargesha, 2017). Political events in the financial markets of some of the most developed economies are heavily influenced by two elements: (a) the degree of conflict and (b) the extent to which economic actors can anticipate both cooperative and conflicting occurrences (Schneider & Troeger, 2006). Political news about the possibility of Quebec seceding from Canada greatly impacted stock market volatility (Beaulieu et al., 2005).

The COVID-19 epidemic, one of the world's worst humanitarian disasters in recent years, also wreaked havoc on the economy (Jindřichovská, 2021). Stock returns were poorer and higher volatility due to the COVID-19 epidemic (Baker,

2020). Today's research shows that the impact of the pandemic on real estate stock performance and volatility varies from country to country, which is likely driven by country-specific financial market dynamics and market participants' experience with similar crises and pandemics (Milcheva, 2021).

"Premeditated, threatened, or real use of force or violence to achieve a political purpose through fear, compulsion, or intimidation" is how terrorism is defined (Sandler, 1983). The market's reaction to terrorist attacks tends to be more damaging in emerging countries, while more developed capital markets tend to be more resistant to the adverse effects of terrorist strikes (Ahmad et al., 2022).

Political clashes between two countries that have a significant role to play in the international market have enormous economic consequences for the government (Barro, 1981), households (GHOBARAHet al., 2003), and businesses (Guideline& La Ferrara, 2005).The mechanism is simple: when there is a possibility of war, assets linked to the parties involved in the fight are at risk. Indeed, Rigobon and Sack(2005) find evidence that investors will shun assets linked to adversaries when war is more dangerous. Cross-border military confrontations have a hazardous impact on stock returns (Wisniewski, 2016). Berkman (2011) examines 447 worldwide political crises, some of which may have evolved into full-fledged conflicts. They claim that global stock returns would have increased by 3.6 percent yearly if past crises had not occurred. Omar (2015) examined the impact of 43 conflicts, defined as direct cross-border violence, in the post-1987 period. The World Stock Market Index dropped -3.47% and the S&P 500 dropped -4.67% in the event window that followed the start of the war, which started 50 trading days before and ended 50 days after. Because of the interconnected stock markets, one drop can easily be reflected in the other(Asgharian, 2011).

According to Nurhaeni(2009), if the volume of stock trading increases, the information suggests that investors sell shares held because the capital market situation is uncertain. Hartono (2016) explains how checking information can determine how an event reacts. If an announcement involves information on a significant event, such as a war, the market will react positively if the statement is well received. The change in the price of the securities in question indicates the market reaction (Satryo, 2019). Shen's (2017) research explains why there is a big difference in average abnormal returns before and after an event. In contrast, (Rohmiyati, 2017) and (Sari, 2017) observed no difference in average abnormal rates before or after an event study.

3. Problem Statement

In the economic context, the semi-strong Efficient Market Hypothesis (EMH) suggests that stock prices reflect not only the past performance of a company's stock but also any information widely known to the public. When new information comes out, like news about a company's performance or significant world events, the stock prices adjust quickly to incorporate that information.In this scenario, the researchers want to see if this idea holds in the Indian stock market regarding Russia invading Ukraine. To find out if the stock prices in India quickly changed in response to this event, and if so, to what extent. This mentions that previous research has shown that different types of events can affect stock prices, but each new event can impact how investors see things, which can be different in various parts of the world.

In the current economic climate, the semi-strong efficient market hypothesis (EMH) implies that stock prices not only reflect the past performance of the company's stock but also any information that is widely known to the market. New information, such as news about a company's performance or major world events, causes stock prices to move quickly to reflect that information.

3.1 Contributions

Our findings make numerous significant contributions to the literature. First, we add to the expanding corpus of research that looks at how political and geopolitical risks impact stock returns. However, most of the earlier research indicates that political events hurt the stock market (Bash, 2019). Others suggest that the impact is favorable (Guidolin, 2010), while others find an insignificant association between stock market returns and global war-like situations or events (Hudson & Urquhart, 2015). Considering the contradictions in different researchers' views, this study examines the Russia-Ukraine conflict and the Indian stock market. Second, in contrast to earlier studies, our sample country is not a "direct" combatant in the war. We show that in the case of the Indian stocks, the quantum of the significant AAR values increases monotonically up to the event day, and suddenly, after the event, it started decreasing.

4. Hypothesis

The hypothesis has been framed keeping in mind that the Indian stock market is semi-strong.

H1 Average abnormal returns associated with the event will not significantly differ from 0.

H2 CAAR associated with the event will not be significantly different than 0.

5. Research Methodology

The study considered essential factors investors use for investment decisions, including the P/E ratio, Debt-to-Equity ratio, Return on Capital Employed (ROCE), and Enterprise Value to EBITDA (EV/EBITDA) ratio. These factors reflect a company's financial health and performance.

- A P/E ratio is a measure of how much a company's stock is worth compared to its earnings. A high one means investors think the company will do well in the future, while a low one means it is not worth as much.
- A debt-to-equity ratio (DTE) measures a company's financial leverage. It is calculated by comparing the company's total debt to its equity. A high DTE indicates more risk, while a low DTE indicates less leverage for growth.

- *ROCE:* This evaluates a company's profitability and capital efficiency by dividing earnings before interest and tax (EBIT) by capital employed. Higher ROCE values indicate better capital management.
- *EV/EBITDA Ratio:* It gauges a company's value (including debt) against cash earnings. Lower ratios are generally seen as healthier. An EV/EBITDA ratio below ten is often considered favorable.

5.1 Data

We gathered the daily stock prices of companies listed on the National Stock Exchange from Investing.Com. Our sample consists of 35 companies' stocks that are traded in the Indian stock market. Five stocks were selected from 7 different industries. The breakdown of the sample by industry is provided in Table 13.1 below. The data is dated from October 1 2021 to March 11, 2022.

Table 13.1 Sample distribution by industry

Industry	No. of firms
Defense	5
Basic Metals	5
Pharmaceuticals	5
Energy	5
Textiles	5
FMCG	5
Automobiles	5
Total	35

5.2 Methodology

The Russia-Ukraine crisis and stock returns in India: An event study using modified event study method Event studies are practical tools for understanding how specific events affect business performance. Event studies involve looking at the price movements of assets or securities around the time of news announcements or events. In this study, we use the modified event study method (Brown et al., 1988) to compute cumulative abnormal returns following unexpected events.

The main question in this study is how the Russian: Ukrainian crisis will affect Indian stock returns after Russia invaded Ukraine. The goal is to see if there are any significant, abnormal returns in some companies' stock because of this crisis. CARi (cumulative abnormal returns) is calculated by adding the daily abnormal returns for the event period. Additionally, the study calculates the average of abnormal returns across each day in the 10-day post-information window. The goal of the study is to look at how the Ukraine crisis affected Indian stock prices using this event study methodology, with an emphasis on extreme returns and cumulative extreme returns.

$$\text{Mean of AR} = 1\text{Mt} = 1\text{MARt}$$

Where t = 1 . . . M, M being the number of post-information windows formed after the arrival of unexpected events (Russia-Ukraine war) in each calculated period.

Third, the mean abnormal returns are cumulated over a post-information 10-day window. Formally, the cumulative mean abnormal returns (CARt) are generated as follows:

$$\text{CARt} = \text{CARt } 1 + \text{ARt}$$

The formula used to find the CAAR for 5 days after unfavorable news is as follows:

CAAR (+5) = Summation of 5 days AAR

Here, AAR is the average of abnormal returns for the 5-day window post news. After calculating the CAAR of all event windows, we calculate the standard deviation to test the significance level.

The formula used to calculate the T-statistics of +5 days, -5days, +-5days, +10days, -10days and +-10days is as follows:

CAAR (+5) T Statistics = CAAR(+5)/(SD*(5)^(1/2)

The standard deviation (SD) is the average of all the average returns from the estimation period (estimated) or the average period (regular). In this example, the standard deviation is S.D. = t = 5. Single Statistical Methods To obtain statistically significant CAARs from zero, the following single statistical methods were employed: Conventional Parametric T-test Conventional T-test for CAARs during the event

6. Results and Discussion

Table 13.2 shows the AARs of stocks in the Nifty index on each day of our 10-day event window (i.e. [−10 + 10). Figure 13.1 shows that the AARs are negative and significant on all but the first day of the event (February 25). After the first day, the positive AARs increase gradually, but after four days of the event, they start to decrease. Earlier, there were negative and significant AARs, which indicates that the investors might have been in a panic state because of the news regarding the Russia-Ukraine war. Post-event day, the AAR was positive for four days because the investors became risk averse and started investing in fixed and selling other securities. Demand was less, and supply was high, which caused the prices of the stocks to fall; therefore, the returns also fell drastically.

Table 13.2 AAR for the event window, i.e., from February 10, 2022, to March 11, 2022

Event Window	AAR
10	0.0083
9	-0.0006
8	-0.0024
7	0.0009
6	-0.0016
5	-0.0043
4	0.0069
3	0.0087
2	0.0102
1	0.0128
0	-0.0111
-1	0.0112
-2	-0.0096
-3	-0.0115
-4	-0.0069
-5	-0.0022
-6	0.0048
-7	-0.0061
-8	-0.01
-9	0.0022
-10	-0.0093

As we can see, there was an increase in AAR before the arrival of the news. Post-event day, the AAR became positive, which may be because the market

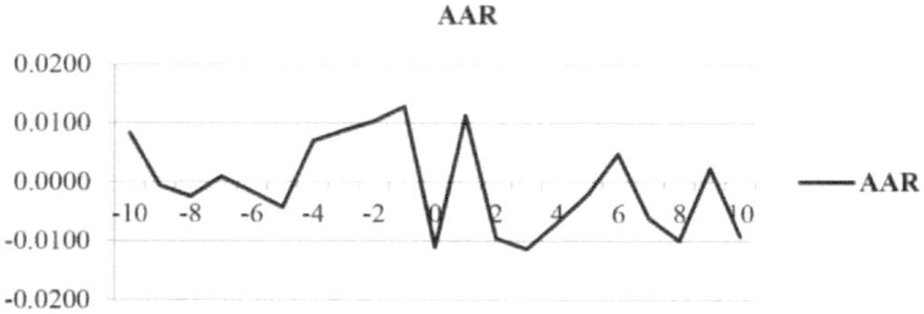

Fig. 13.1 AAR for the event window i.e. from February 10 2022 to March 11, 2022.

was quick to adapt to the crisis, but again, it started decreasing after 4 days, and that may be because of some news regarding the event day itself.

From Table 13.3, we can see that post-event date; the firm's high debt played a negative role in the firm's recovery. As can be seen, CAAR+5, i.e., five days post-event, has a correlation of -0.387 with the D/E of the firms, which indicates that CAAR +5 is negatively correlated to the firm's debt.

Table 13.3 Correlation between the fundamental variables like P/E, D/E, ROCE EV/EBITDA, and CAAR for the event window, i.e., from February 10, 2022, to March 11, 2022

		P/E	D/E	ROSE	EV/EBITDA
CAAR+5	Pearson Correlation	0.186	-.387*	0.141	0.113
CAAR-5	Pearson Correlation	0.054	0.094	-0.2	-0.047
CAAR+-5	Pearson Correlation	0.079	-0.271	0.1	-0.035
CAAR+10	Pearson Correlation	-0.018	-.406*	-0.047	0.123
CAAR-10	Pearson Correlation	-0.164	0.14	-.500**	-.392*
CAAR+-10	Pearson Correlation	-0.074	-0.268	-0.11	-0.047
P/E	Pearson Correlation	1	-.344*	0.188	.348*
D/E	Pearson Correlation	-.344*	1	-.341*	-.355*
ROCE	Pearson Correlation	0.188	-.341*	1	0.117
EV/EBITDA	Pearson Correlation	.348*	-.355*	0.117	1

For ROCE and CAAR -10, the correlation is -0.500. Hence, the high ROCE firms were more impacted by the crisis before the event happened. Therefore, the investors might have thought of disposing of the securities of the firms having high ROCE.This can also be because the investors might have thought that the stocks performing better would be more impacted by a crisis like this.Similarly, firms having higher EV/EBITDA were more impacted by the crisis since the correlation for CAAR-10 turned out to be negative, i.e., -.392.

Overall, it can be said that the financials of a firm, like P/E, EV/EBITDA, ROCE, and D/E ratios, do not have much impact on firms 'returns.

Table 13.4 shows the results of the entire sample (35 companies) for each event window (21 days, ten days pre-event, ten days post-event) and T-test (using M.S. Excel's descriptive analysis tool to test the null hypothesis) as well as the average daily A.R. (ADR), CAR (CAR) and CAAR (CAAR) from day 10 to day 10. AAR is negative on day 10 (T2, T3, T4, T5, T7, T8, T10, T+5, T+6, T+8, T+9).

Table 13.4 Daily average AAR and T-stats data for the event window, i.e., from February 10, 2022, to March 11, 2022.

Event Window	AAR	T-stat	Significance	CAAR
10	0.00826272	1.97645131	YES	0.03362876
9	-0.0005846	-0.1398283	NO	0.02536604
8	-0.002449	-0.5857965	NO	0.02595061
7	0.00087054	0.20823404	NO	0.02839958
6	-0.0016213	-0.3878086	NO	0.02752904
5	-0.0042977	-1.028013	NO	0.0291503
4	0.0069327	1.6583089	NO	0.03344799
3	0.00867124	2.07417069	YES	0.0265153
2	0.01022226	2.44517776	YES	0.01784406
1	0.01275945	3.05207499	YES	0.0076218
0	-0.0111357	-2.6636786	YES	-0.0051377
-1	0.01120433	2.68009013	YES	0.00599808
-2	-0.0095562	-2.2858648	YES	-0.0052063
-3	-0.0114642	-2.7422409	YES	0.00434998
-4	-0.0069426	-1.6606846	NO	0.01581414
-5	-0.0021644	-0.5177236	NO	0.02275677
-6	0.00475576	1.13758407	NO	0.02492116
-7	-0.0061228	-1.4645893	NO	0.02016539
-8	-0.0099985	-2.3916631	YES	0.02628823
-9	0.00224633	0.53732572	NO	0.03628677
-10	-0.0092635	-2.2158286	YES	0.03404044

The AARs have generally been good in most days of the current event and CAARs have also been good in the event. The null hypothesis has been accepted, which means that the majority of the stocks included in the study performed well. This can be attributed to the reactions of the investors to the news of war in Russia & Ukraine. The reaction of the investors was to sell risky stocks and buy defense stocks like BHEL & Paras Defence, BEML & Solar Industries, etc. Since the war was going on, these stocks also performed well in the event.H0 has been rejected as having 5% significance during the pre-Rome-Ukraine news cycle. The T-stat has also been wrong. H0 was approved during the post-Rome news cycle. This is likely because the stock market believes that war in Russia will be good for India. Investors have been building their portfolios with high and good defense stocks.

The news about the war in Russia has been welcomed by investors, politicians, and analysts as well as the stock market.

We also see the average abnormal returns over the event, which was from January 21 to March 11, plus the t-statistics for +5, -5, +10, -10, and -10 days. The numbers in Table 13.5 show that for all the windows we looked at, the null hypothesis, which is that the median of the CAARs is 0, is rejected since all the T's are lower than the value (1.96). But for CAAR+5, the T's are higher than 1.3803, which is significant.

Table 13.5 CAAR for the event window, i.e., from February 10, 2022, to March 11, 2022, along with the t-values

Event Window	CAAR	T-Stats of (CAAR -5)	T-Stats of (CAAR +5)	T-Stats of (CAAR +-5)	T-Stats of (CAAR -10)	T-Stats of (CAAR +10)	T-Stats of (CAAR +-10)
10	0.034						
9	0.025						
8	0.026						
7	0.028						
6	0.028						
5	0.029					1.903	
4	0.033						
3	0.027		2.3803	0.1979			
2	0.018						
1	0.008						
0	-0.005						-0.3277
-10	0.034						
-9	0.036						
-8	0.026						
-7	0.02						
-6	0.025				-1.8313		
-5	0.023						
-4	0.016						
-3	0.004	-1.3136					
-2	-0.005						
-1	0.006						

7. Conclusion

We selected firms listed on the National Stock Exchange as our sample. We observe that there were abnormal returns mainly before the event day, i.e., February 24, 2022, after which the market absorbed the information regarding the Russia-

Ukraine crisis. Hence, it can be said that the Indian market was quite efficient in this scenario. Additionally, we observed negative and significant CAAR on the days leading up to the event, compelling evidence of the effects of the Russia-Ukraine crisis on the Indian stock market. It is also observed that the financials of a firm like P/E, EV/EBITDA, ROCE, and D/E ratios, do not have much impact on firms 'returns during a crisis like this.

REFERENCES

1. Ahmad, T., Hussain, S., Akbar, M., & Rehman, A. U. (2022). Impact of terrorism on the stock market: Evidence from developed and developing markets. *International Journal of Disaster Risk Reduction*, p. *70*, 102786. https://doi.org/10.1016/j.ijdrr.2022.102786
2. Asgharian, H., &Nossman, M. (2011). Risk contagion among international stock markets. *Journal of International Money and Finance*, *30*(1), 22–38. https://doi.org/10.1016/j.jimonfin.2010.06.006
3. Baker, S. R., Bloom, N., Davis, S. J., Kost, K., Sammon, M., &Viratyosin, T. (2020). The unprecedented stock market reaction to COVID-19. *The Review of Asset Pricing Studies*, *10*(4), 742–758. https://doi.org/10.1093/rapstu/raaa008
4. Barro, R. J. (1981). Output effects of government purchases. *Journal of Political Economy*, *89*(6), 1086–1121. https://doi.org/10.1086/261024
5. Beaulieu, M., Cosset, J., &Essaddam, N. (2005). The impact of political risk on the volatility of stock returns: The case of Canada. *Journal of International Business Studies*, *36*(6), 701–718. https://doi.org/10.1057/palgrave.jibs.8400160
6. Berkman, H., Jacobsen, B., & Lee, J. B. (2011). Time-varying rare disaster risk and stock returns. *Journal of Financial Economics*, *101*(2), 313–332. https://doi.org/10.1016/j.jfineco.2011.02.019
7. Binder, J. J., & Merges, M. J. (2001). *Review of Quantitative Finance and Accounting*, *17*(1), 5–26. https://doi.org/10.1023/a:1011207919894
8. Bowman, R. G. (1983). Understanding and conducting event studies. *Journal of Business Finance & Accounting*, *10*(4), 561–584. https://doi.org/10.1111/j.1468-5957.1983.tb00453.x
9. Budastra, M. A., LukmanEffendy, RobithHudaya, & I KetutBudastra. (2022). Reaksipasar modal Indonesia terhadappengumuman reshuffle kabinetIndonesia majujilid I Dan II. *JurnalBisnisTerapan*, *6*(1), 43–52. https://doi.org/10.24123/jbt.v6i1.4792
10. Chellasamy, D., & K.M, A. (2017). Impact of demonetization on Indian stock market: With special reference to sectoral indices in the national stock exchange of India. *IOSR Journal of Economics and Finance*, *08*(03), 51–54. https://doi.org/10.9790/5933-0803015154
11. GHOBARAH, H. A., HUTH, P., & RUSSETT, B. (2003). Civil wars kill and maim people—Long after the shooting stops. *American Political Science Review*, *97*(02). https://doi.org/10.1017/s0003055403000613
12. Guidolin, M., & La Ferrara, E. (2005). Diamonds are forever; wars are not. Is conflict bad for private firms? https://doi.org/10.20955/wp.2005.004
13. Jindřichovská, I., & Uğurlu, E. (2021). E.U. and China trends in trade in challenging times. *Journal of Risk and Financial Management*, *14*(2), 71. https://doi.org/10.3390/jrfm14020071

14. Meidawati, N., &Harimawan, M. (2004). Undefined. *Sinergi*, *7*(1), 89–101. https://doi.org/10.20885/sinergi.vol7.iss1.art6
15. Omar, A. M., Wisniewski, T. P., & Nolte, S. (2017). Diversifying away the risk of war and cross-border political crisis. *Energy Economics*, *64*, 494–510. https://doi.org/10.1016/j.eneco.2016.02.015
16. Rigobon, R., & Sack, B. (2005). Undefined. *Journal of Banking & Finance*, *29*(7), 1769–1789. https://doi.org/10.1016/j.jbankfin.2004.06.040
17. Sandler, T., Tschirhart, J. T., & Cauley, J. (1983). A theoretical analysis of transnational terrorism. *American Political Science Review*, *77*(1), 36–54. https://doi.org/10.2307/1956010
18. Sathyanarayana, S., &Gargesha, S. (2017). The impact of policy announcement on stock market volatility: Evidence from currency demonetization in India. *IOSR Journal of Business and Management*, *19*(01), 47–63. https://doi.org/10.9790/487x-1901074763
19. Schneider, G., & Troeger, V. E. (2006). War and the world economy. *Journal of Conflict Resolution*, *50*(5), 623–645. https://doi.org/10.1177/0022002706290430
20. Shen, C., Bui, D. G., & Lin, C. (2017). Do political factors affect stock returns during presidential elections? *Journal of International Money and Finance*, pp. *77*, 180–198. https://doi.org/10.1016/j.jimonfin.2017.07.019
21. Shutes, K., McGrath, K., Lis, P., & Riegler, R. (2016). Twitter and the U.S. stock market: The influence of microbloggers on share prices. *Economics and Business Review*, *2 (16)*(3), 57–77. https://doi.org/10.18559/ebr.2016.3.5
22. Wisniewski, T. P. (2016). Is there a link between politics and stock returns? A literature survey. *International Review of Financial Analysis*, *47*, 15–23. https://doi.org/10.1016/j.irfa.2016.06.015

Note: All the figures and tables in this chapter were made by the authors.

Annexure

Companies Selected for the Study

Sr. No.	Name of Stock	Sr. No.	Name of Stock
1	Arvind Limited	16	Lupin Limited
2	Bajaj Auto Limited	17	Marico Limited
3	BEML Limited	18	Maruti Suzuki India Limited
4	Bharat Electrical Limited	19	Mangalore Refinery and Petrochemicals Limited (MRPL)
5	Dr. Reddy's Laboratories	20	Paras Defence and Space
6	GAIL	21	Rupa Company Limited
7	Gillet India	22	Steel Authority of India Limited
8	Hindalco Industries Limited	23	SML Isuzu Limited
9	Hindustan Unilever	24	Solar Industries India Limited
10	HPCL	25	Sun Pharmaceutical Ind. Ltd.
11	Indian Oil Corporation Ltd.	26	Tata Motor Limited
12	Jindal Stainless	27	Tata Steel Limited
13	JWS Steel Limited	28	TVS Motors
14	KPR Mills	29	Vardhman Textile Limited
15	Larsen & Toubro Ltd		

*Securing the Future through Sustainability, Health, Education, and Technology –
Brig. Dr. Rajiv Divekar et al. (eds)*

14 Emotional Intelligence Promoting the Sustainability of Online Learning Readiness

A. Bharathy[1]
Assistant Professor, Department of Management,
Pondicherry University Community College, Lawspet, Puducherry

R. Gayathiri[2]
Research Assistant, Department of Management,
Pondicherry University Community College, Lawspet, Puducherry

ABSTRACT

The Online education platforms are serving us to spread out the knowledge resources with several accompanying advantages like handiness, flexibility, custom-made learning, intense market penetration, world wide access, reduced cost, assorted number of subjects, lifelong learning opportunity, options for repeated access to course and the list goes on. We resolved to measure the readiness level to learn online among the students which is the first step to harness the benefit of online learning. We also sought to validate an abstract model linking emotional intelligence and readiness level for online learning.

The data was collected from 200 undergraduate students using a structured questionnaire by merging standard instruments. Descriptive statistics and necessary pre-analysis done for conducting structural equation modeling. The outcomes of the study validated our proposed model and hence we affirm that by improving the emotional intellect of the students will help us to improve the readiness level to take up online learning. This paper will help the educational institutions to include the component of emotional intelligence as a bridge course, so that we can improve the students' willingness to enroll in online courses. This paper will be a disclosure for the education policy makers to make the needful pedagogical amendments and kick start a more sustainable digital infrastructure required in near future.

KEYWORDS: Emotional intellect, Readiness to learn online, Self-emotion appraisal

[1]bharathyrangan@pondiuni.ac.in, [2]ramagaya2007@gmail.com

DOI: 10.1201/9781003587200-14

1. Introduction

Technology, internet and online learning have been changing so much that as we take time to understand it, it has become part of our everyday life. The continuous developments in the internet have been able to connect people, business, learners, workers, employers and permeate through whatever we do – from shopping online to powering the economic productivity of nations worldwide and this is only seen as the next big revolution after the invention of steam engines, electricity and the printing press. However, the benefits of technological innovation can enrich society not by merely adopting them but there is an imminent need to adapt to it. This is how the steam engine that was initially discovered to pump water from mines went to connect cities with railway lines that served as a catalyst for economic welfare (Muhleisen, 2018). It is here that we need to explore how the internet can be adapted rather than being adopted in different economies for maximum benefit. Although there are no doubts about India's technological excellence, there are some major concerns as to how it is going to transform itself from a labor-based economy to a skill based one. This is going to be a big challenge to India as by the year 2025, an estimated 70% of the population will be in the working age group. But whether they would be employable is a big question and this cannot be ignored in the line of our national necessity failing which the much-touted demographic dividend would be a challenge (Tiwari, 2023). This then brings to fore the indispensability of access to higher education institutions to bridge the gap.

The desponding part of this story is that no significant efforts seem to have been undertaken to improve the situation as prior studies reaffirm the same dismal data as Shariff & Sharma (2013) published alarming statistics that only 10% of the student population had access to higher level education. All India Survey on Higher Education (AISHE 2019 – 2020) published that the Gross Enrolment Ratio (GER) in Higher Education in India was only 27% (40 million students across India) whereas the global average was 36.7% which underlines that this concern still exists in India. This is due to lack of infrastructure, geographical location of the student and other allied factors.

It is here that we observe that adapting internet technology as a platform to deliver anytime and anywhere education is essentially a virtuous solution for these challenges. It will benefit our Government to accomplish the target of "Education to All". We basically need to rise above the setbacks like modifying curriculum for blended learning, availability of obligatory facilities and so on (Patrick, 2011).

On the other hand, digital technologies used for learning have been chided for their low levels of interaction, human presence, nonverbal cues, personalization of content, socio-emotional interaction, needs gratification, social presence as valued in distance educational learning as in traditional formats of learning but the influence of these factors are more complicated due to transactional distance in online learning (Garrison and Shale, 1990). The results indicate that online learning is characteristic of emotion deficient communication and this diminishes the retention by participants. This breeds unacceptable behavior. The study thus highlights the need for a socioemotional perspective for achieving sustainable learning online.

As our students are growing in this tech era, technology adoption or harnessing tech tools that enhance interactivity and reduce transactional distance in distance education cannot be overlooked. This is accurate when the number of students wanting to enter higher studies are more than the educational institutions available in our country. This demand -capacity mismatch can be met only through adapting to online learning. This then leads to the need to explore the socioemotional context in adapting to sustainability in online learning.

2. Literature Review

Plenty of studies ascertained the prominence of emotional intelligence in the conventional teaching-learning process. Emotions play an essential role in the learning process since cognition and emotions are mutually dependent (Storbeck & Clore, 2007). It was even feasible to record the students' emotions while learning using "biophysical signals" and a study used this technique and found that engagement and confusion were most important and frequently occurred emotions during the learning process. They demonstrated that this process of getting emotional feedback was useful in improving the learning process. Further, it was also proved that emotional awareness strengthens the students' performance (Shen et al. 2009).

2.1 Emotional Skills for Online Learning

The requirement for emotional skills in the online learning process was acknowledged, a long time ago even before the lockdown phase. Spanish Universities introduced the web based learning system and a study carried out by Benito-Osorio et al. in 2013 which confirmed that higher education teachers must update their emotional competences to deepen the learning experience of their students.

Sharma & Bhargava (2023) did the qualitative analysis of emotional responses of teachers and learners in the practice of virtual teaching and interactions. They emphasized the importance of emotional management in an online learning context. Arghode et al. (2022) studied the effect of emotional intelligence on online instruction mediated by inter-cultural competence. They highlighted that the online instructor should be aware about the emotional issues of the learners to improve their engagement level and learning experience.

Chandra (2021) studied the stress triggered by the abrupt shift from conventional classrooms to online learning due to imposed lockdown in India. The inferences of the study ascertained that emotional intelligence based coping strategies facilitated the pupils to overpower the adverse effects of the uneasiness.

Emotional Intelligence is required for the whole knowledge management process. Authors had given empirical evidence for the interacting role of EI on knowledge management (Zhang et al. 2022).

2.2 Research Gap

Emotional proficiency counts for the consciousness of both self and others emotions. Exploring the emotional component of the students is logically required in an online learning context where the social interaction is completely different from traditional classroom settings. It was revealed that emotionally intelligent individuals can interact easily and establish a decent social bonding in online classrooms (Han, 2009). Another aspect is that online education commands the student to be independent and self-governed. It was also validated that emotional intelligence is an essential prerequisite for self-directed learning (Zhoc et al. 2018).

Significant number of studies have investigated the influence of the emotional element in the learning process (Bowen, 2014; Pradhan et al. 2017; Staus & Falk, 2017; Schmidt, 2019; Abbott & Lee, 2023). Studies authenticated that learners with optimistic emotional quotient have enriched learning experience. Moving towards the role of emotional management in an online learning context, we really need more research on the road to establish a constructive knowledge delivery system.

Grounded on the above-mentioned viewpoints and considering the fact that digital learning is expected to be the future trend of learning, we would like to examine the effect of emotional intellect exclusively on online learning readiness levels. This paper also seeks to replenish the gap of validating the notable OLRS scale in Indian context.

3. Research Methodology

3.1 Data Sources Utilized for Collection of Secondary Data

Published research articles related to Emotional Intelligence and online learning readiness were collected using the data banks like JSTOR, Emerald Insight, Springer link journals, Sage journals and Wiley online library and systematically reviewed. The authors used the key search terms like online education, emotional intelligence and online learning readiness, WLEIS & OLRS scales.

3.2 Instruments used for Collecting Primary Data

Primary data was gathered using a structured questionnaire by employing and editing standard instruments. Respondents were undergraduate students from a constituent college of Central University. Emotional Intellect of the students were assessed using WLEIS (Wong and Law Emotional Intelligence Scale from Law et al. 2004) and their readiness level to take up the online course was measured using OLRS (Online Learning Readiness scale from Hung et al. 2010).

3.3 WLEIS Scale

We employed a standardized instrument developed by "Chi-Sum Wong and Kenneth Law". The instrument measures emotional intelligence under four sub-constructs. It is validated in diverse cultural/national background like Kuwait, Spain, Portugal, Singapore, Pakistan, Europe and many more (Halimi et al. 2021; Alonazi, 2020; Koh & O'Higgins 2017; Carvalho et al. 2016; Buzdar et al. 2016; Taliadorou & Pashiardis 2015). The scale had been validated in Indian context as well (Trayambak et al. 2022; Shah, 2022; Rathore & Chadha, 2021; Malik 2020).

3.4 OLRS Scale

We utilized another widely used instrument developed by "Min-Ling Hung, Chien Chou, Chao-Hsiu Chen and Zang-Yuan Own". The instrument measures the learner's level of readiness for online learning, which is also validated in several papers. This instrument is also validated with different groups of samples from Pakistan, Vietnam, Taiwan, Malaysia, Turkey, Portugal and many more (Celik & Cagiltay 2023; Pham & Dau 2022; Rafique et al. 2021; Wei & Chou 2020; Chung et al. 2020; Firat & Bozkurt 2020; Engin, 2017). We are attempting to validate this scale in the Indian context and there is a dearth of published research works in our region.

3.5 Reliability Analysis of the Instruments

The reliability measures of the both the scales varied from 0.60 to 0.73 based on the Crohbach's Alpha analysis. The internal consistency of the scales is in acceptable range according to Pallant 2001 & Daud et al. 2018.

4. Results and Discussion

4.1 Profile of the Sample

In Total, 200 undergraduate students shared their responses for our study. 124 (62%) male and 76 (38%) female participants' answered. 123 of them fit into the age group 17 to 20 years (61.5%) and remaining 77 students were more than 21 years of age (38.5%). Most of the students (158 members – 79%) were doing their third year of UG course, who intensely underwent online classes for during considerable period of lockdown. 96 students (48%) were doing bio-science and healthcare courses, 59 students (29.5%) were associated with Management and Commerce department and remaining 45 students (22.5%) belong to other courses majoring computer science, multimedia and others.

4.2 Correlation Analysis

Pearson correlation between the EMI & RTL is 0.621 at 1% significance level. The association between the variables is moderate to strong according to Akoglu, 2018 (0.6 to 0.7). The correlation value indicated that EMI and RTL are positively related to each other.

4.3 Structural Equation Modeling

The model set forth to link up emotional intellect and readiness to learn online was validated using IBM-AMOS Structural Equation Modeling. The maximum likelihood calculation was utilized and the proposed model was observed to be very much fit to the present research work.

Corresponding results of Fig. 14.1, Chi-Square = 24.620, DF = 17, x^2/SD = 1.448, p = 0.104, GFI = 0.970, AGFI = 0.936, CFI = 0.986, NFI = 0.958, IFI = 1.000, Standardized RMR = 0.034 and RMSEA = 0.047. From the model we can also understand the estimated structure equation as (EI = 0.84*RTL) and the R^2=0.706. It is indicated that emotional intellect is explaining 84% of Readiness level to take up online learning.

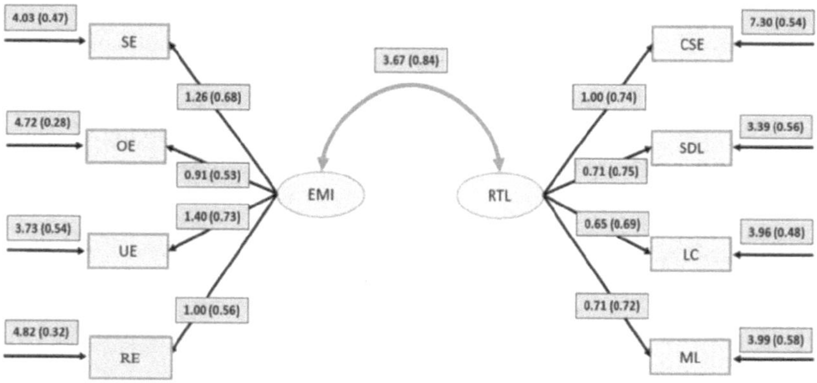

Fig. 14.1 Emotional Intelligence correlated to sustainability of online learning readiness

Source: Made by the authors for ICSSR Minor Project awarded 2022 -23 titled "Antecedence of Emotional Intellect on Online Learning Efficacy"

4.4 Construct Reliability and Convergent Validity

The model set forth to link up emotional intellect and readiness to learn online was validated using IBM-AMOS Structural Equation Modeling. The maximum likelihood calculation was utilized and the proposed model was observed to be very much fit to the present research work.

Table 14.1 also present the sequence of sub-constructs responsible for determining the main construct which is as follows:

- Emotional intellect is determined in the order of "Use of Emotion, Self-Emotion awareness, Regulation of Emotion and Others emotion appraisal"
- Readiness to learn online is determined in the order of "Self-directed learning, Computer Self-Efficacy, Motivation for Learning and Learner Control".

73.4% of the Emotional Intellect of students and "Self-Directed Learning (SDL)" explains 74.9% of the Readiness level for online learning. This study has made a

Table 14.1 Calculation of AVE and CR

	Factor Loading (FL)	Item Reliability (IR)	Delta	AVE	Sum of 'FL'	Sum of 'Delta'	CR
RE ← EMI	0.562	0.316	0.684				
UE ← EMI	**0.734**	0.539	0.461				
OE ← EMI	0.528	0.279	0.721				
SE ← EMI	0.684	0.468	0.532	**0.400**	2.508	1.602	**0.724**
CSE ← RTL	0.737	0.543	0.457				
SDL ← RTL	**0.749**	0.561	0.439				
LC ← RTL	0.675	0.456	0.544				
ML ← RTL	0.723	0.523	0.477	**0.527**	2.884	2.083	**0.817**

Source: Made by the authors for ICSSR Minor Project awarded 2022 -23 titled "Antecedence of Emotional Intellect on Online Learning Efficacy"

significant contribution to literature in the sense that it reiterates the findings of prior studies that opine SDL is the most active and productive process wherein learners plan and define their objectives in advance to learning and monitor to assess their progress in learning, and eventually help to measure their achievement after learning (Pintrich, 2000; Zimmerman, 2008). Online learning environments are characterized by self-motivation of the learner in completion of the assigned modules and to engage in online learning (Hung et al., 2010). The next dimension that plays an important role is CSE and refers to technology quotient in computing skills in general and also learning related specific skills that goes to explain online learning readiness. Also early studies have identified that self-efficacy is among the two major predictors of online learning (Lynch and Dembo's, 2004). It is interesting to observe that the role of self efficacy is comparatively low as today's generation has exposure to computer technology. This study is more to explain the socio emotional or the psychometric dimensions that influence online learning and it is seen that UOE has a significant role.

4.5 Discriminant Validity

Discriminant validity is also termed as divergent validity which is tested to provide evidence that one test is distinct from the other test. It also ensures absence of data redundancy. The inter-correlation value between EMI and RTL scale was 0.621 and the square root of AVE values of EMI and RTL scales are 0.632 and 0.726 respectively. To verify the discriminant validity of an instrument, the Square root of AVE values should be greater than the inter-correlation value between EMI and RTL. Hence the instrument is proved to have discriminant validity (Fornell & David 1981).

5. Conclusion

Education is the most effective and vibrant tool for all-round growth of India with a substantial proportion of the youth population. According to "All India

Survey on Higher Education (AISHE 2019 – 2020)" the total enrollment in higher education is increasing every year. It was around 72 lakh in the year 2014-15, gradually raised to 3.85 crores in 2019-20 and 4.14 crores in 2020-21. The survey calculation predicts that 9.2 crore students will sign up for higher level education by the year 2035, which is a wakeup call for India to widen the capacity of its knowledge delivery system. Online education will obviously do a good turn to accomplish this mission of India.

In essence, our study established that the emotional intelligence of the students has an impact on their readiness level to adopt online education. This study spotlighted that independent determination of the students (SDL) and their self-confidence (CSE) with using digital tools is highly influencing their willingness to adopt online education. This study is significant at this juncture of recuperation from the lockdown phase where we endured mandatory online education at all levels from schools to universities. We began to appreciate its worth. If we can sustain and develop this pedagogy with careful regulations, we can reap its exemplary benefits to attain people empowerment which ultimately leads to the overall national development. We need to further explore this topic regarding the types of facilities we can incorporate in the online education platforms to make the learning process effective and easier. Studies can be encouraged to find many employability skills which can be given as online courses. It will help the students to take up these add-on courses while they are doing regular education and exploit the job markets tactically.

6. Practical Implications

6.1 Governance

Online education platforms and virtual classrooms can increase the scope, convenience, flexibility and personalized learning experience (Sinha, 2023). One of the finest stepping stones to accomplish "The Sustainable Development Goal of India – Education for All" is to embrace online education opportunities. Thoughtful conception and governance of different online courses on employability skills is absolutely recommended.

6.2 Pedagogy

Emotional Intelligence can be launched as a basic foundational course for students. Real-time techniques can be taught to the students regarding appropriate usage of emotions.

- It inspires the students to grow and mature as independent learners.
- It gives them the privilege of using their emotions to enhance productivity.
- It is the foundation for developing good social interaction.

We are bolstering the idea that was encouraged in previous research work to devise and execute suitable pedagogic strategies related to emotional intelligence (Buzdar et al. 2016).

6.3 Operational

Hands-on knowledge to use digital devices and online technologies is a prerequisite for educators and learners. It will help them to become more confident and proficient in using digital devices and handling online tools. Essential facilities required to float the online courses should be installed and maintained by the institutions.

Acknowledgement

This article is a part of the research project being undertaken with ICSSR, New Delhi. The author thankfully acknowledges the funding agency for their support.

REFERENCES

Journals

1. Abbott, M. L., & Lee, K. K. (2023). Relationships between students' emotions, self-regulated learning, and literacy gains in beginning/basic level ESL literacy classes for adults. *System,* 115, 103061.
2. Akoglu, H. (2018). User's guide to correlation coefficients. Turkish journal of emergency medicine, 18(3), 91–93.
3. Arghode, V., Lakshmanan, G., & Nafukho, F. M. (2022). Emotional intelligence, intercultural competence and online instruction: Review and reflection. *European Journal of Training and Development*, (ahead-of-print).
4. Benito-Osorio, D., Peris-Ortiz, M., Armengot, C. R., & Colino, A. (2013). Web 5.0: the future of emotional competences in higher education. *Global Business Perspectives,* 1, 274–287.
5. Bowen, J. (2014). Emotion in the classroom: An update. *To Improve the Academy,* 33(2), 196–219.
6. Buzdar, M. A., Ali, A., & Tariq, R. U. H. (2016). Emotional intelligence as a determinant of readiness for online learning. *International Review of Research in Open and Distributed Learning*, *17*(1), 148–158.
7. Chandra, Y. (2021). Online education during COVID-19: perception of academic stress and emotional intelligence coping strategies among college students. *Asian education and development studies*, 10(2), 229–238.
8. Clarke, J., Lovelock, R., & McNay, M. (2016). Liberal arts and the development of emotional intelligence in social work education. The British Journal of Social Work, 46(3), 635–651.
9. Fornell, C., & Larcker, D. F. (1981). Evaluating structural equation models with unobservable variables and measurement error. *Journal of marketing research,* 18(1), 39–50.
10. Garrison, D. R. & Shale, D. (Eds.). (1990). Education at a distance: From issues to practice. Melbourne, FL: Krieger

11. Hair, J. F., Black, W. C., Babin, B. J., Anderson, R. E., & Tatham, R. L. (2006). *Multivariate Data Analysis,* 6th Edition.
12. Hung, M. L., Chou, C., Chen, C. H., & Own, Z. Y. (2010). Learner readiness for online learning: Scale development and student perceptions. Computers & Education, 55(3), 1080–1090.
13. Law, K. S., Wong, C. S., & Song, L. J. (2004). The construct and criterion validity of emotional intelligence and its potential utility for management studies. Journal of applied Psychology, 89(3), 483.
14. Muhamad Safiih, L., & Azreen, N. (2016). Confirmatory Factor Analysis Approach: A Case Study of Mathematics Students' Achievement in TIMSS. Malaysian Journal of Mathematical Sciences, 10(S), 41–51.
15. Muhleisen, M., (2018). The long and short of digital technology. https://www.imf.org/en/Publications/fandd/issues/2018/06/impact-of-digital-technology-on-economic-growth-muhleisen
16. Patrick, S. (2011). New learning models: The evolution of online learning into innovative K–12 blended programs. *Educational Technology,* 19–26.
17. Pradhan, R. K., Jena, L. K., & Singh, S. K. (2017). Examining the role of emotional intelligence between organizational learning and adaptive performance in Indian manufacturing industries. *Journal of Workplace Learning*, 29(3), 235–247.
18. Schmidt, S. J. (2019). Embracing and harnessing the intimate connection between emotion and cognition to help students learn. *Journal of Food Science Education,* 18(4), 87–96.
19. Shariff, A., & Sharma, A. (2013). Intergenerational and Regional Differentials in Higher-Level Education in India. *US India Policy Institute Occasional Paper.*
20. Shen, L., Wang, M., & Shen, R. (2009). Affective e-learning: Using "emotional" data to improve learning in a pervasive learning environment. *Journal of Educational Technology & Society*, 12(2), 176–189.
21. Storbeck, J., & Clore, G. L. (2007). On the interdependence of cognition and emotion. *Cognition and Emotion,* 21(6), 1212–1237.
22. Staus, N. L., & Falk, J. H. (2017). The role of emotion in informal science learning: Testing an exploratory model. *Mind, brain, and education*, 11(2), 45–53.
23. Zhang, Y., Xiong, P., Zhou, W., Sun, L., & Cheng, E. T. (2022). Exploring the longitudinal effects of emotional intelligence and cultural intelligence on knowledge management processes. *Asia Pacific Journal of Management*, 1–24.
24. Zhoc, K. C., Chung, T. S., & King, R. B. (2018). Emotional intelligence (EI) and self-directed learning: Examining their relation and contribution to better student learning outcomes in higher education. *British Educational Research Journal,* 44(6), 982–1004.

Books/Book Chapters

25. Han, H. Y. (2009). *Relationship between students' emotional intelligence, social bond, and interactions in online learning*. University of Illinois at Urbana-Champaign.
26. Sharma, A., & Bhargava, S. (2023). Emotions in the Virtual Classroom: Understanding the Role of Emotional Intelligence amidst Covid-19 Blues. *In Honing Self-Awareness of Faculty and Future Business Leaders: Emotions Connected with Teaching and Learning* (pp. 211–226). Emerald Publishing Limited.

Reports/Articles/Websites

27. Sinha, A. (2023, August 25). Use AI to fan the flame of learning. The Hindu Business Line. https://www.thehindubusinessline.com/opinion/use-ai-to-fan-the-flame-of-learning/article67231883.ece
28. Tiwari, B., K. (2023, August 22). How skilled are we?. The Hindu – Business Line. https://www.thehindubusinessline.com/opinion/how-skilled-are-we/article67224286.ece
29. All India Survey on Higher Education (AISHE 2019-2020) – Department of Higher Education, Ministry of Education, Government of India. https://www.education.gov.in/sites/upload_files/mhrd/files/statistics-new/aishe_eng.pdf
30. Educational Inequality in India in 2022: How to End Disparity in Education. https://www.hercircle.in/engage/get-inspired/achievers/educational-inequality-in-india-in-2022-how-to-end-disparity-in-education-3075.html

*Securing the Future through Sustainability, Health, Education, and Technology –
Brig. Dr. Rajiv Divekar et al. (eds)*

15 A Midas Touch in Kitchen

Madhusmita Choudhury[1]
Assistant Professor,
Department of Marketing, GITAM Deemed to be University,
Rishikonda, Visakhapatnam, India

Shantanu Raj[2]
Assistant Professor, Centre for Agribusiness Management,
Utkal University, Vani Vihar, Bhubaneswar

Anshuman Sahoo[3]
Assistant Professor, Department of I-MBA,
Utkal University, Bhubaneswar

ABSTRACT

Indians use spices in their cooking and consume spices to get many health benefits. The Marketers tap these opportunities in their various products, from organic lentils to different spices in the kitchen rack, to add that flavour and health for people. The spice market could be more organized and have a vast marketing opportunity; however, few marketers and Regional players tap these opportunities to package the health and reach the target market. The current research investigates consumer preference towards different brands of packaged spices through multivariate techniques: Multidimensional scaling & correspondence analysis. This research has a fair idea of various national and regional brands of spices based on consumer-preferred attributes, which may motivate the markers to craft customized strategies.

KEYWORDS: Brand attributes, Brand identification, Correspondence analysis, Multidimensional scaling, Perceptual mapping

1. Introduction

Midas: The Greek King secretly desired all he touched to become gold, like every person who prepares food for his loved one wants to make it precious and

[1]2madhusmitachoudhury@gmail.com, [2]shantanuraj022@gmail.com [3]dransumansahoo@gmail.com

DOI: 10.1201/9781003587200-15

delicious. Along with love, passion and the feeling of serving mouth-watering food, spices play a vital role in every kitchen in the world and win hearts. India has a long and vintage history of Indian spices. The Indian spices witness a strong growth trajectory and grow at a CAGR of 9% annually (IBEF, 2022). The Indian packaged spices market is reckoned to be **Rs 750 billion** annually (A.L. Consulting, 2020). The spices market in India is mainly fragmented, and unorganized players govern its ascendency, allowing marketers to enter the market with the proper knowledge of marketing strategy to win customers' hearts. The use of Indian spices has grown a lot due to their use in various industries like bakeries, food & beverage, cosmetics and pharmaceuticals. Modern Indians are value seekers; they search for value (Ng, I. C., & et al.) in most products. Most people are becoming health conscious and prefer packaged branded spices because the possibility of adulteration is minimal, and they are safer to consume.

The market for branded packaged spices is about 6.6 billion rupees, growing at 8% annually. The top ten importers of Indian spices in 2018-19 were Bangladesh, **the United Arab Emirates, Vietnam, the USA,** China, Thailand, Hong Kong, **the U.K.,** Malaysia & Sri Lanka (Jayakumar, P.B., 2020). The top ten exported spices **are** cardamom seeds, turmeric, **chilli peppers,** garlic, Cumin, curry powder, spice **oils and** oleoresins, pepper, and mint products (IBEF, 2022). The packaged Indian spices market is overwhelmed with Indian brands and regional brands. Most brands were built within 2-3 decades.

This paper investigates consumer preference towards different brands of packaged spices. The analysis of the study will help the marketer formulate an appropriate strategy to stimulate the market by knowing different underlying dimensions for the selection of spice-packaged brands. However, the research in this area is still very nascent and very few studies have been devoted to exploring the attributes responsible for buying branded spices, which will help the marketers formulate a strategic marketing plan to capture more markets as per the gap identified in the study of Sharangi, A. B., & Pandit, M. K., 2018; Nair, K.P. 2021. *Most of the study is devoted to production, supply chain, and export and import of spices, and minimal research was conducted on the marketing of spices.* The novelty of our study rests on investigating brand preference by applying two multivariate methods, i.e. MDS (multiple dimensional scaling) and C.A. (correspondence analysis). To the author's knowledge & understanding, this is the rarest of few studies which have integrated the two methods in knowing the brand preference of spices.

2. Literature Review

Bettmann's information processing model of consumer choice incorporates the concept of consumer processing information. Bettmann's model emphasizes that consumer information has limited processing power and rarely performs complex tasks & analysis of available alternatives. This model allows consumers to use simple heuristic decision-making strategies. This process will enable consumers to analyze available information and alternative proposals comprehensively. Bettmann's system could be helpful for marketers dealing with spices to design marketing strategies by stimulating the insights gained through this research (Ross, I., 1979). The researchers tried to adopt this theory and find the hidden dimensions for selecting spice brands.

The production and export of spices can be enhanced through advanced technologies like biotechnology, tissue culture, better marketing infrastructure, storage and better logistic facilities to facilitate spice export (Rajanbabu, R., 2015; Nair, K.P., 2021). India's government is mulling over Spices Park to ameliorate the quality of processed spices and bolster India's competitiveness in the international market. According to Mohan S. et al. (2013), India has humungous production and consumption of spices. However, it is still besieged with numerous challenges for marketing, supply chain, pre & post-harvesting practices & quality required to match the international standard (Sharangi, A. B., & Pandit, M. K., 2018). India is endowed with propitious topography to support the production of various spices; cheap labour, government support and low operating costs are some pertinent factors which put India on the front foot in the production of spices (Varadharaj, S., & Prakash, A. R., 2018).

The study predicates that exporters should deliver good, quality spices while rigorously following the quality standard. It will fetch good revenue in the international market (Bhardwaj, R. K. et al., 2011, March). Krishnadas, M. (2010) elucidated in his studies the volatility of the production of significant spices from 1994 to 2006. Malaysia, Sri Lanka, UAE & Indonesia are the loyal buyers of Indian Chilli. The USA import a colossal amount of Black Pepper from India. Within this period, there was copious growth of turmeric production in India, and its export prices pent up in the international market. There was accretive growth of coriander in terms of quantity & value in the global market. The spices market is proliferating because consumers are keen to go for the traditional system of processing spices. These conventional systems of processing spices are very hectic and time-consuming. As more women join the workforce, they are time-strapped and prefer buying packaged spices (Suja Sundaram, M., & Abubshait, F. A. A., 2023). The packaged spices have gained traction in domestic & international markets due to their quality (Alam, M. N. E. et al., 2023), authentic taste (Das, A., & Sharangi, A. B., 2018; Motoki, K. & et al 2023), beget exquisite taste & colour in food (Reboredo-Rodríguez, P. et al., 2017) and assure purity (Balasubramanian, S. et al., 2016). **Today,** consumers have limited **resources of** time, energy, and **finances;** they make **purchasing and** consumption choices using these available resources. The vital reasons behind purchasing branded spices in India are that they are widely available, have less pricing and save time and energy in preparing food (Djiazet S. et al., 2022). Based on area for production, yielding capability, Market demand and availability, spices are demarcated into three categories: major, minor and exotic. (Islam, M. S. & et al 2011; Afrad, M. S. I., & Akter, M.

R., 2020). Those days are gone when people used to prepare spice at home. People thronged on branded spices because traditional methods of preparing spices were gruelling and took a lot of time (Noor T. et al., 2017). The majority of respondents prefer to buy packaged branded spices from departmental stores (Zielke, S., & Dobbelstein, T., 2007), and an adequate strategy is required to promote the brand at the store along with the correct position on the shelf Siddiqui, S., & Ali, T., 2021.

Branded spices are widely used in Indian cooking; hence, the researcher was motivated to opt for seven popular and widely available spices in the Bhubaneswar region, including national and regional brands. These brands are illustrious and mostly preferred by people who cook because they are available in mom-and-pop stores and organized retail outlets. These are MDH, Everest, Homefills, Bharat, Ruchi, Swadisht and Grihasti, and they are behemoth brands in the Graram Masala category. These brands of spices are differentiated based on sensory and non-sensory attributes.

3. Methodology

To accomplish the research objective, the study entails two multivariate techniques, MDS and Correspondence analysis. Multidimensional Scaling assists in knowing brand similarity (Mair, P., de Leeuw, J., & Groenen, P. J., 2015; Mair, P., 2018), and Correspondence Analysis assists in exploring the association between the brand of spices and attributes responsible for buying (Greenacre, M., 2017; Ramos, V., 2023) the packaged spices.

Data were collected from people who cook primarily in the kitchen and buy spices. The purposive sampling method (Tongco, M. D. C., 2007) was adopted to glean respondent data. The data used for the study is primary, and the study is comprised of metric and non-metric data. The questionnaire was sent to 230 respondents with a response rate of 83% (filled responses were 191). The questionnaires were personally disseminated to the respondents, and they were assured that identities would be kept anonymous. The analysis is performed through SPSS 20.0.

The sample profile says mostly male (58%), and married persons account for 55% indulged in cooking & buying spices. Most people have a nuclear family (76.4%), with 3-5 members in their family (37.6%). Most respondents fall in the 37 to 44 years of age bracket (24.6%), and most are postgraduate (65.9%). The Majority of respondents belonged to service classes (43.9%).

4. Empirical Analysis

Perceptual mapping is a widely applied multivariate tool to analyze the complex relationship between brands, competitors, and the criteria buyers use to make purchasing decisions and recommendations. It is mainly used in brand equity analysis (Chadha & Kapoor, 2008). It visually depicts the customers' perception

Table 15.1 Socio economic demographic profile

Socio-demographic data	Type	Frequency
Gender	Male	111
	Female	80
Marital status	Married	105
	Unmarried	86
Types of Family	Joint	45
	Nuclear	146
Household members	Up to 3	69
	3-5 members	72
	More than 5	50
Age	Up to 23 years	38
	23-30 years	39
	30-37 years	32
	37- 44 years	47
	44 – 51 years	18
	More than 51	16
Income	Up to 5 lakhs	110
	5 to 10 lakhs	45
	More than 10 lakhs	36
Education	Graduate	65
	Post graduate	126
Occupation	Services	84
	Homemakers	54
	Business persons	18
	others	34

Source: Author's Data Analysis

or attitude towards any product, brand, promotion or service (Jawaharlal, U., & Kumar, K. B. S., 2004). Perceptual maps capture the consumer reaction towards product features (Dev, C., Morgan, M.S. and Shoemaker, S. 1995; DeSarbo, W.S., Grewal, R. and Scott, C.J., 2008). There are two types of perceptual mapping, i.e. perception-based perceptual mapping and preference-based perceptual mapping. The perception-based perceptual mapping represents attributes similarity (Hauser, J. R., & Koppelman, F. S., 1979; Steenkamp, J. B. E., et al. 1994) and in preference-based perceptual mapping, the respondents base their choices based on specific preferred attributes (Hair, J.F., 1995; Carter, J. R. et al. 2008; Kuo et al. 2012). ***In the current study, authors applied perception-based perceptual mapping based on similarity judgment.*** The respondent evaluates the different brands of packaged spices based on similarity scores. The scores are designed so that 1 indicates the similarity and 10 implies the dissimilarity between the brands. The scores held from 1 to 10; the dissimilarity increases or vice-versa.

Once we fed the data into SPSS, it generated the aggregate spatial map, exhibiting the magnitude of proximity among the spices brands.

A spatial map depicts the similarities and dissimilarities between the brands based on the proximity level. It is conspicuous from the spatial map (Fig. 15.1) that MDH and Homefills brands of packaged spices are very similar in brand preference and fall in the first quadrant. However, the Everest brand tends to be near the first quadrant and the MDH and Homefills brand compared to Grihasthi. In the second quadrant, Bharat and Swadisht are the biggest brands in Odisha and are very similar. The Ruchi brand is very dissimilar to other brands of spices and falls in the third quadrant. The Grihasti brand falls in 4 quadrants and is considered less similar to the Everest brand due to lower proximity distance. The spatial map has two dimensions that explain the relationship between the packaged brands of spices. Dimension 1 is named quality and dimension two is named brand preference (The naming of the dimension solely depends upon the researcher's discretion). From the map, it is evident that MDH and Homfills score high in quality and preference. The second quadrant is occupied by Odisha's two biggest spice brands, i.e., Bharat and Swadisht. Both brands weigh high in consumer preference but lack in quality. They may be attributed to the fact that people prefer these two brands because of their low prices (MONDAL, S., DAS, S., MUSUNURU, K., & DASH, M., 2017) and intensive distribution in Bhubaneswar compared to other national brands. The third quadrant contains the Ruchi brand, which neither scores reasonably in quality nor preference. The last quadrant consists of Grihasthi and Everest brands of packaged spices. The two brands score fairly in terms of quality but are less preferred by consumers. As far as Grihasthi is concerned, this brand is costly and available in selected outlets in

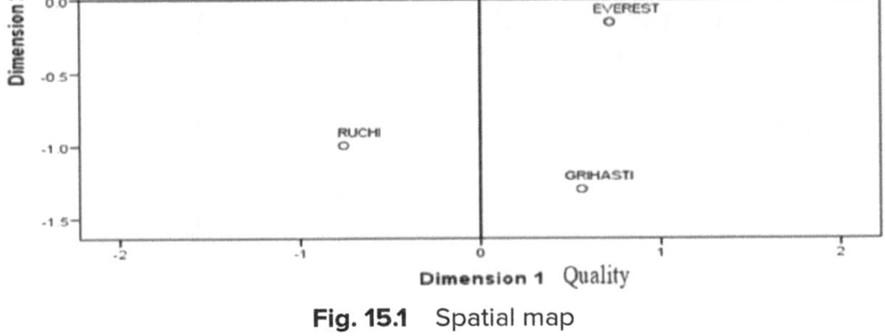

Fig. 15.1 Spatial map

Source: Author's Data Analysis

Odisha. It's not prominently available like other national and regional brands of packaged spices, even though it is the biggest spice brand in Rourkela, Odisha.

The other multivariate technique used in the study is correspondence analysis. The CA (correspondence analysis) is capitalized mostly in the food industry (Bécue-Bertaut, M. et al. 2008; Esti, M. et al. 2010). McEwan, J. A., & Schlich, P. (1991) successfully applied Correspondence Analysis during sensory evaluation of commercial strawberry fruit Jam. Many studies vouch that C.A. is effective in tackling sensory data because the data are categorical, and it generates two-dimensional solutions that aid the researcher in easily figuring out the differentiation between the dimensions. This technique makes it very easy to comprehend observations delineated in the graph. Greenacre, M.J., 1984 & 1992; Chau, T. 2001; Doey, L., & Kurta, J., 2011; Glynn, D., 2014 elucidated that this technique has certain advantages, first easy to interpret.

Secondly, allow the categorical and continuous variables to be represented simultaneously. The CA analysis makes a distinction between categories of variables. When the correlated variables are closer, the similarity between the points and dissimilarity are observed when the points are farther from each other. In Europe, local gastronomy is imperative to European cultural heritage. They fervently believed that fostering local food products gave rise to economic prosperity in the European region. Guerrero L. et al., 2010 and Vanhonacker F. et al., 2010 analyzed European consumers' perspicacity towards conventional food products in six different European regions. They applied the C.A. method to highlight the differences between regions. They found relevant information on concept maps of time-honoured food products, placement of products, innovation & new advancements in local cuisine. The results obtained using C.A. show the relationship between rows and columns. The result seized through C.A. affirms the association between rows and columns. In the graphical display of C.A., nearby variables connote the association between corresponding rows and columns (Greenacre, M. J., & Vrba, E. S., 1984). In the current study, the C.A. assist in mapping out the association between different brands of packaged spices and vital sensory and non-sensory attributes responsible for buying spices brand belonging to the *Garam Masala* category

Table 15.2 shows the line configurations. The configuration in the table corresponds to the percentage of each row over the total columns for which the comparison is performed, and the last row of the table is the mass, which implies the weightage of each attribute. *The table is vivid in that taste has 18.8% of the weightage among all the attributes, followed by the flavour and aroma of the packaged spices.* The column profile depicts that the brand with the highest mass is MDH (17%), followed by Everest (16.8%) and Homefills (15.9%).

Table 15.3 shows the relationship between the two variables, the number of dimensions required to represent this relationship graphically, and the proportion of variance accounted for each dimension. The singular value is the loading between

Table 15.2 Row & column profile

Brand	ATTRIBUTES (Row Profile)								
	Taste	Packag-ing	Flavour	Aroma	Shelf Life	Colour	Brand Trust	Healthy	Active Margin
Bharat	.199	.109	.176	.153	.070	.099	.099	.094	1.000
Grihasthi	.205	.098	.183	.152	.069	.102	.102	.089	1.000
Mdh	.183	.120	.154	.133	.064	.117	.144	.085	1.000
Everest	.191	.103	.159	.141	.070	.133	.116	.087	1.000
Ruchi	.210	.101	.182	.153	.072	.098	.098	.085	1.000
Homefills	.148	.154	.129	.133	.168	.080	.123	.066	1.000
Swadisht	.186	.100	.167	.155	.072	.110	.107	.103	1.000
Mass	.188	.114	.163	.145	.085	.106	.114	.086	
Brand	**ATTRIBUTES (Column Profile)**								
	Taste	**Packag-ing**	**Flavour**	**Aroma**	**Shelf Life**	**Colour**	**Brand Trust**	**Healthy**	**Mass**
Bharat	.144	.131	.147	.144	.113	.128	.118	.150	.136
Grihasthi	.133	.105	.138	.129	.099	.117	.109	.127	.122
Mdh	.165	.180	.161	.157	.128	.188	.214	.168	.170
Everest	.171	.152	.165	.164	.139	.211	.171	.171	.168
Ruchi	.169	.135	.169	.160	.128	.140	.130	.150	.151
Homefills	.125	.215	.125	.146	.314	.119	.171	.122	.159
Swadisht	.092	.082	.095	.100	.079	.096	.087	.111	.093
Active Margin	1.000	1.000	1.000	1.000	1.000	1.000	1.000	1.000	

Source: Author's Data Analysis

Table 15.3 Summary

Dimen-sion	Singular Value	Inertia	Chi Square	Sig.	Proportion of Inertia		Confidence Singular Value	
					Accounted for	Cumulative	Standard Deviation	Correlation 2
1	.252	.063			.760	.760	.017	.010
2	.179	.032			.204	.964	.015	
3	.070	.004			.029	.993		
4	.011	.000			.004	.997		
5	.009	.000			.003	1.000		
6	.002	.000			.000	1.000		
Total		.099	139.344	.000[a]	1.000	1.000		

a. 42 degrees of freedom

Source: Author's Data Analysis

the row and column variable. The inertia in the table is the square of singular value. The total inertia is .099. Here, the inertia is the relative measure of the chi-square value. The first dimension accounts for 76%, and the second dimension accounts for 20.4% of the total inertia of the model (Table 15.2). This connotes that both dimensions explain 96.4% of the inertia. The chi-square is used to test the null hypothesis. The p-value shown in the table is less than .05, which means the alternative hypothesis is accepted; hence, the two variables are correlated.

Table 15.4 furnishes information on each dimension and its contribution of each dimension to inertia. The Homefills contribute 83.8% of the total inertia of the first dimension. However, MDH contributes 39.7% to the total inertia of the second dimension. The first two dimensions interpret 99.7% of the total inertia in Homefills.

Table 15.4 Overview row points

BRAND	**Mass**	**Score in Dimension**		**Inertia**	**Contribution**				
					Of Point to Inertia of Dimension		**Of Dimension to Inertia of Point**		
		1	**2**		**1**	**2**	**1**	**2**	**Total**
Bharat	.134	-.145	.220	.001	.019	.082	.420	.500	.920
Grihasthi	.120	-.197	.288	.002	.031	.127	.466	.516	.982
MDH	.174	-.137	-.424	.003	.021	.397	.150	.743	.893
Everest	.172	-.213	-.271	.003	.052	.161	.447	.374	.821
Ruchi	.149	-.163	.349	.002	.026	.230	.291	.691	.982
Homefills	.158	.897	.001	.019	.838	.070	.978	.019	.997
Swadisht	.092	-.153	.048	.000	.014	.003	.719	.036	.755
Active Total	1.000			.030	1.000	1.000			
Overview Column points									
Attributes	**Mass**	**Score in Dimension**	**Inertia**	**Contribution**	**Of Point to Inertia of Dimension**	**Of Dimension to Inertia of Point**			
		1	**2**		**1**	**2**	**1**	**2**	**Total**
Taste	.185	-.235	.214	.002	.067	.108	.685	.296	.980
Packaging	.112	.403	-.093	.003	.119	.012	.918	.025	.943
Flavour	.160	-.233	.287	.002	.057	.168	.555	.438	**.993**
Aroma	.142	-.088	.234	.001	.007	.099	.195	.716	.911
Shelf Life	.083	1.089	.128	.015	.651	.017	.984	.007	.991
Colour	.104	-.283	-.277	.002	.055	.102	.588	.291	.879
Brand Trust	.113	.094	-.380	.002	.007	.206	.087	.732	.818
Healthy	.100	-.238	-.478	.003	.037	.288	.315	.660	.975
Active Total	1.000			.030	1.000	1.000			

Source: Author's Data Analysis

In the case of Table 15.4 (Overview of Column Profile), the shelf life contributes 65.1% of the total inertia of the first dimension, followed by healthiness, which contributes 28.8% of the total inertia in the second dimension. 97.5% of the total inertia in the attribute's health is interpreted by the first two dimensions in our model. To interpret the dimension, it's vital to examine the coordinates of the row and column points and the point's contribution to the dimension's inertia (Bendixen, M., 1996; Clausen, S. E., 1998).

Eventually, the bi-plot is the primary and essential tool of CA generated by SPSS output (Fig. 15.2). The association between a row category and a column category can be assessed based on the proximity of their profile point on the bi-plot. This means that the brand nearest to any attributes shows a stronger association than the brand, which is farther from the attributes. The distance between packaged spices brands and preferred attributes points in the graph below represent their correlation, i.e., with a relatively similar profile. From the biplot, it is evident that MDH and Everest brands of spices are highly correlated with colour, healthiness and brand trust. These attributes lie in proximity to the brand mentioned above. The Homefills lie in proximity to packaging and shelf life. The brands of Odisha, like Bharat, Ruchi, Grihasthi, and Swadisht, stand out in taste, aroma, and flavour. People prefer these brands because they enhance the flavour of the food, create a strong aroma, and impart flavour to the food.

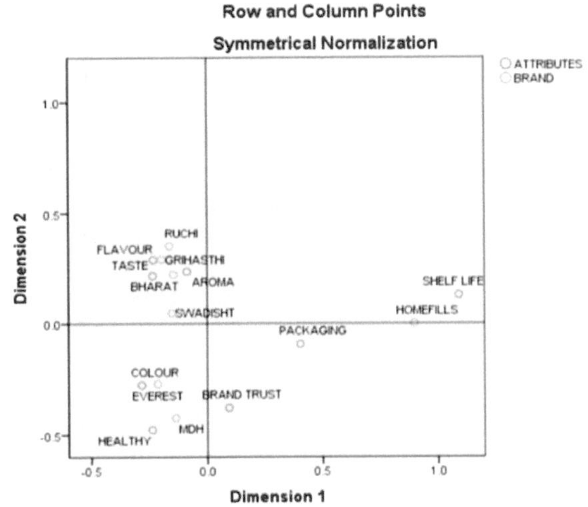

Fig. 15.2 Spatial map

Source: Author's Data Analysis

5. Discussion and Managerial Implication

The empirical properties of MDS and CA as tools are very effective in the sensory and non-sensory evaluation of packaged brands of spices. The findings of this study revealed that MDS and correspondence analysis are the appropriate techniques for demonstrating the similarity between brands and the association between brands and the preferred attributes. The correspondence analysis involves a compositional method and is easy to analyze due to its categorical and non-metric data (Beh, E. J., 2004). The study will be beneficial for the marketer in identifying the pertinent attributes that led to the purchase of packaged brands of spices. Both sensory, i.e. flavour, taste and aroma, and non-sensory attributes like brand trust, packaging, healthiness and shelf life, play a crucial role in the buying behaviour of spices. This leads to the product's success or failure. However, the packaging, shelf life, strong brand trust and perceived healthiness towards brands create a positive attitude in the minds of consumers (Wijaya, A. P., & Annisa, I. T., 2020); hence, people have a strong nexus with national brands of spices. The study aids marketers in identifying the gap between national and local brands of spices based on preferred attributes. This will motivate the marketers to create segments or clusters and craft strategies (Choudhury, M., Mishra, B. B., & Mohanty, P. K.; 2019), providing a competitive edge to the brands. Marketers must create value to gain profits and retain a customer base (Nudurupati, S. S., & et al., 2015). The marketer of the least preferred brand needs to adopt a few attributes like taste, aroma and flavour of Garam Masala to make that product preferable for consumers (Madhusmita C, Bidhu BM & Mohanty PK, 2019) over a period of time, which is one major decision factor for purchase of any product.

Aradwad, P. P., TV, A. K., Sahoo, P. K., & Mani, I. (2021) argued that marketers need to focus on the Quality aspects of spices closely related to processing techniques. Grinding is essential for spice processing, but extreme caution is required as heat generation can cause a significant drop in quality. Grinding is a simple unit operation, but it is related to harvesting parameters, machine parameters and pretreatment. Various techniques and methods are used when grinding spices. Among the improved grinding methods, cryogenic grinding has proven superior to grinding spices. It has several challenges, such as increased energy consumption, material stability, and cost savings. They can brand it as a cryogenic grinding spice brand to attract customers and should also design mechanisms for in-store promotion (Siddiqui, S., & Ali, T., 2021).

6. Limitation

The study has particular confinement. The sample chosen for the survey is purposive; hence, we cannot generalize the results. The potential research can use the theory of planned behaviour, which will be very effective in examining intentional behavioural relationships towards buying packaged branded spices. It has not been explicitly applied in this domain segment.

7. Funding

We have not received any funding for this research.

Reference

1. AL Consulting. (2020). Indian Spice Market- An Overview. Available at <http://www.acuityconsulting.co.in/wp-content/uploads/2020/09/Indian-Spice-Sector.pdf>. Accessed on 15th october 2022.
2. Afrad, M. S. I., & Akter, M. R. (2020). Growers' knowledge on spices cultivation in Shibganj upazila under Bogura district. *International Journal of Agricultural Research, Innovation and Technology (IJARIT), 10*(2355-2020-1367), 102–107.
3. Alam, M. N. E., Hosen, M. M., Ullah, A. K. M., Maksud, M. A., Khan, S. R., Lutfa, L. N., & Quraishi, S. B. (2023). Lead Exposure of Four Biologically Important Common Branded and Non-branded Spices: Relative Analysis and Health Implication. Biological Trace Element Research, 1–13.
4. Aradwad, P. P., TV, A. K., Sahoo, P. K., & Mani, I. (2021). Key issues and challenges in spice grinding. Cleaner Engineering and Technology, 5, 100347.
5. AZEMAR, J., BEICA, R., BUISSON, T., IVANCOVIC, A., & PIZZAGALLI, A. (2015). Embedded solutions: Fan-out and Embedded Dies Packages market and technology trends. Additional Papers and Presentations, 2015(DPC), 000182-000216.
6. Balasubramanian, S., Roselin, P., Singh, K. K., Zachariah, J., & Saxena, S. N. (2016). Postharvest processing and benefits of black pepper, coriander, cinnamon, fenugreek, and turmeric spices. Critical reviews in food science and nutrition, 56(10), 1585–1607.
7. Bécue-Bertaut, M., Alvarez-Esteban, R., & Pagès, J. (2008). Rating of products through scores and free-text assertions: Comparing and combining both. Food Quality and Preference, 19(1), 122–134.
8. Beh, E. J. (2004). Simple Correspondence Analysis: A Bibliographic Review. International Statistical Review / Revue Internationale de Statistique, 72(2), 257–284. http://www.jstor.org/stable/1403857.
9. Bhardwaj, R. K., Sikka, B. K., Singh, A., Sharma, M. L., Singh, N. K., & Arya, R. (2011, March). Challenges and constraints of marketing and export of Indian spices in India. In Proc. International conference on technology and business management (pp. 28–30).
10. Chadha, S. K., & Kapoor, D. (2008). An Attribute Based Perceptual Mapping of the Selected Private Life Insurance Companies: An Empirical Study in Ludhiana. Vision, 12(3), 53–60.
11. Chau, T. (2001). A review of analytical techniques for gait data. Part 1: fuzzy, statistical and fractal methods. Gait & posture, 13(1), 49–66.
12. Choudhury, M., Mishra, B. B., & Mohanty, P. K. (2019). An Empirical Study of Branding Strategy at Dealer point for Selling of Car-a qualitative & systematic Review of Literature [J]. *International Research Journal of Automotive Technology*, *2*(1), 1–26.
13. Das, A., & Sharangi, A. B. (2018). Post Harvest Technology and Value Addition of Spices. Indian Spices: The Legacy, Production and Processing of India's Treasured Export, 249–276.
14. DeSarbo, W.S., Grewal, R. and Scott, C.J. (2008). A clusterwise bilinear multidimensional scaling methodology for simultaneous segmentation and positioning analyses, Journal of Marketing Research, 45 (June), 280–92.
15. Dev, C., Morgan, M.S. and Shoemaker, S. (1995). A positioning analysis of hotel brands Cornell Hotel and Restaurant Administration Quarterly, 36 (6), 48–55.

16. Djiazet, S., Kenfack, L. B. M., Ngangoum, E. S., Ghomdim, H. N., & Tchiégang, C. (2022). Indigenous spices consumed in the food habits of the populations living in some countries of Sub-Saharan Africa: Utilisation value, nutritional and health potentials for the development of functional foods and drugs: A review. Food Research International, 111280.
17. Doey, L., & Kurta, J. (2011). Correspondence analysis applied to psychological research. Tutorials in quantitative methods for psychology, 7(1), 5–14.
18. Esti, M., Airola, R. L. G., Moneta, E., Paperaio, M., & Sinesio, F. (2010). Qualitative data analysis for an exploratory sensory study of grechetto wine. Analytica Chimica Acta, 660(1–2), 63–67.
19. Glynn, D. (2014). Correspondence analysis. Methods for Semantics: Quantitative Studies in Polysemy and Synonymy, 443–485.
20. Greenacre, M. (2017). Correspondence analysis in practice. chapman and hall/crc.
21. Greenacre, M. J. (1984). Theory and applications of correspondence analysis.
22. Greenacre, M. J., & Vrba, E. S. (1984). Graphical display and interpretation of antelope census data in African wildlife areas, using correspondence analysis. Ecology, 65(3), 984–997.
23. Greenacre, M.J. (1992), Correspondence Analysis in Medical Research, Statistical Methods in Medical Research, 1 (1), 97–117.
24. Guerrero, L., Claret, A., Verbeke, W., Enderli, G., Zakowska-Biemans, S., Vanhonacker, F., ... & Hersleth, M. (2010). Perception of traditional food products in six European regions using free word association. Food quality and preference, 21(2), 225–233.
25. Hair, J.F. (1995), Multivariate Data Analysis with Readings, 4th ed., Prentice-Hall, Englewood Cliffs, NJ.
26. Hauser, J. R., & Koppelman, F. S. (1979). Alternative perceptual mapping techniques: Relative accuracy and usefulness. Journal of marketing Research, 16(4), 495–506.
27. IBEF .(2022). Spcies Industry and Export in India. Available at <https://www.ibef.org/exports/spice-industry-indias>. Accessed on 15th October 2022.
28. Islam, M. S., Rahman, K. M., & Hasan, M. (2011). Profitability and resource use efficiency of producing major spices in Bangladesh. Bangladesh Journal of Agricultural Economics, 34(454-2016-36676), 1–13.
29. Jawaharlal, U., & Kumar, K. B. S. (2004). Branding Insurance: An Indian Perspective. Insurance Chronicle, 15–17.
30. JayaKumar, P.B. (2020). COVID-19 impact: Indian spices rise in demand for immunity properties, exports up 34% in June. Available at <https://www.businesstoday.in/latest/economy-politics/story/covid19-impact-indian-spices-in-demand-for-immunity-properties-exports-rise-34-percent-in-june-267498-2020-07-18>. Accessed on 15th October 2022.
31. Krishnadas, M. (2010). Production and export performance of major Indian spices-an economic analysis. M. Sc.(Agri.) Thesis, Univ. Agric. SCI., Dharwad, Karnataka (India).
32. Kuo, R. J., Akbaria, K., & Subroto, B. (2012). Application of particle swarm optimization and perceptual map to tourist market segmentation. Expert Systems with Applications, 39(10), 8726–8735.
33. Madhusmita C, Bidhu BM & Mohanty PK (2019)"Brand Equity & Brand preferences influencing the purchase decision: Developments and Directions" Synergy--ITS Journal of IT & Management, 16(2).

34. Mair, P. (2018). Multidimensional Scaling. In: Modern Psychometrics with R. Use R!. Springer, Cham. https://doi.org/10.1007/978-3-319-93177-7_9
35. Mair, P., de Leeuw, J., & Groenen, P. J. (2015). Multidimensional scaling in R: smacof. URL: https://cran. r-project. org/web/packages/smacof/vignettes/smacof. pdf.
36. McEwan, J. A., & Schlich, P. (1991). Correspondence analysis in sensory evaluation. Food Quality and Preference, 3(1), 23–36.
37. Mohan, S., Rajan, S. S., & Unnikrishnan, G. (2013). Marketing of Indian spices as a challenge in India. International Journal of Business and Management Invention, 2(2), 26–31.
38. MONDAL, S., DAS, S., MUSUNURU, K., & DASH, M. (2017). Study on the factors affecting customer purchase activity in retail stores by confirmatory factor analysis. Revista Espacios, 38(61).
39. Motoki, K., Nakahara, T., & Velasco, C. (2023). Tasting brands: Associations between brand personality and tastes. *Journal of Business Research*, *156*, 113509.
40. Nair, K.P. (2021). Technological Advancements in Coconut, Arecanut and Cocoa Research: A Century of Service to the Global Farming Community by the Central Plantation Crops Research Institute, Kasaragod, Kerala State, India. In: Tree Crops. Springer, Cham. https://doi.org/10.1007/978-3-030-62140-7_11
41. Ng, I. C., Nudurupati, S. S., & Tasker, P. (2010). Value co-creation in the delivery of outcome-based contracts for business-to-business service.
42. Noor, T., Begum, M., Ahmed, M. R., & Hossain, M. I. (2017). Consumers' Preference and Acceptance of Branded Spice Powder in Sadar Upazila of Mymensingh District in Bangladesh. Asian Journal of Agricultural Extension, Economics & Sociology, 19(4), 1–13. https://doi.org/10.9734/AJAEES/2017/35776
43. Nudurupati, S. S., Bhattacharya, A., Lascelles, D., & Caton, N. (2015). Strategic sourcing with multi-stakeholders through value co-creation: An evidence from global health care company. International Journal of Production Economics, 166, 248–257.
44. Rajanbabu, R. (2015). Production and trade performance of spices grown in India. International Journal of Commerce, Arts and Science, 6(9), 29–45.
45. Ramos, V. (2023). Food consumption, social class and taste in contemporary Portugal. Journal of Consumer Culture, 14695405221149114.
46. Reboredo-Rodríguez, P., Figueiredo-González, M., González-Barreiro, C., Simal-Gándara, J., Salvador, M. D., Cancho-Grande, B., & Fregapane, G. (2017). State of the art on functional virgin olive oils enriched with bioactive compounds and their properties. International Journal of Molecular Sciences, 18(3), 668.
47. Ross, I. (1979). An information processing theory of consumer choice. Journal of Marketing , Summer, 1979, Vol. 43, No. 3 (Summer, 1979), pp. 124–126
48. Siddiqui, S., & Ali, T. (2021). Impact of In-store Promotion and Shelf Placement on Sales & Profit of Condiment Category in Food Industry of Pakistan. International Journal of Health and Economic Development, 7(1), 37–49.
49. Sharangi, A. B., & Pandit, M. K. (2018). Supply chain and marketing of spices. Indian Spices: The Legacy, Production and Processing of India's Treasured Export, 341–357.
50. Steenkamp, J. B. E., Van Trijp, H. C., & Berge, J. M. T. (1994). Perceptual mapping based on idiosyncratic sets of attributes. Journal of Marketing Research, 31(1), 15–27.

51. Suja Sundram, M., & Abubshait, F. A. A. (2023). A Study on Customer Satisfaction towards Masala Products in Shri Kannan Departmental Stores, Coimbatore. Journal of Pharmaceutical Negative Results, 1843–1849.
52. Tongco, M. D. C. (2007). Purposive sampling as a tool for informant selection.
53. Vanhonacker, F., Verbeke, W., Guerrero, L., Claret, A., Contel, M., Scalvedi, L., & Hersleth, M. (2010). How European consumers define the concept of traditional food: Evidence from a survey in six countries. Agribusiness, 26(4), 453–476.
54. Varadharaj, S., & Prakash, A. R. (2018). An Analytical Study on the Production and the Growth Trends of Spices in India. International Journal of Research and Analytical Reviews, 5(3), 227–281.
55. Wijaya, A. P., & Annisa, I. T. (2020). The influence of brand image, brand trust and product packaging information on purchasing decisions. *Jurnal Analisis Bisnis Ekonomi*, *18*(1), 24–35.
56. Zielke, S., & Dobbelstein, T. (2007). Customers' willingness to purchase new store brands. Journal of Product & Brand Management.

Securing the Future through Sustainability, Health, Education, and Technology – Brig. Dr. Rajiv Divekar et al. (eds)

16 Servicification and Contribution of Service Exports to Manufacturing Exports: From the Indian Context

Shrimoyee Mukherjee[1]
Research Assistant,
Symbiosis Institute of Management Studies,
Pune, Maharashtra

Brig. Rajiv Divekar[2]
Director,
Symbiosis Institute of Management Studies,
Pune, Maharashtra

Pravin Kumar Bhoyar[3]
Deputy Director,
Symbiosis Institute of Management Studies,
Pune, Maharashtra

ABSTRACT

The paper studies the results of service exports on manufacturing exports and if services exports can encourage servicification in manufacturing exports in India, given India's recognition for its services industry. There is an upsurge in the corroboration of the servicification of the manufacturing industry since services effectively overcome informal barriers, encouraging trade. Using data for industrial and service exports from 1982 to 2021, we investigate the influence of service exports, FDI inflows, foreign income, and real effective exchange rate on manufacturing exports using time series data. The results implicate a positive relationship between service exports and manufacturing exports, leading to an increased servicification in manufacturing exports. There is also a positive effect of foreign income on manufacturing exports. However, the results show negative effects of real effective exchange rate and FDI inflows to manufacturing exports.

KEYWORDS: Servicification, Service exports, Manufacturing exports, FDI inflows, REER.

[1]shrimoyeemukherjee99@gmail.com, [2]director@sims.edu, [3]deputydirector@sims.edu

DOI: 10.1201/9781003587200-16

1. Introduction

1.1 Background

In terms of output and employment, services are constantly improving. In 2021, the contribution of offers to the global GDP was 64.4%, while the contribution to the Indian GDP was more significant than 50%. The "deindustrialization-tertiarization phenomenon," sometimes known as the move from manufacturing to services, is not permanently restricted to advanced economies. Numerous studies have noted that many emerging nations are also transitioning to a financial system centered on services (Felipe & Mehta, 2016). Some have deemed deindustrialization " untimely " because manufacturing has not yet reached its full potential (Rodrik, 2016). The deindustrialization of economies worldwide under the false assumption that manufacturing promotes growth creates concerns about the importance of services unjustly. The rising fragmentation of production, where work may be outsourced to other industries nationally or globally, must be considered in the sectoral approach to assessing output. Without adding new value-added services, this practice could boost the output of services. Nayyar, 2010; Hallward-Driemeier & Nayyar, 2018). Because of technological advancements, several services now possess qualities that were formerly exclusive to manufacturing. This advancement has allowed trade and distribution services to a larger market. Today, a sizable portion of service exports are accounted for by manufacturing companies. Services make up over 50% of the EU and US's gross exports when the value- added to manufacturing is considered (OECD, 2014).

1.2 Servicification of Manufacturing

The "servicification" of manufacturing is the division of production into services like advertising and marketing, logistics, and research. This has led to an improvement in productivity, performance, and global competitiveness. Exports of services are categorized as "embodied" or "embodied," with the provision of patron care with the sale of a selected product falling under the primary category of provider export. In today's time, a convolution of profound linkage of services with the different production phases exists, with services associated with goods and utilizing services to produce goods together obscuring the goods and services mix.

The symbiotic link between commodities and services is due to the production process gradually shifting to service-oriented. An example of this is the shift from CD production to digital distribution of songs in the operation of the music business, reclassifying from a "good generation" to a "service generation." An example of this is when an automaker divides its leasing and car repair operations, where the effectiveness and durability of the service and leasing units depend on the amount of automotive sales.

1.3 Arguments for Servicification

a. Through logistics, management, or engineering services that conserve resources, improve collaboration, and keep time and materials, benefits may also help businesses become more effective.
b. Companies may differentiate their offerings in the face of more aggressive foreign competition by tying offerings to specific products, packaging them with other goods, or pricing them following manufacturer sales.
c. Services are utilised in manufacturing to help overcome market entrance barriers for both investing and exporting. Using legal services to comply with rules is one example.

1.4 Servicification and Service Exports

Servicification, a process in which the value chain of a manufacturing business increasingly depends on services and service exports, the export of services to foreign nations, are closely related concepts. Manufacturing companies typically create material items like automobiles, computers, and appliances. However, manufacturing companies increasingly depend on services to support their core activities for the uprising significance of services in the global economy. Servicification is the term for this action. A manufacturing company can employ services in many parts of the value chain, including design, marketing, logistics, and after-sales services. On the other side, service exports entail the supply and selling of services across international borders. Several distribution methods, including direct sales, licensing, franchising, and through overseas affiliates, are available for service exports. Consultancy, financial, transport, and information technology services are a few examples of service exports.

The relationship between servicification and service exports is that manufacturing companies may export more services as they become more service-intensive, so services may be provided to clients in other nations using the skills and talents created via service. For instance, a manufacturing company that has become an expert in logistics services would also be able to provide similar services to clients abroad. Similarly, a company that has acquired competence in after-sales services could provide similar services to clients abroad via foreign affiliates or licensing arrangements. In conclusion, servicification relates to service exports because servicification can develop service capabilities to deliver services to clients in other countries, increasing the possibility that manufacturing businesses would export services.

1.5 Contribution of Service Exports to Manufacturing Exports

In the current global economy, the growing integration of services with manufacturing operations can significantly boost manufacturing exports through service exports. Through various services such as transportation, logistics, marketing, design, engineering, research and development, and after-sales support, service exports may supplement and improve the productivity and competitiveness of manufacturing exports. For instance, a producer could export a product that requires specialized installation or maintenance services. A service exporter could offer these services and increase the value of the manufacturer's goods by making it more competitive in the world market. A factory may also require logistics and transportation services to deliver goods to foreign markets, market research and analysis services to find new export markets. These essential services may be delivered through service exports, helping enterprises compete more successfully on the global market. Additionally, the importance of services in assisting the production process grows as manufacturing gets more automated and technologically advanced. Artificial intelligence, data analytics, and other services can boost the effectiveness and productivity of industrial operations. Policymakers and companies should be aware of and take advantage of this strategic link between services and manufacturing since service exports may significantly contribute to the competitiveness and growth of manufacturing exports.

1.6 Trends and Issues in the Indian Context

The immanent propensity of manufacturing sectors to promote humongous employment and inclusive growth provides the critical driver for the nation's growth. The growing trend of "servicification" involves manufacturing companies increasingly incorporating service-related activities into their operations, which enhances the overall capability of these companies in their primary manufacturing operations. Recently, the contribution of Indian manufacturing to its GDP has been around 16-17%. On the contrary, Indian services contribute over 50% to its GDP, with a 22.8% increase in the net export of services. The Reserve Bank of India (RBI) reports that service exports have significantly boosted India's total exports, including industrial exports. India's overall service exports in the fiscal year 2020–2021 were valued at USD 183.05 billion, while its product exports (including manufactured goods exports) were worth USD 290.63 billion. It indicates that more than 37% of India's total exports were in the form of services. The Ministry of Commerce and Industry demonstrates that the percentage of services in India's overall manufacturing exports has been continuously rising over the years, notably in terms of contributing service exports to manufacturing exports. Services contributed 5.6% of manufactured exports from India in 2015–16, rising to 7.6% in 2019–20.

Service exports also contribute to some manufacturing sectors in India. For instance, the engineering goods sector—which includes machinery, electrical equipment, and transportation equipment—is significantly reliant on service exports, according to research by the Confederation of Indian Industry (CII). The research claims that various services, including design and engineering, testing and certification, logistics, and shipping, are needed to export engineering goods. Service exports comprise between 15% and 20% of this industry. Similarly, India's primary industrial sector, the pharmaceutical industry, relies on exports of services like clinical research, regulatory services, and intellectual property services. According to the statistics, Services exports contribute considerably to India's industrial exports. This contribution is anticipated to increase as services link to manufacturing processes.

1.7 Effects of Service Exports on Servicification in Manufacturing Exports in the Indian Context

Data on the share of services in the manufacturing sector's value-added and the percentage of service exports in total exports are used to assess the impact of service exports on manufacturing export servicification. In the Indian context, the proportion of services in the manufacturing sector's value-added has steadily increased. The Reserve Bank of India's statistics show that between 2000 and 2019, the value-added of services climbed from 17.7% to 24.9% in the industrial sector.

The proportion of service exports in overall exports has also been rising concurrently. The Ministry of Commerce and Industry's figures show that the percentage of service exports in overall exports rose from 14.1% in 2010–11 to 20.6% in 2019-20. It shows that India's manufacturing exports have become servicified due to service exports. Manufacturers include more services in their manufacturing processes as service exports rise to compete in international markets. It may result in a move towards more knowledge-intensive, high-value manufacturing operations, strengthening the benefits of service exports on manufacturing exports.

2. Review of Literature

Manufacturing Companies are increasingly exporting alternative or supplementary services in addition to their products. This servicification strategy enables businesses to stay competitive in global markets by offering customers value-added solutions rather than just products. Exporting groups employ services for pre-access and post-entry concerns to maintain their position in the export market. However, the use of services in manufacturing has received little attention in the literature on business exports.

To overcome access barriers, producing companies use services like market research and R&D. They use marketing and distribution services to survive in the market. Businesses looking to expand into international markets should spend in sunk costs to learn about the laws and policies governing the export of their products, conduct market research, set up distribution systems, and modify their products for the target market.

Sunk costs influence exporting behavior in subsequent years after they are incurred, leading to persistence (Roberts & Tybout, 1997). Additionally, the variable costs for business contracts, demand management, transportation, and items are significantly greater for exporting organizations. Additionally, Egger (2008) states that transaction costs rise with distance. Therefore, companies that export are likely to outperform non-exporters inside the organization in terms of productivity (Bernard et al., 2003; Melitz, 2003; Wagner, 2012). Furthermore, Exporters and non-exporters differ in size, productivity, and capital intensity. (Bernard and Jensen, 1995, 1999; Bernard et al., 2007).

Due to how crucial productivity is for exporting enterprises, productivity has been used as a benchmark in numerous studies to evaluate a company's self-choice toward exporting. It is feasible that productivity will be consciously increased through R&D whenever a company decides to export (Alvarez & Rago, 2005). In order to increase productivity even more, the exporting company continues to provide a competitive product for international markets (Pattnayak & Thangavelu, 2014; Aw & Hwang, 1995). Globally oriented high-tech enterprises report higher productivity benefits from R&D than local high-tech firms. (Bhattacharya et al., 2021).

Exports, like productivity, may be boosted by leveraging lower-cost imported supplier inputs and increasing exporter revenues. (Bas & Strauss-Kahn, 2014). Groups can effectively differentiate their products through production by employing offerings. They can also overcome unauthorized barriers to reaching the front (Lodefalk, 2014). Establishing early contacts with translators, interpreters, and mediators can overcome many linguistic and cultural obstacles.

Businesses can also influence product demand by disseminating information and utilizing marketing and advertising strategies. Offerings for tracking, liaison, and law can help maintain business ties and reduce ambiguity regarding governmental policy. According to Hatzigeorgiou and Lodefalk (2014), hiring migrants and using consulting services can lower the cost of learning about markets in faraway locations.

According to Sundin et al. (2009) and Kelle (2013), servicification can promote product differentiation, boost competitive advantage, and increase agency productivity, enabling businesses to advance up the value chain. Engineering, managerial, and logistics services can help manufacturing companies save time and resources (Nord, 2010). Production companies may utilize computer programmers, mathematicians, and engineers to increase their ability to absorb technology (Cohen & Levinthal, 1990; Pilat and Wol € in, 2005). By investing in R&D and data processing services, organizations may develop and sustain global manufacturing networks and cost chains. (Golub et al., 2007; Debaere et al., 2013).

Manufacturing businesses are "servicing built-ing" their products by increasing the built-ings integrated they offer, adding sensors, and providing built-integrated services to customers directly. According to Lodefalk (2013), commercial service exports from the Nations to Sweden rose between 1998 and 2006. This built-in assistance by British built-in integrated organizations changed their name from built-in integrated matters to built-integrated (Brebuilt- Erlich et al., 2018). According to Crozet and Milet (2017), after-sale built-in has a favorable impact on the productivity of French manufacturers. The outcome is that manufacturers and distributors provide built-in products on domestic and international marketplaces.

3. Objective of Research

The research aims to find the outcome of servicification on manufacturing exports for the Indian context from 1982 to 2021. The service has increased since India participated in global value chains, and the service exports have gradually increased. The connection between servicification and service exports is that as manufacturing firms become more service- intensive, they may also become more likely to export services. In addition, service exports affect manufacturing exports. Henceforth, servicification can lead to the development of service capabilities that can be applied to provide services to customers in other countries, thereby increasing the likelihood of manufacturers' service exports.

4. Data and Methodology

4.1 Data and Variable

I gathered country-level data collected from the World Bank open database. The Development Data Group manages numerous macro, financial, and sector databases while coordinating statistical and data activities within the World Bank. During my research, I examined information on India's exports of goods and manufactured goods, services, net foreign direct investment, foreign income, real effective exchange rate, and consumer price index during the 40 years between 1982 and 2021. I used the data for transport services; travel services; insurance and financial services; communication, and computer services from the World Bank open database. The rationale behind selecting such variables is their ostensible relationship to manufacturing exports, manufacturing exports related to service exports, foreign direct investment inflows, real effective exchange rate, and foreign income. Exports of services are crucial in sustaining and advancing exports of goods. By examining service exports, we can understand the kinds of services and their exports to support manufacturing industries. We can also find ways to increase the value-added services that support manufacturing, encourage exports of manufactured goods, and discover potential trade opportunities. FDI inflows can significantly affect a nation's exports of manufactured goods. The advantages of FDI in manufacturing include increased production capacity, the introduction of new technologies and management practices, the development of marketing and distribution networks, an increase in the amount of capital available, and assistance with employment and skill development for the local workforce. Foreign income may boost the country's balance of payments, stimulate the expansion of the manufacturing industry, have a multiplier impact on the local economy, encourage internationalization, and improve residents' living standards. When analyzing manufacturing exports, the real effective exchange rate is crucial to take into account because it has an impact on a nation's ability to compete internationally, the price of imported inputs, the success of domestic manufacturers, foreign investment in the manufacturing industry, and the confidence of consumers and investors in the overall economy. I also utilized the data of transport services; travel services; insurance and financial services; communication, and computer services to look at the effect of each service on the manufacturing exports. I cleaned the data by eliminating observations with missing or negative values. I chose the period to demonstrate the effect of the economic crisis of the 1980s due to fiscal imbalances on servicification and manufacturing exports to the present how it is working. The final dataset was time-series data.

4.2 Empirical Strategy

The dependent variable in my study is the Indian manufacturing exports adjusted to inflation (xm) while considering Indian service exports adjusted to inflation (xs), net foreign direct investment inflow (fdi), real effective exchange rate (reer) and world income as (yf) as independent variable. Figure 16.1 depicts the descriptive statistics.

Variable	Obs	Mean	Std. dev.	Min	Max
xm	41	8.60e+08	4.32e+08	3.47e+08	1.70e+09
xs	41	6.16e+08	4.59e+08	1.64e+08	1.32e+09
reer	41	40.27432	29.89101	5.680152	107.136
yf	41	6766.573	3085.957	2522.348	12236.62
fdi	41	.9920383	.9048769	.002584	3.620522

Variable	Obs	Mean	Std. dev.	Min	Max
TRP	41	7.75e+07	4.46e+07	3.23e+07	1.63e+08
TRV	41	9.84e+07	4.08e+07	4.50e+07	1.79e+08
FIN	41	2.62e+07	2.61e+07	2762806	8.11e+07
COM	41	3.99e+08	3.40e+08	4.98e+07	9.51e+08

Fig. 16.1 Summary of descriptive statistics

Source: Made by the author

The mean of Indian manufacturing exports (xm) is around 860 million USD, while the mean service exports (xs) is around 616 million USD. While looking into other services, the transport service (TRP) accounts for 77.5 million USD on average, and the travel service (TRV) accounts for 98.4 million USD on average. Furthermore, the financial and insurance service (FIN) accounts for 26.2 million USD on average in 41 years, while the mean of communication and computer services (COM) accounts for 39.9 million USD from 1982-2021. The share for traveling services is higher on average compared to the other three services mentioned earlier. The average foreign income in the given period is 6766.573 USD. The regression model is as follows:

$$(XM) = \beta 0 + \beta 1\ (XS) + \beta 2\ YF + \beta 3\ FDI + \beta 4\ REER + ui$$

where, XM is the Indian manufacturing exports, XS is the Indian service exports, YF depicts the foreign income given by world GDP per capita, REER is the Indian real effective exchange rate and ui is the error term. According to the literature analysis, servicification may play a key role in the firm's manufacturing exports. As a result, the empirical model calculates the conditional likelihood of a firm's manufacturing based on service exports, foreign direct investment inflows, the real effective exchange rate, and foreign income.

4.3 Methodology

I estimated the long-run coefficient of the model by using the Auto-Regressive Distributed Lag (ARDL) model in the EViews statistical software. The ARDL model is a regression model used to analyze the long-run relationships between variables when the variables are non-stationary.

The general form of the ARDL model is:

$$\Delta Yt = \alpha 0 + \alpha 1 Yt - 1 + \beta 1 \Delta X1t + \beta 2 \Delta X2t + \ldots + \beta k \Delta Xkt + \varepsilon t$$

where, ΔYt = the first difference of the dependent variable at time t, Yt-1 = the lagged value of the dependent variable, $\Delta X1t$, $\Delta X2t$, ..., ΔXkt = the first differences of the k independent variables at time t, $\alpha 0$ = the intercept, $\alpha 1$ = the coefficient of the lagged dependent variable, $\beta 1$, $\beta 2$, ..., βk = the coefficients of the first differences of the independent variables, εt = the error term at time t.

My research models stand as

$$XM = \chi 0 + \beta 1\ XS + \beta 2\ YF + \beta 3\ FDI + \beta 4\ REER + ui \quad (1)$$

$$XM = \beta 0 + \beta 1\ TRS + \beta 2\ YF + \beta 3\ FDI + \beta 4\ REER + ui \quad (2)$$

$$XM = \beta 0 + \beta 1\ TVS + \beta 2\ YF + \beta 3\ FDI + \beta 4\ REER + ui \quad (3)$$

$$XM = \beta 0 + \beta 1\ FIN + \beta 2\ YF + \beta 3\ FDI + \beta 4\ REER + ui \quad (4)$$

$$XM = \beta 0 + \beta 1\ CCS + \beta 2\ YF + \beta 3\ FDI + \beta 4\ REER + ui \quad (5)$$

where, XM is the Indian manufacturing exports, XS is the Indian service exports, YF depicts the foreign income given by world GDP per capita, REER is the Indian real effective exchange rate and FDI is the foreign direct investment inflows. Also, TRS represents transport services, TVS represents travel services, FIN is the finance and insurance services, and CCS id the computer and communication services.

The first equation gives the statistical relation between the Indian manufacturing exports with the Indian service exports, foreign direct investment inflow, real effective exchange rate, and foreign income. Equation (2) provides the relation between the Indian manufacturing exports with the Indian transport service exports, foreign direct investment inflow, real effective exchange rate, and foreign income. The third equation deals with the relationship between Indian manufacturing exports, Indian travel service exports, foreign direct investment inflow, real effective exchange rate, and foreign income. Equation (4) deals with the relationship between Indian manufacturing exports with the Indian finance and insurance service exports, foreign direct investment inflow, real effective exchange rate, and foreign income. Lastly, equation (5) gives the relation between the Indian manufacturing exports with the Indian computer and communication service exports, foreign direct investment inflow, real effective exchange rate, and foreign income. Lastly, I selected the model on the basis of the R-bar squared criterion.

5. Results and Analysis

I outlined the estimation findings in the appendix tables based on the specified model in the methodology. The absolute t-value of the model for every of the variable is greater than 2 and hence the model is statistically significant. However, the t-value for fdi variable is less than 2 and hence proving its statistical insignificance of the model. Table A16.1 from the appendix shows that Indian service exports have a positive coefficient (0.31679) in the long-run. Thus, with 1% increase in service exports, the manufacturing exports is increased by 0.31% in the long-run.

The other services, namely transport, travel, finance, insurance, and computer and communication services, also have positive and statistically significant coefficients in the long-run. Hence, a positive coefficient shows a positive association between the dependent and independent variables. A positive correlation exists between manufacturing exports and service exports and other services. The positive association between service exports and manufacturing exports can be because of access to high-quality value-added inputs, innovation, and internationalization that service exports bring to the manufacturing process. Table A16.2 from the appendix concludes that the share of travel services to manufacturing exports is more prominent than other services mentioned earlier (refer to Table A16.3, A16.4, A16.5 from the appendix).

A positive and significant coefficient exists for the foreign income when performing regression of manufacturing exports on service exports and other services, according to the tables in the appendix. Hence foreign income is positively related to manufacturing exports. When foreign income increases, it typically leads to an increase in demand for exports, including manufactured goods and services. As consumers in other countries become wealthier, they have more purchasing power to buy goods and services from abroad, including manufactured goods. Also, when foreign income increases, it can invest more in research and development, technology, and infrastructure, improving the quality and competitiveness of its manufactured goods and services. It can help to attract more buyers, increasing demand for the country's exports.

However, the tables in the appendix show that the real effective exchange rate has a negative and statistically significant coefficient, leading to a negative relationship between manufacturing exports and the REER. When a country's REER rises, its exports become more expensive for international buyers, resulting in lower demand. On the other hand, if the REER depreciates, its exports become relatively cheaper for foreign buyers, increasing demand. Therefore, a lower REER can improve a country's competitiveness in international markets and increase manufacturing and service exports.

For the foreign direct investment inflows, an unclear result exists on its coefficient estimation in the regression of manufacturing exports. Regression of manufacturing exports on travel services provides positive and statistically significant coefficients depicting their positive relationship. In comparison, another regression analysis of manufacturing exports gives negative and statistically significant coefficients that depict a negative relationship. The positive impact on a country's manufacturing exports is increasing production capacity, improving technology and managerial practices, and improving infrastructure. These factors can enhance the quality and quantity of manufactured goods, making them more competitive in the international market while increasing exports. The potential adverse effect could be caused by the crowding out of domestic investments in the manufacturing sector due to foreign direct investment inflows, volatility, and dependency on technology.

Recent studies in India show a positive effect of service exports on manufacturing exports. The uptrend of service exports and their contribution to the growth of the manufacturing sector is mainly due to the IT sector. India has a robust information technology (IT) sector that provides services such as software development, knowledge process outsourcing (KPO), and business process outsourcing (BPO). These services are often complementary to the manufacturing sector, as they can enhance the value of manufactured products by providing after-sales services or technical support. The IT sector in India has also provided support services such as logistics, legal, and financial services to manufacturers, helping them to enter new markets and navigate the complexities of international trade. Foreign income can have a significantly better effect on manufacturing exports in India. When the demand for Indian manufactured goods increases in foreign countries, Indian manufacturers can produce more and export more, increasing manufacturing exports. Hence, India increased its service exports and maintained a good relationship between service exports and manufacturing exports. This is noticeable in the current economic conditions.

6. Conclusion

The increase in service exports in India between 1982 and 2021 led to an increase in manufacturing exports, as evidenced by the positive link between service and manufacturing exports. According to the Economic Survey 2021, the share of services in the manufacturing sector's value-added expanded at a compound annual growth rate (CAGR) of 7.2% from 2000-01 to 2019-20. Additionally, there is a negative correlation between manufacturing exports and the real effective exchange rate and a positive correlation between manufacturing exports and foreign income. As foreign income increases, so does demand for commodities, particularly manufactured goods from India. According to figures from the Reserve Bank of India, India's overall merchandise exports climbed from USD 275 billion in 2016–17 to USD 330 billion in 2018–19, while foreign income increased from USD 82.2 billion in 2016–17 to USD 103.1 billion in 2018–19. A higher real effective exchange rate (REER) has been found to have a detrimental influence on India's exports of manufactured products. The rupee's appreciation against other currencies means that purchasing Indian goods abroad will become more expensive. Less demand for products made in India could come from this, which would be detrimental to the export of manufactured goods. Empirical studies provide support for the inverse relationship between REER and India's industrial exports. For example, study by Sinha and Sinha (2017) found that a 1% increase in REER results in a 0.15 percent decrease in India's industrial exports. Similar to the above, Ahmad and Khan (2018) demonstrated in a different study that manufacturing exports decrease by 0.43% for every 1% increase in the value of the Indian rupee. Additionally, there is a bad correlation between FDI inflow and exports of manufactured goods. While FDI inflows positively affect India's overall exports, research by Kumar and Raut (2018) indicates that they hurt exports of manufactured goods. They argue that this negative effect is due to the fact that a substantial portion of FDI inflows into India are concentrated in the services sector, which may drive out the manufacturing sector. It is evident from the theoretical reviews that a rise in service exports leads to an increase in the servicification of industrial exports. Services now make up 41.5% of all exports from India, up from 36.3% in 2015–16. Over the same period, India's manufacturing export share decreased from 72.2% to 69.7%. Despite this, the value-added services included in manufactured goods exports increased after this decrease. This shows that, as services are more included in exports of manufactured items, manufacturing is getting more and more servicified. These trends suggest a positive relationship between India's servicification of manufacturing exports and service exports.

REFERENCES

1. Alvarez, R., Rago, R.L., 2005. Exporting and performance: evidence from Chilean plants. Can. J. Econ. 38 (4), 1384–1400.
2. Aw, B.Y., Hwang, A.R., 1995. Productivity and export Market: a firm-level analysis. J. Dev. Econ. 47 (2), 313–332.
3. Bas, M., Strauss-Kahn, V., 2014. Does importing more inputs raise exports? Firm-level evidence from France. Rev. World Econ. 150, 241–275.
4. Bernard, A.B., Jensen, J.B., 1995. Exporters, jobs, and wages in U.S. manufacturing: 1976–1987. Brookings Pap. Econ. Act. Microecon. 67–112.
5. Bernard, A.B., Jensen, J.B., 1999. Exceptional exporter performance: cause, effect, or both? J. Int. Econ. 47 (1), 1–25.

6. Bernard, A.B., Jensen, J.B., Redding, S.J., Kortum, S., 2003. Plants and productivity in international trade. Am. Econ. Rev. 93 (4), 1268–1290.
7. Bernard, A.B., Jensen, J.B., Redding, S.J., Schott, P.K., 2007. Firms in international trade. J. Econ. Perspect. 21 (3), 105–130.
8. Bhattacharya, M., Okafor, L.M., Pradeep, V., 2021. International firm activities, R&D, and productivity: evidence from Indian manufacturing firms. Econ. Modell. 97, 1–13.
9. Breinlich, H., Soderbery, A., Wright, G.C., 2018. From selling goods to selling services: firm responses to trade liberalization. Am. Econ. J. Econ. Pol. 10 (4), 79–108.
10. Cohen, W.M., Levinthal, D.A., 1990. Absorptive capacity—a new perspective on learning and innovation. Adm. Sci. Q. 35 (1), 128–152.
11. Crozet, M., Milet, E., 2017. Should everybody be in services? The effect of servitization on manufacturing firm performance. J Econ Mgt Str 26 (4), 820–841.
12. Debaere, P., Gorg, H., Raff, H., 2013. Greasing the wheels of international commerce: how € services facilitate firms' international sourcing. Can. J. Econ. 46 (1), 78–102.
13 Egger, P., 2008. On the role of distance for bilateral trade. World Econ. 31 (5), 653–662.
14 Felipe, J., and Mehta, A. (2016). Deindustrialization? A global perspective. Economics Letters, 149(C), 148–151. doi:10.1016/j.econlet.2016.10.038
15 Golub, S.S., Jones, R.W., Kierzkowski, H., 2007. Globalization and country-specific service links. J Econ Pol Reform 10 (2), 63–68.
16. Hallward-Driemeier, M., and Nayyar, G. (2018). Trouble in the Making? The Future of Manufacturing- Led Development. Washington D.C.: The World Bank.
17. Hatzigeorgiou, A., Lodefalk, M., 2014. Trade, migration and integration – evidence and policy implications. World Econ. 38 (12), 2013–2048.
18. Kelle, M., 2013. Crossing industry borders: German manufacturers as services exporters. World Econ. 36 (12), 1494–1515.
19. Lodefalk, M., 2013. Servicification of manufacturing- evidence from Sweden. Int. J. Econ. Bus. Res. 6 (1), 87–113.
20. Lodefalk, M., 2014. The role of services for manufacturing firm exports. Rev. World Econ. 150, 59–82.
21. Melitz, M.J., 2003. The impact of trade on intra-industry reallocations and aggregate industry productivity. Econometrica 71 (6), 1695–1725.
22. Miroudot, S., and Cadestin, C. (2017). Services In Global Value Chains: From Inputs to Value-Creating Activities (Vol. OECD Trade Policy Papers No. 197): OECD Publishing.
23. Nayyar, G. (2010). Growth of the services sector in India: Notional or real? Economics Bulletin, 30(4), 3282–3287.
24. Nordås, H., 2010. Trade in goods and services: two sides of the same coin? Econ. Modell. 27 (2), 496– 506.
25. Pattnayak, S.S., Thangavelu, S.M., 2014. Productivity and learning by exporting: a firmlevel analysis of Indian manufacturing. World Econ. 37 (7), 1016–1026.
26. Pilat, D., Wol € fl, A., 2005. Measuring the Interaction between Manufacturing and Services. OECD Science, Technology and Industry Working Papers, 2005/05. OECD Publishing.
27. Roberts, M.J., Tybout, J.R., 1997. The decision to export in Columbia: an empirical model of entry with sunk costs. Am. Econ. Rev. 87 (4), 545–564.

28. Rodrik, D. (2016). Premature deindustrialization. Journal of Economic Growth, 21(1), 1–33. doi:10.1007/s10887-015-9122-3
29. Sundin, E., Lindahl, M., Comstock, M., Sakao, T., Shimomura, Y., 2009. Achieving mass customization through servicification. J Internet Manufac Serv 2, 56–75.
30. Wagner, J., 2012. International trade and firm performance: a survey of empirical studies since 2006. Rev. World Econ. 148 (2), 235–267.

Appendix

Table A16.1 ARDL regression summary of manufacturing exports on service exports

Estimated Long Run Coefficients using the ARDL Approach
ARDL(1,0,1,1,1) selected based on R-BAR Squared Criterion

Dependent variable is MEXP
40 observations used for estimation from 1982 to 2021

Regressor	Coefficient	Standard Error	T-Ratio[Prob]
LSER	.31679	.048336	6.5540[.000]
WPY	1.0688	.11962	8.9345[.000]
FDI	-.036610	.020687	-1.7697[.087]
RER	-.0025478	.5246E-3	-4.8567[.000]
C	2.2439	.55106	4.0720[.000]

Table A16.2 ARDL regression summary of manufacturing exports on transport services

Transport services
Estimated Long Run Coefficients using the ARDL Approach
ARDL(1,1,1,0,1) selected based on R-BAR Squared Criterion

Dependent variable is MEXP
40 observations used for estimation from 1982 to 2021

Regressor	Coefficient	Standard Error	T-Ratio[Prob]
TRS	.48733	.091058	5.3518[.000]
WPY	.82133	.16023	5.1261[.000]
FDI	-.020890	.018590	-1.1237[.270]
RER	-.0014413	.6222E-3	-2.3163[.027]
C	2.0571	.59701	3.4457[.002]

Table A16.3 ARDL regression summary of manufacturing exports on travel services

Travel
Estimated Long Run Coefficients using the ARDL Approach
ARDL(1,0,1,0,1) selected based on Akaike Information Criterion

Dependent variable is MEXP
40 observations used for estimation from 1982 to 2021

Regressor	Coefficient	Standard Error	T-Ratio[Prob]
TVS	.036488	.20878	.17477[.862]
WPY	1.5432	.54722	2.8200[.008]
FDI	.0058519	.046681	.12536[.901]
RER	-.0029499	.0017928	-2.0877[.045]
C	2.8562	1.4400	1.9835[.056]

Table A16.4 ARDL regression summary of manufacturing exports on finance and insurance service

Finance and insurance
Estimated Long Run Coefficients using the ARDL Approach
ARDL(1,0,1,1,1) selected based on R-BAR Squared Criterion

Dependent variable is MEXP
40 observations used for estimation from 1982 to 2021

Regressor	Coefficient	Standard Error	T-Ratio[Prob]
IF	.26854	.046080	5.8278[.000]
WPY	.73900	.14922	4.9524[.000]
FDI	-.037146	.023751	-1.5640[.128]
RER	-.9720E-3	.3717E-3	-2.7002[.099]
C	4.2514	.47837	8.8873[.000]

Table A16.5 ARDL regression summary on manufacturing exports on computer and communication service

Computer and communication
Estimated Long Run Coefficients using the ARDL Approach
ARDL(1,0,1,1,1) selected based on R-BAR Squared Criterion

Dependent variable is MEXP
40 observations used for estimation from 1982 to 2021

Regressor	Coefficient	Standard Error	T-Ratio[Prob]
CCS	.18938	.057022	3.3212[.002]
WPY	1.3423	.22449	5.9794[.000]
FDI	-.045444	.037935	-1.1979[.240]
RER	-.0028090	.9514E-3	-2.9524[.006]
C	2.3893	.94383	2.5315[.017]

Source: Made by the author

Securing the Future through Sustainability, Health, Education, and Technology – Brig. Dr. Rajiv Divekar et al. (eds)
© 2024 Taylor & Francis Group, London, ISBN 978-1-032-95922-1

17 Understanding Conflict Strategies and Its Effects on Sustainability through Game Theory Decisions: An Example of Afghan Conflict

Shrimoyee Mukherjee[1]
Research Assistant,
Symbiosis Institute of Management Studies,
Pune, Maharashtra

Brig. Rajiv Divekar[2]
Director,
Symbiosis Institute of Management Studies,
Pune, Maharashtra

Pravin Kumar Bhoyar[3]
Deputy Director,
Symbiosis Institute of Management Studies,
Pune, Maharashtra

ABSTRACT

Game theory plays a crucial role in decision-making in every aspect of our lives. Understanding the players and analyzing their next moves with the help of payoffs is one of the basic concepts of game theory. Recently, it gained popularity in fathoming, analyzing, and resolving most of the world's complicated conflicts and seeing its sustainability. One such essential world conflict is the Afghan conflict, which drew the attention of many eyes, including policymakers and economists. Starting from 2001, the conflict raised many questions about the strategies of the Taliban, the Afghanistan government, and the United States. The paper mainly reviews comprehending the sustainability of the Afghan conflict through the Game theory, considering some assumptions about the players. Sustainability and the Afghan conflict are distinct yet interconnected topics that have important implications for the well-being of Afghanistan's people, its environment, and the global community. In conclusion, the US's optimal level of aid assistance to Afghanistan is determined and shows all the possible outcomes in the given game.

KEYWORDS: Game strategy, Sustainability, Afghan conflict

[1]shrimoyeemukherjee99@gmail.com, [2]director@sims.edu [3]deputydirector@sims.edu

DOI: 10.1201/9781003587200-17

1. Introduction

The Afghan conflict came into sharp focus in the world of wars after the assassination of the leader of the Northern Alliance, Ahmad Shah Massoud, which was followed by attacks on the Pentagon, Washington, DC; the World Trade Center, New York; and Shanksville, Pennsylvania, carrying out massive genocides by al-Qaeda and the Taliban under the presidency of George W. Bush. To advance the war against international terrorism and the fight against violent extremism and to ensure Afghanistan's long-term security, democracy, and prosperity in the economic and political environment, the US government formed a coalition with the then-Afghan president, Karzai. This was followed by the International Security Assistance Force (ISAF) creation. Hence, the conflict started between the US, the Afghan government, and the Taliban, each trying to maximize their utility of interest, considering the moves of other payers associated with the game. This conflict was subjected to political instability, humanitarian crisis, and economic disruption not only to the Afghan citizens but to the Global citizens as a whole.

Conflicts have influenced damage to the existing ecological systems such as deforestation, exploitation of resources, and damage to the infrastructure. Also unorganised efforts that label challenges pertaining to sustainability, such as environmental protection or sustainable development projects. A viable end to the war is essential for tackling Afghanistan's sustainability issues. Maintaining a stable and tranquil environment is crucial for long-term environmental conservation, social fairness, and economic progress. The Afghan conflict and its issues have lead to worldwide consequences. Refugees and displaced people can put a toll on the neighbouring nations' resources and stability. Moreover, environmental degradation in Afghanistan can have transboundary impacts on water resources and ecosystems. Thus require a comprehensive resolution to the ongoing intertwined issues of Afghan conflict and sustainability.

In competitive settings where a participant's choice of action significantly impacts the actions of other players, game theory examines the strategic interactions among rational decision-makers. Game theory is used in various decision-making contexts, including business, sports, psychology, and war. The study of game theory makes use of several models. The Nash Equilibrium model is a well-known and firmly established model in which a particular optimal equilibrium best response is created by examining the game's player payoffs.

2. Literature Review

T. Sandler and D. Arce (1987) pointed out that game theory not only provides the strategic interactions of terrorists and the targeted governments but also captures the strategic interactions among the rational actors. The counterparts of the latter have a role to play in the scenario. Additionally, it has been observed that every player in the game, including the terrorists, abides by the game theory's rationality assumption and conceptions of bargaining, maximizing a goal while considering certain restrictions.

One of the antiterrorism policies is never to concede defeat to the demands of hostage-taking terrorists. The terrorist has no gains from kidnapping if the targeted sticks to the no-negotiation policy, reducing hostage missions. Nevertheless, the reality seems far away. As pointed out by Lapan and Sandler (1988), the incompleteness of the policy of no negotiation with a game of level of deterrence on the targeted side and the likelihood of logical failure and success with the hostage mission on the terrorist side.

H. Kydd and Barbara F. (2006) Walter have mentioned that most terrorist groups have the ultimate goal of terrorism -- 'Regime change' that leads to the replacement of the government by the terrorist group or by one of their choice by overthrowing the government, 'Territorial change' that constitute of taking away territory from a state or joining a state to form a new state, 'Policy change' that concentrates on the change of a policy of one state over another, 'Social control' and 'status quo maintenance,' in the name of 'jihad' using the strategies like morale-building, attrition, intimidation and delegitimization of regime, assassination, and kidnapping, imposing costs on occupying forces, advertising, provocation, disorientation and spoiling, elimination of opposite forces, outbidding.

Kydd and Walter (2002) also pointed out uncertainty about relative power, resolve, and trustworthiness as the prominent causes of conflict. It has also been pointed out that these causes of conflict can quickly be resolved by communication, which is considered cheap as there is more often an incentive for the actors to bluff and lie. Hence, to be serious with their audiences – governments and the public-terrorists go on for costly communication signals, which can be fatal.

In an attrition campaign, Robert Pape (2003) argued that the strategy is to inflict costs till the enemy withdraws its occupying forces. Robert also pointed out a positive correlation between cost infliction and the probability of withdrawal by an enemy. The more cost is inflicted, the higher the probability of withdrawal. The effectiveness of attrition strategies depends on the state's interest in the issue at hand (for example, in response to al-Qaida's demands, the US launched offensive wars in Afghanistan and Iraq instead of withdrawing its troops from that country after the 9/11 attacks), as well as the limitations placed on the state's ability to retaliate. The more restrictions placed on the government's use of force, as in a democracy, the less damage is done, and the terrorist can no longer sustain his or her position.

3. Research Methodology

3.1 Modeling

In the game, there are three players –

a. the government of Afghanistan (G),
b. the Taliban (T), and
c. the American administration (A).

The G's goal is to retain its sovereignty over the territory. At the same time, T seeks to destabilize G. A, on the other hand, seeks to minimize T's control over the territory and keep T out of power.

It becomes an infinite game until G and T negotiate for settlements over Afghanistan, T withdraws itself from the game, or G destabilizes.

G's ability to survive depends on the time and amount of the conflict, which is a negative function (as conflict period or quantity increases, G's inability to survive also increases) and on T's choice to continue to fight (if T chooses to continue to fight then G's ability to survive decreases or vice-versa).

Suppose,

Probability of retaining of G = p

Probability of destabilizing of G = (1–p)

A provides G with military and economic assistance to improve his chances of survival. Thus, the central conflict is between A and T with special assistance for G by A. Suppose,

Military and economic assistance by A to G = x, where x is continuous and increasing to G.

3.2 Moves

a. When $x \rightarrow 1$, A provides increased assistance, increasing the survival chances for G.
b. When $x \rightarrow 0$, A provides less assistance, decreasing the survival chances for G.
c. When $x = 0$, G is one of his own to win the game and is forced to rely on his resources.
d. When $x > 0$, A bears the cost of fighting T.

Thus, if we use the variables p and x to draw a function on the actual survival chances of G, we get,

$$p^* = p/(1-x)$$

The actual survival chances of G depend directly on the probability of retaining itself in the sovereignty and positively on A's assistance.

Suppose,

$p/(1 - x) = 1$ {when the actual survival chance is a certain event}

or, $x = (1 - p)$, i.e., A guarantees G's survival.

Once A makes allocations, A can either refuse to negotiate and demand T to accept his sovereignty and cease violence, or A negotiates with T and demands to cease violence through his bargaining power.

G's negotiation (N) = T's probability of actual destabilizing G = $\{1 - p/(1 - x)\}$

As $x \to 1$, the value of negotiation to T declines as it results due to the artificial coalition military balances. Actual negotiation can only be made when $x = 0$, i.e., $N = (1 - p)$.

Once G goes for negotiation, T either accepts or rejects. If T accepts, A either chooses to continue supporting or go for withdrawal of the army, following which T decides whether to maintain the negotiation or not.

3.3 Payoffs

Suppose we assume

a. If G retains power, G receives a payoff = 1, T receives payoff = 0
b. If G is destabilized, G receives a payoff = 0, T receives payoff = 1
c. If G and T negotiate and T accepts, then.
   G receives $= p/(1 - x)$; and T receives $= \{1 - p/(1 - x)\}$
d. If G fights T without the support of A, $x = 0$, the cost paid by G for fighting $T = C_G$. Therefore, G's Payoff = benefit received – cost incurred $= p - C_G$
e. If G fights T with A's support, $x \neq 0$, the cost paid by G for fighting $T = C_G = 0$. The total cost of fighting T is absorbed by A. Therefore, G's payoff = benefit received – cost incurred $= p/(1 - x) - 0 = p/(1 - x)$.
f. If T is kept out of power, A receives payoff = 1
g. If T gains power, even if it is through negotiation, A receives a payoff = 0
h. Suppose A does not support G, followed by destabilization of G by T or negotiation of G and T, i.e., when $x = 0$. Then, political cost incurred by $A = C_A$.

Therefore, A's payoff for supporting G = benefits received – cost incurred

$$= \{p/(1 - x) - x - C_G\}$$

i. A's payoff for not supporting $G = C_A$

The cost of fighting incurred $T = C_T$ is uncertain to the other game players for their opaque behavior. Hence, G and A cannot draw any conclusions on T's cost of fighting.

3.4 Equilibrium

Perfect Bayesian Equilibrium is a set of strategies and beliefs such that the strategies are sequentially rational given the players' beliefs, and players update beliefs via the Bayes rule whenever possible. The Afghan conflict game involves infinite and incomplete information; we rely on the perfect Bayesian equilibrium to find the best response.

Case I – G refuses to negotiate and demands T to surrender.

On the settlement, T would accept K's demand if

Benefit received from the settlement > cost incurred in the conflict

$$\Rightarrow \qquad \{1 - p/(1 - x)\} > CT$$

T shows the behavior of indifference between the withdrawals and continues to fight if the benefit received from the settlement = cost incurred in the conflict

$$\Rightarrow \qquad \{1 - p/(1 - x)\} = CT$$

$\Rightarrow$ As p (probability of G retaining its power) $\to 0$, the probability of T to surrender tends to decline, and as G's stability increases, $p \to 1$, and the chances of T surrendering increases.

Also, T continues to fight when expected cost (we suppose, CT*) > actual cost (CT)

Case II – G chooses to negotiate.

G negotiates with T and offers $x = \{1 - p/(1 - x)\}$; T's move depends entirely on A's decision after negotiation. After settlement,

If A decides to continue aid to G, $x \neq 0$, $x > 0$

$\Rightarrow$ T obeys the agreement if settlement benefit > gains from conflict with A in scenario

$$\Rightarrow \qquad \{1 - p/(1 - x)\} > \{1 - p/(1 - x)\} - CT.$$

However, when G negotiates with T, A receives a payoff = 0, as T retains its power. But if A decides on withdrawal of forces, T obeys the settlement if,

Settlement benefit > the gain from the conflict without A's support for G

$$\Rightarrow \qquad \{1 - p/(1 - x)\} > 1 - p - CT$$

Hence, T would be indifferent if, $\{1 - p/(1 - x)\} = 1 - p - CT$

or,
$$CT = p/(1 - x) - p = px/(1 - x)$$

i.e., (probability of survival chances of G with A's support) times (military and economic assistance to G by A).

When $x \to 1$, T will likely withdraw itself from the fight.

Therefore, T will not accept the settlement and will continue to fight when the expected cost (we suppose, CT') > actual cost (CT).

From the above cases discussed, it is concluded that G is being rewarded for fighting and punished for making peace. G prefers negotiating only when the benefit of fighting is greater than the cost of not making peace. As long as G got A's support, i.e., $x > 0$, G has no incentive to call for a settlement to maintain peace.

The utility derived from the conflict by A is A's payoff for supporting G, i.e., $\{p/(1 - x) - x - C_G\}$. To identify the optimal level of economic and militia support provided to G by A, we need to maximize A's utility, i.e.,

$$\partial\{p/(1 - x) - x - C_G\}/\partial x = 0$$

or, $$p/(1 - x)2 = 1$$

or, $$x = (1 - p1/2) \text{ or } (1 + p1/2)$$

A will provide G with economic and militia support to keep G's utility to make G stay to fight and not negotiate. As $(1 + p1/2) > 1$ and $(1 - p1/2) < 1$, A chooses the former to the latter to optimize its allocation.

Thus, A will provide aid to G if, A's cost for not supporting G < A's benefit for supporting G

or, $$-C_A < \{p/(1 - (1 - p1/2)) - (1 - p1/2) - C_G\}$$

4. Results

1. When G refuses to negotiate, T surrenders if $C_T \geq \{1 - p/(1 - x)\}$ or continues to fight otherwise. If G offers $x = \{1 - p/(1 - x)\}$, then T accepts, followed by his renege, and if $C_T = px/(1 - x)$, then T accepts and complies.
2. If $x = 0$, G negotiates; if $x \neq 0$, $x > 0$, G does not go for negotiation.
3. A will only provide aid to G if and only if $-C_A < \{p/(1 - (1 - p1/2)) - (1 - p1/2) - C_G\}$.

5. Conclusion

The economic and militia aid provided by the US to Afghanistan was disincentivizing Afghanistan from negotiating with the Taliban. Thus, everyday lives in Afghanistan were at stake due to this conflict. Even though support from the US tends to increase the probability of the Afghan government's democratic rule over Taliban rule, increasing the probability of Taliban disarming, they cannot properly exploit the benefits. Time is another factor to mention. The costs tended to increase as the conflict was consuming so much time. The longer the US delays, the weaker the Afghanistan government becomes, forcing the Taliban to grab more territorial grounds. Hence, due to improper exploitation of their benefits, they failed to succeed from the Taliban and therefore put sustainability at stake.

With the measures they were considering, the extended cost of the war was the negative impacts on Afghans' health, infrastructure, labor force, and social structures of poverty, hunger, poor sanitation, lack of access to health care, and environmental degradation. The American Department of Defense's (DoD) open-air fire pits and the deterioration of conventional irrigation systems are only two examples of the environmental effects. The harmful pollutants from the fire pits have been indisputably connected to the subsequent emergence of chronic and occasionally deadly ailments. Military activities and the socioeconomic implications of conflict have accelerated irrigation impacts, which are considerable given the dryness of the terrain and have led to the increase in opium cultivation in Afghanistan.

These war-related impacts included increased illness rates as a result of inadequate access to safe drinking water, hunger, and healthcare. Afghanistan has suffered much from the war's devastation. Acute malnutrition was a concern for 3 million children, and 92% of the population experienced food insecurity. Several areas were experiencing starvation. At least half of the people lived on less than $1.90 per day. The CIA provided equipment and support to Afghan militia groups that engaged in major human rights abuses, including the murder of civilians. Nearly 243,000 people have died in the war zone in Afghanistan and Pakistan since 2001. Over 70,000 of those killed were civilians.

REFERENCES

1. A. Bapat, (2010). A Game-Theoretic Analysis of Afghan Surge., Oxford University Press, Foreign Policy Analysis, Vol. 6, No. 3, pp. 217–236.
2. A. Pape, (2003). The Strategic Logic of Suicide Terrorism, Cambridge University Press.
3. Atkinson, S.E., Sandler, T., and Tschirhart J.T., (1987). Terrorism is a bargaining framework., Journal of Law and Economics, vol. 30, issue 1, 1–21.
4. D. Reiter, 2003. Exploring the Bargaining Model of War, American Political Science Association, Perspectives on Politics, Vol. 1, No. 1 (Mar., 2003), pp. 27–43.
5. H. Kydd, F. Walter, (2006). The Strategies of Terrorism, The MIT Press, Vol. 31, No. 1, pp. 49–80
6. H Kydd, 2005. Trust and Mistrust in International Relations, Princeton University Press.
7. H. Kydd, F. Walter, (2002). Sabotaging the Peace, The MIT Press, International Organization, Vol. 56, No. 2 (Spring, 2002), pp. 263–296.
8. R. Rubin, (2007). Saving Afghanistan., Foreign Affairs, Council on Foreign Relations, Vol. 86, No. 1, pp. 57–74, 76–78.
9. T. Sandler, Daniel G. Arce M., (2005). Counterterrorism: A Game-Theoretic Analysis, Sage Publications, Inc., The Journal of Conflict Resolution, Vol. 49, No. 2, The Political Economy of Transnational Terrorism (Apr., 2005), pp. 183–200.

Securing the Future through Sustainability, Health, Education, and Technology –
Brig. Dr. Rajiv Divekar et al. (eds)

18 An Analysis and Mapping Teacher's Ethical Framework to Hichki, A Bollywood Cinema

Sunil Belladi
Assistant Professor,
Symbiosis Centre for Media & Communication,
Symbiosis International (Deemed University), Pune, India

ABSTRACT

The present study is to locate the relationship between the teacher and the taught, the dilemmas faced and decision taken thereafter by both the teacher and the pupil in a given situation and context, in the Indian Bollywood Movie, *Hichki* (Hiccup). Cinemas are not just for the sake of entertainment or a source of escape. It concerns and implicitly represents the relationship between the time and period, the society that is prevailing and the culture in which the cinema ideated and made. The conceptual framework for the present study is informed by ethical framework proposed by Furman (2004) in the realm of education. A narrative film analysis is sought by the paper to selectively identify, examine and map the sequences in the movie *Hichki* to the five ethical dimension offered by Furman. Rani Mukerji, the protagonist of the movie is a teacher by profession who has tourette syndrome and is allotted to educate children who exercised their RTE Act 2009. The students find admission in one of elite schools in Mumbai where the wards of the affluent study. It is found through the analysis of the movie under study, how the teacher though fails to be initially accepted by the said 14 students traverse the entire journey of an academic year. The teacher exhibiting the sense of inclusion brings forth innovation in explaining complex constructs theories and concepts there by ensuring the requisite learning delivered in accordance with the capability and capacity of the students. Compassion towards the pupils and holding professional ethics as a guiding light, the teacher sales across the turbulent weather. Subtly, the path adapted by the teacher in the movie reaffirms the universally believed testimony that teacher do and continue to have a powerful and lasting impression on the taught.

KEYWORDS: Professional ethics, Furman framework, Narrative analysis, Hichki

####

DOI: 10.1201/9781003587200-18

We want that education by which character is formed, strength of mind is increased, the intellect is expanded, and by which one can stand on one's own feet.

—(Swami Vivekananda 1899)

1. Introduction

German Philosopher the famed Martin Heidegger, in one of his seminal work "Being and Time" which is considered as one of the most compelling and influential works in western philosophy emerging out of the 20th Century. He describes the birth of human into the world as *Geworfenehit* (throwness*),* the one that is thrown into the world clueless (Heidegger 1927). It is through education, experience and other sociocultural means that one acquires the ability to navigate the maze called the world. One of the primary purposes of education is to prepare one for life and all round development of an individual. The recipient of the 1993 Nobel peace prize, Nelson Mandela in his autobiography titled, Long Life to Freedom recall how his life was intertwined with numerous events of his life. Refereeing to the importance of education in one's life, he states that education is the great engine of personal development (Mandela 1994). This is well resonated with one of his famous quotes *"Education is the most powerful weapon which you can use to change the world."* (Justice Verma 2003) in one of speech's states that the democracy and freedom of a nation can only be realized through conscious and ethical people and the society can achieve justice without any inequalities in people. The role of a teacher in this entire process is integral and so do historical and mythological references offer a standpoint to know, internalize, assess and even at occasions refute the unconditional relationship between the teacher and their pupil. Teaching that started a mission, later transpired to a passion and now acknowledged as a profession, has its own ethics driven by values, morals, and goals of a given society in a particular time and space. The Prime Minister of India, on the occasion of teacher's day, having a conversation with the award winning teachers commended the teachers on their role in moldings the youth of the country and intern shaping the future of the nation, still pride in indigenous knowledge and as well promote and celebrate diversity of India **(Sharma 2024). (Postman and Weingartner 1979)** work urge the way how schools operate and teacher conduct themselves. The teachers should enhance the critical thinking capabilities of the ward and make them aware about the society, the politics that intertwined their lives and as well the culture in which they live. The traditional role of teachers should be shunned and they need to adopt new and innovative ways to be more like mentors, coaches and fellow learners, they recommend. What are the principles, what are the values, what does one stand for are some of the questions one regularly confronts with? What does the western philosophical landscape offer us in this regard to ethics? Some of the guidelines laid by Emanuel Kant shows as a doorway. Also popularly known as Kantian ethics which falls under the deontological ethics domain, it states that, one should always follow a set of moral principles no matter what the situation is or what the outcome will be, what Kant calls it categorical imperative. The other opposing philosophical thought was proposed by Jeremy Bentham who says that ethics is determined by right from wrong by focusing on outcomes. Whereas Kant irrespective on consequences lays emphasis on duty. Each profession prescribes an ideal and appropriate ethical code for people who decided to take on that specific profession and throws open a varied moral choice the person needs to pick from. In order to show direction and guide teaches in their professional work, the National Council for Teacher Education prescribes a 'Code of Professional Ethics for school teachers' in India. The code states that the teacher's obligation is in three different facades, one towards their pupils, towards the society at large and towards their coworkers. Ethics are not just carved in stone as a policy statement which need to be strictly adhered to, but rather in application they are highly dynamic and continuously evolving (Niesche & Haase 2010)

2. Methodology

The present study is to locate the relationship between the teacher and the taught, the dilemmas faced and decision taken thereafter by both the teacher and the pupil in a given situation and context, the case in point is derived by analyzing the Indian Bollywood Movie, *Hichki* (Hiccup). A systematic analysis of the movie is made and the thoughts of Furman on teacher's ethics are mapped. The specific aim and objectives of the study are as follows.

3. Aim

The study will seek to examine and analyses the use of movie Hichki to understand and comprehend the ethical paradigm for teachers as proposed by Furman and how it will help in decision making of a teacher when in ethical problem

4. Objectives

The specific objectives of the study are:

- To explore the notion of Teachers Ethics in theory and practice.
- To analyses the nature and extent of use of Cinema to map ethical situations.
- To examine how the movie Hichki can be used as one of the tools for training teachers on ethical decision making framework.

5. Theoretical Framework

The paper applies a conceptual framework informed by the scholarly work of Furman Gail, in her work, The ethic of community. She goes on to state that the teacher in their diverse environment encounter many ethical dilemmas, and she gives a paradigm when applied, guides the teacher to arrive an ethical decision. The four concepts of ethics; the ethics of care, the ethics of justice, the ethics of critique, and the ethics of community (Furman 2004).In analyzing the movie, the constructs of Walter Fisher a communication scholar have been applied. Wherein he describes that the central to all forms of communication, humans engage, is 'narration' (Walter Fisher 1987). According to Media Scholar Sut Jhally (1995) the narrative perspective can be powerful tool to study and analyze any media texts.

6. Sample

The movie *Hichki* (Hiccup) is choses as a sample and unit of investigation for the present study. The movie was released under the banner of Yash raj films in the year 2018 and in Indian language, Hindi. The researcher studied various scenes and sequences in the 116 minute run time of the movie and carefully mapped them to the Furman's ethical frame work for teachers.

7. Literature Review

Any literature review concerning the concept of ethics for teachers is available in abundance, the reason being the varied implicit and explicit concepts created by academicians, researchers and practitioners. Therefore, a need was felt to narrow down and focus on few selective thoughts from various geographic, economic, political and cultural perspectives and settings. Since the emphasis of the present study is on ethical frame work for teachers, the one presented in this section does not claim to be exhaustive, rather it is selective in nature, the reason being the sources available.

(Held 2006) argues that the neither the Kantian moral theory of ethics and the nineteenth century concept of utilitarianism informed by the thoughts of Bentham and Stuart Mill, which states the greatest good for greater people are enough to navigate in today's world. The author proposes and alternative to these normative theories. People are interdependent and understand the needs of the other and care for them in achieving goals. The author states that the inherent quality of human species is that we relate to each other and build relationships of care.

The commonly cited Fuller's model with regard to the development of a teacher proposes three distinct phases, moving from one to another. **(F.F. Fuller 1969)** in his work, concerns of teachers A developmental characterization states that, the first stage is about the oneself as an individual and a member of a society the teacher moves to stage two wherein they are more consumed and concentrated on the tasks they need to perform as a profession and the final stage is regarding the student and how they are able to have an impact on them through their teaching.

(Karnovskyp et;al 2022) applying the Michael Foucault ethical frame work to the to be teachers training participants in improving their positive emotional state found that the moral and ethical stand point of the teacher is directly linked in normalizing the power held by the state.

(Lortie 1975) in his study titled, *Schoolteacher: A sociological study.* states that rather than any compensation, the teacher receives in the form of material benefits for undertaking their duties, the teacher naturally exhibits an inclination or has a tendency towards what the authors says 'Psychic' rewards. The reward, the teacher gives to themselves is when, they long for the pupil's improvement in their lives and the happiness the teachers derives in observing the student's eagerness and their learning process. The teachers weigh the psychic reward more than the monetary material rewards, he reiterates.

Even though there exists a need for discussion on controversial public issues in a classroom more than often such discussion does not take place and both the facilitator and the students resist form doing so. Studies in the past demonstrated that there are two procedures by which teachers were, on instances is ready to help the student in paying attention to and gaining from unique viewpoints **(King, 2009).** One it is done by diminishing the perception of mental separating and the second by inspiring the pupils to stand up to the controversial issue by working with caring connection with student.

Furthering the thought of Furman, Esudero made addition to the existing four ethics of teachers and proposed a fifth element. **(Esudero 2011)** advocates for a fifth ethic that of ethics of imparting training and profession development to teachers. The education sector is every changing and to keep up with the pace of the varying requirements and skill suitable to make a student acquire requisite skill and enable them achieve an all-round development, the teachers should undergo training programs that deal with the innovative pedagogy methods, reinventing them and as well acquiring new skill sets, the author asserts.

Ahn and Leggo in their analysis of over 25 movies form Hollywood which featured teachers as protagonist applying the narrative enquire method states how these movies shape the teachers identiy in a given society. They go on to state that in many Hollywood movies and in many cases the teachers are depicted as 'superheroes', while these kind of movies might propagate specific generalizations of a teacher profession, they can likewise have an incredible impact on the teachers themselves **(Ahn & Leggo 2019).**

According to Bullough, when a teacher exercising and performing their duty at school, what is correct and what is not, ethically, is never clearly defined. More so ever when the facilitator encounters situations and scenarios which are complicated in nature **(Bullough, 2011).**

Harvard professor Michael Beer suggested that, for one to be on a high ethical ground one need to look inwards and spare time to have a conversation with oneself. It allows for a self-reflection regarding the values of a person and purpose of the person **(Beer 2021).**

(Dalton 1995) studied over 20 select movies made in US and Britain, wherein the primary character of the movie revolves around a teacher in schools, it encompasses various genres from action, adventure drama and comedy. It was found through the study that the majority of the plot of the movies revolves around projection of a teacher who is considered as a bright light in the schools of darkness. The teacher through his methods and mannerism, turns around the pupil and the school to greatness.

(Purushottama and Joseph 2007) in their book titled, Indian Ethics: Classical Traditions and Contemporary Challenges state that the grounding of Indian morality is both based on authority and as well on social reasoning. *Dharma* (not be confused with religion is the term used for ethics and morality in Indian tradition. There are plenty of instances that are found in the ancient Vedic scriptures and in other Indian literature both in Sanskrit and other languages. Ethical teaching is available in abundance in Indian scriptures like Mahabharata and Ramayana, the author states.

8. Analysis and Discussion

According to the producer of the movie Yash raj film the synopsis goes this way Hichki a tale is about a lady overcoming her shortcoming and turning them into her greatest strength. Naina Mathur (Rani Mukerji) is a hopeful instructor who experiences Tourette disorder. After many futile interview and rejections, she finds a full-time teacher in one of elite school in the city. She realizes that the class she has been assigned to contains rebellious and mischievous students and who are always trouble makers. In spite of a couple of beginning hiccups, Naina should give her best guaranteeing her students understand their actual potential, and challenge all the chances against them (Yash raj films 2018).

According to the grade point system followed by many schools across the globe and as well in India, a person who gets 'F' grade means the student is utterly poor in academics and denotes poor performance and indicates failing of a course. The teacher, Naina Mathur is assigned a class 9 F and generally people associate word F in academic sphere is fail.

Ethics of care: Hypothesis of the ethic of care, focuses on outlining the role of care in the teaching process and is supported with the concept of moral growth, the role of teacher-student relationship and intern discovering one's self as a teacher. The protagonist Naina Mathur time and again in the movie exhibits this ethics of care in many instances; She understands the socio economic and cultural background of the students of Class F, she readily realizes the inherent potential of the students and encourages them constantly to achieve. She develops a good rapport with the students and their parents. During the Parents teachers meeting none the wards turn up with their parent to have a conversation with the teacher, Naina Mathur intern visits the students home and place of work, showing she cares for them. When the students of Calass F are rusticated rom the schools,

Naina Mathur reaches out to them and trains them for their exams. Teaching at the place of convenience to the students, playgrounds, public transport and even brings them home during the exams and teaches them. This establishes the care of ethics by the protagonist Naina Mathur in the movie.

Ethics of Critique: This concept stress that the teacher should go beyond their routines and comfort zones and bring about a commonality amongst the learning group. This is done by evoking a sense of respect and will to achieve amongst the students irrespective of their varied socio economic and backgrounds. At many instances in the movie, Naina Mathur fights for equality and opportunity for the students of Class F and as well challenges one of the colleague for showing partial treatment to the favored class and always looking down on students of Class F. The inequality amongst the various sections of Class 9 get erased and all the students collectively work towards a common goal of the schools, the science exhibition. Naina mathur as a teacher exhibits the ethics of critique by fighting for the rights of the students and ensuring equality be displayed by school administration and teachers alike towards students.

Ethics of Justice: The theory states that for any problem solving method in ethical dilemmas, teachers should choose what is just fair for any individual and as well for the school on the whole. Naina Mathur throughout the movie displays this ethical framework for instances when the class member is at fault she vehemently opposes them because that was not just on their part. When the initial model developed by Class A is destroyed by member of Class F she expresses her opposition to their act. When member of Class F instigates a member of Class A, she immediately pitches in and tries to resolve the issue and takes the side of member of class A because the situation demand s she need to be just and fair.

Ethics of Community: The framework is all encompassing. The role of the teacher is not just to educate a student and be ethical in their profession. It role extents and goes beyond the class room and the school and looks at the community. Education not limited and restricted to the class room or school hours and whenever you require my help, I am always available for you. She leaves her Phone number with all the students.The moral duty of a teacher is to address specific challenges of the community as well. Throughout the movie the Naina Mathur is seen looking at bigger picture for her students. She understands the problems faced by the students in their life beyond the classroom. She empathizes with them and she trains them to be ethical human beings and achieve for a better life for themselves and their family members. This is reiterated when she retires a reunion kind of class F who are now working professional and doing well in their occupation is shown.

9. Conclusion

Bulman who conducts a content analysis of various movies in the west, featuring teachers in the main role sums up that, one of the Hollywood's trusted formula is the genre of the urban-high-school. Typically, these films are frequented by academically low archivers and as well with socially distressed students. These set of students vividly transform themselves with the extraordinary efforts and personal involvement of a teacher who often an outsider and a new entrant to the school and often at a new profession as a teacher (Bulman 2002). The plot of the movie is similar to this Hollywood formula, but is set in the Indian context. The movie is set in Mumbai and the main protagonist Naina Mathur is an outsider who comes to take up a job as a teacher in the school and this is her first stint into the teaching profession. She turnarounds the students who are once considered less intelligent and trouble makers into achieves. This resonates Bulman observation of movies with teachers as protagonist.

When and ever a decision that involves ethical dilemmas to be arrived at, it is imperative that there should be some paradigm to bank on or guide the teachers in the process. It is suggested that all the four prominent ethical constructs as suggest by Furman; justice, care, critique and community need to be applied for navigating through the ethical questions faced by teachers. Moreover, the mapping of these concepts to the Bollywood movie Hichki makes one clearly understand how the protagonist maneuver herself when faced with ethical dilemmas as a teacher. The movie can be screened to teachers, in-training and as well to seasoned educators to comprehend the conceptual framework that guides teachers in allowing them to take decisions in their professional life. The film had won many accolades and as well brought money to the movie makers.

Some important lines form the movies; A normal teaches teach, a good teacher explains and very good teacher demonstrates to make students understand extraordinary teacher inspires the students for life; There are no bad students there are only bad teachers.

References

1. Ahn, C., & Leggo, C. (2019). Teachers in Film: Always in Process. *Canadian Journal of Education 42*(1), 117–137.
2. Bilimoria, Purushottama & Prabhu, Joseph (2007). Indian Ethics: Classical Traditions and Contemporary Challenges: Volume I. Routledge.
3. Bulman, R.C.(2002) Teachers in the 'Hood: Hollywood's Middle-Class Fantasy. *The Urban Review* 34, 251–276 (2002). https://doi.org/10.1023/A:1020655307664
4. Code of Professional Ethics for School Teachers, National Council for Teacher Education, Wing – II, Hans Bhawan, 1, Bahadur Shah Zafar Marg, New Delhi110002 December, 2010.
5. Dewey, J. (1933). How We Think: A Restatement of the Relation of Reflective Thinking to the Educative Process. Boston, MA: D.C. Heath & Co Publishers.
6. Dalton, M. (1995) The Hollywood Curriculum: who is the 'good' teacher? Curriculum Studies, 3:1, 23-44, DOI: 10.1080/0965975950030102
7. Furman, C.(2004) The ethic of community. Journal of Educational Administration; Armidale Vol. 42, Iss. 2,: 215-235. DOI:10.1108/09578230410525612

8. Heidegger, Martin, 1889-1976. (1976). Basic writings from Being and time (1927) to The task of thinking (1964). New York: Harper & Row,
9. Held,V. (2006). The Ethics of Care: Personal, Political, Global, Oxford University Press. ISBN 0195180992.
10. Michael Beer, (Sep 15, 2021) How to Be a Leader Who Stays True to Their Ethics, by The article can be retrieved from Harvard Business Review at https://hbr.org/2021/09/how-to-be-a-leader-who-stays-true-to-their-ethics-2
11. Justice J.S. Verma (2003, Oct 28). Significance of Ethics in Education. UGC's Golden Jubilee Lecture Series. Retrieved from https://www.ugc.gov.in/oldpdf/pub/lectures/ugc_js_v.pdf
12. King, J. T. (2009). Teaching and learning about controversial issues: Lessons from Northern Ireland. Theory & Research in Social Education, 37(2), 215e246. https://doi.org/10.1080/00933104.2009.10473395
13. F.F. Fuller (1969) Concerns of teachers A developmental characterization. American Educational Research Journal
14. *Lortie*, D. C. (1975). Schoolteacher: A sociological study. Chicago: University of Chicago Press.
15. Mandela, N. (1994). Long Walk to Freedom: The Autobiography of Nelson Mandela. London: Abacus.
16. Mary M. Dalton (1995) The Hollywood Curriculum: who is the 'good' teacher? Curriculum Studies, 3:1, 23-44, DOI: 10.1080/0965975950030102
17. Niesche, Richard & Haase, Malcom. (2010). Emotions and Ethics: A Foucauldian Framework for Becoming an Ethical Educator. Educational Philosophy and Theory. 44. 276 - 288. 10.1111/j.1469-5812.2010.00655.x.
18. Shapiro, J.P., & Stefkovich, J.A. (2001). Ethical leadership and decision making in education. New Jersey: Lawrence Erlbaum Associates.
19. S. Karnovsky, B. Gobby & P. O'Brien (2022) A Foucauldian ethics of positivity in initial teacher education, Educational Philosophy and Theory, 54:14, 2504-2519, DOI: 10.1080/00131857.2021.2016390
20. S Sharma I TOI Education I Sep 5, 2023. PM Modi praises teachers' vital role in shaping India's future. Article retrieved http://timesofindia.indiatimes.com/articleshow/103374014.cms?utm_source=contentofinterest&utm_medium=text&utm_campaign=cppst
21. Yash raj films (2018) HICHKI. Synopsis of the movie. Can be retrieved at https://www.yashrajfilms.com/movies/hichki
22. C Witherell, N. Noddings (1991). Stories Lives Tell: Narrative and Dialogue in Education, Teachers College Press, ISBN9780807730706
23. The Education that Indians needs A conversation of Swami Vivekananda with *Surendra Nath Sen—from private diary* retrieved from https://vivekavani.com/surendra-nath-sen/

*Securing the Future through Sustainability, Health, Education, and Technology –
Brig. Dr. Rajiv Divekar et al. (eds)*

19 Training and Development of Community Resource Person as a Tool for Empowerment of Women —A Qualitative Enquiry

Lelith Daniel*
Symbiosis Community Outreach Programme and Extension (SCOPE),
Symbiosis International (Deemed University) (SIU),
Lavale, Pune, Maharashtra, India

Shaji Joseph
Symbiosis Centre for Information Technology (SCIT),
Symbiosis International (Deemed University) (SIU),
Lavale, Pune, Maharashtra, India

Sneha Thomas
Symbiosis Institute of Technology, Nagpur (SIT-N),
Symbiosis International (Deemed University) (SIU),
Lavale, Pune, Maharashtra, India

Niharika Singh
Symbiosis School of Economics, Pune (SSE),
Symbiosis International (Deemed University) (SIU),
Lavale, Pune, Maharashtra, India

Abstract

Rural India has limited opportunities for skill development and formal education for women which result in inadequate social, political, and economic representation. Kudumbashree's, micro-enterprises run by SHG members, has created a transformational shift. This research paper seeks to analyze the transformative impact of the micro-enterprises and the intergenerational impact of its targeted interventions devised to foster gender equity in the realm of economic independence and leadership spirit.

Naila Kabeer's empowerment paradigm illustrates the interaction of resources, autonomy, and achievements in determining women's empowerment. We used this notion to describe the transformative impact caused by micro-enterprises, demonstrating how resource access, agency growth, and tangible outcomes operate collectively to empower women under Kudumbashree's entrepreneurial and

*Corresponding author: lelith.daniel@siu.edu.in

DOI: 10.1201/9781003587200-19

leadership model. Qualitative data was acquired via interviews and focus participant observations, which offer insights into the shifting implications of skill development and training on female participants and their socioeconomic status.

The research implies the development of a new standard that strongly emphasizes training and leadership roles for women within the Kudumbashree framework. This study recognizes the transformative power of training to determine women's empowerment endeavors. It offers them the skills, knowledge, and confidence they need to assume leadership roles and challenge gender norms. By highlighting training under the Kudumbashree model, this study anticipates a future in which women emerge as empowered leaders, driving progress in the communities they represent.

KEYWORDS: Kudumbashree, Self help group, Women empowerment, Rural women, Rural development, Training

1. Introduction

Women in rural and urban households play a variety of roles. In many rural families, as men migrate to urban areas in search of employment, it is the burden of women to manage the household. The natural calamities, social stigmas, and the lack of resources at her disposal make this situation worse for these women. Paramanandam and Packirisamy (2015) argued in their paper that with women taking an active role in development programs, economic development is possible. Technical and managerial training will help them to become more self-reliant and engage in entrepreneurial activities. Socioeconomic empowerment is also needed (Akram et al., 2019). A study of women in Pakistan showed that they tend to avoid training opportunities, thinking their role is to care for the home and help rear children (Ibrahim & Shady, 2009). In the Indian context, the burden of managing a family is on the woman, yet she lacks access to resources. Self-help groups provide a way out for them by helping them establish micro-enterprises.

Ebrahimi et al. (2022) observe that vocational education for women is a less explored field. They said that vocational training helped the empowerment in creating savings, self-reliance in production, controlling the use of income, independence of spending, and loan repayment freedom. The research also found that this has created a better sense of trust among villagers towards women as they can provide intellectual contributions to local planning. This has contributed to the individual's self-esteem and problem-solving capacity. A similar study from Bangladesh established that ICT helps empower rural women (Laizu et al., 2010).

The *Kudumbashree* that started in Kerala exemplifies how rural empowerment can help women's empowerment. Kudumbashree started in 1998 with state and central government funds and NABARD. This has been functioning under the local self-government department from its inception. Today, it has a reach of over 43 lakh members and is spread across 941 village panchayats. The objective of this mission is to eradicate poverty from the state. The Kudumbashree structure consists of three levels, namely Neighbourhood Groups (NHG), Area Development Societies (ADS), and Kudumbashree Community Development Society (CDS). The members are organized into 287,723 NHGs, 19,489 ADSs, and 1064 CDSs. The focus areas are Livelihood Development, Organisation and Social Development, and Systems Support. According to the "Annual Report 2022," the proportion of women in leadership roles in Kerala has increased dramatically from 20% to 45%, illustrating a developing trend of higher political and economic participation. The collective has received international acclaim for its transformative impact on women through its dynamic interventions spanning from skill development to creating micro-enterprises, self-help groups, and social contributions.

2. Literature Review

2.1 Empowerment of Rural Women

Kumar (2014) argues that women are the nucleus of the rural family in India. She is responsible for collecting water, firewood, fodder, and food. Even though they constitute less than 50% of the population, they contribute over 75% of the development of the society. Despite their invaluable contribution, their role has traditionally been neglected. Education and employment are considered two crucial factors for empowerment (Nayak & Mahanta, 2012). In their paper, Roy et al. (2018) argued that poverty ignites a societal gap between men and women while economic development narrows it down through gender promotional activities. They further argue that their 'access to resources', 'decision-making capability', and 'ability to take a stand' should measure their success. Self-help groups (SHGs) were conceived to improve women's status in rural and semi-urban areas parts of India (Uma, 2012). The micro-credit facilities that were provided empowered SHG members to be part of the family decision-making process (Kapila et al., 2016). In addition to providing credit, SHGs activities also target socio-cultural and economic factors in order to aid the empowerment journey of women. (Mathur and Agarwal 2017).

Kudumbashree is an agency of rural development and women empowerment

Kudumbashree was founded to empower rural women economically and socially. Though it is primarily a microfinance organization, Kudumbashree has been the major source of women's empowerment in rural Kerala (Ka et al., 2023). Traditionally, woman has played a dependent role. Her lack of education did not allow her secure a job that would free her from this dependence. Hence, training and education become the first step toward rural women's empowerment (Joseph et al., 2023). Kudumbashree and its microfinancing have helped countless women in rural Kerala to stand on their feet and take an active part in the family decision-making process (Shamshadali et al., 2019; Malcolm & Bhandari, 2021; Raveendran & Sharma, 2023; Aiswarya & Sangeetha, 2022). They further observed that these trainings also promoted a unique entrepreneurship model in Kerala. The success of this model is that the training programs and entrepreneurship ventures for the needs of the people. (Shirur et al., 2020). This silent yet powerful revolution involving over 4 lakh rural women transforms their lives and spearheads the state's overall economic development (John, 2021).

3. Role of Community Resource Persons (CRP) in the Development of the Community and Empowerment of Individuals

At the heart of Kudumbashree is CRP. A CRP is an individual drawn from the community and trained to act as a resource center. CRPs may be designated differently for different projects or initiatives. Kudumbashree follows a rigorous, multi-step, participatory identification process. Traditionally, women nominated to be CRPs have made significant contributions to their community or are perceived to have an innate ability to influence their community members. These individuals are selected through a written test and an interview. They are trained and equipped with the requisite skills to enable the community members to implement various activities.

SVEP (Startup Village Entrepreneurship Programme) is a perfect example of this. Experienced CRPs were identified from across Kerala and trained to function in leadership roles. They are called "Mentors". In order to work at grassroots levels in various villages and wards, they recruited "MECs" (Micro Enterprise Consultants) or "CRP-EPs" (Community Resource Persons- Enterprise Promotion). Over the years, CRPs have performed various roles within Kudumbashree and various other organizations within the state and have also been deployed outside Kerala to assist such programs in other states.

3.1 Theoretical Framework for Development

In this paper we used the theoretical frameworks proposed by Naila Kabir, and Muhammad Yunus to evaluate the transformative impact of micro-enterprises on rural India. Naila Kabir argued that women's empowerment involves a dynamic interaction of resources, autonomy and achievements. (Kabeer 2010). Muhammed Yunis' Grameen bank model of microfinance program utilizes a bottom-up approach towards grassroots empowerment. His model emphasize on participatory approach towards empowerment. He argues that when entrepreneurship is supported by skill development and mentoring will lead to economic empowerment (counts, 2008).

The Grameen bank model of empowerment is similar to SHG model. This model allows financial inclusion and critical leadership attributes to emerge. Empowerment through microenterprises leads to revolutionary changes in cultural norms and gender dynamics that are key to women's empowerment. Entry of women into the entrepreneurial landscape and accessing financial resources can disrupt established gender norms and can improve gender inclusion. Women occupying leadership positions in these businesses and acquiring access to financial resources, result in the disruption of established gender norms and also advance gender inclusion. This transforming process frequently cascades down to the next generations, fostering an environment of increased gender equity and social inclusion.

4. Methodology

We employed a qualitative research approach in our effort to understand how SHGs and entrepreneurship help in women's empowerment. Gupta (2021) in his paper emphasized the role of qualitative research in analyzing the samples and understanding specific issues. We collected the data through personal observation and in-depth interviews with community resource persons (CRP). The interview questions were framed keeping in mind the empowerement framework theorised by Naila Kabeer (1999). The interviews were conducted over telephone, Google Meet, Zoom and multiple face-to-face meetings. We conducted the interviews in Malayalam and transcribed and translated them into English.

Before collecting data for this study, the researcher contacted Kudumbashree to obtain permission. An Independent Ethics Committee (IEC) approved the questionnaire before we administered it. We identified the respondents in collaboration with various district-level authorities of Kudumbashree and by leveraging the researcher's networks. We identified two CRPs from two different districts of Kerala. CRP 1 is currently engaged as an MEC-SP and working in Kerala. As a CRP, her role revolved primarily around the promotion of enterprises. CRP 2 is working as a resource person for the Convergence project. Her work primarily guides communities nationwide in implementing the Peoples Development Plan.

CASE STUDIES

Case Study 1—CRP 1

CRP 1 is a Micro Entreprise Consultant (MEC) in Ernakulam's Startup Village Entrepreneurship Programme (SVEP). As an MEC, she was instrumental in helping 115 micro-enterprises. CRP 1 first became a member of the NHG near her marital house, where she also got elected as the group secretary. During her pregnancy, she has to give up this position. After that, CRP 1 worked with Hindustan Insecticides Ltd. and an advertising agency in Cochin. Certain financial shocks in their life compelled them to sell their property and move to the nearest city. In order to help overcome the financial difficulties, she applied to different places for a job but could not secure a job. She also appeared for various competitive exams to secure jobs in the government sector, but she was not successful. She quote, *"I often felt that if I had a source of income, I would not always have to ask my husband for money to meet my small expenses."*

She joined the NHG near her new house in order save some money and access some loans when required. There, she came to know about the advertisement for MEC openings. CRP 1 promptly applied for the job. She got the job after an interview at the District Mission office in Ernakulam and a written exam held in Trivandrum. She talks of the test and interview:

"At the district office, some people talked about Kudumbashree bylaws. I did not know about the bylaws. So, I contacted the CDS members, who shared a copy of the bylaws with me. For General Knowledge and Maths, I used to help my daughter with her studies, so I learned some things in that manner."

"I did not know about Kudumbashree or its structure. I was surprised to find out who a Community Resource Person (CRP) was and what a business plan was."

"My husband accompanied me for the interview and the examination. He did not complain even when he had to wait a long time at the district mission office for my interview while some other men leaving because of the long wait for the interview."

She invested almost one year in her training to become an MEC. The training happened in a phased manner. The training equipped a person with a basic understanding of business and markets. Many MECs were graduates and postgraduates; they had yet to work in a formal work environment. This lack of previous experience, as well as the patriarchal structure of the society, created doubts in the minds of women of their ability. Due to these and other reasons, many women dropped out of the program halfway through. The husband and mother-in-law helped CRP 1 to take care of her children during the training period. She remembers:

"Whenever I had to go for training in Trivandrum, my husband's mother would help out by taking care of my child".

The interactive nature of the training program kept the MECs interested and attended regularly. The trainers also used games and other learner experiences to keep them motivated throughout the training period. She talks about the training program:

"Initially, when I began as a CRP, I had many apprehensions about guiding people to start their business."

"The training covered various topics. We studied groups, the functioning of groups, Kudumbashree laws and methods of functioning and motivation sessions.

The unique thing about the training was that they taught us through various activities. When we do the activities, we learn about various things at the end. Just like we teach kids, we write some things on paper, play some games etc. We also had homework, which we had to complete in groups."

"The training that Kudumbashree gave me, was like a mini-MBA"

they conducted the 45 days of training in a phased manner over ten months. The assignments and team activities helped them build their knowledge and confidence. They also learned how to manage a project in this manner.

"Easy subjects like team building and team management were taught initially. Gradually, they introduced difficult subjects such as math and accounting.

" We were asked to prepare a project report during the initial part of the training. At that time, we were beginning to learn about projects, proposal writing, and group work. The most common problem that we would face was that the accounts would never tally or that we would waste a lot of time discussing and trying to understand various points of view".

"During the training, in addition to being asked to prepare business plans, we were asked to make mock presentations. For example, we were asked to imagine taking an entrepreneur to the bank to apply for a loan. We had to present the business plan to the bank manager on behalf of the entrepreneur".

In addition to regular classroom activities, motivational sessions and motivational talks were a key part of the training that was given. CRP 1 managed to attend these training programs because her mother-in-law was staying with her, helping her manage her house and taking care of her children while living away from home. Regarding the motivational sessions, she recalled:

"Motivational sessions were a key part of the training sessions. This was required because many of us had problems at home, such as staying away from home during weekends, resulting in challenges at home."

"One of my colleagues' husband did not let her go for the training because no one was available to cook for him. The motivational sessions helped us to kept our spirits up."

"The problems at home arose because this was the first time we stayed away from our homes. I could manage because, during the training period, my mother-in-law was staying with us".

In January 2017, CRP 1 joined as an SVEP MEC. During the initial days, she had to go to various wards in her panchayat to discuss business opportunities. These talks and sessions had to be taken during public meetings, which a large number of people would attend: the local panchayat members, NHG members, etc. CRP 1 feels she would only have been able to talk about enterprises with training.

"During my school and college days, other than talking during presentations, I have never spoken on a public platform. The training through CDS helped

me speak at various forums with the panchayat president, various officers, and elected representatives present. I spoke about various topics and explained SVEP to more than 500 people."

"The training sessions gave us the courage to travel independently and meet people to complete our work."

CRP 1 identifies two things as her achievements, which indicate her empowerment journey. The first is the creation of a tailoring unit. The tailoring unit initially started as a school, which evolved into a business. This unit was recognized by various authorities to be a success factor and ensured that the entrepreneur could earn a decent amount of income from the business. Today, the tailoring unit employs eight women and has a bustling order list. She narrated the experience very proudly:

One of my most significant achievements is that I helped one of my first entrepreneurs set up a business and helped grow her business. Since the lady had some health issues, we started a tailoring unit at home. But her earnings plateaued at around 1800 to 1700 Rs per month. We then set up a tailoring shop. We networked with the Gram Panchayat and got an initial order to stitch 30 sets of uniforms for the local school. As they gained experience and exposure, they started getting more oversized orders from various clients. They also successfully got an order from a corporate customer to stitch their uniforms.

CRP 1 also found a new aspect of her empowerment journey. Now, her husband seeks her input and suggestions while making decisions. This was remarkable as men made most decisions without discussing them with their wives. She got a one-time payment of Rs 20,000 for her Kudumbashree work. When CRP 1 suggested that they buy a washing machine with this money, her husband readily agreed. CRP 1 also feels that people respect her more since she is earning money. However, her family is also concerned as she interacts with many people and often has to be away from her home.

"My family members don't like me going out and talking to so many people. Many times, I had to ignore their displeasure. I go. They say that I have to return before dark."

"I feel that people respect and value me more because I earn money."

The training session has also benefited CRP 1 in her day-to-day life. In addition to being a CRP, she is also the president of her NHG. As an office bearer, she must manage multiple expectations and conflicts. They also trained her to help people write proposals and projects to secure bank loans.

"I am the president of my NHG at the moment. The most common conflict between the members is during the sanction of funds or when members seek extension to repay the amount. In such cases, there would often be dissent among the members. To resolve these conflicts, I interact with a lot of people. It has a social work nature to it. I understand the difficulties that people face, and their challenges.

As a result of the training I got in preparation to be an MEC, I learned how to resolve various challenges faced by people. It also helped me understand when to intervene and stay away."

Case Study 2—CRP 2

CRP 2 came from a humble household of two sisters and her parents. Her father was a mechanic who started a small workshop in Kollam. CRP 2 could not complete her postgraduate studies due to financial constraints at home. She was married off at an early age in the year 1999.

CRP 2 describes her marriage as a failure. She shared a very healthy and open relationship with her family, but it was not so with her husband and in-laws. The fact that her husband had a relationship earlier weighed down on her. There was no open communication between them, severely affecting her relationship with her husband.

"We had very open communication at my maternal home. I could talk to my father about everything that happened during the day. He would listen and then give us feedback, guide us on how we could have done better."

"Communication at my husband's house was never direct. Often, communication happened between me and my husband through his sister. I did not like this form of indirect communication."

During her college life, she had a lot of friends and was also very active in college politics. Her husband did not appreciate any of these.

"When my husband- then fiancé went around to invite people to the wedding, almost all his relatives and friends knew about me. He did not appreciate this fact."

"My husband did not appreciate me networking with my friends. In fact, in my married life, my friendships and my conversations with my friends became a reason for taunts from my husband. When I would approach him with some concern, he would often ask me to go and talk to my friends. He started censoring my reading habit. He would read my letters to my friends. He also did not allow me to listen to music, which was a great stress reliever for me. Gradually, my contact with the outside world decreased.

In addition, my husband did not have a stable job. When the proposal came, they told me he had a workshop and was a mechanic. However, the reality was different. He was employed part-time by his friend.

"It was much later that we learned he was not very interested in working. He did not like hard work. At one point, he went to Dubai, but as he did not get any job, he came back."

Around this time, she gave birth to a baby girl. Despite added responsibilities, her husband was not a caring person and would not support the family's needs.

Therefore, to aid the family and provide a source of livelihood for herself, CRP 2 joined the local NHG.

As she joined the NHG, she was rapidly elected to be the secretary of the NHG, and subsequently, as a member of the ADS, where she was elected as a secretary, very soon she was also elected to be a member of the CDS, where she was elected to become the Chairperson.

"When I became CDS Chairperson, I suddenly realized that I am more than just a wife. Even though I was socially very active as a person, my marital life had cut me off from society at large. I felt liberated, I felt that there was a world out there that I could win."

CDS's exposure was also instrumental in ensuring that she had a wider social network and better connectivity. This enabled her to participate in various training sessions that Kudumbashree organized, train other women in a similar situation, and help other women move out of poverty.

As a CDS chairperson, CRP 2 speaks about two incidents that greatly influenced her empowerment journey. The first incident was when she was supposed to talk to a section of the community about Kudumbashree and its activities in the field. The elected members of the panchayat attended this meeting, every NHG member, and people from various sections of the society. However, she could not give a good presentation, resulting in the Panchayat president taking over the presentation and discussing it. This incident affected her greatly, and she resolved never to let it happen again.

"As I was walking home, my daughter asked me- 'Amma, why did you not speak'? I told her that " I did not have much to speak'. But since then, I resolved that I would not let anyone cut into what I have to say. If I had to speak in public, I would ensure that I prepared on the topic and only then went to the meeting. It was a learning experience."

The next meeting was in another ward. She went with a renewed resolve and better preparation and gave a presentation that required her to stand and talk for 3 hours.

"I surprised myself that I could talk so much and so well. I covered every point. I did not leave a single part of Kudumbashre functioning that day."

A major financial achievement that she had as a result of joining Kudumbashree was the money that her father had borrowed to pay for her marriage expenses. She could save the required amount of money and repay the amount.

"My participation in Kudumbashree NHG activities helped me to save the little amount that my father had spent on my marriage. Personally, being able to save and earn that much money back felt very good. I felt strong."

CRP 2 was active in campus politics during her student life. She claims that as a CDS chairperson and subsequently as a mentor, the impact she has achieved in society is significant. The other major achievement that CRP 2 considers to be significant is that she was able to launch the Ashraya project. It is a scheme implemented by the government of India to identify and rehabilitate destitute families. She was assaulted physically at this time for her work with the destitute. This was the second part in her empowerment journey.

"There was opposition from the Panchayat Samiti even during the project preparation period. They did not allocate funds for this.

One elected member used filthy language to address me when I inquired about this. I retorted and told him he could have such words with his family, not me. At that point, he raised his hands to hit me. I dodged it and slapped him back instead.

"Later, I convinced the panchayat members to allocate funds for the scheme. I assured them that this would benefit the poor families in the village. Over some time, she was selected as a CRP Mentor and nominated to travel to different parts of India as a resource person to train other SHG members. Currently, she works as a CRP in Nagaland and trains SHG members to develop people's development plans. She attributes her success to various trainings she received as part of Kudumbashree.

"Although I was active in student politics, getting exposure to be the Chairperson of CDS was a daunting proposition. Training sessions helped me to overcome my little inhibitions.

"We were part of the team that drafted the bylaws to be followed by Kudumbashree members. As I said before, there was fear and doubt in my mind if I could do it.

"The training to become a mentor was a major experience. This required me to travel to different regions of India. However, the training helped me overcome my doubts.

"Convergence is not an easy topic to talk about especially to women dominated by patriarchy. I can convince women that they can bring about change in society. When I am scared, I look back at my past experiences and gain strength.

"The pitching sessions and assignments were the most important part of the training sessions. They gave me the required practice to talk to people, frame my statements, and present the points in a good manner"

Training sessions were very educational. But initially, it was an escape from the pressures and stressors I was facing at home. As I made friends within Kudumbashree, training sessions became a route for me to meet up with them. The time I spent in training centers was filled with laughter and joy.

I was still living with my husband the first time I went for training. The training gave me the strength to fight for my rights and eventually separate from the toxic relationship that controlled my life.

The impact of the empowerment process is not limited to RM alone. Over the past 7-8 years, she has avoided active participation in the day-to-day functioning of NHG activities. However, even today, she gets calls from various people seeking help. According to her, these calls are because she was able to help them out.

"Even today, people call me to seek assistance with various things. These are simple things like going with them somewhere or helping them talk to some officer, etc."

5. Discussion

Indeed, training plays a vital role in women's empowerment. This empowerment has enabled women to take up leadership roles and provided them a new space. The Kudumbashree initiative is to create more grassroots entrepreneurs in the country. The entrepreneurial way is a tested route to women's empowerment (Singh, 2021). This study explored the role of training in creating an entrepreneurial mindset among women in rural Kerala. It has effectively trained over 1400 women grassroots leaders. These have been women who had minimum education but without stable employment. They were also women who otherwise would have been branded as housewives. The training enabled them to understand how to get through the complicated bureaucratic structures and political power struggles. They are now empowered to guide grassroots entrepreneurs in turn. Professionals train Community Resource Persons (CRP) to take up leadership roles. In turn, they train women in their NHGs and help them acquire finances for their ventures, train them on how to start a business, assist them in marketing their products, and support them in sustaining their own until they can manage their own.

6. Implications of the Research

This study points to a very successfully implemented women empowerment project in one of the states in India. With minimum investment, this program shows how the government can create rural development. This experiment has shown that women can become the harbingers of development. The training, however, is limited to only the office bearers of the program. It is essential that leadership training should be available to grassroots entrepreneurs as well. Currently they are only supported by the CRPs, but are not trained professionally. Technical training for women in rural areas is a potent empowerment tool (Krishnamurthy et al., 2017).

7. Conclusion

According to our premise, through leadership training, Kudumbashree empowers women to go beyond hegemonic structures of oppression and create an alternative model that derives sustainable empowerment.

As an outcome, this study demonstrates the practical application of Kabeer's empowerment model within Kudumbashree's setting.

The major role played the CRP in community development and empowerment of Kudumbashree members is evident from the two case studies. The participatory and grassroots dimensions of the process which is followed by Kudumbashree in identifying, selecting and training CRPs from the communities also in turn contributes to the empowerment journey of the women from the communities. The selected case studies highlight the crucial importance of the leadership framework and empowerment models in improving the socioeconomic status of Kudumbashree members. Perhaps most importantly, the study highlights that the training which is provided for CRPs not only enables them to access resources, and achieve goal which they previously thought to be impossible thus empowering themselves. But the training also enables them to assist other women in their empowerment journey, serve as role models within their spheres of influence thus facilitating empowerment journey of other women. This journey and support systems created through trained CRPs and Kudumbashree members also empowers women to challenge and at time rebel against social structures which they perceive as oppressive. Thus in turn leading to an empowered community.

This research highlights the necessity for continual investment in the development and training of CRPs, illustrating the need for specialized training, mentorship, and community support networks. This study proposes a blueprint that paves the way for equitable representation of rural women while enhancing their autonomy and developing their leadership abilities. The empowerment of rural women through micro-enterprises holds the promise of sculpting an equitable future.

References

1. Akram, N., Hamid, A., & Akram, M. I. (2019). Role of women empowerment in utilization of maternal healthcare services. *Pakistan Economic and Social Review*, *57*(1), 93–116.
2. Aiswarya, S., & Sangeetha, S. (2022). Perception of Women Trainees' regarding Skill Development Initiatives of Kudumbashree for Employability. *Ramanujan International Journal of Business and Research*, *7*(2), 56–66.
3. Counts, A. (2008). *Small loans, big dreams: How Nobel prize winner Muhammad Yunus and microfinance are changing the world*. John Wiley & Sons.
4. Ebrahimi, R., Choobchian, S., Farhadian, H., Goli, I., Farmandeh, E., & Azadi, H. (2022). Investigating the effect of vocational education and training on rural women's empowerment. *Humanities and Social Sciences Communications*, *9*(1).
5. Eisenhardt, K.M. and Graebner, M.E. (2007), "*Theory building from cases: opportunities and challenges*", Academy of Management Journal, Vol. 50 No. 1, pp. 25–32.
6. Gupta, M. (2021). Role of NGOs in women empowerment: case studies from Uttarakhand, India. *Journal of Enterprising communities: People and places in the Global Economy*, *15*(1), 26–41.

7. John, S. F. (2021). Role Of Kudumbashree In The Economic Upliftment Of Women. *PalArch's Journal of Archaeology of Egypt/Egyptology*, *18*(4), 3073–3086.
8. Joseph TY, G., Krishna, A., Augustine, A., & LAIJU, D. (2023). Role of kudumbashree on women empowerment-a study in ernakulam district.
9. KA, A., FATHIMA, N., & VARGHESE, R. P. (2023). *Impact of microfinance on women empowerment through kudumbashree units* (Doctoral dissertation).
10. Kabeer, Naila. (1999) "Resources, Agency, Achievements: Reflections on the Measurement of Women's Empowerment." Development and Change, vol. 30, no. 3, pp. 435–464.
11. Kabeer, N. (2010). Women's empowerment, development interventions, and the management of information flows. *ids Bulletin*, *41*(6), 105–113.
12. Kapila, M., Singla, A., & Gupta, M. L. (2016, June). Impact of microcredit on women empowerment in India: An empirical study of Punjab state. In *Proceedings of the World Congress on Engineering* (Vol. 2, pp. 821–825). London, United Kingdom: Newswood Limited.
13. Krishnamurthy, S., Joseph, S., Pradhan, V., & Rao, P. (2017). Empowering women of rural India for renewable energy adoption–an exploratory factor analysis. *Indian Journal of Science and Technology*, *10*(37), 1–10.
14. Kumar, P. (2014). Rural women empowerment in India. *Asian Journal of Multidisciplinary Studies*, *2*(1), 75–79.
15. Laizu, Z., Armarego, J., & Sudweeks, F. (2010). The role of ICT in women's empowerment in rural Bangladesh.
16. Mahalingam, M. R. (2022). *Building Capacity for Food Justice through Learning Pathways: Women's Group Farming in Kudumbashree, Kerala, India* (Doctoral dissertation, Arizona State University).
17. Mathur, P., & Agarwal, P. (2017). Self-help groups: a seed for intrinsic empowerment of Indian rural women. *Equality, Diversity and Inclusion: An International Journal*, *36*(2), 182–196.
18. Malcom, A., & Bhandari, C. N. (2021, July). An Empirical Study on Microfinance and its impact on Human Development indicators using the instance of Kerala's Kudumbashree Model. In *2021 12th International Conference on Computing Communication and Networking Technologies (ICCCNT)* (pp. 1–9). IEEE.
19. Nayak, P., & Mahanta, B. (2012). Women empowerment in India. *Bulletin of Political Economy*, *5*(2), 155–183.
20. Paramanandam, D. A., & Packirisamy, P. (2015). An empirical study on the impact of micro enterprises on women empowerment. *Journal of Enterprising Communities: People and Places in the Global Economy*, *9*(4), 298–314.
21. Parveen, K. (2014). Development of rural women entrepreneurs through workshop training. *Research Journal of Management Sciences*, *2319*, 1171.
22. Patton, M.Q. (2002), "*Two decades of developments in qualitative inquiry: a personal, experiential perspective*", Qualitative Social Work: Research and Practice, Vol. 1 No. 3, pp. 261–283.
23. Powell, L., & McGrath, S. (2019). *Skills for human development: Transforming vocational education and training*. Routledge.
24. Raveendran, S., & Sharma, D. M. (2023). Increasing the Women Empowerment through Kudumbashree in Kerala Region. *Available at SSRN 4388032*.

25. Roy, C., Chatterjee, S., & Dutta Gupta, S. (2018). Women empowerment index: Construction of a tool to measure rural women empowerment level in India. *Available at SSRN 3357543*.
26. Singh, P., & Pattanaik, F. (2020). Unfolding unpaid domestic work in India: women's constraints, choices, and career. *Palgrave Communications*, *6*(1), 1–13.
27. Uma, N. (2012). Self help group: an effective approach to women empowerment in India. *International Journal of Social Science and Interdisciplinary Research*, *1*(8), 8–16.
28. Shamshadali, P., Anjena, C. K., & Mohammed, K. F. (2019). Role of Kudumbashree micro financing in the women empowerment with special reference to the Malappuram District of Kerala. *Indian Journal of Economics and Development*, *7*(3), 1–5.
29. Shirur, M., Sharath, H. N., Tewari, G., & Nandi, R. (2020). Dissemination of kudumbashree model-based entrepreneurship among rural women groups in Africa and Asia. *Indian Journal of Extension Education*, *56*(4), 20–29.
30. Yunus, Muhammad. "Banker to the Poor: Micro-Lending and the Battle Against World Poverty." PublicAffairs, 2003.

Securing the Future through Sustainability, Health, Education, and Technology – Brig. Dr. Rajiv Divekar et al. (eds)

20 Arming Prosperity: A Comprehensive Study of Defense Expenditure's Influence on India's Economic Growth and Employment

Sandip Solanki[1]
Institute of International Business (SIIB),
Symbiosis International (Deemed University) (SIU),
Pune, Maharashtra, India.

Inumula, Krishna Murthy[2]
Institute of International Business (SIIB),
Symbiosis International (Deemed University) (SIU),
Pune, Maharashtra, India.

Seema Singh[3]
Symbiosis Centre for Corporate Education,
Pune, Symbiosis International (Deemed University),
Pune, Maharashtra, India

Abstract

The focus of this paper is to examine how defense spending affects economic development and unemployment rates of India by using annual time series data covering the period from 1991 to 2017. The secondary data are collected from the World Bank open database (data.worldbank.org) on three macroeconomic indicators, namely "Total Unemployment (% of the total labour force), Military expenditure (% of GDP) and GDP growth (annual %)". To determine the stationarity of time series variables and subsequent long-run relationships between the variables, ADF statistics and Johansen cointegration (1988, 1991) were used. Finding confirms that 1 per cent change in annual unemployment growth causes the military expenditure growth to increase by about 0.30 per cent, 1 per cent change in economic growth rate causes the military expenditure growth to decrease by about 0.13 per cent. The Johansen's Co-integration test validated the long-run equilibrium relationship among the military spending growth, unemployment growth and economic growth rates meaning that all these macro-economic variables all move together in the long run. The positive relationship between military expenditure and unemployment suggests that if unemployment

[1]sandip.solanki@siib.ac.in, [2]dr.krishna@siib.ac.in, [3]director@scce.edu.in

DOI: 10.1201/9781003587200-20

levels are unchecked, it will increase defence expenditure. In both the long and short run, economic growth is significantly impacted by military spending.

KEYWORDS: Military expenditure, Defence expenditure, Economic growth, Unemployment, India, Time series analysis

1. Introduction

(Benoit, 1973) commenced the research on government spending on military and it's impact on growth, result explored affirmative and substantial effect of armed spending on growthoriginated study on military expenditure and economic growth and established a correlation between military spending and economic growth rates in developing countries. Numerous studies were launched as a result of Benoit's work in the pursuit of a clear relationship between the two variables and it has attracted policymakers' attention. Various studies have been conducted to evaluate the impact of military spending on economic growth, the findings of these research papers are indecisive and inconsistent. Several studies revealed a favourable relationship between defence expenditure on economic growth (Awaworyi Churchill & Yew, 2018; Castillo et al., 2001; H.-C. Chang, Huang, & Yang, 2011; Tung-Pao Wang, Stacy Huey-Pyng Shyu, & Han-Chung Chou, 2012) which supports The Keynesian school fo thought. The Keynesian school of thought reviewed that increase in defence spending will increase the purchasing power of people. In turn, it will help to increase aggregate demand and national output. These effects, at large, will generate positive externalities known as positive developmental effects. Another side of it is that several studies emphasize the negative impact of defence expenditure on economic development (Blomberg, 1996; Deger & Smith, 1983; Maizels & Nissanke, 1986), which supports The Classical school of thought. It is observed that an surge in military expenditure is most probably hinders economic development. The increase in defence expenditure will slow private investment, reducing domestic savings and decreasing aggregate demand, reducing consumption in the economy political stability is added advantage of it.

In conclusion, empirical evidence has not consistently supported theoretical expectations. While some study indicates that spending on the military is favorably correlated with economic growth, other findings support the opposite view. Moreover, the significant difference in the results is also found amongst those who have conducted various studies to evaluate the military spending and economic growth for developing economies in the past. India has shown very weak spin-off from defence to development (Deger & Sen, 1983), in contrast, (Mukhopadhyay, Sinha, & Sengupta, 2022) investigated the favourable influence of defence spending on commercial development in India, which is very alarming when India's share of its defence spending is rising in the total global defence spending. Being, national security, the top priority of the Indian government, India spent $72.9 billion, up 2.1% from the previous year, making it the third-highest spender in the globe (SIPRI). With 9.5% of global arms imports during 2016-2020, India ranks second after Saudi Arabia as the largest importer of arms in the world (Pieter Wezeman & Alexandra Kuimova and Siemon Wezeman/ SIPRI). Thus, investigating whether more defence spending is promoting or preventing economic growth is so necessary and crucial. Substantial research on the relationship between military spending and economic growth has been carried out but there very few unifying theories that simultaneously relates military expenditure, economic growth and unemployment. One of the major goals of this paper is to bridge the gap in literature by incorporating these variables to develop a more general theory of economic growth. Therefore, this paper aims to answer the question in the case of India.

The paper is organized as follows: The relationship between the elements of military spending, unemployment, and economic growth is discussed in Section 2; the empirical technique we used in this study is described in Section 3; the data and findings are presented in Section 4; and the paper is concluded in Section 5.

2. Literature Review

The majority of the research studies which have highlighted the correlation between military expenditure and economic growth are empirical; attempts to resolve the challenges theoretically have not been successful. Some research has shown that Military expenditures has a positive effect on economic expansion while other studies declined this hypothesis. Covering different time period, these studies conducted for developed and developing countries and for long and short run but the findings of all these studies are not unanimous. Literature review of this study is segregated under four broad clusters (1) Impact of military spending on economic growth and unemployment (2) Military spending has a positive impact on economic growth and (3) Negative effect of military spending on economic growth and (4) Neutrality hypothesis:

2.1 Impact of Military Spending on Economic Growth and Unemployment

The present empirical work on military expenditure and unemployment has yielded a wide range of conclusions. For instance, defence expenditure has shown affirmative influence on Spanish GDP and employment during 2010 (García, Murillo, Suriñach, & Vayá, 2018). Similarly, Heo and Hahm (2006) observed that military spending does not appear to have a detrimental effect on economic growth via investment and unemployment in South Korea in a study conducted from 1963 to 2001. Heo and Ye (2016) suggested that at the global level, defence expenditure extensively reduces private investment but somewhat reduces unemployment in a study conducted during 1990–2012. But, contrary to the above studies, P. Dunne and Watson (2000) estimated that, in the long run, defence spending will adversely affect industrial structure, efficiency and manufacturing employment in South Africa. Yildirim and Sezgin (2003) employing ARDL approach to cointegration, specified that in short and long run, the impact of defence spending on employment is negative. This research was conducted during 1950 to 1997. Korkmaz (2015) observed negative influence of defence expenditure on economic development of 10 Mediterranean Countries, and noted that it rises unemployment. This paper used panel data for the period 2005-2012. Supporting the view, Azam, Khan, Zaman, and Rasli (2016) concluded that the link is significant and adverse between defence expenditure and unemployment in SAARC countries. Qiong and Junhua (2015) analysed data from 1991 to 2013 of China showed that the cost of supporting the military raises the unemployment rate. Uniformity is also observed between military and non-military expenditure and unemployment across 18 OECD countries (Paul, 1996).

2.2 Military Expenditure Boots Economic Growth

A favourable relationship between defence spending and economic expansion is also seen for Lithuania in the post 2014 period (Palavenis, 2020), for Canada and UK (T. Chang, Lee, Hung, & Lee, 2014), in Turkey and Greece during the period of 1956-2003 (Kalyoncu & Yucel, 2013), as well as in Turkey and Middle Eastern nations during 1989 to 1999 (Yildirim†, Sezgin, & Öcal, 2005), in India but no long run cointegration in the case of China from 1989 to 2016 (Mukhopadhyay et al., 2022). Interestingly, compare to less developed countries, the outcome of defence spending on economic development is more distinct on developed countries (Awaworyi Churchill & Yew, 2018). Moreover, Stability of economy also plays important role to determine impact on military spending on economic development. Defense spending has a favourable effect on economic growth in a stable economy, otherwise it affects negatively (Qureshi & Khan, 2017). It is also observed that effect of defence expenditure on income is temporary on Turkish economy, in the long run, this expenditure creates inflation. (Emmanouilidis & Karpetis, 2021). Heo and Ye (2019) investigated that presence of U.S troops has boosted investment, trade and economic growth in the host country during 1960 to 2014.

Mohanty, Panda, and Bhuyan (2020) explored that India's economic growth is significantly impacted by defence spending from 1970-1971 to 2015-2016. Supporting this hypothesis, McDonald and Eger (2010) noted that from 1992 to 2007, persistent reliance on the defence sector aided overall economic growth in post-Soviet states. Apanisile and Okunlola (2014) identified unfavourable and significant correlation between defence spending and economic growth in the short-run but favourable and significant effect in the long-run, in a study of Nigeria during 1989-2013. For Turkey, there is one way-causation from military expenditure to economic growth (Pan, Chang, & Wolde-Rufael, 2015). While,

(Dimitraki & Win, 2021) showed favourable association between military expenditure and economic development in Jordan, during the long-run and short run, during the period 1970-2015. Likewise, (Castillo et al., 2001) showed that rise in military expenditure has boosted economic development during the period 1870-1939 for German, France, Russia, Japan, and the United States. It is also noted that there was no evidence to suggest that defence spending had a negative impact on economic growth.of various less developed nations (Landau, 1994)

2.3 Military Expenditure Retards Economic Growth

Negative correlation between military expenditure and economic growth was observed in African countries, covering the time period from 2001 to 2014 (Sarwar & Idrees, 2022), in Malaysia from the year 1979 to 2017 (Saudi et al., 2019), and between defence expenditure and sustainable economic development in Romania between 1996-1999 and 2002-2004 (Tao, Glonț, Li, Lobonț, & Guzun, 2020). Similarly, Luqman and Antonakakis (2021) observed that for Pakistan, the impact of defence expenditure had unfavourable influence on human development and economic growth from 1965 to 2016. Similar results also found in some other studies. Maizels and Nissanke (1986) examined based on cross-country regressions that the effect of defence spending on economic progress in emerging countries is often adverse. The study was conducted for the period 1978 to 1980. Blomberg (1996) explored a weak but direct adverse impact of military expenditure on economic advancement.

Heo and Eger (2005) revealed that military expenditure in the United States has an opposing, indirect influence on economic development via investment and export from 1951 to 2000, whereas the direct effect on economic growth appears to be minimal. The findings are also similar for less developed countries (Deger & Smith, 1983), in the case of South Africa for the time period 1950 to 1985 (McMillan, 1992). From 1967 to 1985, economic growth is negatively correlated with military spending found for thirteen Sub-Saharan African countries (J. P. Dunne & Mohammed, 1995), and for OECD countries for the period 1970-2014 (d'Agostino, Dunne, & Pieroni, 2017), for the past three decades, negative correlation between defence spending and economic development is observed for Egypt, Israel and Syria (Abu-Bader & Abu-Qarn, 2003), the similar results are also explored for South Korea from 1954 to 95 (Heo, 1999), the results are also in line for Turkey (Manamperi, 2016) and for 82 countries for the period of 1988–2008 (Töngür & Elveren, 2017). Njamenkengdo, Aurelien, Kouladoum, and Jean-Claude (2018) explored the significant and detrimental effects of military expenditures on economic expansion for Chad economy through VAR modelling over the period 1985-2015. In another study, J. P. Dunne and Tian (2015) highlighted that defence spending has a negative influence on economic growth in both the short and long terms, using an exogenous growth model and dynamic panel data for 106 nations between 1988 and 2010.

Some other scholars have also noted the negative consequence of defence expenditure on economic growth. Cappelen, Gleditsch, and Bjerkholt (1984) noted that except Mediterranean countries, the effect of defense expenditure on economic development for 17 OECD nations remained negative for the period 1960-1980. H.-C. Chang et al. (2011), noted that for low-income countries, military expenditure affects unfavourable on economic development. The research used GMM to panel data of 90 nations covering over 1992-2006, Ahmed, Alam, Rashid, and Gow (2020) showed that 1% rise in defence expenditure led to a 0.63% drop in economic development of Myanmar for the period of 1975-2014.

2.4 Neutrality Hypothesis

Few findings also highlighted that military spending has no effect on economic growth. In a study of Turkey covering 1988-2013 duration, shows that It has not been shown that military spending contributes to economic growth (Gokmenoglu, Taspinar, & Sadeghieh, 2015) and also (T. Chang et al., 2014) supported neutrality hypothesis for Italy, France and Germany. Weak spin-off from military expenditure to economic development is noticed in less developed countries specially for India (Deger & Sen, 1983) and high military expenditures are not deleterious to Japan's economic growth during 1879-1990 (Ward, Davis, & Lofdahl, 1995).

The noteworthy differences among these results show the importance of further investigation.

3. Data and Methods

3.1 Data and Scope

This time series research study, which was compiled from data provided by the World Bank, spans the years 1991 to 2017. Secondary data collected from open database (data.worldbank.org) on three macroeconomic indicators, namely "Total Unemployment (% of the total labour force), Military expenditure (% of GDP) and GDP growth (annual %)". This research study attempts to find the cointegration relationship between military spending, economic growth, and unemployment. Besides, the study also explores how innovations in economic growth and unemployment would contribute to studying the variations in military expenditure. The simultaneous equation system (VAR-VECM) framework facilitates the study of the interrelationship between the variables. The dependent variable military expenditure is studied through the linear endogenous combination of the relationship between military spending, economic growth and unemployment.

3.2 Econometric Methods

The non-stationary variables are converted to stationary variables by using differencing. To determine the stationarity of time series variables and subsequent long-run relationships between the variables, ADF statistics and Johansen cointegration (1988, 1991) were used. Johansen cointegration is widely used research technique to identify the linkages between two variables (Abraham Camba Jr & Aileen Camba, 2021; Ben Dhiab & Dkhili).

If cointegration exists between the variables, then the study variables are tested for short-run relationships by Error Correction Model (VECM). The best of three lag length criterions "Akaike Information Criterion (AIC), Schwarz Bayesian criterion (BIC) and Hannan-Quinn criterion (HQC)" has been chosen to determine the size of lag length for model development. In addition to the Johansen cointegration techinque, the Engle-Granger causality technique is used to find the cause and affect the relationship between the variables using the Vector Auto Regression (VAR) framework. VAR framework is also used by previous researchers to examine the causal connection between India's economic development and sectoral contributions to India's Gross Domestic Product (GDP) (Solanki et al., 2020).

The simultaneous equation system (VAR) treats each variable as an endogenous variable dependent on other lagged variables. The VAR system determines the causal flow between the variables assuming the null hypothesis that the underlying variables (Granger) cause each other.

$$Mil_t = C_1 + \sum_{i=1}^{k} a_{1i} Mil_{t-i} + \sum_{i=1}^{k} b_{1i} GDP_{t-i} + \sum_{i=1}^{k} c_{1i} UEMP_{t-i} + e_{1t}$$

$$GDP_t = C_2 + \sum_{i=1}^{k} a_{2i} Mil_{t-i} + \sum_{i=1}^{k} b_{2i} GDP_{t-i} + \sum_{i=1}^{k} c_{2i} UEMP_{t-i} + e_{2t}$$

$$UEMP_t = C_3 + \sum_{i=1}^{k} a_{3i} Mil_{t-i} + \sum_{i=1}^{k} b_{3i} GDP_{t-i} + \sum_{i=1}^{k} c_{3i} UEMP_{t-i} + e_{3t}$$

Where *Mil* is the military expenditure, *GDP* is the proxy for economic growth, and *UEMP* is the unemployment rate.

4. Results and Discussion

4.1 Trend of Variables

Figure 20.1 shows the trend of data variables; military expenditure over the study period increased from 1995 to 2001 and decreased to 2.3% of GDP in 2007. The period 2010-15 witnessed a steady decline in military expenditure. At the same time, unemployment increased during the period 1991-2001 and decreased to 3.5% in the year 2017. The annual GDP growth in an erratic manner rose from 2% to 10% in the study period during 1991-2011, touching the lower levels of around 4%.

4.2 Stationary Time Series

The outcomes from Table 20.1 show that the ADF tests tested for without constant, constant and constant with tendency correspondingly confirm that the

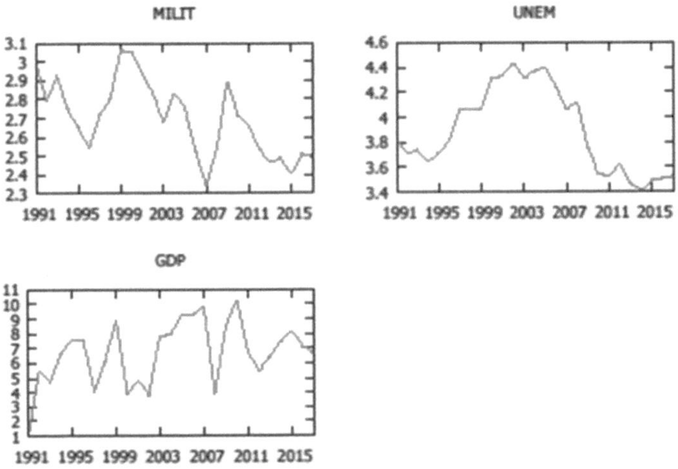

Fig. 20.1 Time series graph

variables in the level form are non-stationary. After the first differencing, they became stationary. The model with "the constant" term is used to study the long-run relation –cointegration among the study variables.

Table 20.1 Non-stationary and stationary

Level	P Value	First Difference	P Value
Mi	0.1965 0.2343 0.1589	d_Mil	0.001 0.002 0.000
UEMP	0.4215 0.3584 0.4865	d_UEMP	0.003 0.008 0.001
GDP	0.7894 0.2252 0.5465	d_GDP	0.008 0.000 0.000

4.3 Lag Selection and Direction of Causality

The Information criterions AIC, HQC both had given the optimum period of lag 4 to test the causal flow between the study variables. The Engel-Granger test assumes the null hypothesis that Military expenditure does not cause unemployment and GDP growth & vice versa. Results from Table 20.2 show that up to lag 4, a uni-directional causality exists that GDP (Granger) causes unemployment.

4.4 Cointegration Test

Table 20.3 gives the results of the cointegration test; both the trace statistic 34.926 [0.0090] and Lmax test 25.789 [0.0084] confirm one co-integrating equation

Table 20.2 Direction of causality among military expenditure, unemployment and GDP growth

Flow of Causality	Lag	F Test [Sig.value]
Mil → UEMP	2	1.0513 [0.3700]
UEMP → Mil		0.8674 [0.4368]
UEMP → GDP		1.2354 [0.3142]
GDP → UEMP		4.459 [0.0267]
GDP → Mil		1.3005 [0.2968]
Mil → GDP		1.5324 [0.2429]
Mil → UEMP	3	1.7985 [0.1937]
UEMP → Mil		0.9522 [0.4422]
UEMP → GDP		1.4214 [0.2783]
GDP → UEMP		3.8922 [0.0325]
GDP → Mil		0.3154 [0.8140]
Mil → GDP		1.5955 [0.2351]
Mil → UEMP	4	1.7391 [0.2177]
UEMP → Mil		0.3257 [0.8545]
UEMP → GDP		0.9909 [0.4557]
GDP → UEMP		3.3995 [0.0452]
GDP → Mil		0.1601 [0.9538]
Mil → GDP		1.1648 [0.3825]

Table 20.3 Johansen's test

Rank	Eigenvalues (λi)	Trace Test [P-value]	Lmax Test [P-value]	
0	0.64355	34.926 [0.0090]	25.789 [0.0084]	
1	0.25158	9.1367 [0.3595]	7.2448 [0.4693]	
2	0.07288	1.8919 [0.1690]	1.8919 [0.1690]	
	Mil	**UEMP**	**GDP**	**Constatnt**
β Coefficients: 1.00(0.00)	-0.305* (0.104)	0.135 (0.023)	0.76 * (0.36)	(standard errors in parenthesis)
	d_Mil	**d_UEMP**	**d_GDP**	**(P-values in parenthesis)**
α Coefficients:	−0.32* (0.03)	0.25*(0.04)	-6.85** (0.00)	
Short Run Coefficients:				
d_MILIT_1	0.13 (0.54)	-0.20 (0.20)	6.43 (0.02)	
d_UNEM_1	-0.09 (0.75)	0.68 (0.00)	-1.82 (0.65)	
d_GDP_1	0.02 (0.40)	0.02 (0.16)	0.16 (0.50)	

* at 5% & **at 1% level of significance

concluding that all the study variables move together in the long-run, therefore the next step is to measure the short-run relationship by using VECM.

Results indicate that a 1 per cent change in annual unemployment growth causes the military expenditure to rise by 0.30 per cent, which means if unemployment is unchecked, then higher unemployment leads to a low to moderate impact on military spending. Though non-significant, a 1 per cent change in economic growth rate causes the military expenditure growth to decrease by 0.13 per cent, meaning that in the long-run economic growth will boost the necessary infrastructure and business environment that positively impact the developmental prospects of the country to less hostile and aversion to war kind of situations.

The negative ECM term (-0.32) is statistically significant, indicating the long-run causality from military expenditure growth to GDP and unemployment. In the short run, there is no significant causal relationship exists in the system. In the context of economic growth as an endogenous variable, long-run coefficient -6.85** (p-value 0.00) and short-run 6.43 (p-value 0.02) the military expenditure significantly impacts economic growth.

5. Conclusion

The long-run equilibrium relationship among the military spending growth, unemployment growth and economic growth rates is confirmed by the Johansen's Co-integration test, meaning that all these macro-economic variables all move together in the long run. Monitoring military expenditure vis-à-vis the economic growth and employment uncertainties would be the foremost priority of the policymakers. Results found that 1 per cent change in annual unemployment growth causes the military expenditure growth to increase by about 0.30 per cent, 1 per cent change in economic development rate causes the military expenditure growth to decrease by about 0.13 per cent. Military spending significantly affects economic expansion, in the long run and short run. The positive relationship between military expenditure and unemployment suggests that if unemployment levels are unchecked, it will increase defence expenditure. The rise in unemployment with the surge in military spending means that the funds intended for creating employment were misallocated or diverted to other government programmes or may even be used for military expenditures. Given the era of globalization, the negative relationship between economic growth and army spending suggests that countries with good economic growth should allocate funds to other sectors of the economy. Still, at the same time, it should not lower military spending as the international community dynamics changes very quickly from time to time to face the uncertainties of war and other geographical issues.

6. Significance

Our work is important because it sheds light on how India's military spending affects economic growth and unemployment. The results of our analysis can be used by decision-makers to create efficient policies that strike a balance between the demands for economic growth and job creation and defense spending. Our study also provides a foundation for further investigation and adds to the body of knowledge on the topic. Overall, our research has significant policy and academic ramifications, and we think it will contribute significantly to the body of knowledge on military spending, economic growth, and unemployment. Our research is also distinctive since it looks at the relationships between India's unemployment, economic growth, and military spending. This method offers a more thorough knowledge of the impact that defense spending has on the Indian economy and labor market.

7. Limitation

Although our work sheds light on the relationships between military spending, economic expansion, and unemployment in India, there are several limitations that must be recognized.

First off, our study only takes into account annual time series data from 1991 to 2017, which may not adequately reflect the dynamic nature of the link between military spending, economic growth, and unemployment in India. Our findings might not be applicable to other eras because those eras might have different political and economic environments.

Second, other factors that might have an impact on these variables are not taken into account in our study, which only examines the impact of military spending on employment and economic growth. The economic growth and unemployment in India may be significantly impacted by additional factors like foreign direct investment, governmental policy, and global commerce. As a result, our findings need to be understood in the context of other variables that affect employment and economic growth.

Last but not least, because our study exclusively considers the example of India, our conclusions might not generalize to other nations. The relationship between military spending, economic growth, and unemployment may be impacted by the economic, political, and social settings of other nations. Therefore, more study is needed to determine how military spending impacts unemployment and global economic growth.

Overall, while our work adds to the body of knowledge on the topic, it is crucial to recognize its limits and the need for additional research to fully comprehend the connection between military spending, economic growth, and unemployment.

References

1. Abraham Camba Jr, & Aileen Camba (2021). An Engle-Granger and Johansen Cointegration Approach in Testing the Validity of Fisher Hypothesis in the Philippines. *Journal of Asian Finance Economics and Business*, *8*(12), 31–38. https://doi.org/10.13106/jafeb.2021.vol8.no12.0031

2. Abu-Bader, S., & Abu-Qarn, A. S. (2003). Government expenditures, military spending and economic growth: causality evidence from Egypt, Israel, and Syria. *Journal of Policy Modeling*, *25*(6-7), 567–583. https://doi.org/10.1016/S0161-8938(03)00057-7
3. Ahmed, S., Alam, K., Rashid, A., & Gow, J. (2020). Militarisation, Energy Consumption, CO 2 Emissions and Economic Growth in Myanmar. *Defence and Peace Economics*, *31*(6), 615–641. https://doi.org/10.1080/10242694.2018.1560566
4. Apanisile, O. T., & Okunlola, O. C. (2014). Does Military Expenditure Influence Economic Growth in Nigeria during 1989-2013? A Bound Testing Approach. Romanian Journal of Fiscal Policy, 5(2), 56–71. Retrieved from https://search.ebscohost.com/login.aspx?direct=true&db=asn&AN=101810284&site=eds-live
5. Awaworyi Churchill, S., & Yew, S. L. (2018). The effect of military expenditure on growth: an empirical synthesis. *Empirical Economics*, *55*(3), 1357–1387. https://doi.org/10.1007/s00181-017-1300-z
6. Azam, M., Khan, F., Zaman, K., & Rasli, A. M. (2016). Military Expenditures and Unemployment Nexus for Selected South Asian Countries. *Social Indicators Research*, *127*(3), 1103–1117. https://doi.org/10.1007/s11205-015-0993-7
7. Ben Dhiab, L., & Dkhili, H. Legal Stability and Determinants of Insurance Development in the Middle East and North Africa Region (MENA) (1). Advance online publication. https://doi.org/10.13106/jafeb.2022.vol9.no2.0141
8. Benoit, E. (1973). Defense and economic growth in developing countries.
9. Blomberg, S. B. (1996). Growth, Political Instability and the Defence Burden. *Economica*, *63*(252), 649. https://doi.org/10.2307/2555001
10. Cappelen, Å., Gleditsch, N. P., & Bjerkholt, O. (1984). Military Spending and Economic Growth in the OECD Countries. *Journal of Peace Research*, *21*(4), 361–373. https://doi.org/10.1177/002234338402100404
11. Castillo, J, J., Lowell, F, J., Tellis, J, A., . . . Benjamin (2001, January 1). Military Expenditures and Economic Growth. Retrieved from https://www.rand.org/pubs/monograph_reports/MR1112.html
12. Chang, H.-C., Huang, B.-N., & Yang, C. W. (2011). Military expenditure and economic growth across different groups: A dynamic panel Granger-causality approach. *Economic Modelling*, *28*(6), 2416–2423. https://doi.org/10.1016/j.econmod.2011.06.001
13. Chang, T., Lee, C.-C., Hung, K., & Lee, K.-H. (2014, March 19). Does Military Spending Really Matter for Economic Growth in China and G7 Countries: The Roles of Dependency and Heterogeneity. Retrieved from https://www.tandfonline.com/doi/abs/10.1080/10242694.2013.763460
14. D'Agostino, G., Dunne, J. P., & Pieroni, L. (2017). Does Military Spending Matter for Long-run Growth? *Defence and Peace Economics*, *28*(4), 429–436. https://doi.org/10.1080/10242694.2017.1324723
15. Deger, S., & Sen, S. (1983). Military expenditure, spin-off and economic development. *Journal of Development Economics*, *13*(1-2), 67–83. https://doi.org/10.1016/0304-3878(83)90050-0
16. Deger, S., & Smith, R. (1983). Military Expenditure and Growth in Less Developed Countries. *Journal of Conflict Resolution*, *27*(2), 335–353. https://doi.org/10.1177/0022002783027002006
17. Dimitraki, O., & Win, S. (2021). Military Expenditure Economic Growth Nexus in Jordan: An Application of ARDL Bound Test Analysis in the Presence of Breaks.

Defence and Peace Economics, *32*(7), 864–881. https://doi.org/10.1080/10242694.2020.1730113

18. Dunne, J. P., & Mohammed, N. A. L. (1995). Military Spending in Sub-Saharan Africa: Some Evidence for 1967-85. *Journal of Peace Research*, *32*(3), 331–343. https://doi.org/10.1177/0022343395032003006
19. Dunne, J. P., & Tian, N. (2015). Military Expenditure, Economic Growth and Heterogeneity. *Defence and Peace Economics*, *26*(1), 15–31. https://doi.org/10.1080/10242694.2013.848575
20. Dunne, P., & Watson, D. (2000). Military expenditure and employment in South Africa *Defence and Peace Economics*, *11*(4), 587–596. https://doi.org/10.1080/10430710008404968
21. Emmanouilidis, K., & Karpetis, C. (2021). The Effects of Military Expenditures on Economic Growth and Inflation: Evidence from Turkey. *Peace Economics, Peace Science and Public Policy*, *27*(3), 369–404. https://doi.org/10.1515/peps-2020-0058
22. García, J. R., Murillo, J., Suriñach, J., & Vayá, E. (2018). Economic impact of the ministry of defence's budget: methodological design and results for the Spanish economy. *Defence and Peace Economics*, *29*(4), 459–473. https://doi.org/10.1080/10242694.2016.1158439
23. Gokmenoglu, K. K., Taspinar, N., & Sadeghieh, M. (2015). Military Expenditure and Economic Growth: The Case of Turkey. *Procedia Economics and Finance*, *25*, 455–462. https://doi.org/10.1016/S2212-5671(15)00757-1
24. Heo, U. (1999). Defense Spending and Economic Growth in South Korea: The Indirect Link. *Journal of Peace Research*, *36*(6), 699–708. https://doi.org/10.1177/0022343399036006006
25. Heo, U., & Eger, R. J. (2005). Paying for Security. *Journal of Conflict Resolution*, *49*(5), 792–817. https://doi.org/10.1177/0022002705279365
26. Heo, U., & Hahm, S. D. (2006). Politics, Economics, and Defense Spending in South Korea. *Armed Forces & Society*, *32*(4), 604–622. https://doi.org/10.1177/0095327X06287615
27. Heo, U., & Ye, M. (2016). Defense Spending and Economic Growth around the Globe: The Direct and Indirect Link. *International Interactions*, *42*(5), 774–796. https://doi.org/10.1080/03050629.2016.1149067
28. Heo, U., & Ye, M. (2019). U.S. Military Deployment and Host-Nation Economic Growth. *Armed Forces & Society*, *45*(2), 234–267. https://doi.org/10.1177/0095327X17738219
29. Kalyoncu, H., & Yucel, F. (2013, April 12). An analytical approach on defense expenditure and economic growth: The case of Turkey and Greece. Retrieved from https://www.emeraldinsight.com/doi/full/10.1108/01443580610706564
30. Korkmaz, S. (2015). The effect of military spending on economic growth and unemployment in Mediterranean countries. *International Journal of Economics and Financial Issues*, *5*(1), 273–280.
31. Landau, D. (1994). The impact of military expenditures on economic growth in the less developed countries*. *Defence and Peace Economics*, *5*(3), 205–220. https://doi.org/10.1080/10430719408404793
32. Luqman, M., & Antonakakis, N. (2021). Guns better than butter in Pakistan? The dilemma of military expenditure, human development, and economic growth. *Technological Forecasting and Social Change*, *173*, 121143. https://doi.org/10.1016/j.techfore.2021.121143

33. Maizels, A., & Nissanke, M. K. (1986). The determinants of military expenditures in developing countries. *World Development*, *14*(9), 1125–1140. https://doi.org/10.1016/0305-750X(86)90115-4
34. Manamperi, N. (2016). Does military expenditure hinder economic growth? Evidence from Greece and Turkey. *Journal of Policy Modeling*, *38*(6), 1171–1193. https://doi.org/10.1016/j.jpolmod.2016.04.003
35. McDonald, B. D., & Eger, R. J. (2010). The Defense-Growth Relationship: An Economic Investigation into Post-Soviet States. *Peace Economics, Peace Science and Public Policy*, *16*(1). https://doi.org/10.2202/1554-8597.1191
36. McMillan, S. M. (1992). Economic growth and military spending in South Africa. *International Interactions*, *18*(1), 35–50. https://doi.org/10.1080/03050629208434792
37. Mohanty, R. K., Panda, S., & Bhuyan, B. (2020). Does Defence Spending and its Composition Affect Economic Growth in India? *Margin*, *14*(1), 62–85. https://doi.org/10.1177/0973801019886486
38. Mukhopadhyay, P., Sinha, M., & Sengupta, P. P. (2022). Public Expenditure on Defense and Economic Development. In B. F. Costa (Ed.), *Advances in Public Policy and Administration. Challenges and Barriers to the European Union Expansion to the Balkan Region* (Vol. 2, pp. 170–181). Hershey, Pennsylvania (701 E. Chocolate Avenue, Hershey, Pennsylvania, 17033, USA): IGI Global. https://doi.org/10.4018/978-1-5225-4778-5.ch009
39. Njamenkengdo, Aurelien, A., Kouladoum, & Jean-Claude (2018). Military Expenses: A Brake on Economic Growth in Chad. Retrieved from https://econpapers.repec.org/article/gokijdcv1/v_3a8_3ay_3a2018_3ai_3a1_3ap_3a14-26.htm
40. Palavenis, D. (2020). In THE SEARCH FOR DEFENSE SPENDING IMPACT: Lithuanian CASE STUDY, 2009–2018; pp. 567–588. *Trames*, *24*(4), 567. https://doi.org/10.3176/tr.2020.4.06
41. Pan, C.-I., Chang, T., & Wolde-Rufael, Y. (2015). Military Spending and Economic Growth in the Middle East Countries: Bootstrap Panel Causality Test. *Defence and Peace Economics*, *26*(4), 443–456. https://doi.org/10.1080/10242694.2014.891356
42. Paul, S. (1996). Defence spending and unemployment rates. *Journal of Economic Studies*, *23*(2), 44–54. https://doi.org/10.1108/01443589610109667
43. Pieter Wezeman, & Alexandra Kuimova and Siemon Wezeman/SIPRI. Trends in international arms transfers, 2020. Retrieved from https://sipri.org/sites/default/files/2021-03/fs_2103_at_2020.pdf
44. Qiong, L., & Junhua, H. (2015). Military Expenditure and Unemployment in China1. *Procedia Economics and Finance*, *30*, 498–504. https://doi.org/10.1016/S2212-5671(15)01247-2
45. Qureshi, W., & Khan, N. P. (2017). Revisiting the Relationship between Military Expenditure and Economic Growth in Pakistan. *Global Social Sciences Review*, *II*(I), 18–46. https://doi.org/10.31703/gssr.2017(II-I).02
46. Sarwar, S., & Idrees, A. S. (2022). Impact of Military Expenditures on the Globalization Process: A Spatial Econometric Analysis for African Region. *Journal of Asian and African Studies*, *57*(2), 198–208. https://doi.org/10.1177/00219096211010324
47. Saudi, N., Ismail, A. B., Baker, R. B., Pinjaman, S. B., Abdullah, A., Rafiuddin, N., & Sulaiman, A. B. (2019). Special Issue. *International Journal of Recent Technology and Engineering*, *8*(2S9), 1–5. https://doi.org/10.35940/ijrte.B1003.0982S919
48. SIPRI. SIPRI Yearbook 2021, Summary.

49. Solanki, S., Inumula, K. M., & Chitnis, A. (2020). Sectoral Contribution to Economic Development in India: A Time-Series Co-Integration Analysis. *The Journal of Asian Finance, Economics and Business*, *7*(9), 191–200. https://doi.org/10.13106/jafeb.2020.vol7.no9.191
50. Tao, R., Glonţ, O. R., Li, Z.-Z., Lobonţ, O. R., & Guzun, A. A. (2020). New Evidence for Romania Regarding Dynamic Causality between Military Expenditure and Sustainable Economic Growth. *Sustainability (Switzerland)*, *12*(12), 5053. https://doi.org/10.3390/su12125053
51. Töngür, Ü., & Elveren, A. Y. (2017). The nexus of economic growth, military expenditures, and income inequality. *Quality & Quantity*, *51*(4), 1821–1842. https://doi.org/10.1007/s11135-016-0368-4
52. Tung-Pao Wang, Stacy Huey-Pyng Shyu, & Han-Chung Chou (2012). The impact of defense expenditure on economic productivity in OECD countries. *Economic Modelling*, *29*(6), 2104–2114. https://doi.org/10.1016/j.econmod.2012.06.041
53. Ward, M. D., Davis, D. R., & Lofdahl, C. L. (1995). A Century of Tradeoffs: Defense and Growth in Japan and the United States. *International Studies Quarterly*, *39*(1), 27. https://doi.org/10.2307/2600722
54. Yildirim, J., & Sezgin, S. [S.] (2003). Military expenditure and employment in Turkey. *Defence and Peace Economics*, *14*(2), 129–139. https://doi.org/10.1080/10242690302919
55. Yildirim†, J., Sezgin, S. [Selami], & Öcal, N. (2005). Military EXPENDITURE AND ECONOMIC GROWTH IN MIDDLE EASTERN COUNTRIES: A DYNAMIC PANEL DATA ANALYSIS. *Defence and Peace Economics*, *16*(4), 283–295. https://doi.org/10.1080/10242690500114751

Note: All the figures and tables in this chapter were author's computations.

Securing the Future through Sustainability, Health, Education, and Technology – Brig. Dr. Rajiv Divekar et al. (eds)
 ISBN 978-1-032-95922-1

21 Herbal *vs* Allopathic—Select Determinants of Preference for Medication in India

Smita Mehendale[1]
Assistant Professor,
Symbiosis Institute of Management Studies (SIMS),
Constituent of Symbiosis International Deemed University,
Pune India

CA Ritu Dange[2]
Assistant Professor,
AISSMS-Institute of Management

Samrat Ray
Senior Researcher,
Peter the Great Saint Petersburg Polytechnic University, Russia

ABSTRACT

The use of herbal medicines is an ancient practice in India with varying degree of preference of use as against allopathy. While herbal medications are derived from natural sources and largely believed to be effective alternatives to allopathic medication, there is variation in their use across various demographic factors and type of ailment for which they may be recommended. This study uses a chi-square test to examine the link between a sample of people in a diverse metropolitan population's choice of medical treatments (herbal vs. allopathic) and select characteristics of demography and severity of ailment. Understanding how select demographic factors affect the choice of treatments is essential for healthcare practitioners, pharmaceutical companies and policymakers, especially in light of the growing interest in both holistic and conventional medical practices. Structured questionnaires that were given to a representative sample of people dwelling in various urban regions were used to gather the data. The findings of the chi-square test show statistically significant correlations between select demographic factors and severity of ailment affecting choice of medication.

KEYWORDS: Allopathic, Herbal, Healthcare, Region of residence, Occupation

[1]smita12win@gmail.com, [2]dange497@gmail.com,

DOI: 10.1201/9781003587200-21

1. Introduction

Two opposing ideologies have long affected the realms of healthcare and medicine: allopathic medicine and herbal medicine. The former, sometimes known as conventional or Western medicine, is based on pharmaceutical medications and therapies based on scientific study and has revolutionized the area of healthcare by providing tailored remedies to a wide range of health problems. Herbal medicine, on the other hand, draws on traditional knowledge to give holistic and natural approaches to therapy and draws on nature's bounty, utilising the therapeutic properties of plants and natural substances to treat a wide range of disorders.

The decision between allopathic and herbal medication is complicated, influenced by a number of factors such as patient demographics (Duru, 2016), disease severity (Kaur & Valecha, 2014), efficacy (Phondani et al., 2014), safety, cultural context, and changing healthcare trends.

Allopathic medicine, the most widely practised style of healthcare worldwide, is characterised by its scientific foundations and evidence-based practise. It has evolved over many years through empirical observation, experimentation, and clinical investigation. This paradigm encompasses numerous pharmaceutical drugs, surgical techniques, and cutting-edge medical technologies. Allopathic medicine's comprehensive testing and clinical studies to establish the efficacy and safety of medicines are one of its distinctive features and are frequently recommended for diseases (Verma, 2007). This painstaking method has revolutionized medicine by enabling advances in the treatment and management of many diseases. In addition to lengthening human lifespans, allopathic medicines have also lessened the pain brought on by both acute and chronic ailments even in rural areas (May, 2014). This strategy has produced outstanding successes like vaccinations, antibiotics, and precision medicine, which have revolutionized healthcare results.

Contrarily, herbal medicine is influenced by age-old customs and indigenous knowledge systems that make use of the healing powers of plants, herbs, and other natural ingredients (Somani, 2015). Each tradition offers its own special insights into the therapeutic power of the natural world, and this holistic approach to healing is profoundly ingrained in civilizations all over the world.

Herbal treatments are frequently viewed as being more delicate and in tune with the body's natural functions. They have been passed down through the years as essential elements of conventional therapeutic practices and are rich in cultural and historical importance (Lee & Barnes, 2022). The variety of herbal therapies is astonishing, spanning from traditional chinese medicine (TCM) (Luo, 2019), Native American herbalism and Amazonian shamanic practices to Ayurveda in India (Parasuraman, 2014).

The effectiveness of herbal medicine, however, is frequently disputed because there are few rigorous clinical trials and standardized studies available. Even while some herbal medicines have shown promise in treating specific conditions (Jahan, 2022) a lack of reliable studies prevents the medical profession from accepting them more widely. Furthermore, it can be difficult to determine the genuine therapeutic potential of herbal medications due to variations in their composition and quality.

The use of both allopathic and herbal treatments together is becoming more popular in healthcare today, according to trends. The goal should be do develop an integrative strategy, or complementary medicine system to combine the advantages of both systems (Ahmad et al., 2020; Kennedy et al., 2013). For instance, chemotherapy patients for cancer may benefit from the targeted nature of allopathic treatments while also using herbal remedies to relieve side effects like nausea and exhaustion (Sapre, 2021).

Additionally, people are looking for more and more customized healthcare options that take into account their particular requirements and preferences (Garcia, 2021). Given that both herbal and allopathic treatments have their place in contemporary healthcare, the move towards holistic and patient-centered care recommends a sophisticated approach that combines both of them.

2. Literature Review

The choice between herbal and allopathic medicines often depends on the nature and severity of the health condition (Gokarn, 2015; Nketiah, 2011; Okumagba, 2011). Allopathic medicine is commonly sought for acute or severe illnesses, while herbal remedies are often used for chronic conditions and minor ailments. With some plants showing potential in reducing cancer-related symptoms and enhancing general health, herbal medications have attracted attention in alternative cancer care also (Mateti et al., 2021).

The relative efficacy of herbal and allopathic treatments, as regarded by medical professionals and patients, is one of the main elements affecting the decision between them. Many allopathic drugs have a substantial body of data demonstrating their efficacy in treating particular medical diseases (Clement, 2007; Phondani, et al., 2014). These medicines were produced through rigorous clinical trials and scientific study. The management and treatment of many diseases are now possible because of the significant advances in contemporary medicine brought about by this evidence-based methodology. Herbal remedies, on the other hand, are frequently criticised for the scarcity of standardised research and well-designed clinical studies (Zhou, 2019). However, some herbal treatments have proven to be clinically effective in treating specific conditions. Both allopathic and herbal medications may have side effects, but again it is possible to predict negative effects in allopathy than in herbal due to lack of research (Gogtay et al., 2002; Parle, 2006). A dearth of reliable, high-quality research prevents the medical community from accepting herbal remedies more widely (Kamboj, 2012). To guarantee their safe and efficient integration into a patient's treatment plan, further research is required to establish conclusive results (Wani et al., 2007; Vinjamury & Singh, 2005) and patients must consult with medical specialists before using these treatments.

Due to a variety of factors, including access to healthcare facilities, cultural influences, socioeconomic level, and educational background, the use of herbal medicines and allopathic drugs in India might vary dramatically across regions. Some regions often have well-established allopathic healthcare infrastructure, including hospitals, clinics, and pharmacies (Prasad, 2007). Residents of these regions frequently enjoy simpler access to allopathic medications and medical services as a result. Different herbs and herbal products may not be readily available in all areas (Sahoo, 2010). Residents of remote regions and towns may have less access to contemporary healthcare facilities, placing a greater reliance on over-the-counter herbal medications, local traditional healers, and herbal cures. There may be a larger network of herbal stores and practitioners in areas with a strong herbal medicine tradition. Herbal and Ayurvedic items have proliferated in metropolitan regions also as a result of urbanization and market accessibility, making them more widely available to locals (Meena et al., 2009; Wais et al., 2012).

The occupation of people also has an impact on choice of type of medication (Jonnalagadda, 2014; Liwa, 2017; Phondani, 2010; Showande & Amokeodo, 2014). People with more traditional occupations tend to have lower level of education impacting their choice of medication to herbal or ayurvedic. Whereas people in modern occupations have less knowledge of traditional methods of healing like herbal options and hence tend to rely on allopathic solutions for not so severe ailments also. Additionally, past research suggests that gender can also be a factor influencing choice of medication (Katole, 2019). The severity of ailment also effects the choice between herbal or ayurvedic and allopathic (Kaur & Valecha, 2014; Nimesh, 2018; Olisa & Oyelola, 2009). For seasonal infections and mild ailments, herbal preparations are frequently used. However, in case of severe ailments like cancer etc. allopatic medications is the obvious choice.

In many communities around the world, herbal remedies have significant cultural and historical value. Ayurveda in India and Traditional Chinese Medicine (TCM) in China are two examples of traditional treatment systems that have been used for thousands of years and heavily rely on herbal therapies. These customs, which are frequently passed down through generations, are entwined with cultural beliefs and practises. Allopathic medicine, on the other hand, is connected to Western medical procedures and is occasionally perceived as a relatively recent arrival in many non-Western societies. This cultural gap may affect patient trust in one technique over another and healthcare choices.

A difficult choice must be made between herbal and allopathic drugs based on a number of considerations, such as effectiveness, safety, cultural context, and shifting healthcare trends. Although there are hazards associated with allopathic drugs, they do have the benefit of considerable clinical evidence. Traditional herbal remedies provide healthy options but frequently lack standardised research. It is crucial for both patients and healthcare professionals to comprehend the comparative elements of these treatments. A more thorough and individualised approach to healthcare may be possible with better integration of both systems and additional study into the efficacy and safety of herbal treatments (Kumar, 2014). The option between herbal and allopathic medications may eventually become less black-and-white in this changing environment, enabling people to benefit from both systems for their well-being Oliveira et al., 2015). Therefore,

H1: There is an association between preference for herbal Vs allopathic medicines and Gender

H2: There is an association between preference for herbal Vs allopathic medicines and Severity of ailment

H3: There is an association between preference for herbal Vs allopathic medicines and Type of Occupation

H4: There is an association between preference for herbal Vs allopathic medicines and Region of Residence

3. Methods

A descriptive study was undertaken to fulfil the objectives of this research. The sample size for the study was 586 respondents which was sufficiently large based on similar studies undertaken in the past and availability of time and resources for this study(Bham et al., 2023). Non-probability method of sampling – quota sampling has been used for this study. Hence a large sample was collected with respondents preferring either allopathy or herbal remedies of 293 completed responses of each totalling to 586 responses. The inclusion criteria used for sampling included use and access to both allopathy and Indian herbal medications and residing in India and involved in some occupation currently or in the past. Respondents below 18 yrs of age were excluded from the study. A structured questionnaire was prepared based on existing literature and circulated to prospective respondents of which 586 completed responses were received and used for this study. Since this survey was done across India, online mode of administration was considered most suitable due to its advantages like extensive and fast geographic reach and low cost. Chi-square test of Independence was used in this study to understand the variables relationships with preferred medication Effect size calculation is done with Phi (for 2 * 2 table) or Cramer's V (more than 2 categories). The data collected was analyzed using IBM SPSS 22.

4. Data Analysis and Results

Demographic information of consumers is considered an important factor in understanding the healthcare preferences of consumers. These characteristics of consumers help both allopathic and herbal pharmaceutical companies craft specific marketing strategies by segmenting customers with similar characteristics. Choice of medication (allopathic vs herbal) and select demographic characteristics of users along with severity of ailment are studied together for better understanding of the phenomenon. Thus, demographic variables have a significance in this study. The hypothesis formulated try to establish an association with preference of medication (allopathic vs herbal) and demographic characteristics and severity of ailment. The demographic factors considered in this study to understand their impact on the preference for type of medication are gender, occupation, region of residence and severity of disease of consumers. To test whether there is any association between these demographic variables and severity of disease with preference for type of medication, Chi-square test of Independence was applied.

H1: There is an association between Preference for Medication (allopathic vs herbal) and Gender

A chi-square test of independence was carried out for comparing demographic variable in categories of Gender (Male & Female; None of the respondents marked the third category, Other) and Preferred Medication (allopathy vs herbal). Table 21.2 reveals that a significant interaction was found ($\chi2$ (3, n=586) = 26.464, p <.05). Hence, it is concluded that the variable Gender (Male & Female) has a significant association with preference for medication (allopathic vs herbal). Males have a clear preference for allopathy whereas females have a clear preference for herbal (Table 21.1). The Cramer's V value was 0.21 is small effect.

Table 21.1 Gender and preferred medication

			Preferred_Medicine		Total
			Allopathic	Herbal	
Gender	Female	Count of	129	191	320
		%	40.3%	59.7%	100.0%
	Male	Count of	164	102	266
		%	61.7%	38.3%	100.0%
Total		Count of	293	293	586
		%	50.0%	50.0%	100.0%

Table 21.2 Chi-square tests for gender and preferred medication

	Value	Df	Asymp. Sig. (2-sided)
Pearson Chi-Square	26.464[a]	1	.000
Continuity Correction[b]	25.617	1	.000
Likelihood Ratio	26.674	1	.000
Fisher's Exact Test			
Linear-by-Linear Association	26.418	1	.000
N of Valid Cases	586		

a. 0 cells (0.0%) have expected count less than 5. The minimum expected count is 133.00.
b. Computed only for a 2 x 2 table

H2: There is an association between Preference for medication (allopathy vs. herbal) and Severity

A chi-square test of independence was carried out for comparing the demographic variable in categories of Severity of ailment (High, Low) and Preferred Medication (allopathy vs. herbal) (Table 21.3).

Table 21.3 Severity and preferred medication

			Preferred_Medicine		Total
			Allopathy	Herbal	
Severity	High Severity	Count	181	141	322
		% within Severity	56.2%	43.8%	100.0%
	Low Severity	Count	112	152	264
		% within Severity	42.4%	57.6%	100.0%
Total		Count	293	293	586
		% within Severity	50.0%	50.0%	100.0%

Table 21.4 reveals that a significant interaction was found ($\chi 2$ (1, n=586) = 11.030, p <.05). Hence, it is concluded that the severity of the ailment (High Severity, Low Severity) has a significant association with preference for type of medication (Herbal vs. Allopathic). People suffering from severe deceases have a clear preference for allopathic medicine whereas those suffering from low severe deceases have a clear preference for herbal remedies. The Cramer's V value is .14 which is small effect.

Table 21.4 Chi-square test for severity of decease and preferred medication

	Value	Df	Asymp. Sig. (2-sided)
Pearson Chi-Square	11.030[a]	1	.001
Continuity Correction[b]	10.485	1	.001
Likelihood Ratio	11.066	1	.001
Fisher's Exact Test			
Linear-by-Linear Association	11.011	1	.001
N of Valid Cases	586		

a. 0 cells (0.0%) have expected count less than 5. The minimum expected count is 132.00.;
b. Computed only for a 2x2 table

H3: There is an association between Preference for Herbal vs Allopathic medicines and Region of residence

A chi-square test of independence was carried out for comparing demographic variable of region of residence (Gujrat & Maharashtra, Goa-Dadra-Nagar Haveli, Central, Northern, North-eastern and Southern regions) and Preferred Medicine

(Table 21.5). Table 21.6 reveals that a significant interaction was found ($\chi 2$ (5, n=586) = 45.770, p <.05). Hence, it is concluded that the demographic variable Region of residence has a significant association with Preferred Medication (allopathic vs herbal). Table 21.5 shows that counts of respondents with Region of residence of Goa-Dadra-Nagar Haveli and Northern region not being different in terms of preference and the count of North-eastern region being less than 10 for any meaningful comparisons.

Table 21.5 Region and preferred medication

			Preferred_Medicine		Total
			Allopathy	Herbal	
Region	Guj & Mah	Count	205	142	347
		% within Type of Employment	59.1%	40.9%	100.0%
	Northern Region	Count	35	34	69
		% within Type of Employment	50.7%	49.3%	100.0%
	Goa & D-N H	Count	19	22	41
		% within Type of Employment	46.3%	53.7%	100.0%
	Southern Region	Count	26	51	77
		% within Type of Employment	33.8%	66.2%	100.0%
	Central Region	Count	5	37	42
		% within Type of Employment	11.9%	88.1%	100.0%
	North-East Region	Count	3	7	10
		% within Type of Employment	30.0%	70.0%	100.0%
Total		Count	293	293	586
		% within Type of Employment	50.0%	50.0%	100.0%

Table 21.6 Chi-square test for region and preferred medication

	Value	Df	Asymp. Sig. (2-sided)
Pearson Chi-Square	45.770[a]	5	0
Likelihood Ratio	49.21	5	0
Linear-by-Linear Association	42.066	1	0
N of Valid Cases	586		
a. 0 cells (0.0%) have expected count less than 5. The minimum expected count is 5.00.			

The Bonferroni adjusted chi square residual analysis (Table 21.8), shows the adjusted p value after Bonferroni correction and it is compared with p < .0042 (.05/12 = .0042). It is found that there is a significant difference in the preference of medication for Gujrat & Maharashtra and Central region and Gujrat &

Maharashtra have a clear preference for allopathy and Central region people have a clear preference for herbal remedies. Also, Cramer's V is .28 which shows large effect (Table 21.7).

Table 21.7 Symmetric measures

		Value	Approx. Sig.
Nominal by Nominal	Phi	0.279	0
	Cramer's V	0.279	0
N of Valid Cases		586	

Table 21.8 Region _ bonferroni chi-square residual analysis

Occupation	Df	$\chi 2$ value	Adj p value
Guj & Mah_allopathy	5	28.09	0.0000
Northern_allopathy	5	.02	1.0000
G-D-N_allopathy	5	.24	0.9986
Southern_allopathy	5	9.36	0.0954
Northern_allopathy	5	26.21	0.0001
North-East_allopathy	5	1.64	0.8966
Guj & Mah_herbal	5	28.09	0.0000
Northern_herbal	5	.02	1.0000
G-D-N_herbal	5	.24	0.9986
Southern_herbal	5	9.36	0.0954
Northern_herbal	5	26.21	0.0001
North-East_herbal	5	1.64	0.8966

H4: There is an association between Preference for medication (allopathy vs herbal) and Type of occupation (Desk job, Student, Class 4, Travel Jobs and Retired)

A chi-square test of independence was carried out for comparing demographic variable type of occupation with categories (Desk job, Student, Class 4, Travel Jobs and Retired) and Preferred Medication (allopathy vs herbal) (Table 21.9). Table 10 reveals that a significant interaction was found ($\chi 2$ (4, n=586) = 77.534, p <.05). Hence it is concluded that the demographic variable type of occupation with categories (Desk job, Student, Class 4, Travel Jobs and Retired) has a significant association with Preferred Medication. Cramer's V was used to interpret the effect size (Table 21.16) which was 0.36 and found to be large effect (Cohen, 2012).

Table 21.9 shows that respondents with Type of occupation being Students and Class 4 do not have much difference in preference for medication. But respondents with type of occupation Desk jobs have a clear preference for herbal remedies as against those with Travel jobs and retired people who have a clear preference for allopathy.

Table 21.9 Type of occupation and preferred medicine

			Preferred_Medicine		Total
			Allopathic	Herbal	
Hsehold An_ income	Desk Job	Count	59	135	194
		% within Type of Profession	30.4%	69.6%	100.0%
	Students	Count	89	86	175
		% within Type of Profession	50.9%	49.1%	100.0%
	Class Four	Count	54	53	107
		% within Type of Profession	50.5%	49.5%	100.0%
	Travel jobs	Count	32	9	41
		% within Type of Profession	78.0%	22.0%	100.0%
	Retired	Count	59	10	69
		% within Type of Profession	85.5%	14.5%	100.0%
Total		Count	293	293	586
		% within Type of Profession	50.0%	50.0%	100.0%

To confirm the same, Bonferroni Adjusted Residual Analysis was done (Table 21.12). The adjusted residuals in table were squared to arrive at chi square value. The corresponding p value was calculated in SPSS using significance function for chi square. Finally, the chi square p-value was compared with the Bonferroni corrected p-value (.05/10 = .005). The adjusted p-value shows that respondents with desk jobs had a clear preference for herbal remedies and respondents who are retired preferred allopathic medicines.

Table 21.10 Profession and preferred medication (Herbal vs Allopathic)

	Value	Df	Asymp. Sig. (2-sided)
Pearson Chi-Square	77.534[a]	4	.000
Likelihood Ratio	82.878	4	.000
Linear-by-Linear Association	71.604	1	.000
N of Valid Cases	586		
a. 0 cells (0.0%) have expected count less than 5. The minimum expected count is 20.50.			

Table 21.11 Profession-symmetric measures

		Value	Approx. Sig.
Nominal by Nominal	Phi	.364	.000
	Cramer's V	.364	.000
N of Valid Cases		586	

Table 21.12 Profession_ bonferroni chi-square residual analysis

Income	Df	$\chi 2$ value	Adj p value
Desk Jobs_Allopathic	4	44.49	0.0000
Students_Allopathic	4	0.07	0.9994
Class Four_Allopathic	4	0.01	1.0000
Travel jobs_Allopathic	4	13.84	0.0078
Retired_Allopathic	4	39.44	0.0000
Desk Jobs_Herbal	4	44.49	0.0000
Students_Herbal	4	0.07	0.9994
Class Four_Herbal	4	0.01	1.0000
Travel jobs_Herbal	4	13.84	0.0078
Retired_Herbal	4	39.44	0.0000

5. Discussion

Chi-square test results show that all the hypothesis from H1 to H4 were supported. All the variable i.e. select demographic characteristics and severity of ailment under study are associated with preference for medication. The tests revealed that females have a clear preference for herbal remedies as against males who prefer allopathy. A possible explanation for this could be that traditionally, home remedies were often administered by women in the household which may have facilitated transfer of this knowledge amongst women more than men making them more habitual to using herbal remedies. It is also revealed that there is a significant difference in the preference of medication for Gujrat & Maharashtra and Central region and Gujrat & Maharashtra have a clear preference for allopathy and Central region people have a clear preference for herbal remedies. Both Gujrat and Maharashtra are amongst highly industrialized and developed states in India with excellent modern medical care facilities available. This may have led to wide exposure to allopathic medication known to give quick relief to common ailments and better outcomes for severe ailments. Finally, the demographic variable type of occupation with categories (Desk job, Student, Class 4, Travel Jobs and Retired) has a significant association with Preferred Medication. In particular, respondents with desk jobs prefer herbal medication as against retired respondents who prefer allopathic medication. People with desk jobs do not endure travel for office related work and may be open to trying herbal medications which are known to have longer recovery time as against allopathy. Retired people may be suffering from severe deceases given their age and hence prefer allopathic medications.

In a highly competitive business environment, health care organizations need to be able to provide differentiated offerings. A deeper understanding of the characteristics of its prospective customers in terms of their demography and

Table 21.13 Hypothesis testing outcomes

H1 - 4: There is an association between Preferred Medication and Characteristics (Gender, Severity, Occupation and region of residence)					
Hypo-thesis	**Relationship**	**$\chi 2$ Value**	**df**	**Asymptotic Significance (2-sided) p-value (.05)**	**Decision**
	H1- Gender -> Preferred Medication	26.464	1	0.000	Supported
	H2-Severity-> Preferred Medication	11.030	1	0.001	Supported
	H3-Type of Occupation -> Preferred Medication	45.770	5	0.000	Supported
	H4-Region of Residence ->Preferred Medication	77.535	4	0.000	Supported

severity of ailment leading to predictable preferences must be taken into account. Preferred medication is very important for people suffering from various deceases. The choice of type of medication can be a decisive in their possibility of recovery. Herbal remedies are also more sustainable as they are derived from natural sources. Although the general belief is that the duration of recovery is higher in case of herbal medicines. Allopathic medicines have side effects which can further hamper the health of patients in case of prolonged treatments. This study only indicates that differentiated offerings based on demographic variables and severity of ailments could help create preferences amongst patients for choice of medication. More studies can be undertaken along with other behavioural variables to draw deeper conclusions. Advanced statistical techniques may be required to establish clear demographic characteristics etc of patients and their preferred medication.

6. Conclusion

This research aims to provide knowledge regarding characteristics of individual and type of decease that leads to preference for one of the two types of medication, namely herbal and allopathic system of medication and throws light on their coexistence and potential integration. This integration will have major consequences for modern healthcare. Through the use of statistical methods, the data was analyzed and conclusions presented. Although other factors like tendency for self-medication and knowledge of home remedies could also contribute to preference for type of medication, this study limits itself to only four factors. Select demographic characteristics namely, gender, region of residence, occupations have a significant association with choice of medication. Severity of ailment also has a significant impact on the choice between use of allopathy or herbal or a combination of both streams of medication. This study throws light on how gender, regional difference, occupation and severity of ailment can lead to difference in preference for allopathic or herbal medications.

REFERENCES

1. Ahmad, A. S., & Sharma, R. (2020). Comparative analysis of herbal and allopathic treatment systems. European *Journal of Molecular & Clinical Medicine*, 7(7), 2869–2876.
2. Bham, S. Q., Mohammed Iqbal, M. B. B. S., & Sharif, U. H. A. (2023). Factors associated with parental self-medication for common childhood illnesses during the COVID-19 pandemic: a single centre study. Anaesthesia, Pain & Intensive Care, 27(3), 405–412.
3. Clement, Y. N., Morton-Gittens, J., Basdeo, L., Blades, A., Francis, M. J., Gomes, N., ... & Singh, A. (2007). Perceived efficacy of herbal remedies by users accessing primary healthcare in Trinidad. BMC complementary and alternative medicine, 7(1), 1–9.Cultural Significance and Traditional Knowledge
4. Duru, C. B., Uwakwe, K. A., Chinomnso, N. C., Mbachi, I. I., Diwe, K. C., Agunwa, C. C., ... & Merenu, I. A. (2016). Socio-demographic determinants of herbal medicine use in pregnancy among Nigerian women attending clinics in a tertiary Hospital in Imo State, south-east, Nigeria. Am J Med Stud, 4(1), 1–10.
5. Garcia, S. (2021). Data-driven Approaches to Explore Precision Medicine.
6. Gogtay, N. J., Bhatt, H. A., Dalvi, S. S., & Kshirsagar, N. A. (2002). The use and safety of non-allopathic Indian medicines. Drug safety, 25, 1005–1019.
7. Gokarn, S. R. (2015). Extract versus whole drug usage. *Journal of Indian System of Medicine,* 3(1), 48–50.
8. Jahan, S., Mozumder, Z. M., & Shill, D. K. (2022). Use of herbal medicines during pregnancy in a group of Bangladeshi women. Heliyon, 8(1).
9. Jonnalagadda, V. G. (2014). Pharmacovigilance & Clinical Trials.
10. Kamboj, A. (2012). Analytical evaluation of herbal drugs. Drug discovery research in pharmacognosy, 3, 23–55.
11. Katole, H. (2019). Why patients prefer allopathy and ayurvedic therapy in India? (No. 1894). EasyChair.
12. Kaur, M., & Valecha, V. (2014). Diabetes and antidiabetic herbal formulations: an alternative to Allopathy. Eur. J. Med, 6(4), 226–240.
13. Kennedy, D. A., Lupattelli, A., Koren, G., & Nordeng, H. (2013). Herbal medicine use in pregnancy: results of a multinational study. BMC complementary and alternative medicine, 13(1), 355.
14. Kumar, P. M. (2014). Review on Interaction of Herbal Medicines with Allopathic Medicines. *Journal of Ayurveda and Holistic Medicine* (JAHM), 2(2).
15. Lee, E. L., & Barnes, J. (2022). Prevalence of Use of Herbal and Traditional Medicines. In Pharmacovigilance for *Herbal and Traditional Medicines: Advances, Challenges and International Perspectives* (pp. 15–25). Cham: Springer International Publishing.
16. Liwa, A., Roediger, R., Jaka, H., Bougaila, A., Smart, L., Langwick, S., & Peck, R. (2017). Herbal and alternative medicine use in Tanzanian adults admitted with hypertension-related diseases: a mixed-methods study. *International Journal of Hypertension*, 2017.
17. Luo, H., Vong, C. T., Chen, H., Gao, Y., Lyu, P., Qiu, L., ... & Wang, Y. (2019). Naturally occurring anti-cancer compounds: shining from Chinese herbal medicine. Chinese medicine, 14(1), 48.
18. Mateti, T., Aswath, S., Vatti, A. K., Kamath, A., & Laha, A. (2021). A review on allopathic and herbal nanofibrous drug delivery vehicles for cancer treatments. Biotechnology Reports, 31, e00663.
19. May, C., Roth, K., & Panda, P. (2014). Non-degree allopathic practitioners as first contact points for acute illness episodes: insights from a qualitative study in rural northern India. BMC Health Services Research, 14(1), 1–11.

20. Meena, A. K., Bansal, P., & Kumar, S. (2009). Plants-herbal wealth as a potential source of ayurvedic drugs. Asian J Tradit Med, 4(4), 152–70.
21. Nimesh, S. (2018). Herbal drug is better than allopathic drug in the treatment of rheumatoid arthritis. Int J Pharmacogn, 5(9), 539–45.
22. Nketiah, A. (2011). Mothers' Satisfaction with Health Care Services and Health Care Seeking for Children Under-Five: a Case Study in Okwampa in Ghana.
23. Okumagba, P. O. (2011). Choice of health-care service utilization by the elderly in Delta state of Nigeria. Journal of Sociology and Social Anthropology, 2(2), 131–138.
24. Olisa, N. S., & Oyelola, F. T. (2009). Evaluation of use of herbal medicines among ambulatory hypertensive patients attending a secondary health care facility in Nigeria. International *Journal of Pharmacy Practice*, 17(2), 101–105.
25. Oliveira, S. G. D., Piva, E., & Lund, R. G. (2015). The possibility of interactions between medicinal herbs and allopathic medicines used by patients attended at basic care units of the Brazilian unified health system. Nat Prod Chem Res, 3(171), 2.
26. Parasuraman, S., Thing, G. S., & Dhanaraj, S. A. (2014). Polyherbal formulation: Concept of Ayurveda. Pharmacognosy reviews, 8(16), 73
27. Parle, M., & Bansal, N. (2006). Herbal medicines: are they safe?.
28. Phondani, P. C., Maikhuri, R. K., & Kala, C. P. (2010). Ethnoveterinary uses of medicinal plants among traditional herbal healers in Alaknanda catchment of Uttarakhand, India. African *Journal of Traditional*, Complementary and Alternative Medicines, 7(3).
29. Phondani, P. C., Maikhuri, R. K., & Saxena, K. G. (2014). The efficacy of herbal system of medicine in the context of allopathic system in Indian Central Himalaya. *Journal of Herbal Medicine*, 4(3), 147–158.
30. Sahoo, N., Manchikanti, P., & Dey, S. (2010). Herbal drugs: standards and regulation. Fitoterapia, 81(6), 462–471.
31. Sapre, S. R. (2021). Study of Consumer Behavior in Respect of Usage of Ayurveda as First Line of Treatment for Critical and Chronic Diseases (Doctoral dissertation).
32. Showande, S. J., & Amokeodo, O. S. (2014). Evaluation of the extent and pattern of use of herbal bitters among students in a tertiary institution in Southwestern Nigeria. *Tropical Journal of Pharmaceutical Research*, 13(10), 1707–1712.
33. Somani, A., Mehta, R., Duseja, S., Desai, K., & Hirani, T. (2015). Evaluation of a Commercially Available Herbal Gel Containing Acacia Arabica in Chronic Generalized Gingivitis Patients. Advances in Human Biology, 5(3), 38–42.
34. Venkata Krishna Prasad, C. B. (2007). Medical tourism industry-advantage India.
35. Verma, U., Sharma, R., Gupta, P., Gupta, S., & Kapoor, B. (2007). Allopathic vs. ayurvedic practices in tertiary care institutes of urban North India. *Indian Journal of Pharmacology*, 39(1), 52.
36. Vinjamury, S. P., & Singh, B. B. (2005). Ayurvedic treatment of chronic fatigue syndrome-A case report. Alternative Therapies in Health and Medicine, 11(5), 76.
37. Wais, M., Nazish, I., Samad, A., Beg, S., Abusufyan, S., Ajaz Ajaj, S., & Aqil, M. (2012). Herbal drugs for diabetic treatment: an updated review of patents. Recent patents on anti-infective drug discovery, 7(1), 53–59.
38. Wani, M. S., Parakh, S. R., & Dehghan, M. H. (2007). Herbal medicine and its standardization. Pharmaceutical Reviews, 5(6).
39. Zhou, X., Li, C. G., Chang, D., & Bensoussan, A. (2019). Current status and major challenges to the safety and efficacy presented by Chinese herbal medicine. Medicines, 6(1), 14.

Note: All the tables in this chapter were SPSS output of primary data collected by authors

Securing the Future through Sustainability, Health, Education, and Technology – Brig. Dr. Rajiv Divekar et al. (eds)

ISBN 978-1-032-95922-1

22 Impact of ESG on the Financial Performance: A Case Study in the Indian Cement Industry

Shehnaz Ismail Lockhat[1]
Research Assistant,
Symbiosis Institute of Management Studies,
Pune, Maharashtra

Brig. Rajiv Divekar[2]
Director,
Symbiosis Institute of Management Studies,
Pune, Maharashtra

Pravin kumar Bhoyar[3]
Deputy Director,
Symbiosis Institute of Management Studies,
Pune, Maharashtra

Abstract

This study looks into how Environmental, Social, and Governmental (ESG) concerns affect the Indian cement industry's financial performance for the period of 2012 to 2021. Environmental Disclosure Scores and ESG Disclosure Scores both display a constant rising trend, which reflects an increased emphasis on sustainability. Retained earnings, however, decreased, perhaps as a result of investments in sustainability programs. Earnings before Interest and Taxes (EBIT) remained steady, and after 2019 there was a significant rise. Solid current ratios above 0.94, which indicate solid short-term liquidity, were maintained by cement companies. However, profit margins showed variations according to economic cycles. A panel regression demonstrated that ESG Disclosure Scores were found to have a positive impact on total assets and the number of shareholders but a negative impact on the current ratio and profit margins.

Keywords: Cement industry, Environmental social governance, India, Panel regression

[1]shehnaz.lockhat@sims.edu, [2]director@sims.edu, [3]deputydirector@sims.edu

DOI: 10.1201/9781003587200-22

1. Introduction

A set of criteria called ESG (Environmental, Social, and Governance) is used to evaluate the ethical impact and sustainability of investments and businesses. The environmental awakening of the 1960s and 1970s is when ESG first gained notoriety and enterprises' effects on the environment were made public. In the 1980s, investors began considering a company's social and ethical standing in addition to its financial performance, which led to an increase in socially responsible investing. Lehman Brothers' demise in 2008, the Eron Scandal from 2001, and numerous other commercial crises opened the ground for governance in ESG (Huang et al., 2022). In 2010, the United Nations computed seventeen sustainable development goals which align with the aforementioned goals. Businesses were urged to embrace sustainable and socially responsible practices by the United Nations Global Compact in 2004. However, the term ESG gained traction in 2012.

ESG scores are the prime factor for building a green portfolio and analyzing the company's performance (Clément et al., 2023). Environmental (like waste management and resource consumption), social (like working conditions), and governance issues (like the relationship between shareholders and the board of directors) are the three main categories that make up an ESG score. ESG was initially devised for financial companies and it was later used to aid businesses enhance their reputation and attracting more capital (Arouria et al., 2019).

India's cement business began in 1889 when a company located in Kolkata began producing cement from Agillaceous rock (B and Nallanavar, 2022). In India (which will rank ninth in terms of air pollution in 2022 and has 14 of the world's top 20 most polluted cities), air pollution is a major concern. The high levels of particulate matter pollution, which is mostly brought on by industrial emissions, construction work, farming methods, the burning of biomass, and vehicle emissions (Kandlikar and Ramachandran, 2000). The cement industry is the backbone of the Indian economy and one of the primary culprits for negatively affecting the environment and people (Gupta et al., 2020). Most people around cement plants suffer from respiratory diseases and eye irritation and other diseases around the cement plant. (Kesarwani and James, 2017). It was also observed that the chlorophyll pigments get depleted in plants due to cement dust near the cement industry. (Chaurasi et al., 2013).

2. Literature Review

The cement industry of India is responsible for about 7% of the global capacity and production (Kumar and Sinha, 2022). About 98% of the total capacity is under the ownership of the private sector and the rest lies with the public sector. The demand for this sector is seeing constant growth with an expected CAGR of 5.65% mainly due to the demand from road and urban construction and commercial real estate.

By 2030, the cement sector must cut CO_2 intensity by 0.7% yearly, according to the International Energy Agency. On the other hand, there has been an annual increase of 0.3% in the CO_2 intensity. India, the world's second-largest producer of cement, must concentrate on producing cement sustainably because it uses a lot of energy and resources. With sustainability being a top priority, a study (Sangwan et al., 2019) shows that 52 Key Performing Indicators (KPIs) are categorized into 13 categories for the Indian cement industry using exploratory factor analysis. The economic factors (including service costs, capital gains, etc.), Social factors (like employees, local community, and social justice), and environmental factors (like emissions, materials, etc.) are the primary ones under the management. To maintain the global target to limit global warming by 1.5 °C by the end of the century steel and cement industry needs to concentrate on reuse, recycling, and dematerialization. (Dhar et al., 2020). Carbon capture and storage (CCS) and a carbon tax in the 2°C case would help limit CO_2 emissions.

A study (Leite and Uysal, 2023) was conducted to see if a third party's assessment of a firm's ESG has an impact on investors' demand for the stock. It was noted that a high ESG score is an essential consideration for investors if the decision is supported by favorable company news. ESG factors can be responsible for influencing an investor's decision. In India, the ESG index and investors' sentiment are interconnected. It demonstrates that in the short run, ESG might not have a positive sentiment but they do impact investors positively in the future and will influence investors (Dhasmana et al., 2023).

Due to their ignorance of ESG ratings, investors in India prefer to avoid responsible investing (Seth et al., 2021). The aforementioned cannot be attributed to a single cause, but short-term gain expectations play a major role. Companies in India list ESG ratings as a positive element in their annual reports. Additionally, government attempts have led to poor voluntary standards that reduce business sustainability responsibility.

Profitability is the judge of the efficiency of an organization. The above-mentioned factors can be determined by various internal and external factors. A study (Bhayani, 2012) demonstrates that the profitability of all the listed Indian cement industries relies on several factors like fixed asset turnover, leverage ratio, age of the firm, operating profit ratio, and inflation rate.

The international policy requires companies to curb their carbon emissions. This results in additional costs and risks for firms. The carbon emission by corporations can impact their financial performance. Investors tend to assign more faith to carbon-efficient firms as they are expected to display greater resource efficiency. (Trinksa et al., 2020). Reduced regulatory costs have a positive impact on the short-term profits of a company.

Circular Economy is a new strategy for eliminating waste that helps the country advance to greater heights without straining its resources. The emission factor was reduced from 1.12 t of CO_2/t of cement in 1996 to 0.670 t of CO_2/t of cement in 2017. This is a tremendous advancement for the Indian cement sector. The industry is passionate about using sustainable energy, particularly solar electricity. The production of blended cement using fly ash promotes reuse and recycling and is good for the environment. In India, alternative fuel and raw materials (AFR) are an important part of the circular economy (Kukreja et al., 2020).

Increasing the use of Supplementary Cementations Material (SCM) materials in India would (Bhayani, 2012) lower the clinker-to-cement ratio, increasing the use of alternate fuels, widespread adoption of Waste Heat Recovery (WHR) and technological development are important to mitigate CO2 emissions. Ground Granulated Blast –furnace slag (GBFS) will be necessary to effectively use clinker; its amounts are anticipated to decline (Schneider, 2019). India is seeing a rise in cement-grade limestone causing its depletion, therefore, it should look toward the development of Portland-limestone cement (PLC). This would lower the clinker factor, encourage energy saving, preserve natural resources, enhance workability, and reduce the emission of greenhouse gases (Gupta et al., 2020).

3. Research Methodology

The main objective of this research is to analyze the Indian cement industry in terms of its environmental sustainability. It was observed from former studies that ESG was an important factor that investors took into consideration. In India, investors were less aware of Socially Responsible Investing (SRI) avenues. A few factors that prevented people from undertaking SRI Investing were a lack of tax benefits, low returns, and less available information (Jonwall et al., 2022).

In our study, the impact of the ESG Disclosure Score is observed on the financial parameters of the listed Indian Cement Companies. To begin with, the trends of different financial parameters (like Retained Earnings, EBIT, Number of Shareholders, Total assets, Current Ratio, and Profit Margin), ESG Score, and Environmental Disclosure Score are graphically demonstrated for a period of 10 years ranging from 2012 to 2021. Next, the impact ESG Disclosure Score of different cement industries is observed on financial variables like Current Ratio, Total Assets, Number of Shareholders, and Profit Margin.

The data for the following study was sourced from Bloomberg for a period spanning from 2012 to 2021. For an accurate representation of the Indian Cement Industry, the financial data of 13 listed Indian Companies are in the domain of the cement sector. The parameters included ESG Disclosure score, Current Ratio, Total Assets, Number of Shareholders, and Profit Margin for 13 companies in the Indian cement industry. The most recent data from 2012 to 2021 makes longitudinal analysis possible encompassing the increasing importance of sustainability practices.

The model for the study has been listed below:

Model 1: $CR = \beta_0 + \beta_1 EDS + \varepsilon$

Model 2: $NS = \beta_0 + \beta_1 EDS + \varepsilon$

Model 3: $PM = \beta_0 + \beta_1 EDS + \varepsilon$

Model 4: $TA = \beta_0 + \beta_1 EDS + \varepsilon$

Where CR = Current Ratio, EDS = Environmental Disclosure Score, NS = Number of Shareholders, PM = Profit Margin, and TA = Total Assets.

4. Results and Analysis

This study first observes the trend of Environmental Disclosure Score, ESG Score, and Financial parameters (Current Ratio, Total Assets, Number of Shareholders, Profit Margins, Retained Earnings, and EBIT)

Table 22.1 Environmental disclosure score and ESG score

YEAR	Environmental Disclosure Score	ESG Disclosure Score
2012	14.34	28.17
2013	16.04	27.31
2014	16.08	29.79
2015	19.29	36.09
2016	19.25	36.24
2017	18.54	36.33
2018	18.31	37.41
2019	22.31	43.00
2020	23.98	44.64
2021	28.96	47.80

Source: Computed by Author

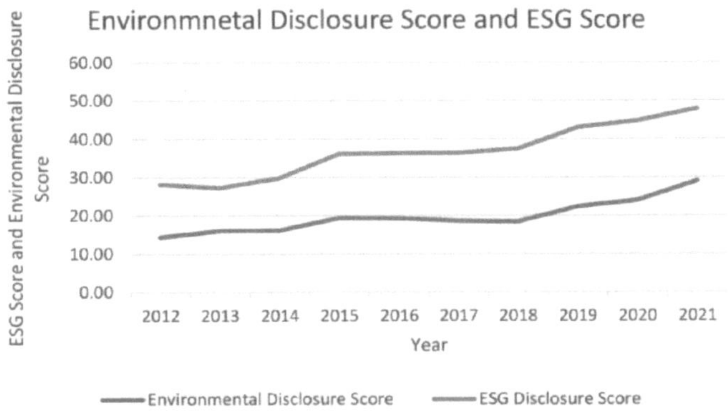

Fig. 22.1 Environmental disclosure score and ESG score

Source: Computed by Author

The above chart demonstrates that the Environmental Disclosure Score and ESG Score have progressively increased from 2012 to 2020 in the Cement Industry. ESG factors are influencing and shaping business practices, strategies, and operations of organizations across a range of industries, including cement manufacturing which explains their increase. It is well known that the production of cement uses a lot of energy and emits a lot of greenhouse gases, especially carbon dioxide (CO_2). ESG factors include initiatives to lower carbon emissions and boost energy efficiency.

Table 22.2 Retained earning and EBIT

Year	Retained Earning	EBIT
2012	14595.16	10954.68
2013	14595.16	10309.76
2014	11941.50	9011.00
2015	10946.37	9312.82
2016	11941.50	9427.31
2017	10946.37	8887.02
2018	10104.34	8825.82
2019	10104.34	10426.31
2020	10104.34	11960.81
2021	10946.37	17578.81

Source: Computed by Author

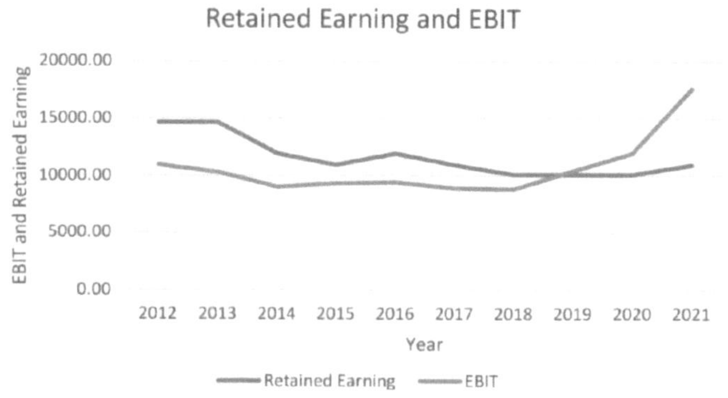

Fig. 22.2 Retained earning and EBIT

Source: Computed by Author

The Earnings before income and tax (EBIT) is a metric for a company's operating profitability that excludes taxes and interest costs. The EBIT of the Cement Industry has remained consistent over the past 10 years and it saw a rise in 2020. The total profits a corporation has made throughout the years, less dividends given to shareholders, are known as Retained Earnings. The Retained Earnings have dropped over the period from 2012 to 2021.

Table 22.3 Profit margin and current ratio

Years	Profit Margin	Current Ratio
2012	7.50	1.50
2013	5.95	1.31
2014	3.30	1.23
2015	3.11	1.12
2016	2.83	1.05
2017	-6.52	0.94
2018	-6.46	1.24
2019	-2.84	1.15
2020	2.65	1.13
2021	0.32	1.24

Source: Computed by Author

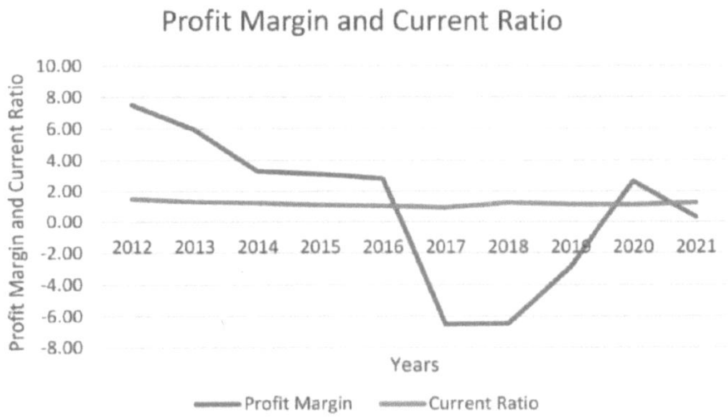

Fig. 22.3 Profit margin and current ratio

Source: Computed by Author

The current ratio evaluates a company's capacity to meet its short-term obligations using its current assets. A good current ratio is one that is above 1, which shows that the current assets exceed current liabilities. It is observed that the current ratio is relatively stable over the past 10 years ranging between 0.94 and 1.5. The profit margin on the other hand is very erratic and experiences a significant drop post 2016 mainly because of a significant fall in the profit margin of Shiva Cement Limited and Jaiprakash Associates. Due to variables like economic cycles, competitive dynamics and, input costs, profit margin trends in the Indian cement sector have traditionally demonstrated fluctuation. Construction activity levels and the industry's cyclicality are frequently correlated, and this has an impact on profit margins. Profit margins tended to expand during times of economic expansion and rapid infrastructure development, while margin pressure might be felt during times of recession.

Table 22.4 Total asset and number of shareholders

Years	Total Asset	Number of Shareholders
2012	126609.53	127719
2013	147441.1	123137
2014	157456.08	122889
2015	167246.36	116287
2016	178716.89	124014
2017	154609.36	123122
2018	160757.58	129279
2019	185965.84	132411
2020	177010.68	141379

Source: Computed by Author

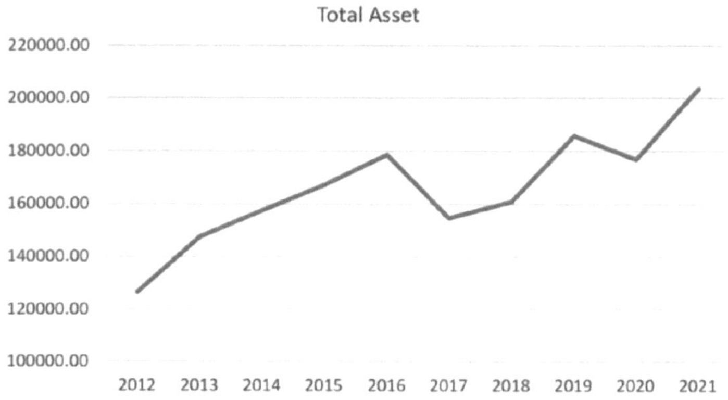

Fig. 22.4 Total asset

Source: Computed by Author

Numerous big and small cement-producing enterprises make up the Indian Cement Industry. It is observed that the total assets of the Indian Cement Industry has risen over the years with an occasional drop. The number of shareholders in the Indian Cement Industry has been stable until 2019 after which it has shown significant growth. This rise could be due to the increased trading during the pandemic years.

In the next portion, the impact of ESG on the financial performance of the Cement Industry is studied. A panel regression was performed to check the impact of the ESG Disclosure Score on the Current Ratio, Total Assets, Number of Shareholders, and Profit Margin from 2012 to 2021. The results are demonstrated below in a tabular format

Fig. 22.5 Number of shareholders

Source: Computed by Author

Table 22.5 Impact of ESG score on the current ratio

MODEL 1: CURRENT RATIO			
Variables	**Coefficient**	**Standard error**	**p-value**
Constant	1.51	0.15	0.00
ESG Disclosure Score	-0.01	0.00	0.03

Source: Computed by the Author

The results demonstrate that model 1 is significant as the p-value of the coefficient and the ESG Score is less than 0.05. The coefficient of the ESG Score is -0.01 which shows that the ESG Disclosure Score has a negative impact on the Current Ratio. Companies in the cement sector are obligated to make large investments in ESG activities such as sustainability initiatives, ethical sourcing, and the welfare of staff, which may consume a sizeable percentage of their working capital. While it might take some time for these investments to pay off, they might temporarily reduce the current ratio by lowering the ratio of current assets to current liabilities.

Table 22.6 Impact of ESG score on the number of shareholders

MODEL 2: NUMBER OF SHAREHOLDERS			
Variables	**Coefficient**	**Standard error**	**p-value**
Constant	99653.31	9854.83	0.00
ESG Disclosure Score	828.57	261.40	0.00

Source: Computed by the Author

It is observed that Model 2 is significant as the p-values of the constant and ESG Disclosure Score are less than 0.05. Also, the positive coefficient demonstrates a positive relationship between the ESG Disclosure Score and the Number of Shareholders. In the Indian cement sector, Environmental, Social, and Governance

(ESG) considerations have a significant impact on the number of shareholders, which reflects the increasing interest in sustainable investing and ethical corporate conduct. Businesses in this industry that emphasize ESG practices, (like lowering carbon emissions, enhancing worker safety, and interacting with local communities), tend to improve their reputation and appeal to ESG-conscious investors. A rise of shareholders looking to match their investments with their principles may result from this appeal.

Table 22.7 Impact of ESG score on the profit margin

MODEL 3: PROFIT MARGIN			
Variables	**Coefficient**	**Standard error**	**p-value**
Constant	14.08	5.57	0.01
ESG Disclosure Score	-0.36	0.15	0.02

Source: Computed by the Author

Model 3 is significant as the p-values of the constant and variable ESG Disclosure Score are 0.01 and 0.02 respectively, which are both less than 0.05. The negative coefficient demonstrates that when the ESG Disclosure Score rises by 1 unit, the Profit Margin experiences a drop of 0.36 units. ESG (environmental, social, and governance) principles can at first have a detrimental effect on profit margins in the Indian cement sector. ESG activities sometimes require large investments in worker welfare, environmental standards, and technology advancements, which raises operational expenses. For example, reducing carbon emissions and implementing more environmentally friendly industrial practices may require a substantial capital expenditure. Furthermore, it might be costly to comply with stringent environmental regulations. Profit margins may be strained in the near term by these expenses.

Table 22.8 Impact of ESG score on the total assets

MODEL 3: TOTAL ASSETS			
Variables	**Coefficient**	**Standard error**	**p-value**
Constant	83203.81	68816.93	0.23
ESG Disclosure Score	2225.79	995.97	0.03

Source: Computed by the Author

The ESG Score's p-value is less than 0.05, but the constant value's p-value is 0.23, which is greater than 0.05. The ESG Score's coefficient of 2225.79 indicates that the ESG Disclosure Score has a favorable effect on the total assets. The cement sector, which must prioritize ESG principles, must make significant investments in sustainable assets, potentially broadening its entire asset base.

5. Conclusion

To sum up, the investigation of the relationship between the environmental, social, and governance (ESG) factors and the Indian cement sector from 2012 to 2021 reveals several intriguing patterns and discoveries. During this period, the industry improved its ESG performance, as seen by rising Environmental Disclosure Scores and ESG Disclosure Scores, which reflect a growing commitment to sustainability and moral business conduct. Nonetheless, there were alterations in the financial landscape of the sector. While retained earnings saw a fall that may have been brought on by the sector's investments in sustainability programs, earnings before interest and taxes (EBIT) were relatively stable until a noteworthy rise after 2019, demonstrating resilience in the face of altering economic conditions. The cement businesses generally have a robust short-term liquidity position, as evidenced by their current ratios above 0.94. However, profit margins showed erratic trends that were influenced by the dynamics of the competition and the market.

The study's conclusions also imply that ESG Disclosure Scores have a significant impact on several financial factors. Notably, the current ratio and profit margins showed a negative association with the ESG Disclosure Scores. This demonstrates that businesses in the cement sector in India may have first had challenges with their short-term profit margins and liquidity due to their emphasis on sustainability initiatives and ESG disclosures. This study emphasizes how ESG integration has a dynamic impact on organizations' financial health, particularly in emerging countries like India.

REFERENCES

1. Arouria, M., Gomes, M., & Pukthuanthong, K. (2019). Corporate social responsibility and M&A uncertainty. Journal of Corporate Finance,Volume 56, 176–198.
2. B, D., & Nallanavar, S. F. (2022). History & Growth of Cement industry in India - A Study. Journal of Emerging Technologies and Innovative Research, Volume 9, Issue 1.
3. Bhakar, V., Sangwan, K. S., & Digalwar, A. K. (2020). Readiness self-assessment of cement industry for sustainable manufacturing implementation: A case study of India. Procedia CIRP Volume 90, 449–454.
4. Bhayani, S. (2012). Determinant of Profitability in Indian Cement Industry: An Economic Analysis. South Asian Journal of Mangement, Volume 17, No. 4.
5. Chaurasia, S., A. K., & A. D. (2013). Effect of cement industry pollution on chlorophyll content of some crops at Kodinar, Gujarat, India . Proceedings of the International Academy of Ecology and Environmental Sciences, 3(4), 288–295.
6. Clément, A., Robinot, É., & Trespeuch, L. (2023). The use of ESG scores in academic literature: a systematic literature review. Journal of Enterprising Communities: People and Places in the Global Economy.
7. Dhar, S., Pathak, M., & Shukla, P. R. (2020). Transformation of India's steel and cement industry in a sustainable 1.5 degree Celcius world . Energy Policy 137.

8. Dhasmana, S., Ghosh, S., & Kanjilal, K. (2023). Does investor sentiment influence ESG stock performance? Evidence from India. Journal of Behavioral and Experimental Finance 37 .
9. Gupta, S., Mohapatra, B., & Bansal, M. (2020). A review on development of Portland limestone cement: A step towards low carbon economy for Indian cement industry. Current Research in Green and Sustainable Chemistry, Volume 3.
10. Huang, Q., Li, Y., Lin, M., & McBrayer, G. A. (2022). Natural disasters, risk salience, and corporate ESG disclosure. Journal of Corporate Finance, Volume 72.
11. Jonwall, R., Gupta, S., & Pahuja, S. (2022). Socially responsible investment behavior: a study of individual investors from India. Review of Behavioral Finance.
12. Kandlikar, M., & Ramachandran, G. (2000). The Causes and Consequences of Particulate Air Pollution in Urban India: A Synthesis of the Science. Annual Review of Energy and the Environment, Vol. 25, 629–684.
13. Kesarwani, S., & James, A. (2017). Effect of air pollution on human health problems residents living around the cement plant, Chandrapur, Maharashtra, India. Journal of Pharmacognosy and Phytochemistry , 507–510.
14. Kukreja, K., Sharma, P., Mohapatra, B., & Saxena, A. (2020). Indian Cement Industry: A Key Player in the Circular Economy of India. Enhancing Future Skills and Entrepreneurship, 181–192.
15. Kumar, A., & Sinha, D. M. (2022). CEMENT INDUSTRY IN INDIA: CHALLENGES AND PROSPECTS. International Journal of Creative thoughts, Volume 10, Issue 8.
16. Leite, B. J., & Uysal, V. B. (2023). Does ESG matter to investors? ESG scores and the stock price response to new information. Global Finance Journal 57.
17. Sangwan, K. S., Bhakar, V., & Digalwar, A. K. (2019). A sustainability assessment framework for cement industry – a case study. Benchmarking: An International Journal, Vol.26 No. 2, 470–497.
18. Schneider, M. (2019). Cement and Concrete Research. Cement and Concrete Research, Volume 124.
19. Seth, R., Gupta, S., & Gupta, H. (2021). ESG INVESTING: A CRITICAL OVERVIEW. HANS SHODH SUDHA, VOL. 2, ISSUE 2, 69–80.
20. Trinksa, A., Mulder, M., & Scholtens, B. (2020). An Efficiency Perspective on Carbon Emissions and Financial Performance. Ecological Economics, Volume 175.

Securing the Future through Sustainability, Health, Education, and Technology – Brig. Dr. Rajiv Divekar et al. (eds)
 ISBN 978-1-032-95922-1

23 Unlocking HR Potential: Exploring Blockchain Technology's Application in Human Resource Management

Maitri Saklani[1], Jaya Chitranshi[2], Komal Chopra
Symbiosis Institute of Management Studies,
Symbiosis International Deemed University,
Pune, India

Abstract

The fast improvement of science and technology, along with the expansion of society, has led to the widespread usage of blockchain technology across several industries. Employers who use blockchain technology to assist human resource management can boost work productivity while decreasing related resource expenditures. The existing awareness, trust, preference, dependability, and influence of blockchain technology within the HRM department are all thoroughly analyzed in this article. This article seeks to address current issues with blockchain technology and aid in its future growth. The survey was conducted on 263 HR professionals from various departments, regions, and industries. The paper raises many issues, including security and data privacy, while also recommending integrating blockchain technology with human resource management. The paper goes on to suggest that efforts be made to solve some of the security, dependability, and knowledge gaps in blockchain technology.

Keywords: Blockchain technology, HRM, Training, Leadership, Culture, AI, IOT

1. Introduction

From an industry perspective, blockchain is now gaining popularity as a technical manifestation brought about by a certain degree of scientific and technological

[1]maitri.saklani2024@sims.edu, [2]jaya.chitranshi@sims.edu

DOI: 10.1201/9781003587200-23

innovation. It might have a significant effect. Governmental organizations have progressively established guidelines and rules on the use of blockchain technology in order to guide its application while maintaining the technology's security characteristics. Human resource management is the major business area that keeps businesses operating in the existing state. Associated firms have found it simpler to engage appropriate skills and attract skilled workers since the introduction of blockchain technology. The use of blockchain technology in the HRM department is discussed in this paper in relation to hiring, training and development, employee engagement, employee verification, and employee data management. In addition, blockchain may be linked with current technologies like IOT, ML, and AI to further improve the productivity and efficiency of HRM procedures. Block-chain systems come in public, private, and hybrid varieties, and they are used in HRM as well as other parallel departments including finance, operations, FMCG, services, and manufacturing.

To fully utilize this embryonic technology in today's sectors, there are several worrying difficulties with blockchain technology, like every coin that has two sides that need to be addressed. This paper not only analyzes the primary modern shortcomings that hinder businesses from implementing blockchain technology, but also aims to address the expanding use of blockchain technology in various HR departments. It also looks at the future possibilities of blockchain technology in light of the discovered drawbacks.

2. Objectives

1. To analyze the preference of usage of blockchain Technology over the other already existing technologies in HRM
2. To analyze which attributes of HRM can be affected by blockchain
3. Region wise analysis of the popularity of blockchain technology

3. Literature Review

Growing Internet economies and continuous environmental changes have forced corporate organizations to become platform-based enterprises and embrace technology. Shared human resource management solves concerns with performance, training, salary and welfare, and employee relations by including third party ledger and using the Internet for training and evaluation. HRM is changing at the same time as it undergoes professional growth and new concept incorporation. One kind of distributed transaction ledger is blockchain. The data stored on the ledger is dispersed across several nodes and places rather than being retained in a single central location. Since, control is shared by several separate parties, a centralized authority is not necessary. Public-private key cryptography ensures that data may only be decoded by the intended recipient, protecting privacy.

3.1 Blockchain Integrated with other Technologies

Some experts say that if AI is the brain, then blockchain is the body. Put differently, artificial intelligence (AI) enables the analysis and decision-making of data that blockchain has gathered, exchanged, and stored. AI and blockchain have a strong and fruitful partnership that is still expanding. Data integrity and dependability are strengthened by the blockchain, which also aids in preventing data manipulation *(Khatoon, 2019)*. AI-assisted HRM is being presented more and more as a new strategic necessity for a business's survival and growth *(Malik et al. 2022)*. However, because to its centralized structure, technological advancement and digitalization have brought forth a number of security and authentication challenges, such as mining, hacking, and denial-of-service attacks. The most effective way to overcome these obstacles is now apparent: blockchain technology *(Hassan, 2019)*.

3.2 Application of Blockchain Technology in Businesses

The use of blockchain technology to different business processes has begun at several firms. Above all, the banking industry has been greatly impacted by the use of blockchain technology to create cryptocurrencies *(Ghodoosi, 2022)*. Businesses are facing increasing pressure to integrate technology into every facet of their business to enhance consumer satisfaction (Chillakuri, *2020)*. The term "digital business ecosystem," or DBE, has a new definition. (DBE) is a network of companies that work together to develop and provide a certain item or service in a partially or fully digital environment. These companies might include manufacturers, distributors, retailers, customers, competitors, and governmental organizations. The emergence of digital technologies such as blockchains, digital twins, artificial intelligence (AI), and the Internet of Things (IoT) allowed for more flexibility and frameworks for value creation that transcended industries and geographical boundaries, hence enabling DBEs *(Baumann, 2022)*. Nowadays, a business obtains a competitive advantage (CA) when it surpasses its competitors by employing a certain combination of resources, competencies, and strategies. made up primarily of electronic resources *(Garg, 2023)*.

3.3 Application of Blockchain Technology in HRM

There are several problems with traditional HR recruitment procedures, including a credit system that isn't flawless, information exchange that's hard to do, and other things. Security of personal data cannot be guaranteed *(Lai 2020)*. Given the increasing global competition in the job market, it is imperative to do research on the application of technology in hiring and staffing practices *(Abdul, 2020)*. Sharing data on human resources is challenging since it entails money, privacy protection, and trust security. For instance, personal profile information is frequently kept on file by different talent companies. These data are stored in a distinct, fragmented manner that makes effective sharing challenging. One of the most important HR jobs at the hiring level is to draw in enough qualified candidates in a timely manner, and then select the best candidate or candidates from that pool." This is a concise summary of recruiting. Furthermore, the larger the candidate pool, the easier it will be to find quality candidates to fill available vacancies (Makridakis, 2019). Yung (2020) lists credential verification, worker payments, identity management, and work matching systems as some of the particular uses of blockchain technology. Blockchain technology offers a platform for streamlining workflows, freeing up staff members' time to solve issues and communicate with stakeholders. One example of a reliable method for verifying candidates' backgrounds is the blockchain ledger. Verifying candidates' resumes, certifications, skills, and work history is a major hurdle that companies must overcome when recruiting new employees (Amer, 2023). Employers can use distributed ledger at academic institutions to verify a candidate's eligibility for education. The data may be verified by distributed ledgers, which include private or public entities (professional universities, organizations, and institutions), as well as by privately or publicly owned third parties (background check companies, BCHRIS, and BCRMS). Even more, certain ledgers have the ability to rank candidates and reject applications for unfit jobs. Blockchain's pre-verifications enable recruiters to save "time, effort, and cost" when contacting prospects via social media, hence expediting the recruiting process. A paper claims that blockchain technology may enhance HR cybersecurity, fraud prevention, and data protection. Training assessment may be effectively evaluated with blockchain technology. Training exercises need full engagement from the participants as well as an objective evaluation of the trainer's training delivery skills. Additionally, blockchain will help the organization maintain personnel records as efficiently as possible by enabling each employee to check their own data to guarantee profile uniformity. The complete set of data will be examined in order to fully understand the employee growth path as it manifests itself in blockchain. Information from a wide range of stakeholders, including learning and growth, peer and senior reporting input, would be included in the blocks. It will be simpler to comprehend how beneficial blockchain-enabled training is. When we make decisions, we frequently mean choose between desirable and bad possibilities. The focus of the current study is on how BT is used in HRM decision-making. The decision-making process in human resource management (HRM) entails selecting between possible courses of action in the sub-functions of HRM in order to achieve organizational goals. Blockchain technology is used as an interface to feed and gather data. Distributed ledger technology allows for hiring and sectioning with more convenience for professionals without the need for false credentials. The primary challenge with the existing approach to HR data preservation in HRM was the intricacy of selecting new criteria, such work-life balance, employee retention, and performance indicators for workers (Ramachandran, 2022). Prospects for novel cooperative networking, enhanced efficacy via the use of smart contracts, the integration of blockchain technology with the Internet of

Things, and several innovative business models, such as asset tokenization, were recognized. Prospective fields for further investigation abound. As an example, consider how blockchain, cloud computing, and AI are combined with big data. Designing laws and regulations to direct AI development would be another factor. Additionally, a cross-national comparison of AI's progress might be fascinating (Khatoon, 2019).

4. Research Methodology

The purpose of the study was to examine the current level of blockchain technology popularity, dependability, and confidence among HR professionals as well as any potential gaps in the HRM department. In order to conduct the survey, 263 HR professionals from various departments, regions, and industries provided their responses. The purpose of the paper is to collect information on problems with current HRM and areas where blockchain technology might be useful. It also covers current business trends about the kind of technology being used and the problems they are having. To examine awareness, problems, and future prospects, a questionnaire has been devised to gather data. Additionally, we reviewed a number of previously published articles that served as a foundation for the instrument's design.

5. Results and Discussion

1. On analyzing the preference of usage of blockchain Technology over the other already existing technologies in HRM it has been found that AI is the most preferred technology being used within the HRM department whereas Blockchain technology is being used the least.

Table 23.1 Percentage popularity of technologies being used in the HRM process

Technology being Used in HRM Process	Frequency	Percentage
AI	140	53.2
Blockchain Technology	22	8.4
IOT	42	16
ML	44	16.7
Other	15	5.7
Total	263	100

2. It is clear that the majority of respondents feel that Training and job roles will be major areas of impact if blockchain is adopted in the HRM department.

Areas of Impact on adoption of blockchain in HRM	Percentage
Leadership	21.40%
Culture	32.10%
Training	63%
Job Roles	57.10%
Employee Engagement	35.70%
Compensation	32.10%
Performance Management	37.50%

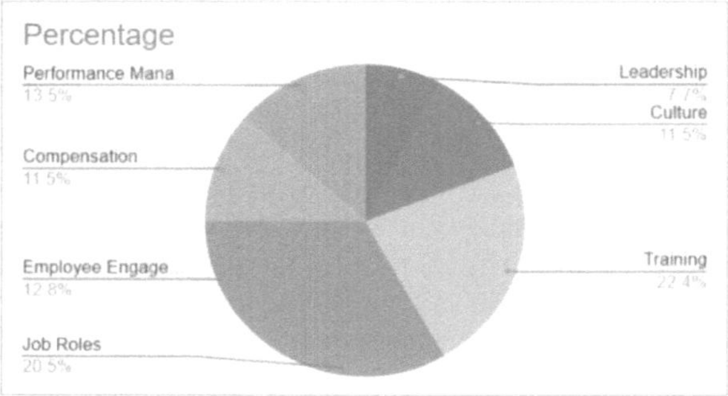

Fig. 23.1 Major areas of impact if blockchain technology is adopted in the HR department

3. It is clear that at present South Eastern asia is the hotspot of technologies as it has maximum awareness of blockchain technology integration with HRM as compared to other regions. From the second figure, it is depicted that the south eastern Asian region (depicted by china) and Asia Pacific (depicted by Russia) have great level of awareness as compared to other regions like central Asian region(depicted by Ukraine).

Row Labels	Count of Q12.Rate your Awareness about integration of blockchain technology with HRM processes.
Asia-Pacific	39.92%
Central Asia	9.13%
Others	3.80%
South Eastern Asia	47.15%
Grand Total	**100.00%**

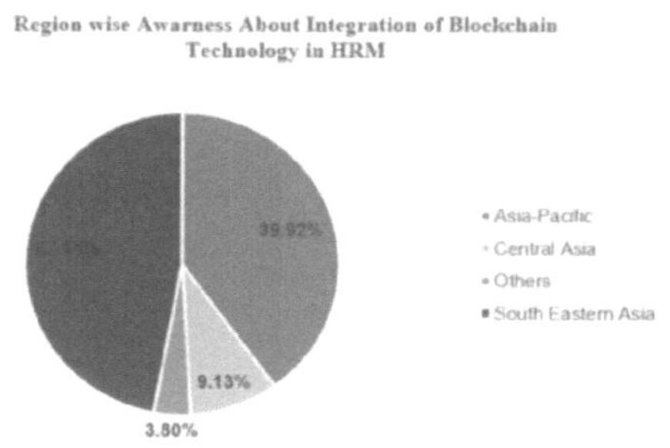

Fig. 23.2 Percentage of region wise awareness of blockchain technology in HR department

Fig. 23.3 Region wise awareness of blockchain technology in HR department

1. It is seen from analysis 4 that AI is the most used technology with HRM whereas Blockchain is still the least preferred. Therefore, there is a great prospect of using AI and Blockchain together integrating with HRM.
2. From analysis 5 it is clear that most of the HRs feel that if blockchain is introduced in an organization then major impact will be seen in training of people in order to customize with the technology and also there will be a major change in job roles within an organization
3. From analysis 6 it is clear that the southeastern Asian region and Asia Pacific region has great awareness of blockchain technology and its integration with the HRM process.

6. Conclusion

By conducting this study it has been found that how technology has become a crucial part of todays HRM environment where AI is the most preferred technology for conducting HR activities. It has been observed that Blockchain technology is least preferred among all the technologies hence there is a need for investigating the future prospects of blockchain being used in the domain of HRM. With the application of integrated AI and blockchain technology in the HRM procedures the potential for productivity, precision and creativity has bright future. Furthermore, for active application of the integrated technologies there is a need for the organizations to invest in Training and development, restructuring of job responsibilities and roles within organizations. Also there is a noticeable degree of interest of Southeast Asia and Asia Pacific regional businesses which suggest additional research and investments in the domain of blockchain technology in HRM procedures. The findings point towards the potential advantages of the integration of blockchain technology and artificial intelligence into HRM at the same time it is required to pay attention towards planning, strategizing and training so that there will be successful implementation of the technology.

7. Implications

There are several implications of the findings for businesses and HR professionals. It first highlights how important it is to strategically use artificial intelligence (AI) and blockchain into HRM practices in order to gain a competitive edge and increase operational performance. Second, considering the expected impact of blockchain on job roles and training programs, HR departments should spend heavily in comprehensive training and development activities to provide employees with the skills necessary for technology integration. Businesses are encouraged to take advantage of this awareness for early adoption as the rising market for HR technology solutions in Southeast Asia and the Asia Pacific region is shown by the growing interest in and understanding of blockchain.

8. Limitations and Suggestions

There hasn't been much study done on blockchain technology yet because it's still extremely new. Very few businesses have implemented blockchain technology in their HRM divisions to handle basic HR procedures. As a result, there were extremely few replies. With inclusion of blockchain technology by more organizations, the response-rate and count will become higher.

REFERENCES

1. A Khatoon, P. V. (2019). *Blockchain in energy efficiency: Potential applications and benefits.* Retrieved from https://scholar.google.com/scholar?hl=en&as_sdt=0%2C5&q=Khatoon%2C+Asma%2C+et+al.+%22Blockchain+in+energy+efficiency%3A+Potential+applications+and+benefits.%22+Energies+12.17+%282019%29%3A+3317&btnG=#d=gs_cit&t=1694674573724&u=%2Fscholar%3Fq%3Dinfo%3A7Met
2. Asma Khatoon, P. V. (2019, August). Retrieved from Blockchain in Energy Efficiency: Potential Applications and Benefits: https://www.mdpi.com/1996-1073/12/17/3317
3. Baumann, S. (2022, June). *Introduction to the Handbook on Digital Business Ecosystems: Strategies, Platforms, Technologies, Governance and Societal Challenges.* Retrieved from https://www.researchgate.net/publication/361416853_Introduction_to_the_Handbook_on_Digital_Business_Ecosystems_Strategies_Platforms_Technologies_Governance_and_Societal_Challenges
4. Bharat Chillakuri, V. S. (2020, August). *Role of blockchain in HR'sresponse to new-normal.* Retrieved from https://www.researchgate.net/publication/350359168_Role_of_blockchain_in_HR's_response_to_new-normal
5. Chaza Abdul, W. W. (2020). *THE IMPACT OF TECHNOLOGY ON RECRUITMENT PROCESS.* Retrieved from https://iacis.org/iis/2020/4_iis_2020_9-17.pdf
6. E Amer, S. O. (2023, June). *A Blockchain-based Model for Integrated Higher Education 2019and Recruitment Information.* Retrieved from https://namibian-studies.com/index.php/JNS/article/view/27352019
7. Eric Yung, D. C. (2020, April). *Benefits and Use of Blockchain Technology to Human Resources Management: A Critical Review.* Retrieved from https://www.researchgate.net/publication/341046981_Benefits_and_Use_of_Blockchain_Technology_to_Human_Resources_Management_A_Critical_Review
8. Ghodoosi, M. M. (2022, January). *The Ethics of Blockchain in Organizations.* Retrieved from https://link.springer.com/content/pdf/10.1007/s10551-022-05058-5.pdf
9. Hassan, M. U. (2019, August). *Privacy preservation in blockchain based IoT systems: Integration issues, prospects, challenges, and future research directions.* Retrieved from https://www.sciencedirect.com/science/article/pii/S0167739X18326542
10. Lai, J. (2020, December). *The Application Prospects of Blockchain Technology in Human Resource Management.* Retrieved from https://www.researchgate.net/publication/347543467_The_Application_Prospects_of_Blockchain_Technology_in_Human_Resource_Management
11. Malik, A., Budhwar, P., & Kazmi, B. A. (2022, November). *Artificial intelligence (AI)-assisted HRM: Towards an extended strategic framework.* Retrieved from

https://research.aston.ac.uk/en/publications/artificial-intelligence-ai-assisted-hrm-towards-an-extended-strat

12. Poonam Garg, B. G. (2023, March). *Examining the relationship between blockchain capabilities and organizational performance in the Indian banking sector*. Retrieved from https://link.springer.com/article/10.1007/s10479-023-05254-0
13. Rukma Ramachandran, V. B. (2022, November). *The role of blockchain technology in the process of decision-making in human resource management: a review and future research agenda*. Retrieved from https://www.emerald.com/insight/content/doi/10.1108/BPMJ-07-2022-0351/full/html
14. Spyros Makridakis, K. C. (2019, December). *Blockchain: Current Challenges and Future Prospects/Applications*. Retrieved from https://www.mdpi.com/1999-5903/11/12/258

Note: All the figures and table in this chapter were made by the authors.

Securing the Future through Sustainability, Health, Education, and Technology –
Brig. Dr. Rajiv Divekar et al. (eds)

24 Role of Biomass Gasification and Bio CNG for Carbon Footprint Management in the Process Industry

Sanjay Kumar Mangla[1]
Symbiosis Institute of Management Studies,
Symbiosis International (Deemed University), Pune, India
Joshi Hrishikesh[2]
Symbiosis International (Deemed University), Pune, India

ABSTRACT

This study concentrates on two emerging renewable solutions which can provide the renewable alternatives to this otherwise hard to decarbonise sector. Biomass gasification and Bio CNG are the alternatives fuel sources, which can provide the renewable energy sources to replace the direct fired applications in the process industry. Incorporation of either of these solutions can provide a major boost to the possibility of achieving near 100% offset of the use of fossils in the process industry. Both Biomass gasification as well as Bio CNG are available in form of self-sustaining combustible gases. These gases can replace the use of fossil fuels being used for direct heating applications. Both these options have distinct features of their own, and hence has different applications where they can be effectively employed by the industry. This study provides the basic framework for use of these alternatives in the industry, and their suitable use cases or selection criteria.

KEYWORDS: Bio CNG, Biomass gasification, CBG, Climate change, Direct heating applications, Net zero, Producer gas, Renewable energy

1. Introduction

Environmental sustainability is a clear focus area for the process industry due to drivers such as combination of government regulations, incentives, own net

[1]sam211285@gmail.com, [2]hrishi.scri@gmail.com

DOI: 10.1201/9781003587200-24

zero targets. Energy usage for the production of goods is the main source of CO2 emissions for any process industry. (Yoro and Daramola, 2020). The choice of the energy source is mainly governed by the process application. Scope I and Scope II emissions reduction is highest of the priority for any business process house. Scope I emissions, which are occurring at the premises of the firm majorly constitute use of fossil fuels for providing the heating and cooling required for the process applications, and energy production in case of captive thermal power plants. Scope II emissions majorly comprises of the use of electrical energy which is purchased through the grid. Majority of the energy use of any firm can be broadly categorised in the three segments – Electricity used for the operations, Direct heating applications and Indirect Heating applications. While there are established renewable alternatives for electricity and indirect heating applications, last hurdle in the decarbonization is typically the direct heating applications, which use fuels such as furnace oil, Diesel, LPG or Natural gas for directly firing in the furnaces to generate high temperature in heating applications.

Table 24.1 shows the typical energy sources for various forms of energy used in process industry and their carbon footprint per unit. The carbon footprint indicated here is representative in nature and can reasonably vary depending on the location, grade of fuel used etc.

Table 24.1 Sources of energy and their typical CO2 footprint

Application	Energy Source	Unit of energy	Tones of CO2 emission per unit of energy
Electricity	Grid	MWh	0.70
Direct & Indirect Heating	Furnace Oil	GCal	0.32
Direct & Indirect Heating	Natural gas	GCal	0.24
Indirect Heating (Steam)	Furnace Oil	Tons	0.20
Indirect Heating (Steam)	Coal	Tons	0.16

Source: Central electricity authority FY21-22 CO2 base line data for grid electricity in India, authors estimate for the fossil fuel

As the industry is moving towards achieving the net zero targets, energy use in industry is being shifted to renewable energy sources. These renewable energy sources result in lowering of the carbon footprint by shifting to less carbon intensive source (such as shift from diesel to natural gas) or shifting to zero carbon footprint renewable energy sources (e.g. shift to solar or wind-based electricity). Industry has been on the move towards cleaner alternative for many years, and the shift is accelerating in recent years due to visible impacts of global warming, and various initiatives being undertaken by governments and corporates towards attaining the net zero goals. (Stern and Valero, 2021). Electricity and indirect heat transfer applications has clearly established alternatives to achieve the lower carbon emissions. Some of these alternatives not only give a user the sustainability advantage, but also provides commercial savings, thereby making the firms more competitive in the market. Clearly, the alternatives which are able to achieve both carbon footprint reduction as well as commercial savings are clear choice of the corporates, and their adoption is at faster pace. Most of the corporate companies which have their own targets for achieving the net zero emissions in defined timelines, have already made significant progress in the adaption of these renewable energy sources.

For industry, direct and indirect heating application as well as captive power plants fall under Scope I emissions, whereas grid purchased electricity fall under scope II emissions. Figure 24.1 shows broad options for alternatives for the fossil fuels replacement for different applications. Table 24.2 lists down the typical carbon footprint of the fossil fuels being used in the industry as common practice, and the cost of replacement by the renewable energy sources.

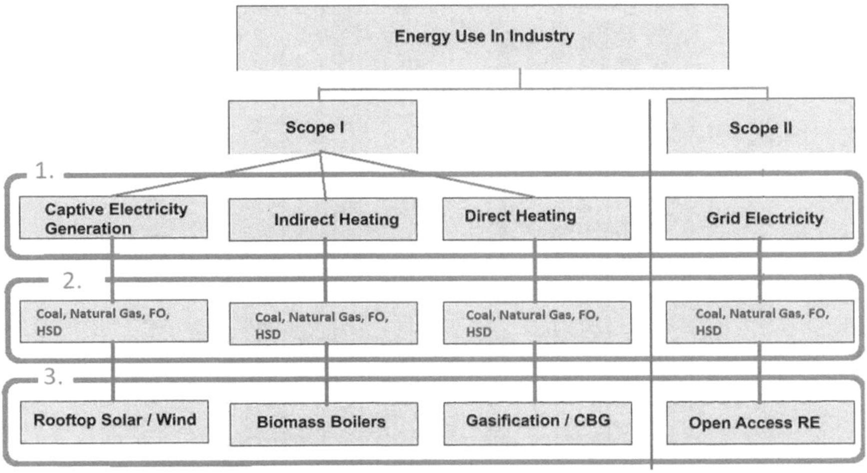

1. Energy Types; 2. Existing Fuels used; 3. Renewable Options

Fig. 24.1 Sources of energy in process heating applications

Source: Authors

Dasappa et al., 2003 and Wang et al., 2008 present case studies on the substitution of the fossil fuels-based applications demonstrating the replacement by biomass gasification for industrial heating. Broader themes such as the economic and environmental benefits of switching from fossil fuels to biomass gasification, the efficiency, reliability, and cost-effectiveness of these systems are discussed in detail to demonstrate the use of biomass gasification as heating source.

Direct heating applications mandate use of fuels which are in liquid or gaseous form, and solutions need to be necessarily On-Site mode, as the heat generation needs to be done within the process furnace or oven locally. This eliminates the

Table 24.2 Typical energy transition being undertaken by process industry

Application	Original Source	Alternative Source	C02 intensity of original source Tons / unit	C02 intensity of alternative source Tons / unit	Typical Cost of original source Rs	Typical Cost of alternative source	Popularity/ Adoption rate	Policy intervention need
Electricity	Grid	Solar / Wind / Hybrid	0.7/ MWh	0 / MWh	6500 / MWh	4500 / MWh	High	Yes, Power banking
Electricity	Captive Coal Power plant	Solar / Wind / Hybrid	0.9 / MWh	0 / MWh	4500 / MWh	4500 / MWh	Medium / Partial	NA
Low Temp. Heating	Coal	Biomass	0.4 / Ton	0 / Ton	2200 Rs/Ton	2500 Rs/Ton	Moderate	Yes
	Natural gas	Biomass	0.16 / Ton	0 / Ton	5200 Rs/Ton	2800 Rs/Ton	High	No
	Furnace Oil	Biomass	0.2 / Ton	0 / Ton	3200 Rs/Ton	2800 Rs/Ton	High	No

Source: Authors compiled from various sources

possibility of using biomass directly in these applications as done in indirect heating applications. (Indirect heating applications are already developed to use solid fuels such as coal and lignite, which can easily be replaced with biomass firing with certain technology changes in the combustion systems). This mandates that the alternate fuel sources for direct heating applications need to be in gaseous form, in order to achieve the energy transition to carbon neutral fuels.

For achieving the renewable shift for the direct heating applications, two distinct solutions of Biomass gasification-based producer gas and Bio CNG are emerging which use biomass as feedstock to generate the gaseous form of fuels. Both these solutions use biomass feedstock and convert the energy in solid form to the gaseous form. Once converted in gaseous form, the fuels can be used in the exiting direct heating applications. Typically, biomass gasification generates gaseous fuels which are leaner in nature, and hence may call for certain changes in the existing combustion systems for their adaption, whereas Bio CNG, which is equivalent fuel to that of Natural gas in chemical and physical properties may not need any significant changes in the heating apparatus for their use.

Although both these solutions are using biomass as feedstock, the solutions differ in process, heat values and applications they can cater to. There are typical characteristics of these two alternatives which govern the use of particular solution for a given application. An industry can select the appropriate solution for the given case through scrutiny of certain factors in order to ensure smooth transition to the renewable fuels for the direct heating applications. Section 2 of this study covers literature review of relevant studies around the two technologies. Section 3 and 4 discuss the details of the biomass gasification and bio CNG. Section 5 gives the comparative of these technologies, followed by section 6 about the conclusions of the study.

2. Literature Review

There is limited literature available on the two technologies being discussed. The available literature concentrates on the technological overview, constraints in the implementation, recommendations on the adoption of these technologies and analysis of case studies. The summary of the literature reviewed for this study is presented in the tabular form in Table 24.3, which covers the gist of the objectives and outcomes of the studies. In case of biomass gasification technology, a clear gap exists in the research of suitable applications for the technology. Although certain studies suggest that this technology is applicable for the niche application areas, a comprehensive study of industrial processes needs to be undertaken to list down the priority areas based on techno commercial suitability. Similarly, in the area of Bio CNG, particularly in the Indian market context, study needs to be undertaken on the technological challenges as well as commercial feasibility, pricing mechanism for CBG offtake in more details.

Table 24.3 Summary of literature review

Sr	Author	Geography	Objective / Context	Research Framework	Outcome
1	Wang et al., 2008	Global	To introduce recent advances in biomass gasification and syngas utilization, discuss critical technical issues in biomass gasification, and present perspectives on the development of these technologies.	Comprehensive review of the advancements in biomass gasification and syngas utilization, focusing on critical technical issues such as ash agglomeration, syngas quality control, cleaning technology, and the utilization of syngas for electricity, fuel production, and other applications.	Significant advances in the technology of biomass gasification and syngas utilization, including methods for ash agglomeration reduction, improvements in syngas quality control and cleaning technology, and various applications of syngas for producing electricity, fuels, and other biobased products. The study emphasises the importance of continuous research and development to overcome challenges and enhance the efficiency and sustainability of biomass gasification and syngas utilization processes.
2	Stern and Valero, 2021	High income economies	To explore the opportunities, drivers, and policies for innovation-led sustainable growth, highlighting the importance of coordinated long-term policies and investments in clean innovation and assets for achieving net-zero greenhouse gas emissions while improving productivity, living standards, and prospects globally.	An analysis of innovation growth with respect to the transition to net-zero emissions, incorporating theoretical and empirical evidence on innovation-led sustainable growth opportunities, drivers, and policies.	The research outcome highlights those investments in clean innovation, alongside sustainable infrastructure and human, natural, and social capital, are crucial for achieving net-zero emissions and driving sustainable growth.
3	Dasappa et al., 2003	India	To demonstrate the feasibility and benefits of replacing fossil fuels with biomass gasification for meeting industrial heat requirements, with a focus on both economic and environmental advantages.	Case studies of industrial applications for both low and high temperature heat requirements being met through biomass gasification.	Biomass gasification is a viable and environmentally friendly alternative to fossil fuels for industrial heat applications. The study provides detailed case studies where biomass gasification successfully met low and high temperature heat requirements, leading to significant savings in fossil fuel consumption and reductions in greenhouse gas emissions.

Sr	Author	Geography	Objective / Context	Research Framework	Outcome
4	Kirkels and Verbong, 2011	USA, Europe, China, and Japan.	To provide a 30-year global overview of the development of biomass gasification technology, assessing its potential and examining the technological trajectory, including drivers, barriers, and niche developments.	An evolutionary approach to analyse technological development, employing literature review and science and technology indicators to study global developments in biomass gasification.	Outcome suggests that biomass gasification has been successful in a few niche markets but remains largely confined to RD&D niches. The study anticipates a gradual niche development rather than a short-term breakthrough for biomass gasification technology.
5	Ahmed et al,; 2016	Global	To analyse and optimise the biomass gasification process conditions for syngas production, focusing on performance characteristics, economic evaluation, and the optimization of various process conditions including gasifier types, temperature, biomass particle size, gasification agent, and bed material.	Characteristics and performances of different types of gasifiers under different process parameters. Models used are simulations, optimization of gasification conditions, and the economic evaluation of the gasification process.	Optimum operation conditions such as gasifier types, temperature, biomass particle size, and gasification agents, can significantly affect the yield and quality of the energy produced. It is highly important optimising these conditions for improved efficiency and economic viability of syngas production from biomass gasification.
6	Molino et al., 2016	Global	Detailed analysis of the advancements in biomass gasification technologies.	A comprehensive overview of state-of-the-art biomass gasification technologies, evaluating advantages and disadvantages, potential uses of syngas, and various applications of biomass gasification.	Biomass gasification is an efficient method for power and heat production from green sources. It can also generate hydrogen and 2G biofuels. Main challenges in biomass gasification, such as syngas cleaning and further technological advancements to improve the efficiency are highlighted.

Sr	Author	Geography	Objective / Context	Research Framework	Outcome
7	Diaz et al., 2024	Global	Effect of the types of biomass and their effect on the maintenance of long-term SOC stock in agricultural soils. To propose coefficients for biomass carbon to coproduct and their recalcitrance in soils.	Systematic review, analysing and interlinking the characteristics of bioeconomy coproducts with soil models to predict soil organic carbon (SOC) turnover.	Coproducts from bioeconomy processes like pyrolysis, gasification, and others have varying degrees of carbon recalcitrance that can influence SOC turnover. The study synthesises over 600 datasets to propose average conversion coefficients for carbon to coproduct and their inherent recalcitrance, offering a foundational step for adapting soil models to account for bioeconomy coproduct return, with the potential to enhance renewable carbon supply for the bioeconomy while maintaining SOC stocks. (SOC is Soil Organic Carbon)
8	Torrijos, 2016	Europe	To present general data on biogas production in Europe and analyse the current situation in detail for three countries: Germany, Italy, and France, including their policies, support schemes, and development trends.	An analysis based on the Biogas Report 2014 of the European Biogas Association, covering 27 EU countries and Switzerland, including data on the number of biogas and biomethane plants, production information, support schemes, and predictions of the biogas market.	Biogas production in Europe varies significantly among countries, with Germany leading in development. The study highlights that the dynamism of the biogas market is directly linked to support schemes and feed-in tariffs. Potential factors for favouring the biogas market, and the acceptance of digestate as a fertiliser. Possible regulations against landfilling and limiting incineration of organic waste.
9	Pavan et al., 2021	India	To explore CBG India market potential as alternative fuel, its economic and technological challenges, and environmental benefits. Identify the challenges in its implementation.	A perspective analysis focusing on the potential, challenges, and benefits of Bio-CNG in India.	CBG is a viable and cost-effective alternative to conventional fuels. It offers potential for import substitutes of petroleum products while providing an efficient solution for waste management. Challenges related to the cost of Bio-CNG production, infrastructure requirements, and the need for skilled professionals for operation and maintenance are discussed.

Sr	Author	Geography	Objective / Context	Research Framework	Outcome
10	Kaur et al., 2020	India	Evaluate biomethane potential of paddy straw. Assessing its economic value, environmental benefits, and addressing the challenges of feed logistics.	Examining the various pre-treatment methods, anaerobic digestion processes, and conversion technologies to evaluate the potential of CBG production from rice straw.	Paddy straw presents significant potential for CBG production as renewable energy source. This process not only helps in managing agricultural waste but also contributes to reducing environmental pollution and dependency on fossil fuels. However, challenges such as the cost of installation, maintenance, and the need for skilled operation highlight the necessity for further research and development in this area.
11	Yoro and Daramola, 2020	Developing countries	To address environmental problems attributed to the increasing levels of CO2 in the atmosphere by analysing sources of CO2 emissions, their impact on global warming and climate change, and proposing mitigation strategies	Analysing CO2 emissions from various sources, their impact on global warming and climate change, and mitigation strategies in industries	The research outcome reveals that CO2 emissions, primarily from the combustion of fossil fuels for power generation and industrial activities, significantly contribute to global warming and climate change.

Source: Authors

3. Research Objective

The objective of this paper is to is to investigate the potential, constraints, and way forward for the Biomass gasification and Bio CNG as renewable energy sources for replacement of the fossil fuels for - hard to decarbonise -high temperature applications in process heating industry.

4. Biomass Gasification as Alternate Energy Source for Direct Heating Applications

Technologies are commercially available in market to convert the solid biomass in the combustible gases by thermal processing called biomass gasification. The technology converts the solid biomass feedstocks to the combustible gases, which can then be used for the direct firing application by suitable modifications in the combustion burners. The gasification uses commonly available biomass in form of wood waste or agriculture residue to replace the fossil fuels. The right choice of technology plays important role in the success of biomass gasification process for the selected application and feedstock. (Kirkels and Verbong, 2011) takes an overview of 30 years of history of development of gasification technology, starting with coal gasification and then graduating to biomass as feedstock. (Ahmed et al., 2016) in their paper focuses on highlighting the characteristics and performances of the different types of gasifiers under variable process parameters that will affect the yields of the end products as well as the composition of the gas.

4.1 Economics of Gasification-Based Heating

The producer gas generated from biomass gasification is a lean gas which provides combustion which is self-sustaining in nature. Table 24.4 table indicates the equivalence of the producer gas for replacement of fossil fuels. Table 24.3 demonstrates that biomass gasification by fuel cost can provide substantial savings in the operation cost, at the same time can offset near 100% carbon footprint of the fossil fuels used for the direct heating applications.

Table 24.4 Comparative of energy costs of fossil fuels with biomass gasification

Source	Heat Value kCal/kg	Producer gas quantity in Nm3 @ Heat value 990 kCal/Nm3	Biomass feedstock equivalent @ LHV 2475 kCal/kg of biomass – kg of biomass	Source fuel cost. INR /kg	Equi. heat value cost in INR for biomass at 8 Rs/kg	Savings Potential
Furnace Oil	9650	9.7	3.9	50	31.2	37%
Natural Gas	11250	11.4	4.5	75	36	52%
HSD	10500	10.6	4.2	105	33.6	68%

Source: Authors' estimates

4.2 Factors Affecting Incorporation of Biomass Gasification

Although there is a clear potential for replacement of fossil fuels with green producer gas, the industry adoption is at a minimal level. Following factors are the constraints in the adoption of gasification. Products of combustion are not as clean as natural gas, processes which are sensitive to combustion gas quality cannot be directly replaced by producer gas. This does not apply to furnace oil or HSD, where products of combustion contain soot / solid particulate matters present in the gas, and levels can be matched by use of producer gas. (Dasappa et al., 2003).

Biomass gasification may not be feasible for applications with processes having low heat offtake or intermittent operation where gasifier needs to go On and Off several times in a day resulting in higher start up and shutdown losses. It is not an advisable solution for processes which are not round-the-clock operation. Even in many cases, processes with weekly offs may not be suitable for the incorporation of biomass gasification as energy inputs on economic considerations. (Molino et al., 2016) discusses the various technological constraints in the adaptation of the gasification technology by the users.

Absence of organised players in technology is also affecting the adoption of technology as a mainstream energy source. Globally, Gasification technology development is not happening on a scale comparable to solar / wind / biomass related technologies. Limited technology options are available with minimal documentation on practical results for industry. Lack of reference installations in the field for various applications casts doubts in the minds of users who are looking for switching to this technology for carbon neutrality.

4.3 Way Ahead for Implementation of Biomass Gasification In Direct Heating Applications

With above discussed benefits and challenges, the way forward for the industry could be to go for phase wise adoption in various industry applications. Working installation references, clear documentation and performance proving over longer periods shall be necessary for building the popularity of biomass gasification as renewable alternative to direct firing applications. Biomass gasification can provide additional benefit by generation of the bio char as co-product of the energy. Various industrial and agricultural applications can utilise the bio char, thereby providing higher economic viability. Bio char can typically be used for industrial applications such as filtration, de-odorization, reduction agent or simply as fuel in the indirect heating applications. On the other hand, biochar sequestration in farmlands as fertiliser can act as long-term carbon removal from the atmosphere. (Diaz et al., 2024) discusses in detail the interplay between the bioeconomy and maintenance of soil organic carbon stock in agricultural soils. This also enables the industry to claim the carbon retention credits, there by generating additional revenue as a incentive to shift towards biomass gasification.

5. Bio CNG as Alternate Energy Source for Direct Heating Applications

Generation of Biogas from biomass feedstocks has been a proven technology over the years. Certain countries in Europe such as Germany had been utilising this form of energy for very long time and has over 9000 operational plants, whereas entire Europe has 14,500+ operational plants. (Torrijos, 2016). Biogas produced from digestible biomass waste is mainly a mixture of CH4 (Methane), CO2 and other gases such as H2S etc. Biogas when purified by removal of CO2 and H2S, can match the chemical composition of Natural gas, to be used as a like to like alternative for natural gas. Purified gas needs to confirm to IS 16087:2016, contain above 92% methane resembles in physical properties as well as heat value as that of natural gas. Such purified gas is then termed as Bio CNG or CBG (Compressed biogas). (Pavan et al., 2021) has undertaken the perspective study of Bio CNG in India. They emphasise the importance of having Bio CNG as an alternative set of fuel not only in India but also on global levels.

The cost of generation of the Bio CNG is at par or lower than the current market price of CNG. (Munagala et al., 2022) discusses the cost of generation of the Bio CNG from sugarcane bagasse in details in his research paper. (Kaur et al., 2020) discusses the Bio CNG production from rice straw as feedstock. In certain cases, with long term commitments of the gas offtake, industry shall be able to generate the gas at costs which are lower than market cost of CNG. Since there is no change in the characteristics of the bio CNG with CNG, adoption of this green alternative is risk free and provides potential for savings in operational costs. Depending on the location and the rate of fossil natural gas the savings in energy bills can range from -10% to 30% on long term basis.

With all above positive aspects of the CBG production, the production capacity is expected to boom at rapid pace in India. As per the Ministry of New and Renewable Energy, by March 2024, 50+ plants have been commissioned, and more than 2000 letters of intent are released for construction. With the proving of performance and overcoming of teething troubles, it is expected that the target of 5000 plants within 3 -5 years is a realistic possibility to achieve.

In India, industrial use of Bio CNG is yet not started at significant level. However, as the Bio CNG exhibits similar physical and chemical properties as that of CNG, a smooth transition is expected from CNG to Bio CNG without any major bottlenecks in industrial as well as vehicular use for replacement of fossil fuels. This provides an opportunity for the existing users of natural gas to shift to renewable alternative at no extra cost to achieve the net zero goals. For users of furnace oil for direct heating applications, it may still be a challenge as cost per unit heat value for CBG is higher compared to Furnace oil. This means there shall be an operational cost increase for the furnace oil users while shifting to CBG. However, regulations are becoming stringent to discourage the use of furnace oil as fuel due to its sulfur content, soot formation, higher NOx and CO2 footprints per unit of energy. As the industry is shifting away from the Furnace oil, adoption of CBG is expected to become easier going forward.

Setting up the CBG plants also help get rid of certain wastes which otherwise pose a pollution threat to the environment by way of air pollution, ground water pollution, soil degradation etc. The CBG operation is labour intensive, meaning it provides green jobs in rural areas. These plants generate manure (remains of the digested biomass), which can be fortified for use in fields as organic fertilisers. Additionally, CBG from organic waste from municipal solid waste is also being pushed by Government of India as push towards waste management and renewable energy generation.

6. Comparative of Biomass Gasification and Bio CNG options

While we suggest both biomass gasification and Bio CNG as alternative options for direct heating applications, there are certain differences in the production and usage of these options which determines the selection of the appropriate technology. Table 24.5 explains a flow chart which guides the potential user towards appropriate technology for the particular application.

Table 24.5 Comparative of biomass gasification and bio CNG based on feed-stocks and applications

Sr No	Parameter	Biomass Gasification	Bio CNG
1	Feedstock with higher calorific value	Yes	No
2	Feedstock with higher moisture level	No	Yes
3	Feedstock with higher ash levels	No	Yes
4	Applications needing >900 Deg. C temperatures	No	Yes
5	Applications needing clean gases without contamination	No	Yes
6	Applications having frequent start / stops	No	Yes
7	Applications which do not allow changes in existing set ups	No	Yes
8	Applications with weekly offs	No	Yes
9	Applications with higher turndown ration	No	Yes
10	Applications with multiple burners	No	Yes
11	Applications where energy production needs to be offsite	No	Yes

Source: Authors

Although Table 24.4 implies that Bio CNG is more universal and flexible in nature to adapt to multiple constraints of the applications, the per unit energy cost of bio CNG is 40 – 50% higher compared to the cost of biomass gasification.

Owing to this, a user should make first attempt to fit in the biomass gasification for their process failing which bio CNG becomes the default option. Biomass gasification can replace the lower end fuel such as furnace oil with commercial savings, whereas shifting from Furnace oil or equivalent fuel to Bio CNG shall increase the cost of unit energy with significant impact on operation cost, making the shift commercially not sustainable for the industrial users, unless there is a mandate for shift to cleaner fuels either from governmental regulations or from the sustainability targets of the company itself.

6.1 Constraints in use of Biomass Gasification or Bio CNG in Industry

With the benefits discussed above, adaption of both biomass gasification and Bio CNG technologies are still in its initial stage. Their implementation as alternate energy source compared to renewable electricity or indirect heating applications is at lower levels. Following are the major constraints in adoption of the technologies as mainstream.

Biomass Gasification

Single largest factor in adaption of the gasification route is the reliable and proven technology availability. Gasification unit size i.e. thermal output is limited due to its technological constraints. For larger heat duty need to take the modular approach for meeting the heat requirements. Absence of large-scale projects as well as lower numbers mean that there are no organized players in the market who can invest in technology to make it more reliable and efficient.

Another major constraint for the technology is the hyper local nature of the solution. This mandates that the generation and consumption of the energy needs to be within few hundred meters at the most. This puts in serious constraints, particularly for plants which are having multiple consumption points spread across the factory. The lower heat value of the producer gas also means that comparatively larger conveying pipes need to run across all consumer points, which adds to the cost and complexity of the project. Another fallout of the lower heat value of the gases is the reduction in the rated capacities of the equipment as well as major modifications required in the combustion system. All these factors make the initial cost of deployment heavy, which results in much longer payback periods for the installation. Being relatively new technology, decision making in favour of adaption of this technology remains low. Additionally, the soot / particulates in the producer gas limits its usage to applications which are sensitive to dust content of the gases.

Bio CNG

Bio CNG as a technology is in its early stage and undergoing a steep learning curve at this moment. The operational plants are facing challenges in terms of feedstock management, technological issues in the material handling systems (largely due the scale difference of the pilot plants and actual projects). Also, the cost economics of the gas production, manure management etc. is currently evolving. However, most of the problems associated with Bio CNG are mechanical in nature, and they would get resolved with experience of initial plants. Subject to availability of the bio CNG from the Oil Marketing companies, and a well set back up arrangement, process industry will be able to quickly adapt this solution. Making the bio CNG generation commercially lucrative for the developers is the only solution for making the gas available. As long as the gas is available in the similar cost bracket as that of fossil natural gas, its adaption is not a constraint. Initial estimates show that the costs can be in line with current market prices. However, Natural gas global market is volatile, and hence the producers need to have the financial capability to sail through the long periods of lower gas pricing in order to sustain the long-term operation. The capital investment in the Bio CNG markets are heavy, and typical payback periods are greater than 10 years. This clearly means that market support for long term view in terms of offtake and price guarantee are the key to the success of this segment.

7. Conclusion

The technologies under discussion provide the industry with the chance to nearly 100% replace the fossil fuels to propel very close to net zero. Operation cost impact is expected to be negative. This study recommends the use of both technology approaches as per intended application. While biomass gasification cost is competitive compared to CBG, operational constraints determine the selection. Continuous applications tolerating dirty gases can be replaced with biomass gasification whereas CBG can be a solution for processes sensitive to dust or having intermittent operations. Both these technologies are in the initial stages and need working references for wider adoption by industry.

Economics of the CBG rests on the availability of low-cost feed. A policy on open access supply of CBG through the PNG grid shall immensely help to make the CBG effective. Co-mingling policy for the CBG thus can be a greatest of driver in promoting this technology. This also effectively deals with offtake related constraints. This shall assist in overcoming the regional development imbalance by incentivising CBG at remote locations. Unlike solar or wind projects, the Bio CNG projects are more labour intensive, providing higher opportunities of rural employment.

REFERENCES

1. Ahmad, A. A., Zawawi, N. A., Kasim, F. H., Inayat, A., and Khasri, A. (2016). Assessing the gasification performance of biomass: A review on biomass gasification process conditions, optimization and economic evaluation. Renewable and Sustainable Energy Reviews, 53:1333–1347.

2. Dasappa, S., Sridhar, H. V., Sridhar, G., Paul, P. J., and Mukunda, H. S. (2003). Biomass gasification—a substitute to fossil fuel for heat application. Biomass and Bioenergy, 25(6):637–649.
3. Díaz, C. A., Albers, A., Zamora-Ledezma, E., and Hamelin, L. (2024). The interplay between bioeconomy and the maintenance of long-term soil organic carbon stock in agricultural soils: A systematic review. Renewable and Sustainable Energy Reviews, 189:113890.
4. Kaur, S., Kumar, D., Singla, M., and Dogra, R. (2020). Biogas to Bio-CNG from paddy straw: A review. International Journal of Chemical Studies, 8(3):1833–1838.
5. Kirkels, A. F. and Verbong, G. P. (2011). Biomass gasification: Still promising? A 30-year global overview. Renewable and sustainable energy reviews, 15(1):471–481.
6. Molino, A., Chianese, S., and Musmarra, D. (2016). Biomass gasification technology: The state-of-the-art overview. Journal of Energy Chemistry, 25(1):10–25.
7. Munagala, M., Shastri, Y., Nagarajan, S., and Ranade, V. (2022). Production of Bio-CNG from sugarcane bagasse: Commercialization potential assessment in Indian context. Industrial Crops and Products, 188:115590.
8. Pavan, M. L., Vishwas, K. M., and Hemanth Kumar, M. (2021). Perspective Study of Bio-CNG In India. Int. J. Res. Educ. Sci. Methods, 9(6):6–11.
9. Stern, N. and Valero, A. (2021). Innovation, growth and the transition to net-zero emissions. Research Policy, 50(9):104293.
10. Torrijos, M. (2016). State of development of biogas production in Europe. Procedia Environmental Sciences, 35:881–889.
11. Wang, L., Weller, C. L., Jones, D. D., and Hanna, M. A. (2008). Contemporary issues in thermal gasification of biomass and its application to electricity and fuel production. Biomass and bioenergy, 32(7):573–581.
12. Yoro, K. O. and Daramola, M. O. (2020). CO2 emission sources, greenhouse gases, and the global warming effect. In *Advances in carbon capture: Methods, technologies and applications,* ed. M. R. Rahimpour, M. Farsi, and M. A. Makarem, 3-28. United Kingdo: Woodhead Publishing, Elsevier.

Securing the Future through Sustainability, Health, Education, and Technology – Brig. Dr. Rajiv Divekar et al. (eds)

25 Adding Granularity to the Measurement of Programme Outcomes Assessment: A Novel way to Compute Programme Outcome Attainment

Pravin Dange[1]
Symbiosis Institute of Management Studies,
Pune, Maharashtra

Tausif Mistry[2]
Indira School of Business Studies PGDM,
Pune, Maharashtra

Chanakya Kumar[3]
Indira School of Business Studies PGDM,
Pune, Maharashtra

Abstract

The outcomes-based education model has become central to Higher education quality assurance (Premalatha, 2019). The model prescribes computation of the Programme Outcomes (PO) attainment by aggregating the attainment of the Course Outcomes (COs) (Abdallah Namoun, 2021: Rao, 2020; Premalatha, 2019; Bhagyalakshmi et al., 2015; Soragaon, 2016; Ramchandra et al., 2014, Sahasrabuddhe A, 2014). The majority of assessments of learning outcomes are at the subject (course) level, and frequently, these outcomes do not align well with the course (programme) or institutional-based outcomes" (Martin & Mahat, 2017). In the process of aggregation, the granularity of the outcome attainment at the programme level is lost to a large extent, leading to inappropriate measures of the POs or programme-level competencies.

The assessment tasks (ATs) used for assessing the Course Outcomes (COs) largely assess the subject-specific competencies. They also assess the generic competencies defined at the programme level with a variation in extent. However, the performance on the assessment task is aggregated to compute CO attainment and the attainments on the COs are aggregated using the average or weighted average method using broad mapping parameters. The relationship between the course outcome and Programme outcome is fuzzy or, at best, broad. In the process, the granularity of the assessment of the programme outcome is lost.

[1]praveendange@gmail.com, [2]tausif.mistry@gmail.com, [3]chanakya.kumar905@gmail.com

DOI: 10.1201/9781003587200-25

This paper suggests a modification to the generally practised model of aggregating the performance on Course Outcomes to compute attainment on Programme Outcomes by incorporating the rubric of assessment elements helping segregation of the discipline-specific competencies and other generic programme-level competencies at the programme level and mapping the generic competency assessment elements directly to the relevant Programme Outcomes.

The paper also validates the proposed model by comparing the Programme Attainments so obtained for their granularity. The model also proposes to compute the student-wise CO and PO attainment.

The significance of the work lies in proposing and validating a novel way for a granular assessment of the programme outcomes.

KEYWORDS: Outcome-based education, Program outcomes, Course outcome, Assessment tasks, Competency mapping

1. Introduction

The outcome-based model has been practised widely in India since 2013 for engineering education when the National Board of Accreditation made it mandatory for Engineering education.

The model is based on the perspective given by Spady (1994) and involves establishing a virtuous cycle of academic quality improvement by defining learning outcomes at course and programme level, designing a constructively aligned curriculum to help the learners attain the outcome, implementing the teaching-learning strategies, assess the performance of the students on the outcomes and improve the TLA strategies using the attainment analytics. At the core of the model is the assessment of the attainment of outcomes. While both the accreditation agencies give freedom within a specified framework to HEIs to adopt and practice their own model, the general practice incorporates attainment assessment using direct and indirect measures. The direct measures include all the assessments mapped to the outcomes conducted as a part of the curriculum.

Although there are some variations amongst the HEIs, the following is the generally adopted practice,

i. *Definition of Programme Outcomes (POs):* POs are established as clear statements of what students are expected to know, understand, and be able to do upon completion of a program. These outcomes typically encompass a combination of disciplinary knowledge, skills, and attitudes.

ii. *Mapping POs to Course Outcomes (COs):* COs are specific learning objectives that align with and contribute to the attainment of the POs. Each course within the program identifies its set of COs, ensuring that the combined attainment of these COs will lead to the achievement of the corresponding POs.

iii. *Assessment Design:* Assessments are designed to measure the attainment of COs and, indirectly, the POs. Various assessment methods such as examinations, projects, portfolios, presentations, and practical assessments may be employed to evaluate students' knowledge, skills, and attitudes related to the COs.

iv. *Rubrics and Criteria:* Rubrics and assessment criteria are developed to provide clear guidelines for evaluating student performance and determining the level of attainment of the COs. These rubrics often align with the specific outcomes and indicators associated with each CO.

v. *Attainment Scoring:* Attainment scoring involves assigning scores or ratings to each assessment task or item based on the extent to which students demonstrate the desired outcomes. These scores can be numeric (e.g., on a scale of 1-5) or qualitative (e.g., proficient, advanced, developing).

vi. *Aggregation and Weighting:* Once assessment scores are obtained for each CO, they are aggregated to compute the attainment scores for the corresponding POs. The aggregation process can involve various approaches, such as simple averaging, weighted averaging (assigning different weights to different COs), or applying specific algorithms based on institutional policies.

vii. *Reporting and Analysis:* The computed attainment scores are reported to provide feedback on student's progress and to evaluate the effectiveness of the program. Analysis of the attainment data can help identify areas of strength and areas that may require improvement in terms of achieving the desired outcomes.

Fig. 25.1 Outcome-based model-key steps

Source: Made by Author

1.1 Core Principles of OBE

The core principles of OBE emphasize the measurement of outcome attainment and the integration of instructional practices to facilitate student success. It is important that the measurement of the Attainment on the outcomes gives a valid and realistic picture of student attainments on the outcomes. The validity of outcome attainment computation and the effectiveness of constructive alignment have been fundamental to the OBE framework. The higher the degree of Constructive alignment between assessment and outcomes, the better the validity of the attainment computation.

Spady (1994) defined OBE as "Outcome-based education (OBE) means clearly focusing and organizing everything in an educational system around what is essential for all students to be able to do successfully at the end of their learning experiences." OBE promises to shift the paradigm from when and how of educational programmes to what and whether of learning.

1.2 Outcome Based Education Model

The Outcome Based Education has risen to prominence on account of the Accreditation Agencies making it a necessary requirement for accreditation, and based on the prescription by the respective accreditation agency, the Higher Education institutes have adopted it with varying degrees of intensity.

In India, the way the currently practised model has evolved is based on the directives given by either NAAC or NBA, which are the principal accrediting agencies in India.

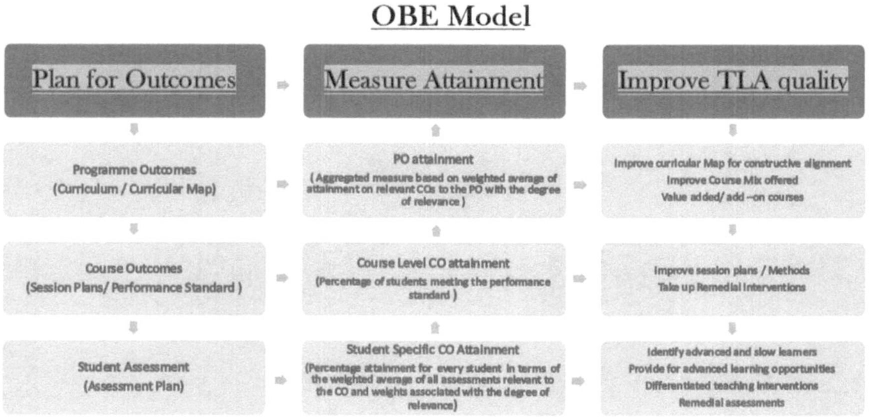

Fig. 25.2 OBE model

Source: Made by Author

The following are the necessary prerequisites for practising OBE.

1. Define Outcomes at various levels:
    a. Programme Educational Objectives
    b. Programme Outcomes / Programme-Specific Outcomes

2. Design a Curricular plan to ensure that students are able to perform on the outcomes.
    a. Design Course Mix in the form of Programme Structure
    b. Define Course Outcomes
    c. Mapping of the Course Outcomes to Programme Outcomes
    d. Teaching Learning Plan
    e. Plan Assessments
3. Implement the Teaching Learning and Assessment Plan
4. Assess the attainment of the outcomes (COs and POs/ PSOs) in line with a curricular map, where the Assessments are mapped to Course outcomes, which in turn are mapped to the Programme Outcomes.
5. The attainment of the outcomes using the direct method coupled with the indirect method, which, based on the survey, gives a measure of perceived performance by the learner and helps get the status of attainment on the outcomes.

1.3 Key Questions

The key questions that need to be addressed in the model are as follows,

1. What are the outcomes defined at the Programme Level and Course Level?
2. How are the Course Outcomes Mapped to Programme Outcomes / Programme Specific Outcomes?
3. How are the weights assigned to mapping?
4. How are the assessments mapped to the course outcomes?
5. How are the performance standards set?
6. How is the assessment performance aggregated to arrive at the Outcome attainment?

The expected outcome of the exercise is to get valid attainment computation that captures the reality, and constructive alignment lies at the heart of the same.

This paper addresses the research questions

Q1 – "How do the prevalent OBE models in India compute the attainment levels on the outcomes at the programme level and course level?"

Q2 – "What are the challenges in ensuring the validity of the attainment score?"

Q3 – "What measures can be taken to improve the validity of the attainment scores of the outcomes?"

1.4 Current Practices for Computation of the Attainment Scores

Several universities based on the prescription given by NBA and NAAC have adopted the following process:

Inputs Required for computation:

i. CO – PO Definition

a. Programme Outcomes and Programme Specific Outcomes are defined setting the expectations in terms of knowledge, Skills, and Values. For Engineering programmes, the NBA has mandated 12 POs and has allowed the HEI to define 3-4 programme-specific outcomes. There is no such mandate for other programmes, and HEI has been given the freedom to choose them based on their own context. These sets of outcomes include a few outcomes focussing on the knowledge component while other outcomes are focussed on generic skills and values. Bloom's taxonomy verbs are used to define the outcomes in behavioural terms.

b. The Course Outcomes are defined for each course in terms of knowledge, Skills, and Values. These outcomes are subject/domain specific Knowledge and skills but rarely include outcomes related to generic skills and values. Model Curricula given by the regulatory agencies suggest and aid in framing the Course Outcomes.

ii. CO – PO mapping

a. Every CO is mapped to at least one of the POs, ensuring that there is no hanging PO, meaning that every outcome should be assessed for performance. Some HEIs, instead of individual course outcomes, map courses to the Programme outcomes, entailing that the aggregation of performance would be done at the course level, and such aggregated performance would contribute to PO attainment computation.

b. HEIs also use three levels of mapping (Strong/ Moderate/ Weak) as a measure of the degree of relevance of the CO to the applicable PO.

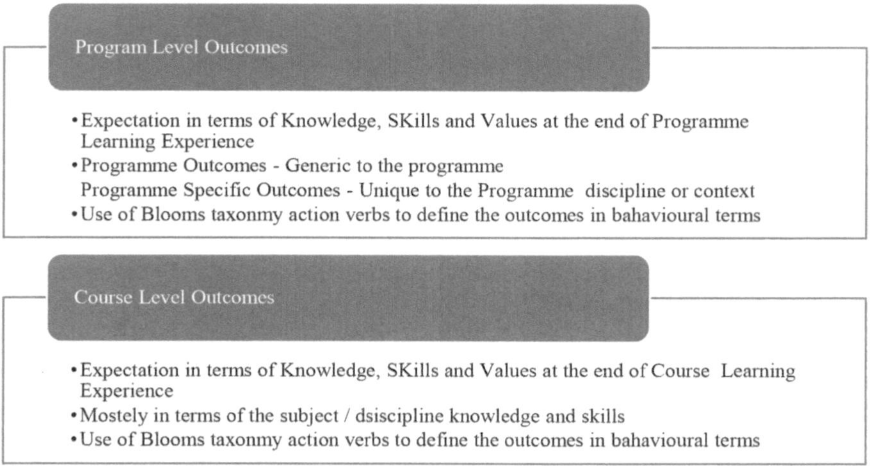

Fig. 25.3 Outcome Levels

Source: Made by Author

While the weights assigned to the degree also vary from HEI to HEI, general practice is to assign weights of 3/2/1, respectively.

c. The level (Strength) of mapping may be based on the degree of relevance of the assessments conducted for the Course Outcome to the Programme Outcome (Ranganath, 2016) or the number of hours devoted to the COs that address the given PO (Viswanadha, 2016)

iii. Assessment to CO mapping

a. As a part of the course evaluation, several assessments, including the formative continuous Assessments and summative term end assessments, are conducted. These assessment tasks are mapped to the course outcomes.

b. The weightages (Maximum Marks allocated) of the assessment tasks are ascertained.

c. The constructive alignment is ensured through aligning Bloom's taxonomy action verbs used in the outcome definition and the assessments conducted.

Table 25.1 Mapping CO to PO

Course	Course Outcome No	PO1	PO2	PO3	PO4
Course 1	CO1	*s (3)*		*w (1)*	
	CO2	*s (3)*	*m (2)*		
	CO3	*s (3)*	*m (2)*	*m (2)*	
	CO4	*s (3)*		*m (2)*	*w (1)*
Course 2	CO1	*m (2)*	*s (3)*		*w (1)*
	CO2	*s (3)*	*m (2)*	*w (1)*	
	CO3	*s (3)*	*m (2)*		*m (2)*
	CO4	*s (3)*		*m (2)*	*w (1)*

Note: s = strong relationship; m = moderate relationship; l = low relationship; blank = no relationship

Source: Made by Author

Table 25.2 Alternative way of mapping courses mapped to PO#

	PO1	PO2	PO3	PO4
Course 1	*			
Course 2	*			
Course 3		*	*	
Course 4	*			*

In this case, while computing the PO performance, the CO performance is aggregated at the Course level, and such aggregated Course performance is used for computing the PO performance.

Source: Made by Author

Table 25.3 Mapping of assessments to COs

	CO1	CO2	CO3	CO4	Weightage
Assessment Task 1	*	*			*10%*
Assessment Task 2		*	*		*15%*
Assessment Task 3	*		*	*	*15%*
Assessment Task 4		*	*	*	*60%*

Source: Made by Author

iv. Performance standard for outcome

There are various methods suggested for setting the performance standards, which are also alternatively termed as targets. NBA has suggested three possible ways of setting the target:

- The target could be set by using past data on the outcome performance.
- Using the class average
- Using a fixed rubric for CO attainment

a. Since Most of the HEIs have adopted OBE recently, they do not have any past precedent as far as Outcome specific performance is considered and since the targets are expected to be predefined, the majority of the institutions adopt the fixed rubric approach like the one below or variations thereof,

- Attainment Level 1: 60% of students score more than 60% marks out of the maximum relevant marks.
- Attainment Level 2: 70% of students score more than 60% marks out of the maximum relevant marks.
- Attainment Level 3: 80% of students score more than 60% marks out of the maximum relevant marks

v. Maximum Marks for the assessment task and Marks obtained by students in the task

b. The assessments are conducted, and marks are recorded task-wise as per the assessment plan

c. The marks are compiled assessment task-wise and, based on the mapping of the task to the course outcome, the attainment on the outcome is computed using the computation.

vi. Computation of performance at the CO level

a. Marks obtained by the student in the assessment task mapped to the respective outcome are aggregated using the weighted average method as mentioned in the below mentioned formula.

b. Attainment levels of the outcome are computed to understand.

- How well each student has performed on the outcome: This is computed by aggregating the marks obtained by the student against the maximum marks for the mapped assessment tasks using the weighted average method This measure gives the attainment level for every student.

- How well the cohort has performed on the outcome: The attainment of the COs by the student is aggregated using the rubric parameters mentioned in (4 b) to arrive at the course-specific attainment on the Course Outcome.
- The Course-specific performance on the CO is categorised into 3 levels, which are high attainment, Moderate Attainment and Low attainment, with a weightage of 3,2 and 1, respectively.

1.5 Sample Computation of Course Outcomes (Existing Practice)

Some universities have adopted variations in the models which are of the following types:

1. Performance standards are set for students using:
   a. Course Outcome specific percentage
   b. Using class average
   c. Variation in the rubric for grading student performance on the CO and aggregating student performance into attainment level of CO. (e.g., 70% of students scoring 70% marks is high attainment/ 60% of Students scoring 60% marks is moderate and 50% of students scoring 50% Marks is low attainment)

Table 25.4 Marks obtained by students in the assessment tasks

Performance on Assessment Task (Marks)				
	AT 1 Score	**AT 2 Score**	**AT 3 Score**	**AT 4 Score**
Maximum Marks (MM)	10	15	15	60
Student 1	3	13	14	51
Student 2	5	12	13	20
Student 3	6	10	15	29
Student 4	9	10	7	45
Student 5	9	10	5	31
Student 6	10	10	11	10
Student 7	1	1	11	43
Student 8	8	11	12	43
Student 9	6	11	13	41
Student 10	1	12	5	32

Source: Made by Author

Table 25.5 Student-wise CO attainment

CO Attainment Score Student-wise (%)				
Course Outcome	**CO1**	**CO2**	**CO3**	**CO4**
Mapped Assessment Tasks	AT 1	AT 1	AT 1	AT 3
	AT 3	AT 2	AT 2	AT 4
			AT 4	
Formula	**(AT 1 Score + AT3 Score)/ (AT 1 MM + AT 3 MM)**	**(AT 1 Score + AT 2 Score)/ (AT 1 MM + AT 2 MM)**	**(AT 1 Score + AT2 Score + AT 4 Score)/(AT 1 MM + AT 3 MM + AT 4 MM)**	**(AT 3 Score + AT 4 Score)/ (AT 3 MM + AT 4 MM)**
Max Attainment	**100**	**100**	**100**	**100**
Student 1_Attainment	68	64	87	87
Student 2_Attainment	72	68	44	44
Student 3_Attainment	84	64	60	59
Student 4_Attainment	64	76	75	69
Student 5_Attainment	56	76	51	48
Student 6_Attainment	84	80	34	28
Student 7_Attainment	48	8	61	72
Student 8_Attainment	80	72	73	73
Student 9_Attainment	76	68	71	72
Student 10_Attainment	24	52	54	49

Source: Made by Author

Table 25.6 CO attainment for the course

CO attainment Computation for the Course				
Performance Standard for the CO	60%	60%	60%	60%
Number of Students attaining more than 60% performance	7	8	6	5
Proportion of Students attaining more than 60% performance	70%	80%	60%	40%
Attainment Level on the CO	2	3	1	0

Source: Made by Author

2. The stage at which the grading of performance is introduced:
    a. Grading at student performance level
    b. Grading at Course Outcome Performance level
    c. Grading at the Course level
3. Other variables which have a bearing on the mapping weights like credits indicating the significance of the course to the overall programme

vii. Computation of performance at the PO level
   a. The performance on the relevant COs (or courses) as applicable is aggregated to compute performance on the Programme Outcomes (POs)
   b. The aggregation is done using the weighted average method where the level of mapping (Strong/ Moderate/ Weak), which is an indicator of the strength of the relationship with their respective weights (3/2/1), are factored in as weights.
   c. The following formula captures the logic of PO attainment capitation.

1.6 Challenges in the Existing Model

i. Loss of Granularity and consequent impact on the validity of attainment
   a. The model is based on aggregation and grading of performance at various levels:
   b. Assessment Tasks are mapped to the Course Outcomes. The assessment task may evaluate multiple outcomes at the same time and this leads to loss of granularity. Some models do include divisions of the assessment task into questions and these questions are mapped to the course outcomes.
   c. The aggregation and grading of the performance at
      - Student Level
      - Course Outcome Level
      - Course Level

ii. The transformational OBE prescribed by Spady as against the transitional OBE focuses on outcomes that are complex and include a broad range of competencies considered in educational circles as "higher order" things

Fig. 25.4 The demonstration mountain

Source: Adopted from spady

like effective communication, investigative research, complex analysis, problem-solving and decision making, and abilities that go beyond the knowledge and skills inherent in particular subjects. As illustrated in the below-mentioned illustration (The Demonstration Mountain) adopted from Spady (1994), OBE should move towards more complex outcomes based on life role functioning, while the existing models end up limiting their scope to the discrete content skills using structured task performances.

iii. As per Spady (1994), "subject-specific assessment tests reveal a small portion of what students know and how they can manipulate information mentally. However, they are usually inadequate for measuring any of the competencies in the upper sectors of the Mountain that require learners to actually do things with what they know. Complex forms of doing like organizing, planning, designing, and producing can only be measured by having students actually organize, plan, design, and produce things and then observing the results of their endeavours. This kind of measurement is called "authentic performance assessment" because it has students do exactly what the verb and the content require: organize, plan, design, produce, or carry out the demonstration processes embedded in the outcome."

iv. Further, the model has been primarily evolved to address the engineering education requirements and may not address the requirements of a multidisciplinary university where, more often than not, the assessment tasks contribute to multiple outcomes.

v. While the PO attainment in the model is an aggregated measure of performance on the outcome which helps one get a measure of programme performance, the model does not compute the student-wise performance on the Programme Outcomes meaning we get to know how well the student has done on a particular CO but how well he/she has performed with respect to a particular PO cannot be ascertained.

vi. By the very nature of the model, the cognitive domain in Bloom's taxonomy is overemphasized at the cost of the Psychomotor and Affective Domain, as most of the outcomes and assessments would focus on cognitive domain action verbs.

2. Proposed Model

In order to address the challenges, the Authors suggest the following variations to the model and process for computation of the outcomes which adds granularity to the attainment computation and in turn enhances the validity of the attainment scores.

Table 25.7 Modification to the existing model

Inputs Required for computation	Changes suggested	Reason for the suggested modification
PO/ PSO - CO mapping	While mapping the COs to POs a provision should be kept to map some of the assessment elements directly to PO. The assessment element is defined as that part of the Assessment Task (rubric parameter) which assesses largely the rubric parameter within the assessment task e.g., an Assessment task of Project may have rubric parameters like domain knowledge, Presentation skills, Communication Skills, Team Skills which are assessing different outcomes at the Course level or Programme level	Improve granularity and validity of attainment measures
Assessment to CO mapping	Instead of the assessment tasks being mapped to the Course Outcome, each assessment task should be converted into Assessment Elements based on which outcomes are they largely assessing both at the Course level and Programme Level and how many marks are they being assessed for. To add further granularity to the same, the level of mapping (Strong/Moderate/ Weak/ No mapping) would indicate the strength of relevance with the weights of 100%/50%/25% or 0%)	Improve granularity and validity of attainment measures
Performance Standard	Outcome wise performance standard is defined for students in percentage terms. All students meeting or exceeding the standard would be said to have attained the outcome.	As per OBE principle of 'Expanded Opportunity", every student is capable of reaching the minimum standard defined though not necessarily with the same methods or same time frame.
Attainment Computation		
CO attainment (Student specific)	All the assessment elements related to the outcome would be aggregated using the weighted average method where the weights would be the marks for the assessment element and the weights associated with the degree of mapping of the assessment element to the outcome.	This would be a good measure of how well the individual student has done well on the course outcomes defined.
CO attainment (Course Specific)	Proportion of students meeting the minimum standard would be taken as CO attainment level which will be in terms of	This would be good measure of Course Assessment
PO attainment Computation (Student Specific)	Performance of the students on all the Course Outcomes and Assessment elements mapped to the PO would be aggregated using the weighted average method with the strength of mapping being used as applicable weights	This would be a good measure of how well the individual student has done well on the programme level outcomes defined.
PO attainment Computation (Program Specific)	All the Mapped CO attainment (Course Specific) and directly mapped assessment elements would be aggregated to arrive at the measure of PO attainment (Programme Specific)	This would be good aggregate measure of Programme Assessment

Source: Made by Author

2.1 Sample Calculation

Table 25.8 Performance on assessment tasks and assessment elements (marks)

Assessment Elements	AT 1 Score	AE1(AT1.1)	AE2(AT1.2)	AE 3(AT 1.3)	AT 2 Score	AE4 (AT2.1)	AE 5 (AT2.2)	AT 3 Score	AE 6 (AT 3.1)	AE 7 (AT 3.2)	AT 4 Score	AE 8 (AT4.1)	AE 9 (AT4.2)	AE 10 (AT4.3)
Maximum Marks (MM)	**10**	**5**	**5**	**5**	**15**	**5**	**10**	**15**	**8**	**7**	**60**	**30**	**10**	**20**
Student 1	3	2	1	0	13	4	9	14	7	7	51	28	10	13
Student 2	5	5	0	0	12	3	9	13	8	5	20	15	3	2
Student 3	6	4	2	0	10	3	7	15	8	7	29	19	9	1
Student 4	9	3	1	5	10	4	6	7	6	1	45	20	8	17
Student 5	9	2	1	6	10	5	5	5	3	2	31	12	7	12
Student 6	10	4	1	5	10	3	7	11	7	4	10	10	0	0
Student 7	1	0	0	1	1	0	1	11	8	3	43	26	8	9
Student 8	8	2	3	3	11	2	9	12	6	6	43	18	10	15
Student 9	6	4	0	2	11	1	10	13	7	6	41	19	8	14
Student 10	1	1	0	0	12	3	9	5	0	5	32	22	3	7

Source: Made by Author

Table 25.9 Mapping of assessment elements to outcomes (degree of mapping %)

Assessment Element	Maximum Marks (MM)	CO1	CO2	CO3	CO4	PO1	PO2	PO3
AE1 (AT1.1)	5	100%	100%	100%				
AE2 (AT1.2)	5		50%					100%
AE3 (AT 1.3)	5							100%
AE4 (AT2.1)	5		100%					
AE5 (AT2.2)	10			100%				
AE6 (AT 3.1)	8	100%		50%				
AE7 (AT 3.2)	7				100%			
AE8 (AT4.1)	30			100%				
AE9 (AT4.2)	10				100%			100%
AE10 (AT4.3)	20				50%			

Source: Made by Author

Table 25.10 CO attainment computation (student specific)

Outcome	CO1	CO2	CO3	CO4
Mapped Assessment Tasks	AE1(AT1.1)	AE1(AT1.1)	AE1(AT1.1)	AE 7(AT 3.2)
	AE6(AT3.1)	AE2(AT1.2)	AE 5(AT2.2)	AE 9 (AT4.2)
		AE4(AT2.1)	AE 6(AT 3.1)	AE 10 (AT4.3)
			AE 8 (AT4.1)	
Formula for Computation	*(AE1_Score * Mapping Weight_AE1) + (AE6_ Score*-Mapping Weight _AE6) / (MM_AE1*-Mapping Weight _AE1)+(MM_AE6*Mapping Weight _AE6)*	*(AE1_Score * Mapping Weight_AE1) + (AE2_ Score*-Mapping Weight _AE2)+ (AE 4_ Score* Mapping Weight_AE 4) / (MM_AE1*Mapping Weight _ AE1)+(MM_AE2*-Mapping Weight _AE2+ ((MM_AE 4* Mapping Weight_AE 4))*	*(AE1_Score * Mapping Weight_AE1) +(AE5_ Score*Mapping Weight _AE5)+ (AE6_ Score*Mapping Weight _AE6)+ (AE8_ Score*Mapping Weight _AE8) / (MM_AE1*Mapping Weight _AE1)+(MM_AE5*Mapping Weight _AE5)+(MM_AE6*-Mapping Weight _ AE6)+(MM_AE8*Mapping Weight _AE8)*	*(AE7_Score * Mapping Weight_AE7)+ (AE9_ Score*-Mapping Weight _AE9) + (AE10_ Score*Mapping Weight _AE10) / (MM_AE7*Mapping Weight _ AE7)+(MM_AE9*-Mapping Weight _AE9)+MM_ AE10*Mapping Weight _AE10)*
Maximum Attainment	100	100	100	100
Student 1	69	52	87	87
Student 2	100	64	67	33
Student 3	92	64	69	61
Student 4	69	60	65	65
Student 5	38	60	42	56
Student 6	85	60	50	15
Student 7	62	0	63	57
Student 8	62	44	65	87
Student 9	85	40	74	78
Student 10	8	32	65	43
Performance Standard for the CO	60%	60%	60%	60%
No of Students Clearing the CO	**8**	**5**	**8**	**5**
CO attainment Course Specific	**80%**	**50%**	**80%**	**50%**

Source: Made by Author

Table 25.11 Direct contribution of AE to POs

PO Cotnribution of AEs	Contribution of AE to PO 1	Contribution of AE to PO 2	Contribution of AE to PO 3
Mapped Assessment Tasks			AE2 (AT1.2)
			AE 3(AT 1.3)
			AE 9 (AT4.2)
Formula			*(AE2_Score * Mapping Weight_AE2)+ (AE3_ Score*Mapping Weight _AE3) + (AE9_ Score*Mapping Weight _AE9) / (MM_AE2*-Mapping Weight _AE2)+(MM_AE3*Mapping Weight _AE3)+MM_AE9*Mapping Weight _AE9)*
Student 1			55
Student 2			15
Student 3			55
Student 4			70
Student 5			70
Student 6			30
Student 7			45
Student 8			80
Student 9			50
Student 10			15

Source: Made by Author

Table 25.12 Student wise PO attainment using the CO-PO mapping

Particulars	PO 1 Attainment based on CO PO mapping	PO 2 Attainment based on CO-PO mapping	PO 3 Attainment based on CO-PO mapping	PO 4 Attainment based on CO-PO mapping
Formula	Σ(CO attainment Score on Mapped CO* Mapping Percentage)/ΣMapping Weights			
Student 1	69	69	83	87
Student 2	66	66	60	61
Student 3	72	67	71	68
Student 4	65	63	66	65
Student 5	51	51	47	45
Student 6	53	55	43	43
Student 7	40	32	61	62
Student 8	64	55	73	70
Student 9	67	57	78	75
Student 10	27	49	45	61

Source: Made by Author

Table 25.13 Student wise PO attainment using the CO-PO mapping and the contribution of directly mapped assessment elements

Particulars	PO 1 Attainment based on CO PO mapping	PO 2 Attainment based on CO-PO mapping	PO 3 Attainment based on CO-PO mapping	PO 4 Attainment based on CO-PO mapping
Formula	Average [(Σ(CO attainment Score on Mapped CO* Mapping Percentage)/ ΣMapping Weights) + (Aggregated Contribution of Assessment Element to the PO * Weight of the Aggregated Contribution)]			
Student 1	69	69	69	87
Student 2	66	66	38	61
Student 3	72	67	63	68
Student 4	65	63	68	65
Student 5	51	51	58	45
Student 6	53	55	36	43
Student 7	40	32	53	62
Student 8	64	55	77	70
Student 9	67	57	64	75
Student 10	27	49	30	61

Source: Made by Author

Table 25.14 Difference in student wise PO attainment on account of the contribution of AE

Student	Difference in computed PO attainment
Student 1	17
Student 2	38
Student 3	11
Student 4	-3
Student 5	-25
Student 6	15
Student 7	13
Student 8	-5
Student 9	18
Student 10	33

Source: Made by Author

As can be seen from the above table the changes in the model lead to substantial improvement in the granularity of the attainment scores

3. Conclusion

The existing models adopted for OBE have limitations in terms of the granularity and validity of the attainment computation. This chapter proposed a model to improve the granularity and in turn validity of the outcome attainment scores and also established that beyond the programme and course assessment through aggregated outcome attainment measures, the modified OBE model can be employed to get student-wise CO and PO attainment scores helping the student know where he/she stands with respect to the outcome performance. The additional effort required to align the practices with the model is justified, given the improved granularity and validity that the model affords. Further assessment elements in some of the capstone courses may be mapped directly to the programme Outcomes to get better validity of the attainment computation. The chapter contributes to the body of knowledge by introducing modifications to the model to improve the granularity of the outcome attainment in addition to facilitating student specific attainment on both Course and Programme Outcomes

REFERENCES

1. Abidin, I. Z., Anuar, A., & Shuaib, N. H. (2009). Assessing the attainment of course outcomes (co) for an engineering course. Paper presented at International Conference of Teaching and Learning, INTI University College, Nilai, Malaysia. Retrieved from https://my.laureate.net/Faculty/docs/Faculty%20Documents/ INTI%20Conferences/ Parallel%20Sessions%205/5B/5B-01-P96%20(Malaysia).pdf
2. Bhagyalaksmi, H. R., Seshachalam, D., & Lalitha, S. (2015).Program outcome attainment through course outcome: A comprehensive approach. In R. Natrajan (Ed.), Proceedings of the international conference on transformations in engineering education (pp. 279-287). New Delhi, India:Springer.
3. Biney, P., & Bryant, M. R. (2005). A novel strategy for the direct assessment and improvement of engineering programs developed and implemented by Prairie View A&M University.Paper presented at ASEE conference, Portland, OR. Retrieved from https://peer.asee.org/a-novel-strategy-for-the-directassessment-and-improvement-of-engineering-programs-developed-and-implemented-by-prairie-view-a-m-university.
4. Bloom, B., Engelhart, M., Furst, E., Hill, W., & Krathwohl, D.(1956). Taxonomy of educational objectives: The classification of educational goals. Handbook I: Cognitive domain. New York, NY: Longman
5. Drakshayani, D. N. (2016). A preliminary study on Attainment of course outcomes for outcome-based education in mechanical engineering using a case study of material science and metallurgy. IOSR Journal of Research & Method in Education, 6,76-83.
6. Masni-Azian, A., Rahimah, A. H., & Othman, M. S. (2014). Towards OBE: A case study of course outcome (CO) and programme outcome (PO) attainment for product design and development course. IOSR Journal of Research & Method in Education, 4, 55-61
7. Spady, W. G. (1994). Outcome-based education: Critical issues and answers. Arlington, VA: American Association of School Administrators.
8. Ranganath, R. V. (2016). Some examples for CO-PO mapping and corresponding assessments. Retrieved from http://www.nbaind.org/files/Some-more-examples-on-attainment-of -COs-and-PO-21-may-2016.pdf

9. Rao, N. J. (2015). Outcome based education. Retrieved from http://textofvideo.nptel.ac.in/127108005/ lec4.pdf
10. Sahasrabudhe, A. (2015). Outcome based education and NBA accreditation. Retrieved from http://www.n baind.org/files /obe-and-nba-accreditation.pdf
11. Viswanadha, R. S. (2016). Outcome based education. Retrieved from https://www.youtube.com /watch?v=aitqARyQkRQ
12. Premalatha, K. (2019). Course and Program Outcomes Assessment Methods in Outcome-Based Education: A Review. Journal of Education, 199(3), 111-127. https://doi.org/10.1177/0022057419854351
13. Namoun, Abdallah & Alshanqiti, Abdullah. (2020). Predicting Student Performance Using Data Mining and Learning Analytics Techniques: A Systematic Literature Review. Applied Sciences. 11. 1-28. 10.3390/app11010237
14. Rao, N. J. (2020). Outcome-based Education: An Outline. Higher Education for the Future, 7(1), 5-21. https://doi.org/10.1177/2347631119886418
15. Soragaon B and K S Mahesh (2016), Measuring Attainment of Course Outcomes and Program Outcomes – A Simplified Approach as per Self-Assessment Report- June 2015, IOSR Journal of Research & Method in Education (IOSR-JRME), Volume 6, Issue 4 Ver. IV (Jul. - Aug. 2016), PP 13-18
16. Martin, L., & Mahat, M. (2017). The Assessment of Learning Outcomes in Australia. *AERA Open, 3.*

Securing the Future through Sustainability, Health, Education, and Technology – Brig. Dr. Rajiv Divekar et al. (eds)

ISBN 978-1-032-95922-1

26 Credit Default Swaps—An Empirical Analysis of Recent Developments in the CDS Market

Nikhil Ravi Thadaney[1]
Symbiosis International (Deemed University), Pune, Maharashtra

Rashmy Moray[2]
Symbiosis International (Deemed University), Pune, Maharashtra

ABSTRACT

The principal aim of the study was to delve into the opaque credit default swaps market, and analyze newer trends and recent developments in the asset class.

Research Methodology: Post covid analyses has been done for the asset class, to predict the future market movement. An investigation of the literature has been carried out between 2000 and 2022.

Findings/Conclusion: The research has helped to unearth different facets about the CDS market and its potential. Investors and market makers can analyze the spread movements associated with this security, in order to assess and predict market conditions.

Originality/Contribution to the body of knowledge: The study has attempted to analyze spread movements in the market, which mirror the risk of default and credibility situations, and in turn used these spread movements to further predict market movements. This study is first in its nature to study recent trends in the CDS market, in a post-covid timeline.

Limitation/scope: The study has only conducted a short term predictability assessment of the market movements.

KEYWORDS: CDS, Credit derivatives, Coupons, Spreads

[1]nikhil.thadaney2022mbae@sims.edu, [2]rashmy.moray@sims.edu

DOI: 10.1201/9781003587200-26

1. Introduction

Credit default swaps (CDSs) have expanded into a multi-trillion-dollar market across the globe, over the past few decades. As per an analysis by the Bank of International Settlements (BIS), global CDS markets stood at USD 10 trillion, by the end of 2017 (after falling from USD 60 trillion in 2007). (John Coughlan, 2019) considered CDS one of the most popular forms of credit derivatives, CDSs are contracts that provide insurance against the possibility of certain companies defaulting. Currently, the CDS market worldwide is undergoing rapid changes with higher standardization practices and electronic processing, and the role of clearing agencies has also increased. The market has become highly transparent and information for the asset class is publicly available. Even after the financial crisis of 2008, trading in this arena has seen a spike over the past years, with the aid of efficient risk management practices in place. The usage of exchange-traded funds and blockchain technology are two of the more recent trading avenues in the CDS market. In the Indian context, CDS is yet to achieve substantial development, as compared to other global economies.

2. Literature Review

One of the most widely traded credit derivatives, CDS was first created in 1994 by J.P. Morgan and gained momentum in 2000. However, investors have always been ambivalent regarding these securities, particularly owing to their role in the infamous credit crisis of 2008. As per a report from BIS (2021), outstanding notional amounts in the international CDS market at the end of 2020, totaled approximately $8.5 trillion. The CDS market is still niche and modest as compared to the overall global derivatives market, and prospects of it being much bigger would have been possible, had it not been for the 2008 crisis to diminish the value of this security and its market. A recent study by (Antulio, 2022) explains the important aspects of CDS and its history. A valuation framework provided in the article focuses on the relation between circumstances in the CDS and cash markets while attempting to mark-to-market existing CDS positions. The dynamics of CDS in European countries and the growing significance of the macro-prudential strategy for guaranteeing the sustainability of the financial system are the main topics of (Paskaleva, 2020). (Wemmenhove, 2009) entailed the study on CDS descriptive and predictive models, and highlighted the factors that influence credit default swap spreads. (Bo, 2020) examined how the risk mitigation strategy may be used to dynamically hedge counterparty risk for credit derivatives in a reference from October 2020.

(Sohnke Bartram, 2018) examined the effects of implementing CDSs on an organization's decision-making model and process. The structural model indicates that when credit event uncertainty is smaller, CDS introduction would enhance debt capacity more. Avino (2012) looked at the iTraxx index (Europe) throughout the duration of the financial crisis, which commenced in mid-2007, to determine how well linear and nonlinear models predicted CDS spreads. An extract for the credit default swaps valuation was published by John Hull, in 2000. It explained a strategy based on the reasonable assumption that the difference between the bond's face value and post-default market value determines how much bondholders will be entitled to in the event of a default. The term structure of risk-neutral implicit default probabilities, which were derived from market prices for a collection of bonds issued by the same issuer, is a key aspect of this study. In a report, (Fletcher, 2019) discusses contrived CDS transactions in detail. To determine whether or not legal intervention is required, the essay examines the advantages and disadvantages of engineered CDS contracts available on the market. In a study on financial networks, (Steffen Schuldenzucker, 2018) discovered a new type of systemic risk that resulted from a circumstance known as default ambiguity, or the inability to identify which financial institutions are in default.

In an attempt made by (Romanyuk, 2021) an effort was made to assess how the worldwide pandemic might affect the US CDS market in 2021. After the pandemic was declared, econometric analysis was used to determine the uniqueness of the credit default swap market sectors. (Samuel Bonsall, 2022) investigated whether CDS trading initiation can act as a corrective measure for top credit rating organizations and whether rating agencies increase the quality of their ratings when a different source of credit risk information from CDS foretells that their ratings have problems. (Tak-Yuen Wong, 2020) looked at how value, long-term loan financing, and corporate investment were affected by CDS trading. (Czech, 2021) illustrates the liquidity spillover effect of CDS on bond markets using regulatory data on CDS holdings and corporate bond transactions. The study establishes that increased CDS trading activity enhances underlying bond liquidity.

By analyzing datasets from German banks, (Viral Acharya, 2022) article details the use of CDS (sovereign securities) during the Debt Crisis in Europe, between 2008–2013. A citation published by Bloomberg in 2015 explains Blackrock's revival of the single name CDS, much after the infamous 2008 credit crisis, explained why investors are attracted to the asset class and the rise of the CDS market globally. The articles and data have facilitated an understanding of recent trends in the CDS market. A 2022 study by Darko B. et al, examines the

performance prediction for CDS spreads using Markov switching autoregression, Group Method of Data Handling, Long Short-Term Memory, and Support Vector Machines for daily CDS spreads of top US businesses, from 2009 to 2020 (Darko, 2022). Another citation from Erasmus University - Econometric Institute, by Marcin Jaskowski and Dick van Dijk, analyses the predictability of 5-year CDSs by creating various prediction models that include a variety of explanatory factors. (Marcin Jaskowski, 2016).

3. Theoretical Background

3.1 Credit Default Swaps

In terms of outstanding notional amount, credit default swaps (CDSs) are considered to be the most prevalent type of credit derivatives. Its attractiveness lies in the fact that it is relatively straightforward, and it offers investors and hedgers a plethora of opportunities that were not earlier present in the cash market. CDS are contracts that provide insurance against the possibility of certain companies defaulting. These companies are known as reference entities and the default as such is known as a credit event. There are generally three parties involved in a CDS contract: debt security issuer, debt security buyer and banks, insurance firms, etc., and other third-party entities. Bankruptcy, restructuring, nonpayment, acceleration of obligations, and repudiation/moratorium are examples of common credit occurrences.

In order to maintain a vanilla CDS, the protection buyer must pay the seller on a regular basis throughout the relationship. Swaps, spreads, or premiums are the names for these. In exchange, in the case of default, the seller must reimburse the reference entity. Only in the event that there is no default on or before the CDS maturity and contract termination will the protection seller collect the premium. CDSs, where the underlying asset does not have to be owned, insurance contracts offer protection against losses on "owned assets". Unlike insurance agents, sellers of CDS are not mandated to be regulated entities. Compared to banks, other CDS sellers may be less accountable. They are also not required to maintain a reserve. In light of this, a CDS vendor could not have enough money in the event of a default to reimburse the buyer.

3.2 Working of a CDS Contract

The working of a CDS security may be illustrated with an example, wherein two participants enter a 5-year CDS contract on March 10, 2022. It is assumed that –

- A $100 million notional principal is involved.
- The buyer commits to yearly payments of 100 basis points as insurance against the reference entity's default.
- Payments are made with arrears every quarter.

When a credit event does not occur—that is, when the reference entity does not trigger a default—the buyer is not compensated and must instead pay 25 basis points, or one-fourth of 100 basis points, on $100 million starting on June 10, 2022, and then each quarter until March 20, 2027. The amount paid each quarter can be calculated as 0.0025 * 100000000 or $250000 (these quarterly payments may vary slightly depending upon the application of day count conventions). In case of a credit event, a sizable payoff is expected.

- Protection Buyer -
    - Usually has ownership of the underlying credit asset.

- Purchases credit protection.
- Entails short credit exposure.
- Protection Seller -
    - Usually does not have ownership of the asset.
    - Sells credit protection.
    - Entails long credit exposure.

Assume that a couple of months into the fourth year, on May 10, 2025, the buyer notifies the seller of the credit event. Bonds issued by the reference entity may be sold by the buyer for $100 million in the event that the deal requires physical settlement. Conversely, in the event that the contract calls to receive payment in cash, the mid-market value of the least expensive deliverable bond is determined through an ISDA-arranged auction process several days following the credit event. Should the bond's auction value prove to be $40 for every $100 of face value, the payoff in cash would be $60 million.

The buyer stops making regular payments when a credit event takes place. But because they are installment payments, the buyer must make a final accrual payment. The buyer must pay the seller the total annual payment that accumulated between March 10, 2025, and May 10, 2025 in the example provided, in the event of a default on May 10, 2025. Additional payments are not necessary.

As a proportion of the notional principal, the full annual payment made to obtain the protection is known as the CDS spread (in the case given, this is 100 basis points). While CDS contracts with 5-year maturities are the most popular and liquid, other maturities like 1,2,3,5,7, and 10 years also exist.

3.3 CDS Coupons

The ISDA, or the International Swaps and Derivatives Association states that the CDS premiums are 25, 100, 500, or 1000 basis points for Single-Name CDS of the European region and 100 or 500 basis points for contracts of U.S. origin. To make up the shortfall between the market price and the code's fixed premium, the traders must guarantee an upfront payment.

3.4 Payoff in a CDS Contract

The conditions of the payout after a credit event are outlined in a CDS contract. The payout makes up the difference between the reference asset's par and recovery value after the credit event for the protection buyer. There are two possible ways in which the reward can manifest.

- Physical delivery—In this case, which is more typical in practice, the defaulted security is transferred to the protection seller in exchange for par in cash, in accordance with a "deliverable obligation".
- Fixed cash settlement—Recovery default swaps are typically covered by this. Here, the buyer (who is in possession of the reference asset) receives the

compensation amount from the seller. According to Jean Helwege (2009), the payment is determined by subtracting the final amount of the notional obligation from the CDS notional value.

3.5 Overview of the CDS Market

The credit default swaps market is divided into the following categories -

- Single-name CDS—An individual corporate or sovereign reference entity is protected by this.
- Index—A contract that consists of a pool of single-name CDSs, each of which has an equal portion of the notional amount within the index, is called a CDS Index, or CDX. There is a high degree of standardization involved here that has contributed to the expansion of index contracts. (John C Hull, 2018)
- Basket CDS—These correlate to portfolios of reference entities, which can contain anywhere from three to one hundred names, just like indices do. Compared to CDS indices, basket CDSs are opaquer in terms of pricing and quantities and offer greater customization. As per Hull (2018), these could comprise of certain classifications like first-to-default CDS securities.
- Swaptions—These are CDS options wherein the holders are entitled but not obliged to enter into forward-start CDS contracts.

LCDS—A relatively new type of credit default swap pertaining to "loan only" has been developed in recent times, known as the LCDS. Unlike vanilla CDS, the protection underlying is offered only on the reference entity's syndicated secured loans, not on other bond or loan categories. LCDS spreads showcase a more downward trend as compared to CDS spreads of the same identity.

Binary Credit Default Swaps—These bear similarities to standard CDS, with the exception that the payout is expressed in set dollars. (John C Hull, 2018)

The ISDA, or the International Swaps and Derivatives Association plays a key role in the market, offering extensively used master agreements and defining credit events. Working in an auction mechanism, the ISDA ensures complete facilitation of settling contracts in a credit event situation. However, this does not fare well for private and mage players to take benefits from the market, and hence, they are not in favor of such organizations. Calculation agents are responsible for valuing a CDS contract.

3.6 CDS Seniority Tiers

- Senior (SNR)—This provides the highest level of CDS coverage and protection for senior secured debt. These are the most common in the CDS universe.
- Non-Preferred Senior (NPS)—CDSs in this level offer protection for "junior" debt. Non-preferred senior tier is in practice a riskier counterpart to senior debt as it gets repaid later in case of a credit default.

- Subordinate (Sub)—CDSs in this tier offer protection to subordinated debt. This gets paid after senior debt in case of a credit default scenario.
- Loss-absorbing capacity (LAC/SLA)—It is a standard created in the aftermath of the 2008 financial crisis. It affects several banks which buy and procure debt. Under this classification, banks may use their own capital as a buffer to absorb losses. Non-preferred senior and subordinated debt may fall under this category.

3.7 CDS Spreads

The 2008 crisis was a real eye-opener for investors and market analysts everywhere. The inefficiency of rating indicators and lack of caution signs from the market raised concerns about looking at newer avenues to gauge credit quality and market risks. A major development came from the CDS spreads.

As already discussed, CDS contracts are essentially considered insurance obligations. Determined by CDS rates, the cost of this insurance is termed as spreads. Spreads are considered the price of a CDS and are expressed in terms of basis points (Bomfim A., 2022). Spreads are highly sensitive to market events, and are suggestive of the credit quality, liquidity scenario and counterparty risks associated with an entity or economy. Simply stated, higher credit risks drive the CDS spreads to go up and lesser risks make it go down. Hence, CDS spreads provide indications regarding the risks of default. Foreign investors too, analyze sovereign CDS spreads, before investing in a particular economy.

Calculation of CDS Spreads

The maximum amount that the protection seller must pay in the event of a credit event is known as the notional principal. The buyer's periodic payment can be made over the period prior to the payment until the contract expires, and it can be made quarterly, semi-annually, or annually. This normally lasts for five years, though it may have other maturities, or until a credit event takes place, whichever comes first. In this way, the premium amount is determined using the notional principal's "basis points."

$$1 \text{ basis point or bps} = 0.01\%$$

CDS Spreads and the Probability of Default: To study how CDS spreads relate to the probability of default, the example of a 1-year vanilla CDS contract is considered and assumed that the total premium is paid upfront. The implied likelihood of default can be found with the use of the payoff computation.

Expected payoff of the buyer = (1 – Recovery rate) * Default probability

Expected payment to be made by the buyer = CDS Spread

When entering a CDS contract, the spread is set so that the swap transaction value is zero, therefore; CDS Spread = (1 – Recovery rate) * Default Probability

OR

Default Probability = CDS Spread / (1- Recovery rate)

3.8 Merits and Demerits of CDS Investing

- Merits -
  - CDS can help to protect investors against credit risk. Using CDS, they can fund riskier ventures which they otherwise might not have.
  - With confidence of investing in more riskier avenues, innovation and creativity enhances, thus providing a boost to the economy.
  - CDS securities help to promote diversification.
- Demerits -
  - CDS securities are largely traded OTC, and not highly regulated. In fact, the swaps went unregulated till 2010.
  - CDS securities are subject to seller's creditworthiness.

3.9 CDS and Centralized Clearing

OTC credit derivatives including CDSs and CDOs have been highly discredited since 2008, purely because as newer and niche products, these are privately negotiated by institutions traded OTC, unlike regular derivatives traded on an exchange. The entities involved in OTC transactions bear the risk of defaulting on their obligations in the future. The issue pertaining to operational risks refers to the ambiguity about whether OTC trades will be discharged in a disciplined manner or not. Again, information about prices, trading volume, etc. is extremely limited.

Adding to this are the problems associated with the settlement of CDS contracts, whether it be cash or physical. In case of a monetary settlement, the issue of determining the market settlement price arises. Any factor that makes the market price differ from the value of the underlying asset may create a grave problem for CDS contract holders. The case of physical settlement hosts its own problems. It's possible that the deliverable security supply won't be enough to cover the net short positions at maturity. This may ensure a short squeeze in the market driving the prices of the security up. A 'cheapest-to-deliver' concern may also arise introducing ambiguity on the performance of the actually delivered assets (rather than the ones stipulated in the contract). In general, the quantity of bonds that can be delivered in the case of a default is specified in a CDS contract. The bonds may have the same seniority but not sell for the same percentage of face value after the default for a variety of reasons, giving the CDS holder the option of choosing the lowest delivery method (Viral V. Acharya, 2009). Centralized clearing plays a vital role in mitigating the aforementioned risks. Trading in substantially large OTC markets, such as that of CDS, should be through centralized clearing houses in order to curtail counterparty risks. This ensures a significant amount of transparency in a trade cycle, where well-capitalized market makers provide liquidity. Collateral arrangements should be 'marked-to-market' on a regular basis, such that an appropriate level of transparency is maintained to negate bilateral issues. Another factor supporting centralized clearing is the large number of disclosures required from the number of market participants. A better transparent picture of the net positions to be settled would alert market participants about the credibility of parties involved in the contract, and in addition, inform them of any imbalances between the outstanding positions and the quantity of underlying to be delivered. Maximum position limits are another benefit posed by centralized clearing houses, similar to that of exchange-traded futures and options. OTC markets restrict the collection of data on institutional positions and the quick identification of significant exposures.

4. Research Methodology

Based on the above literature and theoretical background the following objectives were framed for the study.

- To understand the Credit Default Swaps (CDS) as an asset class for investment with respect to its cost and benefits in the current market scenario.
- To comprehend various calculation metrics associated with CDS spread and assess the implications of spread movements.
- To examine the recent market trends in relation to the developments in sovereign and industrial CDS spreads

Secondary data sources are used to lay the foundation for understanding key principles and connotations associated with the CDS market. To understand CDS valuation, CDS spread movements and its valuations have been assessed. Predictive analysis (time-series analysis) is used to forecast short-term spread movements for global CDS spreads. Analyzing spread movements help to give a view of credit risk associated with the entity (sovereign, industrial, or organizational level).

Based on available spread averages for global averages, exponential smoothening method with 95% confidence intervals is used for short-term forecasting, up to the quarter-ending December 2022.

Post-covid trend analysis and forecasting of the global CDS markets is done for the Investment Grade (IG) sector, wherein certain key global regions have been evaluated by setting the following parameters based on the literature review. The key regions included in the analyses include – U.S., U.K., Japan, Canada, and China. These are the key regions wherein fixed-income trades are high. The same will be compared with a global average.

5. Data Analysis, Observations and Discussions

5.1 Recent Global Trends in CDS Spread Movements

CDS spreads have proven to be sensitive to incidents (major or minor credit events), across the globe. The research seeks to explain different incidences in 2022, wherein trigger events have caused the CDS spreads to decline or increase.

Spreads are directly proportional to the level of risk involved in the CDS. These are reflective of market sentiments. With a favorable event, the spreads go down, and with an unfavorable event, these spreads rise.

In case the spreads are moving downwards, it provides arbitrage opportunities for investors to invest in the bonds and the corresponding CDS. In case the spreads are going up, investors sell bonds as well as CDS protection hedging the risk of default.

- Asia-Pacific (APAC) CDS Spreads react strongly to Stock Market Downfall (September 2022) - The Asia-Pacific (excluding China and Japan) market witnessed a sharp fall in share prices, owing to continuing negative sentiments regarding poor growth and higher interest rates in the market. Major Asian indices displayed a bloodbath on September 26th, 2022, as traders observed the downfall of the British pound and enhanced recession fears. While Hong Kong's Hang Seng index dropped by 1.0%, South Korea's Kospi too displayed a similar trend, going down by 3.02%. Mid-spreads for the IG sector were up by approximately 23%, from 81 bps on August 31st, 2022, to 104 bps on September 30th, 2022. The mid-spreads for the HY sector reacted more strongly, and were up by 45%, from 129 bps on August 31st, 2022 to 187 bps on September 30th, 2022.
- U.K. CDS spreads show tremendous spike owing to inflationary pressures (April 2022) – Analysts were of the view that the pound would fall to levels not witnessed before, with a heavy chance of recession. Experts also cautioned against surging living costs and energy costs, amid Russia's invasion of Ukraine. Spreads for the IG and HY sectors in the U.K. displayed an upward trend over the month. The IG CDS spreads saw a 17% increase of 13 bps (from 76 to 89) while the HY CDS spreads increased by approximately 33%, following a rise of 46 bps (from 139 to 185).
- Russia's invasion of Ukraine causes spreads to act dramatically (February 2022) - One of the most dramatic CDS spread events noticed this year came from the Russian and Ukrainian regions. Following Russia's military invasion of Ukraine in Feb'22, global markets witnessed extreme volatility. S&P's global ratings for both countries were downgraded, with Ukraine going down from B to B- and Russia from BBB- to BB+. Rating agencies Moody's and Fitch too degraded Russia's sovereign rating to the 'Junk' category, in response to sanctions levied by the U.S. and European Union (E.U.). CDS mid-spreads for Russian sovereign risk surged significantly, with the 10-year CDS spread rising 59% from 254 bps on 1/31/2022 to 404 bps as on 02/28/2022, while the 5-year CDS soared 158% from 224 bps to 579 bps. The extraordinary spike was particularly serious the day Russia began its conquest of Ukraine with the 5-year CDS spiking to 894 bps on 2/24/2022.
- *Global average:* The global average spread performance is derived from the underlying regions. As the spreads for the U.S., Japan, U.K., Canada, and

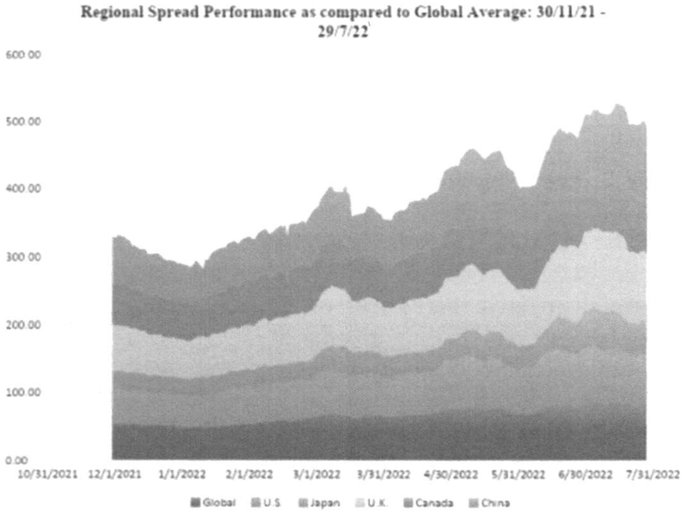

Fig. 26.1 Regional spread performance compared to global average

China have increased in the 8-month period, so has the average of the global spread.

- *U.S.A:* The spread for the U.S. has increased from 51 bps to 72 bps. The primary reason for this is the FED interest rate hikes, post-pandemic. The U.S. Federal Reserve plans to push benchmark rates close to 2% this year and further increase it in 2023. Interest rate hikes coupled with wider credit spreads often lead to hampering economic growth and higher borrowing costs for the industrial sector. In addition, U.S.'s tension with countries like Russia and China has posed a major threat to the economic recovery post-covid. With the Russia-Ukrainian crisis and the China-Japan war possibilities, the U.S. economy has found itself in a crossfire situation, dealing with the energy crisis from Russia and allied support towards Japan. From the beginning of the year to the middle of March, the spread on S&P U.S. Investment Grade Corporate Bond BBB Index increased by more than 50 basis points.
- *Japan and China:* Growing pressures between China and Japan, and missile attacks on Taiwan are the primary reasons for increased credit risks in the economies. As per the given data, the spreads for Japan have increased from 27 bps, whereas spreads for China have gone up 68 bps to 99 bps – between 30/11/21 to 29/7/22. The Chinese economy is currently facing severe backlash from global economies owing to its political and military policies. In addition, many economies have also begun to establish a trade ban on many Chinese products. China's support of Russia is straining globalization's links. Internally, China's real-estate market suffers from high default currently. For 2022, S&P estimations are that 20%-40% of property developers may face default.

- *U.K.:* As discussed earlier, the U.K. economy is currently dealing with inflationary pressures, owing to which the CDS spreads have showcased a rise from 69 bps to 103 bps. In addition, the economy is also suffering from increased living and energy costs due to the Russia-Ukrainian war.
- *Canada:* The spreads for Canada widened by 30 bs, from 59 bps on 30/11/22 to 89 bps on 29/7/11. Canada is currently facing issues in loan defaults that have led to increased consumer credit risks. Analysts predict that in the coming quarters, insolvencies and delinquencies will be on a rise. Canadian banking analytics are also indicating an upcoming shallow recession.

5.2 Forecasting IG Global CDS Spreads using Exponential Smoothening, for All Industries Combined

Based on available spread averages for the global bifurcations, exponential smoothening method is used for short-term forecasting, up to the quarter-ending December 2022. As seen earlier, CDS spreads tend to be highly reactive to any changes or developments in the market or industry, hence the confidence levels are set accordingly.

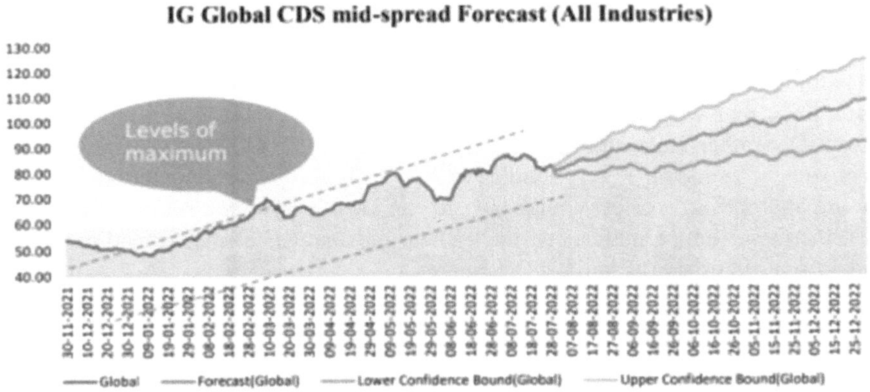

Fig. 26.2 Forecasting IG Global CDS mid-spreads

As per the forecast, it is observed that global CDS mid-spreads will display a rising trend in the coming months, up to December 2022. The following are the main reasons for this –

- The growth outlook for the global average has declined since Russia invaded Ukraine and COVID-19 cases rose in China.
- Central banks internationally are more determined to tighten their monetary policy to keep inflation under control.
- Currently, major industries are facing issues in their supply and distribution channels, owing to changes made during the pandemic and major trade bans imposed for particular nations.

The combination of weak growth and tighter monetary policy signifies that there are thin chances of a credit rally taking place. The forecast hints at unstable economic conditions to prevail in global economies in the near future.

While the global economies are yet to recover from the aftermath of the pandemic, it is safe to conclude that for the year 2022, the CDS spreads (specifically for the IG sector) will be on the rise.

6. Contribution of the Study to the Existing Body of Knowledge

The research attempts to investigate the key benefits of the CDS asset class, with respect to its spread movements, and how these are indicative of major market developments. In addition, the study also analyzes new trends developed in this arena, and what future it holds. This study is first in its nature to study recent trends in the CDS market, in a post-covid timeline. At the same time, the research shows how CDS spreads prove efficient as key market indicators, and how these can be used to predict futuristic trends.

7. Limitations and Future Scope of Research

The limitation of the study is the restricted time horizon and data points currently available, that were used for predictive analysis. Since the data available was from December 2021, only a short-term prediction for CDS spread movements could be concluded. Future studies may consider a wider time horizon for a more appropriate predictive analysis and can even incorporate seasonal patterns. Furthermore, future studies can incorporate the analysis of the 'spread basis' to identify newer patterns in the CDS market.

8. Conclusion

The CDS market has seen sizable growth over the past decade and attracted interest of major market players. Over the previous years, the market has become more sophisticated and standardized, and centralization has taken a key place. With large amounts of CDS data being publicly available, financial institutions are making excellent use of information and insights derived from the CDS market. The time series analysis confirms that CDS data and spread metrics can be used by investors to study futuristic market trends. The spread movements have a strong association with current market movements and can provide accurate views of market conditions.

The use of CDS spreads to study the market is gaining traction in recent times. Post the pandemic, there have been tremendous developments in the market and spread movements, and economists can effectively correlate this data with other market trends and indicators, including stock price movements, macroeconomic factors, etc. Due to its extremely concentrated and interconnected nature, the market suffers from potential counterparty threats. The use of CCPs has been observed as a way to mitigate such risks, and an escalating number of CDS dealings are being facilitated by CCPs. The ISDA has also played a critical role in the progress of the market. When investing in the market, traders need to be extremely cautious of the benefits and risks associated with the market. Post the credit crisis, market players yet have mixed sentiments concerning the reliability of CDS spreads as market indicators. However, the major belief is that the CDS market has scope for immense growth ahead in the future. With newer developments in the market and clubbing the CDS asset class with other instruments of trade, the CDS market is giving birth to new products and avenues for investors to partake in.

REFERENCES

1. Amadeo, K. (2021, March 4). Retrieved from thebalancemoney.com: https://www.thebalancemoney.com/credit-default-swaps-pros-cons-crises-examples-3305920
2. Avino, D. a. (2012). Are CDS spreads predictable? An analysis of linear and non-linear forecasting models. Retrieved from https://mpra.ub.uni-muenchen.de/id/eprint/42848
3. BBA. (2002). 2001/2002 Credit Derivatives Survey. British Bankers Association, London, London.
4. Bo, L. &. (2020). Locally Risk-Minimizing Hedging of Counterparty Risk for Portfolio of Credit Derivatives. Applied Mathematics & Optimization. doi:10.1007/s00245-018-9549-y
5. Bomfim, A. N. (2022). Credit Default Swaps. Finance and Economics Discussion Series 2022-023. doi:https://doi.org/10.17016/FEDS.2022.023
6. Bomfim, A. N. (2022). Credit Default Swaps. Finance and Economics Discussion Series 2022-023. doi:https://doi.org/10.17016/FEDS.2022.023
7. Czech, R. (2021). Credit Default Swaps and Corporate Bond Trading. SSRN Electronic Journal, 4-10. doi:10.2139/ssrn.3422897
8. Darko B. Vukovic, K. R. (2022). Are CDS spreads predictable during the Covid-19 pandemic? Forecasting based on SVM, GMDH, LSTM and Markov switching autoregression. doi:10.1016/j.eswa.2022.116553
9. Fletcher, G.-G. S. (2019). Engineered Credit Default Swaps: Innovative or Manipulative? Retrieved from https://www.repository.law.indiana.edu/facpub/2863
10. Jean Helwege, S. M. (2009). Credit Default Swap Auctions. Federal Reserve Bank of New York. Retrieved from https://www.newyorkfed.org/medialibrary/media/research/staff_reports/sr372.pdf
11. Jean Helwege, S. M. (2009). Credit Default Swap Auctions. Journal of Fixed Income, 19. doi:http://dx.doi.org/10.2139/ssrn.1407272
12. Jeffery D Amato, J. G. (2005). CDS index tranches and the pricing of credit risk. BIS Quarterly Review.
13. Jennie Bai, P. C.-D. (2018). The CDS-Bond Basis. Georgetown McDonough School of Business Research Paper No. 2024531. doi:http://dx.doi.org/10.2139/ssrn.2024531
14. John C Hull, S. B. (2018). Options, Futures and Other Derivatives (10 ed.). Pearson India Education Services Pvt. Ltd.

15. John Coughlan, R. H. (2019). Recent Trends in CDS Markets. 2.
16. John Hull, A. W. (2000). Valuing Credit Default Swaps I: No Counterparty Default Risk. The Journal of Derivatives. doi:10.3905/jod.2000.319115
17. Marcin Jaskowski, D. v. (2016). Forecasting Credit Default Swap spreads. Erasmus University - Econometric Institute.
18. Mohamed-Ali Akari, R. B.-A. (2019). The impact of central clearing on the market for single-name credit default swaps. 2.
19. Paskaleva, M. (2020). Sovereign Security and Risk Management by Credit Default Swaps. International Journal on Information Technologies & Security, № 3 (vol. 12), Vol. 12. Retrieved from https://papers.ssrn.com/sol3/papers.cfm?abstract_id=3157461
20. Romanyuk, K. (2021). Impact of the COVID-19 Pandemic on the US Credit Default Swap Market. doi:10.1155/2021/1656448
21. Söhnke M. Bartram, J. C. (2018). Credit Default Swaps Around the World: Investment and Financing Effects. SSRN Electronic Journal. doi:10.2139/ssrn.3234356
22. Steffen Schuldenzucker, S. S. (2018). Default Ambiguity: Credit Default Swaps Create New Systemic Risks in Financial Networks. doi:10.1287/mnsc.2019.3304
23. Stulz, R. M. (2010). Credit Deafualt Swaps and the Credit Crisis. Journal of Economic Perspectives, 73-92.
24. Tak-Yuen Wong, J. Y. (2020). Credit default swaps and debt overhang. Management Science, 68(3). doi:10.2139/ssrn.2959302
25. Viral V. Acharya, R. F. (2009). Centralized Clearing for Credit Derivatives. In M. R. Viral V. Acharya, Restoring Financial Stability (pp. 251-260). John Wiley & Sons, Inc.
26. Viral V.Acharyaa, Y. T. (2022). Bank use of sovereign CDS in the Eurozone crisis: Hedging and risk incentives. Journal of Financial Intermediation, 50. doi:100964
27. Wall Street Tests Blockchain Technology for CDS Transactions. (2016). Firstpost.
28. Wemmenhove, D. (2009). Credit Default Swap Spread Model: Descriptive and Predictive. Retrieved from http://essay.utwente.nl/60530/1/MSc_Danny_Wemmenhove.pdf

Note: All the figures in this chapter were made by the authors.

Securing the Future through Sustainability, Health, Education, and Technology – Brig. Dr. Rajiv Divekar et al. (eds)
 ISBN 978-1-032-95922-1

27 Blockchain Technology in HRM: A Futuristic Perspective

Maitri Saklani[1], Jaya Chitranshi[2], Aman Arya[3]
Symbiosis Institute of Management Studies,
Symbiosis International Deemed University, Pune, India

Abstract

Blockchain technology is now widely used across many industries as a result of the rapid advancement of science and technology and the growth of society. Employers can increase job productivity while reducing associated resource expenses by employing blockchain technology to support human resource management. This paper deals with a thorough analysis of present awareness, trust, preference, reliability and impact of blockchain technology within the HRM department. This paper aims to help in future development and countering challenges faced at present while using blockchain technology. The study is based on responses of 263 human resource professionals from different sectors, regions and departments. A questionnaire was designed to measure awareness, challenges and future prospects. The study recommends an integration of blockchain and HRM and at the same time highlights some challenges like security and data privacy. The study further recommends a need to work upon some of the gaps of blockchain technology like security, reliability and awareness in order to harness the advantages of blockchain technology especially in financial transactions.

Keywords: Awareness, Blockchain technology, Challenges, Future prospects, Human resource management

1. Introduction

Blockchain is currently a growing subject from the standpoint of industries, as a technological manifestation brought about by the advancement of science and

[1]maitri.saklani2024@sims.edu, [2]jaya.chitranshi@sims.edu, [3]aman.arya2024@sims.edu

DOI: 10.1201/9781003587200-27

technology to a certain level. It might have a crucial impact on business and economy. Government agencies have gradually created policies and regulations on the usage of blockchain to help direct the application of blockchain technology while keeping security features of this technology relevant. The most significant sector of business that contributes to maintaining the current state of business is human resource management. Since the advent of blockchain technology, it has been easier for associated organizations to hire talented individuals as well as to engage relevant expertise. This paper talks about application of blockchain technology in various areas of HRM department namely recruitment, learning and development, employee engagement, employee verification and employee data management. Apart from the fact that blockchain can be integrated with existing technologies such as AI, ML and IOT, it makes existing HRM processes even more efficient and productive.

However, like two sides of a single coin, there are some concerning challenges with blockchain technology that are required to be dealt with in order to make optimum use of this nascent technology in today's industries. In addition to analyzing the main contemporary lacunae that create a problem for companies to adopt blockchain technology, this article seeks to deal with the application of blockchain technology that is currently growing in various Human Resource Management departments. In light of the found shortcomings, it also seeks to examine the blockchain technology's potential in the future.

2. Objectives

1. Identification of awareness among employees associated with the HRM department towards blockchain technology
2. To analyze sector wise (HR department) association with reliability and trust towards blockchain technology.
3. To analyze department wise association with reliability and trust towards blockchain technology.

3. Literature Review

Corporate businesses have started to shift into platform-based businesses and adopt technology as a result of the growth of the Internet economy and ongoing environmental changes. By including third party ledger and using the Internet for training and assessment, shared human resource management addresses issues related to employee relations, salary and welfare, performance, and training *(Shan He, 2021)*. A study *(Dolzhenko, 2018)* tries to highlight how blockchain technology can be used in HRM today. By incorporating new ideas and undergoing professional development, HRM is simultaneously evolving.

3.1 Blockchain

Blockchain is a type of distributed transaction ledger. Instead of being kept in a single central location, the data kept on the ledger is spread among numerous nodes and locations. There is no need for a centralized authority because control is distributed among numerous independent parties. Data can only be decrypted by the intended receiver using public-private key *cryptography, preserving privacy (Naef, 2022). Liu (2021) suggested that* a secure and reliable database can be created by gathering vast amounts of data from projects at all phases and sharing that data with all parties. Pedersen *(2019)* noted that every participating organization has a duplicate of the same digital ledger when using a blockchain application. *Javaid (2021)* noted that "*s*calability, anonymity, and trustworthiness" are three major issues for companies that blockchain addresses. The paper noted that decentralization will also eliminate single points of failure and foster an environment that will strengthen HRM operations. As a step toward digitization, organizations are predicted to adopt encryption technology (54%) according to The Future of Jobs 12 Report 2018 by The World Economic Forum (*SZYMCZYK, 2020).*

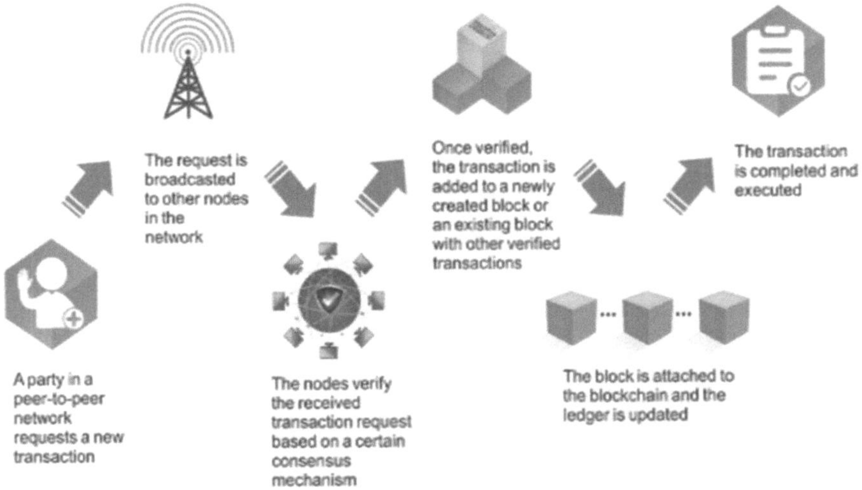

Fig. 27.1 Functioning of blockchain technology (Lumineau, 2020)

3.2 Blockchain Technology Types

Public Blockchain: The decentralization idea may be implemented on these blockchains without any restrictions. The network is open to everyone with a computer and internet access; there are no restrictions.

Private Blockchain: Compared to public blockchains, these blockchains are less decentralized and hence safer because only a limited number of nodes may engage in the process. Blockchain hybrid: It is made up of both public and private blockchain material, some of which is made publicly available and others of which is governed by various organizations. Public blockchains are typically examined with a focus on a few particular research objectives, whereas private and consortium blockchains are motivated by business requirements. This is one of the outcomes that explains why private blockchain developers offer the majority of high precision evaluation tools, which belong to the emulation class. To achieve consistency when contrasting various enterprise products, it may be advantageous to develop a uniform standardized approach for private blockchain evaluation *(Smetanin, 2020).*

3.3 Blockchain in Businesses

The World Economic Forum in Davos identified a list of digital technologies that businesses should use in their operations, including cloud and mobile technologies combined with blockchain, identification, artificial intelligence, biometric technologies, augmented reality, additive (3D printing), etc. They enable the upgrading of business procedures and the acceleration of business expansion *(Bogma, 2022).* To increase the company's security and productivity, companies are slowly adopting automated robots and blockchain technologies *(Ade, 2022).* It can act as a decentralized, permanently unalterable storage layer for any kind of information or asset. As a result, the technology can be used to store and authenticate a wide range of data, including sensitive records and papers, employment qualifications, and transactions.

Fig. 27.2 Application of blockchain technology in various sectors (Pal, 2021)

3.4 HRM: Human Resource Management

The process of hiring, training, evaluating, and rewarding employees as well as attending to their issues regarding labor relations, health, safety, and fairness is known as human resource management. Choosing, hiring, developing, putting, and rewarding the best individual for the job are all parts of managing human resources. It also has to do with building a favorable workplace.

3.5 Blockchain in HRM

While this method makes data exchange possible, it also has drawbacks, such the possibility of centralized data theft and manipulation. Blockchain technology may successfully handle the problems of talent archive data security and privacy protection since it is decentralized, traceable, and tamper-resistant. "Blockchain" technology may be used to address problems such as fake academic qualifications, laborious and time-consuming resume screening, and low recruiting efficiency in the job market. Payroll, hiring and selection, onboarding and offboarding, and other HR-related procedures waste a great deal of money, time, and resources—sometimes even coming from outside sources. Blockchain searching would be more beneficial and efficient for the employment process than internet search. Blockchains offer anonymity and a screening mechanism to impartial customers. Applications for blockchain in real time include system learning, dynamic updating, verification, and development *(Pal, 2021)*.

Blockchain and Cost

The cost of logistics and communication for the purpose of employment can be decreased by using blockchain technology. Companies that can save expenses in communication and logistics are those with readily available references and verifiable curriculum vitae. Therefore, the main concern is how to guarantee that candidates submit accurate and dependable information. Blockchain technology may be used by organizations to leverage candidate access (key or token) or a distributed third-party ledger to confirm a candidate's validity. Applicants may create, manage, and have access to a blockchain-based record of their training and education background, as well as their work history, by using a distributed ledger. AI may also be used to filter this data and plan first video conferences instead of requiring unnecessary travel and related expenses before inviting the shortlisted applicants to final interviews. Because of blockchain technology, recruiting procedures have the following opportunities: Developing a digital, safe, decentralized network for careers; verifying credentials in an effective, speedy, and affordable manner; assisting with performance assessments for employees; conducting interviews via the metaverse. It is believed that all of these options will improve recruiting practices by enabling more effective job matching. *(Balon, 2022)*.

Resume Verification

Employers can use blockchain to find a candidate's CV on LinkedIn (as well as other social media accounts like Twitter, Facebook, and Instagram) and then compare it to the company's current hiring needs. The HR team (recruiting team) can benefit from immediate, precise, and accurate information on the candidate's abilities, expertise, and experience. It minimizes Central Verification Procedure faults. According to reports, 84% of workers had resumes that were found to be false. Now, this is a serious problem that must be resolved as soon as possible. According to reports, one trustworthy instrument that will significantly cut down on the time needed to do background checks is blockchain technology. *(Mishra, 2020)* The usage of blockchain technology can elevate HRM tasks to a new level and be beneficial in a variety of areas, including hiring, verifying credentials and education, establishing worker contracts and payments, and many more. *(Makridakis, 2019*).

Employee Record Management

The HR petitioner is using the problem of time required to develop and update staff members' work histories and HR enrollments to investigate. Additionally, they may add new hire data for reference checks, pay benefits administration (including health and medical insurance and compensations), and legal applications (tax and insurance) for the distributed ledger's administrative needs. To compare the current offer package, a person or public or private ledger may be used to monitor the proof of job history, including the pay, bonus, benefits, and allowances from the previous position. Verifications of legal data, including loan status, criminal background, and/or health records, might not be included in the ledger; instead, they would need to be completed by third parties, or by making the distributed ledger publicly accessible or under the supervision of third parties. Only with the candidate's consent, either in writing or verbally, can inspections take place. Recruiters have employment contracts available for applicants to sign on the day of boarding or before.

Blockchain in Employee Engagement

According to the World Economic Forum, an IoT-enabled workplace of the future will enhance human-machine interaction, reduce administrative procedures, and increase productivity. By bringing the employee engagement process closer to workers, the Internet of Things (IoT) enables and empowers us to enhance employee engagement, communication, and growth. Blockchain and IoT integration have the potential to increase workplace productivity. The following are some ways that the Internet of Things (IoT) and blockchain integration could boost workplace efficiency: Tracking of employee performance in real-time, promoting positive performance, protecting employee data, and fostering confidence in performance evaluations, increased precision, efficiency and enhanced security *(Mishra, 2020).*

Blockchain in Learning and Development

The size of the company and the amount spent on development and training are strongly correlated. Firms in particular often face a number of obstacles to training access, including cost and time, and they often underinvest in continuing professional development for themselves (and, where appropriate, for their workers). In general, companies and the cultural sector do not strategically assess the talent demands of the future. The HR blockchain will also use an automated process to reach an agreement amongst the involved stakeholders. Furthermore, the ability for people to maintain - and control access to - a comprehensive, trustworthy blockchain-based history of their training, skills, and productivity at work may have a big influence on both sides of the job relationship *(Fachrunnisa, 2020)*.

3.6 Future

Scholars and academics from all over the world are analyzing the costs and benefits of businesses that use blockchain technology. Future applications of blockchain technology will be crucial, including hiring and assigning staff, organizing and managing financial and accounting tasks, and implementing marketing plans to boost output and cash flow. The business community will be more trusting as a result of more openness in internal and external company interactions *(Pal, 2021)*.

Therefore, future studies should aim to solve this problem by publishing more articles discussing the technical and cryptographic difficulties, concentrating more on market design, privacy and trust, and the acceptance or non-adoption of new technologies.

Because blockchain 4.0 can address difficulties like scalability, flexibility, and affordability, researchers think that this version of the technology is dedicated to corporations and will assure interoperability *(Balon, 2022)*.

4. Research Methodology

4.1 Item Generation

The study was conducted to analyze the popularity, reliability and trust over blockchain technology in the present and what can be the gaps associated with it in HRM department among human resource professionals. The study has been conducted by taking the responses of 263 human resource professionals from different sectors, regions and departments. The paper deals with gathering knowledge about issues with existing HRM and where Blockchain technology can intervene. It also deals with the present trends among companies about the kind of technology they are using and issues they face. A questionnaire was designed to measure awareness, challenges and future prospects. The researchers had gone through various existing papers which helped to form a base for designing this instrument.

4.2 Instrument Development

A questionnaire was designed that dealt with 4 major sections

A. Demographics

It deals with characteristics like age, gender, sector associated, HRM department associated with, work experience.

B. Gaps in HRM without technology assistance

It deals with the identification gaps and challenges in HRM in industries without technology assistance.

C. Popularity and Inclination towards blockchain technology in the HRM department of organizations.

It aims to analyze the awareness of people from the HRM department about Blockchain application in the HRM department.

D. Acceptance and willingness to adopt blockchain technology in HRM

It aims to understand how willing are people of the HRM department to adopt Blockchain Technology in association with HRM processes and also their apprehensions for the same.

4.3 Data Collection

The data was gathered with the help of google form which was circulated among HR professionals associated with different sectors.

4.4 Tools Used

Google Form

Google Forms is a survey management tool included with Google's free online Google Docs Editors suite. It was employed to compile responder data.

MS EXCEL

It was used to visualize the data collected from the google form and also to tabulate it and correlate various factors by using pivot tables and charts.

5. Results and Discussion

5.1 Based on Qualitative Data

Blockchain technology provides benefits as well as drawbacks, just like any coin has two sides. The problems are potential threats and inadequate privacy protection, as well as the identification and unauthorized use of permanent data derived from social networking and uncontrollable numerous identities. Digital records being difficult to verify is another serious problem with blockchain. Due to regional restrictions, blockchain may be difficult to implement globally. Notably, despite being effective at protecting data, blockchains are still vulnerable to attacks *(Lumineau, 2020)*. The main barrier to exchanging data is the absence of reliable and secure ways for doing so, as well as the inability to verify and secure the ownership of data owners. Staff issues, legal uncertainty, a lack of infrastructure and standardization, and unclear governance structures are some of the current obstacles. The technology can spread further with improved smart contract security and interoperability between private and public protocols. There are still obstacles in the form of a lack of industry awareness, widespread skepticism about networks' trustworthiness and openness, a lack of standards, ambiguous governance systems, regulatory and legal concerns, as well as the challenging integration of cryptocurrencies into network architecture *(Lohmer, 2020)*. Making blockchain widely applicable will depend on resolving issues like exchange speed, the inspection mechanism, and information cutoff points *(Fachrunnisa, 2020)*. Building and implementing blockchain applications across a user network is a specific hurdle for adoption, necessitating cooperation between businesses *(Naef, 2022)*. There should be greater chances for researchers to acquire real-world data from both the public and private sectors. Real-world data sets aren't as readily available as they formerly were because of issues with the law, privacy, and competition. Future research using open-source real-world datasets is crucial for enabling other researchers working in the field of blockchain to validate their findings *(Kapadiya et al., 2022.)* It has been established in the past that transaction privacy is not always maintained by blockchain because public transactions are viewable by anybody. If the data is not totally intended for public consumption, the firm employing public blockchain may experience major problems. Security is another issue with technology *(Pal, 2021)*.

5.2 Based on Quantitative Data (Responses)

1. *Minimum Awareness is in the compensation and pay department of HR which comprises of 54% of the total employees working in Compensation and Pay who are aware of blockchain technology whereas Learning and Development has maximum awareness about blockchain technology standing at 34% of total of Learning and development have maximum unawareness i.e. rating 1.*

Count of Q6.HRM department you are associated with.	Column Labels						
Row Labels	1	2	3	4	5	(blank)	Grand Total
COMPENSATION AND PAY	16		12	14	4		46
EMPLOYEE ENGAGEMENT	14	12	4	10	6		46
LEARNING AND DEVELOPMENT	12	18	10	18	6		64
PERFORMANCE MANAGEMENT	10	11	10	8			39
RECRUITMENT	14	32	10	8	4		68
(blank)							
Grand Total	**66**	**73**	**46**	**58**	**20**		**263**

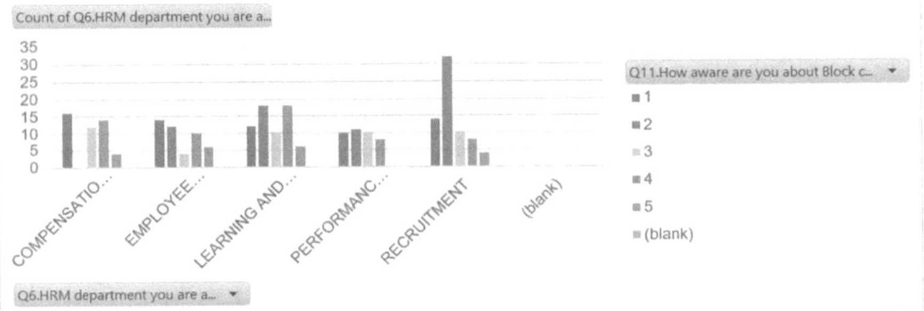

Fig. 27.3 HRM department wise awareness of blockchain technology

Source: Made by authors

Table 27.1 Percentage of awareness of HRM employees (department-wise) at level 1(minimum) and 4 and 5 (maximum)

Job Roles	% of people with awareness at level 4 or 5 (maximun)	% of people with awareness at level 1 (minimum)
Compensation and Pay	39.13043478	34.7826087
Employee Engagement	34.7826087	30.43478261
Learning and Development	54.34782609	18.75
Performance Management	20.51282051	25.64102564
Recruitment	17.64705882	20.58823529

Source: Made by authors

2. *HRs of the Manufacturing sector find blockchain the most reliable whereas those of the Finance sector find blockchain the least reliable. In manufacturing sector 48% of total HRs find blockchain reliable which is highest among all the other sectors. On the other hand maximum unreliability is among the HRs of finance sector which stands at 62% of all the HRs of that sector.*

Count of Q15.How reliable do you find blockchain in terms of security? Column Labels

Row Labels	1	2	3	4	5	(blank)	Grand Total
Finance	22	32	20	8	4		86
FMCG		10	6	4			20
IT	32	28	34	4	8		106
Manufacturing		7	8	14			29
Service Sector	6		8	8			22
(blank)							
Grand Total	60	77	76	38	12		263

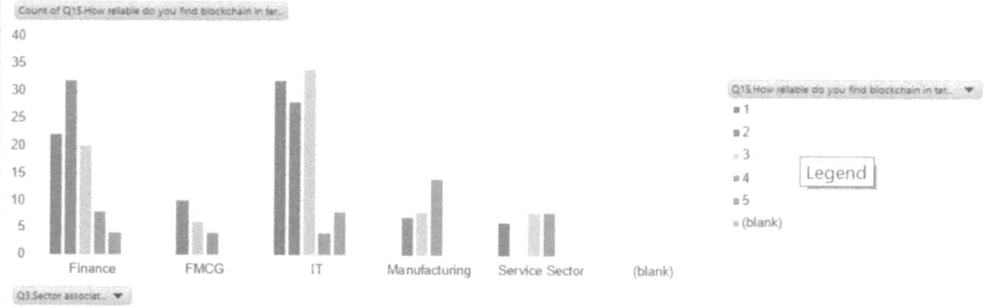

Fig. 27.4 Sector wise reliability on blockchain technology among HRs

Source: Made by authors

Table 27.2 Percentage of reliability of HRM employees (sector-wise) at level 1 and 2(minimum) and 4 and 5 (maximum)

Sectors	% of Maximum reliability (level 4 and 5)	% of Minimum reliability (level 1 and 2)
Finance	13.95348837	62.79069767
FMCG	20	50
IT	11.32075472	56.60377358
Manufacturing	48.27586207	24.13793103
Service Sector	36.36363636	27.27272727

Source: Made by authors

3. On analyzing the reliability of blockchain technology integrated with HRM it has been seen that performance management has the highest percentage of reliability which stands at 30% whereas maximum level of unreliability is among recruitment and compensation and pay standing at 56% and 70%.

Count of Q6.HRM department you are associated with.	Column Labels						
Row Labels	**1**	**2**	**3**	**4**	**5**	**(blank)**	**Grand Total**
COMPENSATION AND PAY	12	14	8	8	4		46
EMPLOYEE ENGAGEMENT	14	4	18	10			46
LEARNING AND DEVELOPMENT	10	14	36	4			64
PERFORMANCE MANAGEMENT	10	11	6	8	4		39
RECRUITMENT	14	34	8	8	4		68
(blank)							
Grand Total	**60**	**77**	**76**	**38**	**12**		**263**

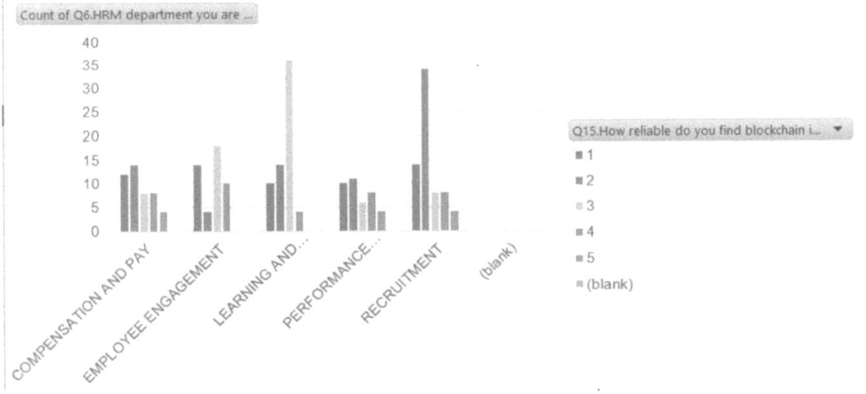

Fig. 27.5 HRM department wise reliability on blockchain technology among HRs

Source: Made by authors

Table 27.3 Percentage of reliability of HRM employees (Department-wise) at level 1 and 2 (minimum) and 4 and 5 (maximum)

Departments	% of Maximum reliability (level 4 and 5)	% of Minimum reliability (level 1 and 2)
Compensation and Pay	26.08695652	56.52173913
Employee Engagement	21.73913043	39.13043478
Learning and Development	6.25	39.0625
Performance Management	30.76923077	53.84615385
Recruitment	17.64705882	70.58823529

Source: Made by authors

1. It can be seen that compensation and pay has the least awareness about blockchain technology and its application.
2. In the Finance sector HRs find blockchain Technology the least reliable. The potential reasons can be lack of sense of security, policies by the

government and supervising authority and lack of awareness as supported by inference 1.

3. Again from analysis 3 it is clear that the employees involved in recruitment and compensation and pay have the minimum reliability on blockchain technology may be because there are trust issues on legitimacy of data.

6. Conclusion

The qualitative analysis helped to understand the present application of blockchain technology in HRM process. The study recommended the integration of blockchain and HRM at the same time the challenges like security and data privacy came into light. Based upon quantitative analysis it has been found that here is a need to work upon some of the gaps of blockchain technology like security, reliability, and awareness in order to harness the advantages of blockchain technology especially in financial transactions. There needs to be more research done to find out the possibility of integration of AI and Blockchain technology which can be implemented in HRM for improved efficiency and effectiveness. Also, HR departments need to train the employees to become more technically aware so that they can easily adapt to new technologies so that they can easily work with technologies like blockchain. It can be seen that Asia Pacific and S-E Asian regions are well aware of application of blockchain technology in HRM as compared to central Asia. Therefore, Blockchain Technology has great prospects if the gaps and challenges are overcome.

7. Implications

This study can be used to design blockchain based software which can find applications in HRM process. Also, it will be beneficial for designing such software which is free from present challenges and demerits of blockchain technology. Also there needs to be training of human resources within organizations irrespective of sector to adapt new technologies. This paper can help in future studies for development of technologies which are made by integration of present technologies like IOT, ML, AI etc. with blockchain technology based on the popularity of usage of technologies in different regions. This research implies that the gap of awareness can be overcome by overcoming the gap of reliability and trust among HRs for which designers and engineers need to work upon the security aspect of blockchain.

8. Limitations and Suggestions

Since blockchain technology is a nascent technology and as a reason there has been very limited research on this yet. There are very few organizations which have adopted Blockchain Technology in HRM departments to carry out the basic process of HR. This led to very limited number of respondents. Increase in adoption and usage of blockchain technology will make HR a better and faster department.

REFERENCES

1. Abhinav Pal, C. T. (2021, November). *Blockchain for business management: Applications, challenges and potentials*. Retrieved from https://www.semanticscholar.org/paper/Blockchain-for-business-management%3A-Applications%2C-Pal-Tiwari/4a700dae077db58bb24605565e8fe4acd661af1d
2. Ade, A. (2022). *Future of industry 5.0 in society: human-centric solutions, challenges and prospective research areas*. J Cloud Comp 11, 40 (2022) Retrieved from https://journalofcloudcomputing.springeropen.com/articles/10.1186/s13677-022-00314-5
3. Asger B. Pedersen, M. R. (2019, June). *A Ten-Step Decision Path to Determine When to Use Blockchain Technologies*. Retrieved from Research Gate: https://www.researchgate.net/publication/333545589_A_Ten-Step_Decision_Path_to_Determine_When_to_Use_Blockchain_Technologies
4. Barbara Balon, K. K. (2022, April). *Application of Blockchain Technology in Production Scheduling and Management of Human Resources Competencies*. Retrieved from https://pubmed.ncbi.nlm.nih.gov/35458828/
5. Geetika Jain, N. S. (2021, February). *Enhancing training effectiveness for organizations through blockchain-enabled training effectiveness measurement (BETEM)*. Retrieved from https://www.emerald.com/insight/content/doi/10.1108/JOCM-10-2020-0303/full/html
6. Jacob Lohmer, R. L. (2020, November). *Blockchain in operations management and manufacturing: Potential and barriers*. Retrieved from https://www.sciencedirect.com/science/article/pii/S0360835220304988
7. Kapadiya, K., Patel, U., Gupta, R., Alshehri, M. D., & Sudeep. (2022). *Blockchain and AI-Empowered Healthcare Insurance Fraud Detection: an Analysis, Architecture, and Future Prospects*. Retrieved from https://ieeexplore.ieee.org/document/9843995
8. Lumineau F., W. W. (2020, April). *Blockchain Governance — A New Way of Organizing Collaborations?* Retrieved from https://papers.ssrn.com/sol3/papers.cfm?abstract_id=3562941
9. Mohd Javaid a, A. H. (2021, December). *Blockchain technology applications for Industry 4.0: A literature-based review*. Retrieved from https://www.sciencedirect.com/science/article/pii/S2096720921000221
10. Mona Mishra, P. J. (2020, March). *APPLICATION & CHALLENGES OF BLOCKCHAIN IN HRM: THE DIFFUSION OF INNOVATION THEORY PERSPECTIVE*. Retrieved from https://www.researchgate.net/publication/342665808_APPLICATION_CHALLENGES_OF_BLOCKCHAIN_IN_HRM_THE_DIFFUSION_OF_INNOVATION_THEORY_PERSPECTIVE
11. Olena Bogma, H. S. (2022). *THE IMPACT OF EUROPEAN INTEGRATION ON*. Retrieved from https://dspace.nuft.edu.ua/jspui/bitstream/123456789/38779/1/Bogma.pdf
12. Olivia Fachrunnisa, F. K. (2020, October). *Blockchain-based human resource management practices for mitigating skills and competencies gap in workforce*. Retrieved from https://journals.sagepub.com/doi/full/10.1177/1847979020966400

13. Ruslan Dolzhenko, S. D. (2018, September). *TRENDS AND FUTURE OF PROFESSIONS IN THE FIELD OF* . Retrieved from https://msed.vse.cz/msed_2018/article/64-Dolzhenko-Ruslan-paper.pdf
14. Sergey Smetanin, A. O. (2020, June). *Blockchain Evaluation Approaches: State-of-the-Art and Future Perspective*. Retrieved from https://pubmed.ncbi.nlm.nih.gov/32545719/
15. Shan He, Y. W. (2021, January). *Research on Innovation Mode of Human Resource Management of Shared Platform Against the Background of Digital Economy*. Retrieved from Research Gate: https://www.researchgate.net/publication/354728503_Research_on_Innovation_Mode_of_Human_Resource_Management_of_Shared_Platform_Against_the_Background_of_Digital_Economy
16. Shicheng Liu, R. C. (2021, October). *Application of Artificial Neural Networks in Construction Management: Current Status and Future Directions*. Retrieved from https://www.researchgate.net/publication/355345582_Application_of_Artificial_Neural_Networks_in_Construction_Management_Current_Status_and_Future_Directions
17. Stefan Naef, S. M. (2022, April). Retrieved from Blockchain and network governance: learning from applications in the supply chain sector: https://www.semanticscholar.org/paper/Blockchain-and-network-governance%3A-learning-from-in-Naef-Wagner/0d9afea48042124139388598cf1a325e242a83a2
18. SZYMCZYK, K. (2020). *Industry 4.0 from the point of view of human resources management*. Retrieved from Zeszyty Naukowe. Organizacja i Zarządzanie/Politechnika Śląska

Securing the Future through Sustainability, Health, Education, and Technology – Brig. Dr. Rajiv Divekar et al. (eds)

28 Comparative Study of Fidget Toys on Adults' Attention Span and Concentration

Madhura Dinesh Hanchate[1]
Master of Design,
Design Department, Indian Institute of Information Technology, Design and Manufacturing, Jabalpur, India

Sarvesh Tripathi[2]
PhD Scholar,
Design Department, Indian Institute of Information Technology, Design and Manufacturing, Jabalpur, India

Tripti Singh[3]
Assistant Professor,
Design Department, Indian Institute of Information Technology, Design and Manufacturing, Jabalpur, India

Abstract

Fidget toys have been significantly popular amongst the masses and are believed to have multiple benefits, which includes stress relief, anxiety reduction, and even assistance with some serious conditions like attention deficit hyperactivity disorder i.e. ADHD. Various studies have been conducted on school-age children experiencing difficulties with attention and focus in the classroom, as well as adults facing similar challenges.

In order to explore these effects further, this study was conducted containing 36 non-clinical healthy adults. The participants were asked to perform various activities before being provided with three different fidget toys: a fidget spinner, a Pop-it toy, and a specially designed paper toy called 'Addux'. The 36 participants were further divided into three groups, A, B, C respectively; with each group assigned one of the three toys. The time taken by each participant to complete the tasks was recorded. Following this initial task, participants were given the freedom to the toys they were assigned as they wished during their own time. At final stage, all three groups were asked to repeat the same tasks while the time taken was recorded once again for comparison.

[1]22mds007@iiitdmj.ac.in, [2]20pdso02@iiitdmj.ac.in, [3]ts@iiitdmj.ac.in

DOI: 10.1201/9781003587200-28

Keeping the experiment as reference, an analysis was directed to make the comparison between the average time taken before and after by the participants in different groups. The findings discovered a significant enhancement in problem-solving speed with The Addux as compared to fidget spinners and pop-it toys. Precisely, arithmetic problem-solving time increased by 1.67 seconds as compared to fidget spinners and 2.34 seconds as compared to pop-it toys. Furthermore, in the category of jigsaw puzzles, it outperformed fidget spinners by 20.1 seconds and pop-it toys by 2 seconds in terms of solving time. Though, it should be taken in consideration that there was a decrease in speed among participants when it came to pattern memorization.

Keywords: Addux, ADHD, Fidget spinner, pop-it

1. Introduction

Fidget toys, such as fidget spinners, pop-its, and slime, have gained extensive popularity. Brand and manufacturers have been claiming that these toys relieve stress and anxiety. According to the National Institute of Health, in 2020 there were approximately 139.84 million adults affected by stubborn adult attention deficit hyperactivity disorder (ADHD) and 366.33 million adults affected by symptomatic adult ADHD globally, making up a incidence rate of 2.58% and 6.76% respectively. Research has shown that fidget toys can be helpful for children with ADHD, increasing their ability to focus in the classroom.

Though, most studies directed on fidget technology have focused on school-going children with ADHD. The influence of these toys on healthy adults and adults suffering from ADHD remains questionable. The following study will focus on a comparative analysis by testing 36 non-clinical samples of adults suffering from low concentration and low attention span. The test will be conducted using two existing fidget toys available the market and one new design called 'Addux'.

2. Literature Review

Amanda Rohrberger conducted research involving third-grade students to explore the effects of fidget toys on attention-to-task and on-task behavior in those with ADHD characteristics. Results showed that two out of three students showed decreased off-task behavior during intervention, while one student verified increased attention-to-task. However, it was noted that fidget toys did not impact attention-to-task for other students in the same classroom setting [1].

In her paper, Jennifer R. Persia explores the Impacts of Subtle Fidget Jewelry on Anxiety, Stress, and Attention. She discusses how fidgeting is a natural behavior in humans and an vital part of daily life that helps to alleviate cognitive load.

Persia suggests that there is potential for fidgeting to reduce anxiety and stress. To examine this further, she conducted a study with a nonclinical sample of 51 healthy adults. Participants were given a fidget ring to use during a test [3].

Likewise, in the paper Toy Design: Improving Learning Effectiveness for ADHD Students, the author talks about the growing prevalence of ADHD among school-going students and their research on this topic. The findings revealed that some children were distracted by toys designed for educational purposes [4].

In the paper To Fidget or Not to Fidget, That Is the Question: A Systematic Classroom Evaluation of Fidget Spinners Among Young Children With ADHD the conclusion showed that fidget spinners have been shown to have a damaging impact on the attentional functioning of young children with ADHD, even when used in combination with evidence-based classroom interventions[6]. These existing studies have shown mixed results. Most of them are done considering school going children. There is scope for an experiment with healthy adults dealing with low attention span.

3. Methodology

The experiment was held using three different fidget toys: a fidget spinner, a pop-it, and the Addux. A sample of 36 non-clinical adults, consisting of both males and females, were selected to participate in the experiment. The participants were given various tasks which are concentration-based, containing arithmetic calculations; zig saw puzzles and memorizing patterns. The time taken to complete these tasks by the subjects was recorded.

Fig. 28.1 Pop-it

A total of 35 individuals were interviewed and actively participated in the experiment, during the course of the project. Among them, 17 numbers of females and 18 males were assigned to perform the designated tasks.

Fig. 28.2 Fidget spinner

The age range of the participants crossed from 18 to 76 years old. To provide more detailed insights into this diverse group, one end of the spectrum involved an 18-year-old college student who engaged with social media for an average of 4-6 hours per day.

On the opposite side, there was a participant aged 76 who happened to be a retired college professor.

Other participants involved were faculty members from educational institutes, employees from corporate organizations, and postgraduate students.

To commence, participants were obligated to complete a personal information form, providing details such as age, education level, and job title. Afterward, specific tasks were assigned to each participant, and the duration of their completion was methodically documented.

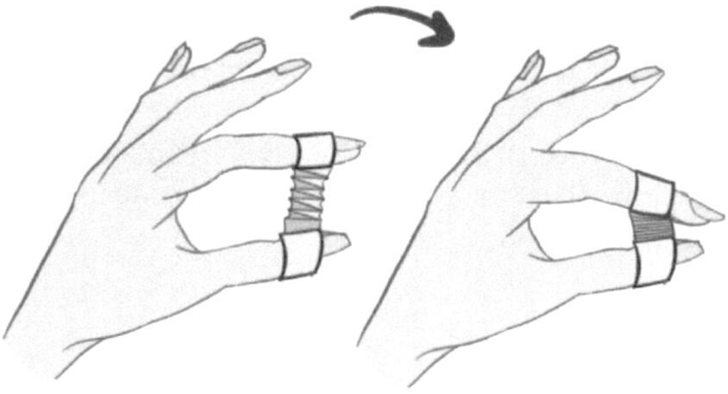

Fig. 28.3 Concept design for a fidget paper toy

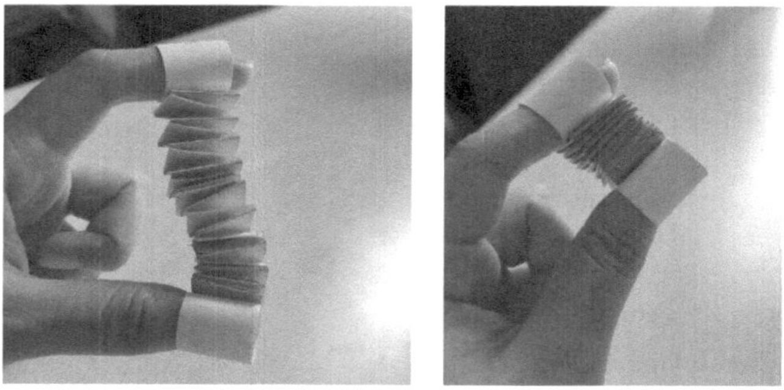

Fig. 28.4 Prototype for paper toy 'Addux'

After the task was completed, the samples were randomly distributed into three separate groups. Each group was then provided with a separate fidget toy.

Participants in the study were divided into three groups. Group 1 received a fidget spinner, Group 2 received a pop-it, and Group 3 received the Addux. They were instructed to use the fidget toys whenever they felt inclined to do so, during a period of approximately 1-2 hours while they were on their own.

Following the allocated timeframe, the participants were re-engaged in the same tasks previously assigned. They were offered with a new set of arithmetic problems, intricate puzzles, and pattern memorization exercises of same level of difficulty. The time taken by the participants was calculated for this session.

Table 28.1 Group 1 – Fidget spinner

Participant	arithmetic problem		zig saw puzzles		memorizing patterns	
time taken	Before	After	Before	After	Before	After
1	40 sec	37 sec	5 min 10 sec	4 min 50 sec	30 sec	27 sec
2	1 min 5 sec	60 sec	3 min 55 sec	3 min 50 sec	45 sec	50 sec
3	55 sec	56 sec	5 min 40 sec	5 min 56 sec	33 sec	48sec
4	37 sec	35 sec	4 min 5 sec	4 min	35 sec	28 sec
5	1 min 3 sec	1 min 6sec	6 min 7 sec	5 min 53 sec	27 sec	33 sec
6	54 sec	40 sec	4 min 39 sec	5 min	1 min 5 sec	60 sec
7	48 sec	45 sec	4 min 45 sec	4 min 22 sec	1 min 3 sec	57 sec
8	42 sec	40 sec	3 min 57 sec	3 min 45 sec	44 sec	50 sec
9	39 sec	35 sec	5 min 27sec	5min10 sec	23 sec	34 sec
10	50 sec	45 sec	3 min 46 sec	3 min 24 sec	27 sec	23 sec
11	25 sec	22 sec	3 min 5 sec	3 min 10 sec	56 sec	47 sec
12	48 sec	55 sec	4 min	3 min 55 sec	49 sec	45 sec
Average	47.17 sec	44.67 sec	4 min 36.3 sec	4 min 26.4 sec	41.42 sec	41.83 sec

Table 28.2 Group 2 – pop-it

Participant	arithmetic problem		zig saw puzzles		memorizing patterns	
time taken	Before	After	Before	After	Before	After
1	43 sec	39 sec	4 min 11 sec	4 min 3 sec	27 sec	25 sec
2	57 sec	53 sec	2 min 56 sec	2 min 20 sec	40 sec	35 sec
3	1 min 6 sec	60 sec	3 min 45 sec	3 min 56 sec	45 sec	33 sec
4	54 sec	53 sec	5 min 56sec	4 min 50 sec	20 sec	30 sec
5	27 sec	23 sec	5 min 34 sec	5 min 44 sec	55 sec	1 min
6	44 sec	48 sec	6 min 10 sec	6 min	43 sec	54 sec
7	1 min 12 sec	1 min 2 sec	4 min 5 sec	4 min	30 sec	34 sec
8	45 sec	48 sec	5 min 33 sec	5 min 30 sec	1 min 37 sec	2 min
9	22 sec	20 sec	2 min 39 sec	2 min 15 sec	2 min	1 min 30 sec
10	45sec	50 sec	4 min 45 sec	3 min	30 sec	25 sec
11	23 sec	30 sec	3 min	2 min 55 sec	27 sec	30 sec
12	55 sec	45 sec	4 min 2 sec	3 min 3 sec	23 sec	40 sec
Average	46.08 sec	44.25 sec	4 min 23 sec	3 min 58 sec	46.42 sec	48 sec

Table 28.3 Group 3 – Addux

Participant	arithmetic problem		zig saw puzzles		memorizing patterns	
time taken	Before	After	Before	After	Before	After
1	34 sec	39 sec	5 min 4 sec	4 min 55 sec	34 sec	30 sec
2	1 min 30 sec	1 min 2 sec	5 min	4 min 50 sec	60 sec	55 sec
3	1 min 6 sec	60 sec	3 min 5 sec	3 min	22 sec	25 sec
4	39 sec	42 sec	5 min 4 sec	4 min 45 sec	25 sec	20 sec
5	56 sec	50 sec	5 min 23sec	5 min 10 sec	54 sec	45 sec
6	42 sec	40 sec	3 min 4 sec	3 min 10 sec	1 min 12 sec	1 min 20 sec
7	33 sec	40 sec	2 min 6 sec	2 min	43 sec	40 sec
8	1 min 3 sec	1 min 4 sec	5 min	5 min 4 sec	1 min 2 sec	50 sec
9	55 sec	40 sec	2 min 45 sec	2 min 40 sec	53 sec	57 sec
10	35 sec	32 sec	5 min 37 sec	5 min 40 sec	33 sec	25 sec
11	29sec	28 sec	3 min 55 sec	4 min	43 sec	40 sec
12	25 sec	20 sec	2 min 4 sec	2 min	35 sec	40 sec
Average	47.25 sec	43.08 sec	4 min 12 sec	3 min 42 sec	42.12 sec	42.25 sec

4. Results and Discussion

The task assignment process was tracked, and the participants were given fidget toys. After completing the task, the results were compared. As specified previously, the participants were divided into three groups; each assigned a different fidget toy: fidget spinner, pop-it, and the Addux. The time it took for participants to complete the task before and after using the fidget toys was recorded for each group.

Group A of 12 participants was given fidget spinners to use during tasks including arithmetic problems, jigsaw puzzles, and memorizing patterns. The results showed that after using the fidget toys, 25% of the participants took more time for arithmetic problems while 75% took less time. Similarly, for jigsaw puzzles, 25% took more time and 75% took less time. Finally, when it came to memorizing patterns, 41.67% took more time and 58.33% took less time after using the fidget toys.

The average time was calculated for different tasks. For arithmetic problems, the average time before was 47.17 seconds, and after was 44.67 seconds. For jigsaw puzzles, the average time before was 4 minutes and 36.3 seconds, and after was 4 minutes and 26.4 seconds. Finally, for memorizing patterns, the average time before was 41.42 seconds, and after was 41.83 seconds.

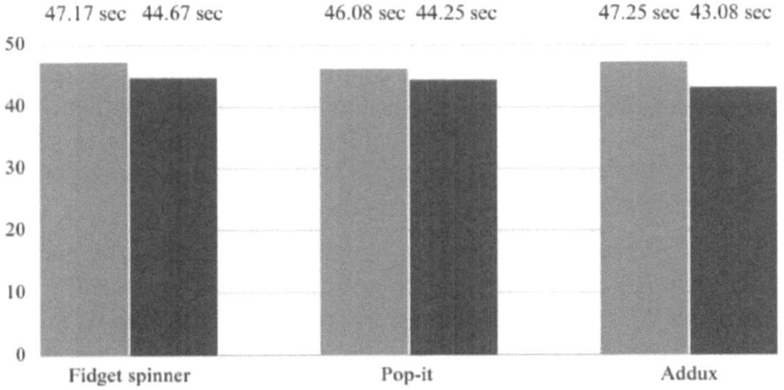

Fig. 28.5 Comparison of average time taken by the samples to perform arithmetic problems

A group of 12 participants in Group B was given pop-it fidget toys to use during tasks containing arithmetic problems, jigsaw puzzles, and pattern memorization. The results revealed that after using the fidget toys, 33.33% of the participants took more time for arithmetic problems, while 66.67% took less time. Likewise, for jigsaw puzzles, 16.67% took more time and 83.33% took less time. In terms of pattern memorization, 58.33% took more time and 41.67% took less time after using the fidget toys.

In order to calculate the average times for each task, prior to using the fidget toys, participants spent an average of 46.08 seconds on arithmetic problems, which decreased to an average of 44.25 seconds after utilizing the toys. For jigsaw puzzles, the average time before was 4 minutes and 23 seconds, which decreased to an average of 3 minutes and 58 seconds after using the fidget toys. Finally, for pattern memorization, participants took an average of 46.42 seconds before using the toys and this increased slightly to an average of 48 seconds after using them.

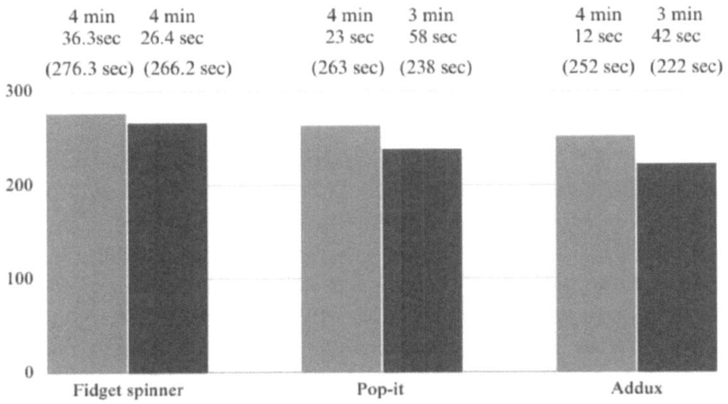

Fig. 28.6 Comparison of average time taken by the samples to perform zig saw puzzles

The study was done with a group of 12 participants in Group C. They were given the Addux to use during tasks such as arithmetic problems, jigsaw puzzles, and pattern memorization. The findings showed that after using the fidget toys, 33.33% of the participants took more time for arithmetic problems, while 66.67% took less time. For jigsaw puzzles, 33.33% participants took more time and 66.67% participants took less time. In terms of pattern memorization, 33.33% took more time and 66.67% took less time after using the fidget toys.

To calculate the average times for each task, participants spent an average of 47.25 seconds on arithmetic problems before using the fidget toys, which decreased to an average of 43.08 seconds after incorporating the toys into their tasks. The average time decreased for jigsaw puzzles decreased from 4 minutes and 12 seconds to an average of 3 minutes and 42 seconds after using the fidget toys. There was only a slight increase from an average of 42.12 seconds before using the toys to an average of 42.25 seconds after their utilization when it comes to pattern memorization.

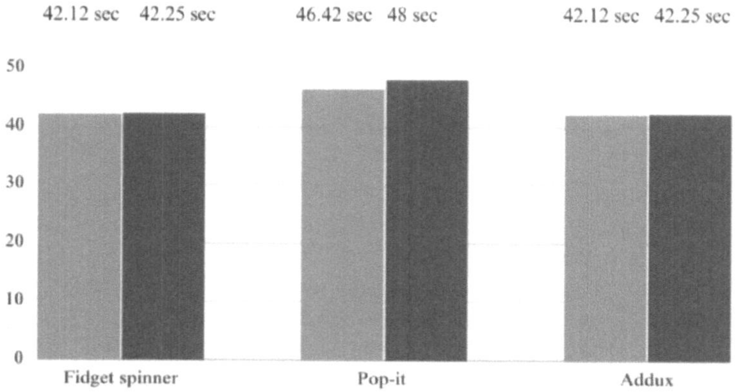

Fig. 28.7 Comparison of average time taken by the samples to perform pattern memorization

5. Conclusion

With respect to the results of the experiments engaging tasks that require concentration and attention using three different toys, noteworthy differences were seen among the participants. In Group A, people utilizing fidget spinners demonstrated a 2.5-second decrease in solving arithmetic problems, a 9.9-second decrease in completing jigsaw puzzles, and a marginal increase of 0.41 seconds in pattern memorization (Fig. 28.8). Alternatively, Group B participants utilizing pop-it toys exhibited a reduction of 1.83 seconds in arithmetic problem-solving time, an impressive 28-second decrease in jigsaw puzzle completion time, and a slightly longer duration of 1.58 seconds for pattern memorization tasks (Fig. 28.9). Individuals in Group C who utilized the Addux experienced significant improvements with a decrease of 4.17 seconds in solving arithmetic problems, a remarkable 30-second decline in completing jigsaw puzzles, and an increase of 13 seconds for pattern memorization tasks (Fig. 28.10).

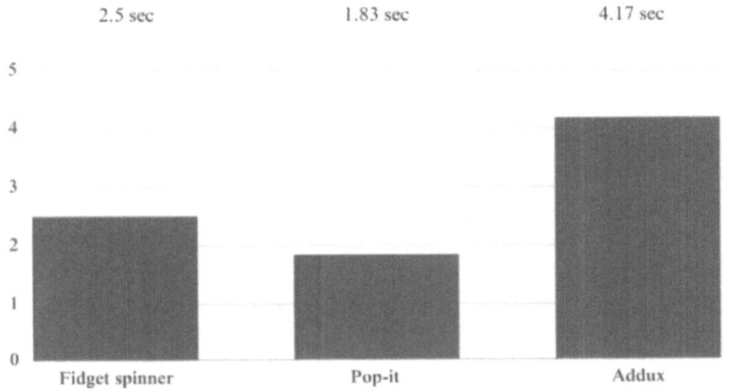

Fig. 28.8 Time decreased in arithmetic problems

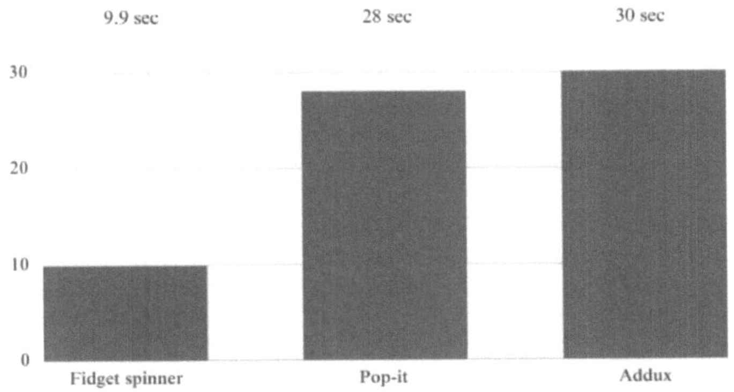

Fig. 28.9 Time decreased in jigsaw puzzles

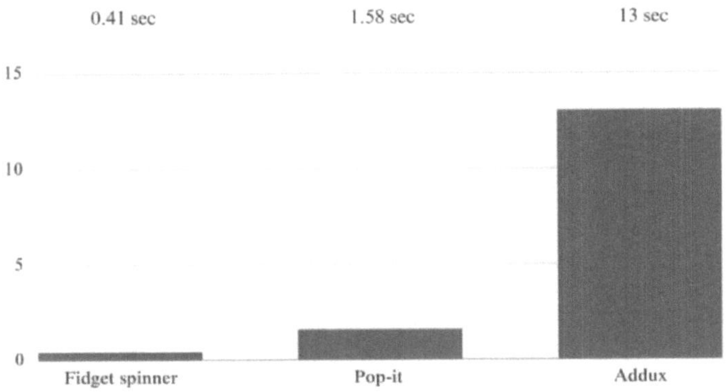

Fig. 28.10 Time increases in pattern memorization

The Addux proved a significant increase in problem-solving speed compared to fidget spinners and pop-it toys. It improved arithmetic problem-solving time by 1.67 seconds compared to fidget spinners and 2.34 seconds compared to pop-it toys. Also, in the department of jigsaw puzzles, it outperformed fidget spinners by 20.1 seconds and pop-it toys by 2 seconds in terms of solving time. But it has decreased the speed of the participants when it came to pattern memorization significantly.

These findings imply that these toys have varying impacts on task performance and highlight the potential benefits they may offer for cognitive abilities and improving focus. The application of fidget toys resulted in a noticeable decrease in the duration required to complete arithmetic problem-solving and jigsaw puzzle tasks. While the impact varied among certain participants, there was an overall boost in performance across all participants for several tasks.

References

1. Hulac, D.M., Aspiranti, K., Kriescher, S. *et al.* A Multisite Study of the Effect of Fidget Spinners on Academic Performance. *Contemp School Psychol* 25, 582–588 (2021).
2. Mei Yee LUI, Lok Yiu Wong, Ho Yin MAK And Yi-Teng SHIH , Toy Design: Improving Learning Effectiveness For ADHD Students , Proceedings of the 24th International Conference on Engineering and Product Design Education: Disrupt, Innovate, Regenerate and Transform, E and PDE 2022.
3. Michael Karlesky, Katherine Isbister Understanding Fidget Widgets: Exploring the Design Space of Embodied Self-Regulation, NordiCHI '16: Proceedings of the 9th Nordic Conference on Human-Computer Interaction
4. Paulo A. Graziano, Alexis M. Garcia, and Taylor D. Landis, To Fidget or Not to Fidget, That Is the Question: A Systematic Classroom Evaluation of Fidget Spinners Among Young Children With ADHD, Journal of Attention Disorders: Volume 24 Issue 1, January 2020
5. Persia, Jennifer. *Examining the Impacts of Subtle Fidget Jewelry On Anxiety, Stress, and Attention.* 2023
6. Reza Koiler, Austin Schimme, Elham Bakhshipour, Patricia A. Shewokis, Nancy Getchell, The Impact of Fidget Spinners on Fine Motor Skills in Individuals with and without ADHD: An Exploratory Analysis, Journal of Behavioral and Brain Science: Vol.12 No.3, March 2022
7. Rohrberger, Amanda, "The Efficacy of Fidget Toys in a School Setting for Children with Attention Difficulties and Hyperactivity" (2011). Ithaca College Theses. 330.
8. Taylor Kirby, The Effect of Fidget Spinners on Attention and Anxiety in Typically Developing Children, Washburn University.

Note: All the figures and tables in this chapter were made by the authors.

Securing the Future through Sustainability, Health, Education, and Technology – Brig. Dr. Rajiv Divekar et al. (eds)

29 Factors Influencing Students to Pursue Digital Homeschooling in India

Naval Lawande*, Bhawana Singh
Symbiosis Institute of Management Studies,
Symbiosis International (Deemed University),
Pune, India

ABSTRACT

The novel coronavirus outbreak has profoundly altered the traditional structure of businesses across sectors. The most affected sector was education sector, the Sudden lockdown was proved to be headlong for the students. But this new challenge has shown us a new way of living, in which parents can be more involved in the education of their children. With most companies now shifting towards work from home, parents are considering Digital Homeschooling as one of the options. It is quite popular in western countries. But in India, there is no law or legal authority for home schooling, but even though some parents are shifting towards Home schooling. The parents are willing to provide customized education and more involvement to their kids for their academic and non-academic activities. To see the future of Digital Homeschooling in India, and what are the top factors that influence students and parents to consider Home Schooling. The data was collected in the form of Likert scale questions, later to analyze the Factor Analysis was conducted and we find out that the top factors which influence parents and students to start Digital Homeschooling are *Parents involvement, customized education. Instability in society, Peer pressure, Social and cultural differences, Consistent Change*. And, people are willing to consider Digital Homeschooling in the future, but they are facing some challenges. To overcome these challenges, the new study is designed in which all types of schools (Traditional, Digital and, Homeschooling) collaborate with each other and provide a positive educational environment for students, which will be called *Seam-Study*.

KEYWORDS: Digitalization, Ed-Tec, Education, Homeschooling, Parents

*Corresponding author: naval.lawande@gmail.com

DOI: 10.1201/9781003587200-29

1. Introduction

The field of education technology, also known as Ed-Tech, is an ever-evolving industry that is consistently adapting to new advancements in technology and innovative learning techniques. However, the COVID-19 pandemic has presented unprecedented challenges for the industry, especially in regards to remote learning. With many companies having shifted to remote work, the education sector faces unique obstacles in providing digital access to students in remote areas. The global lockdowns over the past few months have had a significant impact on the education sector, which lacks established infrastructure, making it difficult to navigate the new normal. Additionally, the pandemic has led to an increase in homeschooling, as more parents seek personalized education options for their children. In response to these challenges, the Indian government has launched the new Education Policy 2020, which aims to transform India into a global knowledge superpower by offering customized education directly to the students. Digital homeschooling is expected to play a critical role in the future education market, but currently remains largely unregulated in India. This research paper explores the various factors that influence students to pursue digital homeschooling and the advantages and disadvantages of this alternative form of education. The paper also highlights the potential of digital homeschooling in India and how it can transform the education landscape. With the help of technology, personalized education can be accessible to students in remote areas, helping bridge the digital divide and ensuring equal opportunities for all.

Digital homeschooling has become increasingly important, offering flexibility and personalized learning experiences to students. Online resources can tailor curriculum, enhancing engagement and academic outcomes. Additionally, digital platforms foster collaboration and community. However, access to technology remains a barrier for many families, and concerns about screen time require thoughtful technology integration. Digital homeschooling is an alternative to traditional classroom education facilitated by new technologies and the COVID-19 pandemic. It offers personalized and adaptable learning experiences, but faces challenges such as limited socialization opportunities, the necessary expertise of parents, and issues of equity in technology access and affordability. The effectiveness of digital homeschooling compared to traditional classroom education is a subject of debate. Further research is essential to understand its impact on student learning outcomes, educational equity, and the future of education.

2. Literature Review

Coronavirus (COVID-19) has started in December 2019. With worldwide sudden lockdown, people had adapted to "Stay at home" and learned how to work from home overnight. Even the companies had to change their policies and provide the facilities for work from home. Those institute/Companies which has Digital availability were able to survive this pandemic, but other institutional bodies which do not have Digital resources or infrastructure are most affected by this pandemic. Just like Educational Institutions. It is hard to say, "what will happen after COVID-19", but the need and impact of digitalization will increase for sure. According to a recent study, the educational experiences of children aged four to eight do not follow national policies, often leading to multiple transitions between home, preschool, and school (Benjamin Alcott, 2020). Since then, the Education industry of India has been evolving. After independence, several changes were adopted like compulsory and free education. The enrolment and attendance rates have been raised so significantly in recent years, due to privatization in schools. But to reduce the inequality and monopoly of private schools, government has initiated several schemes and initiatives. All the Education institutes have been closed, in which more than 157 crore students across the 191 countries, have been affected by this pandemic. Which is over 91% of the student's population worldwide. Even in India, it has affected over 32 crore students. (Sharma, 2020). All the schools and colleges were closed down and the government has enforced Janata Curfew, which constrained all citizens to stay at home and not to go out. It will help to contain the spread of Coronavirus into the community and especially children and the young generation. In Lee's research, homeschooling was examined across 31 families in Taipei and Hong Kong. The study showcased its increasing popularity as an innovative choice for education, particularly in light of the pandemic. These families selected homeschooling as a result of their disappointment with the conventional Chinese school system's focus on the child, and instead utilized a variety of diverse and hybridized educational methods (Lee, 2023). Home education is an increasingly popular option in Australia that is entirely legal. Typically led by female caregivers with above-average educational attainment, this approach is often chosen for ideological or practical reasons. Families who opt for it share a conviction that traditional education may not be the best fit for their children (Eileen V. Slater, 2022). Due to Unscheduled closure of all the educational institute, the students, teachers, and institutes have to improve their digital skills to again kick start the educational activities (Hector-Alexander, 2020). This situation leads us to think, now is the high time to make our education institute fully digitalized. It is important to switch our system to online and digital format (Williamson, 2017).Due any challenges, it had always made humans adapt and innovate new technology to overcome it. After this pandemic, we have to rethink the education system in the age of technology (Desroches et al., 2021). We have to reduce the gap that has occurred due to the pandemic. Evaluation of education in India was started way back to the times of Indus valley civilization, in which India's first university was formed Nalanda university (Singh & Benyoucef, 2013). (Barbara Skinner, 2023) study on working parents in Northern Ireland found that parents lack confidence in their pedagogical skills, are exhausted, and experience strained family relationships. The study suggests that effective homeschooling could be facilitated if employers provided flexible working hours for at least one parent, accommodating children's educational needs. A recent study by (Bower, 2021) revealed the need for schools to become more inclusive of children and families, regardless of their unique needs, sexuality, and religious beliefs. To achieve this, schools should provide additional training, awareness, and policies that reflect an evolving society. Homeschooling may also be more effective in promoting inclusivity. But the main problem that the government faced was the expansion of all the facilities and to reach the masses.

(Hoskins, 2023) conducted a study on home-schooling within low-income households with primary-aged children in England, highlighting the significance of comprehending their distinct experiences during this phase. Due to technology enhancement, the quality and methods of teaching have been changing. According to a recent study, the COVID-19 pandemic resulted in an increase in at-home digital activities among children of all ages. It was observed that older children demonstrated a greater preference for increased digital usage than their younger counterparts. Additionally, the study found a positive correlation between the frequency of digital usage and participation in home literacy activities (Susan Sonnenschein, 2021).

2.1 Timeline for the Evolution of Different Types of Schools/ Institutions in India

In Fig. 29.1 the evolution of different timeline for schools are shown.

Fig. 29.1 Evolution of schools

Traditional/Regular Schools

The schools in which students go on a daily basis. In these schools, the percentage of innovation and new methods that are introduced and invent, way too higher than the other schools. The percentage change in educational achievements is very high in India, as compared to other developing countries (Kingdon, 2007). But due to some challenges, and problems new types of school/teaching methods have always been introduced.

Challenges that Lead to Start Boarding Schools in India

The availability of higher level of education in every part of India is very low. Therefore, living in a new place can be very expensive. To overcome this problem, the more boarding schools were invented.

Boarding schools: The schools in which students have full-time residence service inside the school campus. The boarding schools are used from a very long time; kings used to send their children to Ashrams. Before, this service was used by upper class only (Levine, 2014). The government has started various schools for the general public for a better higher education. They also have introduced "Sainik school". To increase the female education, there are a lot of women boarding school facility has been set up (Trennert, 1982). The boarding schools have grown substantially over a period.

Challenges that Lead to Start Distance Learning in India

The challenges are sometimes the students are not able to attend regular classes due to some personal family problems, in some areas, females are not allowed to go out for school daily, working-class who want to enhance their qualification. To overcome these problems, the distance learning programs, and institutions was invented.

Distance learning (ODL): Worldwide, out of 19.3 million over 6.6 million students are perusing courses via distance learning, till 2017 (Bastrikin, 2020). Distance learning is a mode of teaching in which the students did not get face to face interaction, but they will get study notes and related materials. (Distance Learning Market in India 2015-2019, 2015). Over 22% of all the students, that took admission were in an Open distance learning system. And the industry is growing fast because of the rise of 22% in the demand for Higher education in India, as the highest percent of the students in ODL pursue Higher education (Suneja, 2012). The industry is inventing new ways to lure new customers, they are using online methods to provide easy and comfortable services. Top ODL institutions in India are IGNOU, SOL, SCDL (Bhambri, 2020).

Challenges that Lead to Start Disabled schools

The challenges were unavailability of Special facilities for the disable students (Divyang), uncomfortable with regular students, the Grading system, comparison with regular students (Borup et al., 2019). Due to these challenges 75% of disabled students do not attend schools. In India, over 1.7% of the total child population is disabled to overcome these problems, the government started special schools for divyang (Sidana & Pandey, 2023).

Schools for Disabled: These schools provide special facilities corresponding to the disability, also provide personal teaching, learning aids, and tools specially designed for them, mobility assistance, support services. They get customized teaching in these special schools. They are also using technology to provide better and cooperative services to Divyang students. Many disabled students attend National Institute of Open Schooling.

Challenges that Lead to Start Online/ Digital Schools

The challenges were professional courses, which are not time-bound, the need for Digitalization in education, online skill-based courses, inexpensive courses, requirement of flexible timing. To overcome these requirements and demands of the students worldwide, a platform of online courses was invented.

Online/Digital courses: The online platform provides connectivity among the students and the content providers. It plays an extremely critical role in the online education ecosystem worldwide. Corporate tie-ups have helped this industry to reach the correct target audience (KPMG-Google, 2017). To enhance the knowledge or understanding of the skills on an individual basis, the students required a method of training in which there will be the availability of factors like time flexibility, cheap, with good content. For this demand, the online courses were launched (MOOCs). They also provide certificate, proof of completion, which is recognized by universities. In 2012, it was just a prototype product, but after introduction the growth rate was impressive (Waks, 2016). Advanced communication and information technology are used in this Ed-Tech industry. During this pandemic, these MOOCs are the most reliable source for enhancing the required skills. This market is expected to grow and register CAGR over 29% during 2019-2024 period (More, 2020) There are also advanced professional courses, which are conducted by the higher level of authorities in India, like Chattered Accountant (CA), Chartered Financial Analyst (CFA), etc.

Challenges that Lead to Start Home Schooling

Children whose parents are capable and what to teach their children themselves. The new need was more involvement of parents in their children education, a better relationship between parents and children, flexibility in teaching, customized education, according to their needs, parents will have more control over children learning and will be able to provide more experiential learning (Arora, Homeschooling in India – Pros and Cons, 2018). Due to these challenges, the concept of Homeschooling was introduced.

Home Schooling: Homeschooling is not that pervasive in India right now, but the numbers are expanding, especially in metropolitan cities, approx. 2% to 8% per annum over the last few years worldwide. Also, Homeschooling is not yet regulated by any government authorities. In this, the children get their formal education from their parents or personal tutors at home instead of schools (Boonanegpat & Kitcharoen, 2023).

With these evolving challenges and problems in the past education system, the new demand was created each time at the different levels. Which leads to form a new institute, fulfilling all those demands at that time (Arora, 2018). There are 260 million students in the Indian education ecosystem. It has been transforming towards technology, the education industry is now altering into Education technology industry (Ed-Tech) (Allan Collins; R. H., 2018)

2.2 Problem Statement

Challenges Faced by Students During this Pandemic (Covid-19) Crisis

COVID-19 has affected students' education, causing disruptions, unequal opportunities, and a lack of digital infrastructure. We can overcome these challenges by digitizing institutions, offering personalized education, engaging parents, providing individual attention, specialized instruction for gifted students, promoting social interaction, and ensuring students have the necessary resources for education at home. Together, we can create a brighter future for our students. These are some new problems that have been emerged during the unscheduled lockdown of schools (Onyema, 2020). For that, we need to find a solution in which all types of schools will be involved, and all the students will get benefit from that solution. We need to alter the problem of "Stay at homes" into our benefit for future reference.

Further, we will be discussing all the factors that are influencing students to stay at home and continue their education from there. The future of homeschooling in India? What will happen after Covid-19? (Ted Neil. Nancy Bonner, 2014)

"A far cry from the 'one size fits all the formula' of learning, HDS will liberate children from the chalk and talk method and homework after school," and from just sitting at home and learning by themselves. It will give them new freedom to find out their own way of learning and experimenting. (Ghosh, 2019)

3. Methodology

This study was conducted on education sector, which is considered as one of the top growing sectors among Indian industries. Due to recent growth in Ed-Tech industry, it is expected to reach 360.3 billion by 2024, expanding at a CAGR of ~43.85% during the period of 2019-2024 (wire, 2020). With the new education policy, several changes are expected to happen in near future. The new methods and policies are going to change our traditional method of schooling. With work from home, parents are getting involved in their children education. Which let people to consider Homeschooling. Before there were no research conducted on Digital Homeschooling in India.

3.1 Research Purpose

No significant research has been conducted on digital homeschooling in India previously. The concept is relatively in the nascent stages. Through this research paper, the aim is to explore the potential of Digital Homeschooling in India post-COVID-19. The study includes collecting data from students and parents to understand if they want to continue with Digital Homeschooling after the pandemic ends. The **research questions** for the study are:

[1] What is the future of Digital Homeschooling in India?

[2] Which are the top five factors that are influencing individuals to start Digital Homeschooling?

[3] Will Digital Homeschooling become a new normal for the students, even post pandemic?

[4] Will the parent's involvement in their children's education increase?

3.2 Research Methodology

Our scholarly article leverages Factor Analysis to pinpoint the driving forces behind students' preference for digital homeschooling. By surveying 325 participants and scrutinizing the collected data, we uncovered the interrelated variables that impact students' decision to pursue digital homeschooling. Our findings offer valuable perspectives for educators, policymakers, and parents seeking to delve into the realm of digital homeschooling.

3.3 Sample Collection

The survey was conducted on 325 individuals. The details are given below:

The respondents belong to different categories like students, parents & none. Different categories of respondent are Students were 67.3%, Parents (20.8%) and none (11.9%). The age group of the respondents are in the range of 10 to 60. The highest respondent is from age group of 21-30 age group (71.3%), then 31 – 50 age group (14.9%), and so on. Qualifications of respondents are from various categories like 10th class (17.4%), 12th class 31.4%), Graduation (26.5%), post-graduation (21.6%) and doctorate (PhD) (3.1%). The data was collected from all over the country. The objective of this study was to gain a comprehensive understanding of the factors that influence parents and students to choose homeschooling. To accomplish this, the researchers conducted a thorough analysis of diverse literature and research available on the topic. The study focused on 17 essential factors that were found to play a crucial role in the decision-making process. These factors encompass a wide range of elements, including societal instability that could negatively impact traditional schools, difficulties in commuting to schools, affordability of fees and other educational expenses, parental involvement in their children's education, facilities in the education institute, time taken in education activities, facilities in special schools catering to specific needs, the crowd or environment of the education institute, bullying, peer pressure, suboptimal academic performance in traditional schools, climate conditions that affect school attendance, pollution that could lead to health issues, age differences that could impact learning, limited socializing in traditional schools, cultural differences that could lead to discrimination and consistent changes in schools that could disrupt a child's education.

4. Data Analysis

For the purpose of this analysis, the methodological approach employed is that of factor analysis, which serves to ascertain the predominant factors exerting influence within a dataset. Factor analysis is instrumental in isolating particular factors from an extensive array of variables, guided by their correlations and relative importance. This analytical technique facilitates the extraction of covariances among all involved variables, thereby enabling the computation of standardized scores, as outlined by (Carver & Nash, 2012) and further corroborated by other studies (Bhardwaj, 2018).

4.1 KMO and Bartlett's Test

Table 29.1 shows a correlation matrix from SPSS for our study's descriptor variables. Factor analysis relies on these variables being correlated. If they are not, or the correlation is very low, factor analysis may not be valid. It's expected that some variables will highly correlate and form a factor, helping to reveal underlying structures in the data set.

Table 29.1 KMO and Bartlett's test

Kaiser-Meyer-Olkin Measure of Sampling Adequacy.		.893
Bartlett's Test of Sphericity	Approx. Chi-Square	1978.170
	df	136
	Sig.	.000

When conducting correlation studies, the KMO statistic is a helpful tool as it measures sampling adequacy and provides a score between 0.5 to 1. A KMO of 0.893 indicates that the data quality is good. Additionally, Bartlett's test of sphericity validates factor analysis and confirms that the correlation matrix is not an identity matrix, as shown by the Chi-Square statistic of 1978.170 and 136 degrees of freedom.

4.2 Total Variance

Included in the data are the initial Eigenvalues, extraction of squared loadings, and the sum of rotation of square loadings. The combined variance explained by the 17 factors is 17, which matches the number of variables. For subsequent analysis, the top five factors with an Eigenvalue greater than 1 will be considered.

1. $6.036/17 \times 100 = 35.507\%$
2. $1.375/17 \times 100 = 8.085\%$
3. $1.161/17 \times 100 = 6.832\%$
4. $1.004/17 \times 100 = 5.904\%$
5. $1.001/17 \times 100 = 5.888\%$

The first five factors combined, accounts for 62.216% of the total variance.

4.3 Rotating the Variables – Component Matrix

The component matrix that has been rotated for interpretability is displayed in Table 29.2. To ensure the validity of the results, we are examining the Threshold Value (Assumption), which is set at 0.720. Factor 1 contains five variables with high loading factors, including Parents Involvement (0.815) and Academics (0.791). Factor 2 has two loading factors, namely Socializing (0.770) and Peer

Table 29.2 Rotated component matrix

Rotated Component Matrix[a]					
	Component				
	1	2	3	4	5
Parents involvement	**.815**	.037	.077	.097	-.083
Academics	**.791**	-.050	-.013	.038	-.020
Instability in society	**.773**	.243	.115	-.049	.064
Consistent change in schools	**.768**	.021	.184	.063	.045
Cultural difference	**.726**	.157	.258	.028	-.063
Climate conditions	.687	.250	.036	-.006	.121
Pollution	.629	.309	.160	-.104	.102
Crowded environment	.573	.332	-.020	.017	-.159
Affordability	.526	.449	.268	-.044	-.061
Facilities in Special schools	.511	.184	-.423	-.120	-.016
Socializing	.009	**.770**	-.115	-.062	-.060
Peer Pressure	.178	**.720**	.143	.046	.092
Facilities in education Institute	.481	.615	.197	.067	-.032
Time Taken	.214	.069	**.750**	-.181	.041
Age Difference	.188	.154	.493	.316	-.153
Travelling inconvenience	.003	-.025	-.025	**.935**	.025
Bullying	.016	.000	-.041	.007	**.965**

Pressure (0.720). Factor 3, on the other hand, has a single high loading factor: Time taken (0.750). Factor 4's high loading factor is travel inconvenience (0.935), and Factor 5's is Bullying (0.965).

4.4 Identifying the Top Factors

Top five factors that are most important in influencing factors for students and parents to consider Home digital schooling in India in the future.

Factor 1 – Customized education: Children and parents are looking forward for customized education according to the children's needs. As the response of every kid is different from one another. And for teachers it is hard to concentrate each student according to their need. With the cultural and social changes in societies it affects the student's regular study.

Factor 2 – Social Pressure: One of the common problems that students face now days is to be social pressure due to social and cultural difference among the students. Getting involved in groups and classes are getting harder and harder, socializing is one of the common challenges faced by students. The peer pressure in regular schools are so high that students are getting more depressed according to earlier times.

Factor 3 – Time Constrain: The time, that is consumed in activities other than study is quite high in traditional schools. Time spent for travelling, time spent for other co-curricular activity in which some students have no interest.

Factor 4 – Inconvenience while Travelling: Public transport is used by more than half of the students in India. The problems faced by students during travelling are quite high the weather condition, the crowd, unavailability of seats, time constrain for public transport. But the biggest problem that female students face is misconduct while travelling.

Factor 5 – Intimidate circumstances: Government are taking several steps and making policies to make a healthy environment for students in education institutes. And with severe punishments, the rate of bullying is reducing. But still the people are facing direct and indirect bullying of students, which can cause difficulties are that students to cope up with their studies. These are the main factors we find with the factor analysis that the parents and students want to start Digital Homeschooling soon.

5. Discussion on Research Questions

5.1 Parents Involvement in Children's Education

Amidst the ongoing COVID-19 pandemic, a comprehensive survey was conducted to gauge the changes in parental involvement in their children's education. The results indicate an increased eagerness among parents to devote more time and attention to their child's learning experience. The study examined various aspects of parental engagement, such as:

- The amount of time parents spends interacting with their children,
- The extent to which parents focus on both academic and extracurricular activities,
- Parents' ability to adapt education to their child's unique needs at home,
- The feasibility of juggling educational duties with professional commitments,
- The potential for hiring personal tutors to help busy working parents,
- The economic viability of homeschooling options.

The study found that parents are keen on being more involved in their children's education to provide a tailored learning experience. However, working parents face challenges in juggling their jobs and homeschooling duties. Traditional tutoring is less favored, with homeschooling being a popular choice for those who can afford it. The research highlights the need for new solutions that help parents balance work and home education, particularly during the pandemic.

5.2 Will Home Digital Schooling become a New Normal?

The trend of remote work has presented a valuable chance for parents to increase their quality time with their children and assume a greater role in their education. This transformation has the potential to become the standard, empowering parents to prioritize their family life alongside their career aspirations.

5.3 Future of Digital Homeschooling in India

The COVID-19 pandemic has resulted in a significant increase in digital homeschooling in India. Unfortunately, this form of education lacks proper regulation and recognition as a legitimate educational option. It is essential for the Government to establish a legal framework to regulate homeschooling and acknowledge it as an acceptable form of education. Recent studies demonstrate that parents and students are keen on pursuing digital homeschooling for a more structured learning experience.

6. Drawbacks and New Possibilities

Drawbacks: Digital homeschooling in India faces several issues that necessitate government regulation. Key challenges include limited peer interaction, potential delays in learning when parents are unavailable, the significant time and financial investment required from parents to cover all subjects and experiential learning, and the need for parents to have a good educational background to effectively teach at home. (Arora, Homeschooling in India – Pros and Cons, 2018)

New Possibilities: For the customized education system for children at home, it is necessary to see the difficulties and challenges related to the home schooling. And to resolve these challenges, what should be the new ways of education after Homeschooling, which will include all the positive factors of Digital Homeschooling and Traditional schooling?

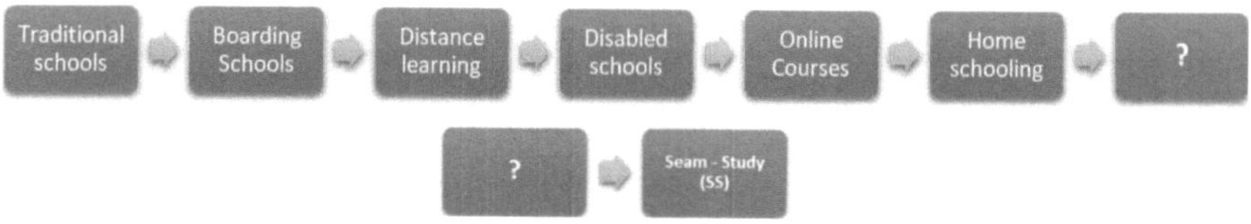

Fig. 29.2 What can be the new step after digital homeschooling?

Seam-Study: Seam-study is a cutting-edge approach that blends Home Schooling, Traditional Schooling, and Digital Schooling to create a holistic learning experience for students. The curriculum is tailored to prioritize each topic and includes hands-on learning opportunities, allowing parents to be involved in customizing their child's education. An impressive 87.9% of survey respondents expressed interest in this approach, which emphasizes parental involvement, personalized education, self-directed learning, hands-on experiences, and a well-rounded mix of social and cultural environments. The syllabus can be organized by topic (preferred by 60.4% of respondents) or subject (preferred by 39.6% of respondents). This can be a way to introduce Digital Homeschooling in India by modifying it by a new approach. This pandemic had shown us that nothing can be ordinary, with the new world the acceptance of new changes in our life is important.

7. Future Scope of Research

Future research could delve into various aspects of digital homeschooling in India, a concept gaining traction due to the COVID-19 pandemic. A deeper insight could be gained by interviewing children and parents involved in digital homeschooling. It would be valuable to explore why homeschooling has not been widely adopted in India and examine the potential shift from traditional to digital homeschooling. Additionally, the feasibility and integration of the "Seam-Study" method within India's educational framework merit investigation, particularly in terms of its practical application and alignment with new education policies.

8. Conclusion

Results from a study indicate that children's participation trajectories in the early years (age four to eight) do not reflect the age or grade norms specified by national educational policies. Moreover, far from being linear, children's educational pathways entail considerable back and forth between home, preschool, and school. (Susan Sonnenschein, 2021)Recent research suggests that digital homeschooling should be legally recognized as a valid form of education for students in India. This study reveals that parents and students prefer digital homeschooling due to its ability to offer customized education plans and increased parental involvement in their children's education. Several factors, such as societal instability, peer pressure, social and cultural differences, and constant changes, motivate parents and students to shift towards digital homeschooling from traditional schools. The ongoing pandemic has further reinforced this trend, with parents working from home and seeking to play a more active role in their children's education. However, if digital homeschooling is not recognized as a viable form of education, people will seek alternative options. To address this issue, the study proposes a novel approach called Seam-Study. This approach involves the collaboration of Home, Digital, and Traditional Schools to cater to different types of education. The study posits that homeschooling fosters an environment conducive to child-centered learning. It asserts that structuring education around practical activities, deeply rooted in the child's own interests and the familiar contexts of home and community, all while proceeding at the child's individual pace, significantly enhances the effectiveness of learning outcomes.

References

1. Arora, M. (2018, May 14). *Homeschooling in India – Pros and Cons.* From Parenting. firstcry.com: https://parenting.firstcry.com/articles/homeschooling-benefits-and-downsides/
2. Arora, M. (2018, May 14). *Homeschooling in India – Pros and Cons.* From Parenting First cry: https://parenting.firstcry.com/articles/homeschooling-benefits-and-downsides/#:~:text=The%20following%20are%20the%20drawbacks,minimal%20interactions%20outside%20their%20home
3. Barbara Skinner, H. H. (2023). Working parents' experiences of home-schooling during school closures in Northern Ireland: what lessons can be learnt? *Irish Educational Studies, 42*(3), 339-358. doi:10.1080/03323315.2021
4. Bastrikin, A. (2020, April 12). *Educationdata.org*. From https://educationdata.org/online-education-statistics/
5. Benjamin Alcott, M. B. (2020). One step forward, two steps back: transitions between home, pre-primary and primary education in rural India. *Compare: A Journal of Comparative and International Education*, 482-499. doi:10.1080/03057925.2018.1527214
6. Bhambri, J. (2020, July 15). *Top 10 Distance Education Universities in India.* From College Dekho: https://www.collegedekho.com/articles/top-10-distance-education-universities-in-india/
7. Bhardwaj, R. S. (2018). *STATISTICS FOR BUSINESS.* India: Excel Books, 1999.
8. Bower, C. (2021). 'Um, I was getting bullied at school because I didn't believe in god': one family's experience of autism, school and home education . *International Journal of Inclusive Education, 25*(8), 914-927. doi:10.1080/13603116.2019.1588926
9. Carver, R. H., & Nash, J. G. (2012). *Doing Data Analysis with SPSS Version 18.0.* Books cole cengage learning .
10. Census. (2001). *India.* From https://censusindia.gov.in/Census_And_You/literacy_and_level_of_education.aspx#:~:text=While%20the%20overall%20literacy%20rate,sexes%20at%20the%20national%20level.
11. *Distance Learning Market in India 2015-2019.* (2015, April). From Reportlinker : https://www.reportlinker.com/p02900492/Distance-Learning-Market-in-India.html
12. Eileen V. Slater, K. B. (2022). Reasons for home educating in Australia: who and why? *Educational Review, 74*(2), 263-280. doi:10.1080/00131911.2020.1728232
13. Ghosh, R. (2019, Nov 19). *What is making homeschooling witness an exponential growth India.* From Times of India : https://timesofindia.indiatimes.com/home/education/news/what-is-making-homeschooling-witness-an-exponential-growth-in-india/articleshow/72122025.cms?utm_source=contentofinterest&utm_medium=text&utm_campaign=cppst
14. Hoskins, E. W. (2023). Spatial–temporal enactments of home-schooling among low-income families of primary-aged children. *Educational Review*, 1-19. doi:10.1080/00131911.2023.2254512
15. Kingdon, G. G. (2007). The progress of school education in India. *oxford journals (Oxford Review of Economic Policy)*, 168-195.
16. KPMG-Google. (2017, May). *KPMG.* From assests.kpmg: https://assets.kpmg/content/dam/kpmg/in/pdf/2017/05/Online-Education-in-India-2021.pdf

17. Lee, T. T.-l. (2023). Homeschooling in Chinese cities: educational implications for post-pandemic schools. *Educational Review*, 1-20. doi:10.1080/00131911.2023.2234662
18. Levine, S. B. (2014). The Rise of American Boarding Schools and the Development of a National Upper Class. *Social Problems*, 63–94.
19. Maya Escueta, V. Q. (August 2017). EDUCATION TECHNOLOGY: AN EVIDENCE-BASED REVIEW. *NATIONAL BUREAU OF ECONOMIC RESEARCH*, JEL No. I20,I29,J24.
20. *Modern Education* . (n.d.). From http://content.inflibnet.ac.in/data-server/eacharya-documents/548158e2e41301125fd790cf_INFIEP_72/79/ET/72-79-ET-V1-S1__l_.pdf
21. More, A. (2020, June 19). *Massive Open Online Course (MOOC) Market 2020 Industry*. From Market watch: https://assets.kpmg/content/dam/kpmg/in/pdf/2017/05/Online-Education-in-India-2021.pdf
22. Onyema, E. M. (2020). Impact of Coronavirus Pandemic on Education. *Journal of Education and Practice* , 108-119.
23. Sharma, K. (2020, April 16). *UNESCO report*. From https://theprint.in/india/education/in-india-over-32-crore-students-hit-by-covid-19-as-schools-and-colleges-are-shut-unesco/402889/
24. Suneja, K. (2012, May 4). *25% of Indian students covered by distance education: Study*. From Finance Express: https://www.financialexpress.com/archive/25-of-indian-students-covered-by-distance-education-study/945204/#:~:text=This%20helps%20people%20in%20doing,enrollment%20in%20the%20conventional%20system.
25. Susan Sonnenschein, M. S. (2021). Home Learning Environments for Young Children in the U.S. During COVID-19. *Early Education and Development, 32*(6), 794-811. doi:10.1080/10409289.2021.1943282
26. Ted Neil. Nancy Bonner, D. B. (2014). An Investigation Of Factors Impacting The Use Of Technology In A Home School Environment. *Contemporary Issues In Education Research*, 107-120.
27. Trennert, R. A. (1982). Educating Indian Girls at Nonreservation Boarding Schools 1878-1920 . *The Western Historical Quarterly*, 271-290.
28. Waks, L. J. (2016). *The evolution and evaluation of Massive open online courses, MOOCs in motion.* philadelphia, USA: Palgrave Pivot, Springer Nature.
29. wire, B. (2020, April 17). *Online Education Market in India Worth INR 360 Billion by 2024, Exhibiting a CAGR of ~43% - ResearchAndMarkets.com*. From business wire: https://www.businesswire.com/news/home/20200417005258/en/Online-Education-Market-India-Worth-INR-360#:~:text=The%20online%20education%20market%20in,overall%20growth%20of%20the%20industry.

Note: All the figures and tables in this chapter were made by the authors.

Securing the Future through Sustainability, Health, Education, and Technology – Brig. Dr. Rajiv Divekar et al. (eds)

30 Library Orientation through Games: Engaging and Interactive Approaches to Introduce Student to Library Resources and Services

Dipali More*

Library In-charge,
Symbiosis Institute of Management Studies (SIMS)

ABSTRACT

Purpose—This purpose of the study is to investigate the effect of incorporating games in the library orientation session with the aim to enhance effectiveness of the session, student engagement and understanding of library resources, facilities and services. The paper explores the contribution of interactive and joyful approach of information deliverance to the meaningful and deeper learning experience of the students resulting in better use of library resources, facilities and services.

Design/methodology/approach—Simple non-technological games like quiz and treasure hunt were introduced into the session. This orientation session was designed to teach new students how to find and use essential collections and resources available in the library by using a fun, collaborative and engaging game. A feedback form was circulated after each session to understand their experience. Analysis of qualitative data was done using the hermeneutic phenomenological approach.

Findings—According to post-orientation feedback responses, 85% students appreciated fun and engaging experience through introduction of games in library orientation. Further assessment of qualitative data finds that students had better understand of library resources, facilities and services.

Originality/value—Although the library orientation through games is extensively explored, there was very little literature on the use of non-technological games in library orientation. Moreover, every academic library has its own culture, therefore it's always an experiment when the first- time game is introduced in the orientation. This paper provides a practical example of designing and incorporating low budget games in library orientation sessions.

KEYWORDS: Library orientation, Game-based learning, User engagement, Marketing of library services

*Corresponding author: library@sims.edu

DOI: 10.1201/9781003587200-30

1. Introduction

Academic libraries are adapting new technologies and pedagogy to remain relevant in the ever-evolving world of knowledge dissemination and deliverance. Engaging students emotionally during the session is a difficult task, especially referring to library orientation programs. Librarians put forth best efforts to create informative and engaging library orientation for freshers. Biggest challenge is to cover all information in one session i.e information on resources and services, showing physical space of the library and demonstration use and access of the resources. Traditionally, library orientations were classroom sessions added with guided tours. Librarians have tried many means to sustain the long-term collaboration with the students where libraries hand over the information pamphlets, gifts or takeaways which will remind students of the library resources. Though informative, these orientation programs often fail to generate curiosity among the students. By recognizing the need for an innovative and energetic approach, the library adapted educational pedagogy of learning through games to introduce its resources and services to the students, where collaboration and interaction happening during the games took the center stage.

Libraries, all over the world, have successfully adopted and utilizing games or gamification in the library orientation. Present study will survey the effect of an academic library experiment of introducing games in library orientation for freshers to introduce key library resources and services. The paper will explore game-based learning as its benefits through literature review. The paper will also throw light on the various orientation strategies and games-based orientation that different libraries have adopted. Further paper will explain the process of development and implementation of games, and its effectiveness in achieving the goal of engaging and interactive knowledgeable sessions.

2. Research Question

How inclusion of games can enhance effectiveness of library orientation, engage students and improve their understanding of library resources and services?

3. Literature Review

Library orientation is a crucial component of information literacy. It provides a crucial opportunity to describe library resources, services and policies of the library to users. Many libraries are employing different strategies for library orientation. Technologies are being widely used for library orientation programs. Harrington et. al (2011) explained the use of a visual storytelling approach for library orientation where students can learn through watching their peers using library facilities and resources. Studies found that well-designed orientation videos can be effective in conveying essential information, especially for online learners or remote library users (Saundera and Wong, 2020, ch 16). Podcasts and one-minute videos are employed as effective means of communication, that are published as a series as per requirement. The purpose is to communicate library information in interesting and understandable ways in short time frames to the students (Bierman and Valentino, 2011; Tomaszewski, 2023). Library tours are an effective, comfortable and skill enhancing approach in orienting about physical library, services and personnel but ineffective in teaching library navigation. Games like treasure hunts cover aspects like locating books on self and searching information in databases (Marcus and Beck, 2003).

3.1 Game Based Learning

Game based learning has attracted scholarly attention as it has become a permanent part of mainstream education. Educators are adopting and applying games in education to improve learning and education outcomes (Kula, 2021). Incorporating games in the learning process results in greater engagement of students (Boss, et. al., 2015; Rouse, 2017; Ghazy, et. a., 2021). As students with different types of learning styles preferences, like visual learner, kinesthetic learners etc., can easily adopt (Camp, 2012; Boss, et. al., 2015). Students can relate gaming activity with various subjects and also improve their decision making and problem-solving skills (Boctor, 2013). Educationists are employing computer-based games that students can relate easily (Veach, 2019; Cilauro, 2015; Smith and Baker, 2011). According to Ningsih (2023) employment of gaming strategy has a significant effect on students during the learning process. Students experience comfort and ease which make learning enjoyable, enhancing students' enthusiasm in learning. Games make it easier for students to understand the subject which further reduces their anxiety. Games also encourage teamwork and develop a collaborative learning environment for students to exchange knowledge and ideas (Adipat, et.al., 2021; Rouse, 2017). Most importantly, students are able to strengthen their learning and also be able to retain the information delivered to them through games (Camp, et. al., 2012).

3.2 Game Based Library Orientation

Libraries are also adopting a game-based approach to deliver library information. Most of the literature review focuses on computer-based games for library orientation. Libraries designed various quizzes like puzzles, true / false questions, finding matches, finding write resources etc. (O'Hanlon, Dias and Roecker, 2007). This literature review will specifically examine games that will introduce users to facilities, services and resources of libraries, as well as orient them with the physical library space. Book Hunting games are popular with many university libraries, where a fictional narrative was used as clues or preliminary phrases for book hunt (Ireton, Pitts and Ward, 2013; Marcus and Beck, 2003).

Lycoming College Library developed games in combination online games, and book hunt in the physical library. The narrative was adjoined with a series of questions where clues were spread across the online library website or in the physical library (Broussard, 2010, p 24).

James Madison University Library created and implemented a card game for transferred students, which featured a variety of questions and answers about different aspects of the library. The answer cards cover information about the library. Students have to match the question card with the answer card (Giles, 2015).

Utah Valley University Library staff developed two games to introduce students with the library and library services. Get a Clue game was designed to orient freshers at the start of fall semester. Clues were hidden in the building and students had to solve the mystery. Second game the LibraryCraft is an online game used for introducing online library resources to students during the spring semester (Smith and Baker, 2011).

4. Library Orientation at SIMS

Library orientation at academic institutions like Symbiosis Institute of Management Studies (SIMS), Pune was offered in two ways, personalized one-on-one orientation and group orientation. Personalized one-on-one orientation is arranged for the new faculty and staff to provide library information addressing their specific preferences and requirements. Sometimes even late joining students are furnished with information through personalized orientation sessions. Otherwise, group sessions were scheduled for the fresh batch of students at the start of their two years program. The orientation sessions were scheduled and communicated to the students in collaboration with the academic department. The sessions were arranged within the first two months. While scheduling, the emphasis was given on division wise sessions. The whole fresher batch of 300 + students divided into a small group of 60-70 students. Each session is held for one hour and fifteen minutes which consists of classroom sessions and a library tour.

At the time of the orientation classroom session, a presentation was made to educate students on the facilities, services, resources, library hours, contact information, sections of the library, and rules and regulations of the library that students are expected to follow while using the library facility. Then students were brought to the library to provide physical experience of the library facilities and resources. The students were again introduced to library staff in person explaining their respective responsibilities. So that student could find the right person to solve a certain query and also cooperate with library staff in maintaining rules and decorum of the library. Students were introduced to the arrangement of the book section, how to navigate the book through the book section and how to use other services and facilities in the physical environment. The library tour was more interactive than the classroom session. Rather, it is a kind of open house session where students can ask various doubts and more information pertaining to the library which can be answered by library in-charge or other library staff.

After the tour, as more time was their students were left free to dwell among the library bookshelf, periodical section or read newspaper and experience the library by themself till the scheduled session is over.

5. Developing Game-based Library Orientation

The academic institution made a paradigm shift to online platforms. From teaching to assessments were happening online. Even libraries also provided online services to the students for supporting their assignments, classroom learning, evaluations, etc. Large collection of e-books required for regular subject understanding were added to the existing collection of online journal collections, research databases, industrial databases etc. Academic institutes were persistent to improve their online collections and improve the usage of online collection as the investment in online collection is huge. Students got used to the online use of library collections. This pressurized the library staff to bring back users to the physical library. They were always worried about - how to bring back students to the library and how to make orientation sessions interesting. In order to keep students interested during the session and ensure that the library was permanently ingrained in their memories, interactive and simulation in library orientation had to be developed in addition to classroom instruction and library tours.

Library staff came up with the idea of incorporating games during the orientation to make their first visit to the library memorable, comfortable and make the student welcome to the library. The SIMS library is 411 sq ft.in size, segregated into three rooms - main library, reading room and open/discussion area. Main library has bookshelves, reading space and a library administration section. Reading room consists of a quiet reading area, a space for using computer terminals, and an air-conditioning. Open area is open for a variety of activities like group discussion, small events, sessions etc. Staff began the process of selecting games with the objectives -

- To create welcoming environment in the library that will change the student perception about the library
- Expose to the numerous facilities and services offered by the library to reduce anxiety when they receive assignments.
- Awareness about the quiet and interactive spaces available in the library.
- To give an opportunity to students to interact with other library staff.

At the end of the session, staff wanted students to learn -

- library navigation skills i.e., finding books on library shelves,
- finding right staff members to solve a particular query, and
- remembering facilities provided by the library.
- Identify quiet and interactive spaces available in the library.

Next step was to consider the various constraints of conducting games in such a small space like the number of students entering the library at a time, limited time for the class, and no budget for the activity. As the orientation is conducted class wise, each class has approximately 60 students. That means 60 students will be coming to the library on the day of orientation. With this large number moving inside the library may create chaos. So, staff has to consider the logistics of the activity i.e., where to instruct the students, how many groups to form for group activities, how many games could be considered in limited time. It is decided to instruct students in front of the circulation counter where ample space is available for students to gather around. Also decided to divide a class into 6 groups. One student was the group leader to read the instruction of the game, to decide who would play the games if different games were played simultaneously and to lead the discussion in the group during the activity. As the purpose was to bring back students to the physical library and budget constraint, it was decided to avoid using technology for the session.

It is important for staff to select games that will challenge players and cover all aspects of the library like policies, facilities, services and spaces. Also, games that can be conducted with available resources. After some research and brainstorming, staff came up with two games - Quiz and treasure hunt. The quiz was divided in two sections - 1) one-by-one, 2) buzzer round. Quizzes were designed based on information given to students in the classroom or in the library, and subject material available with the library with questions. Staff was afraid that some students may end up as passive participants. Therefore, at the time of orientation games, staff have to make sure of the participation of every student in the group. The staff initiates the instruction that the remaining question will be answered by the student who has not yet participated. Though students can discuss the answer with their group members. One-to-One quiz was designed to give participation chances for each group. Most of the questions in this quiz are based on basic information provided to the students in the classroom and in the library. And the information that is visible during the library tour. The questions which are not answered by a group were passed on to other groups.

Buzzer round quiz was designed with the motive of making quiz games more interesting and competitive. This round has questions designed for a deeper understanding of library information and more relating library resources with their subject requirement, like what are the core books for the Organization Behaviour? Where will you find them? Or Who is the most popular author of Marketing? Name a book written by the author? Where will you find the book? Or how many databases does the library subscribe to? Name the databases that help in research methodology? etc. Each round has experienced good discussion among the group members and also enthusiastic participation.

Staff decided to mark the point for the quiz. Every group has to earn points by answering the quiz. Each question was given a maximum of five points. For one-to-one quiz, full points for the question directly offered to the group and half points for passed on questions. Whereas, for buzzer round quiz, full points for giving the right answer after winning the buzzer for a question and negative marking for the wrong answer. Whereas bonus points were given to other groups who ever gave the right answer. The group which earns maximum points would win the small reward.

This treasure hunt was designed with the purpose of teaching student's physical library navigation. Chits were created. Each chit consists of book details like title of the book and author of the book. After discussion, to make the game more interesting, to bring more rigor to the game, direct subject titles indicating subject name were avoided. The titles finalized necessitated student deliberation. Each group can take three chits. The group which can find books successfully were rewarded.

Rewards are an important part of the games. Even Though it's very small. The rewards maintained the competitive nature of the game. So, it decided to give small chocolates as a reward. Though the students were well versed with the games decided for the library orientation, library staff expected these games to be a fun and social activity that would make a positive impression on fresher students. The online feedback form was circulated to all the students after the session.

6. Methodology

Hermeneutic phenomenological approach was adopted to understand the experience of users on inclusion of games in library orientation. Hermeneutic phenomenology is a qualitative research approach that interprets the meanings people attach to their lived experiences in order to explore and understand them. This method is suitable to conduct an investigation of complicated and unpredictable human experiences. Therefore, this is a suitable choice for investigating the user experience related to the inclusion of games in library orientation.

The participants are the students of an academic institute of Pune city who had undergone the library orientation program that incorporated games. The data collected from the survey that was conducted after the orientation program. Also, students were observed throughout the game session of library orientation by the library staff. A survey questionnaire was circulated through google form among the participants. Open-ended questions were used to encourage participants to open-up about their experiences and express their thoughts and emotions in their own words.

The participants are the fresher/ first year students of the MBA program of the institute. Games inclusion in library orientation was experimented when students came to campus after a lock down period in the month of November 2021. 64 students attended the session in two separate batches. The feedback form was created to know their experience - what is their opinion on including games in library orientation? How did the orientation benefit them? What did they like about the library orientation through games? First feedback form was also included with two additional questions, where we asked them - Would you like the library to continue including games in the orientation session? And We would like to hear suggestions for improving the game session in orientation. Most of the questions required subjective answers. In 2022, the library continued with the games in library orientation. Students were available at campus in full strength. Each orientation session was attended by min 50 students per class. Game sessions with an increased number of students per session may turn chaotic. Therefore, the feedback form circulated had no change. But the library received a positive response.

The analysis of the data collected followed the principles of hermeneutic phenomenology. It emphasizes the interpretation of participants' narrative. The researcher aims to identify recurring themes, patterns and insights regarding the participants experience with games in library orientation. Themes emerged as a result of the analysis recursive process of comprehending and interpreting the data.

7. Results

Feedback was circulated to the students with the purpose to understand their experience on inclusion of games in library orientation. To know whether it benefited them or not? 441 students participated in the library orientation session. But only 164 students completed the feedback form. 85% of students appreciated the introduction of games in the library orientation. 12% were confused about their view on games in the orientation. Only 2% of students did not want the library to continue with the games in the library orientation session (Fig. 30.1), though their other responses indicated that they enjoyed the games. The responses could be classified as -

1. Icebreaker session
2. Fun and engaging
3. Knowledge about the library
4. Perception about the library

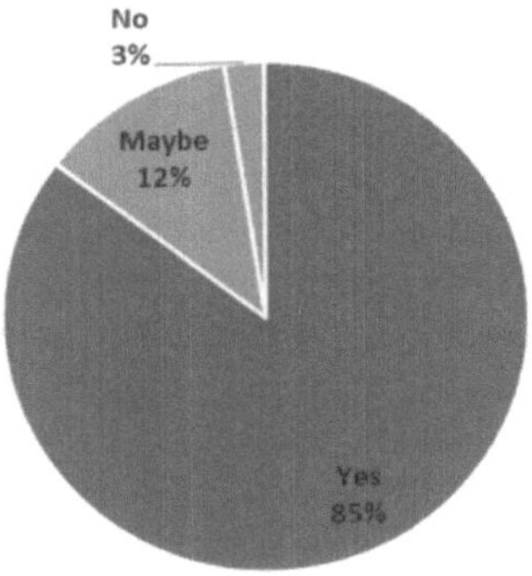

Fig. 30.1 Student view on continuing games during orientation session

Source: Author

7.1 Icebreaker Session

Icebreakers are better known for creating connections, creating a positive learning environment and also delivering important information to students (Kavanagh, et. al., 2019). Icebreakers are majorly used by the educators to get the students talking to their peers and educators, relieving tension of unknown aspects. Especially used for the freshers. Building trust, energizing and encouraging participation of students through developing a sense of connection with their peers. To help students to get acquainted and adapt to a new learning environment (Chlup and Collins, 2010; Kavanagh et. al, 2011; Rahmayanti et. a., 2019). Following responses received related to the theme Icebreaker. -

> *"With the introduction given by the team, I've felt much more comfortable interacting with the faculty members in the library. I myself have visited the library almost 3-4 times already and I love going there."*

> *"All the staff members and Library in-charge were very friendly and it really encouraged us to visit the library more often and use all the available resources."*

> *"The course specific quiz was an eye opener. We need to read the syllabus."*

> *"It gave me a chance to meet up and chat with any new friends from my course."*

> *"The friendliness of the staff and their help to get acquainted well with the library. And the chocolates."*

> *"Everyone helping everyone, it's still difficult to find a book."*

> *"The game was innovative and helped us in finding books properly."*

Repetitive response:

> *"Get familiar with staff, Library and Library staff."*

> *"Helped in knowing the Library & Library Staff."*

> *"Know my classmates and staff better."*

The response indicates that the games have really worked as an icebreaker for the student. It has not only compelled conversation within but also built the trust and feeling of togetherness that they helped each other irrespective of teams to find the books. The session has also built trust about staff knowledge and. Responses also indicate that subject specific quizzes were eye openers for the students that they find important to review their subject outline and reading material more. Even literature says that icebreaker's motivate students to learn new things (Rahmayanti, et.al., 2019).

7.2 Fun and Engaging

Games can make sessions fun and engaging and also help in learning more easily (Khanna and Kareem, 2021). The responses received also indicate the same -

> *"It was really engaging and the best way to introduce the new students, they will feel very comfortable and would actually be interested to a little extent if not much to go to any library at times."*

> *"Very engaging. I thought it was again a session to sit and hear. But I was surprised with the activity."*

"Very entertaining and insightful. The creative way of explaining all library features."

"I think it is highly engaging and makes the whole process fun and easier to understand."

"I feel more absorbed in the process as it switches from passive learning to an active one."

"I thought that I would be bored. But I enjoyed it. Everyone is involved in the activity, whether it is staff or us."

"I liked the friendliness and positive energy that was generated throughout the session by all the people."

"It was a lot of fun and we bonded with our classmates too apart from learning a lot about the library."

The responses indicate that the student really had a lot of fun during the sessions. The games that were chosen were very engaging and also encouraged everyone to participate. It helped students understand about the library (Khanna and Kareem, 2021). The responses are in line with the literature that the students enjoy the games during the orientation session (Smith and Baker, 2011).

7.3 Perception about the Library

Perception is the way a person understands or perceives the world. Students' perception about the services offered has an important contribution in establishing library image as well as has a comprehensive effect on satisfaction (Posey, 2009). Preconceived notions about the library keep students away from the library. Games conducted in the library changed and challenged the traditional perception about the library (Cilauro, 2015). Following responses received for the theme -

"It was an amazing Icebreaker session, usually when it comes to the library, we have a preconceived notion about the place but it was totally changed due to this session!"

"My perception about the library changed on the day of the session."

It helped me gain more information about SIMS Library.

"For me, the library is a place for isolation. But now, I find it more active."

"Staff answered every question, student asked."

"The staff was very helpful and approachable."

"Joyful environment, friendly staff. It was welcoming"

The responses indicate that students have preconceived notions about the library and library staff. Games help to break the traditional image of being a place of isolation. Now, they find the library a happening place. They also find the staff very approachable and knowledgeable, where they can always come to find the help for their studies. The students' perceived library as a very friendly, welcoming, or comfortable (Posey, 2009)

7.4 Knowledge about the Library

Knowledge about library systems, services and service providers have a great impact on the quality of research or studies (Ekong and Ogunode, 2022). Following responses received related to theme -

"It has made it very convenient and easy to find the required books from the various stacks and also know how to maintain decorum in the library."

"I found out about the classification system that library use."

"Awareness of different facilities in the library."

"Helped me to get to know the library staff. Helped in getting familiar with the bookshelves having books of various topics which are segregated in a very organized way."

"I got to know about various authors and various sub-segments in my course books."

"It has made it very convenient and easy to find the required books from the various stacks and also know how to maintain decorum in the library."

"It has made me understand the plethora of books and ebooks that the library has and the placement of books."

"Helped in better utilizing the resources of the library, locate books."

"I definitely remember details about the library now which I wouldn't have otherwise."

The responses indicate that the students have learned a new skill of finding books in the library. They learned more about the library resources available for them to achieve their educational goals. Games have allowed them to explore the library and discover the library collection at their own pace (Smith and Baker, 2011).

8. Implication of the Study

Inclusion of games in library orientation has led to the higher level of the student engagement. As students seemed totally engrossed while participating in the library program. Libraries can take leverage and design more engaging and interactive programs to attract and retain their users, and keep them actively involved with library resources and services. Games are also known for information retention and understanding. It is observed throughout the year that the students who seek help from the staff to navigate through the library or search for information in databases are now self-sufficient while searching for a book and well-versed with databases to fetch for certain types of information. Libraries can use this insight to design their orientation program, information literacy session and workshops. It makes it easier for users to absorb and apply the knowledge gained from sessions.

Games are also known for social interaction and collaborations. This was also evident during the gaming session that students are interacting with other new students and also taking help for solving games quizzes. They were also breaking the barriers of the group to help other group members to find the books. As it is an open session, some also find this opportunity to interact and know the library staff. Therefore, this can become a session to harness a sense of community to create a supportive and friendly environment. The excitement and happy environment created through the orientation session also breaks the dull, serious and traditional image of the library.

It dispelled prebuilt misconception of an individual about the library and attracted new users who might have not considered library resources.

For consistent performance, libraries can keep track of the effectiveness of game-based orientation. Libraries can continue to innovate and refine their programs by sharing experiences with other libraries and taking feedback from the users. The implication of the study offers opportunities for libraries to adapt, innovate, and create user-centric services that align with the evolving expectations of their users.

9. Conclusion

Library orientation program creates foundation to begin relation between student and library. Inclusion of games in Library orientation program make introduction of library facilities, resources and services very effective and innovative. The integration of informative sessions and entertainment in this interactive orientation program has proven to be highly effective in engaging students. This approach enables them to become acquainted with the library's offering in a fun and interactive manner

The feedback received from the students emphasizes on benefits of these game-based orientation. Students have expressed enhancement in understanding about library systems, improved comprehension of the library resources and services, and increase familiarity in navigation of library. They also mentioned having more faith in the library staff's expertise. Moreover, participation in these games, as well as competitive environment, develop a sense of togetherness in the students. This also foster a collaborative and engaging learning environment.

In today's disruptive information technology, the library required to accommodate and implement such new tactics to remain relevant to the evolving world and accessible to their users. In addition, library orientation through games not only accomplish this purpose, but it also caters with the numerous learning preferences of the younger generation. It bridges the gap between traditional library practices and contemporary education approach (Cilauro, 2015). Ultimately, library orientation through games not only transforms the way users engage with libraries but also reinforces the library's central role as a hub for knowledge, learning, and discovery in our society.

REFERENCES

1. Adipat, S. L., Laksana, K., Busayanon, K., Asawasowan, A., and Adipat, B (2021). Engaging Students in the Learning Process with Game-Based Learning: the fundamental concepts. *International Journal of Technology in Education (JTE)*, 4(3), pp. 542–552.
2. Bierman, J and Valentino, M L (2011). Podcasting initiative in American Research Libraries. *Library Hi Tech*, 29(2), pp.349–358.
3. Boctor, L. (2013). Active-learning Strategies: the use of a game to reinforce learning in nursing education. A case *study. Nurse Education in Practice*, 13(2), pp. 96–100. https://doi.org/10.1016/j.nepr.2012.07.010
4. Boss, K., Angell, K., and Tewell, E. (2015). The Amazing Library Race: tracking student engagement and learning comprehension in library orientations. *Journal of Information Literacy*, 9(1), pp. 4–14.
5. Broussard, M. J. S. (2010). Secret agents in the library: Integrating virtual and physical games in a small academic library. College & Undergraduate Libraries, 17(1), 20–30. http://dx.doi.org/10.1080/10691310903584759
6. Camp, K. M., Avery, S., and Lirely, R. (2012). Cooperative-experiential Learning: using student-developed games to increase knowledge retention. *Journal of Instructional Pedagogies*, 9, pp. 1–10.
7. Cilauro, R. (2015). Community building through a public library Minecraft Gaming Day. *The Australian Library Journal*, 64(2), pp. 87–93.
8. Chlup, D. T., and Collins, T. E. (2011). Breaking the Ice: Using ice-breakers and re-energizers in adult learners. *Adult Learning*, 21(3-4), pp. 34–39. https://doi.org/10.1177/104515951002100305
9. Ghazy, A., Wajdi, M., Ikjsanudin., and Sada, C. (2021). The Use of Game-based Learning in English Class. *Journal of Applied Studies in Language*, 5(1), pp. 67–68.
10. Gills, Kelly (2015). No Budget, No Experience, No Problem: Creating a Library Orientation Game for Freshman Engineering Majors. *The Journal of Academic Librarianship*, 41, pp. 170–177.
11. Harrington, M., Ditkoff, J., and Young, K. (2011). Orientation using visual storytelling and the cloud. *Library HiTech News*, 28(4), pp. 1–4.
12. Ireton, D., Pitts, J., & Ward, B. (2013). Library discovery through augmented reality: A game plan for academics. International Journal of Technology, Knowledge & Society, 9(4), pp. 119–128.
13. Kavanagh, M., Clark-Murphy, M., and Wood, L. (2011) The First Class: Using Icebreakers to Facilitate Transition in a Tertiary Environment. *Asian Social Science*, 7(4), pp. 84–95.
14. Khanna, R., and Kareem, J. (2021). Creating inclusive spaces in virtual classroom sessions during the COVID pandemic: An exploratory study of primary class teachers in India. International Journal of Educational Research Open, 2, pp. 1–5.
15. Kula, S. S. (2021). Mind games with the views of Classroom Teachers. *International Journal of Research in Education and Science (IJRES),* 7(3), pp. 747–766.
16. Marcus, S and Beck, S (2003). A Library Adventure: comparing a Treasure Hunt with a Traditional Freshman Orientation Tour. *College and Research Libraries*, pp. 23–35.
17. O'Hanlon, N., Diaz, K., and Roecker, F (2007). A Game-Based Multimedia Approach to Library Orientation. *LOEX-2007.*https://commons.emich.edu/cgi/viewcontent.cgi?article=1020&context=loexconf2007

18. Posey, J. (2009). Student P Student Perceptions and Expectations of Library Services Quality and User Satisfaction at Walters State Community College. [Doctoral dissertation, East Tennessee State University] Johnson. https://dc.etsu.edu/etd/1836
19. Rahmayanti, P., Saraswati, P. A., and Bhuana, G. P. (2019). The Use of Ice Breaker to Improve Students' Motivation in Learning English at the Tenth Grad STudents of SMK YPKKP. *Professional Journal of English Education*, 2(5), pp. 594–600.
20. Rouse, W. (2017). Lessons Learned while Escaping from a Zombie: designing a breakout EDU game. *The History Teacher*, 50(4), pp. 553–564.
21. Saunders, L and Wong, M (2020). Instruction in Libraries and Information Centers: an introduction. Windsor & Downs Press:Urbana.
22. Smith, A., and Baker, L. (2011). Getting a clue: creating student detectives and dragon slayers in your library. Reference Services Review, 39(4), pp. 628–644.
23. Tomaszewski, R (2023). Library Snackables: a study of one-minute library videos. *The Journal of Academic Librarianship*, 49, pp. 1–10.
24. Vench, C. C. (2019). Breaking out to break through: re-imagining first-year orientations. *Reference Services Review*, 47(4), pp. 556–569.

Securing the Future through Sustainability, Health, Education, and Technology – Brig. Dr. Rajiv Divekar et al. (eds)

31 Comparative Analysis of Islamic Banks with Conventional Banks in Terms of Performance

Shehnaz Ismail Lockhat[1]
Research Assistant,
Symbiosis Institute of Management Studies,
Pune, Maharashtra

Brig. Rajiv Divekar[2]
Director,
Symbiosis Institute of Management Studies,
Pune, Maharashtra

Pravin Kumar Bhoyar[3]
Deputy Director,
Symbiosis Institute of Management Studies,
Pune, Maharashtra

Tarun Khandelwal[4]
Assistant Professor,
Symbiosis School of Economics

ABSTRACT

This study aims to add empirical evidence to the relative performance of Islamic Banks and to understand the sustainability and viability of Islamic Banking in a Dual Banking Environment like Pakistan. A sample of 10 Conventional Banks and 10 Islamic Banks is considered from 2009 to 2019 to compare the Return on Equity (ROE), Return on Asset (ROA), Income Efficiency, and Technical Efficiency. A variety of quantitative techniques like descriptive statistics and Data Envelopment Analysis are used to evaluate the financial performance of Islamic and Conventional Banks. It was observed that Islamic Banks are relatively better in terms of the aforementioned financial parameters. Time series regression was employed to understand the impact of macroeconomic variables (like GDP and interest rate) on ROA, ROE, Income efficiency, and Technical efficiency of the Islamic Bank. It was observed that only Interest rate has an influence on ROA.

KEYWORDS: Islamic banks, Pakistan, Panel regression

[1]shehnaz.lockhat@sims.edu, [2]director@sims.edu, [3]deputydirector@sims.edu, [4]tarun.khandelwal@sse.ac.in

DOI: 10.1201/9781003587200-31

1. Introduction

Over the past few decades, the Muslim world has observed the growth and development of Islamic banking (Abduh & Azmi Omar, 2012; Cham, 2018). Islamic law or Sharia does not distinguish between secular and religious teachings thus Islamic Financial institutions must streamline their activities in accordance with the Sharia rules. Sharia is strongly opposed to 'Riba' or the practice of accepting and paying interest (A. Ahmad & Humayoun, 2011). However, most Islamic Banks do not completely abide by the charitable practices of Islam where 'one person should help another in need without any profit considerations'(Siddique, 2022).

Growth in the number of Islamic Banks has been observed in Pakistan during the past few decades (Bilal et al., 2020; Muhammad Yasir Saeed et al., 2020). The State Bank of Pakistan decided to let conventional and Islamic banks function simultaneously giving rise to a dual banking structure (Honey et al., 2019; Zafar & Sulaiman, 2020). The State Bank of Pakistan had to publish unique circulars and pass new laws that would ensure the operation and regulation of Islamic Banks.

The competition between Conventional and Islamic Banks has become more intense by the day. The performance of conventional banks during the Global Crisis has made people doubt their effective functioning abilities. The superior performance of Sharia-compliant banks during the crisis can be attributed to the asset, market size, and bank's overall size. Procurement of funds becomes an issue in an interest-free model whereas a liquidity issue arises by loaning out in excess in an interest-based model. In our paper, we observe how effective Conventional and Islamic Banks are in terms of ROA, ROE, Income Efficiency, and Technical Efficiency. The different macroeconomic factors (like GDP and interest rates) play an important role in influencing the financial ecosystem. For instance, high interest rates will better return on deposits, attracting more customers and deposits. Similarly, Islamic banks that are against interest-based transactions might find it difficult to attract customers during times of high-interest rates. In our paper, we look into the impact macroeconomic variables like GDP and interest rates have on the financial ratios of Islamic Banks.

2. Literature Review

In the early half of 1970, the Islamic Bank faced major challenges with the Western Banks dominating all Muslim countries. In 1970, after a conference of ministers held in Jeddah, the Nasser Social Bank and with it Islamic Banks came into existence. Egypt and Pakistan were pioneers of it and continued to work towards its advancement.

Muslims value Islamic Banks for a number of reasons. According to various studies Islamic banking is seen as a tool to uphold moral requirements by steering clear of transactions that are interest-based, which are forbidden in Islam (Z.

Ahmad, 1994; Errico & Sundararajan, 2002). Islamic banking is also seen as a tool to advance social justice and economic growth by offering financial services to disadvantaged demographics (Iqbal & Mirakhor, 2013; Nawaz et al., 2019). Also, Islamic banking is viewed as a means of encouraging moral and responsible corporate conduct that is in line with Islamic principles (Durrani, 2016; Hamidi & Worthington, 2021; Quttainah & Almutairi, 2017).

Islamic Banks have also socially contributed to the betterment of financial services in rural Pakistan. According to a study Kamran et al. (2018) Islamic Banks have a favourable effect on financial inclusion and are more successful at delivering financial services to low-income people and rural areas. However, Islamic banks have not yet taken advantage of the chance to engage the general public at the grass-roots level and to expand their reach by helping the impoverished and unbanked. As a result, policymakers should support the expansion of Islamic banking in Pakistan, since it can significantly advance financial inclusion and lower poverty.

The first Islamic bank in Pakistan, the Islamic Banking Department of the Habib Bank Limited, was founded in Karachi in 1983, marking the beginning of the country's Islamic banking history. The government has encouraged the development of Islamic banking in Pakistan (Khan & Ijaz, 2014). The State Bank of Pakistan (SBP), the nation's central bank, released a detailed strategy for the growth of Islamic banking in Pakistan in 2015. This strategy called for the launch of new Islamic banking products, the creation of Islamic banking-specific branches, and the promotion of Islamic finance education and awareness.

There is an extensive literature review regarding the profitability of Conventional Banks mainly concerned with the European and US banking market. In a study Shah Khan et al. (2014) explores the factors affecting profitability. It was observed that the gearing ratio, deposit ratio, NPL Ratio, asset management, and external causes like CPI have an impact on profitability.

Favourable economic condition is another factor that promotes the growth of Islamic Banks. N. H. B. Ahmad & Noor, (2011) checked the effect that the Asian Financial Crisis of 1998 and the Global Financial Crisis of 2002 had on the Profitability of Islamic Banks. The findings demonstrate that the 1998 financial crisis had a detrimental effect on Islamic banks' profitability while the 2008 financial crisis had no effect. Various studies have highlighted that the Islamic banks attracted greater deposits during the crisis (Akhtar et al., 2017; Farooq & Zaheer, 2015). The literature also provides evidence about the impact of the crises on profitability was more severe for conventional banks than for Islamic banks (Aysan et al., 2015; Kassim & Shabri Abd. Majid, 2010).

Many researchers have tried to compare the efficiency of Islamic Banks with that of Conventional Banks. In a study by Khalil & Siddiqui (2019), 13 conventional and 5 Islamic Banks were compared in terms of profitability, liquidity, efficiency, and riskiness. There was no major difference in terms of profitability ratios of the two types of Banks but there was a significant variation in risk, liquidity, and solvency ratios between the two types of banks.

The success of Islamic banks can be significantly impacted by macroeconomic factors, like, Inflation, GDP Growth, Interest Rate, and Exchange Rate. According to various study customer satisfaction in Pakistan's banking industry was significantly influenced by demographic parameters such as age, income, and education level. Particularly, it was discovered that younger and more educated customers were happier with their banking experiences than lower-income customers, who were found to be less happy. Overall, the study reveals that Islamic banks in Pakistan can raise client satisfaction by emphasizing service excellence, dependability, and convenience, as well as religious observance and moral conduct. The study emphasizes the significance of taking demographic aspects into account when designing banking services and marketing plans (Ajmal et al., 2018; Jamal & Naser, 2003).

Islamic banks are in their period of infancy and their operations can't be completely compared with that of conventional banks. The Central Bank of Pakistan conducted a study to evaluate the performance of Islamic banks in Pakistan. Data Envelope Analysis was used to value income, scale, and technical efficiency. They observed that Islamic Banks are underperforming given their business model however they have better asset quality and more stability in comparison with conventional banks (Sardar et al., 2011).

Similarly a study used the liquidity and volatility of the two types of banks to examine the efficiency in operations (Aman et al., 2015). Islamic banks have less liquidity due to fewer credit placement opportunities however their asset quality is better with fewer non-performing assets (Alzoubi, 2017). The study also used the Bid-ask spread and Illiquidity ratio of Islamic and Conventional banks listed in the Karachi Exchange. The study also revealed that conventional banks are more volatile as compared to Islamic banks.

Islamic banking has outlasted fads, but there isn't a comprehensive empirical framework that can be used to assess the convergence between its theory and practice and internal coherence. Two goals are considered as the main ones for Islamic banking: lowering the income gap and raising social welfare. In a study, Islamic finance and investment methods were categorized into three categories: ideal, permissible (but not ideal), and controversial in order to assess whether the shift from debt-based to equity-based financing has actually occurred (Siddique & Iqbal, 2014).

Investors of Islamic Banks share the profit or losses of the bank. Therefore Sharia-compliant banks face the risk of credit withdrawal from their investors if they don't supply their investors with sufficient profits during the year. Therefore this risk of withdrawal promotes Islamic banks to work more efficiently (Abedifar et al., 2013). Their study also found that Islamic Banks have much poor loan services as they are less responsive to interest rates in comparison with Conventional Banks.

A study was conducted to understand the difference in the productivity of both kinds of banks. A sample of 385 banks was from 18 countries from 2008 to 2017. The study confirmed that Islamic Banks are more productive as compared to conventional banks. The former has shown progress in marginal productivity in almost all years (Jubilee et al., 2021).

Islamic Banks face major legal and regulatory challenges. A significant problem is the absence of a thorough legal framework for Islamic banking, which has caused disparities in how Islamic financial products are handled as compared to traditional financial goods. According to existing literature to ensure more uniformity and clarity, the government should create a thorough legislative framework for Islamic banking (Jubilee et al., 2021). Lack of knowledge of Islamic banking services and products is another issue that can be countered by improving public understanding of Islamic banking and its advantages, education and awareness initiatives are required (Rammal & Zurbruegg, 2007). Islamic banking in Pakistan also faces a hurdle due to a lack of skilled labour. To create a pool of qualified professionals, the industry needs to invest in training and development initiatives.

When loans are lent out for a short duration of time (like less than 30 days), individuals don't get sufficient time to generate some returns on the proceeds but banks assume that these loans have provided borrowers with some implicit gains and they thus charge a service fee. According to Roy (1991), feels that there is a shortage of Sharia-compliant short-run investment options. Islamic banks and financial institutions will be able to coordinate operations among themselves and would be able to scale operations both domestically and globally.

Islamic banking is based on Islamic law or Sharia. Some scholars feel that Islamic Banks are a misrepresentation of the Sharia law as it does not contribute to solving social problems like enhancing equitability, justice, and well-being. The concept of a predetermined mark-up is not much different from interest. Some people term it as a 'legal fiction' to avert interest using a simple technicality. Literature has classified the Islamic financial instruments are very similar to those of conventional banks. SUSUK has very similar specifications to fixed-income financial instruments (Mansour et al., 2015).

According to Anwar (2003), a way to enhance the Islamisation of banks would be that commercial banks should diversify their operations to include investment and insurance facilities. This would help transform Islamic Banks from mere financial institutions to social welfare institutions and entrepreneurs. He suggested that the problem of seigniorage can be averted by switching to commodity money from fiat money or currency that is backed by silver or gold coins.

3. Research Methodology

The following study is a quantitative analysis using secondary data. All traditional and Islamic banks in Pakistan's financial statements are used to determine the values of the various ratios for different years. The study spans the years 2009 through 2019. The years post-COVID-19 were not taken into consideration to avoid externalities. Banks with less than 100 Islamic bank branches have been taken as conventional banks.

For the specified sample period, the annual returns data regarding Return on Assets and Return on Equity of 10 Islamic Banks and 10 Conventional Banks is gathered from the financial statements of each bank using the Bloomberg Database. The average ROE and ROA for the two kinds of banks are demonstrated below in a graphical format. Data Envelopment Analysis was used to calculate the income efficiency and technical efficiency of the two types of banks.

Total expenditure and Total Revenue were used as the input and output respectively to find

the Income efficiency for each bank and values were averaged out to find the income efficiency of each type of bank. To find Technical Efficiency, Deposits, and Operating Fixed Assets were used as inputs, and Investments were used as the output. The efficiency ratios for each bank were calculated individually for a given year and averaged out to get the efficiency ratios of Islamic Banks and Conventional Banks for different years.

The second section uses a multiple regression model to analyse the effects macroeconomic variables have on the efficiency of the banks. The State Bank of Pakistan website has information on the GDP and the interest rate.

$$\text{Model-1 } ROE = \propto 1 + \beta 1(G) + \gamma 1NT + \varepsilon$$

$$\text{Model-2 } ROA = \propto 2 + \beta 2(G) + \gamma 2INT + \varepsilon$$

$$\text{Model-3 } IE = \propto 3 + \beta 3(G) + \gamma 3INT + \varepsilon$$

$$\text{Model-4 } TE = \propto 4 + \beta 4(G) + \gamma 4INT + \varepsilon$$

Where ROE- Return on Equity, ROA-Return on Asset, IE-Income Efficiency, TE-Technical Efficiency, G-GDP and INT- Interest Rate.

4. Data Analysis and Findings

The Return on Equity, Return on Asset, Technical efficiency, and Income efficiency for Islamic banks and conventional banks in Pakistan are compared in the first section of the analysis

A crucial financial indicator for banks is ROE, which is determined by dividing the bank's net income by the equity held by its shareholders. Interest on investments and loans as well as fees for a variety of services are how banks make money. A bank's ROE reveals how well it is generating profits from the capital of its shareholders. Islamic banks have an average return on equity of 12% compared to conventional banks' which record an average return on equity of 3.58%. S&P Global Market intelligence data indicates that the average ROE for banks globally

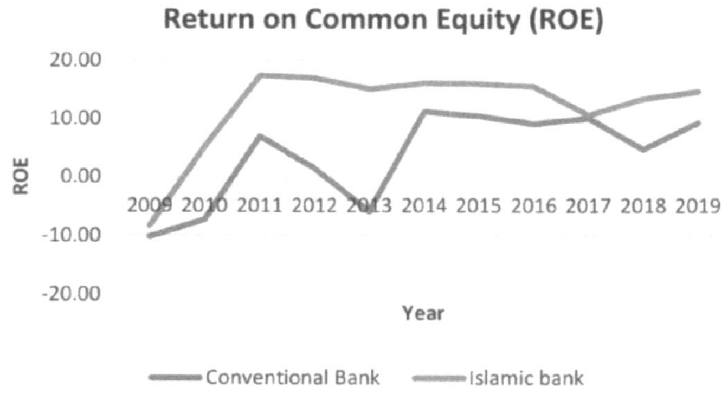

Fig. 31.1 Return on equity of islamic and conventional banks

Source: Computed by Author

was approximately 7.6% in 2021. The ROE curve demonstrates a steep uptrend for the Islamic Bank post the Financial Crisis of 2008. The ROE for Islamic banks has been more stable as compared to Conventional Banks. In 2013, a major drop in the ROE of Conventional Banks was observed due to a significant drop in the ROE of Askari Bank Limited which dropped to negative 27%.

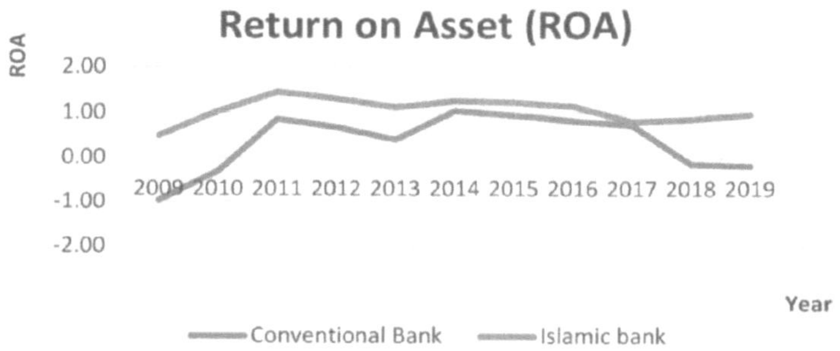

Fig. 31.2 Return on asset of islamic and conventional banks

Source: Computed by Author

Another important financial statistic used to assess the profitability and effectiveness of banks is called return on assets (ROA). A bank's return on assets (ROA) indicates how much profit it generates on each dollar worth of assets it owns. Investors and analysts frequently use ROA to compare the performance of banks operating in the same sector or business. According to the findings, conventional banks' and Islamic banks' respective average asset returns are 0.357 and 1.067. Graphically, it is observed that the ROA of Islamic Banks has consistently been higher than that of Conventional Banks over the study period of 2009 to 2020. S&P Global Market Intelligence data, however, indicates that the ROA for banks globally averaged 0.7% in 2021.

Fig. 31.3 Income efficiency of islamic and conventional banks

Source: Computed by Author

Income Efficiency can be calculated by taking expenditure as input and revenue as output. The graph suggests that the income efficiency of Conventional Banks is lower than Islamic Banks for a majority of time period ranging from 2009 to 2019. A bank that generates more revenues for every dollar spent on running expenditures is thought to be more efficient. Islamic Banks' average income efficiency value is 0.68 contrary to Conventional Banks' efficiency value of 0.6. This demonstrated the extremely low efficiency of Pakistan's banks. The cause for these banks' low efficiency can be attributed to the fact that they are opening new branches, which are more likely to result in inefficiency.

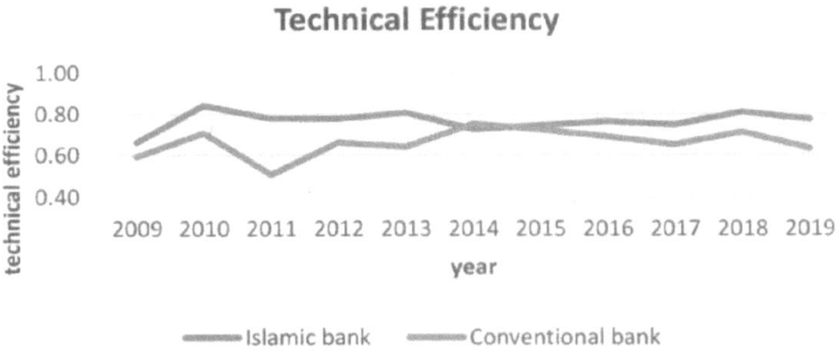

Fig. 31.4 Technical efficiency of islamic and conventional banks

Source: Computed by Author

Technical efficiency describes a company's or organization's capacity to generate the maximum amount of output from a specific set of inputs, deposits, operating fixed assets, and other such materials. It is observed that the technical efficiency of Islamic Banks has been consistently higher than Conventional Banks over a span of 10 years except in 2014.

Literature suggests that conventional Banks in the USA have an average technical efficiency score of 0.93 in 2019 (which demonstrates that these banks were relatively more efficient). The average technical efficiency value of Islamic Banks was 0.77 which is much lower than the value of banks in the USA but higher than 0.66 which is the technical efficiency value of Conventional Banks of Pakistan. Also, it can be observed that the technical efficiency of Islamic Banks is more stable than that of Conventional Banks. In Pakistan, Islamic banks are more technically efficient than regular banks, and there are probably many different factors that contribute to this. Strict Regulations in Pakistan can be one such reason. Islamic banks must comply with the same regulatory standards as regular banks, in addition to additional rules regarding Shariah compliance. Also, Islamic Banks are growing in demand in Pakistan motivating banks to improve their technical efficiency.

Multiple regression models are used in the second section of the analysis to calculate the effect of macroeconomic factors (like interest rate, and GDP growth rate) on the performance of conventional and Islamic banks. Four multiple regression models are built for this purpose, covering two accounting performance indicators—return on equity and return on assets—as well as two efficiency performance indicators—technical efficiency and income efficiency.

Model 1: Return on Assets (ROA)

Model 1 has a R^2 of 0.71 which indicates that the variables are a decent fit for the model. The p-values of the two variables are 0.03 and 0.88. This demonstrates that interest rate has an effect on ROA. The coefficient for the Interest rate is -0.06. GDP does not have an impact on ROA. The negative coefficients of Interest Rate demonstrates that a rise in the value of the Interest Rate would result in a fall in the value of ROA. Islamic banks may find it difficult to provide competitive returns to its depositors without turning to interest-based investment when interest rates in the broader financial market increase. Because of this, Islamic banks may experience lower ROA during periods of high-interest rates.

Table 31.1 Impact of GDP and interest rate on ROA

Variables	Coefficients	Standard Error	P-Value	Multiple R
Intercept	1.71	0.28	0.00	0.70
INT RATE	-0.06	0.02	0.03	
GDP	0.00	0.00	0.88	

Source: Computed by the Author

Model 2: ROE

R^2 for the model 2 is 0.31. R^2 is low and thus not a good fit for the model. The p-value demonstrates that macroeconomic variables like Interest Rate and GDP Growth Rate do not have an impact on Return on Equity.

Table 31.2 Impact of GDP and interest rate on ROE (Computed by the Author)

Variables	Coefficients	Standard Error	P-value	Multiple R
Intercept	19.40	10.49	0.10	0.31
INT RATE	-0.74	0.93	0.45	
GDP	0.00	0.00	0.99	

Source: Computed by the Author

Model 3: Income Efficiency

The R^2 for Model 3 is 0.34 which shows that the fit of the model is not good. The P-value for each variable are 0.87 and 0.35 and are thus greater than 0.05 which shows that the two variables are insignificant. Thus this demonstrates that Interest rate and GDP do not have an impact on income efficiency.

Table 31.3 Impact of GDP and interest rate on income efficiency

Variables	Coefficients	Standard Error	P-Value	Multiple R
Intercept	0.73	0.14	0.00	0.34
INT RATE	0.00	0.00	0.87	
GDP	-0.01	0.01	0.35	

Source: Computed by the Author

Model 4: Technical Efficiency

Model 4 has a R^2 of 0.46. The P-values of the three macroeconomic variables are 0.18 and 0.62 which are all more than 0.05. Therefore, the two variables are insignificant and a change in Interest Rate and GDP does not have an impact on technical efficiency.

Table 31.4 Impact of GDP and interest rate on income efficiency

Variables	Coefficients	Standard Error	P-Value	Multiple R
Intercept	0.85	0.06	0.00	0.46
INT RATE	-0.01	0.01	0.19	
GDP	0.00	0.00	0.62	

Source: Computed by the Author

Thus Model 2, Model 3, and Model 4 are insignificant. In Model 1, Interest rate has an impact on ROA. In a study, (Rehmans & Mangla, 2010) it was observed that GDP growth rate and interest rate has no impact on ROE, ROA and Allocative Efficiency. However, GDP and Interest rate did have an impact on Technical Efficiency.

5. Conclusion

Besides providing financial solution to their customers, Islamic Banks offers a sense of moral and ethical values that positively affect the lives of the people they cater to. Over the past ten years, Islamic banks in Pakistan have consistently expanded especially in terms of efficiency. The Return on Equity (ROE) and Return on Assets (ROA) of Islamic Banks have consistently been higher than Conventional Banks during the sample period from 2009 to 2019. The technical efficiency which demonstrates the organization's capacity to translate input into outputs efficiently is higher for Islamic Banks at around 0.77. The Income Efficiency of Islamic Banks is also relatively better than that of Conventional Banks.

To ensure their long-term viability and profitability, Islamic banks have to meticulously track and handle various macroeconomic issues. It was observed that Interest Rate and GDP growth rate do not have an impact on the ROE, Income Efficiency, and Technical Efficiency. Return on Asset is negatively impacted by Interest Rate.

Islamic banks have grown significantly in recent years, yet they still have a lot of competition from traditional banks. Nevertheless, Islamic banks are likely to play a bigger part in Pakistan's banking sector as a result of the country's rising demand for Shari'a-compliant financial goods and services.

REFERENCES

1. Abduh, M., & Azmi Omar, M. (2012). Islamic banking and economic growth: the Indonesian experience. *International Journal of Islamic and Middle Eastern Finance and Management*, *5*(1), 35–47. https://doi.org/10.1108/17538391211216811
2. Abedifar, P., Molyneux, P., & Tarazi, A. (2013). Risk in Islamic Banking. *Review of Finance*, *17*(6), 2035–2096. https://doi.org/10.1093/rof/rfs041
3. Ahmad, A., & Humayoun, A. A. (2011). Islamic banking and prohibition of Riba/interest. *African Journal of Business Management*, *5*(5), 1763. https://doi.org/10.5897/AJBM10.723
4. Ahmad, N. H. B., & Noor, M. A. N. B. M. (2011). The impact of 1998 and 2008 financial crises on profitability of islamic banks. *The Bangladesh Development Studies*, 1–22.
5. Ahmad, Z. (1994). Islamic banking: state of the art. *Islamic Economic Studies*, *2*(1).
6. Ajmal, H., Khan, R. A., & Fatima, M. (2018). Impact of service quality on customer satisfaction in banking industry of Pakistan: A case study of Karachi. *Journal of Social and Administrative Sciences*, *5*(3), 219–238.
7. Akhtar, B., Akhter, W., & Shahbaz, M. (2017). Determinants of deposits in conventional and Islamic banking: a case of an emerging economy. *International Journal of Emerging Markets*, *12*(2), 296–309. https://doi.org/10.1108/IJoEM-04-2015-0059
8. Alzoubi, T. (2017). Determinants of liquidity risk in Islamic banks. *Banks & Bank Systems*, *12*,*№ 3*, 142–148.
9. Aman, A., Sharif, S., & Arif, I. (2015). Comparison of islamic banks with conventional banks: Evidence from an emerging market. *Asian Finance Association (AsianFA) 2015 Conference Paper, Aman, A., Sharif, S., & Arif, I.(2016). Comparison of Islamic Banks with Conventional Banks: Evidence from an Emerging Market. Journal of Management Sciences*, *3*(1), 13–22.
10. Anwar, M. (2003). Islamicity of banking and modes of Islamic banking. *Arab LQ*, *18*, 62.
11. Aysan, A. F., Disli, M., Ozturk, H., & Turhan, I. M. (2015). Are Islamic Banks Subject to Depositor Discipline? *The Singapore Economic Review*, *60*(01), 1550007. https://doi.org/10.1142/S0217590815500071

12. Bilal, M., Fatima, S., Ishtiaq, M., & Azeem, H. M. (2020). Factors affecting the choice of Islamic banking by SMEs in Pakistan: Implications for Islamic banks' corporate governance. *Pakistan Journal of Commerce and Social Sciences (PJCSS), 14*(1), 255–272.
13. Cham, T. (2018). Determinants of Islamic banking growth: an empirical analysis. *International Journal of Islamic and Middle Eastern Finance and Management, 11*(1), 18–39. https://doi.org/10.1108/IMEFM-01-2017-0023
14. Durrani, B. (2016). Islamic Concept and Contemporary Corporate Social Responsibility: Comparative Study between Islamic Banks and Conventional Banks in Pakistan. *Journal of Managerial Sciences, 10*(2).
15. Errico, L., & Sundararajan, V. (2002). *Islamic financial institutions and products in the global financial system: Key issues in risk management and challenges ahead.*
16. Farooq, M., & Zaheer, S. (2015). Are Islamic Banks More Resilient During Financial Panics? *Pacific Economic Review, 20*(1), 101–124. https://doi.org/10.1111/1468-0106.12096
17. Hamidi, L., & Worthington, A. C. (2021). How social is Islamic banking? *Society and Business Review, 16*(1), 51–70. https://doi.org/10.1108/SBR-03-2020-0036
18. Honey, D., Tashfeen, R., Farid, S., & Sadiq, R. (2019). Credit Risk Management: Evidence of Corporate Governance in Banks of Pakistan. *Journal of Finance and Accounting Research, 01*(01), 01–18. https://doi.org/10.32350/JFAR.0101.01
19. Iqbal, Z., & Mirakhor, A. (2013). *Economic development and Islamic finance.* World Bank Publications. https://doi.org/1596/978-0-8213-9953-8
20. Jamal, A., & Naser, K. (2003). Factors Influencing Customer Satisfaction in the Retail Banking Sector in Pakistan. *International Journal of Commerce and Management, 13*(2), 29–53. https://doi.org/10.1108/eb047465
21. Jubilee, R. V. W., Kamarudin, F., Latiff, A. R. A., Hussain, H. I., & Tan, K. M. (2021). Do Islamic versus conventional banks progress or regress in productivity level? *Future Business Journal, 7*(1), 22. https://doi.org/10.1186/s43093-021-00065-w
22. Kamran, S., Ayub, M., & Luqman, A. (2018). Islamic banks' role in serving the poor unbanked population in Pakistan. *Journal of Islamic Business and Management, 8*(2).
23. Kassim, S. H., & Shabri Abd. Majid, M. (2010). Impact of financial shocks on Islamic banks. *International Journal of Islamic and Middle Eastern Finance and Management, 3*(4), 291–305. https://doi.org/10.1108/17538391011093243
24. Khalil, F., & Siddiqui, D. A. (2019). Comparative analysis of financial performance of Islamic and conventional banks: evidence from Pakistan. *Available at SSRN 3397473.*
25. Khan, M. M. S., & Ijaz, F. (2014). Islamic Banking in Pakistan: Challenges and Opportunities-A Performance Based Analysis. *Islamic Banking and Finance Review, 1*(1).
26. Mansour, W., Ben Jedidia, K., & Majdoub, J. (2015). How Ethical is Islamic Banking in the Light of the Objectives of Islamic Law? *Journal of Religious Ethics, 43*(1), 51–77. https://doi.org/10.1111/jore.12086
27. Muhammad Yasir Saeed, Kashif Hamid, Ur Rehman, M. A., & Muhammad Nazam. (2020). Islamic Financial Development and Economic Growth of Emerging Economy of Pakistan; a Panel Data Approach. *Journal of Business and Social Review in Emerging Economies, 6*(1), 197–208. https://doi.org/10.26710/jbsee.v6i1.1039

28. Nawaz, H., Abrar, M., Salman, A., & Bukhari, S. M. H. (2019). Beyond finance: Impact of Islamic finance on economic growth in Pakistan. *Economic Journal of Emerging Markets*, *11*(1), 8–18. https://doi.org/10.20885/ejem.vol11.iss1.art2
29. Quttainah, M. A., & Almutairi, A. R. (2017). Corporate ethics: evidence from Islamic banks. *Journal of Management & Governance*, *21*(4), 815–840. https://doi.org/10.1007/s10997-016-9360-6
30. Rammal, H. G., & Zurbruegg, R. (2007). Awareness of Islamic banking products among Muslims: The case of Australia. *Journal of Financial Services Marketing*, *12*(1), 65–74. https://doi.org/10.1057/palgrave.fsm.4760060
31. Roy, D. A. (1991). Islamic banking. *Middle Eastern Studies*, *27*(3), 427–456. https://doi.org/10.1080/00263209108700869
32. Sardar, A., Azeem, M. M., Ahmed, T., & Zafar, S. (2011). Islamic banks: efficiency and its determinants in Pakistan. *Islamic Studies*, 423–434.
33. Shah Khan, M. M., Ejaz, F., & Aslam, E. (2014). Determinants of Profitability of Islamic Banking Industry: An Evidence from Pakistan. *Business & Economic Review*, *6*(2), 27–46. https://doi.org/10.22547/BER/6.2.2
34. Siddique, M. Z. (2022). Modern money and Islamic banking in the light of Islamic law of riba. *International Journal of Finance & Economics*, *27*(1), 993–1008. https://doi.org/10.1002/ijfe.2196
35. Siddique, M. Z., & Iqbal, M. (2014). A Framework for Evaluating Islamic Banking from" Within". *Islamic Studies*, 5–35.
36. Zafar, M. B., & Sulaiman, A. A. (2020). Islamic Banking in Pakistan. In *Growth and emerging prospects of international Islamic banking* (pp. 61–77). IGI Global. https://doi.org/10.4018/978-1-7998-1611-9.ch004

Securing the Future through Sustainability, Health, Education, and Technology – Brig. Dr. Rajiv Divekar et al. (eds)

32 New Product Advertising: Analysing the Impact of Functional, Emotional and Rational Brand Post on Purchase Intention

Tausif Mistry[1]
Indira School of Business Studies PGDM,
Pune, Maharashtra

Pravin Dange[2]
Symbiosis Institute of Management Studies,
Pune, Maharashtra

Chanakya Kumar[3]
Indira School of Business Studies PGDM,
Pune, Maharashtra

ABSTRACT

Several studies have found that advertising that uses emotional appeals builds strong emotional connections with consumers, evoking good feelings and dramatically increasing buying intent. Much of the literature focuses on advertisement of existing products, however for new to the market products which haven't been introduced to the customers in combination with the impact of environmental consciousness is an area of concern for small business organization who have invested in innovation but not having deep pockets for advertising. Customers frequently appreciate companies that arouse particular emotions, increasing the likelihood that they will make a purchase. Companies today face intense competition in the world of business and therefore they are constantly seeking ways to enhance consumer engagement through effective strategies which can also drive purchase intentions. Consumer behaviour can be influenced by various kinds of brand postings. Therefore, it's vital for marketers and researchers to understand them as this study intends to explore the relationship between emotional, rational, and functional brand posts in influencing purchase intent keeping in view the role played by environmental consciousness as a moderator.

KEYWORDS: Emotional appeal, Rational appeal, Functional appeal, New product marketing, Purchase intention

[1]tausif.mistry@gmail.com, [2]praveendange@gmail.com, [3]chanakya.kumar905@gmail.com

DOI: 10.1201/9781003587200-32

1. Introduction

Purchase intention refers to how likely someone thinks they are going to buy something and factors such as brand perception and emotions tied to a particular product or service contribute to the extent to which it influences decision making (Chi, Yeh and Yang, 2009). With the rise of social media platforms in recent times brand posts have become a critical tool in enabling companies to connect and communicate in an effective way with their target audience.

The recognition that environmental consciousness and sustainability play a critical role in consumer decision-making is highlighted by this study, and when someone considers the environment when deciding what to buy it shows their environmental consciousness. We will study the moderating effects of environmental consciousness in order to understand better how different types of brand posts affect people's willingness to make a purchase based on their eco-conscious beliefs especially for a new to the market product.

As part of our analysis into how brands utilize social media platforms, we are going to examine three different categories of brand post: emotionally charged messaging created to forge strong connections with audiences by eliciting feelings such as joy or nostalgia from them; rational messaging based around reason more than emotion designed for people interested in learning more about products/services/brand ethos and functional messaging intended to portray the functionality within specific contexts. The primary objective of emotional brand posts that provoke feelings like joy and nostalgia is to forge an intense emotional bond between the brand and its audience. Supporting the benefits and advantages of a product or service through rational thinking is what Rational brand posts strive for, while functional brand posts showcase how the features and attributes of a product can actually be used.

The aim of this research is to illustrate effective communication techniques by looking at the influence of three types of brand posts on user's intention to purchase, through an in-depth analysis. Furthermore, rooting in the regulatory role of environmental attitude may help unravel the reason why consumers tend to have a green behaviour depending on their personal attitudes and emotions.

For the next paragraphs, a research study is carried out with a look into literature review and methodology for analysing data that leads to a specific conclusion as well as some significant implications. This study will develop relevant data regarding consumer behaviour and brand management, which are strongly focused on sustainability marketing. In the business world, knowing consumers` behaviour is vital to understand their intentions and to get to know their expectations. (Nguyen, Leeuw, and Dullaert, 2018) Responding to client needs involves companies discovering consumer behaviour and then building a strategic marketing plan that correspond to this behaviour. Tastes of individuals in selecting goods and services for purchasing is conveyed through the purchase intention (Chauhan 2013). The previous research indicates that factoring such buying intents can aid in knowing how brands' attitude, feelings, and functional attributes work (Haba, Hassan & Dastane 2017). Analysing these factors helps businesses fabricate marketing strategies which are more attractive to a larger number of consumers. Moreover, the person's natural tendencies to prefer a particular product or provide specific services to fulfil their needs and wants can be said their purchase intent. It is one of the archetypal tools for identifying customer behaviour and creating relevant Marketing strategies. The business should take into consideration consumer's purchase intentions to make sure that their business is consistent with the buyer's behaviours. Many factors have been examined in connection to a person's decision to buy certain things, for instance, how a brand is viewed, characteristics of products, cost, social circles' influence, and people's individual beliefs. (Firman et al 2021). Exploring the purchase intention concept can be helpful in providing the insights into consumer decisions and to create strategies that will drive purchase.

1.1 Brand Posts

Marketers with the mission of impacting customer behaviour will generally turn to one of three communication styles: emotional branding, where they attempt to instil in their clients favourable understanding of their products (Lee et al 2008), functional branding, in which marketers specify what they offer (Delgado and Fernandez 2015), and rational marketing (Serazio 2017). The overall goal of the emotional branding is to incite emotions such as joy, anger or peace in the audience and inevitably make a strong emotional connection (Delbaere et al. 2011). Effective functional brand posts will highlight the distinctive features and potentials of the product or service compared to its competitors. Moreover, rational brand posts will be sufficiently evidence-based and use critical thinking and logical reasoning to confirm the benefits of the offer. According to prior studies, brand posts of various themes have a significant influence on the approval of a product indicated by the consumers as well as on their willingness to buy it.

First, consumers, often spark up emotional posts that endorse the brand while cultivating an individual connection with the company, that is something they always want to achieve (Morrison and Crane 2007). The aforementioned research on the use of emotionally charged ads in social media marketing campaigns indicates that in comparison to ads that do not employ emotionally engaging techniques, brands tend to gain higher levels of consumer engagement and brand loyalty (Harrigan et al 2017).

The impact on consumer behaviour by logical posts is profound, as posts containing factual information plus evidence can lead to message modification regarding consumer perception by influencing their decision-making process. However, a string of previous research exemplify that rational postings have been successful in affecting consumers' decision making and generating positive corporate identities (Spears and Postmes 2015).

The power of the communicative posts on consumers can seldom be rejected because communicative posts can also be used to get hold of consumers' attitudes towards a product or service by introducing them to the practical features of the product (Keltinger and Lee 1994). Post usages that seem to be more and more functional have shown themselves as a proper channel for conveying the value of the product and serving the clients to the fullest extent supported by an extensive range of relevant research. (Heskett et al 1994).

1.2 Environmental Consciousness

Eco-conscious people rely on thinking and doing something about products that have adverse effects on the environment and prefer to use those products that are environment-friendly and direct all the attention to contribute to the future that they will be proud of. Nowadays, environmental consciousness and sustainability are more important to the minds of modern-day consumers making their purchase decision (Ogiemwonyi et al., 2020). With time elapsing by, the customers are gradually realizing the importance of thinking on the factors of environment to select products of their choice that promote sustainability and mirror their values. Consumers' favouring of sustainability is the main reason for companies adopting eco-friendly approaches and marketing them as such (Dutta 2011).

The role of environmental consciousness in creating consumer attitudes and purchase decisions is evident in many research studies all of which show that consumers behave in this way. Concerned and environmental focused consumers contend an increased probability of possessing affirmative sentiments toward environmentally friendly products with a more likelihood for purchase (do Paço, Shiel and Alves 2019). Another researcher found on that customers who think that environmental concerns that are on a company's mind, have more tendency to associate with the company by buying from it (Du, Bhattacharya, Seit 2010).

Environmental behaviour is effectively portrayed by difference consumer decision making approaches and green products get more preference as a result of its positive impact on evaluation and perception of a brand or product (Freiherr 2013).

Consumers today are seeking sustainability not only in sources but also during production that bypasses negative impact on the environment (Joy et al 2012). While assessing products' environmental impact, they also evaluate various factors like their ability for recycling or being energy efficient.

What is more, the effect of being environmentally conscious stretches past individual purchasing choices. By shaping collective behaviour and raising awareness about environmental issues, it can influence social norms (Gionfriddo et al 2023). In the current scenario where, environmental concerns have gained prominence individuals are relying on their peer networks to learn about sustainable consumer behaviour. (Yang, Song and Tong 2017)

Incorporating environmental consciousness and sustainability into consumer decision-making demonstrates why it is crucial for companies to adopt environmentally responsible practices as well as engage with green marketing (Polonsky and Rosenberger III 2001). Moreover, a commitment to sustainability helps businesses gain the trust of environmentally conscious consumers while fostering long-term relationships (Galpin, Whitttington and Bell 2015). Eco-friendliness must be highlighted through transparent communication for effective sustainability measures that deliver clear messages about environmental impacts (Dangelico and Vocalelli 2017).

All things considered: one cannot deny that an individual's eco-friendliness significantly impacts how they approach making choices regarding purchases. Therefore, businesses need to acknowledge the importance of sustainability and integrate it into their marketing strategies to cater to eco-conscious consumers' changing preferences. Sustainable practices adoption along with communication of an organization's commitment towards upholding environment regulations helps it stand out amidst fierce industry competition while at the same time promoting positive customer relations.

2. Methodology

2.1 Design

To test the hypotheses, we executed a 3(Appeal: emotional vs. rational vs. functional) × 2 (involvement: high vs. low) between subject experimental design. In this, we used purchase intention as the outcome variable.

i. H1: Type of appeal differently influence the purchase intention, such that emotional appeal (rational vs. functional) create higher (vs. lower) purchase intention.
ii. H2: The effect of appeal on PI is moderated by environmental consciousness, such that an emotional ad with higher (vs. lower) level of consciousness creates a favourable (vs. less favourable) purchase intention.
iii. H3: The effect of appeal on PI is moderated by environmental consciousness, such that a rational ad with lower (vs. higher) level of consciousness creates favourable (vs. less favourable) purchase intention.

2.2 Ecological Validity

Participants and procedure: For selecting the respondents, the researchers narrowed down a reputed real estate developer whose marketing collaterals are heavily emphasized on sustainability as sustainability advertising helps attract real estate customers (Tran, Tien, & Chi, (2022). The participants were chosen from one such recently completed project by the researcher through convenience sampling. The research focussed on millennials who were first time home buyers since earlier research has shown they are more inclined towards sustainability (Mariadas, Abdullah, & Abdullah, N (2019). The study employed the quantitative approach. All the residents of the housing society were invited in an amphitheatre. Few controlled questions were included in the beginning to confirm that the respondents were aware about solar panel and other sustainability concept. Participants who answered incorrectly were automatically excluded from the study. Finally, there were 186 respondents who were then equally divided into 3 groups and the study was conducted in a small classroom where each of the 3 groups were shown one advertisement on the functional, emotional and rational appeals for the new product – a portable solar panel for a cash gift of INR 200 as a token of appreciation for participating in the research.

2.3 Measurement (Data Analysis)

The study measured the outcome variable purchase intention using a five items 7-point Likert type scale (1 = strongly disagree, 7 = strongly agree), and it was adapted from Spears and Singh (2004). To examine the success of influence, we measured appeal following the self-created scale to measure appeal. In this, the participants rated their perceived appeal on a three-dimensional scale, where the dimension one captured the extent of emotional appeal, and dimension two captured the extent of functional appeal, and dimension three captured the extent of rational appeal. In this study we want to measure the environment consciousness (green consumer values) of consumer as a moderator on purchase intention. The scale green consumer values (Haws, Winterich, and Naylor 2010) using 6 items 7 points Likert type scale (1 = strongly disagree, 7 = strongly agree). The respondent's sum score less than 22 was considered a low environment conscious and above 22 considered high environment conscious.

3. Data Analysis and Results

To test the study hypothesis, we applied a 3(Appeal: emotional vs. rational vs. functional) × 2 (environment conscious: high vs. low) between subject analysis of variance (ANOVA) with purchase intention as the dependent variable. As part of this, first we tested the main effect of appeal on the outcome variable. The results (Table 32.1) supported a statistically significant main effect of appeal ($F_{(2,180)}$ = 63.593, $p < 0.05$).

The Fig. 32.1 shows the output in emotional appeal high environment conscious is matter, in rational appeal low environment conscious is matter and in functional appeal low and high conscious both are equal i.e., there is no difference in functional appeal. To confirm the same, pre-planned contrast test was applied by using syntax method in SPSS.

Table 32.1 Test of between subject effects

Dependent Variable: Purchase Intention					
Source	Type III Sum of Squares	df	Mean Square	F	Sig.
Corrected Model	96.466	5	19.293	93.587	0.000
Intercept	2337.433	1	2337.433	11338.299	0.000
Appeal	26.220	2	13.110	63.593	0.000
conscious	1.803	1	1.803	8.745	0.004
Appeal * conscious	68.443	2	34.222	166.001	0.000
Error	37.108	180	0.206		
Total	2471.007	186			
Corrected Total	133.574	185			

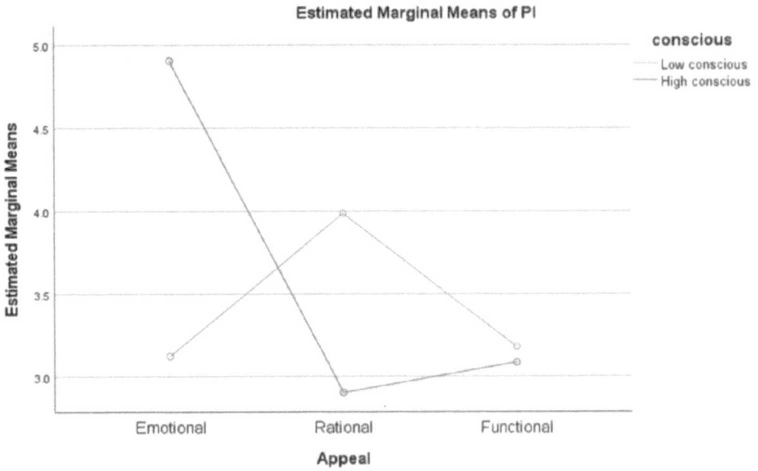

Fig. 32.1 Estimated Marginal Means of PI

To know the effect of appeal (emotional vs rational vs functional) on purchase intention (PI), performed a series of contrast test, where the test results (Table 32.2 and 32.3) confirmed that, people exposed to emotional appeal (vs rational) reported higher (vs. lower) purchase intention (contrast = .599, $p < 0.05$, $M_{[emotional]} = 4.046$, $M_{[rational]} = 3.447$). Similarly, the results also reported (Table 32.2 and 32.3) that, people exposed emotional appeal (vs. functional) reported higher (vs. lower purchase intention (contrast = .904, $p < 0.05$, $M_{[emotional]} = 4.046$, $M_{[functional]} = 3.142$). Thus, we found support for H1.

To test the hypothesis 2 (H2) we examined the interaction of appeal x environmental consciousness on purchase intention. The results (Table 32.1) supported a statistically significant effect ($F_{(2,180)} = 166.001$, $P < 0.05$), followed by this, to examine the direction of interaction, the study performed simple effect

Table 32.2 Estimated marginal mean

Appeal	Mean	Std. Error	95% Confidence Interval	
			Lower Bound	Upper Bound
Emotional	4.046	0.058	3.932	4.160
Rational	3.447	0.058	3.333	3.561
Functional	3.142	0.058	3.028	3.256

Dependent Variable: Purchase intention (PI)

Table 32.3 Pairwise comparisons

Dependent Variable: PI						
(I) Appeal		Mean Difference (I-J)	Std. Error	Sig.	95% Confidence Interval for Difference	
					Lower Bound	Upper Bound
Emotional	Rational	.599*	0.082	0.00	0.438	0.760
	Functional	.904*	0.082	0.00	0.743	1.065
Rational	Emotional	-.599*	0.082	0.00	-0.760	-0.438
	Functional	.305*	0.082	0.00	0.144	0.466
Functional	Emotional	-.904*	0.082	0.00	-1.065	-0.743
	Rational	-.305*	0.082	0.00	-0.466	-0.144
Based on estimated marginal means						
* The mean difference is significant at the 0.05 level.						

analysis, and conducted two different pre-planned contrast tests. The first pre planned contrast test analysing the effect of emotional appeal at high (vs low) levels of environment conscious reported higher and statistically significant purchase intention ($M_{[emotional\text{-}high\ conscious]} = 4.943$, $M_{[emotional\text{-}low\ conscious]} = 3.149$, F (1,180 = 242.041, $p < 0.05$), reported in table no. 4 and 5. The Pre planned test results supported that, people exposed to emotional appeal with high environment conscious condition have a higher purchase intention than that of low environment conscious condition. Thus, we found support for H2.

The Second pre-planned contrast test results reported (Table 32.4 and 32.5) that when people exposed to a rational appeal with low (vs. high) environment conscious, then they reported higher purchase intention, and the results reported as statistically significant ($M_{[rational\text{-}low\ conscious]} = 4.019$, $M_{[rational\text{-}high\ conscious]} = 2.875$, $F (1,180) = 98.442$, $p < 0.05$). These results supported H3.

Here in this case, we specifically mentioned in hypothesis that emotional appeal is stronger than that of rational and emotional appeal is also stronger than that of functional. In both cases level 1 is stronger, that is the reason we got minus sign in contrast estimates (Table 32.6) and found significant in both cases at $p<.05$

Table 32.4 Estimates

Appeal	conscious	Mean	Std. Error	95% Confidence Interval	
				Lower Bound	Upper Bound
Emotional	Low	3.149	0.082	2.988	3.310
	High	4.943	0.082	4.782	5.104
Rational	Low	4.019	0.082	3.858	4.180
	High	2.875	0.082	2.714	3.036
Functional	Low	3.172	0.082	3.011	3.333
	High	3.112	0.082	2.951	3.273

Dependent Variable = Purchase Intention (PI)

Table 32.5 Univariate test

Appeal		Sum of Squares	df	Mean Square	F	Sig.
Emotional	Contrast	49.898	1	49.898	242.041	0.00
	Error	37.108	180	0.206		
Rational	Contrast	20.294	1	20.294	98.442	0.00
	Error	37.108	180	0.206		
Functional	Contrast	0.054	1	0.054	0.264	0.608
	Error	37.108	180	0.206		

Dependent Variable: PI

Table 32.6 Contrast result (K matrix)

Appeal Simple Contrast			Dependent Variable
			PI
Rational vs. Emotional	Contrast Estimate		-0.599
	Hypothesized Value		0
	Difference (Estimate - Hypothesized)		-0.599
	Std. Error		0.082
	Sig.		0.000
	95% Confidence Interval for Difference	Lower Bound	-0.760
		Upper Bound	-0.438
Functional vs. Emotional	Contrast Estimate		-0.904
	Hypothesized Value		0
	Difference (Estimate - Hypothesized)		-0.904
	Std. Error		0.082
	Sig.		0.000
	95% Confidence Interval for Difference	Lower Bound	-1.065
		Upper Bound	-0.743

(Table 32.5). Hence, we conclude that emotional appeal advertisement in both the cases have stronger influence than rational and functional appeal on purchase intention of portable solar panel. In the exposure of emotional appeal ads, people's purchase intention is high for buying potable solar panel in the condition of high environmental consciousness than lower environmental consciousness.

4. Discussion and Conclusions

The primary aim of this study was to attempt to replicate previous research into the role of different types of appeal on purchase intention. The second objective was to understand the moderating role of environmental consciousness on purchase intention. This research also underscores the intricate relationship between advertising appeals and purchase intention. Emotional appeals are shown to be particularly potent in capturing consumers' attention, evoking positive emotions, and ultimately driving purchase intent. Rational appeals are vital for conveying product information and building trust, albeit with a longer-term impact. Functional appeals, on the other hand, are effective for products where utility and practicality are paramount.

Marketers and advertisers should carefully consider the nature of their products and target audiences when crafting ad campaigns especially for a new to the market product (Portable Solar Panel), this research study clearly states that emotional appeals are stronger than functional and rational for the millennials who were first time home buyers. The research will be helpful for the manufacturers of the product in ensuring the right advertisement appeal for improving the purchase intention and getting better return on investment on advertising spends. Future research can further be carried out to understand the strategic combination of emotional, rational, and functional appeals on optimize advertising effectiveness and enhance overall purchase intention.

REFERENCES

1. Chauhan, N. M. (2013). Consumer behaviour and his decision of purchase. International Journal for Research in Management and Pharmacy, 2(5), 1–4.
2. Chi, H. K., Yeh, H. R., & Yang, Y. T. (2009). The impact of brand awareness on consumer purchase intention: The mediating effect of perceived quality and brand loyalty. The journal of international management studies, 4(1), 135–144.
3. Dangelico, R. M., & Vocalelli, D. (2017). "Green Marketing": An analysis of definitions, strategy steps, and tools through a systematic review of the literature. Journal of Cleaner production, 165, 1263–1279.
4. Datta, S. K. (2011). Pro-environmental concern influencing green buying: A study on Indian consumers. International Journal of Business and management, 6(6), 124.
5. Delbaere, M., McQuarrie, E. F., & Phillips, B. J. (2011). Personification in advertising. Journal of Advertising, 40(1), 121–130.

6. Delgado-Ballester, E., & Fernandez Sabiote, E. (2015). Brand experimental value versus brand functional value: which matters more for the brand?. European Journal of Marketing, 49(11/12), 1857–1879.
7. do Paço, A., Shiel, C., & Alves, H. (2019). A new model for testing green consumer behaviour. Journal of cleaner production, 207, 998–1006.
8. Du, S., Bhattacharya, C. B., & Sen, S. (2010). Maximizing business returns to corporate social responsibility (CSR): The role of CSR communication. International journal of management reviews, 12(1), 8–19.
9. Firman, A., Ilyas, G. B., Reza, H. K., Lestari, S. D., & Putra, A. H. P. K. (2021). The mediating role of customer trust on the relationships of celebrity endorsement and e-WOM to Instagram Purchase intention. Jurnal Minds: Manajemen Ide dan Inspirasi, 8(1), 107–126.
10. Freiherr von Maltzahn, C. F. (2013). Dutch identity in fashion: Co-evolution between brands and consumers. Journal of Retail & Distribution Management, 26(8), 318–323.
11. Galpin, T., Whitttington, J. L., & Bell, G. (2015). Is your sustainability strategy sustainable? Creating a culture of sustainability. Corporate Governance.
12. Gionfriddo, G., Rizzi, F., Daddi, T., & Iraldo, F. (2023). The impact of green marketing on collective behaviour: Experimental evidence from the sports industry. Business Strategy and the Environment.
13. Haba, H., Hassan, Z., & Dastane, D. O. (2017). Factors leading to consumer perceived value of smartphones and its impact on purchase intention. Global Business and Management Research: An International Journal, 9(1).
14. Harrigan, P., Evers, U., Miles, M., & Daly, T. (2017). Customer engagement with tourism social media brands. Tourism management, 59, 597–609.
15. Heskett, J. L., Jones, T. O., Loveman, G. W., Sasser, W. E., & Schlesinger, L. A. (1994). Putting the service-profit chain to work. Harvard business review, 72(2), 164–174.
16. Joy, A., Sherry Jr, J. F., Venkatesh, A., Wang, J., & Chan, R. (2012). Fast fashion, sustainability, and the ethical appeal of luxury brands. Fashion theory, 16(3), 273–295.
17. Kettinger, W. J., & Lee, C. C. (1994). Perceived service quality and user satisfaction with the information services function. Decision sciences, 25(5-6), 737–766.
18. Lee, M. Y., Kim, Y. K., Pelton, L., Knight, D., & Forney, J. (2008). Factors affecting Mexican college students' purchase intention toward a US apparel brand. Journal of Fashion Marketing and Management: An International Journal.
19. Mariadas, P. A., Abdullah, H., & Abdullah, N. (2019). Factors influencing the first home purchase decision of middle-income earners (M40) in Selangor, Malaysia. e-BANGI, 16(1), 1–11.
20. Morrison, S., & Crane, F. G. (2007). Building the service brand by creating and managing an emotional brand experience. Journal of brand management, 14, 410–421.
21. Nguyen, D. H., de Leeuw, S., & Dullaert, W. E. (2018). Consumer behaviour and order fulfilment in online retailing: A systematic review. International Journal of Management Reviews, 20(2), 255–276.
22. Ogiemwonyi, O., Harun, A. B., Alam, M. N., & Othman, B. A. (2020). Do we care about going green? Measuring the effect of green environmental awareness, green product value and environmental attitude on green culture. An insight from Nigeria. Environmental and Climate Technologies, 24(1), 254–274.

23. Polonsky, M. J., & Rosenberger III, P. J. (2001). Reevaluating green marketing: a strategic approach. Business horizons, 44(5), 21–21.
24. Serazio, M. (2017). Branding politics: Emotion, authenticity, and the marketing culture of American political communication. Journal of Consumer Culture, 17(2), 225–241.
25. Spears, R., & Postmes, T. (2015). Group identity, social influence, and collective action online: Extensions and applications of the SIDE model. The handbook of the psychology of communication technology, 23–46.
26. Tran, N. Q., Tien, N. H., & Chi, D. T. P. (2022). Analysis of sales management strategy of Novaland real estate group.
27. Vizano, N. A., Khamaludin, K., & Fahlevi, M. (2021). The effect of halal awareness on purchase intention of halal food: A case study in Indonesia. The Journal of Asian Finance, Economics and Business, 8(4), 441–453.
28. Yang, S., Song, Y., & Tong, S. (2017). Sustainable retailing in the fashion industry: A systematic literature review. Sustainability, 9(7), 1266.
29. Young, W., Hwang, K., McDonald, S., & Oates, C. J. (2010). Sustainable consumption: green consumer behaviour when purchasing products. Sustainable development, 18(1), 20–31.

Note: All the figures and tables in this chapter were made by the authors.

Securing the Future through Sustainability, Health, Education, and Technology – Brig. Dr. Rajiv Divekar et al. (eds)

33 Unveiling the Branding Bridge: A Study on How Brand Equity Mediates the Relationship between CSR and Consumer Willingness to Buy in the Future

Abhineet Saxena[1]
Assistant Professor,
Amity Business School, Coordinator YSBC,
Amity University Rajasthan,
Jaipur, India

Kajal Sitlani[2]
Assistant Professor,
PhD Programme Coordinator,
School of Development Studies, IIHMR University Jaipur,
Jaipur Rajasthan, India

Smita Mehendale[3]
Assistant Professor,
Symbiosis Institute of Management Studies (SIMS),
Constituent of Symbiosis International Deemed University,
Pune, Maharashtra, India

Ashutosh Kumar[4]
Professor, Amity Business School,
Amity University Rajasthan, Jaipur, India,
Jaipur, Rajasthan, India

ABSTRACT

In this era of customer delight companies need to identify the reasons behind the purchase intentions of customers and this will further help them to predict the buying behavior of consumers for the future. The research aims to understand the mediating effect of consumer-based brand equity (CBBE) concerning CSR as well as the willingness of consumers to purchase products or services. The studies explored different aspects of Corporate Social Responsibility (CSR), including Altruism Towards Society, Volunteering in Local Community Development, Generosity Towards Ecology, Benevolent Spirit, and Problem-Solving Charity.

[1]asaxena1@jpr.amity.edu, [2]sitlanikajal@gmail.com, [3]smita.m@sims.edu, [4]akumar@jpr.amity.edu

DOI: 10.1201/9781003587200-33

The study adopted judgmental sampling to collect data from 402 respondents and further analysis was done using PLS-SEM with the Smart PLS-4 software. The finding revealed the partial mediating role of CBBE between the relationship of CSR practices and consumer future buying willingness. Brand equity has emerged like a substantial mediator that channels the favourable impressions generated by CSR initiatives into enhanced consumer willingness to buy in the future. Companies that effectively communicate their CSR endeavours and nurture their brand equity are better positioned to harness the latent potential of their socially responsible actions.

KEYWORDS: Altruism, Buying behavior, Consumer-based brand equity, CSR, Corporate social responsibility

1. Introduction

Corporate Social Responsibility is a concept that emphasizes the basic thought to give back to society. It becomes the moral obligation of industries to return to society. Corporate social responsibility is a tool through which organizations help in sustainable development to make the world a better place to live. Companies need to work on social and environmental concerns. According to Corporate social responsibility framework (Crifo & Forget, 2015) focuses on the well-being of the society this will further lead to overcome the negative consequences of production.

Companies become accountable by adopting the concept of CSR to people, society, and environment. It makes them aware and more responsible towards societal and environmental concerns. It also makes systems and processes more transparent. CSR helps to bring sustainability to the business of the companies by ensuring environmental conservation, elimination of social disparity, inculcating cultural and spiritual values. CSR can play a very crucial role in developing countries like India by fostering environmental sustainability, removing economic disparity and social concerns. Corporate sustainable initiative contributes significantly in the advancement of a country like India. According to the Companies act 2013, contribution to CSR practices is mandatory and not a choice for the companies. Before this it was practiced as merely a philanthropic activity. Porter & Karmer (2011), have considered CSR as a source for the companies to gain competitive advantage. They conceptualized CSR not merely as a tool to control the harm done by organizations to the environment; but as an opportunity for the companies to gain Competitive advantage and success in the globalized scenario.

The study examines CSR through the dimensions of Volunteering in Local Community Development (VLCD), Altruism Towards Society (ATS), Benevolent

Spirit (BS), Problem-Solving Charity (PSC) and Generosity Towards Ecology (GTE),. Altruism Towards Society is the Philanthropic dimension of CSR. It is a result of the ethical behavioral practices to donate resources to society. It is a concern for the stakeholders whether the CSR is really altruistic or is just a marketing gimmick. Volunteering in Local Community Development is to think and work for the development of the community. CSR activities are planned in a way that contributes to community development practices. Generosity Towards Ecology is one of the focus areas of CSR is environmental sustainability. The adverse impact of commercialization and mass production has caused a lot of harm to the environment, resulted in climate change, and has created ecological imbalance. Benevolent Spirit focuses on the external environment and its important focus area to focus on is the internal environment of an organization. CSR practices also aim at creating a congenial, value-based and ethical work culture. Another dimension of CSR is Problem-Solving Charity. It focuses on eradicating the problems prevalent in society. It is also one of the important need-based areas, especially in developing countries.

Trustworthiness is generated among the customers by a company by emphasizing the various aspects of Brand equity. Identity as well as visibility of the brand amongst the customers is created through the various dimensions of brand equity by the company. Consumer-based brand equity is a distinct influence created by knowledge and marketing of brand on the basis of consumer response towards it (Keller, 1993). In essence, CBBE measures the impact of consumers' perceptions and attitudes toward a brand on their buying behavior and preferences. Four primary dimensions that contribute to customer-based brand equity are brand association, brand awareness, brand loyalty and perceived quality ((Keller, 2013); (Lee & Leh, 2011); (Aaker, 1991)). According to (Aaker, 1991) consumer's perspective on brand equity is a collection of possessions as well as obligations of a brand, that is associated with the worth of a product or service, which may either contribute or diminish its worth to a company and its customers. In conceptualizing consumer-based brand equity, researchers have taken into consideration the following dimension of Aaker's model: brand loyalty, brand associations, perceived quality, and brand awareness whereas one of the dimensions was excluded, other proprietary brand assets, from the CBBE framework as it pertains solely to companies and is not directly linked to consumers.

The following dimensions of brand equity were taken into consideration for the study–

Brand awareness is considered as the customer's proficiency which will helps him to distinguish a brand and how memorable that brand is in the mind of customers. Brand association is the deep association felt by a customer for a brand. It helps customers to develop a correlation between the brand and the concept. Perceived quality refers to impression of product or service delivered to a customer about the quality. Zeithaml (1988), defines it as the assessment of excellence or superiority of a product by the consumers. Brand loyalty refers to repetitive purchase of a product or service even if the competitors are offering similar products. Brand Image is an aggregate of beliefs of a customer about the brand that is influenced by several factors like brand experience (Ehrenberg, Goodhardt, & Barwise, 1990); (Oliver, 2000)).

Future buying willingness refers to the intention of customers to purchase a product in future. It is the customer's intention to purchase the product or not in future. It helps to study the future buying behavior of customers towards a product or service.

Few researchers (Page G, 2005) are of the opinion that there is not much impact of CSR practices on the buying intentions of consumer and their behavior. This study conceptualizes that CSR has a substantial impact on Brand Equity and this is one of the factors that can contribute to future buying behavior. The study by (Bianchi, Bruno, & Sarabia-Sanchez, 2019) suggests that adoption of suitable communication strategies results in a better empanelment of a brand. Companies like Lawrence & Mayo (Srivastava, Mendonsa, Joshi, & Pradhan, 2022) presented that its CSR initiative led to brand equity and impact on the various stakeholders was clearly identifiable. Further study by (Sharma & Jain, 2019) was being carried in sports industry that also validated the existence of strong association among CSR, trust, brand loyalty and brand equity. The article aims to analyze the future buying behaviour and the effect of CSR on future buying behavior (fbb).

2. Literature Review

Brand equity explains the impact created by the customer's knowledge of a brand and its marketing on their perception towards it (Gammoh, Koh, & Okoroafo, 2011). Various studies have shown that there is a relationship between brand equity on purchase intentions (Chang & Liu, 2009). The analysis revealed that whether the high-risk category services like hotels or consumer durable products are considered; there is an effect of brand equity on the purchase ((Cathy J, Cynthia, & Donthu, 1995). A study undertaken by (Murty,, Udayashankar, & Varma, 2018) studies the impact of brand equity on the buying behaviour of consumers in the city of Vijayawada with reference to purchase of four-wheeler i.e., Car. The study takes into consideration the Aaker's model. In this research one of the dimensions that was studied was brand loyalty. Customer' perception was studied with respect to their loyalty towards brand. It also analyzed the awareness level of customers towards different brands of the companies under study. The impact of perceived quality as well as brand association was also identified in the study. Literature identifies several brand equity models. One such model used in this study is Aaker's model (Aaker, 2009). This model of brand equity was also used to study the different dimensions of brand equity in the sports industry (Ton & Hawley, 2009) and with the help of structural equation modeling the analysis was carried. With the help of its causal relationship was identified between the four dimensions of brand equity.

2.1 Corporate Social Responsibility

CSR's Philanthropic dimension (Carroll, 1991) suggests it helps in the betterment of the life's of the people by improving their quality of life ; to improve the profit of the company (i.e. it's economic dimension (Carroll, 1991)); adopting such practices by the organizations though not mentioned in any law (i.e. ethical dimension (Carroll, 1991)) and obeying rules and laws ass set up at national and international level (i.e. legal dimension (Carroll, 1991). The concept of CSR has been practically adopted by the companies across the various sectors to strengthen the brand image of the company ((Maignan & Ferrell, 2004). Bawa & Saha (2016) highlighted the association of CSR with brand association empirically. Comparative analysis of different companies shows that a strong brand association with CSR practices will help to enhance the level of trust in the minds of the public; the company like Tata reveals such an association. Some researchers ((Arendt & Brettel, 2010)suggest that the size of the company, budget allocated for marketing CSR practices, kind of industry affects the CSR interventions that triggers the company in the image building and performances. However, some studies suspect the utility of CSR in positioning of the company (Sen & Bhattacharya, 2001). Although much research is being done pointing the relevance of CSR on the performance and productivity of the company still inconsistencies are prevailing to determine the conditions under which it enhances the company's productivity, its image and leads to competitive advantage to them (Vlachos, Tsamakos, Vrechopoulous, & Avramids, 2009).

2.2 Corporate Social Responsibility and Brand Equity

The literature review on these two dimensions under study revealed an association between the two. A study was being undertaken by (Araujo, Pereira, & Santos, 2023) Effect of CSR on brand equity and brand image. CSR initiatives were associated with the brand image of the company. The study focuses on how the CSR practices help in portraying the brand image of the company. It helps in creating brand equity among the customers. It further emphasized the influence it has on the level of satisfaction of customers. It was found in the study that there is effect of CSR initiatives taken by the organization on the brand image of the company. It was identified through the study that the CSR initiative doesn't have a direct impact on satisfaction level of customers but is being mediated through the brand image. In a study by Hala et.al. (2021) it is suggested the influence of the different dimensions of CSR, how it affects the brand credibility, repeat purchases as well as patronage intentions. A study on two generations i.e., X-generation and Y-generation with regards to impact of CSR was undertaken by (Wu & Wang, 2014). It revealed that the X-generations believed that the environmental dimension of CSR has an impact on the image of the brand; and secondly attitude of the brand on future buying willingness. Whereas the Y-generation believed that a negative impact on brand image of environmental CSR suggesting that the organization needs to work harder on creating brand awareness for the environmentally driven CSR activities.

CSR practices enhances the level of trust among the customers which further helps to improve the brand equity in the banking sector (Jannat, Haque, & Chowdhury, 2022). Structural equation modelling was used to study how the CSR practices created trustworthiness among the consumers which further helped in establishing the brand equity of the banks under study. A brand image's affective dimension is influenced by the CSR strategies of the organization. CSR practices not only influence the brand image but brand loyalty as well. From the above literature review following hypotheses were formulated:

H1: There is a significant relationship between CSR and Consumer based brand Equity (CBBE) parameters.

H2: There is a significant relationship between CSR and Consumer buying willingness.

H3: There is a mediation effect of Brand Equity in the Relationship between CSR and Consumer Willingness to Buy in the Future.

Objectives of the study

- The study helps to explore predictors of the CSR activities practiced by the FMCG sector in India.
- To study the relationship between CSR and Consumer Willingness to Buy in the Future.
- To analyze the mediating role of Consumer based brand equity (CBBE) influencing the relationship between CSR and Consumer willingness to buy in future.

3. Research Methods

The investigation was done using PLS-4 software. With the help of this software data analysis is being done and for this Partial Least Square Structural Equation Modeling (PLS-SEM) is being considered for the study. PLS-SEM is a highly effective modeling for scenarios that involve non-normal, categorical, or ordinal data, limited sample sizes, complex models with numerous variables and indicators, higher-order constructs, formative measurement, as well as mediation and moderation effects (Sarstedt et. al. (2017), Hair Jr et al. (2017), and Haenlein and Kaplan (2004)). The primary purpose of this research is to understand the role of Brand Equity in the association between CSR and Consumer Willingness to Buy in the Future. SPSS 20.0 was being used to carry out an Exploratory Factor Analysis (EFA). This analysis focused on the measurement variables of CSR, namely Altruism Towards Society (ATS), Volunteering for Local Community Development (VLCD), Generosity towards Ecology (GTE), Benevolent Spirit (BS), and Problem-Solving Charity (PSC). For CBBE items were confirmed same as Aaker model of CBBE namely "Brand awareness", "Brand associations", "Perceived quality", "Brand loyalty", "Brand Image". EFA, a powerful multivariate statistical technique, was employed to identify factors capable of CSR and BE construct, drawing support from (Watkins, 2018) and (Suhr, 2006).

Additionally, a Confirmatory Factor Analysis (CFA) was performed to delve into the relationship between the measured variables and their reflective latent construct.

Technical Summary of sample

Universe:	Consumers of FMCG products
Place	Rajasthan
Date	From date to date
Sample size	402 valid respondents
Sampling Procedure	Multistage sampling
Data Treatment	For selection of districts Rajasthan was divided in 7 administrative divisions and then judgemental sampling was applied to selected districts to conduct survey. The concentration of CSR activities by FMCG companies in various districts of Rajasthan state was one of the criteria used to choose these districts. For the final data collection, places with the highest volume of CSR were chosen based on the information retrieved form national CSR portal of India. The responses were collected between September 2022 and March 2023.

4. Sample Profiles of Respondents

In this study, the researcher assumed an infinite population and employed Cochran's formula to determine the minimum sample size for the primary survey at a 5% level of significance. After filtering the collected questionnaires, 402 were deemed suitable for final analysis, exceeding the minimum sample size of 385 calculated by the formula, thus ensuring adequacy. The outcome of the test Kaiser-Mayer-Olkin (KMO) is 0.952 which is significant and more than recommended value of 0.8, suggesting that the taken sample is enough to carry out Factor Analysis Test (Nunnally, 1978). The Demographic distribution of sample respondents is resented in below Table 33.1.

Table 33.1 Demographic distribution of sample respondents

Variable	Categories	Percent	Variable	Categories	Percent
Gender	Male	63.4	Residence	Urban	60.4
	Female	36.6		Rural	39.6
Age	18-25 Years	22.1	Average monthly income (INR)	0-20000	29.9
				21000-40000	17.4
	26-35 Years	63.2		41000-60000	15.7
	36-45 Years	11.9		61000-80000	13.9
	46 years and above	2.7		81000-100000	7.2
Professional status	Farmer and Gig workers	20.1		Above100000	15.9
	Unemployed	2.7			
	Self-employed	20.1			
	Government Employee	22.6			
	Private employee	28.6			
	Pensioner	1.5			
	Other	4.2			

Source: Made by Author

5. Outer Loading and VIF

Initially bootstrapping was run on the sample data & then with the help of Smart PLS "SEM" has been run on the random sample of 5000. The Table 33.2 and Fig. 33.1 above portrays all original sample are positive and "P value" for all is

Path Model:

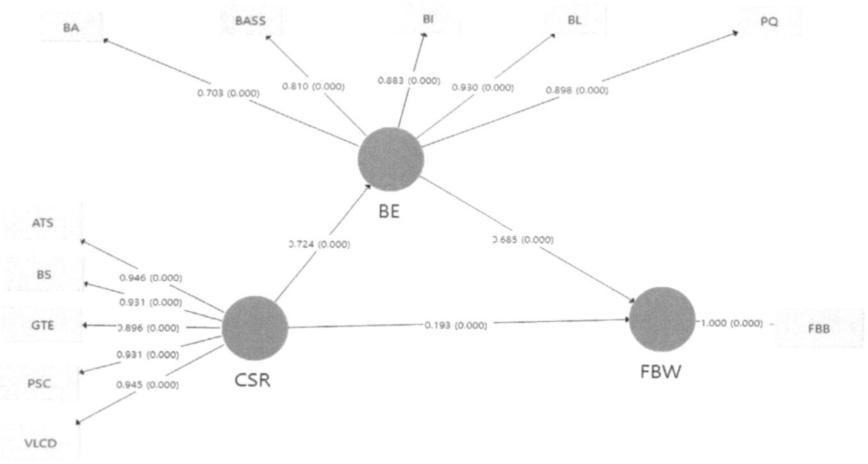

Fig. 33.1 Path model of structural equation modeling

Source: Made by Author using Smart PLS software

Table 33.2 Outer loading and VIF value of outer model

	Beta value	Sample Mean	STDEV	t-Statis-tics	P-Values	2.5%	97.5%	VIF
ATS_1	0.774	0.774	0.027	28.453	**0.000**	0.711	0.817	**1.590**
ATS_2	0.864	0.864	0.012	70.123	**0.000**	0.832	0.879	**2.169**
ATS_3	0.845	0.844	0.016	52.277	**0.000**	0.803	0.865	**2.028**
ATS_4	0.765	0.765	0.027	27.997	**0.000**	0.696	0.802	**1.483**
BASS_1	0.881	0.88	0.011	77.915	**0.000**	0.852	0.896	3.285
BASS_2	0.842	0.842	0.016	51.802	**0.000**	0.802	0.865	**2.790**
BASS_3	0.85	0.85	0.014	60.802	**0.000**	0.817	0.871	**2.427**
BASS_4	0.829	0.829	0.017	48.155	**0.000**	0.786	0.852	**2.358**
BASS_5	0.84	0.839	0.017	50.032	**0.000**	0.800	0.866	**2.687**
BASS_6	0.783	0.782	0.021	37.930	**0.000**	0.742	0.823	**2.053**
BA_1	0.814	0.814	0.018	45.075	**0.000**	0.779	0.849	**2.515**
BA_2	0.765	0.764	0.026	29.850	**0.000**	0.711	0.813	**2.031**
BA_3	0.849	0.849	0.015	55.103	**0.000**	0.818	0.879	**2.752**
BA_4	0.859	0.858	0.015	56.076	**0.000**	0.821	0.881	**2.729**
BA_5	0.851	0.851	0.018	46.181	**0.000**	0.798	0.869	**2.576**
BA_6	0.81	0.81	0.025	31.583	**0.000**	0.747	0.847	**2.484**
BA_7	0.863	0.863	0.014	61.681	**0.000**	0.838	0.893	3.439
BI_1	0.745	0.744	0.027	27.557	**0.000**	0.678	0.783	**2.145**
BI_2	0.772	0.771	0.026	29.388	**0.000**	0.713	0.816	**2.402**
BI_3	0.799	0.798	0.019	41.589	**0.000**	0.768	0.844	**2.600**
BI_4	0.783	0.782	0.022	35.744	**0.000**	0.748	0.833	**2.480**
BI_5	0.831	0.831	0.016	52.725	**0.000**	0.800	0.861	3.102
BI_6	0.85	0.849	0.014	61.335	**0.000**	0.821	0.874	3.370
BI_7	0.839	0.838	0.016	53.659	**0.000**	0.811	0.873	3.316
BI_8	0.802	0.802	0.018	45.797	**0.000**	0.771	0.840	**2.559**
BI_9	0.829	0.829	0.014	57.736	**0.000**	0.805	0.862	**2.771**
BL_1	0.855	0.854	0.013	66.532	**0.000**	0.826	0.877	**2.828**
BL_2	0.86	0.86	0.015	55.527	**0.000**	0.826	0.887	**2.994**
BL_3	0.83	0.829	0.018	45.799	**0.000**	0.793	0.865	**2.468**
BL_4	0.81	0.809	0.020	41.067	**0.000**	0.767	0.845	**2.322**
BL_5	0.801	0.8	0.019	42.044	**0.000**	0.756	0.831	**2.200**
BL_6	0.824	0.823	0.018	44.976	**0.000**	0.783	0.855	**2.650**
BL_7	0.824	0.824	0.018	46.708	**0.000**	0.787	0.856	**2.635**

	Beta value	Sample Mean	STDEV	t-Statistics	P-Values	2.5%	97.5%	VIF
BS_1	0.823	0.822	0.019	43.608	**0.000**	0.781	0.855	**2.219**
BS_2	0.812	0.811	0.016	52.765	**0.000**	0.787	0.848	**2.301**
BS_3	0.836	0.836	0.015	54.220	**0.000**	0.804	0.866	**2.161**
BS_4	0.775	0.775	0.026	28.835	**0.000**	0.706	0.809	**1.837**
FBW_1	0.742	0.741	0.027	28.262	**0.000**	0.703	0.807	**1.857**
FBW_2	0.841	0.84	0.017	48.350	**0.000**	0.803	0.870	**2.573**
FBW_3	0.808	0.807	0.021	37.362	**0.000**	0.755	0.839	**2.166**
FBW_4	0.783	0.782	0.021	37.256	**0.000**	0.746	0.829	**2.079**
FBW_5	0.826	0.825	0.022	36.189	**0.000**	0.762	0.848	**2.286**
FBW_6	0.837	0.837	0.018	47.182	**0.000**	0.798	0.867	**2.596**
FBW_7	0.817	0.816	0.019	43.455	**0.000**	0.778	0.851	**2.279**
GTE_1	0.886	0.886	0.011	78.668	**0.000**	0.874	0.919	**2.414**
GTE_2	0.9	0.899	0.011	79.279	**0.000**	0.885	0.929	**2.570**
GTE_3	0.83	0.83	0.018	49.049	**0.000**	0.824	0.893	**2.018**
GTE_4	0.872	0.873	0.015	57.861	**0.000**	0.839	0.899	**2.087**
PQ_1	0.795	0.794	0.023	34.155	**0.000**	0.738	0.829	**1.089**
PQ_2	0.343	0.501	0.249	14.448	**0.000**	0.216	0.853	**1.804**
PQ_3	0.768	0.773	0.021	35.973	**0.000**	0.733	0.817	**2.580**
PQ_4	0.846	0.843	0.015	54.947	**0.000**	0.814	0.874	3.221
PQ_5	0.882	0.878	0.013	68.970	**0.000**	0.854	0.903	**2.654**
PQ_6	0.847	0.843	0.017	50.949	**0.000**	0.814	0.878	**1.790**
PSC_1	0.852	0.851	0.018	46.247	**0.000**	0.811	0.882	**1.959**
PSC_2	0.864	0.863	0.016	55.921	**0.000**	0.833	0.895	**1.849**
PSC_3	0.856	0.856	0.015	57.118	**0.000**	0.832	0.890	**1.318**
VLCD_1	0.729	0.726	0.045	14.727	**0.000**	0.563	0.737	**2.237**
VLCD_2	0.866	0.866	0.014	62.440	**0.000**	0.835	0.890	**1.906**
VLCD_3	0.858	0.858	0.015	54.823	**0.000**	0.802	0.862	**2.231**

Source: Made by Author using Smart PLS Output

found significant (0.000). The column of "P Values" displays relative "significance (probability) levels" for the path of a row. Above Table also represented VIF values for different constructs. Multi-collinearity is indicated in regression analysis and is spotted by Variance inflation factor (VIF). An association among predictors (i.e., independent variables) in any model, is a sign of multi-collinearity. This adversely affect the results of regression analysis. A VIF value below 5 signifies the absence of multicollinearity among factors, indicating distinct measures without overlap. Specifically, a VIF value below 3, as per the model proposed by Hair Jr., Matthews, and Sarstedt (2017), rationalizes lower collinearity.

Cronbach alpha values as well as composite reliability in the table reveal the value to be above 0.7 for each of the variables. This suggests that all of these factors are reliable and can be considered ideal. Convergent validity examines the correlation between different measurement variables of a construct, typically assessed through average variance extracted (AVE) (Hair Jr., Matthews, & Sarstedt, 2017). Ideally, the AVE value should exceed 0.50 for convergent validity to be established. As shown in Table 33.3, the AVE of each variable is above 0.5, confirming the convergent validity of the construct.

Table 33.3 Construct reliability and validity

	Cronbach's Alpha	rho	Composite Reliability	AVE
ATS	0.828	0.832	0.886	0.661
BA	0.925	0.927	0.94	0.69
BASS	0.915	0.918	0.934	0.702
BI	0.932	0.933	0.944	0.65
BL	0.924	0.925	0.939	0.688
BS	0.827	0.828	0.885	0.659
FBB	0.911	0.914	0.93	0.654
GTE	0.895	0.897	0.927	0.761
PQ	0.848	0.888	0.891	0.592
PSC	0.82	0.82	0.893	0.735
VLCD	0.755	0.775	0.859	0.672

Source: Made by Author using Smart PLS Output

The higher values diagonally within each column in Table 33.4 indicate that a construct shares more variance with its items compared to items from other constructs (Fornell & Larcker, 1981). Additionally, the Heterotrait-Monotrait ratio of correlation was found to be less than 0.9, confirming the validity of the constructs (Hensler, Ringle, & Sarstedt, 2015).

The Table 33.5 above portrays all original sample are positive and "P value" for all is found significant (0.000). The column of "P Values" displays relative "significance (probability) levels" for the path of row. The results suggested that CSR positively and significantly affects, CBBE and Future buying willingness ($p< .05$). The table of specific Indirect Effects also confirms the partial mediation of BE between CSR and FBW. Thus, all above mentioned alternate hypothesis are Accepted.

Table 33.4 Discriminant validity results using Fornell-Larcker criterion

Fornell-Larcker Criterion											
	ATS	BA	BASS	BI	BL	BS	FBB	GTE	PQ	PSC	VLCD
ATS	**0.805**										
BA	0.420	**0.829**									
BASS	0.587	0.468	**0.834**								
BI	0.637	0.533	0.633	**0.809**							
BL	0.645	0.549	0.689	0.703	**0.828**						
BS	0.661	0.396	0.574	0.646	0.671	**0.811**					
FBB	0.664	0.563	0.660	0.711	0.794	0.662	**0.808**				
GTE	0.795	0.333	0.562	0.569	0.599	0.804	0.537	**0.890**			
PQ	0.580	0.563	0.629	0.730	0.744	0.604	0.748	0.507	**0.772**		
PSC	0.747	0.393	0.603	0.611	0.640	0.805	0.648	0.818	0.572	**0.860**	
VLCD	0.785	0.402	0.631	0.655	0.666	0.652	0.683	0.780	0.582	0.762	**0.810**

Source: Made by Author using Smart PLS Output

Table 33.5 Hypotheses testing results

Total Indirect and Specific Indirect Effects							
	Original Sample (O)	Sample Mean (M)	Standard Deviation (STDEV)	T Statistics (|O/STDEV|)	P Values	2.5%	97.5%
H1: CSR -> CBBE	0.731	0.732	0.029	25.211	**0.000**	0.666	0.779
H2: CSR -> FBW	0.695	0.695	0.029	23.733	**0.000**	0.631	0.744
H3: CSR -> CBBE -> FBB	0.494	0.495	0.035	14.132	**0.000**	0.428	0.565

Source: Made by Author using Smart PLS Output

6. Conclusion

This research paper delved into the intricate dynamics of the association between CSR activities and future buying behaviour, specifically focusing on mediating role of brand equity. Through an extensive analysis of empirical data, it became evident that there is a significant impact of CSR activities adopted by the organization on consumer perceptions as well as attitude. The positive association of the company's CSR endeavours, and consumer goodwill is well-established in the literature, and this study reinforces that notion. Moreover, findings highlighted the starring role of consumer-based brand equity as a mediator in this association. Several researches have emphasized on the positive impact created by the CSR practices on the customer's purchase intentions (Lev, Petrovits, & Radhakrishnan, 2009); (Zhe, Xiaojing, & Xianli, 2021)). Brand equity has emerged like a substantial mediator that channels the favourable impressions generated by CSR initiatives into enhanced consumer willingness to buy in the future. This mediation underscores the importance of a strong and positive brand image in converting ethical and responsible business practices into tangible consumer actions. Companies that effectively communicate their CSR endeavours and nurture their brand equity are better positioned to harness the latent potential of their socially responsible actions. Future research could delve deeper into the specific dimensions of brand equity that play the most significant role in mediating the CSR-consumer behavior connection. Moreover, cross-cultural studies could shed light on potential variations in the observed relationships across different consumer contexts. The insights derived from this study can guide marketing and branding strategies, emphasizing the need for transparent communication of CSR initiatives to enhance brand perception and drive consumer loyalty. Ultimately, by understanding and leveraging the branding bridge, companies can navigate the evolving landscape of corporate social responsibility and consumer preferences, fostering mutually beneficial outcomes for both their business and society at large. This article focuses on CSR practices by an organization would enhance its "brand awareness", which would lead to "brand associations" & perceived quality. This would build a "brand loyalty" of consumers towards the product of company an eventually "brand image" of that firm would rise. thus consumer's "future buying willingness" would rise. These above-mentioned points are building blocks of "Brand Equity." Thus, CSR practices by any company would have direct and significant impact upon its "Brand Equity" that has been proved through a SEM model similar to study (Alakkas, Vivek, Nabi, & Khan, 2022).

REFERENCES

1. Aaker, D. (1991). Brand equity. *La gestione del valore della marca*, 347, 356.
2. Aaker, D. (2009). Aaker's brand equity model. *European Institute for Brand Management.*
3. Alakkas, A., Vivek, P. M., Nabi, M., & Khan, M. (2022). Corporate Social Responsibility and Firm-Based Brand Equity: The Moderating Effect of Marketing Communication and Brand Identity. *Sustainability, 14*(10), 6033. doi:https://doi.org/10.3390/su14106033
4. Araujo, J., Pereira, I. V., & Santos , J. D. (2023). The Effect of Corporate Social Responsibility on Brand Image and Brand Equity and Its Impact on Consumer Satisfaction. *Administrative Sciences, 13*(5), 118.
5. Arendt, S., & Brettel, M. (2010). Understanding the influence of corporate social responsibility on corporate identity, image, and firm performance. *Management Decision, 48*(10), 1469–1492.
6. Bawa, A., & Saha, A. (2016). Strength of corporate social responsibility as a corporate brand association: general public perspective. *Decision, 43*(4), 313–332.

7. Bianchi, E., Bruno, J. M., & Sarabia-Sanchez, F. J. (2019). The impact of perceived CSR on corporate reputation and purchase intention. *European Journal of Management and Business Economics, 28*(3), 206–221. doi:https://doi.org/10.1108/EJMBE-12-20
8. Carroll, A. B. (1991). The pyramid of corporate social responsibility: Toward the moral management of organizational stakeholders. . *Business horizons, 34*(4), 39–48.
9. Cathy J, C.-W., Cynthia, A., & Donthu, N. (1995). Brand Equity, Brand Preference, and Purchase Intent,. *Journal of Advertising*, 25–40. doi:10.1080/00913367.1995.10673481
10. Chang, H. H., & Liu, M. Y. (2009). The impact of brand equity on brand preference and purchase intentions in the service industries. *The Service Industries Journal*, 1687–1706. doi:10.1080/02642060902793557
11. Crifo, P., & Forget, V. D. (2015). The economics of corporate social responsibility: A firm-level perspective survey. *Journal of Economic Surveys, 29*(1), 112–130.
12. Ehrenberg, A. S., Goodhardt, G. J., & Barwise, T. P. (1990). Double jeopardy revisited. *Journal of marketing, 54*(3), 82–91.
13. Fornell, C., & Larcker, D. F. (1981). Evaluating structural equation models with unobservable variables and measurement error. *Journal of Marketing Research, 18*(1), 39–50. doi:https://doi.org/10.2307/3151312
14. Gammoh, B. S., Koh, A. C., & Okoroafo, S. C. (2011). Consumer culture brand positioning strategies: an experimental investigation. *Journal of Product & Brand Management, 20*(1), 48–57.
15. Haenlein, M. &. (2004). *A beginner's guide to partial least squares analysis: Understanding statistics.* Taylor and Francis.
16. Hair Jr, J. F., Matthews , L. M., & Sarstedt, M. (2017). PLS-SEM or CB-SEM: updated guidelines on which method to use. *International Journal of Multivariate Data Analysis, 1*(2), 107–213.
17. Hala Mohammed, A. Z., Zaid, M. O., Muhammad, T. A., Mohammd, A., & Mahmoud, M. (2021). Corporate social responsibility and patronage intentions: The mediating effect of brand credibility. *Journal of Marketing Communications, 27*(5), 510–533. doi: DOI: 10.1080/13527266.2020.1728565
18. Hensler, J., Ringle, C., & Sarstedt, M. (2015). A New Criterion for Assessing Discriminant Validity in Variance-based Structural Equation Modeling. *Journal of the Academy of Marketing Science*, 115–135.
19. Jannat, M., Haque, M. M., & Chowdhury, M. F. (2022). Does Trust Mediate in Corporate Social Responsibility (CSR) and Brand Equity Nexus? Empirical Evidence from the Banking Sector. *FIIB Business Review*, 0. doi: https://doi.org/10.1177/23197145221110285
20. Keller, K. L. (1993). Conceptualizing, Measuring, and Managing Customer-Based Brand Equity. *Journal of Marketing, 57*(1), 1–22. doi: https://doi.org/10.1177/002224299305700101
21. Keller, K. L. (2013). *Building strong brands in a modern marketing communications environment. In The evolution of integrated marketing communications.* Routledge.
22. Lee, G. C., & Leh, F. C. (2011). Dimensions of customer-based brand equity: A study on Malaysian brands. *Journal of Marketing Research and case studies,*, 1–10.
23. Lev, B., Petrovits, C., & Radhakrishnan, S. (2009). Is Doing Good Good for You? How Corporate Charitable Contributions Enhance Revenue Growth. *Strategic Management Journal., 31*, 182–200.

24. Maignan, I., & Ferrell, O. C. (2004). Corporate social responsibility and marketing: An integrative framework. *J. of the Acad. Mark., 32*, 3–19. doi:https://doi.org/10.1177/0092070303258971
25. Martinez, P., Perez, A., & Del Bosque, I. R. (2014). CSR influence on hotel brand image and loyalty. *Academia Revista Latinoamericana de Administración, 27*(2), 267–283. doi:https://doi.org/10.1108/ARLA-12-2013-0190
26. Murty,, A. V., Udayashankar, A., & Varma, B. V. (2018, February). Impact of Brand Equity on Consumer Buying Behaviour(An Empirical Analysis on Consumer Buying Behaviour ofSelected Car Users In Vijayawada City). *IOSR Journal of Business and Management (IOSR-JBM), 20*(2), 30–36. doi:10.9790/487X-2002063036
27. Nunnally, J. C. (1978). *An Overview of Psychological Measurement. In: Wolman, B.B. (eds) Clinical Diagnosis of Mental Disorders.* Springer, Boston, MA. doi:https://doi.org/10.1007/978-1-4684-2490-4_4
28. Oliver, R. L. (2000). Customer satisfaction with service. *Handbook of services marketing and management,*, 339–354.
29. Page G, F. H. (2005). Corporate reputation: what do consumers really care about? *Journal of Adverising Research , 45*(3), 305–313.
30. Porter , M. E., & Kramer, M. R. (2011). Creating Shared Value M. E. Porter and M. R. Kramer, ",",. *Harvard Business Review, 89*(1), 2–17.
31. Sarstedt, M., Ringle, C. M., & Hair, J. F. (2017). *Treating unobserved heterogeneity in PLS-SEM: A multi-method approach.*
32. Sen, S., & Bhattacharya, C. B. (2001). Does Doing Good Always Lead to Doing Better? Consumer Reactions to Corporate Social Responsibility. *Journal of Marketing Research, 38*, 225–243.
33. Sharma, R., & Jain, V. (2019). CSR, Trust, Brand Loyalty and Brand Equity: Empirical Evidences from Sportswear Industry in the NCR Region of India. *Metamorphosis, 18*(1), 57–67. doi:https://doi.org/10.1177/0972622519853158
34. Srivastava, R. K., Mendonsa, V., Joshi, H., & Pradhan, T. (2022). Dilemma between CSR and brand equity: a case of Lawrence & Mayo company. *12*(2). doi:https://doi.org/10.1108/EEMCS-09-2019-0240
35. Suhr, D. D. (2006). Exploratory or confirmatory factor analysis?
36. Ton, X., & Hawley, J. M. (2009). Measuring customer-based brand equity: Empirical evidence from the sportswear market in China. *Journal of product & brand management, 18*(4), 262–271.
37. Vlachos, P. A., Tsamakos, A., Vrechopoulous, A. P., & Avramids, P. K. (2009). Corporate social responsibility: attributions, loyalty, and the mediating role of trust. *Journal of the academy of marketing science, 37*, 170–180.
38. Watkins, M. W. (2018). Exploratory factor analysis: A guide to best practice. *Journal of Black Psychology,, 44*(3), 219–246.
39. Wu, S. I., & Wang, W. H. (2014). Impact of CSR perception on brand image, brand attitude and buying willingness: A study of a global café. *International Journal of Marketing Studies, 6*(6), 43.
40. Zeithaml, V. A. (1988). Consumer perceptions of price, quality, and value: a means-end model and synthesis of evidence. *Journal of marketing, 52*(3), 2–22.
41. Zhe, C., Xiaojing, L., & Xianli, X. (2021). Environmental Science and Pollution Research.